Lecture Notes in Computer ~

Edited by G. Goos and J. Hartmanis

Advisory Board: W. Brauer   D. Gries

Peter A. Fritzson (Ed.)

Compiler Construction

5th International Conference, CC '94
Edinburgh, U.K., April 7-9, 1994
Proceedings

Springer-Verlag
Berlin Heidelberg New York
London Paris Tokyo
Hong Kong Barcelona
Budapest

Series Editors

Gerhard Goos
Universität Karlsruhe
Postfach 69 80
Vincenz-Priessnitz-Straße 1
D-76131 Karlsruhe, Germany

Juris Hartmanis
Cornell University
Department of Computer Science
4130 Upson Hall
Ithaca, NY 14853, USA

Volume Editor

Peter A. Fritzson
Department of Computer and Information Science, Linköping University
S-58183 Linköping, Sweden

CR Subject Classification (1991): D.3.4, D.3.1, F.4.2, D.2.6, I.2.2

ISBN 3-540-57877-3 Springer-Verlag Berlin Heidelberg New York
ISBN 0-387-57877-3 Springer-Verlag New York Berlin Heidelberg

© Springer-Verlag Berlin Heidelberg 1994
Printed in Germany

Typesetting: Camera-ready by author
SPIN: 10131984   45/3140-543210 - Printed on acid-free paper

Preface

The International Conference on Compiler Construction (CC) provides a forum for presentation and discussion of recent developments in the area of compiler construction, language implementation and language design.

Its scope ranges from compilation methods and tools to implementation techniques for specific requirements on languages and target architectures. It also includes language design and programming environments issues which are related to language translation. There is an emphasis on practical and efficient techniques.

This volume contains a selection of the papers which were accepted for presentation at CC'94, the fifth International Conference on Compiler Construction, held in Edinburgh, Scotland, 7-9 April 1994. This is a continuation of the CC series of workshops which was started in Germany in 1986, and has lately grown into a regular conference. In October 1992 the CC program committe decided to synchronize the CC conferences with the ESOP/CAAP conferences, in order to provide a European conference week covering a range of subjects, both practical and theoretical, related to programming languages and their implementation. CC'94 is the first in the CC series to be co-located in this way.

The good response to the call for papers shows the need for a forum on compiler construction and language implementation: 77 papers were submitted, of which the program committe selected 29 for presentation and inclusion in this volume. Further contributions were selected to be presented at a poster and demo session, where also a number of tools and systems were shown. The poster papers were printed in a technical report at the Department of Computer and Information Science, Linköping University, Linköping, Sweden. The conference program started with a keynote speech by Professor Kristen Nygaard on the subject: "The Language Designer - the Implementor's Friend or Foe?".

On behalf of the Program Committee, the Program Chairman would like to thank all those who submitted papers to CC'94. Thanks also go to the Program Committee and others who helped in reviewing and evaluating the papers. Also, special thanks to the invited keynote speaker, Professor Kristen Nygaard from the University of Oslo in Norway. Last but not the least, the effort of all those who helped in organizing the conference, especially the local organizers in Edinburgh, is gratefully acknowledged. CC'94 was hosted by the University of Edinburgh.

Linköping, January 1994   Peter Fritzson

Program Chairman:

Peter Fritzson　　　　　　　(Linköping University, Sweden)

Program Committee:

Boris Babaian	(Moscow Center for Sparc Technology, Russia)
Peter Fritzson	(Linköping University, Sweden)
Allen Goldberg	(Kestrel Institute, Palo Alto, USA)
Rajiv Gupta	(University of Pittsburgh, USA)
Tibor Gyimóthy	(Academy of Sciences, Szeged, Hungary)
Seif Haridi	(KTH, Stockholm, Sweden)
Laurie Hendren	(McGill University, Canada)
Nigel Horspool	(University of Victoria, Canada)
Francois Irigoin	(Ecoles des Mines, Paris, France)
Thomas Johnsson	(Chalmers, Gothenburgh, Sweden)
Martin Jourdan	(INRIA-Rocquencourt, Paris, France)
Uwe Kastens	(University of Paderborn, Germany)
Kai Koskimies	(University of Tampere, Finland)
Monica Lam	(Stanford University, USA)
Ole Lehrmann-Madsen	(Aarhus University, Denmark)
David Padua	(University of Illinois, USA)
Gunter Riedewald	(University of Rostock, Germany)
Sergei Romanenko	(Russian Academy of Sciences, Russia)

List of Referees

Many other referees helped the program committe in evaluating the papers. Their assistance is gratefully acknowledged.

Zoltan Alexin
Erik Altman
Corinne Ancourt
Beatrice Apvrille
Lennart Augustsson
Miklos Bartha
David Berson
William Blume
Urban Boquist
Ding-Kai Chen
Fabien Coelho
Alexandr Drozdov
Evelyn Duesterwald
Robin Duquette
Christine Eisenbeis
Keith Faigin
William Gardner
Chun Gong
Thomas Hallgren
John Hughes
Pierre Jouvelot
Justiani
Mariam Kamkar
Kent Karlsson
Ronan Keryell
Brian Koehler
Herbert Kuchen
Jean-Marie Larchevêque
Ai Li
Luis Lozano
Dmitry Maslennikov

Sharad Mehrotra
Michael Miller
Ilya Mukhin
Henrik Nilsson
Alexandr Ostanevich
Jukka Paakki
Didier Parigot
Mikael Pettersson
Lori Pollock
KVS Prasad
Lawrence Rauchwerger
Niklas Röjemo
Sergey Rozhkov
Dan Sahlin
Sriram Sankar
Eljas Soisalon-Soininen.
Jan Sparud
V.C. Sreedhar
Kevin Theobald
Valentin Tikhonov
Vladimir Tikhorski
Steve Tjiang
Janos Toczki
Mei-Chin Tsai
James Uhl
Vladimir Volkonski
Tia Watts
Stephen Westfold
Bob Wilson
Yingwei Zhang

Table of Contents

Semantics Specification II

Mixed topics

Parallelization

Data-Flow Analysis

Optimization II

OASIS: An Optimizing Action-based Compiler Generator

Peter Ørbæk*

Computer Science Department, Aarhus University
Ny Munkegade Bldg. 540, DK-8000 Aarhus C, Denmark

Abstract. Action Semantics is a new and interesting foundation for semantics based compiler generation. In this paper we present several analyses of actions, and apply them in a compiler generator capable of generating efficient, optimizing compilers for procedural and functional languages with higher order recursive functions. The automatically generated compilers produce code that is comparable with code produced by handwritten compilers.

1 Introduction

Semantics based compiler generation has long been a goal in computer science. Automatic generation of compilers from semantic descriptions of programming languages relieves programmers and language theorists from much of the burden of writing compilers.

We describe the OASIS (Optimizing Action-based Semantic Implementation System) compiler generator, and especially the analyses that provide the information enabling the code generator to produce good quality code.

The generated compilers expand a given abstract syntax tree to the equivalent action by way of the action semantics for the language. All analyses are applied to the expanded action. The system is capable of generating compilers for procedural, functional (lazy and eager) and object oriented languages. After analysis, the action is translated to native SPARC code. For further details, see [18].

A short introduction to Action Notation is given first, and in the following section we describe a type-checker for actions, whose *raison d'être* is to allow us to dispense with all run-time type checks.

We then proceed to describe the various analyses that are carried out on the type checked action. Most of the analyses are set up in an abstract interpretation framework. The analyses annotate the action with approximate information about its run-time behavior.

The results of the analyses are used by a code generator, generating code for the SPARC processor. The code generator also employs a couple of optimization techniques on its own, namely a storage cache used to avoid dummy stores and reloads, and a peephole optimizer responsible for filling delayslots and removing no-op code.

Finally we compare the performance of the generated compilers for a procedural and a functional language with handwritten compilers for similar languages, and relate our results to previous approaches to compiler generation.

---

* The authors Internet address: poe@daimi.aau.dk

The results are very encouraging as our automatically generated compilers emit code that performs within a factor 2 of code produced by handwritten compilers. This is a major performance enhancement in relation to earlier approaches to compiler generation based on Action Semantics [20, 19, 3], as well as compared to other semantics based compiler generators.

2 Action Notation

Action Semantics is a formalism for the description of the dynamic semantics of programming languages, developed by Mosses and Watt [17]. Based on an order-sorted algebraic framework, an action semantic description of a programming language specifies a translation from abstract terms of the source language to Action Notation.

Action Notation is designed to allow comprehensible and accessible semantic descriptions of programming languages; readability and modularity are emphasized over conciseness. Action semantic descriptions scale up well, and considerable reuse of descriptions is possible among related languages. An informal introduction to Action Notation, as well as the formal semantics of the notation, can be found in [17].

The semantics of Action Notation is itself defined by a structural operational semantics, and actions reflect the gradual, stepwise, execution of programs. The performance of an action can terminate in one of three ways: It may *complete*, indicating normal termination; it may *fail*, to indicate the abortion of the current alternative; or it may *escape*, corresponding to exceptional termination which may trapped. Finally, the performance of an action may *diverge*, ie. end up in an infinite loop.

Actions may be classified according to which *facet* of Action Notation they belong. There are five facets:

- the *basic* facet, dealing with control flow regardless of data.
- the *functional* facet, processing *transient* information, actions are *given* and *give* data.
- the *declarative* facet, dealing with bindings (*scoped information*), actions *receive* and *produce* bindings.
- the *imperative* facet, dealing with loads and stores in memory (*stable information*), actions may *reserve* and *unreserve* cells of the storage, and change the contents of the cells.
- the *communicative* facet, processing *permanent information*, actions may *send* and *receive* messages communicated between processes.

In general, imperative and communicative actions actions are *committing*, which prevents backtracking to alternative actions on failure. There are also hybrid actions that deal with more than one facet. Below are some example action constructs:

- 'complete': the simplest action. Unconditionally completes, gives no data and produces no bindings. Not committing.
- 'A_1 and A_2': a basic action construct. Each sub-action is given the same data as the combined action, and each receives the same bindings as the combined construct. The data given by the two sub-actions is tupled to form the data given

by the combined action, (the construct is said to be *functionally conducting*). The performance of the two sub-actions may be interleaved.

- 'A_1 or A_2': a basic action construct, represents non-deterministic choice between the two sub-actions. Either A_1 or A_2 is performed. If A_1 fails without committing A_2 is performed, and vice versa.
- 'store Y_1 in Y_2': an imperative action. Evaluates the yielder Y_1 and stores the result in the cell yielded by Y_2. Commits and completes when Y_1 evaluates to a storable and Y_2 evaluates to a cell.

An action term consists of constructs from two syntactic categories, there are action constructs like those described above, and there are yielders that we will describe below. Yielders may be evaluated in one step to yield a value. Below are a few example yielders:

- 'sum(Y_1, Y_2)': evaluates the yielders Y_1 and Y_2 and forms the sum of the two numbers.
- 'the given $D\#n$': picks out the n'th element of the tuple of data given to the containing action. Yields the empty sort nothing unless the n'th item of the given data is of sort D.
- 'the D stored in Y': provided that Y yields a cell, it yields the intersection of the contents of that cell and the sort D.

As an example we give below an action semantics for a simple call-by-value λ-calculus with constants.

2.1 Abstract Syntax

needs: Numbers/Integers(integer), Strings(string) .
grammar:
(1)   Expr = [["lambda" Var "." Expr]] | [[Expr "(" Expr ")"]] |
            [[Expr "+" Expr]] | integer | Var .
(2)   Var = string .

2.2 Semantic Functions

includes: Abstract Syntax .
introduces: evaluate _ .
- evaluate _ :: Expr → action .
(1)   evaluate I:integer = give I .
(2)   evaluate V:Var = give the datum bound to V .
(3)   evaluate [["lambda" V:Var "." E:Expr]] =
            give the closure abstraction of
            |furthermore bind V to the given datum#1
            |hence evaluate E .
(4)   evaluate [[E_1:Expr "(" E_2:Expr ")"]] =
            |evaluate E_1 and evaluate E_2
            then enact application the given abstraction#1 to the given datum#2 .

(5)   evaluate $[\![\ E_1:\text{Expr "+"}\ E_2:\text{Expr}\ ]\!]$ =
         |evaluate E_1 and evaluate E_2
         then give the sum of them .

2.3   Semantic Entities

includes: Action Notation .
- datum   = abstraction | integer | $\square$.
- bindable = datum .
- token   = string .

3   Type Checking

The main purpose of the type-checker for action notation is to eliminate the need for run-time type-checking. If we hope to gain a run-time performance comparable to traditional compiled languages such as C and Pascal, we need to eliminate run-time type-checks, otherwise values would have to carry tags around identifying their type, and we would immediately suffer the penalty of having to load and store the tags as well as the actual values. We are thus lead to choose a wholly static type system.

Our type-checker is related to the one given by Palsberg in [20], but our type-checker is also capable of handing unfoldings that are not tail-recursive. This imposes some problems, since fixpoints have to be computed in the type lattice. Like Palsberg's type-checker, our type-checker can be viewed as an abstract interpretation of the action over the type lattice.

The type-checker has been proved *safe* with respect to the structural operational semantics of a small subset of Action Notation [18], but we will not go into details about the proof here, we just give the structure of the proof. It should be straightforward, but tedious, to extend the proof to the larger subset accepted by OASIS.

First a type inference system for a small subset of Action Notation is defined. It is shown that the inference system has the Subject Reduction property with respect to the operational semantics of Action Notation. Second, the type checking *algorithm* is proved *sound* with respect to the inference system. Finally subject reduction and soundness are combined to prove the safety of the type checker. Below we state the main safety result:

> *The type-checker is safe in the sense that, if the type-checker infers a certain type for the outcome of an action then, when that action is actually performed, the outcome indeed has the inferred type.*

As a corollary to the safety property, we have proved that all run-time type-checks can be omitted.

4   Analyses

The main reason for the good run-times that we are able to achieve for the produced code, is the analyses that we apply to the action generated from the semantics. The analyses consist of the following stages:

- **forward analysis**, incorporating constant analysis, constant propagation, commitment analysis and termination analysis.
- **backwards flow analysis**, used to shorten the lifetime of registers.
- **heap analysis**, determines which frames can be allocated on the stack, and which need to be allocated on the heap.
- **tail-recursion detection**, checking whether unfoldings are tail-recursive or not.

4.1 Forward Flow Analysis

The forward flow analysis is essentially an abstract interpretation of the action over a product of several complete lattices. The various parts of the analysis are interleaved in order to obtain better results than would be possible had the analyses been done one after the other.

The forward analyses can be divided up into the following parts:

- **constant analysis**, determines whether bound values are static or dynamic.
- **constant propagation and folding**, propagates constants and folds expressions with constant arguments into constants.
- **commitment analysis**, approximates the commitment nature of the action.
- **termination analysis**, approximates the termination mode of the action.

All of the analyses are set up in an abstract interpretation framework [5]. They are all essentially intra-procedural, so each abstraction is not analyzed in relation of all of its enactions (calls).

Constant propagation and folding is a well-known technique often used in compilers to reduce constant expressions to constants. There is nothing special about our constant propagation technique for actions. For example if the two arguments propagated to a "sum" yielder are constant, the sum is folded into a constant at compile time, and propagated further as a constant. The other parts of the forward analysis are more interesting.

4.1.1 Constant Analysis Since the constant analysis is integrated with the constant propagation, we use the following lattice of abstract values for this part of the analysis:

$$SD = (\{(Static, v), Dynamic\}, \leq)$$

where for all values v : $(Static, v) \leq Dynamic$.

The above lattice differs from the traditional lattice used in binding time analyses (eg. in [1]) by incorporating the statically known value with the Static tag. This only buys us a marginal benefit, but it is simply the obvious thing to do when the constant analysis and constant propagation are integrated.

A binding of a constant (Static) value need not have space allocated in the frame of the enclosing abstraction, as the bound value can be inserted statically wherever it is referenced. Bindings of dynamic values are associated with a cell (a memory location) in the relevant frame, and when a value is bound at run-time, it is stored in the cell, and it is retrieved from that cell whenever the bound value is referenced.

Arguments to abstractions are assumed to be dynamic. We do not attempt to do inter-procedural constant analysis. The need for such an analysis is not too great for ordinary imperative languages, where fewer and larger procedural abstractions dominate. Also, an intra-procedural analysis can be done more efficiently. We avoid the compile-time performance problems often associated with inter-procedural abstract interpretations.

Likewise, the analysis assumes that the contents of memory cells are dynamic. All loads and stores in Action Notation go through pointers, and storing a value to wherever a dynamic pointer points may over-write the contents of any cell of the same type. This problem with dynamic pointers is usually known as *aliasing* problems in traditional compilers. Since the performance of sub-actions may be interleaved, it is hard to guarantee that the contents of a cell has not been over-written by an unknown value at any given point of the performance.

4.1.2 Commitment Analysis Actions may or may not *commit*. If an action commits it means that it has made some irreversible change to the state of the machine, such as having stored a value in a cell or having sent a message to another process.

We are interested in knowing whether an action may commit and subsequently fail (ie. err) within an "A_1 or A_2" construct. If this is the case, the "or" can't trap the failure, a run-time error should be indicated and the program stopped (in the absence of commitment, an alternative action may be performed). In the CANTOR system [20, 19], a significant amount of run-time is used to check for such committed failures. Our analysis is able to statically determine the possibility of committed failures in most cases, thus much fewer run-time checks need to be inserted. The lattice used by the commitment analysis looks like this:

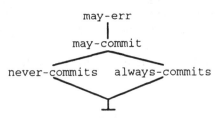

Commitment of ground actions such as "**store** Y_1 **in** Y_2" is determined by the type checker. Commitment of combined actions such as "A_1 **and** A_2" is determined by commitment of the sub-actions and the results of the termination analysis on the sub-actions. For unfoldings a fixed point is computed.

4.1.3 Termination Analysis The termination analysis computes approximate knowledge about the termination mode of sub-actions. There are many benefits to be drawn from such knowledge. For example, suppose we have the action "A_1 **then** A_2". If the termination analysis is able to guarantee that the sub-action A_1 always fails, no code need to be generated for A_2!

The termination analysis abstractly interprets the action over the power-set of the four possible termination modes (*complete, fail, escape* and *diverge*) ordered by subset inclusion:

$$\mathsf{CFED} = (\mathcal{P}\{\mathsf{AC}, \mathsf{AF}, \mathsf{AE}, \mathsf{AD}\}, \subseteq)$$

The termination mode of ground actions is determined by the type checker and influenced by the propagated constants. The termination mode of combined actions is determined by the termination mode of the sub-actions.

The termination- and commitment analyses have been formally specified in [18], although soundness still remains to be proven.

4.2 Backwards Analysis

The backwards analysis is used to shorten the lifetime of transient values. This analysis traces the data-flow backwards and increases counters in the abstract compile-time representations of values each time such values are used, ie. stored to memory, written to standard output or passed as parameters to an abstraction.

During code generation, the same counters are decreased at each point of usage and when the counter reaches zero, the register holding the value can safely be discarded for eventual re-use. This analysis is similar to the computation of *live variables* in traditional optimizing compilers.

4.3 Heap Analysis

Since abstractions are first class values in action notation, they can be given as transient data, returned from abstractions and stored in memory. As we deal with statically scoped languages, we need to provide abstractions with their correct static environment when they are enacted (called).

In traditional languages with first class abstractions, such as Scheme, all frames (or activation records) are typically allocated on the heap and it is up to a garbage collector to release the associated memory when it is no longer used. In order to avoid spending lots of time doing garbage collection, and to avoid heap allocated frames for programs in traditional imperative languages such as Pascal, we employ the heap analysis[2]. The heap analysis is yet another abstract interpretation of the action, this time over the following domain:

$$(\mathcal{P}(\{\mathsf{SA}, \mathsf{PC}\}), \subseteq)$$

The analysis traverses the action and marks each abstraction with an element from the above domain as explained in the following:

SA stands for *stores abstraction*, it means that the abstraction may store, give, or escape with an abstraction, ie. an abstraction may leak out of scope. PC stands for *provides closure*, it means that the abstraction provides (part of) the closure for another abstraction, ie. it has a syntactically nested abstraction. Only if an abstraction is marked $\{\mathsf{SA}, \mathsf{PC}\}$ need the corresponding frame be allocated on the heap. Note that the top-most

---

[2] This analysis was initially called *closure analysis* for obvious reasons, but that term has a more specific and different meaning in Copenhagen, so it was renamed.

or global frame can always be allocated on the stack as it will exist until the program terminates.

Thanks to this analysis, an action semantics for full Pascal will never give rise to code needing heap allocated closures, as it is impossible for a procedure in Pascal to leak out of scope.

4.4 Tail Recursion

In order to implement standard while loops efficiently by the "unfolding" construct, we need to be able to detect tail-recursive unfoldings, so as not to incur the overhead of a procedure call for each iteration of the loop. The action semantic equation for a while construct would typically look something like:

execute ⟦ "while" E:Expression "do" S:Statements ⟧ =
    evaluate E then
    |unfolding
    |||check the given truth-value then execute S then unfold
    |or
    |||check not the given truth-value .

In full generality, "unfold" may cause a recursive call. The tail-recursion detector traverses the body of the unfolding and marks "unfolds" as tail-recursive or recursive depending on whether any part of the loop-body may be executed after the "unfold". If there is just one recursive "unfold" in the body of a loop, then all "unfolds" in that loop are treated as recursive.

5 Code Generation

The code generator generates assembly code for the SPARC processor from the action tree annotated by the preceding analyses. The assembly code is generated in one pass, and registers are allocated on an as-needed basis.

As much of the code generator as possible is kept machine-independent, to facilitate easy porting of the code generator to other RISC processors. One machine-independent part of the code generator is the storage cache. It serves the purpose of minimizing the number of load and store operations in basic blocks. When a value is loaded from a known memory location into a register, an association between the register and the location is kept, such that a later load from the same address can be coded as a cheap register copy. Storing the contents of a register in a known memory location keeps the association between the location and the register in the same way, and the actual store is delayed until the last possible moment within the same basic block to avoid two stores to the same location just after each other. (This may not be entirely beneficial on a RISC architecture, where loads and stores should be spread out, but it was easier to implement than a full graph-coloring register allocation algorithm).

A machine-dependent part of the code generator is the peephole optimizer. A peephole optimizer is a traditional optimization technique, that is often used to remove dummy instruction sequences and to simplify instructions. Our peephole optimizer does not attempt to eliminate all dummy instructions, but is geared towards fixing deficiencies in the code generated by our specific code generator.

The code generator is pretty intricate, as there are lots of special cases to consider when one tries to generate good code for a realistic machine such as the SPARC. Perhaps a code generator generator such as iBurg [8] could be used clean this up.

6 Overview

The action compiler and compiler generator consists of many parts written in different languages[3]. This section gives an overview of the different parts and their interaction.

The compiler generator (gencomp) takes an action semantics written as a Scheme [4] program, and produces a compiler written in Perl [24]. Scheme was chosen because it was easy to implement a few macros in Scheme that make it painless to write a semantics using Scheme syntax. Also, it was felt that not too much time should be spent on this part of the compiler generator, as work is in progress that will make it possible to write action semantics in the ASF+SDF system [11].

The generated compiler driver (or front-end) is written in Perl for ease of implementation. The driver parses command-line options, calls the different parts of the compiler and takes care of cleaning up if something goes wrong, such as a syntax error in the given program etc.

The compiler takes a textual representation of an abstract syntax tree (AST) for a program in the source language, and produces, if all goes well, executable code for the SPARC processor. The AST could easily be produced by, say, a YACC or Bison generated parser for the source language.

The first step of the compiler is to massage the input AST into something resembling a Scheme program, and combine it with the Scheme representation of the semantics for the source language.

The second step runs a Scheme interpreter on the semantics and the munged program, and writes a textual representation of the action corresponding to the program to a file. Currently, the free scm implementation of the Scheme standard [4] is used.

Step three runs the action compiler on the produced action, and produces assembly code for the SPARC processor. This is the major step of the process. The action compiler consists of approximately 10,000 lines of C++ code [21], plus a lexical analyzer generated by Flex and an action parser generated by Bison.

The fourth step of the compiler assembles the output from the action compiler and links the object module with a small run-time support library providing primitive input/output routines. The run-time library is written in traditional C [10].

The produced object program reads from standard input and writes to standard output.

---

[3] The OASIS system is available by anonymous ftp from ftp.daimi.aau.dk in the directory /pub/action/systems/

7 Comparisons

Here we compare the performance of our compiler generator with handwritten compilers and other approaches to compiler generation. We consider two example languages: HypoPL and FunImp.

The procedural language HypoPL contains integers, booleans, arrays, the usual control structures (while-loops and conditionals) and generally nested procedures. The syntax and semantics for HypoPL can be found in [12, 19, 18]. The functional (eager) language FunImp contains higher order recursive functions as well as mutable data. The syntax and semantics for FunImp is derived from the language considered in [22], and is defined in [18].

All our timings, except for the run-times of the generated code, are made on an ordinary 33 MHz 386-based PC with 20 MB RAM, running the Linux operating system (version 0.99). The generated SPARC code was run on a Sun Microsystems SparcStation ELC running SunOS 4.1.1.

Generating a compiler for Lee's HypoPL language [12, 13] takes 0.8 seconds. Using the generated compiler to compile the HypoPL bubblesort program takes 3.9 seconds. As explained in a previous section, this involves running the Perl interpreter, the Scheme interpreter and the action compiler, and the result is an assembly file suitable for the SPARC assembler. The assembly code consists of roughly 250 instructions, ie. 1000 bytes when assembled.

Comparing these figures with what Palsberg obtained with the CANTOR system [20, 19] shows that the compilers we generate are two orders of magnitude faster than his, and that the code size is also two orders of magnitude smaller than his. It should be noted that Palsberg's tests were also run on a Sun SparcStation ELC.

The tables below show some results from using the generated HypoPL compiler to compile some example programs (the same programs as used in [20, 19]):

- **bubble:** A bubblesort program, bubblesorts 500 integers.
- **sieve:** The sieve of Eratosthenes, finds all primes below 512, repeated 400 times.
- **euclid:** Euclid's method of finding the greatest common divisor of two numbers (1023 and 37), repeated 30,000 times.
- **fib:** Computes the 46'th Fibonacci number 10,000 times. (The 46'th number in the series is the largest that will fit in a 32 bit twos complement integer.)

The table below lists the compile times of various programs. The first column lists the time it takes to compile the HypoPL program to assembly, the second column lists the time it takes to compile the action generated from the HypoPL program, and the last column lists the time it takes to compile an equivalent C program with optimization turned on. All times are in seconds.

Program	HypoPL	Action	C-opt
bubble	3.9	0.9	0.6
sieve	3.4	0.9	0.5
euclid	2.3	0.4	0.4
fib	2.1	0.4	0.3

The figures above indicate that something could be gained by integrating the processing of the semantic functions with the action compiler, instead of relying on a Scheme interpreter to expand the program to an action.

The generated HypoPL compiler is on average 6.5 times slower than the hand-written C compiler. Much of this slowdown stems from the Scheme interpreter. The action compiler itself compiles an action within a factor two of the time it takes to compile the equivalent C program. This is what one would expect, as the action is at least twice as large (textually) as the corresponding C program.

The "code size" column in the table below is a simple line count of the generated assembly files. The actual number of instructions is smaller because of a little overhead, such as assembler directives, labels and so forth. All times are in seconds. The fourth column gives the run-time for an equivalent program written in C and compiled with the GNU C compiler (gcc 2.4.3). The last column states the run-time for the C program compiled with full optimization turned on.

Program	Code size	Run-time	C-runtime	C-opt
bubble	254	0.4	0.4	0.2
sieve	211	1.2	0.7	0.3
euclid	144	2.1	1.4	0.7
fib	93	0.8	0.7	0.5

The above table shows that the run-times for all four programs are within a factor 1.7 of code generated by a hand-written C compiler. If we let the C compiler do its best at optimizing the program, our code is still at most 4 times slower. The main reason why our code is so much slower than optimized C code is the lack of a global register allocator. Another reason is that HypoPL allows general nesting of procedures, something that C doesn't. This has an impact on performance, since a HypoPL compiler (in the absence of a corresponding analysis) cannot take the same shortcuts as a C compiler can when accessing variables.

Unrolling the sieve program a number of times, to obtain a source program ten times as large (539 lines) yield compile times (19 seconds) about ten times longer than for the small program (2 seconds), as one would expect, since the analyses are of linear complexity. Keeping the actual amount of computation constant, we get the same run-times for the small and large program. The code size scales linearly too, of course.

The figures show that code generated with the OASIS system is about two orders of magnitude faster than code generated with the CANTOR system

7.1 FUNIMP versus scm

Here we make a performance comparison between Scheme and the generated FUNIMP compiler. The example program is a recursive Fibonacci function.

The first column below shows the number of seconds it takes to compute the result in interpreted Scheme, the second column is for the Scheme program compiled to C and then to machine code by the Hobbit [23] compiler. The last column shows the run-time for the OASIS-compiled FUNIMP program. Again our results are within a factor two of a hand-written compiler.

s cm	Compiled Scheme	FunImp
84.8	3.4	5.7

The main difference between the code we generate for fib and the code that Hobbit/C generates, is that our implementation of the conditional is less than optimal, due to the symmetric nature of the "or" action construct and our non-optimal implementation of the "check" construct. Our code actually computes the truth value, whereas C need only test the condition. Comparing against an optimized, equivalent hand-written C program, shows that our code is about 3 times slower.

7.2 Lee and Pleban

Comparing performance against Lee's system [12, 13] is difficult since it ran on much slower hardware than what is available today. Comparing the time that it took for that system to compile a HypoPL program to the time it takes for OASIS on more modern hardware would be unfair. Also, traditional compiler technology has improved since his comparisons with the traditional compilers of then, making a comparison based on those relative figures difficult.

Lee's system is based on High Level Semantics, where the static semantics is separated from the dynamic semantics, and he explicitly gives a so-called micro semantics tailored for the processor. Giving a new micro-semantics in his system would equal writing a new code generator part to the action compiler. If one were to write a micro-semantics targeting the SPARC processor, then it would be realistic to assume that code produced by a HypoPL compiler generated from the high level semantics system could be as good as the code produced by a HypoPL compiler generated by the OASIS system.

However, it seems that all optimizations in Lee's system happens at the micro-semantic level, hence a new micro semantics will be difficult to write.

7.3 Kelsey and Hudak

In [9] Kelsey and Hudak describe their compiler generator based on denotational semantics. In their system one writes denotational descriptions of languages in a variant of Scheme, and the system then performs several transformations on the resulting Scheme program, eventually arriving at assembly code for the Motorola 68020 processor.

They evaluate the performance of their system by comparing code produced by a generated Pascal compiler with code produced by the standard Pascal compiler on the Apollo workstation they used. The quality of the produced code is as good as what the standard Pascal compiler can generate, all performance figures lie within a factor 1.5 of the Pascal-generated code. Assuming that the standard Pascal compiler on the Apollo is comparable to a standard C compiler, one will have to say that the performance of their system is on a par with the OASIS system.

Apart from being based on denotational semantics, the main difference between their system and OASIS, is that their system *transforms* the meta-language (Scheme) until they reach something that is close enough to assembly to warrant a mechanical substitution from Scheme terms to assembly code. In OASIS the meta-language (Action

Notation) is not transformed, but merely annotated by the various phases of analysis, and then ultimately an intricate code generator is invoked to generate assembly.

7.4 Bondorf and Palsberg

Using the same subset of Action Notation as in [20], Bondorf and Palsberg in [2] present another compiler generator based on Action Semantics. The compiler generator partially evaluates a Scheme representation of the action generated from the semantics. The generated compilers are compared with compilers generated by the CANTOR system. In comparison with the CANTOR system, run-times of the produced Scheme code are improved by at most a factor of 4, including a hypothetical factor 5 that the authors think they would achieve, had they used a Scheme compiler instead of an interpreter. Since the produced object code from the OASIS system is two orders of magnitude faster than what the CANTOR generated compilers produce, our system is clearly superior to this partial evaluation approach to compiler generation.

7.5 Actress

Comparing performance against the ACTRESS system is difficult since only one small test program with timings is given in [3]. For the system that they had implemented at the time, they write that the code they produce (C code) is 69 times slower than the equivalent Pascal program compiled with a standard compiler. This is certainly slower than our system. With certain mechanical optimizations, that were not implemented at the time of their article, they improve performance to within a factor two of the Pascal compiler. No timings are given for how long it takes to compile a program with the generated compilers.

The Actress approach to action compilation is closer to the approach by Kelsey and Hudak than it is to ours, in that they *transform* the action generated by the semantics to gain better run-times.

8 Concluding Remarks and Future Work

We have described several analyses based on Action Semantics, and have shown how they can be applied in a compiler generator capable of generating compilers that produce code comparable to code produced by handwritten compilers for similar languages.

Even though Action Semantics was developed from a semantic perspective without regard for compilability and run-time efficiency, we have demonstrated that efficient compilers can be automatically generated from Action Semantic descriptions.

However, there are various shortcomings of the current version of the system. The type system is probably too strict, and some sort of type inference like the system by Even and Schmidt [7] would be an advantage, if it could be modified in a way that would allow us to dispense with – most or all – run-time type checks. Moreover, many useful data-types are not easily expressible in the system, such as lists and records. Again the type system would have to be extended to cater for them.

There is still ample room for improvements of the code quality. The contents of memory cells should be tracked, and loop optimizations such as strength reduction could be applied. One possible way to obtain better code would be to transform the action tree to some other internal form better suited for low level optimizations, such as RTL (Register Transfer Language) [16, 15] or structured RTL [14].

A few experiments have been made with the specification and generation of compilers for object oriented languages. A small language with classes, objects, block structure and inheritance has been specified and a compiler has been generated. We simply employ the ability of OASIS to handle higher order abstractions to model objects and methods. However, the current system is not capable of resolving non-virtual method-calls at compile time, as further analysis would be needed to accomplish that.

Work is currently going on to formally specify the various analyses described in this paper, and to prove their safety with respect to the operational semantics of Action Notation.

Further work could go in the direction of using the results of analyses on actions to say something about the source program. It would also be useful to analyze the semantic equations themselves (akin to the work by Doh and Schmidt [6]), this could perhaps cut down on the time it takes to compile actions to assembly. Generally it would be advantageous to analyze as much as possible in the compiler *generation* phase, as opposed the *compilation* phase. Typically one will apply the generated compilers more often that the compiler generator.

9   Acknowledgements

I want to thank Peter D. Mosses for encouragements and guidance in the preparation of the article. I also want to thank Ole L. Madsen for reading a draft of the paper. I must also thank the anonymous referees for useful and guiding feedback.

References

1. A. Bondorf. Automatic Autoprojection of Higher Order Recursive Equations. In N. Jones, editor, *Proceedings of the 3rd European Symposium on Programming (ESOP 90)*, volume 432 of LNCS, pages 70–87, Copenhagen, May 1990. Springer-Verlag.
2. A. Bondorf and J. Palsberg. Compiling Actions by Partial Evaluation. In *Proceedings of Conference on Functional Programming Languages and Computer Architecture (FPCA '93)*, 1993.
3. D. F. Brown, H. Moura, and D. A. Watt. ACTRESS: an Action Semantics Directed Compiler Generator. In *Proceedings of the 1992 Workshop on Compiler Construction, Paderborn, Germany*, volume 641 of LNCS. Springer-Verlag, 1992.
4. W. Clinger and J. R. (editors). Revised[4] Report on the Algorithmic Language Scheme. Technical report, MIT, 1991.
5. P. Cousot and R. Cousot. Abstract Interpretation: A Unified Lattice Model for Static Analysis of Programs by Construction or Approximation of Fixpoints. In *Conference Proceedings of the Fourth ACM Symposium on Principles of Programming Languages*, pages 238–252, Los Angeles, January 1977.

6. K.-G. Doh and D. A. Schmidt. Extraction of Strong Typing Laws from Action Semantics Definitions. In B. Krieg-Brückner, editor, *Proceedings of the 4th European Symposium on Programming (ESOP 92)*, volume 582 of LNCS, pages 151–166, Rennes, February 1992. Springer-Verlag.

7. S. Even and D. A. Schmidt. Type Inference for Action Semantics. In N. Jones, editor, *Proceedings of the 3rd European Symposium on Programming (ESOP 90)*, volume 432 of LNCS, pages 118–133, Copenhagen, May 1990. Springer-Verlag.

8. C. W. Fraser, D. R. Hanson, and T. A. Proebsting. Engineering a Simple, Efficient Code Generator Generator. Technical report, AT&T Bell Labs, 1992.

9. R. Kelsey and P. Hudak. Realistic Compilation by Program Transformation. In *Proceedings of the 16'th ACM Symposium on Principles of Programming Languages*, pages 281–292, January 1989.

10. B. W. Kernighan and D. M. Richie. *The C Programming Language*. Prentice-Hall, 1978.

11. P. Klint. A meta-environment for generating programming environments. In J. A. Bergstra and L. M. G. Feijs, editors, *Algebraic Methods II: Theory, Tools and Applications*, volume 490 of LNCS, pages 105–124, Mierlo, September 1989. Springer-Verlag.

12. P. Lee and U. F. Pleban. A Realistic Compiler Generator on High-Level Semantics. In *Proceedings of the 14th ACM Symposium on Principles of Programming Languages*, pages 284–295, 1987.

13. P. Lee and U. F. Pleban. An Automatically Generated, Realistic Compiler for an Imperative Programming Language. In *Proceedings of the ACM SIGPLAN'88 Conference on Programming Language Design and Implementation*, pages 222–232, June 1988.

14. C. McConnel. *Tree-Based Code Optimization*. PhD thesis, University of Illinois Urbana Champaign, March 1992. Draft.

15. C. McConnel and R. E. Johnson. Using SSA Form in a Code Optimizer. Technical report, UIUC, 1991.

16. C. McConnel, J. D. Roberts, and C. B. Schoening. The RTL System. Technical report, UIUC, October 1990.

17. P. D. Mosses. *Action Semantics*. Cambridge University Press, 1992. Number 26 in the Cambridge Tracts in Theoretical Computer Science series.

18. P. Ørbæk. Analysis and Optimization of Actions. M.Sc. dissertation, Computer Science Department, Aarhus University, Denmark, September 1993.

19. J. Palsberg. A Provably Correct Compiler Generator. In B. Krieg-Brückner, editor, *Proceedings of the 4th European Symposium on Programming (ESOP 92)*, volume 582 of LNCS, pages 418–434, Rennes, February 1992. Springer-Verlag.

20. J. Palsberg. *Provably Correct Compiler Generation*. PhD thesis, Computer Science Department at Aarhus University, January 1992.

21. B. Stroustrup and M. A. Ellis. *The Annotated C++ Reference Manual*. Addison-Wesley, 1990.

22. J.-P. Talpin and P. Jouvelot. Polymorphic type, region and effect inference. *Journal of Functional Programming*, 2(3):245–271, July 1992.

23. T. Tammet. Hobbit: A Scheme to C compiler. Unpublished, (available by ftp from nexus.yorku.ca:/pub/scheme), 1993.

24. L. Wall and R. L. Schwartz. *Programming Perl*. O'Reilly and Associates, 1991.

Action Transformations in the ACTRESS Compiler Generator

Hermano Moura*, David A. Watt**

Abstract. Given the action-semantic description of a source language, ACTRESS generates a compiler. The generated compiler translates its source program first to an action, and then to object code. Transformations of the intermediate action greatly improve the efficiency of the object code. This paper studies these transformations.

1   Introduction

ACTRESS [2] is an *action-semantics directed compiler generator*. That is to say, it accepts a formal description of the syntax and action semantics of a particular programming language, the *source language*, and from this it automatically generates a compiler that translates the source language to C object code. The generated compiler translates each source program to an action, which we call the *program action*, and thereafter translates the program action to object code.

We have used ACTRESS to generate compilers for a small functional language, MINI-ML, and a small imperative language, MINI-△. The preliminary version of ACTRESS[2] generated compilers whose object code was rather inefficient. However, significant improvements have since been achieved.

Inspection of typical program actions reveals many opportunities for simplification. For example, actions obey simple algebraic laws [7], which can be exploited to simplify them. However, more sophisticated transformations are needed to achieve major simplifications. Our recent work has been directed to discovering, formalising, and implementing such transformations. Our ultimate aim is to make ACTRESS generate compilers whose object code is only about 2–4 times slower than that of hand-crafted compilers.

This paper describes our recent work. The rest of the paper is structured as follows. Section 2 is a very brief summary of the ACTRESS subset of action notation. Section 3 is a brief description of ACTRESS itself. Section 4 motivates the need for action transformations in generated compilers, focusing on algebraic simplification, transient elimination, binding elimination, and storage allocation. Section 5 shows how we formalise these transformations. Section 6 outlines how we implement them, and includes a worked example of action transformations in the generated MINI-△ compiler. Section 7 concludes. Appendix A outlines an

---

* Caixa Econômica Federal, Brazil. E-mail: `hermano@di.ufpe.br`. Work supported by CNPq, Brazil.

** Department of Computing Science, University of Glasgow, Glasgow G12 8QQ, Scotland. E-mail: `daw@dcs.glasgow.ac.uk`.

action-semantic description of MINI-$\triangle$, which we use as a running example in this paper.

A fuller version of this paper is available as [10].

2   Action Notation

Action semantics was developed by Mosses and Watt [7, 8, 16]. Action semantics has very good pragmatic qualities: language descriptions are unusually easy to read, to write, and to modify.

Action notation provides a number of action primitives, action combinators, and yielders. An *action primitive* represents a single computational step, such as giving a datum (transient), binding an identifier to a datum, or storing a datum in a cell. An *action combinator* combines sub-actions into a composite action, and governs the control flow and the data flow (transients, bindings, and storage) between these sub-actions. There are action combinators· that correspond to sequential composition, functional composition, choice, iteration, and so on. Finally, some primitive actions include *yielders*, which are used to access data flowing into the action. Some of the more common action primitives, action combinators, and yielders are summarised in Table 1.

An *action-semantic description* of a programming language $\mathcal{L}$ specifies a mapping from the phrases of $\mathcal{L}$ to action notation. An action-semantic description is structured like a denotational description, with semantic functions and semantic equations, but the denotations of phrases are expressed in action notation. Extracts from an action-semantic description of MINI-$\triangle$ may be found in Appendix A.

3   The ACTRESS Compiler Generator

ACTRESS is a compiler generation system developed at the University of Glasgow by Brown, Moura, and Watt [2]. It provides a collection of modules operating on actions (represented internally as trees). These modules include the following.

$Check_\mathcal{A}$ is the action notation sort checker.[3] This infers the sort of a given action and each of its sub-actions. It annotates each action with its sort.

$Encode_\mathcal{A}$ is the action notation code generator. This translates the (annotated) action to C object code.

Other modules are generated by ACTRESS from the formal description of a particular source language $\mathcal{L}$.

$Parse_\mathcal{L}$ is a parser for $\mathcal{L}$. This parser is generated from a syntactic description of $\mathcal{L}$, $syntax_\mathcal{L}$, using the standard parser generator, *mlyacc*:

$$parse_\mathcal{L} = mlyacc\ (syntax_\mathcal{L}) \tag{1}$$

---

[3] A *sort* in action semantics is roughly equivalent to a type. The sort of an action includes the sorts of all transients and bindings passed into and out of that action.

Primitive action	Meaning
complete	Completes immediately (i.e., does nothing).
fail	Fails immediately.
give Y	Gives the datum yielded by Y, labelled 0.
give Y label #n	Gives the datum yielded by Y, labelled n.
bind k to Y	Produces a single binding, of identifier k to the datum yielded by Y.
recursively bind k to Y	As 'bind', but allows the binding of k to be used in evaluating Y.
store Y_1 in Y_2	Stores the datum yielded by Y_1 in the cell yielded by Y_2.
allocate a S	Finds an unreserved cell of sort S, reserves it, and gives it.
enact Y	Performs the action incorporated by the abstraction yielded by Y.

Composite action	Meaning
A_1 or A_2	Performs either A_1 or A_2. If the chosen sub-action fails, the other sub-action is chosen.
A_1 else A_2	Tests the given truth value, and then performs A_1 if it is true or A_2 if it is false.
unfolding A	Performs A. Dummy action 'unfold', whenever encountered inside A, is replaced by A. Used for iteration.
A_1 and A_2	Performs both A_1 and A_2 collaterally. Any transients given by A_1 and A_2 are merged. Any bindings produced by A_1 and A_2 are merged.
A_1 and then A_2	Performs A_1 and A_2 sequentially. Otherwise behaves like 'A_1 and A_2'.
A_1 then A_2	Performs A_1 and A_2 sequentially. Transients given by A_1 are given to A_2.
A_1 hence A_2	Performs A_1 and A_2 sequentially. Bindings produced by A_1 propagate to A_2.
A_1 before A_2	Performs A_1 and A_2 sequentially. Bindings produced by A_1 and A_2 are accumulated.
furthermore A	Performs A. Bindings produced by A override received bindings.

Yielder	Meaning
the S	The given transient datum labeled 0. It must be of sort S.
the S #n	The given transient datum labeled n. It must be of sort S.
the S bound to k	The datum currently bound to identifier k. It must be of sort S.
the S stored in Y	The datum currently contained in the cell yielded by Y. It must be of sort S.
abstraction A	The abstraction that incorporates action A.
closure Y	The abstraction yielded by Y, with the current bindings supplied to the incorporated action.
Y_1 with Y_2	The abstraction yielded by Y_1, with the transient datum yielded by Y_2 supplied to the incorporated action.

Table 1. Some primitive actions, composite actions, and yielders.

Actioneer$_\mathcal{L}$ is a module that translates a parsed $\mathcal{L}$ program to the corresponding program action. This module is generated from a semantic description of $\mathcal{L}$, *semantics$_\mathcal{L}$*, using the actioneer generator, *actgen*:

$$actioneer_\mathcal{L} = actgen\ (semantics_\mathcal{L}) \tag{2}$$

The actioneer generator treats *semantics$_\mathcal{L}$* as a syntax-directed translation from $\mathcal{L}$ to action notation.

Composition of the generated parser and actioneer for $\mathcal{L}$ with the action notation sort checker and code generator yields a compiler for language $\mathcal{L}$:

$$compile_\mathcal{L} = encode_\mathcal{A} \circ check_\mathcal{A} \circ actioneer_\mathcal{L} \circ parse_\mathcal{L} \tag{3}$$

We have recently added a new module to ACTRESS. *Transform$_\mathcal{A}$* is the action transformer, which attempts to simplify a given (annotated) action. This module may be used to construct a compiler that generates more efficient object code:

$$compile'_\mathcal{L} = encode_\mathcal{A} \circ transform_\mathcal{A} \circ check_\mathcal{A} \circ actioneer_\mathcal{L} \circ parse_\mathcal{L} \tag{4}$$

4 Action Transformations

When a source program is translated to a program action, the latter is generated by piecing together fragments of action notation from different semantic equations in the action-semantic description. Examination of the program action tends to reveal many opportunities for simplification. In this section we introduce some of the more common possibilities.

Algebraic Simplification

Actions enjoy a variety of nice algebraic properties [7]. For example: 'and then' is associative, and has 'complete' as a unit; 'or' is associative, commutative, and idempotent, and has 'fail' as a unit.

These algebraic laws are used by the sort checker and transformer to simplify progam actions. Consider the following MINI-Δ command:

    let var n: **int**   **in** ... n

The command is mapped to the following action:

```
furthermore
| allocate a cell then bind "n" to the cell
hence
|
| | . . .
| |
| | give the value bound to "n" or
| | give the value stored in the cell bound to "n"
```

The sub-action on the last two lines is 'evaluate $[\![$ "n" $]\!]$' – see semantic equation A.2(6). In the context of the above action, the sort checker infers that the sub-action receives a binding of identifier "n" to a cell. It follows that 'give the value bound to "n"' must fail (since a cell is not a value) and can be replaced by 'fail':

```
    ...
  | fail or
  | give the value stored in the cell bound to "n"
```

Now we can apply algebraic simplification, 'fail' being a unit of 'or':

```
    ...
  give the value stored in the cell bound to "n"
```

In fact, the sub-actions 'give the value bound to I' and 'give the value stored in the cell bound to I' in equation A.2(6) are mutually exclusive, since the sorts value and cell are mutually disjoint. At least one of the sub-actions must fail. This point is important because it allows ACTRESS to infer automatically that this 'or' corresponds to a *static* (compile-time) choice.

In addition to any opportunities for algebraic simplification in the original program action, such as the above, we shall see that other action transformations tend to expose further opportunities for algebraic simplification.

Transient Elimination

Program actions often contain 'give' actions that can easily be eliminated. For example, the MINI-Δ constant declaration "**const** $n \sim 10$" is mapped by semantic equations A.2(5, 8) to the following action:

```
give 10 then bind "n" to the value
```

It should be clear that we can simplify the action to:

```
bind "n" to 10
```

This is an example of *transient elimination*.

Binding Elimination

A typical program action contains many 'bind' actions, arising from the translation of declarations, and other actions that use these bindings. Immediate translation of the program action generates object code that explicitly manipulates sets of bindings – a large overhead. Fortunately, we can avoid this overhead in most cases, using an action transformation called *binding elimination*.

Consider the following action:

```
bind "x" to 7 hence ... the value bound to "x"
```

The sub-action 'bind "x" to 7' produces a binding of the identifier "x" to the datum 7. The scope of this binding is the sub-action following 'hence'. Within this sub-action, the yielder 'the value bound to "x"' is an *applied occurrence* of the identifier "x". Clearly, this yielder will yield 7 whenever it is evaluated, so we can simply replace it by '7'. Now the 'bind' action becomes redundant, and we can replace it by 'complete':

```
complete hence ... 7
```

This action can now be algebraically simplified.

Binding elimination can also be applied in more complicated situations. Consider the following action:

```
bind "y" to the value hence
... the value bound to "y"
```

which might be the body of an abstraction (which is given an argument value). The sub-action 'bind "y" to the value' produces a binding of the identifier "y" to a (statically) unknown datum – all we know about this datum is that it must be of sort value. Thus we cannot simply replace applied occurrences of "y" by the datum to which "y" is bound. What we *can* do is to store the unknown datum in a known cell, say cell$(1,4)$[4], and replace each applied occurrence of "y" by a fetch from that cell:

```
store the value in cell(1,4) hence
... the value stored in cell(1,4)
```

We define an action to be *statically scoped* if, for every applied occurrence of an identifier k in the action, we can uniquely identify the 'bind' action that produced the current binding of k.

We define a programming language to be *statically scoped* if every program in the language is mapped to an action that is statically scoped. Otherwise the programming language is *dynamically scoped*.

Action semantics is quite capable of specifying the semantics of both statically and dynamically scoped languages. In general, binding elimination will be fully effective in program actions generated from statically scoped languages, but only partly effective in those generated from dynamically scoped languages.

Moura's thesis [9] proposes the following sufficient condition for static-scopedness. A language $\mathcal{L}$ is statically scoped if in an action-semantic description of $\mathcal{L}$:

- 'abstraction A' always occurs in the context 'closure (abstraction A)';
- in any occurrence of 'abstraction A', 'unfolding A', or 'A_1 or A_2', the sub-actions A, A_1, and A_2 produce no bindings.

This condition is of theoretical interest because it offers, for the first time as far as we know, a definition of static-scopedness related to the programming language's *formal* description. It is also of practical interest because it will be used in a future version of ACTRESS. If ACTRESS finds the source language to be statically scoped, it will build that useful knowledge into the generated compiler and its run-time system. (Even if it finds the source language to be dynamically scoped, ACTRESS will still generate a compiler, but the overhead of manipulating sets of bindings at run-time will, inevitably, still be there.)

---

[4] This notation will be explained later.

Static Allocation

Another important transformation is concerned with storage allocation. The action 'allocate a cell' finds and reserves an unused cell; in other words, it is *dynamic allocation*. This is in fact the *only* form of storage allocation provided by standard action notation.[5]

As is well known, however, storage space for global and local variables can be more efficiently allocated in *frames* (or *activation records*). The basis of such *static allocation*[6] is as follows. All the variables local to a particular procedure P are allocated together in a frame, which is essentially a sequence of contiguous cells, and the position q of each variable within the frame is statically known. The static nesting level l of P is also known. (For the main program, $l = 0$.) At run-time, the lth display register points to the frame within which these local variables have been allocated, whenever P is active and these variables are accessible. Thus the address of each local variable is completely determined by the pair (l, q), which is statically known.

In the context of action notation, for 'procedure' read 'abstraction', and for 'main program' read 'program action'. For the purposes of the transformation about to be described, we extend action notation with a non-standard yielder, cell(l,q). When evaluated at run-time, this will yield the qth cell in the frame currently at display level l.

The MINI-Δ command "**let var** v: **bool in** $v := true$" is mapped to the following action:

furthermore
| allocate a cell then bind "v" to the cell
hence
| give true then store the value in the cell bound to "v"

Suppose, for the moment, that this action is part of the program action, i.e., it is at level 0. Instead of dynamically allocating a cell, we can statically allocate a known cell, say cell(0,5), and transform the action to:

furthermore
| give cell(0,5) then bind "v" to the cell
hence
| give true then store the value in the cell bound to "v"

Now we can apply transient and binding elimination, taking advantage of the fact that "v" is bound to a known cell:

furthermore complete
hence store true in cell(0,5)

---

[5] Action notation could be enhanced with explicit static allocation, but that would make the notation more complicated, harder to formalise, and more implementation-oriented.

[6] Some authors use *static allocation* more restrictively, to mean the allocation of fixed addresses to global variables. In this paper, however, we shall use the same term to include allocation of frame-based addresses to local variables.

If the same action occurs as the body of an abstraction, i.e., at a level greater than 0, similar transformations are still possible.

Not all 'allocate' actions can be transformed in this way. Some source language constructs demand dynamic allocation, an example being the *new* allocator in PASCAL. So we must be able to distinguish between static and dynamic allocations.

Consider an 'allocate' action contained in action A, where A is either the program action or the body of an abstraction. Let l be the static nesting level of A. Then:

– If this 'allocate' action occurs in a static context within A, replace the 'allocate' action by 'give cell(l,q)', choosing q such that cell(l,q) is not used for any other purpose in A.

In action notation it is rather easy to distinguish between static and dynamic contexts within A. Basically, sub-actions of the combinators 'or', 'else', and 'unfolding' are in dynamic contexts; all other sub-actions are in static contexts. This is, admittedly, a fairly crude test, although always erring on the side of safety.

5 Formalisation

Having motivated the principal action transformations in Section 4, our next step is to formalise them. We shall do this by means of inference rules. To formalise an action transformation we use the judgment:

$$\mathcal{K}, \mathcal{T}, \mathcal{B}, \mathcal{S} \vdash A \leadsto A', \mathcal{T}', \mathcal{B}', \mathcal{S}' \tag{5}$$

where:

– A is the original action, and A' is the transformed action.
– $\mathcal{K}$ is *sort information*, from which the sort of A can be determined.
– $\mathcal{T}$ and $\mathcal{T}'$ are *transient substitutions* applicable to the transients flowing into and out of A, respectively. The transient substitution:

$$\mathcal{T} = [d/n, d'/n', \ldots] \tag{6}$$

indicates that 'the S #n' is to be replaced by the known datum d, 'the S #n'' is to be replaced by the known datum d', and so on.
– $\mathcal{B}$ and $\mathcal{B}'$ are *binding substitutions* applicable to the bindings flowing into and out of A, respectively. The binding substitution:

$$\mathcal{B} = [d/k, \text{the } \_ \text{ stored in } c'/k', \ldots] \tag{7}$$

indicates that a scoped applied occurrence of 'the S bound to k' is to be replaced by the known datum d, a scoped applied occurrence of 'the S bound to k'' is to be replaced by 'the S stored in c'', and so on.

– S and S' are the *storage allocation contexts* before and after transforming A, respectively. The storage allocation context:

$$S = (l, q, sd) \tag{8}$$

indicates that action A is at scope level l, that q cells have been allocated statically in the current scope, and that sd indicates whether A is in a it static or it dynamic context.

Similarly, to formalise a yielder transformation, we use the judgment:

$$\mathcal{K}, \mathcal{T}, \mathcal{B}, \mathcal{S} \vdash Y \leadsto Y' \tag{9}$$

Binding Elimination

Binding elimination is formalised by the following inference rules:

$$\frac{\mathcal{K} \vdash \text{bind } k \text{ to } Y : (\tau, \beta) \hookrightarrow (\{\}, \{k : d\})}{\mathcal{K}, \mathcal{T}, \mathcal{B}, \mathcal{S} \vdash \text{bind } k \text{ to } Y \leadsto \text{complete}, [], [d/k], \mathcal{S}} \tag{10}$$

$$\frac{\mathcal{K} \vdash \text{bind } k \text{ to } Y : (\tau, \beta) \hookrightarrow (\{\}, \{k : S\}) \qquad \mathcal{K}, \mathcal{T}, \mathcal{B}, \mathcal{S} \vdash Y \leadsto Y'}{\substack{\mathcal{K}, \mathcal{T}, \mathcal{B}, (l, q, stat) \vdash \text{bind } k \text{ to } Y \leadsto \\ \text{store } Y' \text{ in cell}(l, q), [], [\text{the } \_ \text{ stored in cell}(l, q)/k], (l, q+1, stat)}} \tag{11}$$

$$\overline{\mathcal{K}, \mathcal{T}, [d/k, \ldots], \mathcal{S} \vdash \text{ the } S \text{ bound to } k \leadsto \text{ the } S \text{ yielded by } d} \tag{12}$$

$$\overline{\mathcal{K}, \mathcal{T}, [\text{the } \_ \text{ stored in } c/k, \ldots], \mathcal{S} \vdash \text{ the } S \text{ bound to } k \leadsto \text{ the } S \text{ stored in } c} \tag{13}$$

$$\frac{\mathcal{K}, \mathcal{T}, \mathcal{B}, \mathcal{S} \vdash A_1 \leadsto A_1', \mathcal{T}_1', \mathcal{B}_1', \mathcal{S}_1' \qquad \mathcal{K}, \mathcal{T}, \mathcal{B}_1', \mathcal{S}_1' \vdash A_2 \leadsto A_2', \mathcal{T}_2', \mathcal{B}_2', \mathcal{S}_2'}{\mathcal{K}, \mathcal{T}, \mathcal{B}, \mathcal{S} \vdash A_1 \text{ hence } A_2 \leadsto A_1' \text{ hence } A_2', \mathcal{T}_1' \oplus \mathcal{T}_2', \mathcal{B}_2', \mathcal{S}_2'} \tag{14}$$

Rule (10) applies when the action 'bind k to Y' binds identifier k to a known datum d.[7] The 'bind' action is replaced by 'complete', and the output binding substitution contains the information that scoped applied occurrences of 'the S bound to k' are to be replaced by d. Rule (12) formalises the latter transformation.

Rule (11) applies when the action 'bind k to Y' binds identifier k to an unknown datum. In (11), The 'bind' action is replaced by 'store Y' in cell(l,q)', and the output binding substitution contains the information that scoped applied occurrences of 'the S bound to k' are to be replaced by 'the S stored in cell(l,q)'. Rule (13) formalises the latter transformation. Rule (11) takes (l, q) from the storage allocation context, in the same way as (15) discussed below.

Rule (14) links together rules (10–11) and (12–13). In the action 'A_1 hence A_2', the bindings produced by A_1 are propagated into A_2. Therefore, A_1's output binding substitution $\mathcal{B}_1'$ becomes A_2's input binding substitution.

---

[7] This case and that of rule (11) are distinguished by whether the sort of the 'bind' action associates k to an individual d or to a proper sort S.

Static Allocation

Static allocation is formalised by the following inference rule:

$$\overline{\mathcal{K}, \mathcal{T}, \mathcal{B}, (l, q, stat) \vdash \text{allocate a cell} \rightsquigarrow \text{give cell}(l, q), [\,], [\,], (l, q+1, stat)} \quad (15)$$

Rule (15) applies when the action 'allocate a cell' occurs in a static context, where it is safe to allocate a known address (l, q). Here (l, q) is taken from the input storage allocation context. In the output storage allocation context the cell count is incremented to $q + 1$.

When we transform the program action, we take its input storage allocation context to be $(0, 0, stat)$. When we transform the body A of an abstraction 'abstraction A', we take its input storage allocation context to be $(l + 1, 0, stat)$, where l is the scope nesting level of the surrounding action.

6 Implementation

The action transformer accepts an action (annotated with sort information), and returns a simplified action.

Algebraic simplification is implemented by a simple ML function, *law*. Given an (annotated) action A, *law* A returns an equivalent but simplified action.

The more complicated transformations (transient and binding elimination, and static allocation) are implemented by ML functions *simpAction* and *simpYielder*. Given an (annotated) action A, *simpActionATBS* returns a quadruple (A', T', B', S'), in accordance with judgment (5).[8] Similarly, *simpYielderYTB S* returns a transformed yielder Y', in accordance with judgment (9).

Here now is a complete worked example of action transformations. Consider the following MINI-Δ source program:

```
let const c ~ 7;
    var x : int;
    proc p (n : int) ~ begin x := n end
in  begin x := 3; p(c) end
```

This is mapped by the parser, actioneer, and sort checker[9] to the following program action:

furthermore

---

[8] $\mathcal{K}$ corresponds to the sort information with which the action has been annotated.

[9] The sort checker replaces failing actions by 'fail' and then algebraically simplifies the result.

```
| give 7 then bind "c" to the value
before
| allocate a cell then bind "x" to the cell
before
|   recursively bind "p" to closure abstraction
|                           furthermore bind "n" to the value
|                           hence
|                           | give the value bound to "n" then
|                           | store the value in the cell bound to "x"
hence
| | give 3 then store the value in the cell bound to "x"
| and then
| | give the value bound to "c" then
| | enact (the abstraction bound to "p" with the argument)
```

This program action is simplified by the transformer to the following:

```
| store abstraction
|       | store the value in cell(1,0) hence
|       | | give the value stored in cell(1,0) then
|       | | store the value in cell(0,0)
|       in cell(0,1)
hence
| store 3 in cell(0,0) and then
| enact (the abstraction stored in cell(0,1) with 7)
```

Note the complete elimination of bindings and of dynamic allocation. The transformed program action is about half the size of the original program action.

When the transformed program action is passed to the action notation code generator, inspection of the object code (not shown here) reveals that it is structurally very similar to the object code that would be generated by a simple hand-crafted compiler. It runs about twice as fast as the object code generated without action transformations.

Larger programs show larger speedups. The more declarations the program contains, the greater the benefit of binding elimination; and the more variables the program contains, the greater the benefit of static allocation. A small set of benchmarks [9] suggests that incorporating the action transformer improves generated compilers' object code from 15–100 times slower to only 7–30 times slower than the object code of hand-crafted compilers. (These figures exclude other code improvements, such as elimination of run-time sort checks, outside the scope of this paper.)

7   Conclusion

The transformations we have discussed in this paper are not the ones found in ordinary 'optimising' compilers. The need for these transformations is a consequence of generating compilers automatically from semantic descriptions. The need for binding elimination, for instance, is a consequence of the presence of bindings in the source language's semantic description. This factor applies not only to action semantics but also to denotational semantics and other formalisms.

Denotational semantics maps source programs to λ-notation, in which environments and stores are passed around like ordinary values. Sophisticated analysis is needed to detect rather basic properties such as storage single-threadedness and block structure [14, 15]. Environment elimination can be achieved by partial evaluation [5, 6]. Any realistic denotational-semantics directed compiler generator must, however, impose some structure on the semantic descriptions it accepts. For example, the DML system [13] imposes the continuation-passing style, which guarantees storage single-threadedness.

We believe that action semantics is particularly well-suited to semantics-directed compiler generation. Action notation has much more structure than λ-notation. The concept of bindings is built in, and bindings have definite scope; the concept of storage is also built in, and is guaranteed to be single-threaded. This structure gives action-semantics directed compiler generators a better handle on the problem than other compiler generators. Equally important, the good pragmatic qualities of action semantics make it feasible for the same semantic description to be used by language designers, implementors, and programmers – which is not true of other semantic formalisms!

Other important work on action-semantics directed compiler generation has been done by Palsberg [12], Ørbæk [11], and Doh [3]. Palsberg's compiler generator CANTOR is broadly similar to ACTRESS, but it restricts itself to statically-scoped source languages. Nevertheless, the current version does not actually eliminate bindings. Ørbæk's system OASIS includes an action notation code generator that incorporates a variety of forward and backward analyses, enabling it to eliminate many time-consuming run-time checks from the generated object code.

Doh's prototyping system, based on a category-sorted algebraic model for action semantics [4], extracts a binding-time semantics from an action-semantic description. It generates a syntax-directed translator that translates the source program to a program action annotated with binding-time information. This annotation will assist a static evaluator to identify which parts of the program action can be statically performed. As compared with Doh's method, it seems that our method can eliminate more bindings, and is applicable to a larger subset of action notation.

An ACTRESS-generated compiler cannot yet match the quality of a competent hand-crafted compiler. If the source language is statically scoped, the compiler writer will *know* that every applied occurrence of an identifier I can be substituted, whereas the ACTRESS-generated compiler tests each applied occurrence individually to determine whether substitution is possible. Similarly, if the source language is block-structured, the compiler writer will *know* that variable declarations can be implemented by static allocation, whereas the ACTRESS-generated compiler tests each allocation individually to determine whether it is dynamic or static.

The compiler writer acquires this knowledge by studying the source language's description, and inferring key properties such as whether the language is statically scoped and block structured. We postulate that a future version of ACTRESS will be able to infer such properties automatically from the action-semantic description[10], and will be able to build its knowledge of these properties into the generated compiler. In effect, it will transform the semantic equations (and hence the generated actioneer) at compiler generation time, rather than transform every program action at compilation time.

The program action serves as an intermediate representation of the source program's semantics. Of course, it is commonplace for hand-crafted compilers to use intermediate representations at the interface between their front and back ends [1]. Compared to these *ad hoc* intermediate representations, however, action notation has several important advantages:

- Action notation is independent of both source and target languages. Thus it can serve as a universal intermediate representation.
- Action notation is formally specified [7]. This will allow us (at least in principle) to prove the correctness of our transformations with respect to the formal semantics of the actions.

Another intriguing possibility is to express the standard compiler transformations – such as common subexpression elimination and code motion – in terms of action notation. This would allow us to formalise the standard transformations and (at least in principle) to prove their correctness. It would also have the practical benefit of enabling us to implement the standard transformations, once and for all, in the form of a module that could optionally be plugged into ACTRESS-generated compilers.

Acknowledgments

Deryck Brown, the third member of the ACTRESS group, has made innumerable comments and suggestions on the work reported here. Peter Mosses, Simon Peyton Jones, David Schmidt, and Phil Wadler have also, at various times, provided valuable contributions. We are happy to acknowledge them all.

References

1. A. Aho, R. Sethi, and J. Ullman. *Compilers – Principles, Techniques, and Tools.* Addison-Wesley, 1986.
2. D. F. Brown, H. Moura, and D. A. Watt. ACTRESS: an action semantics directed compiler generator. In U. Kastens and P. Pfahler, editors, *Compiler Construction*, 95–109. Springer-Verlag, 1992.
3. K.-G. Doh. Action semantics-directed prototyping. PhD thesis, Kansas State University, 1992.

---

[10] We already know how to test for static-scopedness — see Section 4.

4. S. Even and D. A. Schmidt. Category sorted algebra-based action semantics. *Theoretical Computer Science*, (77):73–96, 1990.

5. C. K. Gomard and N. D. Jones. A partial evaluator for the untyped lambda-calculus. *Journal of Functional Programmming*, 1(1):21–69, 1991.

6. N. D. Jones, C. K. Gomard, and P. Sestoft. *Partial Evaluation and Automatic Program Generation*. Prentice Hall International, 1993.

7. P. D. Mosses. *Action Semantics*. Cambridge University Press, 1992.

8. P. D. Mosses and D. A. Watt. The use of action semantics. In M. Wirsing, editor, *Formal Description of Programming Concepts*, 135–163. North Holland, 1987.

9. H. Moura. Action notation transformations. PhD thesis, University of Glasgow, 1993.

10. H. Moura and D. A. Watt. Action transformations in the ACTRESS compiler generator. Report FM-94-02, Department of Computing Science, University of Glasgow, 1994.

11. P. Ørbæk. Analysis and optimisation of actions. MSc dissertation, Aarhus University, 1993.

12. J. Palsberg. Provably correct compiler generation. PhD thesis, Aarhus University, 1992.

13. M. Pettersson and P. Fritzson. DML – a meta-language and system for the generation of practical and efficient compilers from denotational specifications. In *International Conference on Computer Languages*, Oakland, California, 1992.

14. D. A. Schmidt. Detecting global variables in denotational specifications. *ACM Transactions on Programming Languages and Systems*, 7(2):299–310, 1985.

15. D. A. Schmidt. Detecting stack-based environments in denotational definitions. *Science of Computer Programming*, 11:107–131, 1988.

16. D. A. Watt. *Programming Language Syntax and Semantics*. Prentice Hall International, 1991.

A Action-Semantic Description of MINI-$\triangle$

The following are extracts from the action-semantic description of MINI-$\triangle$. Only those parts of it referred to in the paper are shown.

A.1 Semantic Entities

(1) value = truth-value | integer .
(2) argument = value | cell .
(3) bindable = value | cell | abstraction .
(4) storable = value .

A.2 Semantic Functions

- execute _ :: Command →
      action [storing] [using current bindings | current storage] .
(1) execute [[I ":=" E]] =
      evaluate E then store the value in the cell bound to I .

(2)   execute ⟦ I:Identifier "(" A:Actual ")" ⟧ =
        give-argument A then
        enact (the abstraction bound to I with the argument) .

(3)   execute ⟦ C_1 ";" C_2 ⟧ =
        execute C_1 and then execute C_2 .

(4)   execute ⟦ "let" D:Declaration "in" C:Command ⟧ =
        furthermore elaborate D
        hence execute C .

- evaluate _ :: Expression →
        action [giving a value] [using current bindings | current storage] .

(5)   evaluate N:Numeral =
        give integer-valuation N .

(6)   evaluate I:Identifier =
        give the value bound to I or
        give the value stored in the cell bound to I .

- elaborate _ :: Declaration →
        action [binding | storing] [using current bindings | current storage] .

(7)   elaborate ⟦ "const" I:Identifier "~" E:Expression ⟧ =
        evaluate E then bind I to the value .

(8)   elaborate ⟦ "var" I ":" T ⟧ =
        allocate a cell then bind I to the cell .

(9)   elaborate ⟦ "proc" I:Identifier "(" F:Formal ")" "~" C:Command ⟧ =
        recursively bind I to closure abstraction
             | furthermore bind-parameter F
             | hence execute C .

(10) elaborate ⟦ D_1:Declaration ";" D_2:Declaration ⟧ =
        elaborate D_1 before elaborate D_2 .

- bind-parameter _ :: Formal → action [binding] .

(11) bind-parameter ⟦ I:Identifier ":" T:Type ⟧ =
        bind I to the value .

- give-argument _ :: Actual →
        action [giving an argument] [using current bindings | current storage] .

(12) give-argument ⟦ E:Expression ⟧ =
        evaluate E .

An Overview of Door Attribute Grammars

Görel Hedin

Dept. of Computer Science, Lund University
Box 118, S-221 00 Lund, Sweden
e-mail: Gorel.Hedin@dna.lth.se

Abstract. An extension to attribute grammars is introduced which allows objects and references to be specified as part of a syntax tree attribution. Practical advantages of these grammars include a simpler specification of many problems in static-semantic analysis, including the specification of object-oriented languages, and a highly reduced number of affected attributes after syntax tree modifications. The resulting attributions are space-efficient and allow efficient incremental attribute evaluation in interactive language-based editors.

1 Introduction

Attribute grammars [16] and incremental attribute evaluation is a well-studied technique for implementing interactive language-based editors where static-semantic checking is performed incrementally during editing [20]. The principal idea of using AGs for incremental updates is very attractive: the attribution of a syntax tree is described declaratively, and an incremental attribute evaluator can be derived automatically from the specification. However, as is well known, there are several problems with using standard AGs [2, 3, 5, 10, 11, 12, 13, 14, 21, 24].

One problem is that standard AGs lead to low-level complex specifications for many problems in static-semantic checking. An example of this is the specification of languages with homogeneous name spaces, i.e. where declaration-sites and use-sites may appear in any order. Another example is the specification of languages with advanced scope rules, e.g. object-oriented languages where name analysis depends on the classification hierarchy and not only on block structure.

Another problem is that, even for simple languages, there are common situations where a small syntactic change results in very many affected attributes, i.e. attributes which require new values. This leads to poor performance during incremental evaluation. The typical example of this is the addition of a new global declaration which affects the environment attributes of essentially all nodes in the syntax tree.

In this paper we introduce *Door attribute grammars*, an extension to standard AGs which provides a solution to the above problems by allowing objects and reference attributes to be specified as part of an attribution. Door AGs allow complex problems to be specified in a simpler way than do standard AGs. Furthermore, the number of affected attributes after a syntax tree modification is substantially lower than for a standard AG and the potential for effective incremental evaluation correspondingly higher.

Many other researchers have also suggested solutions to the problems of using AGs for incremental evaluation, primarily to solve the problems occurring for simple block-structured languages, and to some extent modular languages. In contrast, we have addressed the more complex problems arising from specifying object-oriented languages. Our solution is more general than the earlier solutions in that more advanced attributions can be handled.

This work was done within the Mjølner project [17] and a more detailed account of Door AGs is given in the author's thesis [7]. A more elaborate example of Door AGs applied to an object-oriented language is given in [9].

This paper is organized as follows. Section 2 describes the elements of a Door AG specification. Section 3 gives an example of using Door AGs. Section 4 describes an incremental attribute evaluator for Door AGs, based on visit procedures. Section 5 describes a systematic method for constructing the visit procedures. Section 6 discusses our experience with constructing Door AG specifications and evaluators, and compares the approach to standard AGs. Section 7 discusses related work, and section 8 concludes the paper.

2 Door attribute grammars

2.1 Extended syntax trees

Door attribute grammars are based on the view of a syntax tree as a tree of objects where each object is an instance of a *node class* [6]. Rather than expressing the context-free grammar as a set of nonterminals and productions we express it as a set of node classes where superclasses correspond to nonterminals and subclasses to productions. An attributed syntax tree defined by a Door AG consists of three kinds of objects:

- syntax node objects (instances of node classes)
- door objects (instances of door classes)
- semantic objects (instances of other classes)

The *semantic objects* can be used for representing static-semantic structures, for example symbol tables. As we shall see later, it is often advantageous to model the structured attributes used in a standard AG by semantic objects in a Door AG. The *door objects* serve as interface objects between the syntax nodes and the semantic objects in order to encapsulate the non-local attribute dependencies which occur in Door AGs (this is treated in more detail below). Both door objects and semantic objects are introduced by defining them as direct or indirect *part-objects* of syntax nodes. An object denotes its part-objects by means of *static references* (references which cannot be changed to denote other objects). Part-objects and static references have the same semantics as in BETA [19].

The Door AG fragment below shows the introduction of part objects. For any A object a unique D object is created at the same time as the A object, and the

A object can refer to its D object by the static reference x. The A object is said to be the *owner* of the D object.

A: **nodeclass**
{ x: **object** D;   -- *the static reference x denotes an object of class D*
}

By adding part-objects, the complete set of objects forms an *extended syntax tree*, or *EST*, as shown in figure 1.

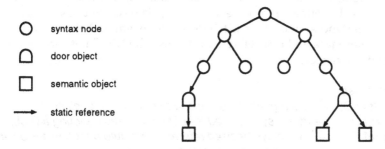

○ syntax node

◠ door object

☐ semantic object

➤ static reference

Figure 1   *An extended syntax tree*

2.2 Attributes and equations

All of the objects in the EST can have attributes. As for standard AGs the attributes are defined by equations of the form

$$a_0 := f(a_1, \ldots a_n)$$

where the attribute a_0 is defined by the side-effect-free function f applied to the attributes $a_1, \ldots a_n$. Attributes are declared as inherited, synthesized, or local. For syntax nodes, inherited attributes are defined by equations in the father node, whereas synthesized and local attributes are defined by equations in the node itself. Similarly for door objects, inherited attributes are defined by equations in the owning syntax node, whereas the door object itself defines its local and synthesized attributes. Semantic objects have only local attributes and no equations. The attributes of a semantic object are instead defined by equations in its owning door object.

We use the term "inherited" in the sense of attribute grammars, and will use the term *oo-inherited* to mean inherited in the sense of object-oriented programming. Attributes and equations defined in a class are oo-inherited by all its subclasses.

2.3 Reference attributes

Door AGs extend standard AGs by allowing attributes to be *references* to other objects. A reference attribute is declared as follows:

r: **ref** Q;

where Q is a class. The reference attribute r is said to be *qualified by* Q, i.e. it may only denote objects of class Q (objects of subclasses to Q are also considered to be Q-objects). The value of r is the *object identity* for a Q-object. Each object has a unique identity which is immutable and not affected by changes to the attributes of the object (the state of the object). Two reference attributes are considered equal if and only if they have the same object identity value, i.e. they denote the *same* object.

Reference attributes can be used to denote node objects, door objects, and semantic objects. To define a reference attribute, it is possible to use static references, self references, and other attributes. The example below shows the use of static references and self references. We use the "this"-notation of Simula [4] for self references.

```
P: nodeclass
{ x: object D;      -- x is a (static reference to a) part object of class D
  ↑rd: ref D;       -- rd is a synthesized reference attribute denoting a D object
  ↑rp: ref P;       -- rp is a synthesized reference attribute denoting a P object
  rd := x;          -- rd is defined to denote the object x
  rp := this P;     -- rp is defined to denote this P object
}
```

By using reference attributes it is possible to propagate a reference from one part to another in the EST. This allows objects to have references to other objects arbitrarily far away in the tree and thereby gives the possibility to define arbitrary directed graphs on top of the EST substrate. Figure 2 shows an example of such a graph. Note that the graphs may be cyclic. This possibility to use objects and reference attributes to define graphs is very powerful. It allows, for example, use sites to be connected directly to declaration sites and vice versa. In the specification of object-oriented languages it allows subclasses to be directly connected to superclasses. It also allows mutually recursive types to be conveniently described as objects containing references to each other.

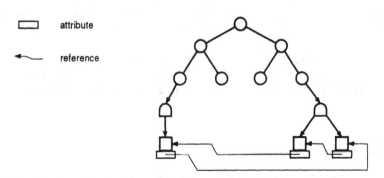

Figure 2   *Graph formed by reference attributes*

2.4 Accesses via references

An object in an EST may be connected to the following objects:

- to its son nodes (in case of a node object) via its son references
- to its part objects via its static references
- to arbitrary other objects in the EST via its reference attributes

The object may access the attributes of these connected objects using the usual dot-notation "r.a", where r is a reference and a is an attribute of the object denoted by r. The access is said to be a *local access* if r is a son reference or a static reference, and a *non-local access* if r is a reference attribute. The use of non-local accesses leads to *non-local dependencies*. Consider the following Door AG fragment:

```
D: doorclass
{  ↓ r: ref Q;      -- r is an inherited reference attribute, denoting a Q object
   ↑ b: integer;    -- b is a synthesized integer attribute
   b := r.a;        -- b is defined using a non-local access
}
```

This grammar defines the attribute b in terms of the non-local access to the attribute a. Thus, there is a dependency from a to b, but since a is located in a Q object which can be arbitrarily far away from the D object in the EST, this is a non-local dependency.

Non-local dependencies are difficult to handle in an incremental attribute evaluator: whenever the attribute a is updated we need to locate the b attribute to update it as well. To make the incremental attribute evaluation practical, Door AGs restrict the use of non-local access to occur only in the door objects. Furthermore, only attributes of semantic or door objects may be accessed non-locally. From this follows an important property:

There are no non-local dependencies involving attributes in the syntax nodes.

Thus, in order to access non-local information, or provide information for non-local access, it is necessary to introduce a door object. This design of the Door AG makes it possible to use standard attribute evaluation algorithms for the syntax nodes, while new algorithms are needed to handle the door objects.

To summarize, the communication of information between objects takes place locally from neighbor to neighbor within the EST, but can also go non-locally from a door object to another door object arbitrarily far away in the EST.

2.5 Handling large attribute values

In standard AGs it is usually necessary to have some attributes with very large structured values. Typically, such attributes are used to describe symbol tables and declarative environments in order to define name analysis. Such large attributes are problematic in many ways. From a specification point of view they are problematic because one needs to introduce auxiliary attributes which are threaded around in the syntax tree to gather all the "small" attribute values that contribute to the large value. This leads to low-level complex specifications. From the point of view of incremental evaluation, the large attributes are also problematic: Using the common evaluation technique of evaluating all attributes which depend on changed attributes, a small change to the large attribute leads to subsequent re-evaluation of all "client" attributes using the large attribute even if most of these client attributes are not affected by the change.

In Door AGs there are two mechanisms for handling the problems of large attribute values:

- Break up a large value by representing it as several small objects
- Define "collection-valued" attributes by membership declarations rather than by equations

To illustrate the first mechanism, consider the definition of a symbol table attribute. In a standard AG, a symbol table might be represented as a set of (STRING, TYPE) pairs:

ST: **set** (STRING × TYPE)

Each time the type of a declared identifier is changed, the symbol table attribute ST will get a new value. In a Door AG, a symbol table might instead be represented as a set of references to Decl objects

ST: **set** (**ref** Decl)

where each Decl object has STRING and TYPE attributes. Using this definition, a change to the type of a declared identifier does not affect the value of the symbol table attribute – its value is still the same set of references.

To split large values into small objects reduces the number of affected attributes and also the number of attributes which need to be re-evaluated (i.e., attributes which depend on affected attributes). To also simplify the specification, Door AGs have a special mechanism for defining collection-valued attributes, which we describe in the next section.

2.6 Collection-valued attributes

Symbol tables and declarative environments are usually represented by some kind of collection-valued attribute, i.e. a set, bag, sequence, finite function, or similar type. Often, there are many attributes which contribute to the collection-valued attribute independently of each other. But to define the collection-valued attribute in a standard AG, one needs to introduce auxiliary attributes which are propagated around in the tree, gathering the attribute values which should contribute to the final collection-value, leading to a complex low-level specification.

To avoid this, Door AGs have a mechanism for defining collection-valued attributes by so called *conditions* which allow objects to be declared as members of a collection. The collection-valued attribute is placed in a *collection object*, which is a semantic object but differs from ordinary semantic objects in that its attributes are defined by conditions rather than by equations in its owning door object. Collections are similar to the *set* attributes introduced by Kaiser [14] and to the *maintained* attributes introduced by Beshers [3]. See section 7 for a comparison.

The following example illustrates the mechanism. Symbol tables are represented by the class SymbolTable. A door class D1 defines a collection object of class SymbolTable and uses a synthesized attribute tbl to propagate a reference to the symbol table into the syntax tree.

```
D1: doorclass
{ collection myTable: object SymbolTable;
   ↑ tbl: ref SymbolTable;
   tbl := myTable;
};
```

The reference to the symbol table object is propagated using synthesized and inherited attributes through the tree and into zero or more door objects of class D2. A D2 object has a condition reg (for "register") to define itself as a member of the symbol table:

```
D2: doorclass
{ ↓ tbl: ref SymbolTable;
   reg: cond tbl.hasMember(this D2);
};
```

A condition has a boolean expression which must evaluate to *true* in a correctly attributed tree. In the above example, hasMember is a boolean function in class SymbolTable, and the boolean expression tbl.hasMember(**this** D2) will evaluate to true if the D2 object is a member of tbl. To maintain the condition, two operations need to be implemented in class D2:

- evalReg This operation should add the D2 object to tbl, to make the condition expression hold.
- deevalReg This operation should remove the D2 object from tbl, to undo the effects of a previous call to evalReg.

2.7 Constant objects

In addition to node, door, and semantic classes, a Door AG may also contain *constant* semantic object definitions. Such objects are declared globally and are not part of the EST. All their attributes are constant (i.e., they do not depend on any part of the EST). As an example of the use of constant objects, consider representing use-declaration bindings as reference attributes. To handle missing declarations one could declare a constant object noDecl. Each use site could have a reference attribute binding which would normally denote a declaration object in the EST. But in case there is no matching declaration for the use site, the binding attribute would denote the constant object noDecl.

3 An example

Figure 3 shows an example of an attributed EST for the following tiny Algol program:

```
begin
    integer x;
    x := 1;
end;
```

The Door AG specification of the door classes used is given in the appendix. For brevity, our example ignores multiple declarations of the same identifier. See [7] for an example of how that could be added to the specification.

- **BlockDoor** objects are used for extending the syntax tree at each block statement in the program. A BlockDoor object has two semantic part objects: a symbol table object (which is a collection of DeclDoor objects) and a so called "path" object which represents the declarative environment for use sites within the block. The path object has two attributes local and encl which connect the path object to the local symbol table (reference 1) and to the enclosing declarative environment (reference 2). In

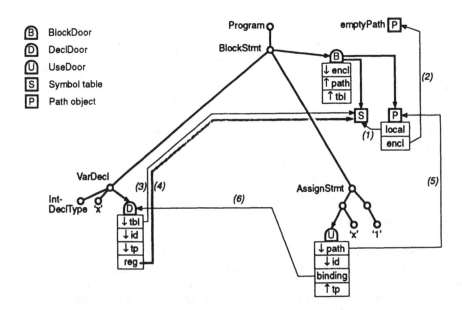

Figure 3 *Attributed EST for a tiny Algol program*

this case, the block is at the topmost level in the program and the enclosing environment is represented by the constant object emptyPath.

- **DeclDoor** objects are used for extending the syntax tree at each declaration. A DeclDoor object declares itself as a member of a symbol table tbl (reference 3) by using a condition reg (membership 4). The tbl attribute is inherited and defined by propagating the synthesized tbl attribute of a BlockDoor to each DeclDoor in the block (these propagation attributes are not shown in the figure).

- **UseDoor** objects are used for extending the syntax tree at each identifier use site. A UseDoor object has an attribute path (reference 5) which represents the declarative environment of the use site. The path attribute is inherited and defined by propagating the synthesized path attribute of a BlockDoor to each UseDoor in the block (these propagation attributes are not shown in the figure).

The path attribute is used for defining the binding attribute (reference 6) which denotes the matching DeclDoor object. The definition of binding uses a lookup function which traverses the symbol table objects reachable from path. This lookup function performs non-local accesses to attributes in the DeclDoor objects collected by the symbol tables.

3.1 Supporting an object-oriented language

The space here is too limited to give more than a sketch of how object-oriented languages can be supported by Door AGs. For details, we refer the reader to [7] and [9].

We are considering object-oriented programming languages in the style of Simula, C++, and Eiffel which all have similar scope and type rules. The basic constructs which need to be addressed for these languages are *subclassing* (in combination with block structure), *qualified access* (e.g., message sending), and *reference assignments* (doing type checking while taking the hierarchical type system into account). We have successfully specified a small example object-oriented language containing these constructs, and constructed an efficient incremental Door AG evaluator for it.

Subclassing To handle subclassing, we attribute each class with a ClassDoor which is similar to the BlockDoor above. The Path object of the ClassDoor contains reference attributes not only to the local and enclosing symbol tables, but also to the chain of symbol tables of its superclasses. This way, the Path object describes the visibility rules for free use sites occurring inside the class: first look in the local symbol table, next in the chain of superclasses, and finally according to the Path of the enclosing block. Methods inside the class are also attributed with a door similar to BlockDoor and have a Path object combining the local symbol table of the method with the Path of the enclosing class. Methods are registered as members of the enclosing class' symboltable using DeclDoor objects, in the same way as is done for variables in the Algol example.

Qualified access To handle qualified access, each class is (via its ClassDoor) attributed with a RefType object which represents the type of references qualified by that class. The RefType object is connected to another Path object, qual-Path, which describes the chain of symbol tables of the class and its superclasses. Consider a message-send "r.m" where r is a reference qualified by class C and m is a method in C. The Path object describing the environment for m is then tp.qualPath, where tp is the type of r (i.e., a RefType object). UseDoor objects are used for binding both r and m to their appropriate declarations.

Reference assignment In a reference assignment "r1 := r2", the qualifications of r1 and r2 must be compared, taking the type hierarchy resulting from subclassing into account. To support this, each RefType object is connected to the RefType object of the corresponding superclass. However, these connections may change if the user changes the class hierarchy in the program. The comparison is thus dependent on non-local information, and therefore embedded in a CompareDoor. The syntax tree propagates the reference types of r1 and r2 into the CompareDoor, and obtains the result of the comparison as a synthesized attribute of the door.

4 Incremental attribute evaluation

We have developed a systematic technique for constructing efficient incremental attribute evaluators for Door AGs. The evaluation is driven by visit procedures which are added to the node classes and door classes in the grammar. A visit procedure evaluates attributes and calls visit procedures of other objects in order to propagate the evaluation according to the attribute dependencies.

4.1 Main grammar and door package

We use the terms *main grammar* to refer to the set of node classes, and *door package* to refer to the set of door and semantic classes of a Door AG.

From an implementation point of view, the main grammar is very similar to a standard AG. Although it differs from a standard AG by allowing reference attributes, it contains no non-local dependencies, and the reference attributes can therefore be treated just like any other attributes in the dependency analysis. This allows the visit procedures for the main grammar to be constructed automatically, using standard AG methods. A door object can be treated as a special kind of son node since a syntax node communicates with its door objects in exactly the same way as with its son nodes – using inherited and synthesized attributes.

The visit procedures for the door package are more difficult to construct due to the non-local dependencies present between the door objects. We have developed a systematic method for constructing these visit procedures, but this method involves manual decisions.

The partitioning of a Door AG into a main grammar and a door package is very important from a practical point of view: the part which can be implemented automatically (the main grammar) is isolated from the part which requires manual implementation (the door package). This allows door packages to be viewed as tool boxes which extend standard AGs. Advanced facilities for common problems in static semantics can be implemented in a door package which can be used by many main grammars describing different languages.

4.2 Evaluator architecture

The attribute evaluator is implemented as a global object with operations to be called by the editor. Basic operations are: replace a subtree, insert/delete a sublist, and evaluate a whole new syntax tree. We will only discuss the replace-subtree operation since the other operations can be seen as special cases of this operation.

The evaluator starts the attribute evaluation by calling visit procedures in the syntax nodes and door objects. Syntax nodes propagate the evaluation by calling visit procedures of their neighbors in the EST. Door objects may call visit procedures of other door objects, arbitrarily far away in the EST, in order to propagate the evaluation along non-local dependencies.

The evaluator keeps a worklist of non-locally dependent doors. When evaluation propagates to a non-locally dependent door, appropriate attributes and conditions in that door are re-evaluated, but the evaluation is not immediately propagated into the owning syntax node. Instead, the door is put on the worklist and the evaluation at this site is resumed at a later stage in the evaluation. This ensures that the different evaluation threads do not collide (i.e., it is ensured that a visit procedure is never called in an object where there is already an active visit procedure).

The evaluation after a subtree replacement proceeds in the following four steps. During each of these steps, the evaluation may propagate to non-local dependent doors which are then put on the evaluator's worklist.

1. **Exhaustive de-evaluation** The conditions in the doors of the replaced subtree are de-evaluated. I.e., objects in the replaced subtree which are members of collection objects are removed from those collections.
2. **Exhaustive evaluation** All attributes and conditions in the inserted subtree are evaluated.
3. **Local incremental evaluation** Incremental evaluation proceeds in the syntax tree, starting at the successors of the synthesized attributes of the root of the inserted subtree.
4. **Non-local incremental evaluation** For each door on the worklist, the evaluation is propagated into the owning syntax node, and from there further on into the tree.

4.3 Visit procedure protocol

The different evaluation steps make use of different visit procedures as shown in figure 4. Currently, we use a simple 1-visit algorithm for the main grammar, but this could easily be generalized to any standard AG algorithm. Below, we summarize the tasks of the different visit procedures.

- **d.exhDeEvalVisit** De-evaluates all the conditions in the door object d.

- **n.exhVisit** Evaluates all the equations in the node n.
- **d.exhEvalVisit** Evaluates all equations and conditions in the door d.

- **n.incDoorVisit**(d) Re-evaluates equations in node n which depend on the synthesized attributes of its door d.
- **n.incSonVisit**(s) Re-evaluates equations in node n which depend on the synthesized attributes of its son node s.
- **n.incFatherVisit** Re-evaluates equations in node n which depend on the inherited attributes of n.
- **d.incOwnerVisit** Re-evaluates equations and conditions in door d which depend on inherited attributes in d.

- **d.deEval$_L$**, **d.eval$_L$** This pair of door procedures models a non-local visit to a door d from another door. They de-evaluate and evaluate equations and conditions according to a given non-local dependency labelled L.

5 Construction of visit procedures

We now show in some detail how the visit procedures for a Door AG are constructed. The full details are available in [7].

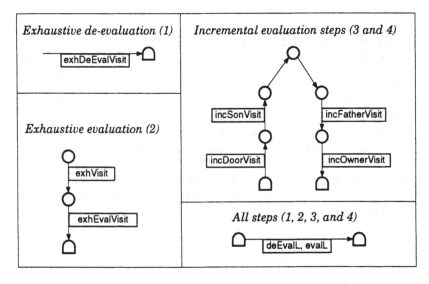

Figure 4 *Visit procedure calls*

5.1 Main grammar visit procedures

As mentioned earlier, the visit procedures for the main grammar can be constructed automatically from the grammar. In our implementation, the visit procedures implement a 1-visit evaluator (i.e. similar to an Ordered AG [15] but requiring only one visit to each node). As discussed in [7], it is possible to adapt any standard AG algorithm to the main grammars, in order to handle more advanced dependencies. This would imply merging of the exhaustive evaluation and local incremental evaluation steps. However, we have found that for our example languages we need only a 1-visit evaluator, even though the languages we have implemented would require general Ordered AGs, had the semantics been defined using a standard AG. This is because the use of references and objects in Door AGs reduces the need for complex local attribute dependencies.

5.2 Door dependency graphs

The construction of the visit procedures for the door package follows a systematic method where a dependency graph is constructed for each door class. Special *send* and *receive* vertices are added to represent the outgoing and incoming non-local dependencies. For each send vertex, a function is implemented which returns the actual set of dependent door objects. In order to implement these functions efficiently one may add so called *dependency attributes* to the door classes. These attributes are defined using equations or conditions, just like ordinary attributes, but their purpose is to make the incremental evaluator run faster. Time/space trade-offs can be made by choosing different dependency attributes.

Figure 5 shows dependency graphs constructed for our example door package. Receive vertices are added to represent the incoming non-local dependencies resulting from non-local attribute access. For example, the attribute tp in UseDoor is defined by a non-local access binding.tp. This dependency is represented by the receive vertex tpChanged. Similarly, a receive vertex lookupChanged is added to represent the non-local dependencies in the definition of the binding attribute.

For each receive vertex one or many send vertices are added, to represent matching outgoing non-local dependencies. In the DeclDoor graph, a send vertex (tpChanged, UseDoor, fUses) is added. Here, fUses is a dependency function which computes the set of UseDoors affected by a change to the tp attribute of the DeclDoor. To be able to compute this set efficiently at evaluation time, we need to add dependency attributes (see the appendix). We have added a collection uses to the DeclDoor which collects all UseDoors whose binding denotes the DeclDoor. This collection is defined by a new condition cUses in UseDoor.

To handle the lookupChanged dependency, we partly rely on the uses collection, but to efficiently handle the case of inserting a new declaration, we also add a collection attempted to the symbol tables. It collects UseDoors that have attempted to find a declaration for a given identifier in the symbol table, and is defined by the condition cAttempted in UseDoor.

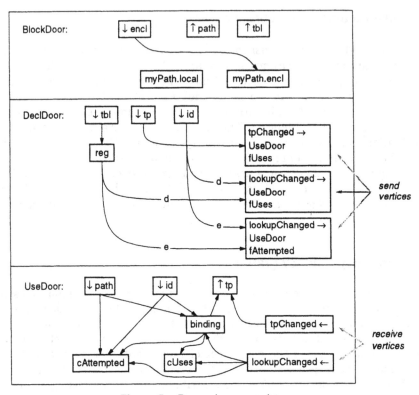

Figure 5 *Dependency graphs*

De-evaluation and evaluation edges A dependency graph edge (x,y) indicates that a change to x may affect y. An edge labelled d indicates that only the de-evaluation of x affects y. For example, id's outgoing d-labelled edge indicates that if the attribute id is changed, it is the absence of its old value which affects the UseDoors computed by uses. The outgoing e-edge indicates that the presence of the new value affects the UseDoors computed by fAffected.

Fix attributes In order to simplify the implementation of a door package, synthesized and inherited attributes of the door classes may be declared as *fix*. This indicates that the specification must be such that the attribute value will never be affected by modifications to the syntax tree, assuming that subtree replacement or list insertions/deletions are the only legal syntax tree modifications. This allows the dependencies from fix attributes to be ignored for incremental evaluation, and results in simpler dependency graphs and simpler door visit procedures. For example, we have declared the attribute encl of BlockDoor as fix. This allows us to ignore the effects of a change to this attribute, which explains why there are no send vertices in the dependency graph for BlockDoor.

5.3 Door visit procedures

Once the door dependency graphs have been constructed, the construction of the door visit procedures is straight-forward. For each of the different procedures (exhDeEvalVisit, exhEvalVisit, incOwnerVisit, deEval$_L$/eval$_L$) a characteristic subgraph of the dependency graph is considered, and the visit procedure is constructed according to the following basic outline:

1. Compute the sets of dependent doors according to the send vertices.
2. Call deEvalL for each dependent door (L is the appropriate send vertex label)
3. De-evaluate local conditions
4. Evaluate local conditions and equations
5. Call evalL for each dependent door
6. Add the dependent doors to the evaluator's worklist

For example, to construct the exhDeEvalVisit procedure one considers a characteristic subgraph containing all the condition vertices, none of the local equation vertices, and only those send vertices which have an incoming d-edge reachable from a condition vertex.

6 Practical experience

We have specified and implemented Door AGs for both block-structured and object-oriented languages with homogeneous namespaces. In addition, an earlier variant of the technique was used for implementing the incremental static-semantic analyzer for Simula in the Mjølner Orm environment [18]. Both Orm and the Door AG evaluators are implemented in Simula and run on SUN SPARC stations. Below, we summarize our experience by comparing our example Door AGs with corresponding standard AGs.

Number of attributes   The number of attributes is about the same for Door AGs and standard AGs. The Door AGs have additional dependency attributes which are not present in the standard AGs. On the other hand, the standard AGs have additional auxiliary attributes used to compute the symbol tables.

Number of affected attributes   For changes to declarations, the number of affected attributes in our Door AGs is proportional to the number of affected use sites, i.e. use sites which need to be rebound or re-typechecked. For the standard AGs, the number of affected attributes is much larger and grows with the size of the syntax tree. For other changes, the number of affected attributes is about the same for Door AGs and standard AGs.

Attribute dependencies   The main grammars for our Door AGs have only 1-visit dependencies whereas the corresponding standard AGs are Ordered AGs. The reason for this is of course that the standard AGs build up the symbol table by using auxiliary attributes which in effect correspond to the passes of a batch compiler. The Door AGs use collection objects instead.

By considering also the non-local dependencies, Door AGs may have circular dependencies, which indeed our Door AGs have. However, although the grammar as a whole is circular, the simple and efficient 1-visit evaluation technique can still be used for the main grammar. The circular evaluation is handled during the non-local incremental evaluation (step 4) by the iteration over the worklist. A non-locally dependent door on a cycle may be added multiple times to the worklist during this iteration.

Space consumption In our Door AG implementations, we have made heavy use of *demand attributes*, i.e. attributes whose values are not stored, but instead computed each time they are accessed. As a general rule, we store only those attributes where something non-trivial is computed, whereas all attributes defined by copy rules are implemented as demand attributes.

The resulting space consumption for the Door AGs is very low, approaching that of commercial hand-coded systems. The Rational Ada system [27] (a commercial incrementally compiling programming environment) is reported to use an average of 35 bytes per syntax node for syntactic and static-semantic information. By assuming a 12 byte overhead per object for the implementation language,[1] we have calculated the space required for our Door AGs to be an average of 60 bytes per syntax node. (This includes the dependency attributes.) The space consumption in our actual implementation is higher, due to a higher object overhead in our implementation language.

Efficiency of evaluator Optimality of incremental attribute evaluators is usually defined in terms of the number of attributes re-evaluated as compared to the number of actually affected attributes [20]. Using this criterion our Door AG evaluators are close to optimal for normal programs. We have some suboptimality due the following factors:

- Demand attributes
- Dependency functions which sometimes locate a few too many dependents.[2]
- Uncoordinated evaluation threads in the non-local incremental evaluation.
- Updating of dependency attributes

While it is possible to construct pathological programs where these factors do make a difference, it is our experience that they are negligible for normal programs.

For practical purposes the usual optimality criterion is not necessarily a very useful measure. From a system perspective, there are only some of the attributes that are actually interesting, whereas many other attributes are present only in order to define the interesting attributes. The problem is that all these uninteresting attributes are included in the traditional optimality

---

1. This would cover one pointer to the class template, one for the static link, and one for garbage collection. For an implementation language like C++, our figures would be even lower.

2. This happens in the Door AG for the object-oriented language when the class hierarchy is changed. See [8] for details.

criterion. Thus, an optimal algorithm may then optimally evaluate a lot of uninteresting attributes, which is exactly the problem with the standard AG optimal incremental evaluators.

A more practically interesting optimality criterion is to compare the evaluator performance with the number of interesting attributes which are affected. If we consider all the attributes of the door packages (excluding dependency attributes) to be interesting, our Door AG evaluators are still close to optimal for normal programs. The evaluators for standard AGs which are optional in terms of the usual criterion, are on the other hand not anywhere near optimality using this measure.

From a practical point of view our Door AG evaluators are fast. This is because they are close to optimal, using the interesting optimality criterion, and because they are based on static dependency analysis and visit procedures which have a very low overhead during evaluation. Although our actual implementations leave much to be optimized, we have split-second response-times on changes to global declarations regardless of program sizes (the largest tested programs are around 1000 lines).

7 Related work

Nonlocal productions Johnson and Fischer suggested extending AGs with *non-local productions* [12, 13]. A nonlocal production connects a number of "interface" syntax nodes which may be distant from each other in the syntax tree, and allows attribute values to propagate directly along these connections. For example, type-changes can be propagated directly from declared identifiers to their corresponding uses. However, they do not provide any general technique for updating the non-local productions incrementally, and the technique does therefore not improve on standard AGs in the case of added and removed declarations.

Predefined finite function types Hoover and others [10, 11, 21] have developed mechanisms for improving incremental evaluation without extending or changing the standard AG formalism as such. They provide special evaluation support for a built-in abstract data type for finite functions which is useful for defining symbol table attributes. The technique allows changes, additions, and deletions of declarations to be propagated directly to the affected use sites, thus solving the basic performance problems of standard AGs in the case of simple block-structured languages. However, the finite function values are not first class values and may not be stored as a part of another value. This prevents them from being used in lookup of identifiers whose environment depends on other identifier lookups, which is precisely what is needed to handle subclassing and qualified access.

Collections The collections and conditions used in Door AGs are similar to the *set* and *membership* constructs of Kaiser [14], and to the *maintained* and *constructor* attributes of Beshers [3]. These techniques all allow the distributed definition of a collection-valued attribute. However, the two latter approaches are limited compared to Door AGs because they allow non-local access (declaration site memberships or use site lookups) only if the set/maintained attribute is located in an ancestor syntax node. Since collections in Door AGs are accessed via reference attributes, there are no such restrictions on the location of the collection objects. This is important in order to support subclassing and qualified access, where the symbol tables used in lookup are, in general, not in the use site's chain of ancestor nodes.

Visibility networks   Vorthmann has developed a graphical technique called *visibility networks* (VN) for describing name visibility and bindings in programming languages [24, 25]. He has exemplified the power of the technique by specifying complex visibility rules of Ada. The technique has several similarities to Door AGs. The VN language is analogous to an advanced generic door package for name analysis which can be parametrized to support different languages. Vorthmann has also implemented an efficient incremental VN evaluator which is analogous to a door package evaluator. Combining the two approaches seems like a fruitful line of further research. If the VN language can in fact be formulated as a real generic door package it would become a very powerful library component in a Door AG-based system. From the VN perspective, Door AGs would provide an attractive way of formalizing the connections between the VNs and the syntax tree. We are currently investigating these possibilities together with Vorthmann.

Attributed Graph Specifications   Alpern et al. have developed a specification technique called *attributed graph specifications* (AGS) which generalizes attribute grammars by supporting the specification of attributed general graphs rather than attributed trees [1]. This is useful if the underlying edited structure is a general graph rather than an abstract syntax tree. Example applications include hardware designs and module interconnection graphs. AGSs and Door AGs thus aim at solving different problems and extend standard AGs in different ways: AGSs by extending the edited substrate from a tree to a graph, Door AGs by extending the domain of attribute values to include references. The graph formed by the reference attributes in a Door AG syntax tree is thus derived from the syntax tree, whereas the graph in an AGS system is constructed explicitly by the user.

Higher-Order AGs   In Higher-Order AGs [26, 23], a syntax tree may define subordinate syntax trees as attributes, installed as so called *nonterminal attributes*. The syntax trees of the nonterminal attributes are themselves attributed and may define their own nonterminal attributes, and so on. This scheme is useful for modelling transformations to intermediate languages, macro processing, and many other interesting applications. Door AGs may at first sight seem related to HAGs because the syntax tree is extended by additional objects. However, the existence of the door objects and semantic objects depend solely on the class of their owning syntax node, and do not at all depend on attribute values. Thus, Door AGs is a first-order formalism, and the mechanisms of HAGs are orthogonal to those presented here.

Syntactic references   The Synthesizer Generator (SG) supports *syntactic references*, i.e., references to syntax nodes can be used to define attribute values [22]. This is convenient because it allows, e.g., the declaration part of a block's syntax tree to be used directly as a symboltable attribute, rather than building a corresponding structure in the attribute domain. However, an SG syntactic reference stands for a complete syntax subtree, viewed as a structured value. This is fundamentally different from Door AGs where a reference stands only for the identity of an object, and the contents of the object is not included in the reference value. Thus, the number of affected attributes does not decrease by using SG syntactic references, and they cannot be used to construct cyclic structures. Furthermore, the SG syntactic references are considered to stand for *unattributed* subtrees. An extension to view them as *attributed* subtrees was proposed in [23], but the implementational consequences of such an extension were not investigated.

8 Concluding remarks

In this paper we have given an overview of Door AGs and the implementation of incremental attribute evaluators for such grammars. Our experience is that the use of references and objects in the syntax tree attributions is very powerful and greatly facilitates the specification of complex problems, in particular name analysis. Due to limited space we had to focus on a simple example of a block-structured language, but the advantages are even more apparent when specifying more complex languages like object-oriented languages. We sketched how the technique can be used to specify subclassing, qualified access, and type checking of reference assignments. The resulting attributions have a low cost in space and the incremental attribute evaluators we have constructed are fast in practice.

There are many interesting possibilities for future work. One is to work on automatizing the implementation of the door packages, either for arbitrary packages, or for some suitable subcategories. Another important issue is to develop more examples, both in the direction of providing general door packages which are applicable to many different languages, and in the direction of supporting more advanced language constructs, e.g. the virtual classes of BETA [19]. We also believe that the use of references and objects in specifications has a wider general applicability.

Acknowledgments
I would like to thank Boris Magnusson, Bill Maddox, and the anonymous referees for useful comments on an earlier draft of this paper.

References

[1]   B. Alpern, A. Carle, B. Rosen, P. Sweeney, and K. Zadeck. Graph attribution as a specification paradigm. In *Proceedings of the ACM SIGSOFT/SIGPLAN Software Engineering Symposium on Practical Software Development Environments*, pp 121–129. Boston, Ma., 1988. ACM SIGPLAN Notices 24(2).

[2]   R. A. Ballance. *Syntactic and Semantic Checking in Language-Based Editing Systems*. PhD thesis, Computer Science Division – EECS, Univ. of California, Berkeley, 1989. TR UCB/CSD 89/548.

[3]   G. M. Beshers and R. H. Campbell. Maintained and constructor attributes. In *Proceedings of the SIGPLAN 85 Symposium on Language Issues in Programming Environments*, pages 34–42, Seattle, Wa., 1985. ACM. SIGPLAN Notices, 20(7).

[4]   O.-J. Dahl, B. Myhrhaug, and K. Nygaard. SIMULA 67 common base language. NCC Publ. S-2, Norwegian Computing Centre, Oslo, May 1968. Revised 1970 (Publ. S-22), 1972, and 1984. Swedish Standard SS 63 61 14, 1987.

[5]   A. Demers, A. Rogers, and F. K. Zadeck. Attribute propagation by message passing. In *Proceedings of the SIGPLAN 85 Symposium on Language Issues in Programming Environments*, pp 43–59, 1985. ACM. SIGPLAN Notices, 20(7).

[6]   G. Hedin. An object-oriented notation for attribute grammars. In S. Cook, editor, *Proceedings of the 3rd European Conference on Object-Oriented Programming (ECOOP'89)*, BCS Workshop Series, pages 329–345, Nottingham, U.K., July 1989. Cambridge University Press.

[7]   G. Hedin. *Incremental semantic analysis*. PhD thesis, Lund University, Lund, Sweden, 1992. Tech. Rep. LUTEDX/(TECS-1003)/1-276/(1992).

[8]   G. Hedin. Incremental name analysis for object-oriented langauges. In [17].

[9]   G. Hedin. Using door attribute grammars for incremental name analysis. In [17].

[10] R. Hoover. *Incremental Graph Evaluation*. PhD thesis, Cornell University, Ithaca, N.Y., May 1987. Tech. Rep. 87-836.

[11] R. Hoover and T. Teitelbaum. Efficient incremental evaluation of aggregate values in attribute grammars. In *Proceedings of the SIGPLAN '86 Symposium on Compiler Construction*, pages 39–50, July 1986. ACM SIGPLAN Notices, 21(7).

[12] G. F. Johnson and C. N. Fischer. Non-syntactic attribute flow in language based editors. In *Proc. 9th POPL*, pp 185–195, Albuquerque, N.M., January 1982. ACM.

[13] G. F. Johnson and C. N. Fischer. A meta-language and system for nonlocal incremental attribute evaluation in language-based editors. In *Proc. 12th POPL*, pages 141–151, New Orleans, La., January 1985. ACM.

[14] G. Kaiser. *Semantics for Structure Editing Environments*. PhD thesis, Carnegie-Mellon University, Pittsburgh, Pa., May 1985. CMU-CS-85-131.

[15] U. Kastens. Ordered attribute grammars. *Acta Informatica*, 13:229–256, 1980.

[16] D. E. Knuth. Semantics of context-free languages. *Mathematical Systems Theory*, 2(2):127–145, June 1968.

[17] J. L. Knudsen, M. Löfgren, O. L. Madsen, and B. Magnusson. *Object oriented environments: the Mjølner approach*. Prentice Hall, 1993.

[18] B. Magnusson. The Mjølner Orm system. In [17].

[19] O. L. Madsen, B. Møller-Pedersen, and K. Nygaard. *Object Oriented Programming in the BETA Programming Language*. ACM Press, 1993.

[20] T. Reps. *Generating Language-Based Environments*. MIT Press, 1984.

[21] T. Reps, C. Marceau, and T. Teitelbaum. Remote attribute updating for language-based editors. In *Proc. 13th POPL*, pages 1–13, January 1986. ACM.

[22] T. W. Reps and T. Teitelbaum. The Synthesizer Generator. *A system for constructing language-based editors*. Springer-Verlag, 1988.

[23] T. Teitelbaum and R. Chapman. Higher-order attribute grammars and editing environments. In *Proceedings of the ACM SIGPLAN'90 Conference on Programming Language Design and Implementation*, pages 197–208. White Plains, N. Y., June 1990.

[24] S. A. Vorthmann. *Syntax-Directed Editor Support for Incremental Consistency Maintenance*. PhD thesis, Georgia Institute of Technology, Atlanta, Ga., June 1990. TR GIT-ICS-90/03.

[25] S. A. Vorthmann. *Modelling and Specifying Name Visibility and Binding Semantics*. CMU-CS-93-158. Carnegie Mellon University, Pittsburgh, Pa., July 1993.

[26] H. H. Vogt, S. D. Swierstra, and M. F. Kuiper. Higher-order attribute grammars. In *Proceedings of the ACM SIGPLAN '89 Conference on Programming Language Design and Implementation*, pages 131-145, Portland, Or., June 1989. ACM SIGPLAN Notices, 24(7).

[27] T. Wilcox and H. Larsen. The interactive and incremental compilation of ADA using Diana. Internal report, Rational, 1986.

Appendix

Door package

Path: **class**
{ lookup: **ref** (DeclDoor) **func** (id: STRING);
};

BlockPath: **class** Path
{ local: **ref** SymbolTable;
  encl: **ref** Path;
  impl lookup
    := **let** res := local.lookup(id) **in**
        if res = **none**
        then encl.lookup(id)
        else res;
};

emptyPath: **object** Path
{ **impl** lookup
    := **none**;
};

SymbolTable: **class**
{ state: **seq**(**ref** DeclDoor);
  add: **proc**(d: **ref** DeclDoor) { ... };
  rem: **proc**(d: **ref** DeclDoor) { ... };
  hasMember: boolean **func**
    (d: **ref** DeclDoor) := ...;
  lookup: **ref** (DeclDoor) **func**
    (id: STRING) := ...;
};

BlockDoor: **doorclass**
{ ↓ encl: **ref** Path **fix**;
  ↑ path: **ref** Path **fix**;
  ↑ tbl: **ref** SymbolTable **fix**;
  collection myTable: **object** SymbolTable;
  myPath: **object** BlockPath;
  myPath.local := myTable;
  myPath.encl := encl;
  path := myPath;
  tbl := myTable;
};

DeclDoor: **doorclass**
{ ↓ tbl: **ref** SymbolTable **fix**;
  ↓ tp: TYPE;
  ↓ id: STRING;
  reg: **cond** tbl.hasMember(**this** DeclDoor);
};

UseDoor: **doorclass**
{ ↓ path: **ref** Path;
  ↓ id: STRING;
  ↑ tp: TYPE;
  binding: **ref** DeclDoor;
  binding := path.lookup(id);
  tp :=   **if** binding = **none**
           then unknownType
           else binding.tp;
};

Dependency attributes and functions

addto SymbolTable
{ **collection** attempted: **object**
  { state: **set**(STRING × **set** (**ref** UseDoor));
    hasMember: boolean **func** (id: STRING, u: **ref** UseDoor) := ... ;
    attemptsAt: **set**(**ref** UseDoor) **func** (id: STRING)
      := ... *returns the set of* UseDoors *associated with* id;
  };
};

addto DeclDoor
{ **collection** uses: **object**
  { state: **set** (**ref** UseDoor);
    hasMember: boolean **func** (u: **ref** UseDoor) := ... ;
  };
  fUses: **set** (**ref** UseDoor) **func** := uses.state;
  fAttempted: **set** (**ref** UseDoor) **func**(id: STRING) := tbl.attempted.attemptsAt(id);
};

addto UseDoor
{ cUses: **cond**
    if binding ≠ **none**
    then binding.uses.hasMember(**this** UseDoor)
    else true;
  cAttempted: **cond**
    the expression t.attempted.hasMember(id, **this** UseDoor) *is true for each symbol
    table* t *occurring on* path *before the symbol table where* binding *is found (or for all the
    symbol tables on* path *in case* binding = **none**).
};

Coupling Evaluators
for Attribute Coupled Grammars*

Gilles ROUSSEL, Didier PARIGOT & Martin JOURDAN

INRIA
Projet "ChLoE", Bât. 13, Domaine de Voluceau, Rocquencourt, BP 105
F-78153 Le Chesnay Cedex, France
E-mail: {Gilles.Roussel,Didier.Parigot,Martin.Jourdan}@inria.fr

Abstract. Some years ago, the notion of attribute coupled grammars
was introduced by Ganzinger and Giegerich [4], together with descriptional composition. The latter works essentially at the specification level,
i.e., it produces an attribute grammar which specifies the composition of
two attribute coupled grammars.

We introduce a new approach to this composition of attribute coupled
grammars. This composition no longer works at the specification level but
at the evaluator level. It produces a special kind of attribute evaluator.
For this purpose we have introduced the notion of coupling evaluator.

The main advantage of this new approach, compared with descriptional
composition, is that it is possible to build separately the coupling evaluator of each attribute coupled grammar; in other words it allows real
separate compilation of AG modules.

Another important advantage is that we do not need to check the attribute grammar class in order to construct the final sequence of evaluators; thus, this construction produces a new sort of evaluator.

1 Introduction

Since Knuth's seminal paper introducing attribute grammars (AGs) [10], it has
been widely recognized that this method is quite attractive for specifying every
kind of syntax-directed computation, the most obvious application being compiler construction. Apart from pure specification-level features —declarativeness,
structure, locality of reference— an important advantage of AGs is that they are
executable, i.e., it is possible to automatically construct, from an AG specifying
some computation, a program which implements it. One could thus expect that
they are used heavily to develop practical, production-quality, applications.

Unfortunately, it appears that this is not yet the case, although AGs have
been around for quite a long time and although powerful AG-processing systems
are now available (e.g., FNC-2 [9], which is the base of the present work; see also
[1] for a good list of other systems). In our opinion, the main reason for this is
that AGs still cruelly lack the same support for modularity as the one which is
offered by most programming languages, even the oldest ones [8].

* This work was supported in part by ESPRIT Project #5399 "COMPARE".

This is the reason why Attribute Coupled Grammars and Attribute Couplings (AC) were introduced in [4] to allow modularity in AG specifications. An application can be decomposed into several attribute couplings, each of which transforms an input syntax tree into a new output syntax tree. This has been widely recognized as a very important concept for attribute grammar modularization.

As separate compilation of each AC into a classical evaluator leads to a loss of efficiency compared to non-modular specifications (because of intermediate tree constructions), descriptional composition has been introduced to create, from a modular specification, a large attribute grammar which avoids any intermediate tree construction.

In our system based on Strongly Non-Circular (SNC) attribute grammars [9], this construction looses a bit of power because the SNC class is not closed under descriptional composition [6]: the attribute grammar resulting from the descriptional composition of SNC modules is not necessarily SNC. Moreover, in the context of attribute grammar reuse [3], descriptional composition appeared to be limited due to the need for complete reconstruction of the resulting attribute grammar before any evaluator construction: separate compilation is impossible.

These observations and our personal work on attribute grammars reusability [7,11] have led us to introduce a new technique allowing separate compilation of modules as in [3] but with no intermediate tree construction. This technique is based on the simple but powerful idea of descriptional composition, i.e. attaching computations of an attribute grammar to the tree construction actions of the attribute coupling which precedes it in a sequence. The main difference between descriptional composition and our technique is that we do not work at the specification level but at the evaluator level. To do so, we introduce new sorts of evaluators, called *coupling evaluators* and *parameterizable evaluators*.

Given a sequence of ACs, we construct a parameterizable evaluator for the last AC. This evaluator is very similar to a classical evaluator, except that it only sees one special production instance of its input tree at each time. When placed at the end of a sequence, when it wants to move in its input tree (change to a neighbouring node, i.e. another production instance), it queries the "visit selector" mechanism which performs the move in the input tree of the first grammar in the sequence. The result is a new production instance which is passed through the coupling evaluators attached to the different ACs of the sequence. Each of them transforms its input production instance into a new production instance for its output grammar. The last created production instance is the production instance that the parameterizable evaluator requires.

Beside good properties of separate compilation and efficiency, this technique brings an interesting result for attribute grammar evaluators: since it avoids all problems of class closure under descriptional compilation, it can construct an evaluator based on visit sequences for a non-SNC attribute grammar, provided that it is correctly modularized [6]. This method essentially differs from the approach in [3], by providing separate compilation while keeping the property of the descriptional composition that the intermediate trees are not constructed.

2 Outline of Attribute Couplings and their Descriptional Composition

First, we recall some notations and definitions on Attribute Grammars and Attribute Couplings, but for complete definitions readers should refer to the excellent paper by Ganzinger and Giegerich [4].

Definition 1. A *context-free grammar* is a tuple $G = (N, T, Z, P)$ in which:

- N is a set of non-terminals;
- T is a set of terminals, $N \cap T = \emptyset$;
- Z is the root non-terminal (start symbol), $Z \in N$;
- P is a set of productions,
  $p : X_0 \to X_1 \ldots X_n$ with $X_0 \in N$ and $X_i \in (T \cup N)$.

Notations for a grammar G:

t denotes a syntax tree of G;
u denotes a node of t;
$label(u)$ notes the non-terminal at u;
$prod(u)$ denotes the production at u;
$Pos(u, i)$ denotes the child of node u at position i.

Other notations will be defined as needed, but most of them are quite well-known or hopefully self-explanatory. To introduce our coupling evaluators, we first recall the definition of attribute grammars where the attributes are typed by sorts.

Definition 2 (Attribute Grammar). An *Attribute Grammar* is a tuple $AG = (G, S, A, F)$ where:

- $G = (N, T, Z, P)$ is a context-free grammar as in definition 1.
- S is a set of sorts;
- $A = \bigcup A(X)$ is a set of attributes attached to $X \in N$, noted $X.a$, with $type(a) \in S$;
- $F = \bigcup F(p)$ is a set of attribute rules where f_{p,a,X_i} designates the attribute rule defining the attribute a of non-terminal X_i in production p.

Non-terminals and terminals of a given grammar can be sorts for some attribute grammar, whose result is then one or more trees of this grammar. Productions are constructors for non-terminal sorts, and terminal sorts are identified with the single constant they contain.

We introduce a simple definition of Attribute Couplings, derived from the one by Ganzinger and Giegerich [4]. Our definition is a restriction of the latter; it disallows any semantic computation and forbids the attribute rules of F to be complex tree-construction rules. We say that this kind of AC is a *purely syntactic AC*. With these restrictions, the definition of descriptional composition and our construction of coupling evaluators are simpler. At the end of this paper we give an informal presentation of how to relax these restrictions.

Definition 3 (Attribute Coupling). We call *Attribute Coupling* of G_1 and G_2, noted $\alpha : G_1 \rightarrow G_2$, an attribute grammar $\alpha = (G_1, S_\alpha, A_\alpha, F_\alpha)$ such that:

- $S_\alpha \subset (N_2 \cup T_2)$;
- each $f_{p,a,X_i} \in F_\alpha$ is either a copy rule or a tree-construction rule associated with a production of P_2;
- the root non-terminal Z_1 has a unique attribute z_2 of type Z_2.

An AC $\alpha : G_1 \rightarrow G_2$ takes as input a tree of G_1 and gives as output a tree of G_2.

For descriptional composition to be well defined, we require that each attribute occurrence of a given production appears once and only once in the attribute rules, either in the LHS (if it is defined) or in the RHS (if it is used). Each attribute occurrence of a given production can thus be associated with a unique attribute rule in this production.

In the sequel, for the sake of simplicity, we consider the copy rules, of the form $X.a := Y.b$, as tree-construction rules $X.a := Id_{type(a)}(Y.b)$. So we assume that each attribute coupling is extended with an identity construction Id_X for each non-terminal X in the input grammar. The attribute rules attached to these new productions are only composed of copy rules between the same attributes of the left hand side and the right hand side non-terminal. Thus, in the following definitions, we do not need to add a special case for copy rules.

Example of attribute coupling We have rephrased the example of the list inversion AG [5] using our notation, see figure 1. The input and the output grammar of this AG are the same list grammar. In the next section, we also use this example to construct a coupling evaluator. $\diamond$

$$type(z) = Z;$$
$$type(s) = type(h) = L;$$

$p_1 : Z \rightarrow L$ $L.h := p_3();$ $Z.z := p_1(L.s);$

$p_2 : L_0 \rightarrow L_1 D$ $L_1.h := p_2(L_0.h, D);$ $L_0.s := Id_L(L_1.s);$

$p_3 : L \rightarrow$ $L.s := Id_L(L.h);$

Added production for copy rules:

$$Id_L : L_0 \rightarrow L_1 \quad L_0.s := Id_L(L_1.s); \quad L_1.h := Id_L(L_0.h);$$

Fig. 1. Attribute coupling performing list inversion

The aim of descriptional composition is to construct, for a given sequence of two attribute couplings, a new attribute coupling which has the same semantics as this AC sequence. This new AC has the advantage of not performing the construction of the intermediate tree of G_2.

The basic idea of the descriptional composition algorithm is, given two ACs $\alpha : G_1 \to G_2$ and $\beta : G_2 \to G_3$, to project the attribute rules of a given production p_2 of G_2 onto the productions of G_1 where there exists an attribute rule performing the construction of p_2. This projection follows the structure of this attribute rule. Descriptional composition is a purely syntactic construction. It does not take into account the semantics of the projected attribute rules.

Moreover the descriptional composition creates a new set of attributes. The attribute names are composed of an attribute name of the first grammar followed by an attribute of the second one. In our construction of coupling evaluators we find the same notion of attribute names (although the attributes are not really declared).

Definition 4 (Descriptional Composition). [2] Let $\alpha : G_1 \to G_2$ and $\beta : G_2 \to G_3$ be attribute couplings. The *Descriptional Composition* of α and β generates an attribute coupling $\gamma : G_1 \to G_3 = (G_1, S_\gamma, A_\gamma, F_\gamma)$ such that:

1. $S_\gamma = S_\beta$;
2. for each attribute $a_\alpha \in A_\alpha(X^1)$ with $type(a_\alpha) = X^2$ and for each attribute $a_\beta \in A_\beta(X^2)$ the attribute $a_\alpha.a_\beta$ is declared in $A_\gamma(X^1)$ with $type(a_\alpha.a_\beta) = type(a_\beta)$;
3. for each production $p^1 : X_0 \to X_1 \ldots X_n \in P_1$ and for each attribute rule $f_{p^1,x^0,X^0} \in F_\alpha(p^1)$ with form $X^0.x^0 = p^2(X^1.x^1, \ldots, X^l.x^l)$, and for each attribute rule $f_{p^2,y^0,Y^0} \in F_\beta(p^2)$ with form $Y^0.y^0 = f(Y^1.y^1, \ldots, Y^m.y^m)$ on the production p^2 with the form $p^2 : Y_0 \to Y_1 \ldots Y_l$, we define the attribute rule f_{p^1,t^0,T^0} in $F_\gamma(p^1)$ with the form $T^0.t^0 = f(T^1.t^1, \ldots, T^m.t^m)$ such that, for each $j \in [0..m]$, $T^j = X_i$ and $t^j = x^i.y^j$ if $Y^j = Y_k$ and $X^k = X_i$ with $k \in [0..l]$ and $i \in [0..n]$.

We do not consider terminals in the previous definitions because their behavior is the same as classical attribute occurrences if we assume them to have a unique attribute with an empty name and the same type as the terminal itself, see [4].

The AG resulting from the descriptional composition of the list inversion AG of Fig. 1 with itself is presented in Fig. 2. As expected, it constructs a copy of the input list, albeit in a rather complicated manner.

3 Coupling Evaluators

The basic idea of coupling evaluators is very similar to that of descriptional composition, except that we work directly on the evaluators and not on the AG specifications. The basic goal for the coupling evaluator for $\alpha : G_1 \to G_2$ is to

---

[2] Please take care that X^i and X_i do not represent the same non-terminal in the various definitions.

$$p_1 : Z \to L \qquad L.h.s := Id_L(L.h.h);$$
$$Z.z.z := p_1(L.s.s); \qquad L.s.h := p_3();$$

$$p_2 : L_0 \to L_1 D \quad L_0.h.h := p_2(L_1.h.h, D); \; L_1.h.s := Id_L(L_0.h.s);$$
$$L_0.s.s := Id_L(L_1.s.s); \qquad L_1.h.s := Id_L(L_0.h.s);$$

$$p_3 : L \to \qquad L.s.s := Id_L(L.h.s); \qquad L.h.h := Id_L(L.s.h);$$

Fig. 2. Descriptional composition of the list inversion AG with itself

allow to run the evaluator of $\beta : G_2 \to G_3$ directly on an input syntax tree of G_1. The coupling evaluator transforms an instance of a production of G_1 into the relevant production instance for the evaluator of β, according to the attribute rules of α. We call this constructed production instance, a *virtual production instance*. As these coupling evaluators are to be used in any context of attribute coupling sequences, we introduce the formal definition of the latter.

Definition 5 (Attribute Coupling Sequence). An *Attribute Coupling Sequence*, noted $\Sigma_i^j = G^i \overset{AG^i}{\to} G^{i+1} \ldots G^j \overset{AG^j}{\to} G^{j+1}$ is a sequence of attribute couplings AG^k such that $AG^k : G^k \to G^{k+1}$ for $k \in [i..j]$.

Given an AC sequence Σ, our goal is to build a coupling evaluator for each AC of Σ except the last one. For the last one, we introduce the notion of parameterizable evaluator (see section 4) which is able to work with the result of the sequence of coupling evaluators, i.e., not only the current node, but a virtual production instance. A coupling evaluator transforms a virtual production instance according to tree-construction rules of its associated AC specification. A parameterizable evaluator accesses its "virtual" syntax tree through constructed virtual production instances which are passed as parameters. Thus the intermediate syntax trees are never physically constructed. See the end of section 5 for a discussion about this special last evaluator and separate compilation.

The following definitions of virtual objects (nodes, production instances, etc.) are parametrized by a given AC sequence Σ, for the sake of correctness ("type checking"). These virtual objects are then used to define and construct the coupling evaluators. We'll see however that the coupling evaluator of a given AC is independent from the AC sequence it is embedded in.

A virtual production instance is an object that the coupling evaluator can consider as a production instance of a real tree of its input grammar. Virtual production instances are composed of complex objects, called *virtual nodes*.

A virtual node is associated with a real node of the input tree and with an attribute sequence composed by attributes of each AC in the preceding subsequence, i.e. the calling context of this coupling evaluator. This attribute sequence accounts for the sequence of transformations of virtual productions which are performed through the preceding sequence of coupling evaluators.

Definition 6 (Virtual node). Given a sequence Σ_1^i, we define a *Virtual Node*, noted v, as a sequence $v = u.a^1. \cdots .a^{i-1}$, and its label, noted $label(v)$, such that:

1. if $i = 1$ then $v = u$ and $label(v) = label(u)$ with:
   - u a node for G^1;
   - $label(u) \in N^1 \cup T^1$;
2. if $i > 1$ then $v = v'.a^{i-1}$ and $label(v) = type(a^{i-1})$ with
   - v' is a virtual node for Σ_1^{i-1};
   - a^{i-1} is an attribute of $label(v')$ in AG^{i-1}.

For a given node in the input syntax tree, there exists more than one virtual node. In the virtual nodes, the node part indicates the real node of input syntax tree, and the attribute part specifies to which attribute it refers according to descriptional composition. In fact, if we draw a parallel with descriptional composition, then the attribute part is exactly the name of an attribute in the attribute grammar resulting from descriptional composition of all ACs in the sequence Σ except the last one.

Then the size of the data structure needed is exactly the size of the data structure used in the AG resulting from the descriptional composition. Moreover the virtual nodes are just the input nodes renamed; we insist on the fact that they do not exist physically.

Definition 7 Virtual Production Instance. Given a sequence Σ_1^i and production $p : X_0 \rightarrow X_1 \ldots X_n$ of G^i, a *Virtual Production Instance* of p is of the form $V(p) : v_0 \rightarrow v_1 \ldots v_n$, such that, for each $k \in [0..n]$:

1. v_k is a virtual node for the sequence Σ_1^i;
2. $label(v_k) = X_k$.

Now we explain the mechanism, called *virtual construction*, which transforms a virtual production instance of an input syntax tree into a virtual production instance of an output syntax tree according to an attribute occurrence of the input production. This transformation derives from the tree-construction rule in which the attribute occurrence appears; it instantiates this tree-construction on the input virtual production instance, and this gives the output instance production. This transformation also records the position of the attribute occurrence instantiation in the output virtual instance production for further transformations.

Definition 8 (Virtual Construction). Let $AG : G \rightarrow G'$ be a attribute coupling in a sequence Σ. We define a *Virtual Construction* on $p : X_0 \rightarrow X_1 \ldots X_n$ according to an attribute a, noted $< V(p), j > \underset{a}{\Longrightarrow} < V(p'), j' >$. It takes as input a virtual instance production $V(p) : v_0 \rightarrow v_1 \ldots v_n$ of p and a position j in p. It returns the pair $< V(p'), j' >$ such that:

1. Let $f_{p,y^0,Y^0} \in F$ be the unique attribute rule referencing attribute occurrence $X_j.a$ in p; it is of the form $Y^0.y^0 = p'(Y^1.y^1, \ldots, Y^l.y^l)$, with p' a production of G' and $Y^{j'}.y^{j'} = X_j.a$;

2. $V(p') : w_0 \rightarrow w_1 \ldots w_l$ where $w_s = v_k.y^s$ if $Y^s = X_k$ for $s \in [0..l]$.

As we have qssumed that each attribute occurrence was associated with a unique attribute rule, this virtual construction is well defined.

The virtual construction only depends on AG, not on its context in the sequence Σ.

We introduce another notion, the *virtual attribute*, to complete our construction of a coupling evaluator. A virtual attribute is a sequence of attributes composed of one attribute of each AC in the sequence. It is used to direct the sequence of virtual constructions. We will see later that such a virtual attribute represents the name of the calling virtual node in the parameterizable evaluator of the last AC of the sequence.

Definition 9 (Virtual Attribute). Given a sequence Σ_j^m, we define a *Virtual Attribute*, noted $v(a^j)$, as a sequence of attributes $v(a^j) = a^j. \cdots .a^{m-1}$, such that:

1. if $j = m$ then $v(\epsilon) = \epsilon$ (empty sequence[3]) is the only possible virtual attribute;
2. if $j < m$ then $v(a^j) = a^j.v(a^{j+1})$ where $v(a^{j+1})$ is a virtual attribute for the sequence Σ_{j+1}^m and a^{j+1} is either ϵ or an attribute of AG^{j+1} such that $a^{j+1} \in A(type(a^j))$.

At the beginning of a virtual construction sequence we suppose that we know a virtual attribute. We will see later that this virtual attribute is given by the last evaluator.

The coupling evaluator takes as input a virtual production instance, a virtual attribute and a position; the virtual attribute and the position give the virtual construction to be applied on the virtual production instance. The coupling evaluator gives as output the virtual attribute for the rest of the sequence and the output of the virtual construction, i.e. the new virtual production instance and the new position.

Definition 10 (Coupling Evaluator). Let $AG : G \rightarrow G'$ be an attribute coupling. The *Coupling Evaluator* of AG, noted CE, is a set of *virtual transitions* defined as follows:

1. for each production $p : X_0 \rightarrow X_1 \ldots X_n$,
2. for each attribute rule $f_{p,y^0,Y^0} : Y^0.y^0 = p'(Y^1.y^1, \ldots, Y^l.y^l)$ on p,
3. for each attribute occurrence $Y^{j'}.y^{j'} = X_j.a, j' \in [0..l]$, of this rule,

we create the virtual transition $< V(p), v(a), j > \Longrightarrow < V(p'), v(a'), j' >$ where:

$V(p)$ is a virtual production instance for some sequence of attribute couplings ending with AG,

---

[3] for convenience we define that $a.\epsilon = a$.

$v(a)$ is a virtual attribute for some sequence of attribute grammars starting with
AG,

j is a position in p,

and such that:

- $v(a) = a.v(a')$, and
- $< V(p), j > \underset{a}{\Longrightarrow} < V(p'), j' >$.

This definition is completely independent of the sequence Σ in which this attribute coupling is used. So we reach our aim to have a separately constructible evaluator.

The position j in the virtual transition represents the position of the calling virtual node in the current virtual production instance. This position can change at each step.

Fig. 3 presents the coupling evaluator for our running example of AC.

4 Parameterizable Evaluator

The type of parameterizable evaluator is not relevant to our construction, i.e., these parameterizable evaluators can be based on different evaluation methods. So, for simplification, we do not give a formal definition of such an evaluator and we limit our presentation to the use of evaluators based on visit sequences (see figure 4). A parameterizable evaluator is the part of a classical evaluator where attribute computations are made. It takes information about its input tree through parameters.

In the different definitions, for the sake of simplicity, we did not introduce the visit numbers, but it is easy to introduce them, passing the visit number through the different coupling evaluators.

5 Evaluation Strategy

Now, to complete our construction of a sequence of coupling evaluators, we must define the *visit selector*, which finds the real production in the input syntax tree and calls the first coupling evaluator on this production.

The virtual node on which the current visit is called gives the real node of the current call and the virtual attribute which will direct the subsequent sequence of virtual constructions.

For convenience, we assume that we know the father node, noted u^J, of the current production instance. It allows us to find the new production instance and the position of the call node in it.

Definition 11 (Visit Selector). Given a parameterizable evaluator based on visit sequences for the AG which ends a sequence Σ_1^m, we define a *Visit Selector*, noted VS, such that:

For a given tuple of form $< V(p), v(a), j >$
the coupling evaluator has the following form:

case p is

$p_1 : Z \rightarrow L$ $< V(p) = V(p_1) : v_0 \rightarrow v_1, v(a) = a.v(a'), j >$
case a.j is
$z.0 :< V(p_1) : v_0.z \rightarrow v_1.s, v(a'), 0 >$
$s.1 :< V(p_1) : v_0.s \rightarrow v_1.s, v(a'), 1 >$
$h.1 :< V(p_3) : v_1.h \rightarrow, v(a'), 0 >$

$p_2 : L_0 \rightarrow L_1 D$ $< V(p) = V(p_2) : v_0 \rightarrow v_1 D, v(a) = a.v(a'), j >$
case a.j is
$s.0 :< V(Id_L) : v_0.s \rightarrow v_1.s, v(a'), 0 >$
$s.1 :< V(Id_L) : v_0.s \rightarrow v_1.s, v(a'), 1 >$
$h.1 :< V(p_2) : v_1.h \rightarrow v_0.hD, v(a'), 0 >$
$h.0 :< V(p_2) : v_1.h \rightarrow v_0.hD, v(a'), 1 >$

$p_3 : L \rightarrow$ $< V(p) = V(p_3) : v \rightarrow, v(a) = a.v(a'), j >$
case a.j is
$s.0 :< V(Id_L) : v.s \rightarrow v.h, v(a'), 0 >$
$h.0 :< V(Id_L) : v.s \rightarrow v.h, v(a'), 1 >$

$Id_L : L_0 \longrightarrow L_1$ $< V(p) = V(Id_L) : v_0 \rightarrow v_1, v(a) = a.v(a'), j >$
case a.j is
$s.0 :< V(Id_L) : v_0.s \rightarrow v_1.s, v(a'), 0 >$
$s.1 :< V(Id_L) : v_0.s \rightarrow v_1.s, v(a'), 1 >$
$h.1 :< V(Id_L) : v_1.h \rightarrow v_0.h, v(a'), 0 >$
$h.0 :< V(Id_L) : v_1.h \rightarrow v_0.h, v(a'), 1 >$

Fig. 3. Coupling Evaluator for the List Inversion AG

- given a calling virtual node $v = u.a^1. \cdots .a^{m-1}$ for the sequence Σ,
- given the father node u^f of the current production instance of G^1,

we build a starting tuple for the sequence, noted $< V(p), v(a), j >$, and the new u^f where:

1. $v(a) = a^1. \cdots .a^{m-1}$;
2. if the real calling node u is equal to u^f then we go up in the input tree, $u^f \leftarrow father(u)$, and the calling node position j in this new production is such that $u = Pos(u^f, j)$; otherwise, i.e. if u is different from u^f, then we go down in the input tree, $u^f \leftarrow u$, and the calling node position j in this new production is 0;
3. $V(p) : u^f \rightarrow Pos(u^f, 1) \cdots Pos(u^f, n)$ with $p = prod(u^f)$.

Starting State Given a sequence of attribute couplings Σ_1^m, we now have all the elements to construct the whole evaluator; we just need to define the starting

The evaluator of List Inversion based on visit sequences is parameterized by the tuple $< V(p), \epsilon, 0 >$. The calling position is always equal to zero because we use a top-down evaluator. This evaluator does not perform multiple visits to a same node, so we do not introduce visit numbers.

$$\text{case } p \text{ is}$$

$$p_1 : Z \rightarrow L \qquad < V(p) = V(p_1) : v_0 \rightarrow v_1, \epsilon, 0 >$$
$$v_1.h := p_3();$$
$$\text{visit } v_1;$$
$$v_0.z := p_1(v_1.s);$$

$$p_2 : L_0 \rightarrow L_1 D \quad < V(p) = V(p_2) : v_0 \rightarrow v_1 D, \epsilon, 0 >$$
$$v_1.h := p_2(v_0.h, D);$$
$$\text{visit } v_1;$$
$$v_0.s := Id_L(v_1.s);$$

$$p_3 : L \rightarrow \qquad < V(p) = V(p_3) : v \rightarrow, \epsilon, 0 >$$
$$v_0.s := Id_L(v_0.h);$$

$$Id_L : L_0 \longrightarrow L_1 \quad < V(p) = V(Id_L) : v_0 \rightarrow v_1, \epsilon, 0 >$$
$$v_0.s := Id_L(v_1.s);$$
$$\text{visit } v_1;$$
$$v_1.h := Id_L(v_0.h);$$

Fig. 4. Parameterizable Evaluator for the List Inversion AG

state. At the beginning of the process, the first tuple $< V(p), v(a), j >$ is defined as follows:

1. $V(p)$ is the root production of the input tree;
2. $v(a)$ is composed of the sequence of the synthesized attributes of the start symbol (root) of each attribute coupling except the last one, $z^1.z^2.\cdots.z^{m-1}$;
3. j is equal to 0.

The starting current node u^j is the root node.

Evaluator Chaining Given a sequence Σ_1^m, the call of the parameterizable evaluator PE^m of AG^m on the input syntax tree of G^1 is made using the different coupling evaluators CE^i. The call of the new visit sequence by PE^m is passed to CE^1 using the visit selector VS. This process is illustrated in Fig. 5. The links between these different entities lead to an evaluation method which can walk up and down in the input syntax tree.

The status of the last evaluator seems to conflict with the idea of separate compilation (an AC by itself should not know that it is the last in some sequence). This is not true if we consider that, for each AC, we have to construct both a coupling evaluator and a parametrizable evaluator. We claim that this will be

The call on the virtual node $v = u.v(a^1)$ is performed as follows:

$$u.v(a^1)$$
$$\downarrow^{VS}$$
$$< V(p^1), v(a^1), j^1 >$$
$$\downarrow^{CE^1}$$
$$\vdots$$
$$\downarrow^{CE^{m-2}}$$
$$< V(p^{m-1}), v(a^{m-1}), j^{m-1} >$$
$$\downarrow^{CE^{m-1}}$$
$$< V(p^m), \epsilon, 0 >$$
$$\downarrow^{PE^m}$$
$$u'.v(a'^1)$$

Fig. 5. Example of evaluation sequence

the case in practice because, in the course of the development of a whole AC sequence, you have to test each AC in turn and hence have to construct its parametrizable evaluator.

6 Extended Coupling Evaluators

In this section, we give a brief idea of how to introduce semantic computations in an AC while keeping our notion of coupling evaluator. We also briefly present how to introduce complex tree-construction rules, such as conditionals.

We have presented the coupling evaluator only for purely syntactic ACs, in which each set of attribute rules is composed only of (simple) tree-construction rules. We would like to accept a sequence of ACs with some semantic rules. First we suppose that we have a mechanism able to separate each AC into two AGs. In [6] we can find such a decomposition, called *e-t-Decomposition*. The first one only contains semantic rules and is called the semantic AG; the second one, called the syntactic AG, is purely syntactic and contains only tree-construction rules. Our construction can be applied to the syntactic AG.

For these two AGs, we construct their evaluators, a parameterizable evaluator for the semantic AG, and a coupling evaluator for the syntactic AG. Then the introduction of the semantic part is reduced to correctly calling the parameterizable evaluator of the semantic AG before any call to the coupling evaluator of the syntactic AG. To do so, it is necessary to correctly store some attribute instance values of semantic AGs at the real nodes of the real input tree. Indeed, several calls of the same coupling evaluator can use a same attribute instance value in different contexts but on the same input tree. However, it must be clear that each semantic attribute of each AC is directly attached to the real node corresponding to the virtual node that carries it; no additional data structure is needed.

To accept complex tree-construction rules, such as conditionals, we introduce into the coupling evaluators complex expressions of the same form to regroup virtual transitions. Then the idea is simple: the complex tree-construction rules are decomposed into simple tree-construction rules, to which our virtual transition construction can be applied; then we recombine the results into a complex virtual transition using the previously introduced complex expressions. Details can be found in [13].

We have also eliminated many useless operations introduced by identity rules creating non-local virtual production instances. The details of this elimination can be found in [12].

7 Related work

In [6], there exists a preliminary approach which constructs directly from the evaluators of an AG sequence, an evaluator associated to the AG resulting from the descriptional composition of the sequence. But this approach only applies to purely synthesized syntactic AGs[4]. More precisely, "directly" means that there is no need to compute the attribute dependencies for the composed AGs; however the need to completely construct the evaluator still exists. Our approach has some similarities with this construction, except that we work directly on the evaluators and we accept non-purely-synthesized AGs.

In [3], the authors present the notion of separable AGs. They want to have separate compilation of these AGs, hence they do not use descriptional composition. They propose an adaptation of the classical evaluation scheme which allows separate compilation, but the construction of (some) intermediate trees is necessary. The aim of our approach is to allow separate compilation while avoiding the construction of any intermediate tree. From the external point of view, then, both works appear to have similar expressive power (separable AGs) but it is from an evaluation point of view that our approach is very different, essentially because we do not construct the intermediate trees.

8 Conclusion and Future Work

The main advantage of the notion of coupling evaluator is certainly that there is no class constraint on the coupling evaluators. The class of the resulting (complete) evaluator is the class of the parameterizable evaluator of the last AG of a given sequence Σ. Thus, to construct an evaluator based on visit sequences, for a given AC sequence, only the last AG needs to have such an evaluator.

---

[4] See proposition 8 in [6] for more details.

In fact, the resolution of class constraints in descriptional composition was the first motivation of this work. In the same way, it is possible to see our coupling evaluator as a generalization of the classical AG transformations for class reduction (e.g. from SNC to l-ordered [2]; see also [1]) which often work at the specification level.

The second advantage is the possibility to construct the coupling evaluators separately while keeping the good properties of descriptional composition, i.e. the fact that the intermediate trees are not constructed. However, only practical experience with a real implementation (which we don't have yet) will show whether this is indeed valuable.

Regarding the size of the data structures needed for our Coupling Evaluator, we notice that it is equivalent to the size of the data structures which is needed for descriptional composition. Since our Coupling Evaluators only work on the part of a grammar which is really necessary, the size of their data structure is smaller than the one needed for a sequence of classical evaluators which construct the whole intermediate trees.

We must notice that, if we are not interested in separate compilation, we can obtain much more efficient combined evaluators. Indeed, if we know the sequence of ACs, we can directly code the different tests into the coupling evaluators, because the number of cases which are really used is very small. This is a form of specialization by partial evaluation. This also reduces the size of the evaluator. More precisely, it is possible to apply a transformation on a given sequence of Coupling Evaluators which produces a particular evaluator where only revelant cases are present and where a sequence of calls of coupling evaluators is reduced to a unique call. This new evaluator retains the advantage of the descriptional composition and it is also always possible to construct it.

Moreover, we presented a first approach to the construction of Coupling Evaluators, where the main goal was not the efficiency of this kind of evaluator, but rather "simplicity".

In this paper we have assumed that each attribute occurrence was used only once in each production of the attribute coupling. We think that this restriction can be relaxed rather simply, by remembering which attribute occurrence has been chosen until a visit returns.

We also hope to eliminate many useless operations introduced by identity rules, by creating non-local virtual production instances and trying to find statically useless copy rules; this analysis will apply the results and techniques of [12] to descriptional composition.

From a theoretical point of view, it is very difficult to formally compare sequential implementation with this new technique, beside the fact that intermediate trees are not to be constructed. The only good (but partly false) view which we could give, is a comparison with factoring in mathematics: with coupling evaluators we factor out moves into one tree (see Fig. 6).

66

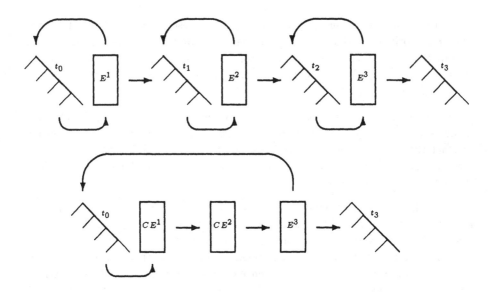

Fig. 6. Factorization of moves

References

1. Deransart, P., Jourdan, M. and Lorho, B. *Attribute Grammars: Definitions, Systems and Bibliography*. Lect. Notes in Comp. Sci., vol. 323, Springer-Verlag, New York–Heidelberg–Berlin, Aug. 1988.

2. Engelfriet, J. and Filè, G. Simple Multi-Visit Attribute Grammars. *J. Comput. System Sci. 24*, 3 (June 1982), 283–314.

3. Farrow, R., Marlowe, T. J. and Yellin, D. M. Composable Attribute Grammars: Support for Modularity in Translator Design and Implementation. In *19th ACM Symp. on Principles of Progr. Languages* (Albuquerque, NM, Jan. 1992). pp. 223–234.

4. Ganzinger, H. and Giegerich, R. Attribute Coupled Grammars. In *ACM SIGPLAN '84 Symp. on Compiler Construction* (Montréal, June 1984). *ACM SIGPLAN Notices 19*, 6 (June 1984), 157–170.

5. Ganzinger, H., Giegerich, R. and Vach, M. MARVIN: a Tool for Applicative and Modular Compiler Specifications. Forschungsbericht 220, Fachbereich Informatik, Univ. Dortmund, July 1986.

6. Giegerich, R. Composition and Evaluation of Attribute Coupled Grammars. *Acta Inform. 25* (1988), 355–423.

7. Jourdan, M., Le Bellec, C., Parigot, D. and Roussel, G. Specification and Implementation of Grammar Couplings using Attribute Grammars. In *Programming Languages Implementation and Logic Programming* (Tallinn, Aug. 1993), M. Bruynooghe and J. Penjam, Eds. Lect. Notes in Comp. Sci., vol. 714, Springer-Verlag, New York–Heidelberg–Berlin, pp. 123–136.

8. Jourdan, M. and Parigot, D. Application Development with the FNC-2 Attribute Grammar System. In *Compiler Compilers '90* (Schwerin, Oct. 1990), D. Hammer, Ed. Lect. Notes in Comp. Sci., vol. 477, Springer-Verlag, New York–Heidelberg–Berlin, pp. 11–25.

9. Jourdan, M., Parigot, D., Julié, C., Le Bellec, C. and Durin, O. Design, Implementation and Evaluation of the FNC-2 Attribute Grammar System. In *ACM SIGPLAN '90 Conf. on Progr. Languages Design and Implementation* (White Plains, NY, July 1990). ACM SIGPLAN Notices, vol. 25, no. 6, pp. 209–222.

10. Knuth, D. E. Semantics of Context-free Languages. *Math. Systems Theory 2*, 2 (June 1968), 127–145. Correction: *Math. Systems Theory 5*, 1, pp. 95-96 (Mar. 1971)..

11. Le Bellec, C. La généricité et les grammaires attribuées. Thèse de doctorat, Dépt. d'Informatique, Univ. d'Orléans, June 1993.

12. Roussel, G. A Transformation of Attribute Grammars for Eliminating Useless Copy Rules. Research report to appear, INRIA, 1994.

13. Roussel, G. Différentes transformations de grammaires attribuées. Thèse de doctorat, Dépt. d'Informatique, Univ. de Paris VI, Mar. 1994.

Towards the Global Optimization of Functional Logic Programs*

Michael Hanus

Max-Planck-Institut für Informatik
Im Stadtwald, D-66123 Saarbrücken, Germany.
michael@mpi-sb.mpg.de

Abstract. Functional logic languages amalgamate functional and logic programming paradigms. They can be efficiently implemented by extending techniques known from logic programming. In this paper we show how global information about the call modes of functions can be used to optimize the compilation of functional logic programs. Since mode information has been successfully used to improve the implementation of pure logic programs and these techniques can be applied to implementations of functional logic programs as well, we concentrate on optimizations which are unique to the operational semantics of functional logic programs. We define a suitable notion of modes for functional logic programs and present compile-time techniques to optimize the normalization process during the execution of functional logic programs.

1 Introduction

In recent years, a lot of proposals have been made to amalgamate functional and logic programming languages [7, 17]. Functional logic languages with a sound and complete operational semantics are based on narrowing (e.g., [10, 12, 26, 28]), a combination of the reduction principle of functional languages and the resolution principle of logic languages. Narrowing, originally introduced in automated theorem proving [29], is used to *solve* equations by finding appropriate values for variables occurring in arguments of functions. This is done by unifying (rather than matching) an input term with the left-hand side of some rule and then replacing the instantiated input term by the instantiated right-hand side of the rule.

Example 1. Consider the following rules defining the addition of two natural numbers which are represented by terms built from 0 and s:

$$0 + N \rightarrow N \qquad (R_1)$$
$$s(M) + N \rightarrow s(M + N) \qquad (R_2)$$

The equation X+s(0)=s(s(0)) can be solved by a narrowing step with rule R_2 followed by a narrowing step with rule R_1 so that X is instantiated to s(0) and the instantiated equation is reduced to s(s(0))=s(s(0)) which is trivially true. Hence we have found the solution X↦s(0) to the given equation. □

---

* The research described in this paper was supported by the German Ministry for Research and Technology (BMFT) under grant ITS 9103. The responsibility for the contents of this publication lies with the author.

In order to ensure completeness in general, *each* rule must be unified with *each* non-variable subterm of the given equation which yields a huge search space. This situation can be improved by particular narrowing strategies which restrict the possible positions for the application of the next narrowing step (see [17] for a detailed survey). In this paper we are interested in an *innermost narrowing* strategy where a narrowing step is performed at the leftmost innermost position. This corresponds to eager evaluation in functional languages.

However, the restriction to particular narrowing positions is not sufficient to avoid a lot of useless derivations since the uncontrolled instantiation of variables may cause infinite loops. For instance, consider the rules in Example 1 and the equation (X+Y)+Z=0. Applying innermost narrowing to this equation using rule R_2 produces the following infinite derivation (the instantiation of variables occurring in the equation is recorded at the derivation arrow):

$$(X+Y)+Z = 0 \rightsquigarrow_{\{X\mapsto s(X1)\}} \quad s(X1+Y)+Z = 0$$
$$\rightsquigarrow_{\{X1\mapsto s(X2)\}} \quad s(s(X2+Y))+Z = 0$$
$$\rightsquigarrow_{\{X2\mapsto s(X3)\}} \quad \cdots$$

To avoid such useless derivations, narrowing can be combined with simplification (evaluation of a term): Before a narrowing step is applied, the equation is rewritten to normal form w.r.t. the given rules [9, 10] (thus this strategy is also called *normalizing narrowing*). The infinite narrowing derivation above is avoided by rewriting the first derived equation to normal form:

$$s(X1+Y)+Z = 0 \rightarrow s((X1+Y)+Z) = 0$$

The last equation can never be satisfied since the terms s((X1+Y)+Z) and 0 are always different due to the absence of rules for the symbols s and 0. Hence we can safely terminate the unsuccessful narrowing derivation at this point. The integration of rewriting into narrowing derivations has the following advantages:

1. The search space is reduced since useless narrowing derivations can be detected. As a consequence, functional logic programs are more efficiently executable than equivalent Prolog programs [10, 13, 14].[2]

2. There is a preference for deterministic computations. Since we assume a confluent and terminating set of rules, normal forms are unique and can be computed by any simplification strategy. Hence normalization can be deterministically implemented. Since rewriting is executed before each nondeterministic narrowing step, the goal is computed in a deterministic way as long as possible. The preference of deterministic computations can save a lot of time and space as shown in [13].

Therefore we consider in this paper a *normalizing innermost narrowing* strategy where the computation of the normal form between narrowing steps is performed by applying rewrite rules from innermost to outermost positions, i.e., a rewrite rule is applied to a term only if each of its subterms is in normal form. Such an operational semantics can be efficiently implemented by extending compilation techniques known from logic programming [12, 13].

---

[2] It is easy to see that the Prolog program corresponding to the above example would run into an infinite loop.

The integration of normalization into narrowing derivations has also one disadvantage. Since the entire goal must be reduced to normal form after each narrowing step, the normalization process may be costly. Fortunately, it is possible to normalize the terms in an incremental manner [15] since normalization steps after a narrowing step can only be performed at positions where some variables have been instantiated. However, better optimizations could be performed if the evaluation modes for functions are known at compile time. In this paper we define the notion of evaluation modes, which is different from logic programs [35], and show possible compile-time optimizations using these modes. We are not interested in low-level code optimizations to improve primitive unification instructions since such techniques, which have been developed for pure logic programs (e.g., [24, 25, 31, 32, 33, 34, 35]), can be applied to functional logic programs as well due to the similarities between WAM-based Prolog implementations and implementations of functional logic languages [12, 13, 23]. We limit our discussion to optimizations which are unique to functional logic programs based on an eager evaluation strategy like ALF [12, 13], LPG [1], or SLOG [10]. The automatic derivation of mode information for functional logic programs is a different topic which will be addressed in a forthcoming paper [18].

After a precise definition of the operational semantics in Section 2, we define the notion of modes for functional logic programs in Section 3. Section 4 discusses the optimization techniques using particular mode information. Experimental results for these optimization techniques are presented in Section 5, and some peculiarities of the automatic mode derivation for functional logic programs are discussed in Section 6.

2   Normalizing narrowing

To define the operational semantics considered in this paper in a precise way, we recall basic notions of term rewriting [8].

A *signature* is a set $\mathcal{F}$ of *function symbols*. Every $f \in \mathcal{F}$ is associated with an *arity* n, denoted f/n. Let $\mathcal{X}$ be a countably infinite set of *variables*. Then the set $\mathcal{T}(\mathcal{F}, \mathcal{X})$ of *terms* built from $\mathcal{F}$ and $\mathcal{X}$ is the smallest set containing $\mathcal{X}$ such that $f(t_1, \ldots, t_n) \in \mathcal{T}(\mathcal{F}, \mathcal{X})$ whenever $f \in \mathcal{F}$ has arity n and $t_1, \ldots, t_n \in \mathcal{T}(\mathcal{F}, \mathcal{X})$. We write f instead of $f()$ whenever f has arity 0. We denote by $\mathcal{T}(\mathcal{F}, \mathcal{X})^n$ the set $\{\langle t_1, \ldots, t_n \rangle \mid t_i \in \mathcal{T}(\mathcal{F}, \mathcal{X}), i = 1, \ldots, n\}$ of n-tuples of terms ($n \geq 0$). The set of variables occurring in a term t is denoted by $\mathcal{V}ar(t)$. A term t is called *ground* if $\mathcal{V}ar(t) = \emptyset$.

Usually, functional logic programs are *constructor-based*, i.e., a distinction is made between operation symbols to construct data terms, called *constructors*, and operation symbols to operate on data terms, called *defined functions* or *operations* (see, for instance, the functional logic languages ALF [12], BABEL [26], K-LEAF [11], SLOG [10]). Hence we assume that the signature $\mathcal{F}$ is partitioned into two sets $\mathcal{F} = \mathcal{C} \cup \mathcal{D}$ with $\mathcal{C} \cap \mathcal{D} = \emptyset$. A *constructor term* t is built from constructors and variables, i.e., $t \in \mathcal{T}(\mathcal{C}, \mathcal{X})$. An *innermost term* t [10] is an operation applied to constructor terms, i.e., $t = f(t_1, \ldots, t_n)$ with $f \in \mathcal{D}$ and $t_1, \ldots, t_n \in \mathcal{T}(\mathcal{C}, \mathcal{X})$. A *function call* $f(t_1, \ldots, t_n)$ is an operation $f \in \mathcal{D}$ applied to arbitrary terms. Such a term is also called *f-rooted term*.

A *(rewrite) rule* $l \rightarrow r$ is a pair of an innermost term l and a term r satisfying $Var(r) \subseteq Var(l)$ where l and r are called *left-hand side* and *right-hand side*, respectively.[3] A rule is called a *variant* of another rule if it is obtained by a unique replacement of variables by other variables. A *term rewriting system* $\mathcal{R}$ is a set of rules.[4] In the following we assume a given *term rewriting system* $\mathcal{R}$.

The execution of functional logic programs requires notions like substitution, unifier, position etc. A *substitution* σ is a mapping from $\mathcal{X}$ into $\mathcal{T}(\mathcal{F}, \mathcal{X})$ such that the set $\{x \in \mathcal{X} \mid \sigma(x) \neq x\}$ is finite. We frequently identify a substitution σ with the set $\{x \mapsto \sigma(x) \mid \sigma(x) \neq x\}$. Substitutions are extended to morphisms on $\mathcal{T}(\mathcal{F}, \mathcal{X})$ by $\sigma(f(t_1, \ldots, t_n)) = f(\sigma(t_1), \ldots, \sigma(t_n))$ for every term $f(t_1, \ldots, t_n)$. A *unifier* of two terms s and t is a substitution σ with $\sigma(s) = \sigma(t)$. A unifier σ is called *most general* (*mgu*) if for every other unifier σ' there is a substitution ϕ with $\sigma' = \phi \circ \sigma$ (concatenation of σ and ϕ). Most general unifiers are unique up to variable renaming. By introducing a total ordering on variables we can uniquely choose *the* most general unifier of two terms. A *position* p in a term t is represented by a sequence of natural numbers, $t|_p$ denotes the *subterm* of t at position p, and $t[s]_p$ denotes the result of *replacing the subterm* $t|_p$ by the term s (see [8] for details).

A *rewrite step* is an application of a rewrite rule to a term, i.e., $t \rightarrow_\mathcal{R} s$ if there exist a position p in t, a rewrite rule $l \rightarrow r$ and a substitution σ with $t|_p = \sigma(l)$ and $s = t[\sigma(r)]_p$. In this case we say t is *reducible* (at position p). A term t is called *irreducible* or in *normal form* if there is no term s with $t \rightarrow_\mathcal{R} s$.

$\rightarrow_\mathcal{R}^*$ denotes the transitive-reflexive closure of the rewrite relation $\rightarrow_\mathcal{R}$. $\mathcal{R}$ is called *terminating* if there are no infinite rewrite sequences $t_1 \rightarrow_\mathcal{R} t_2 \rightarrow_\mathcal{R} t_3 \rightarrow_\mathcal{R} \cdots$. $\mathcal{R}$ is called *confluent* if for all terms t, t_1, t_2 with $t \rightarrow_\mathcal{R}^* t_1$ and $t \rightarrow_\mathcal{R}^* t_2$ there exists a term t_3 with $t_1 \rightarrow_\mathcal{R}^* t_3$ and $t_2 \rightarrow_\mathcal{R}^* t_3$. A terminating and confluent term rewriting system $\mathcal{R}$ is called *convergent*.

If $\mathcal{R}$ is convergent, we can decide the validity of an equation $s =_\mathcal{R} t$ (where $=_\mathcal{R}$ denotes validity w.r.t. the equations $\{l \doteq r \mid l \rightarrow r \in \mathcal{R}\}$) by computing the normal form of both sides using an arbitrary sequence of rewrite steps. In order to *solve* an equation, we have to find appropriate instantiations for the variables in s and t. This can be done by *narrowing*. A term t is *narrowable* into a term t' if there exist a non-variable position p in t (i.e., $t|_p \notin \mathcal{X}$), a variant $l \rightarrow r$ of a rewrite rule and a substitution σ such that σ is a most general unifier of $t|_p$ and l and $t' = \sigma(t[r]_p)$. In this case we write $t \leadsto_\sigma t'$. If there is a narrowing sequence $t_1 \leadsto_{\sigma_1} t_2 \leadsto_{\sigma_2} \cdots \leadsto_{\sigma_{n-1}} t_n$, we write $t_1 \leadsto_\sigma^* t_n$ with $\sigma = \sigma_{n-1} \circ \cdots \circ \sigma_2 \circ \sigma_1$.

Narrowing is able to solve equations w.r.t. $\mathcal{R}$. For this purpose we introduce a new operation symbol = and a new constructor **true** and add the rewrite rule

---

[3] For the sake of simplicity we consider only unconditional rules, but our results can easily be extended to conditional rules.

[4] We will apply rules in two ways: (a) in rewrite steps to evaluate terms, and (b) in narrowing steps to solve equations. Therefore we will sometimes distinguish between *rewrite rules* and *narrowing rules*. Usually, the set of rewrite rules and the set of narrowing rules are identical, but in some languages it is also possible to use some rules only for rewrite steps or only for narrowing steps (e.g., in ALF [12, 13] or SLOG [10]).

$x=x \to$ **true** to $\mathcal{R}$. Then the following theorem states soundness and completeness of narrowing.

Theorem 1 [20]. *Let $\mathcal{R}$ be a convergent term rewriting system.*
1. *If $s=t \leadsto_\sigma^*$ **true**, then $\sigma(s) =_\mathcal{R} \sigma(t)$.*
2. *If $\sigma'(s) =_\mathcal{R} \sigma'(t)$, then there exist a narrowing derivation $s=t \leadsto_\sigma^*$ **true** and a substitution ϕ with $\phi(\sigma(x)) =_\mathcal{R} \sigma'(x)$ for all $x \in Var(s) \cup Var(t)$.*

Thus to compute all solutions to an equation $s=t$, we apply narrowing steps to it until we obtain an equation $s'=t'$ where s' and t' are unifiable. Since this simple narrowing procedure (enumerating all narrowing derivations) has a huge search space, several authors have improved it by restricting the admissible narrowing derivations (see [17] for a detailed survey). In the following we consider *normalizing innermost narrowing* derivations [10] where

- the narrowing step is performed at the leftmost innermost subterm, and
- the term is simplified to its normal form before a narrowing step is performed by applying rewrite rules from innermost to outermost positions.

The *innermost* strategy provides an efficient implementation [12, 13, 21, 23] while the *normalization* process is important since it prefers deterministic computations: rewriting a term to normal form can be done in a deterministic way since every rewrite sequence yields the same result (because $\mathcal{R}$ is convergent) whereas different narrowing steps may lead to different solutions and therefore all admissible narrowing steps must be considered. Hence in a sequential implementation rewriting can be efficiently implemented like reductions in functional languages whereas narrowing steps need costly backtracking management as in Prolog. For instance, if the equation $s =_\mathcal{R} t$ is valid, normalizing narrowing will prove it by a pure deterministic computation (reducing s and t to the same normal form) whereas simple narrowing would compute the normal form of s and t by costly narrowing steps.

Normalizing innermost narrowing is complete if $\mathcal{R}$ is convergent and all functions are totally defined, i.e., reducible on all appropriate constructor terms [10]. This is a reasonable class from the functional programming point of view. But it is also possible to extend this strategy to incompletely defined operations. In this case a so-called *innermost reflection* rule must be added which skips an innermost function call that cannot be evaluated [19]. For the sake of simplicity we assume in the following that all functions are totally defined, i.e., normalizing innermost narrowing is sufficient to compute all solutions.

3 Modes for functional logic programs

In pure logic programs, the *mode* for a predicate is a description of the possible arguments of a predicate when it is called [35]. E.g., the mode $p(g, f, a)$ specifies that the first argument is a ground term, the second argument is a free variable, and the third argument is an arbitrary term for all calls to predicate p. The mode information is useful to optimize the compiled code, i.e., to specialize the unification instructions and indexing scheme for a predicate [24, 25, 32, 34, 35]. Since functional logic languages are usually based on narrowing which uses unification to apply a function to a subterm, mode information could also be useful to optimize functional logic programs. However, the notion of "mode" in functional logic programs is different from pure logic programs if normalization is included in the narrowing process because functions are evaluated by narrowing as well as by rewriting. In the following we discuss this problem and define a new notion of modes for functional logic programs which will be used in Section 4 to optimize functional logic programs.

Example 2. In this example we discuss a derivation w.r.t. our narrowing strategy. Consider the rules of Example 1 together with the following rewrite rules:

$$
\begin{array}{ll}
\texttt{double(0)} \rightarrow \texttt{0} & (R_3) \\
\texttt{double(s(N))} \rightarrow \texttt{s(s(double(N)))} & (R_4) \\
\texttt{quad(N)} \rightarrow \texttt{(N+N)+double(N)} & (R_5)
\end{array}
$$

We want to compute solutions to the initial equation $\texttt{quad(X)=4}$ by our strategy, where 4 denotes the term $\texttt{s(s(s(s(0))))}$. Before applying any narrowing step, the equation is reduced to its normal form by rewrite steps. Hence we apply rule R_5 to the subterm $\texttt{quad(X)}$:

$$\texttt{quad(X)=4} \quad \rightarrow_{\mathcal{R}} \quad \texttt{(X+X)+double(X)=4}$$

Then the resulting equation is normalized by trying to apply rewrite rules to the three operation symbols, but no rewrite rule is applicable due to the free variable X. Hence the equation is already in normal form. Now a narrowing step is applied at the leftmost innermost position, i.e., the subterm $\texttt{X+X}$. Both rules R_1 and R_2 are applicable. We choose rule R_2 so that X is instantiated to $\texttt{s(Y)}$:

$$\texttt{(X+X)+double(X)=4} \quad \rightsquigarrow_{\{X \mapsto s(Y)\}} \quad \texttt{s(Y+s(Y))+double(s(Y))=4}$$

The resulting equation must be reduced to its normal form by trying to apply rewrite steps from innermost to outermost positions. A rewrite rule is not applicable to the leftmost innermost subterm $\texttt{Y+s(Y)}$ since the first argument Y is a free variable. But we can apply rule R_4 to the subterm $\texttt{double(s(Y))}$ and rule R_2 to the outer occurrence of +:

$$
\begin{array}{ll}
\texttt{s(Y+s(Y))+double(s(Y))=4} & \rightarrow_{\mathcal{R}} \quad \texttt{s(Y+s(Y))+s(s(double(Y)))=4} \\
& \rightarrow_{\mathcal{R}} \quad \texttt{s((Y+s(Y))+s(s(double(Y))))=4}
\end{array}
$$

The latter equation is in normal form. Therefore we apply a narrowing step to the leftmost innermost subterm $\texttt{Y+s(Y)}$. We choose rule R_1 so that Y is instantiated to 0:

$$\texttt{s((Y+s(Y))+s(s(double(Y))))=4} \quad \rightsquigarrow_{\{Y \mapsto 0\}} \quad \texttt{s(s(0)+s(s(double(0))))=4}$$

We normalize the resulting equation by applying rule R_3 to $\texttt{double(0)}$ and rules R_2 and R_1 to the remaining occurrence of +:

$$
\begin{array}{ll}
\texttt{s(s(0)+s(s(double(0))))=4} & \rightarrow_{\mathcal{R}} \quad \texttt{s(s(0)+s(s(0)))=4} \\
& \rightarrow_{\mathcal{R}} \quad \texttt{s(s(0+s(s(0))))=4} \\
& \rightarrow_{\mathcal{R}} \quad \texttt{s(s(s(s(0))))=4}
\end{array}
$$

Thus we have computed the solution $\{X \mapsto \texttt{s(0)}\}$ since the left- and right-hand side of the final equation are identical. A closer look to the narrowing and rewrite attempts in this derivation yields the following facts:

1. The operation + is evaluated both by narrowing and rewrite steps.

2. If a narrowing step is applied to +, the first argument is always free and the second argument may be partially instantiated.
3. If a rewrite step is applied to +, both arguments may be partially instantiated.
4. At the time when a narrowing step could be applied to double (i.e., if all functions to the left of double are evaluated), its argument is ground. Hence double is evaluated by rewriting and not by narrowing.
5. If a rewrite step is applied to double, its argument may be partially instantiated.
6. If a rewrite or narrowing step is applied to quad, its argument is always a free variable. Hence no rewrite rules can be applied to any function call in the right-hand side of rule R_5 immediately after the application of these rule, i.e., the rewrite attempts for these function calls can be skipped.

In order to have a formal representation of these properties, we assign to each operation a *narrowing mode* (+(f,a), double(g), quad(f) in this example) and a *rewrite mode* (+(a,a), double(a), quad(f)). Using this kind of mode information it is possible to avoid unnecessary rewrite attempts, compile rewrite derivations in a more efficient way, delete unnecessary rewrite or narrowing rules etc. (see Section 4). □

In the following we give a precise definition of the possible modes for functional logic programs w.r.t. a normalizing narrowing semantics. In this definition we consider a mode as a (possibly infinite) set of term tuples. Such a set contains all possible parameters which may occur in a function call. In subsequent sections we abstract such a set to a finite representation like g, f or a. Since there are also other useful abstractions (e.g., type approximations [4]), we do not restrict the general definition of modes.

Definition 2. Let f/n be an operation symbol and $N, R \subseteq T(\mathcal{F}, \mathcal{X})^n$.
(a) N is called $\mathcal{N}$-mode (*narrowing mode*) for f/n whenever $\langle t_1, \ldots, t_n \rangle \in N$ if a narrowing step should be applied to the subterm $f(t_1, \ldots, t_n)$ during program execution.
(b) R is called $\mathcal{R}$-mode (*rewrite mode*) for f/n whenever $\langle t_1, \ldots, t_n \rangle \in R$ if a rewrite step should be applied to the subterm $f(t_1, \ldots, t_n)$ during program execution. □

We have defined modes w.r.t. arbitrary program executions. However, for the sake of good program optimizations it is desirable to consider only executions w.r.t. a given class of initial goals. In this case the modes are computed by a top-down analysis of the program starting from the initial goals.

4   Optimization of functional logic programs using modes

As mentioned in the previous section, we are not interested in the precise term sets contained in the modes, but we abstract these term sets into a finite number of *abstract values*. For the optimizations techniques we have in mind the abstract values g, f and a are sufficient, where g denotes the set $T(\mathcal{F}, \varnothing)$ of ground terms, f the set $\mathcal{X}$ of free variables and a the set $T(\mathcal{F}, \mathcal{X})$ of all terms. Hence the $\mathcal{N}$-mode $\langle g, a, f \rangle$ for the operation $f/3$ specifies that the first argument is ground and the third argument is a free variable if a narrowing rule should be applied to this operation. Such modes can be specified by the programmer, but it is more reliable to derive the modes automatically from the given program (w.r.t. a mode for the initial goal). Automatic mode inference has been investigated for pure logic programming (e.g., [3, 5, 6, 25, 30]) and similar schemes for functional logic programs are under development [18]. In the following we show possible optimization techniques w.r.t. given modes for a functional logic program.

4.1 Using freeness information

We have seen in Example 2 that rewrite steps cannot be applied to function calls if some arguments are not sufficiently instantiated. Hence we can omit all rewrite attempts to a function call if an argument that is required in all rewrite rules has $\mathcal{R}$-mode f.

We say an operation f *requires argument* i if $t_i \notin \mathcal{X}$ for all rewrite rules $f(t_1, \ldots, t_n) \rightarrow r$, i.e., t_i has a constructor at the top. Our optimization w.r.t. freeness is based on the following proposition.

Proposition 3. *If an operation f has $\mathcal{R}$-mode $\langle m_1, \ldots, m_n \rangle$ with $m_i = f$ and requires argument i, then no rewrite step can be applied to an f-rooted term during execution.*

In this case all rewrite rules for f can be deleted in the compiled program and all attempts to rewrite f-rooted subterms can be immediately skipped. However, in practice this case rarely occurs since rewrite steps are always applied to the entire goal before each single narrowing step. Therefore function arguments are usually not definitely free for all rewrite attempts but become more and more instantiated while narrowing steps are performed. But we can see in Example 2 that there is an interesting situation where unnecessary rewrite attempts occur. After applying a narrowing step with rule $l \rightarrow r$ to the leftmost innermost subterm, due to the eager normalization strategy, applications of rewrite rules are tried to all functions occurring in r. Since a narrowing step is only applied because of the insufficient instantiation of arguments (otherwise the subterm would be evaluated by rewriting), it is often the case that the function calls in r are not sufficiently instantiated to apply rewrite rules. Hence the rewrite attempts immediately after a narrowing step could be avoided.

In order to give a precise definition of this optimization, we define a special kind of rewrite mode which is valid immediately after a narrowing step.

Definition 4. Let $f(t_1, \ldots, t_n) \rightarrow r$ be a narrowing rule and N be a $\mathcal{N}$-mode for f/n. Let $g(s_1, \ldots, s_m)$ be a function call in r and $R_f \subseteq T(\mathcal{F}, \mathcal{X})^m$. Then R_f is called $\mathcal{R}/\mathcal{N}$-mode (w.r.t. to N) *(rewrite mode w.r.t. narrowing)* for the function call $g(s_1, \ldots, s_m)$ iff $\sigma(\langle s_1, \ldots, s_n \rangle) \in R_f$ for each most general unifier σ of $\langle t_1, \ldots, t_n \rangle$ and some $\langle t'_1, \ldots, t'_n \rangle \in N$. □

Note that suitable $\mathcal{R}/\mathcal{N}$-modes can be easily derived from a given $\mathcal{N}$-mode of an operation. Since Proposition 3 is also valid w.r.t. $\mathcal{R}/\mathcal{N}$-modes and the immediate rewrite attempts after a narrowing step, we can use $\mathcal{R}/\mathcal{N}$-modes to avoid unnecessary rewrite attempts. For instance, consider Example 2 and the rule

$$s(M) + N \rightarrow s(M + N) \qquad (R_2)$$

Since + has $\mathcal{N}$-mode $\langle f, a \rangle$, a suitable $\mathcal{R}/\mathcal{N}$-mode of the function call M+N in the right-hand side is $\langle f, a \rangle$. Therefore no rewrite rule is applicable to M+N immediately after a narrowing step with R_2 because + requires its first argument.

In the case of nested function calls, we can also skip rewrite attempts to function calls which contain function calls in normal form at a required argument position. For instance, if (X+Y)+Z occurs in the right-hand side of a narrowing rule and the $\mathcal{N}$-mode implies that X is always a free variable, then rewrite attempts to both occurrences of + can be neglected.

The realization of this optimization in a compiler-based implementation of normalizing innermost narrowing is easy. In order to avoid a dynamic search in the current goal for the leftmost innermost subterm, it is useful to manage an *occurrence stack* at run time [13]. This stack contains references to all functions calls in a goal in leftmost innermost order, i.e., the top element refers to the leftmost innermost subterm. If a narrowing rule $l \rightarrow r$ is applied, the top element of the occurrence stack is deleted, references to all function calls in r are added, and the application of rewrite rules are tried to all subterms referred by the occurrence stack.[5] The management of the occurrence stack provides an efficient implementation and causes nearly no overhead (see [13] for benchmarks). Moreover, it provides a simple realization of the freeness optimization. To skip unnecessary rewrite attempts in the right-hand side of a narrowing rule, the occurrences of the corresponding subterms are not pushed onto the occurrence stack. Although this optimization is simple, it has measurable effects on the execution time if the portion of narrowing steps in the computation is not too low (see Section 5 for benchmarks). In extreme cases all unnecessary rewrite attempts are avoided by this optimization.

4.2 Using groundness information

An implementation of normalizing narrowing requires the application of rewrite rules to all function calls in a goal before a narrowing step is performed. Therefore function calls cannot be represented by pieces of code similarly to predicate calls in the WAM [36], but they must be explicitly represented as a term structure. For instance, if the quad rule R_5 of Example 2 is applied in a narrowing or rewrite step, the term representation of the right-hand side (N+N)+double(N) is created in the heap area (which contains all term structures during program execution [13, 36].)[6] This implementation has the disadvantage that many terms are created on the heap which are garbage after the evaluation of the function calls. The situation can be improved if it is known that some functions are completely evaluable by rewriting. A sufficient criterion is the groundness of some arguments.[7]

---

[5] This explanation is slightly simplified. In the concrete implementation, a second so-called *copy occurrence stack* is used in the rewrite process. See [13] for more details.

[6] It is not necessary to create a term representation for all functions calls. Since the leftmost innermost function call N+N is evaluated in the next step, a representation of this term is only necessary if no rewrite rule is applicable to it. Therefore the creation of this term is delayed in [13]. This results in an implementation similar to WAM-based Prolog systems.

[7] Note that we assume that all narrowing rules are also used for rewriting, otherwise the proposition does not hold.

Proposition 5. *If an operation f has R-mode ⟨g, ..., g⟩, then all f-rooted sub-terms are completely evaluated by rewriting during execution.*

This property holds since a narrowing step is only performed at an innermost position if some arguments are not sufficiently instantiated, but the latter condition can never be satisfied if it is a ground function call. Consequently, ground function calls can be implemented by a fixed sequence of function calls which do not require a representation on the heap. For instance, if quad has R-mode ⟨g⟩, then the rewrite rule quad(N)→(N+N)+double(N) could be translated similarly to functions in imperative or functional languages according to the following code sequence:

```
N   := A1          % Register A1 contains the actual argument of quad
N1  := N+N         % call operation +
N2  := double(N)   % call operation double
N3  := N1+N2       % call operation +
return(N3)         % return the computed value
```

The intermediate values could be stored in an environment on the local stack which can be deleted after the **return** (or before, if last call optimization is implemented). Thus, if groundness information is available, we could optimize the code such that function calls need not be represented on the heap and intermediate results are stored on the local stack instead of the heap. This has the advantage that the used memory space on the local stack is automatically released after deterministic computations while the heap is cleaned up only after a garbage collection phase. Some results to this optimization are shown in Section 5.

4.3 Code elimination using mode information

Rewrite steps and narrowing steps differ in the application of the left-hand side to a subterm: while the subterm is *matched* with the left-hand side in a rewrite step, it is *unified* with the left-hand side in a narrowing step. Due to this different behavior (and some other reasons, cf. [13]), rewrite rules and narrowing rules are compiled into separate instructions. In particular, if the program rules defining operations are used both as narrowing rules and rewrite rules, each rule is compiled in two ways. This has a positive effect on the time efficiency of the compiled code, but it doubles the code space. On the other hand, only a few rules are actually used both for narrowing and rewriting in practical programs. Some rules are only used in rewrite steps, while others are exclusively used in narrowing steps. Information about modes can help to detect these cases at compile time so that unnecessary code can be avoided in the target program. The following conditions are sufficient criteria to omit rules in the target program:

1. If f has R-mode $\langle m_1, \ldots, m_n \rangle$ with $m_i = f$, then rewrite rules of the form $f(t_1, \ldots, t_n) \rightarrow r$ with $t_i \notin \mathcal{X}$ are superfluous (by Proposition 3).
2. Narrowing rule $f(t_1, \ldots, t_n) \rightarrow r$ is superfluous if f has N-mode $\langle m_1, \ldots, m_n \rangle$ and for each $t_i \notin \mathcal{X}$ and each $t_i \in Var(t_j)$ (for some $j \neq i$) $m_i = g$ holds (since in this case the rule is always applicable in a preceding rewrite step.)[8]

---

[8] Note that the case $t_i \in Var(t_j)$ is necessary since we allow multiple occurrences of the same variable in the left-hand side of a rule. E.g., the rule f(X,X)→X is not applicable to the term f(Y,Z) in a rewrite step, thus this rule must be kept as a narrowing rule.

Extreme cases of 2 are rules of the form $f(X_1, \ldots, X_n) \to r$ where $X_1, \ldots, X_n$ are pairwise different variables, or all narrowing rules for a function f which has $\mathcal{N}$-mode $\langle g, \ldots, g \rangle$.

For instance, in Example 2 we can delete R_3, R_4, R_5 as narrowing rules. These rules are only used in rewrite steps, while rules R_1 and R_2 are used both in rewrite and narrowing steps.

5 Experimental results

In order to obtain results about the practical usefulness of the optimizations discussed so far, we have applied these optimizations to some functional logic programs. These optimizations were performed with the ALF system [12, 13] which uses normalizing innermost narrowing as the operational semantics. We have not introduced any new low-level instructions into the abstract machine A-WAM on which the ALF system is based. All the optimizations discussed in Section 4 are implemented using the standard instruction set of the A-WAM which is the simplest, but not the most efficient way to implement these optimizations. Therefore it is obvious that better results can be obtained if the A-WAM would be redesigned according to the availability of mode information.

Table 1 shows the difference of the execution time between programs compiled without and with the optimizations w.r.t. freeness information as discussed in Section 4.1. All programs were executed on a Sparc 1. The programs are small but typical functional logic programs in the sense that functions are called with non-ground arguments so that narrowing rules must be applied to evaluate these functions. arith is a program that solves the equation X+X=10 on natural numbers (where natural numbers are represented by terms built from the constructors 0 and s). hamilton computes a Hamiltonian path in a graph. last computes the last element of a given list with 10 elements by solving the equation append(_,[E])=[···]. path computes a complete path through a graph. permsort is the functional version of the permutation sort program, a typical generate-and-test program which demonstrates the advantages of functional logic programs compared to pure logic programs [14].

Program	Standard	Optimized	Improvement
arith	2.70	2.42	11.5%
hamilton	1180	980	20.4%
last	5.40	4.80	12.5%
path	1400	1120	25.0%
permsort	1680	1480	13.5%

Table 1. Execution times (in msec) for optimized programs w.r.t. freeness information

Although freeness information is only used to avoid some unnecessary rewrite attempts for the right-hand side after a narrowing step (and not for other more

	Standard		Optimized	
Program	local stack	heap	local stack	heap
fac	104	441168	161380	370104
fib	104	1145148	780	926248
zero	104	655620	636	280

Table 2. Maximum memory usage for optimized programs w.r.t. groundness information (in bytes)

primitive optimizations [24, 31, 32, 34, 35]), the table presents interesting improvements in the execution time. The variations show that it is difficult to state a general factor of improvement using freeness information. This factor largely depends on the number of function calls which can be safely skipped in the normalization process after the application of a narrowing rule.

Table 2 shows the memory usage for unoptimized and optimized programs w.r.t. groundness information as discussed in Section 4.2. The programs are recursive functions on natural numbers where natural numbers are represented by terms built from the constructors 0 and s. fac computes the factorial of 8, fib computes the 20'th Fibonacci number, and zero is a function which maps all inputs to the constant 0 but it is recursively defined similarly to fib.

Since we have not changed the instruction set of the A-WAM, we could only simulate the optimizations with the existing instruction set. But we can see in Table 2 that the heap space is reduced while the local stack increases. This is a desirable property since the local stack is automatically cleaned up after deterministic computations while the heap space must be reclaimed by a garbage collector. In the optimized version, no function calls are created on the heap. The remaining heap cells are occupied by constructor terms created during execution (in these examples: s-terms representing natural numbers). An extreme case is the recursive function zero which creates no constructor terms. The large heap space in the unoptimized version is due to the representation of recursive function calls in the heap.

6   Automatic derivation of modes

The main motivation of this paper is to show opportunities to optimize functional logic programs. For this purpose we have defined a notion of modes which is suitable for the particular operational semantics. However, the automatic derivation of these modes is another complex topic which will be addressed in a forthcoming paper [18]. In this section we will discuss some peculiarities related to the automatic derivation of modes.

Innermost narrowing without normalization is equivalent to SLD-resolution if the functional logic program is transformed into a flat program without nested function calls [2]. For instance, we could transform the rules of Example 1 into the flat logic program

```
add(0,N,N).
add(s(M),N,s(Z)) :- add(M,N,Z).
```

where the predicate **add** corresponds to the function + with its result value. The nested function call in the right-hand side of rule R_2 has been replaced by the new variable Z and the additional condition **add(M,N,Z)**. Now each innermost narrowing derivation w.r.t. rules R_1 and R_2 corresponds to one SLD-derivation w.r.t. the transformed logic program.

Due to these similarities of narrowing and SLD-resolution, one could try to apply abstract interpretation techniques developed for logic programming (e.g., [3, 22, 27]) to derive the desired information. E.g., to derive the narrowing mode of the function + w.r.t. to the class of initial goals $x+y=z$, where x and y are always ground and z is a free variable, we could use an abstract interpretation framework for logic programming to infer the call modes of the predicate **add** w.r.t. the class of initial goals **add**(x,y,z). In this case we infer that the call mode is $\langle g, g, f \rangle$ and the argument z of the initial goal will be bound to a ground term at the end of a successful computation. Hence we could deduce that $\langle g, g \rangle$ is the narrowing mode of the function +.

However, normalizing narrowing, which we have considered in this paper, does not directly correspond to SLD-resolution because of the intermediate normalization process. These normalization steps between narrowing steps may delete entire subterms or change the order of subterms. These subtleties require more sophisticated analysis techniques than those developed for pure logic programming. E.g., consider the rules

$$f(0,Z) \rightarrow 0 \qquad\qquad\qquad g(0) \rightarrow 0$$

and the initial equation $f(g(X),g(Y))=0$. Using normalizing innermost narrowing, this equation is solved by applying a narrowing step to the innermost subterm $g(X)$ followed by a rewrite step:

$$
\begin{aligned}
f(g(X),g(Y)) = 0 \;&\leadsto_{\{X \mapsto 0\}}\; f(0,g(Y)) = 0 \\
&\rightarrow_{\mathcal{R}} \quad\; 0 = 0
\end{aligned}
$$

Hence variable Y remains unbound at the end of the computation. On the other hand, the flattening transformation yields the following corresponding logic program:

```
f(0,Z,0).
g(0,0).
?- g(X,Z1), g(Y,Z2), f(Z1,Z2,0).
```

But this logic program has another behavior than the functional logic program since the variable Y will be bound by SLD-resolution! Therefore we can apply abstract interpretation frameworks for logic programming in our context only if there are no rewrite rules which may delete or permute arguments. Such rewrite rules require a special treatment in the abstract interpretation procedure which will be described in a forthcoming paper [18]. Another approach to abstract interpretation of functional logic programs based on an alternative operational semantics is described in [16].

7 Conclusions

In this paper we have shown optimization techniques in the presence of mode information which are unique to the execution mechanism of functional logic programs. We have considered normalizing innermost narrowing as the operational semantics since it has been shown that this strategy is a reasonable improvement over Prolog's left-to-right resolution strategy [10, 14]. We have defined the notion of modes for functional logic programs. These modes can be used to optimize the normalization process. On the one hand, the normalization process is the reason for the operational improvements of functional logic languages compared to pure logic languages. On the other hand, the normalization process may add unnecessary work. This can be improved using modes: freeness information avoids superfluous rewrite attempts, and groundness information provides for a better implementation (in terms of memory consumption) of the normalization process. Moreover, information about modes can also be used to avoid the generation of code for rewrite or narrowing rules which will never be used at run time.

Future work includes a refinement of the abstract machine for the execution of functional logic programs following the lines presented in [32, 34], the development of appropriate abstract interpretation frameworks to derive mode information at compile time [18], and refined applicability conditions for rewrite rules using type information [4].

References

1. D. Bert and R. Echahed. Design and Implementation of a Generic, Logic and Functional Programming Language. In *Proc. ESOP'86*, pp. 119–132. Springer LNCS 213, 1986.
2. P.G. Bosco, E. Giovannetti, and C. Moiso. Narrowing vs. SLD-Resolution. *Theoretical Computer Science 59*, pp. 3–23, 1988.
3. M. Bruynooghe. A Practical Framework for the Abstract Interpretation of Logic Programs. *Journal of Logic Programming (10)*, pp. 91–124, 1991.
4. M. Bruynooghe and G. Janssens. An Instance of Abstract Interpretation Integrating Type and Mode Inferencing. In *Proc. 5th Conference on Logic Programming & 5th Symposium on Logic Programming (Seattle)*, pp. 669–683, 1988.
5. S.K. Debray. Static Inference of Modes and Data Dependencies in Logic Programs. *ACM TOPLAS*, Vol. 11, No. 3, pp. 418–450, 1989.
6. S.K. Debray and D.S. Warren. Automatic Mode Inference for Logic Programs. *Journal of Logic Programming (5)*, pp. 207–229, 1988.
7. D. DeGroot and G. Lindstrom, editors. *Logic Programming, Functions, Relations, and Equations*. Prentice Hall, 1986.
8. N. Dershowitz and J.-P. Jouannaud. Rewrite Systems. In J. van Leeuwen, editor, *Handbook of Theoretical Computer Science, Vol. B*, pp. 243–320. Elsevier, 1990.
9. M.J. Fay. First-Order Unification in an Equational Theory. In *Proc. 4th Workshop on Automated Deduction*, pp. 161–167, Austin (Texas), 1979. Academic Press.
10. L. Fribourg. SLOG: A Logic Programming Language Interpreter Based on Clausal Superposition and Rewriting. In *Proc. IEEE Int. Symp. on Logic Programming*, pp. 172–184, Boston, 1985.
11. E. Giovannetti, G. Levi, C. Moiso, and C. Palamidessi. Kernel LEAF: A Logic plus Functional Language. *Journal of Computer and System Sciences*, Vol. 42, No. 2, pp. 139–185, 1991.
12. M. Hanus. Compiling Logic Programs with Equality. In *Proc. PLILP'90*, pp. 387–401. Springer LNCS 456, 1990.
13. M. Hanus. Efficient Implementation of Narrowing and Rewriting. In *Proc. PDK'91*, pp. 344–365. Springer LNAI 567, 1991.

14. M. Hanus. Improving Control of Logic Programs by Using Functional Logic Languages. In *Proc. PLILP'92*, pp. 1–23. Springer LNCS 631, 1992.

15. M. Hanus. Incremental Rewriting in Narrowing Derivations. In *Proc. ALP'92*, pp. 228–243. Springer LNCS 632, 1992.

16. M. Hanus. On the Completeness of Residuation. In *Proc. of the 1992 Joint Int. Conf. and Symp. on Logic Programming*, pp. 192–206. MIT Press, 1992.

17. M. Hanus. The Integration of Functions into Logic Programming: From Theory to Practice. *To appear in Journal of Logic Programming*, 1994.

18. M. Hanus and F. Zartmann. Automatic derivation of modes for functional logic programs. Max-Planck-Institut für Informatik, Saarbrücken (in preparation), 1994.

19. S. Hölldobler. *Foundations of Equational Logic Programming*. Springer LNCS 353, 1989.

20. J.-M. Hullot. Canonical Forms and Unification. In *Proc. 5th Conference on Automated Deduction*, pp. 318–334. Springer LNCS 87, 1980.

21. H. Kuchen, R. Loogen, J.J. Moreno-Navarro, and M. Rodríguez-Artalejo. Graph-based Implementation of a Functional Logic Language. In *Proc. ESOP'90*, pp. 271–290. Springer LNCS 432, 1990.

22. B. Le Charlier, K. Musumbu, and P. Van Hentenryck. A Generic Abstract Interpretation Algorithm and its Complexity Analysis. In *Proc. International Conference on Logic Programming*, pp. 64–78. MIT Press, 1991.

23. R. Loogen. Relating the Implementation Techniques of Functional and Functional Logic Languages. *New Generation Computing*, Vol. 11, pp. 179–215, 1993.

24. A. Marien, G. Janssens, A. Mulkers, and M. Bruynooghe. The impact of abstract interpretation: an experiment in code generation. In *Proc. Sixth International Conference on Logic Programming (Lisboa)*, pp. 33–47. MIT Press, 1989.

25. C.S. Mellish. Some Global Optimizations for a Prolog Compiler. *Journal of Logic Programming (1)*, pp. 43–66, 1985.

26. J.J. Moreno-Navarro and M. Rodríguez-Artalejo. Logic Programming with Functions and Predicates: The Language BABEL. *Journal of Logic Programming*, Vol. 12, pp. 191–223, 1992.

27. U. Nilsson. Systematic Semantic Approximations of Logic Programs. In *Proc. PLILP'90*, pp. 293–306. Springer LNCS 456, 1990.

28. U.S. Reddy. Narrowing as the Operational Semantics of Functional Languages. In *Proc. IEEE Int. Symp. on Logic Programming*, pp. 138–151, Boston, 1985.

29. J.R. Slagle. Automated Theorem-Proving for Theories with Simplifiers, Commutativity, and Associativity. *Journal of the ACM*, Vol. 21, No. 4, pp. 622–642, 1974.

30. Z. Somogyi. A system of precise modes for logic programs. In *Proc. Fourth Int. Conf. on Logic Programming*, pp. 769–787. MIT Press, 1987.

31. A. Taylor. Removal of Dereferencing and Trailing in Prolog Compilation. In *Proc. Sixth Int. Conf. on Logic Programming*, pp. 48–60. MIT Press, 1989.

32. A. Taylor. LIPS on a MIPS: Results form a Prolog Compiler for a RISC. In *Proc. Seventh Int. Conf. on Logic Programming*, pp. 174–185. MIT Press, 1990.

33. P. Van Roy. An Intermediate Language to Support Prolog's Unification. In *Proc. 1989 North American Conf. on Logic Programming*, pp. 1148–1164. MIT Press, 1989.

34. P.L. Van Roy. *Can Logic Programming Execute as Fast as Imperative Programming?* PhD thesis, Univ. of California Berkeley, 1990. Report No. UCB/CSD 90/600.

35. D.H.D. Warren. Implementing PROLOG - Compiling Logic Programs. 1 and 2. D.A.I. Research Report No. 39 and 40, University of Edinburgh, 1977.

36. D.H.D. Warren. An Abstract Prolog Instruction Set. Technical Note 309, SRI International, Stanford, 1983.

A Portable and Optimizing Back End for the SML/NJ Compiler

Lal George[1], Florent Guillame[2], John H. Reppy[1]

[1] AT&T Bell Laboratories, 600 Mountain Ave., Murray Hill, NJ 07974, USA
[2] École Normale Supérieure, 45, rue d'Ulm, 75005 Paris, France
Email: {george, jhr}@research.att.com, guillaum@clipper.ens.fr

Abstract. There are two major goals that must be addressed in a portable back end: a good sequence of instructions must be selected making full use of the capabilities of the machine, and it must be possible to orchestrate target-specific optimizations. A key to the first problem is the language MLRISC, intended in part, to represent the simplest and most basic operations implementable in hardware. The importance of MLRISC is that it provides a common representation for expressing the instruction set of any hardware platform. Bottom-up tree pattern matching with dynamic programming, expressed using succinct and clear specifications of the target instruction set, is used to generate target machine code from an MLRISC program. Target-specific optimizations are performed by parameterizing *off-the-shelf* optimization modules with concepts common across architectures. The specification of a variety of architectures, and the ability to mix and match sophisticated optimization algorithms are shown. The resulting back end is independent of the intermediate language used in SML/NJ, and could in principle be used in a compiler for a source language quite different from SML. We argue that porting the compiler to a new architecture requires substantially less effort than the existing abstract machine approach, and report significant gains from preliminary architecture description driven optimizations.

1 Introduction

Portability is crucial to the widespread use and acceptance of any new language. Not only must the compiler be readily portable to a wide variety of architectures, but it must also generate code that is competitive with one where portability is not an issue. The compiler cannot be biased towards one architecture.

The Standard ML of New Jersey system (SML/NJ)[3, 4] is a highly optimizing compiler that uses the Continuation Passing Style (CPS) intermediate form for optimization[2]. Most of the optimizations in the compiler are done at this level. The code generation model has been based on an abstract machine called the **cmachine** for *code machine*. The **cmachine** has a small set of registers, and a fairly high level instruction set. There is a **cmachine** instruction that can expand to several hundred instructions. Registers include: an *allocation pointer* representing the next available location in the heap, a *limit register* representing the highest address in the heap, a set of *miscellaneous registers* for parameter passing, and others. The compiler is ported to a new architecture by providing a mapping of the cmachine registers to physical registers, and *templates* that macro-expand cmachine instructions into target machine instructions. Such a port is unsatisfactory in several ways: useful low level optimizations are omitted in the translation to machine code; it may not be possible to use the full capabilities of the target architecture and its instruction set, and it is sometimes difficult to incorporate target-specific optimizations. The back end is responsible for linking, scheduling, span-dependency analysis, and binary instruction output. There is no dependence on the host assembler and linker. Various target specific optimizations, such as scheduling are manually implemented for each architecture.

Two major problems must be addressed in a portable back end, namely: a good sequence of instructions must be selected for the task, making full use of the available registers and instructions, and it must be possible to orchestrate optimizations specific to the architecture, without compromising portability.

2 Overview of Our Approach

Our new approach is not biased towards any architecture. CPS is compiled to a tree language called MLRISC; intended in part, to describe the simplest kinds of operations implementable in hardware. No assumptions are made regarding addressing modes or types of instructions, and because of our register allocation scheme, there are few assumptions made about physical registers. The MLRISC is then converted to a flow graph of target machine instructions, which is optimized using generic optimization modules parameterized over a machine description.

The importance of MLRISC is that it provides a common medium for the specification of any instruction set. There are basic operations implementable in hardware, and instructions are made up of these operations. An instruction ought to be definable using these basic operations.

Bottom-up tree pattern matching with dynamic programming (BURG) is central to our approach. The translation from CPS to target machine code proceeds in three major phases, two of which involve BURG specifications (Figure 1). The high level CPS is first translated into a simpler form called ctrees, suitable as input to BURG. Several optimizations are performed during this simplification. Using the BURG specification Ψ, the ctree language is rewritten to MLRISC trees, optimizing the tagging and untagging of arithmetic operations along the way. BURG is used once again to translate MLRISC to a flowgraph of target machine instructions. The specification Φ is a description of the target architecture *instruction set* and *registers*. Various optimizations such as liveness analysis, scheduling, span-dependency analysis, and graph-coloring register allocation are performed on the target machine instructions. The optimization phase is parameterized over a machine description represented as a set of SML modules. The back end is constructed by a series of functor applications and is a nice demonstration of the flexibility provided by the module system[15]. The concise description of the instruction set in terms of MLRISC, and the ability to perform architecture description driven optimizations, are the key contributions.

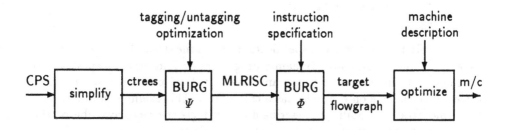

Fig. 1. Flowchart of new code generation model

3 ML-Burg

The new code generation strategy is implemented using a SML version of iBurg[10, 13]. Given a tree rewriting system augmented with costs, ML-Burg generates a program to perform bottom-up tree pattern matching with dynamic programming. A successful reduction of the input tree, corresponds to rewriting the input tree to a special non-terminal symbol called the *start non-terminal*. Upon successful reduction, facilities are provided to walk the tree emitting semantic actions associated with the rules that matched.

Consider the rewrite system specified below:

```
reg :    LI_i               (1)  ;
reg :    ADD(reg,LI_i)      (1)  ;
reg :    ADD(reg,reg)       (1)  ;
```

ADD is a binary node with the usual meaning, and LI$_i$ is a leaf node representing the *integer immediate i*. The integer i is not used in pattern matching and is not part of the rewrite rule, but it is an attribute that may be used in semantic actions . This grammar specifies that: an input tree matching LI$_i$ can be reduced to the *non-terminal* reg with a cost of one; an input tree matching ADD(reg,LI$_i$), where the first child can be reduced to reg, can also be reduced to the non-terminal reg. The grammar above is clearly ambiguous as there are two ways to reduce the tree ADD(LI$_3$,LI$_4$) to the non-terminal reg. The two reductions are shown below, where each reduction is annotated with SPARC assembly code. The registers, %t1, %t2, and %t3 are pseudo-registers that are assigned to physical registers in a later register allocation pass.

```
ADD(LI₃,LI₄)                              ADD(LI₃,LI₄)
    ↓     ;; add %g0,3,%t1                    ↓     ;; add %go,3,%t1
ADD(reg,LI₄)                              ADD(reg,LI₄)
    ↓     ;; add %g0,4,%t2                    ↓     ;; add %t1,4,%t2
ADD(reg,reg)                                  reg
    ↓     ;; add %t1,%t2,%t3
    reg
```

It is precisely this ambiguity in specification that is the strength of tree rewriting code generation techniques. Dynamic programming finds the cheapest set of instructions to implement the program. The reduction on the left has a cost of three, while the one on the right has a cost of two. This example however, does not demonstrate the ability to describe different register classes available on the target architecture, or non-regular register sets (Section 6).

4 MLRISC

Figure 2 shows the SML signature for MLRISC. The instruction set, described by the datatype mlrisc, makes no assumptions about addressing modes on the target machine. It is possible to JMP to *anything*, and LOAD/STORE from *anything*. Each mlrisc instruction defines a basic combinator that will be used to describe the target instruction set. A BURG grammar is used to define the instruction set, and the associated semantic actions can be used to effectively utilize the hardware.

Non-commutative arithmetic operations specify the order of evaluation of arguments, using the type order. The order of evaluation must be recorded to preserve the semantics with respect to arithmetic exceptions. Thus instructions like SUB and DIV, etc., specify the order of evaluation. The order is assumed to be left-to-right for commutative operators.

There is a commitment to general purpose and floating point registers, REG and FREG respectively. Nearly all processors today have these sets of registers and provide dedicated instructions to operate on them. This does not preclude the Motorola 68000 that does not have general purpose registers. BURG nonterminals may be used to represent the Motorola 68000, address and data registers (Section 6).

Lastly, MLRISC has no connection to the CPS intermediate representation or dedicated registers, and can be easily divorced from SML/NJ system.

5 Ctree and MLRISC Generation

The ctree representation is used to simplify the high level semantics of CPS, and provide a suitable tree representation for input to BURG. Generating a tree representation from the linear CPS input must observe the semantics with respect to arithmetic exceptions and memory. Several low level optimizations may be performed on the ctree representation, such as:

```
structure Label : sig
                    datatype label =
                        ...
                    end =
struct  ... end

signature MLRISC = sig
    datatype order = LR | RL                    (* order of evaluation *)
    datatype bcond  = LT | LE | EQ | GEU        (* branch conditions *)
    datatype mlrisc                             (* instructions *)
        = REG  of int                           (* register *)
        | FREG of int                           (* floating register *)
        | LI   of int                           (* integer constant *)
        | MV   of mlrisc * mlrisc               (* move *)
        | FMV  of mlrisc * mlrisc       (* floating point move *)
        | ADD  of mlrisc * mlrisc               (* addition *)
        | SUB  of mlrisc * mlrisc * order       (* subtraction *)
        ...
        | ANDB  of mlrisc * mlrisc              (* logical AND *)
        ...
        | LOAD  of mlrisc                       (* memory operations *)
        | STORE of mlrisc * mlrisc
        ...
        | CVTI2D of mlrisc           (* convert integer to double *)
        | FADDD of mlrisc * mlrisc   (* floating point addition *)
        ...
        | BR    of Label.label                  (* branch instructions *)
        | JMP   of mlrisc
        | BCC   of bcond * mlrisc * mlrisc * Label.label * order
        | FBCC  of bcond * mlrisc * mlrisc * Label.label * order
        | SEQ of mlrisc * mlrisc                (* sequencing *)
    end
```

Fig. 2. MLRISC specification

- The detection of situations where a record creation in the heap can be implemented as a tight loop copying consecutive locations from one memory area to the record being created.
- Propagating increments to the allocation pointer, so that it is performed only once at the function exit points.

Dynamic programming is used to optimize the tagging and untagging of arithmetic expressions, in the translation of ctrees to MLRISC. Integers in SML are tagged with their lowest bit set to one, (i.e., the integer n is represented as $2n + 1$). On the MIPS, the old code generator expands the CPS program (x:=a-b; z:=x+y) to:

```
sub    a,b,t1        % t1 := a - b
add    t1,1,x        % x := t1 + 1
sub    x,1,t2        % t2 := x - 1
add    t2,y,z        % z := t2 + y
```

Clearly the intermediate tagging and untagging is unnecessary. Dynamic programming using BURG is a fast and elegant solution to this problem. Peterson's min-cut algorithm is more thorough but expensive $(O(n^3))$[16]. The BURG specification Ψ contains 124 rules (details appear in an extended version[11]).

The resulting MLRISC program represents the simplest set of operations required to implement the CPS program. The burden of various optimizations till this point, in the abstract machine model, would have been on the person porting the compiler. These optimizations would be repeated for each architecture. Now, it has been transferred once and for all, to a person that is an expert on the internals of the compiler. These basic operations must now be combined to match instructions on the target machine.

6   Instruction Set Specification

As a concrete example, Figure 3 introduces a fragment of the SPARC specification. An effective address on the SPARC can either be a *register+displacement* or a *register+register*. This is specified using the non-terminal **ea**. The semantic actions associated with rules that reduce to **ea**, return a value of type **eaValue**. The operand to a **LOAD** must be reduced to the non-terminal **ea**, and the code to emit is a simple case statement over the various **eaValue** constructors. Fortunately, no restrictions were imposed on the operand to **LOAD** in the MLRISC design. This example extends to handle the full set of addressing modes and instructions found on CISC machines such as the Intel i486 or Motorola 68000. A description of the i486 addressing modes involves just 10 lines of BURG specification.

An example from the Motorola 68000, illustrates how simple specifications can later on yield high quality code, and the use of non-terminals to denote various kinds of register classes. On the 68000, certain kinds of registers are not permitted as operands to instructions. For example, the operand to **LOAD** must be reducible to an address register. The result of the load may be either an address or data register. This is fairly easy to specify by devoting a non-terminal to address registers. A possible fragment of the 68000 specification is shown in Figure 4.

For correctness, a **movl** is required in the implementation of **ADD**. Since we assume an infinite number of registers, which are later assigned to physical registers, these moves normally turn out to be harmless. Coalescing non-interfering live ranges in a graph-coloring register allocation algorithm[9], collapses **rd** and **dreg**$_1$ to the same physical register where possible, eliminating the redundant move. This technique is used quite effectively to handle the non-regular register set on the Intel i486. These specifications and semantic actions are very simple, yet they describe quite varied and complex systems.

```
datatype eaValue = DISPea of register * int
                 | INDXea of register * register
...
ea:    ADD(reg,LIᵢ)      (0) DISPea(reg,i) ;;
ea:    ADD(reg₁,reg₂)    (0) INDXea(reg₁,reg₂) ;;
ea:    SUB(reg,LIᵢ)      (0) DISPea(reg,~i) ;;
ea:    reg               (0) DISPea(reg,0) ;;
reg:   LOAD(ea)     (1) let val rd : register = newReg()
                        in
                            case ea
                              of DISPea(rt,n) => emit(ld(rt,IMMED n,rd))
                               | INDXea(rs,rt)=> emit(ld(rs,REG rt,rd))
                            (* esac *);
                            rd
                        end ;;
```

Fig. 3. SPARC instruction set specification

```
areg:   LOAD(areg)         (1) ...
dreg:   LOAD(areg)         (1) ...
dreg:   ADD(dreg₁,dreg₂)   (1) let val rd = newDreg()
                               in
                                   emit(movl(rd,dreg₁));
                                   emit(addl(rd,dreg₂))
                               end
```

Fig. 4. Motorola 68000 instruction set specification

The combination of ML-Burg and MLRISC is an elegant way to solve the instruction selection problem. BURG is expressive enough to allow the concise specification of most instruction set. A similar observation was reported by Appel[5], who wrote TWIG[1] specifications for the VAX and Motorola 68000; detailed information was encoded in the cost function to aid in the selection of the best rule. Porting the compiler does not require knowledge of any compiler internals, such as tagging schemes, runtime representations, and semantics of high level abstract instructions (often specific to SML). The instruction set must be specifiable in MLRISC, which is then used to pick the cheapest instructions to emit with respect to the cost function. Since the generated MLRISC data structure is larger than the source CPS, the instruction selection is done in small units.

7 Target Machine Architectural Description

Once instruction selection has been performed, facilities exist to generate a generic control flowgraph, where the nodes contain target machine instructions. It is not possible to directly output the binary representation of instructions as they contain pseudo-registers and symbolic labels. Instruction scheduling, span-dependency resolution, and further optimizations, may be necessary before final binary code emission. Writing target-specific optimizations for each architecture would be a portability nightmare. Instead, we use a scheme where *off-the-shelf* optimization modules are parameterized over a description of the target machine.

While all machines are different in detail, they are all very similar in concept. The idea behind our machine description is to describe those concepts that are common across architectures, and use them in generic optimization modules. The structure of the machine description is shown in Figure 5. At the lowest level of the module dependency is a description of the storage units on the machine, specified by the signature CELLS. Several dataflow problems require efficient operations over sets of cells, so we require the type **cellset** and the usual set operations over them. These are easily constructed using modules defined in the SML/NJ Library[6]. The signature INSTRUCTION is a specification of the available instructions on the machine in terms of its cells. This hierarchy corresponds to the fundamental design of von Neumann machines. Lastly, the signature INSN_PROPERTIES contains the bulk of the machine description. Useful properties of the instruction set are collected here, and used in generic optimizations modules. For example: the type **kind**, returned by the function **instrKind**, is used to classify instructions as being either a NOP (IK_NOP), a jump instruction (IK_JUMP), or any other (IK_INSTR); the type **target** returned by **branchTargets** is used to describe the target of branch instructions. **instrKind** and **branchTargets** are used to implement a generic module that produces a flowgraph specialized over instructions of the target machine.

Figure 6 shows the machine description for the SPARC. The type **cell** includes: an unlimited supply of general and floating point registers (**Reg** and **Freg**, respectively), the condition code register (CC), and the floating point condition code register (FCC). The stack (STACK) and memory (MEM), which are not normally considered to be in the same category as registers, are also included. Instructions that access the memory or stack, will be marked as accessing the MEM or STACK resource. This information is used during instruction scheduling. **SparcInstr** is the module matching INSTRUCTION in the machine description. The type operand has been simplified for expository purposes. **SparcProps** shows a fragment of the module matching INSN_PROPERTIES. The module is a total of 460 lines, most of which is boiler-plate.

As additional optimization modules are developed, one may expect the signature for INSN_PROPERTIES to grow, in order to meet the demands for more information about the target architecture. After a certain point in this evolution, generating high quality code for a new architecture will involve mixing and matching off-the-shelf optimization modules to suit the architecture.

```
signature CELLS = sig
  type cell
  type cellset
  val cardinality : cellset -> int
  val union       : cellset * cellset -> cellset
  val add         : cell * cellset -> cellset
  ...
end

signature INSTRUCTION = sig
  structure C : CELLS
  type instruction
end

signature INSN_PROPERTIES = sig
  structure I : INSTRUCTION
  structure C : CELLS
  sharing I.C = C

  datatype kind = IK_NOP | IK_JUMP | IK_INSTR
  datatype target = LABELED of Label.label | FALLTHROUGH | ESCAPES
  val instrKind     : I.instruction -> kind
  val defUse        : I.instruction -> C.cellset * C.cellset
  val branchTargets : I.instruction -> target list
  ...
end
```

Fig. 5. Machine description

8 Target Machine Optimization

A generic basic block scheduler that is parameterized by a machine description, described above, has been developed. Figure 7 shows the machine properties required for this purpose. We describe each component individually in more detail to illustrate their complexity (or more appropriately, lack of):

branchDelayedArch is a boolean flag that indicates if the architecture requires a branch delay slot. Special considerations are used for picking this instruction if needed.

latency(*instr*) is a function that returns the number of cycles needed to execute the instruction *instr*.

needsNop(*instr*,*instrs*) during scheduling there may not be enough instructions available to keep the pipeline busy while executing high latency instructions. Further, some architectures require an explicit NOP (No OPeration) instruction between two instructions under such circumstances. For example, on the MIPS, a **MFHI** instruction must occur at least two instructions after a

```
structure SparcCells = struct
  structure S = SortedList
  datatype cell = Reg of int
                | Freg of int
                | CC | FCC | STACK | MEM
  type cellset = int list * int list * int list
  fun cardinality(r,f,e) = length r + length f + length e
  fun union((r1,f1,e1),(r2,f2,e2)) =
      (S.merge(r1,r2),S.merge(f1,f2),S.merge(e1,e2))
  ...
end

structure SparcInstr = struct
  structure C = SparcCells
  datatype operand = REGrand of int
                   | IMrand of int
                   | LABrand of Label.label
  datatype cond_code = CC_A | CC_E  | CC_NE | CC_G | CC_GE
                     | CC_L | CC_LE | CC_GEU | CC_LEU
  datatype instruction
    = NOP
    | LD    of int * operand * int
    | ADD   of int * operand * int
    | ADDCC of int * operand * int
    | JMPL  of int * Label.label list
    | BCC   of cond_code * Label.label
    | FBCC  of cond_code * Label.label
    ...
end

structure SparcProps = struct
  structure I = SparcInstr
  structure C = SparcCells
  datatype kind = IK_NOP | IK_JUMP | IK_INSTR
  datatype target = LABELED of Label.label | FALLTHROUGH | ESCAPES
  fun instrKind(I.NOP)      = IK_NOP
    | instrKind(I.BCC _)    = IK_JUMP
    | instrKind(I.JMPL _)   = IK_JUMP
    | instrKind(I.FBCC _)   = IK_JUMP
    | instrKind _           = IK_INSTR
  fun branchTargets(I.BCC(I.CC_A,lab)) = [LABELLED lab]
    | branchTargets(I.BCC(_,lab))      = [LABELLED lab,FALLTHROUGH]
    ...
    ...
end
```

Fig. 6. SPARC machine description

```
val branchDelayedArch : bool
val latency  : I.instruction -> int
val needsNop : I.instruction * I.instruction list -> int
val defUse   : I.instruction -> int list * int list
val isSdi    : I.instruction -> bool
val minSize  : I.instruction -> int
val maxSize  : I.instruction -> int
val sdiSize  : I.instruction * (int -> int) * int -> int
val expand   : I.instruction * int * (int -> int) ->
                                       I.instruction list
```

Fig. 7. Machine properties for basic block scheduling

MULT instruction. needsNop returns the number of NOPs required between *instr* (the instruction being emitted), and *instrs* (the previous instructions emitted).

defUse(*instr*) returns list of resources defined and used by the instruction. This is used to construct the data dependency graph.

isSdi(*instr*) returns true if *instr* is a span-dependent instruction whose size is determined by the final value of labels.

minSize/maxSize(*instr*) returns the minimum/maximum size of the instruction *instr*. These two functions are used to schedule blocks with span-dependent instructions. The value of labels is calculated assuming all instructions expand to their minimum size. Another calculation is performed assuming all labels expand to their maximum size. If the size of a span-dependent instruction does not vary under these extremities, then it may be expanded, and scheduled along with the other instructions in that block. Such a block is said to be *stable*. Scheduling a basic block refines the value of labels under these two extremities and may stablize an otherwise unstable block. If unstable blocks still persist, then there is no option but to expand the span-dependent instructions to their maximum size.

sdiSize(*instr*, *labMap*, *loc*) returns the size of the span-dependent instruction *instr*, under the assignment of labels given by *labMap*, where the current location counter is *loc*.

expand(*instr*, *size*, *labMap*) returns the sequence of instructions when the span-dependent instruction *instr* is expanded to *size* number of instructions, assuming the assignment of labels given by *labMap*.

The generic basic block scheduler is 397 lines of SML code. The module to perform span-dependency analysis is 384 lines. In a similar fashion to basic block scheduling, we have developed a generic graph-coloring register allocator used to allocate general purpose and floating point registers on most target machines. In addition, on the IBM RS/6000 it is used to allocate pseudo condition code registers among the eight condition code registers available. More optimizations are planned in the near future.

9   Mix and Match

Figure 8 shows the construction of the SPARC code generator, which is formed by linking several optimization phases. The **FlowGraph** functor produces a flowgraph data structure specialized over the SPARC instructions. The **Liveness** functor exports a function called **liveness**, which will annotate the flowgraph with liveness information at block boundaries. Optimizations are mixed and matched using functor applications. The functors **RegAllocator** and **FlowGraphGen** implement a certain optimization, and requires a function **codegen** that will be invoked to perform the rest of the optimizations. The functor **BBSched** that performs basic block scheduling, is the last in the chain, and exports a function called **finish** that does the final machine code output. The SPARC code generator, in Figure 8, strings together: flowgraph generation that includes liveness analysis (**FlowGen**); integer register allocation (**IntRAlloc**); floating point register allocation (**FloatRAlloc**), and finally basic block scheduling (**BBsched**). The various parameters to these functors are unimportant except to note that they are specified by signatures that describe generic properties of architectures. The example illustrates that the use of functor application makes it easy to mix and match generic optimization modules to suit the SPARC architecture.

```
structure SparcFlow = FlowGraph(structure Instr = SparcInstr)

structure SparcLive = Liveness(structure Flowgraph = SparcFlow
                               structure InsnProps = SparcProps)

structure BBsched = BBSched(structure Flowgraph = SparcFlow
                            structure InsnProps = SparcProps
                            structure Emitter   = SparcMCEmitter)

structure FloatRAlloc = RegAllocator(structure Ra = FloatRA_Arg
                                     val codegen = BBsched.bbsched)

structure IntRAlloc =   RegAllocator(structure Ra = IntRA_Arg
                                     val codegen = FloatRAlloc.ra)

structure FlowGen = FlowGraphGen(
                        structure Flowgraph = SparcFlow
                        structure InsnProps = SparcProps
                        val codegen = SparcLive.liveness)
```

Fig. 8. Gluing the SPARC code generator together

10   Results

At the time of writing, we have working code generators for the MIPS, IBM RS/6000 and SPARC, an an untested specification for the Intel i486. The preliminary results reported here are only for the SPARC.

A fairly standard set of SML benchmarks are used[2]. We first measure the improvements from using a more sophisticated register allocation scheme. SML/NJ supports a register passing style for parameters, and it is essential that operands be computed in the *right* register. Register constraints may require that the operand be first computed into a temporary and later moved into the correct register before a function call. The first column of Figure 9 shows the number of register-register moves required at function call boundaries in the existing compiler (version 0.93). The second column shows the performance of our new graph-coloring register allocator. At least 40% of the original register-register moves are removed.

Figure 10 shows the improvements from dynamic programming and the allocation pointer optimization described (Section 5). The first column shows the static code size (in number of instructions) without any optimization, and the second with these optimizations. There is a static code size improvement of 2-5%. In terms of dynamic instruction counts, this corresponds to roughly 1-3% improvement. This is encouraging as these improvements have come largely for free in our attempt to improve portability. Machines such as the Dec Alpha or the IBM RS/6000, should do even better, because multiple overflow checks may be collapsed into one.

While compile time speeds are acceptable, we do not report them since the new system is not tuned or optimized for this. The back end in the current SML/NJ compiler takes about 25% of the total compilation time. This percentage does not include CPS optimization. The new back end is currently about 3-4 times slower.

11   Future Work

Machine descriptions are required for all the architectures that the SML/NJ compiler currently supports, which include, the Motorola 68000, and the HPPA. Work is in progress on a DEC Alpha port. The main areas for future work relate to the speed of compilation, and further optimizations relevant to RISC processors. Our compilation scheme is highly symbolic — developing fast table driven optimizations[17] derived from a more concise machine description, and the use of partial evaluation[7] ought to produce a faster backend. Composing BURG specifications similar to that done for attribute grammars may also prove worthwhile[8]. Lastly, a pre-pass global scheduler is extremely important for superpiplined and superscalar machines[12, 14].

	SML/NJ 0.93	New back end	ratio
mandelbrot	46	5	0.11
life	299	212	0.71
kbendix	968	594	0.61
simple	1089	657	0.60
lexgen	1965	1121	0.57
yacc	4090	2222	0.54

Fig. 9. register-register moves with 6 callee-save registers

	static code size			dynamic instruction count
	before	after	% improvement	% improvement
mandelbrot	625	561	11.4	16.2
life	6333	6032	5.0	0.8
kbendix	13209	12808	3.1	3.2
simple	30492	29263	4.2	1.9
lexgen	24671	24217	1.9	2.2
yacc	96925	94666	2.4	2.3

Fig. 10. Static code size and dynamic instruction count improvements

12 Conclusions

A highly portable and optimizing back end has been described. It addresses the problems of target machine instruction selection and machine specific optimization. Porting the compiler to a new architectural platform is expected to be trivial for someone ignorant of the internal of the compiler, but familiar with the architecture. Off-the-shelf optimization modules can be easily constructed to suit a particular machine. The set of optimizations currently implemented show encouraging results.

References

1. AHO, A., GANAPATHI, M., AND TJIANG, S. Code generation using tree matching and dynamic programming. *ACM Transactions on Programming Languages and Systems 11*, 4 (Oct. 1989), 491–516.
2. APPEL, A. *Compiling with Continuations.* Cambridge Univ. Press, 1992.
3. APPEL, A., AND MACQUEEN, D. A Standard ML compiler. In *Functional Programming Languages and Computer Architecture*, G. Kahn, Ed. Springer-Verlag, 1987, pp. 301–324. LCNS No.274.
4. APPEL, A., AND MACQUEEN, D. Standard ML of New Jersey. In *Third Int'l Symp. on Prog. Lang. Implementation and Logic Programming* (New York, August 1991), M. Wirsing, Ed., Springer-Verlag. (in press).

5. APPEL, A. W. Concise specifiations of locally optimal code generators. Tech. Rep. CS-TR-080-87, Princeton University, Feb. 1987. Dept. of Computer Science.

6. AT&T. *The Standard ML of New Jersey Library, Reference Manual*, 0.2 ed. AT&T Bell Laboratories, 600 Mountain Ave, Murray Hill, NJ 07974, 1993.

7. BIRKEDAL, L., AND WELINDER, M. Partial evaluation of Standard ML. Master's thesis, University of Copenhagen, October 22 1993. Dept. of Computer Science.

8. BOYLAND, J., AND GRAHAM, S. Composing tree attributions. In *POPL '94: 21st ACM SIGPLAN-SIGACT symposium on principles of programming languages* (January 1994), ACM, pp. 375–388. Portland,Oregon.

9. CHAITIN, G. Register allocation and spilling via graph coloring. *SIGPLAN Notices 17(6)* (June 1982), 98–105. Proceeding of the ACM SIGPLAN '82 Symposium on Compiler Construction.

10. FRASER, C., HANSON, D., AND PROEBSTING, T. Engineering a simple, efficient code generator generator. In *Letters on Programming Languages and Systems* (1992), ACM.

11. GEORGE, L., GUILLAME, F., AND REPPY, J. A portable and optimizing back end for the SML/NJ compiler. Tech. Rep. BL112610-931103-38TM, AT&T Bell Laboratories, November 1993.

12. GOODMAN, J., AND HSU, W.-C. Code scheduling and register allocation in large basic blocks. In *Proceedings of the 1988 International Conference on Supercomputing* (July 1988), ACM, pp. 442–452.

13. GUILLAUME, F., AND GEORGE, L. *ML-Burg — Documentation*, 1.0 ed. AT&T Bell Laboratories, 600 Mountain Ave, Murray Hill, NJ 07974, 1993.

14. GWENNAP, L. Cyrix describes pentium competitor. *Microprocessor Report 7*, 14 (October 1993), 5–10.

15. MACQUEEN, D. Modules for Standard ML. In *Proc. 1984 ACM Conf. on LISP and Functional Programming* (New York, 1984), ACM Press, pp. 198–207.

16. PETERSON, J. Untagged data in tagged environments: Choosing optimal representations at compile time. In *Functional programming languages and computer architecture* (September 1989), ACM, pp. 89–99.

17. PROEBSTING, T., AND FRASER, C. Detecting pipeline structural hazards quickly. In *Principles of Programming Languages* (January 1994), ACM.

Efficient Organization of Control Structures in Distributed Implementations

Guido Hogen[1] and Rita Loogen[2]

[1] RWTH Aachen, Lehrstuhl für Informatik II
Ahornstraße 55, D-52056 Aachen, Germany
email: ghogen@zeus.informatik.rwth-aachen.de
[2] Philipps-Universität Marburg, Fachgebiet Informatik
Hans Meerwein Straße, Lahnberge, D-35032 Marburg, Germany
email: loogen@informatik.uni-marburg.de

Abstract. A new technique for the management of control structures in distributed implementations of dynamic process systems is presented. Instead of storing the runtime stacks of parallel processes as linked lists of activation blocks in a heap structure, the local stacks of several parallel processes, which are executed on the same processor element, are stored in an interleaved manner on a single physical stack (within each processor element), called the *meshed stack*. The technique ensures that there is almost no overhead for the evaluation of single processes due to the parallel environment. In principle, the meshed stack technique is independent of the implemented language. We explain it for the parallel implementation of functional languages.

1   Introduction

In purely sequential implementations of most programming languages a *runtime stack* is used for the control of recursive function or procedure calls. Such calls lead to the allocation of control information (activation blocks) on top of the stack. When the call terminates, this information is removed and control is given back to the calling environment. A graph or heap structure is only used for the representation of dynamic data structures.

For parallel implementations, which support dynamic processes, as it is the case in parallel implementations of functional or logic languages, the efficient realization of the runtime stack is one of the most important problems. The use of a global contiguous array of activation blocks is no longer advisable, because each parallel task or process needs its own stack structure. Furthermore a suspension mechanism must be implemented to save the state of tasks which are waiting for the result of some parallel subtask. This led to the idea of allocating runtime structures in a graph or heap instead of on a stack. The runtime stack of each process is implemented as a linked list of activation blocks in the heap [Goldberg, Hudak 86], [Loogen et al. 89], [Augustsson, Johnsson 89], [Kingdon et al. 91]. Spawning of parallel processes yields a tree structure of such linked lists, which represents a so-called *cactus stack*.

A main advantage of this *graph organization* is the *decentralization* which is especially suited for distributed systems, as the bottleneck of a global central stack is avoided. Context switches can simply be achieved by redirecting the pointer to the currently active process. Note that heap *allocation* can be done as efficiently as stack allocation by the incrementation of a heap pointer [Appel 87]. There are however two important disadvantages:

1. the increased organizational overhead for the *deallocation* (garbage collection) of runtime information and

2. the overhead that is imposed on the purely sequential evaluations within processes.

In this paper we present an alternative management of the runtime structures which tends to support parallel and sequential evaluations equally well. Instead of representing the cactus stack as a linked tree of activation blocks, we allocate the activation blocks, within each processor element of the parallel system, on a single *meshed stack*, which is organized as a contiguous array, but shared by several processes. The heap is only used for the representation of migrated parallel processes, structured data, closures and suspensions. Evaluation is controlled by the stack. During the sequential evaluation of processes the meshed stack is used as in conventional implementations. Activation blocks are allocated on top of it, when function or procedure calls are executed, and removed, when the calls terminate. Central issues of the new stack technique are the generation and suspension of parallel processes.

The meshed stack technique is independent of the implemented language. We will explain it for the distributed implementation of a functional language.

The paper is organized as follows. In the next section, we introduce a simple first order functional language which is sufficient for the explanation of our approach. Section 3 explains a simple *sequential* reduction machine which will be the sequential kernel of the parallel implementation. Section 4 introduces parallelism information into the functional language and explains the problems that must be solved to provide a distributed implementation of the parallel functional language. Section 5 is devoted to the explanation of the meshed stack technique. In Section 6 we develop a parallel abstract reduction machine. A special garbage collection method for the meshed stack is described in Section 7. Results from a transputer implementation of our system are contained in Section 8. Finally related work is discussed and some conclusions are drawn.

2 FUN — A Simple FUNctional Language

FUN is a first order monomorphically typed functional language with algebraic data structures. We do not consider higher order functions and polymorphism, as the treatment of these features is orthogonal to our implementation technique.

A *FUN-program* consists of a finite set of defining rules for function symbols. FS denotes the set of function symbols defined in a program. The *defining rule for an element* $f \in FS$ has the form: $f(x_1, \ldots, x_n) := e$, where x_i are variables and e is a FUN-expression. The definition of FUN-expressions is given in Fig. 1.

Function symbols in applications may be basic operation symbols $\phi \in \Omega$, data constructors $\phi \in \Gamma$ or defined function symbols $\phi \in FS$. case-expressions define a complete case analysis on the top level constructor of a data structure expression. The predefined projection operator enables the selection of data

$$
\begin{aligned}
e ::= \; & x & & \% \; x \in Var^t \\
| \; & \phi(e_1,\dots,e_n) & & \% \; \phi \in (\Omega \cup \Gamma \cup FS)^{t_1 \times \dots \times t_n \to t}, e_i \in Exp^{t_i} \\
| \; & \text{if } b \text{ then } e_1 \text{ else } e_2 & & \% \; b \in Exp^{bool}, e_1, e_2 \in Exp^t \quad \text{conditional expr.} \\
| \; & \text{case } e \text{ of} & & \% \; e \in Exp^d, \qquad\qquad\qquad \text{case expression} \\
& \quad c_1 : e_1; \dots c_k : e_k & & \% \; c_i \in \Gamma^{\dots \to d}, e_i \in Exp^t \\
& \text{end} \\
| \; & \mathbf{proj}(j, e) & & \% \; e \in Exp^d \qquad\qquad\qquad\quad \text{projection to } j\text{th} \\
& & & \qquad\qquad\qquad\qquad\qquad\quad \text{component} \\
| \; & \text{let } y_1 = e_1 \text{ and} & & \% \; y_i \in Var^{t_i}, e_i \in Exp^{t_i} \quad \text{local definitions} \\
& \quad \dots \qquad \text{and} \\
& \quad y_k = e_k \\
& \text{in } e & & \% \; e \in Exp^t
\end{aligned}
$$

Fig. 1. FUN-Expressions

structure components. let-expressions define sharing of arbitrary subexpressions. We always assume that rules and expressions are well-typed.

The semantics of FUN programs are the usual lazy reduction semantics with strict interpretations of basic operations. The program rules are used as rewrite rules for the evaluation of applications of defined function symbols.

In our example programs we assume the predefined base types *integer* and *boolean* with the usual arithmetic and boolean operation symbols, for which we allow infix notation.

The definition of the function symbol *tower* assumes the data structure *tree* with constructors *leaf* of type *int* → *tree* and *node* of type *tree* × *int* × *tree* → *tree*. *append* is the well known list concatenation function.

$$
\begin{aligned}
psum(l, h) := \; & \text{if } l = h \text{ then } l \text{ else if } l + 1 = h \text{ then } l + h \\
& \text{else let } m = (l + h)/2 \text{ in } psum(l, m) + psum(m + 1, h) \\
tower(n, sour, help, dest) := \; & \\
& \text{let } move = 10 * sour + dest \\
& \text{in if } n = 1 \text{ then } leaf(move) \\
& \qquad\quad \text{else } node(\, tower(n - 1, sour, dest, help), move, \\
& \qquad\qquad\qquad\qquad tower(n - 1, help, sour, dest)) \\
append(l_1, l_2) := \; & \text{case } l_1 \text{ of } nil : \quad l_2; \\
& \qquad\qquad\quad cons : cons(\mathbf{proj}(1, l_1), append(\mathbf{proj}(2, l_1), l_2)) \\
& \text{end}
\end{aligned}
$$

3 Implementation of Functional Languages

In this section we shortly describe the structure and the behaviour of a simple reduction machine for the implementation of functional languages. This reduction machine is the sequential kernel of the parallel implementation.

3.1 Structure of the Reduction Machine

The store of the reduction machine is illustrated in Fig. 2. Its central component is the function stack which contains the activation blocks of recursive function calls. Structured data, basic values, and arguments, whose evaluation

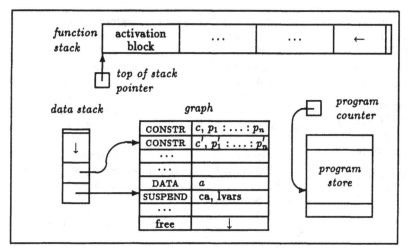

Fig. 2. Structure of a Sequential Reduction Machine

is postponed in case of a lazy evaluation strategy, are represented in the graph. Consequently, we distinguish between *constructor nodes, data nodes,* and *suspension nodes* (see Fig. 2). Constructor nodes contain the constructor name c and pointers to the graph representation of the components. Data nodes simply contain a basic value. Suspension nodes contain a code address ca, which is the address, at which the code for the evaluation of the delayed or suspended argument starts, and a list *lvars* of parameters to which some instructions in the code may refer.

3.2 Behaviour of the Reduction Machine

In order to evaluate a function application, the addresses of the graph representations of the arguments are written on top of the data stack and a function call is executed. The instruction CALL (ca, n, k) creates a new activation block on top of the function stack, moves n pointers to the function arguments from the data stack to the function stack, reserves k cells for local variables, writes the value of the instruction pointer as return address and the dynamic link to the previously active activation block into the new activation block and finally jumps to the program address ca.

The code for each function f consists of the code for the body expression e of f's defining rule and a RETURN instruction:

$$\text{Code for } f : exptrans(e); \text{ RETURN.}$$

The return instruction terminates a function call by removing the top level activation block from the stack and jumping to the saved return address. The result of the function call is given on top of the data stack.

The compilation of expressions is shown in Fig. 3. For simplicity, we do not consider any optimization techniques as e.g. tail recursive function calls.

The reduction machine is capable of carrying out an innermost and a lazy strategy. Which strategy is chosen to execute a program, depends on the compilation of argument expressions. In case of an innermost strategy, arguments are translated by the *exptrans*-scheme. This implies that expressions are evaluated

$exptrans(x_i)$
:= LOAD i
  INITIATE
$exptrans(op(e_1, ..., e_n))$
:= $exptrans(e_1)$
    ⋮
  $exptrans(e_n)$
  EXEC (op, n)
$exptrans(c(e_1, ..., e_n))$
:= $argtrans(e_1)$
    ⋮
  $argtrans(e_n)$
  CNODE (c, n)

$exptrans($if b then e_1 else $e_2)$
:= $exptrans(b)$
  JMF l_2
  $exptrans(e_1)$
  JMP l_3
 $l_2 : exptrans(e_2)$
 $l_3 :$
$exptrans($case e of
    $..c_j : e_j..$ end$)$
:= $exptrans(e)$
  SWITCH $(... c_j : l_j ...)$
$l_1 : ...$
$l_j : exptrans(e_j)$
  JMP l
$l_{j+1} : ...$
 $l :$

$exptrans($proj $(j, e))$
:= $exptrans(e)$
  PROJ j
$exptrans($let $..y_k = e_k..$
        in $e)$
:= ...
  $argtrans(e_k)$
  STORE k
  ...
  $exptrans(e)$
$exptrans(f(e_1, ..., e_n))$
:= $argtrans(e_1)$
    ⋮
  $argtrans(e_n)$
  CALL $(ca(f), n, loc(f))$

~~~~~~~~~

$delaytrans(x_i)$
:= LOAD i
$delaytrans(c(e_1, ..., e_n))$
:= $delaytrans(e_1)$
    ⋮
  $delaytrans(e_n)$
  CNODE (c, n)

otherwise:
$delaytrans(e)$
:= SUSPEND l
  JUMP l'
$l: exptrans(e)$
  UPDATE
$l':$

$argtrans(M)$

$argtrans(M) := \begin{cases} exptrans(M) & \text{for an "eager" strategy} \\ delaytrans(M) & \text{for a "lazy" strategy} \end{cases}$

Fig. 3. Sequential Code for Expressions

to normal form and INITIATE instructions, which are necessary to force the evaluation of suspended arguments, can be omitted. In case of a lazy evaluation strategy, arguments are translated by the *delaytrans*-scheme, which generates suspension nodes for the representation of arguments not evaluated yet, using the instruction SUSPEND. Furthermore, code for the evaluation of the suspension is generated using the *exptrans*-scheme. This code is concluded by the instruction UPDATE, which writes the result of the evaluation into the suspension node and gives control back to the calling environment.

4   Parallelism in Functional Languages

The *implicit parallelism* within FUN-programs consists of the reduction of independent subexpressions which is possible due to the side effect free nature of the reduction semantics. The eager evaluation strategy allows the parallel evaluation of arbitrary subexpressions. In case of the lazy reduction strategy, strictness analysis can be used to find out subexpressions which can be safely evaluated in parallel. Usually annotations or special syntactic constructs are used to show the implicit parallelism within programs [Goldberg, Hudak 86], [Augustsson, Johnson 89]. An automatic parallelizing compiler for lazy functional languages is described in [Hogen et al. 92]. This compiler translates functional programs into a parallelized form where the construct

    letpar $y_1 = f_1(e_{11}, ..., e_{1n_1})$ **and** $\cdots$ **and** $y_p = f_p(e_{p1}, ..., e_{pn_p})$ **in** e

is used to indicate parallelism. Such a **letpar**-expression means that the function applications $f_i(e_{i1}, \ldots, e_{in_i})$ *may be* evaluated in parallel with the main stream of evaluation, e. Whether a parallel evaluation really takes place at runtime, depends on the workload of the distributed system. Evaluation of a **letpar**-expression first leads to the parallel activation of the function applications. Then the evaluation of the body e proceeds until the result of a parallel subexpression, represented by y_j, is needed but not available yet. In this case, the evaluation of e will be suspended until the parallel subprocess sends its result. In the meantime, the processor should be free to evaluate some other process.

The resulting process system is hierarchical. The execution of a parallelized functional program starts with the evaluation of a main expression. **letpar**-expressions generate parallel subprocesses, that can be executed on other processor elements. By the execution of parallel processes, further processes may be generated. When a process terminates, its result is communicated to the father process, i.e. the process that generated the subprocess, and all other processes waiting for the result.

A parallelization of the first two example functions of Section 2 is:

$$psum(l,h) := \textbf{if } l = h \textbf{ then } l \textbf{ else if } l+1 = h \textbf{ then } l+h$$
$$\textbf{else let } m = (l+h)/2 \textbf{ in letpar } y_1 = psum(l,m)$$
$$\textbf{in } psum(m+1,h) + y_1$$

$$tower(n, sour, help, dest) :=$$
$$\textbf{let } move = 10 * sour + dest$$
$$\textbf{in if } n = 1 \textbf{ then } leaf(move)$$
$$\textbf{else letpar } y_1 = tower(n-1, help, sour, dest)$$
$$\textbf{in } node(\, tower(n-1, sour, dest, help), move, y_1)$$

The process system that will be created for the expression $psum(1,6)$ is shown in Fig. 4. It shows already the shape of the cactus stack the parallel system has to cope with. Most of the existing parallel implementations of functional languages generate for each recursive function call a new activation block, called task node or VAP (variable sized application) node, in the heap [Augustsson, Johnson 89], [Loogen et al. 89], [Kingdon et al 91]. The activation blocks in the heap contain all the information and substructures that are necessary for the evaluation of the corresponding function call. A parallel evaluation can simply be achieved by the migration of a block to another processor element.

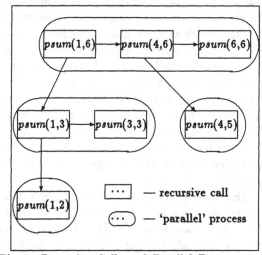

Fig. 4. Recursive Calls and Parallel Processes of the *psum*-Program

The dynamic extension of activation blocks in case of tail recursive function calls can be avoided by the use of the stacklessness analysis of [Lester 89a], which allows to create activation blocks large enough to evaluate all tail recursive calls that may occur in a reduction sequence.

In this paper we claim that this "linked list"-realization of the cactus stack is not natural, because it does not support the sequential evaluations within processes in an optimal way. The knowledge about the stack behaviour of the various local stacks is lost and general garbage collection techniques must be used to collect the activation blocks of terminated tasks.

[Goldberg, Hudak 86] already pointed out that the graph allocation of activation blocks should be avoided for purely sequential functions which do not spawn parallel subtasks and may not be suspended due to parallel subtasks. They proposed a hybrid system which assumes an analysis and decomposition of the program into sequential and non-sequential functions. For sequential functions an ordinary stack-based evaluation is arranged. For non-sequential function calls the more expensive allocation of runtime information in the heap must be chosen to support parallel evaluations.

In the following, we will present a new stack technique that is a combination of the heap organization of parallel processes and the stack management of sequential evaluation sequences. It works for arbitrary dynamic process systems.

5 The Meshed Stack Technique

From an abstract point of view, each parallel process will be executed on a sequential reduction machine, which is capable of the generation of new parallel processes. Thus, each process works on its own function stack area. For sequential recursive function calls, new activation blocks are generated on top of this private function stack. Parallel processes are spawned by generating a special node in the graph, which serves as a placeholder for the result of the process. The characteristic information of the process is embedded into a so-called *process message*, which contains also the address of the placeholder node. This message will be sent to another reduction machine. The placeholder for the result of the parallel process can be seen as a graph representation of the migrated evaluation.

In a concrete parallel system there will, of course, be only a finite number of processor elements. As processes are created dynamically, i.e. there is no restriction on the number of processes, this implies that each reduction machine within a parallel environment must be capable of *multitasking*. It must be possible to evaluate several parallel processes in a single reduction unit. In particular, a machine must be able to organize the interleaved evaluation of several active processes.

The main problem is how to organize the runtime information of several parallel processes in a space- and time-efficient way. One possibility is the pure graph organization which leads to a linked-list realization of local function stacks, which we already rejected. Another possibility is the allocation of private contiguous stack areas within a reserved memory area for the function stack. This approach is very time-efficient, but it leads to a fragmentation of the function stack area and there will be a restriction on the number of parallel processes which can be executed in a single reduction unit or there must be some mechanism to split stack areas if more processes than available stack areas are created. Furthermore there must be some mechanism for the dynamic extension of stack areas, if processes run out of stack space and there is still free space.

Because of these difficulties, we decided to try another approach which originated from the organization of runtime information in the Warren Abstract Machine (WAM), which has been developed for the implementation of logic languages [Warren 83]. This might be surprising, but there is the following analogy. In the WAM the runtime information of several alternative computation sequences is kept on a single stack. This stack is not a stack in the conventional sense. Due to the information that is kept for alternative computation branches, the active activation block (environment) is not always on top of the stack and on termination of "procedure" calls the activation blocks can only be removed from the stack if they are on top of it.

Our meshed stack keeps the runtime information of several parallel processes on a single stack. Its main property is that the current activation block need not be on top of the stack. New activation blocks will always be generated on top of the stack, but if a function call terminates and its activation block is not on top of the stack, it will not be removed, but simply marked as garbage. If a parallel process is suspended, because it has to wait for some information that is not locally available, its activation blocks are kept on the stack until its evaluation can continue. In the meantime, the reduction machine can proceed with the evaluation of another parallel process, whose activation blocks will simply be allocated on top of the activation blocks of the suspended process. If the new process will eventually be suspended and the process is reactivated, newly created activation blocks of this evaluation will be allocated on top of the activation blocks of the previous evaluation. Thus we will get a mixture of activation blocks belonging to different parallel processes on the stack, which is the reason for calling it a meshed stack. This explains the main idea of the meshed stack technique.

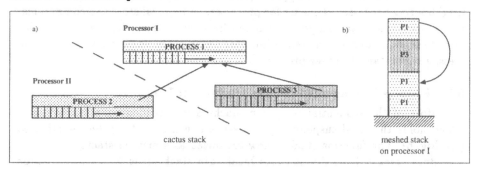

Fig. 5. Implementation of a Cactus Stack on a Meshed Stack

In Fig. 5 a cactus stack and its implementation with a meshed stack is shown. In the cactus stack each node represents one parallel task including sequential function calls. So each node represents a number of activation blocks. Process

1 and 3 are executed in the same reduction machine. If we look at the meshed stack of this reduction machine, we find the activation blocks of these processes interleaved.

But, what happens when function calls terminate and the corresponding blocks can be deallocated. The deallocation of blocks on top of the stack is of course no problem. Inner activation blocks which can be removed are marked as garbage. They are collected, i.e. removed, as soon as there is no valid, i.e. active or suspended activation block on top of them. If the stack runs out of space, a special garbage collector is invoked. This garbage collector simply crunches the stack *in place* in one pass. Details will be given in Section 7.

6 Development of a Parallel Reduction Machine

In this section we develop a parallel reduction machine by embedding extended sequential reduction machines in a parallel environment.

6.1 General structure

The parallel reduction machine consists of a finite number of identical processor elements, each with a local storage. An interconnection network enables the processor elements to communicate by exchanging messages. Each processor element consists of two independent processing units, which communicate via the exchange of messages in a local shared memory (see Fig. 6).

- The *communication unit* handles the organization of the parallel aspects of the reduction process.
- The *reduction unit* is a sequential reduction machine which has been extended by capabilities for multitasking and for the processing of messages.

The main task of the communication unit is the distribution of parallel processes and the organization of the message traffic. We will not go into the details of the communication processor, as task distribution and routing strategies are out of the scope of this paper. We assume a simple static routing scheme and a passive process distribution strategy, i.e. processor elements without work ask their neighbouring processor elements for processes. In its local store the communication processor maintains a process queue which contains parallel processes which have been generated by the reduction unit and a static table for the routing of messages from and to other processor elements.

6.2 Process Management in the Reduction Units

The store of the sequential reduction machine is extended by a *ready queue*, which holds the local suspended processes which are ready to be re-activated (see Fig. 6). The function stack is now organized as a meshed stack.

The data stack will be divided into local data stack areas for each activation block. This is necessary to avoid the saving of data stack entries on process switches. Each function call gets an activation block on the function stack and its own "private" data stack. For allocation purposes one has to know the maximum storage demands of each local data stack. These can be estimated during compile

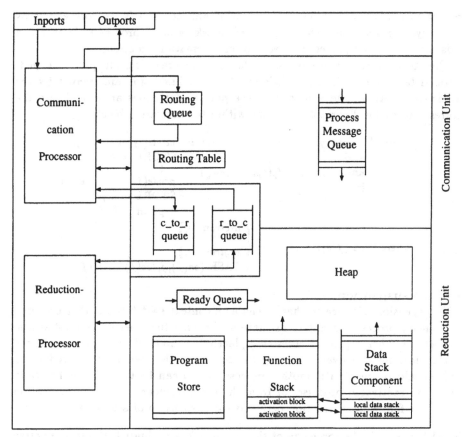

Fig. 6. Global Structure of a Single Processor Unit

time and passed as a parameter in the instructions which generate new activation blocks, as e.g. CALL. The heap component is extended by placeholder nodes for the results of parallel processes.

Process creation

For spawning a parallel function call a new instruction, similar to the CALL-instruction, is introduced:

TASK (ca, n, k, $size$) produces a process that can be executed in parallel. ca is the code address, n the number of arguments, k the number of local variables in the definition of the corresponding function and $size$ the maximal data stack size that will be necessary during the execution of the function. In the heap component, a placeholder node for the result is created. A process message containing the code address and parameters of the parallel function call and the address of the placeholder node is sent to the communication unit. The computation of the actual task proceeds, until there is a demand for the result of a parallel subtask.

The communication unit stores the process message in its *process queue*, as processes are only distributed to other processor elements on demand. If the reduction unit runs idle, the communication unit can satisfy its workrequest by an entry from its own process queue before asking other processor elements. In this case, a parallel process is executed on its creation processor.

Let us consider now program compilation: When reaching a letpar-construct, parallel tasks for all function calls on the right hand side are created by the TASK-instruction. The addresses of the placeholder nodes are stored into the corresponding local variable positions within the activation block.

$$exptrans \; [\![\; \textbf{letpar} \; y_{m+1} = f_1(e_{11},\ldots,e_{1l_1}) \quad := \quad pcode(f_1(e_{11},\ldots,e_{1l_1}))$$

$$\textbf{and} \quad \ldots \qquad\qquad\qquad\qquad STORE \; m+1;$$

$$\textbf{and} \quad y_{m+p} = f_p(e_{p1},\ldots,e_{pl_p}) \qquad \vdots$$

$$\textbf{in} \quad e \;]\!] \qquad\qquad\qquad pcode(f_p(e_{p1},\ldots,e_{pl_p}))$$

$$STORE \; m+p;$$

$$exptrans \; [\![e]\!]$$

$$\text{where } pcode(f(e_1,\ldots,e_j)) := \left\{ \begin{array}{l} argtrans[\![e_1]\!] \\ \vdots \\ argtrans[\![e_j]\!] \\ TASK \; (ca(f),j,loc(f),dsize(f)); \end{array} \right.$$

Process suspension

The suspension of processes has to enable a context switch to another process.

When a process encounters a situation where a value is needed but not available yet, i.e. when a process accesses a placeholder node, it has to wait until the placeholder node is overwritten by the result. In the meantime the reduction unit should proceed with another process, which can be taken from the ready queue of reactivated processes or from the process queue in the communication unit. The following instruction performs the suspension of a process.

WAIT checks if the top entry of the data stack is evaluated. If not, the active process is suspended until the result is available. Therefore, the stack address of the current activation block is added to the list of waiting tasks within the placeholder node of the argument. When the result is delivered, the waiting list of a placeholder node is moved to the ready queue.

The WAIT-instruction is used for the compilation of variables in a context where the result of the variable is needed.

$$exptrans \; [\![y_i]\!] := \left\{ \begin{array}{ll} LOAD \; i; & \\ WAIT; & \text{if } y_i \text{ is a variable introduced using } \textbf{letpar} \\ & \\ LOAD \; i; & \\ INITIATE; & \text{else} \end{array} \right.$$

We have to distinguish between variables introduced by the letpar-construct and others (formal parameters and local variables introduced by let). The latter are always locally available and can be accessed directly. The result of parallel processes may not be available, so one has to suspend the actual evaluation.

Process termination

As in the sequential machine, the RETURN instruction terminates a function call. It returns the result to the calling process and marks the actual activation block and data stack as garbage. Due to parallel execution, the calling task can be local (so one can put the pointer onto the calling data stack and continue computing the calling task) or global (the result is sent to the placeholder node on the other processor element).

6.3 Message Handling in the Reduction Units

During the execution of processes, the reduction units will produce

- *process messages* when parallel processes are spawned,
- *memory request messages* when graph nodes which are allocated in the heap of another reduction unit are needed,
- *answer messages* in order to reply to process and memory request messages.
- *work requests* to ask the communication unit for new processes.

In detail, the reduction units behave as follows on incoming messages:

A *process message* represents a parallel ready-to-run process. It will be received after a work request message has been sent to the communication processor. A new activation block is created and its stack pointer is added to the ready queue. One cannot start the process directly (although demanded by the work request) because in the time between the work request and the task message, a result could have been delivered which triggered other activations. Also, due to different scheduling strategies, several processes could be delivered on demand.

A *memory request message* forces the reduction unit to look up a value for another processor element and to send the value in form of an answer message back to the inquiring processor. If the requested graph node is a suspension, the reduction unit will first initiate its local evaluation. The request message will be answered as soon as this evaluation finishes.

Finally, *answer messages* overwrite the placeholder nodes and activate the waiting tasks.

7 Garbage-Collection in the Meshed Stack

Due to the distinction between *control information* (in the stack component) and *data information* (stored in the heap component), one can handle each component with an appropriate garbage collection mechanism. E.g., the problem of data sharing needs only to be handled by the garbage collector of the heap component and causes no unnecessary administration overhead in the stack garbage collector. One major advantage of our approach is the fact, that the knowledge of the special stack structure can be used to develop a simple and efficient garbage collector for this component.

In general, activation blocks can only be released immediately from the top-of-stack pointer until one finds a non-garbage block. Inbetween the stack, there may be still some "holes" left (see Fig. 7). If we had an infinite stack space, the above strategy would be sufficient to eventually release all blocks. Since our stack space is limited, the stack can run out of space while there are still garbage holes within the stack.

Each block contains an individual block id, all references to the activation block are made through this id. The actual address of the block can be found in a table which maps id's to stack addresses. If the garbage collector is invoked, the stack is simply crunched *in place*, deleting the holes. The main procedure is outlined in Fig. 8. Starting from the bottom, garbage blocks are skipped and their id's are released. Once a valid block is encountered, it is moved "down" the stack and the address entry in the table is updated[1]. This process is iterated until the top of the stack is reached.

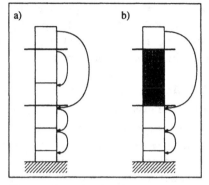

Fig. 7. Function Stack Structure

References to the stack occur *only* locally as *waiting task id's*, attached to the placeholder nodes. So, at the moment a waiting task is activated, it looks up its actual stack position in the table. Therefore the garbage collection process is completely transparent to the rest of the environment. The indirection introduced by the address table causes no significant overhead, since the mapping of id's to actual addresses is only resolved during context switches.

Details of the stack garbage collector are given in [Schmidt 93].

```
procedure crunch_stack;
{ to = from = bottom_of_stack;          % start at bottom
  while (from < top_of_stack)
    { while (garbage(from))             % garbage blocks:
        { release_table_entry(id(from));  % release id and
          from = nextblock(from) }      % skip holes
      mem_copy(from, to, size(from));   % copy from-block
      rewrite_table_entry(id(from), to); % new address entry
      to += size(from);
      from = nextblock(from) }          % examine block above
  top_of_stack = to                     % new Top of Stack
}
```

Fig. 8. The Main Procedure for Garbage Collecting the Stack

8   Implementation Results

The implementation of an interpreter version of the machine on a transputer system under Helios C is still in progress. Therefore, we will only present runtime results for some simple example programs.

In a real system the length of the process message queue, which is managed by the communication unit is limited and may overflow. First of all, the question

---

[1] The functions **size**, **id** and **garbage** yield the size, id and garbage information of the actual block, resp. **nextblock** sets the pointer to the activation block on top of the actual one.

arises, what to do in that case. Obviously, too much tasks are generated. So we introduce a flag *pmq_full* which is set by the communication unit and can be read by the reduction unit. If the reduction process encounters a TASK-instruction, it first checks the boolean flag. If the queue is full, instead of sparking a new task, a CALL-instruction is simulated, causing the generation of a *local* activation block. The introduction of this flag has two interesting side-effects:

1. If only one processor is involved (the total amount of processors in the system is known by every processor), the *pmqfull*-flag can simply be set to *true*, thus suppressing any task generation.

2. The maximum number of process message queue entries can be changed during runtime according to statistics about the system behaviour. So the system can adjust itself dynamically and the generation of too much tasks flooding the system can be prevented.

In our system we have implemented the first feature, which results in a runtime behaviour of a parallel program on one processor that is very similar to the sequential version of the program.

In Fig. 9 runtime measurements (in seconds) of the parallel example programs of Section 4 and the well known *nfib*-program

$$nfib(x) := \text{if } x < 2 \text{ then } 1 \text{ else letpar } y_1 = nfib(x-2) \text{ in } nfib(x-1) + y_1 + 1$$

on 1, 2 and 4 processor elements (*PE*) are presented.

Program	n	Runtimes (in seconds) sequential 1 PE	parallel 1 PE	parallel 2 PE	parallel 4 PE	Speedups (parallel) 2 PE	Speedups (parallel) 4 PE
psum	10,000	3.70	3.99	2.37	1.22	1.68	3.27
	20,000	7.40	7.96	4.75	2.41	1.68	3.30
	50,000	19.97	21.53	12.19	6.18	1.77	3.48
towers	11	0.70	0.74	0.47	0.28	1.57	2.64
	12	1.37	1.47	0.90	0.46	1.63	3.20
	13	2.74	2.95	1.80	0.91	1.64	3.24
nfib	20	4.49	4.99	3.03	1.62	1.65	3.08
	21	7.24	8.07	4.44	2.44	1.82	3.31
	22	11.72	13.06	7.50	3.83	1.74	3.41

Fig. 9. Runtimes and Speedups for Example Programs on the Parallel Machine

9 Related Work and Conclusions

Most parallel implementations of functional languages rely on the graph-based model of reduction ($\langle \nu, G \rangle$-machine of [Augustsson, Johnsson 89], the HDG-machine of [Kingdon et al. 91], ALFALFA [Goldberg, Hudak 86], PAM [Loogen et al. 89]). There have been attempts to incorporate stack techniques ([Koopman et al. 90], [Peyton-Jones 91]), but only on the sequential level. We presented an alternative extended stack technique for the management of control structures in distributed implementation of dynamic process systems. The technique has been presented in the context of functional languages, but in principle it is independent of the chosen programming language.

A similar approach has been taken in [Hofman et al. 92], but there only activation blocks on top of the stack are allowed to be executed. So inner activation blocks may be ready to be reactivated, but are blocked by the top-of-stack task. Note that they consider a fork/join task model. In our environment, where sharing of subtasks is allowed, this approach could result in deadlock situations. Nevertheless, their approach yields a good cache behaviour, which should also be observed in our machine.

Our technique allows for a special efficient garbage collection of control structures. For garbage collection of the heap, the approach of [Lester 89b], a combined scheme of a (local) copying and a (global) reference counting garbage collector, seems appropriate and will be implemented in the future.

References

[Appel 87] A.W. Appel: *Garbage Collection can be faster than stack allocation*, Information Processing Letters, 21(4):275–279, 1987.

[Augustsson, Johnsson 89] L. Augustsson, Th. Johnsson: *Parallel Graph Reduction with the $\langle \nu, G \rangle$-Machine*, Conf. on Functional Progr. Lang. and Comp. Arch. (FPCA), Addison-Wesley 1989.

[Goldberg, Hudak 86] B. Goldberg, P. Hudak: *ALFALFA — Distributed Graph Reduction on a Hypercube Multiprocessor*, Workshop on Graph Reduction, LNCS 279, Springer 1986.

[Hogen et al. 92] G. Hogen, A. Kindler, R. Loogen: *Automatic Parallelization of Lazy Functional Programs*, Europ. Symp. on Progr. (ESOP '92), LNCS 582, Springer 1992.

[Hofman et al. 92] R. Hofmann, K. Langendoen, W.G. Vree: *Scheduling Consequences of Keeping Parents at Home*, Proceedings of ICPADS'92, December 1992.

[Kingdon et al. 91] H. Kingdon, D. Lester, G. Burn: *The HDG-Machine: a highly distributed graph-reducer for a transputer network*, Computer Journal 34 (4), 1991.

[Koopman et al. 90] P. Koopman, M. van Eekelen, E. Nöcker, J. Smeetsers, R. Plasmeijer: *The ABC-machine: A Sequential Stack-based Machine for Graph Rewriting*, Technical Report 90–22, University of Nijmegen 1990.

[Lester 89a] D. Lester: *Stacklessness: Compiling Recursion for a Distributed Architecture*, Conf. on Functional Progr. Lang. and Comp. Arch. (FPCA), Addison-Wesley 1989.

[Lester 89b] D. Lester: *An Efficient Distributed Garbage Collection Algorithm*, Conf. on Parallel Arch. and Lang. Europe (PARLE) 1989, LNCS 365, Springer 1989.

[Loogen et al. 89] R. Loogen, H. Kuchen, K. Indermark, W. Damm: *Distributed Implementation of Programmed Graph Reduction*, Conf. on Parallel Arch. and Lang. Europe (PARLE) 1989, LNCS 365, Springer 1989.

[Peyton-Jones 91] S.L. Peyton-Jones: *The Spineless tagless G-machine: Second Attempt*, Proceedings of the Workshop on Parallel Impl. of Functional Lang. , Technical Report CSTR 91-07, University of Southhampton 1991.

[Schmidt 93] A. Schmidt: *Garbage Collection of Meshed Stacks*, Diploma Thesis, RWTH Aachen 1994.

[Warren 83] D.H.D. Warren: *An abstract Prolog instruction set*, Technical Report 309, SRI International 1983.

Implementing 2DT on a Multiprocessor

Yosi Ben-Asher   Gudula Rünger   Reinhard Wilhelm   Assaf Schuster
Haifa University   Universität des Saarlandes   Technion IIT
yosi@cs.huji.ac.il   {ruenger,wilhelm}@cs.uni-sb.de   assafs@cs.technion.ac.il

Abstract

The implementation of a parallel functional language is discussed. 2DT-programs are composed of local SPMD-computations and global transformations of 2-dimensional data structures leading to a coarse grain compute-communicate scheme. The implementation is made up of virtual processes doing the local computations and abstract processors emulating several virtual processes and taking care of communication. Code and data structures which are common to virtual processes are shared and allocated to abstract processes in order to make context switches cheap. Code that would be executed redundantly by logical processes is converted to abstract code and executed only once. Aims of this effort are maximizing the amount of parallelism, keeping communication cheap and managing parallelism efficiently.

1   Introduction

2DT (*2-dimensional transformations*) is a general paradigm for the design of parallel SPMD (single-program-multiple-data) languages for multiprocessor systems proposed in [BRSW93a]. 2DT programs are composed of two levels of computation, local computations on local data and global transformations on ordered combinations of local data (*2D-arrays*). The local computations are performed by an existing sequential base language and modify all local data in a SPMD-ic fashion. For the parallel functional language 2DT-FP, Backus FP [Bac78] is chosen to be the base language [BRSW93a]. The global transformations serve as a communication mechanism. They may reshape a 2D-array thereby rearranging its components, exchanging the components of a 2D-array, splitting one 2D-array into several new 2D-arrays, or reglueing some 2D-arrays together. Thus, 2DT programs reflect a coarse grain compute-communicate scheme which is appropriate for the formulation of loosely synchronous algorithms which, e.g., arise in numerical problems. In addition to the parallelism on local data, operations on different 2D-arrays can be performed in parallel. Thus, a high degree of parallelism is provided.

An implementation of 2DT on a distributed multiprocessor network should be efficient and should preserve the degree of parallelism. We will achieve this by an implementation with the following *design goals*:

- Maximal amount of parallelism
- Cheap communication
- Efficient management of parallelism
- Portability
- Efficiency on the target machine

For the implementation, we associate each local data with a *virtual process*. Such a virtual process performs the local (FP) computations and, at least conceptually, is responsible for the communication realizing its part of global transformations. Virtual processes are executed by *abstract processors* each running on one physical processor. Abstract processors have to do *virtual process management*, i.e. creation, deletion, allocation, and scheduling of virtual processes. We will see that for efficiency reasons they also take over communication from their respective virtual processes. The group parallelism is handled by *process group management*, i.e. allocation, scheduling of groups of processes.

In order to exploit high amount of parallelism and since array sizes are dynamic, we have to employ dynamic load-balancing. But due to the regular SPMD-mode, load-balancing is relatively simple. Cheap communication is attained by the combination of small messages to large ones. This is feasible because in communication stemming from global transformations lots of local data are involved. Efficient management of parallelism is achieved by *context sharing* of virtual processes and clever process group management. Context sharing means that all the common components of the virtual processes of a 2D-array are shared leaving very small contexts to be switched. The implementation of global transformations consists in a topology independent message-preparation phase to be performed on each single abstract processor and a communication phase between the abstract processors. This scheme supports portability for the preparation phase. Efficiency is achieved by using specific communication algorithms provided on the physical target machine.

FP–type functional languages are attractive for parallel implementation and for parallel programming. The apply–to–all–operator can easily be given a parallel implementation. This is essentially, what has been done in the implementation of FP* [BW91]. However, FP*–programs are translated into some data parallel version of Fortran. No direct, efficient implementation on a multicomputer is realized.

[DP93] describe an interesting approach to the parallel implementation of FP. They correctly argue, that the code generated for a function should depend on the way, the data are distributed, on which the function operates. There are only a fixed set of functionals in FP. Thus, [DP93] propose to define a code template for essentially any way a functional can be used. This template contains an analytical formula for the costs connected with executing the corresponding code. A complex compiler organization is described to find out the best combination of templates for a given FP program. The approach looks nice, but hasn't been tested in practice. In addition, the templates have only static parameters including the problem size. This we consider unrealistic.

The equivalent of apply–to–all in lazy functional languages is *map*. It has also been regarded as a natural parallel operator [Hil93][Jou91]. Both papers consider the compilation of functional languages with aggregate data types and corresponding *map* functions to SIMD architectures. The stated assumption, that any monolithic operation, whose individual operation takes $O(1)$, when applied to on an aggregate of size n executed on a SIMD computer of size p takes also constant time, is not shared by these authors. Working on the increasingly popular MIMD machines under more realistic assumptions about execution and communication times is of great importance.

The paper is organized as follows. Section 2 introduces the general 2DT-paradigm and the language 2DT-FP. The association of local data with virtual processes is described in section 3. Section 4 contains allocation strategies and the abstract machine model. The code-generating function is given in section 5. Finally, section 6 presents some 2D-transformation and their intended communication behavior.

2 Overview of the Language 2DT-FP

The 2DT-Paradigm : The essential concept of 2DT-languages is a two-level hier-archy of local and global computations which are performed on parts or on the entire set of the problem-data. The execution of a 2DT-program $\mathcal{P}$ consists of a sequence of consecutive operations $\mathcal{P} = T_k ; \dots ; T_1$ in which local and global functions alternate. The semicolon ";" denotes function composition. A 2DT-program $\mathcal{P}$ is applied to problem data which are divided into disjoint parts L_i, $i = 0, \dots, m-1$, called **local data** *(LoDa)*. The whole set of problem data is represented as a **tuple of local data**, i.e. $L = (L_0, \dots, L_{m-1})$. Depending on the currently executed local or global function of the program $\mathcal{P}$ the view on the data is different.

Local computations are performed on the lower level of the data representation by applying the same local function F to each component L_i of the data-tuple in parallel, see Fig.1a (**apply-to-all parallelism**). The data-structure of the *local data (LoDa)* is inherited from the original data according to the considered algorithm, e.g. input data forming a matrix may be subdivided into blocks with two-dimensional structure or columns with one-dimensional structure.

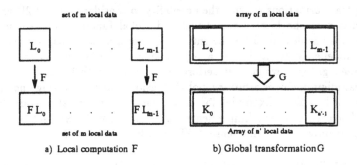

a) Local computation F   b) Global transformation G

Figure1: *2DT computations*

Global transformations G are applied to the upper level, the entire tuple of data L, see Fig.1b. In contrast to local computations, where we don't assume a special form of the *LoDa* L_i, 2-dimensional transformations are only defined on 2-dimensional (rectangular) data-structures. Thus, all local data L_i are described as *linear data* $L_i = (L_i^1 , \dots , L_i^n)$ of the same length n. The structure of the data L_i^j is left unspecified in the general case and has to be designed according to the special algorithm. The two-dimensional rectangular "data in a global state" is called **2D-array of shape (n,m)** (see Fig.2).

Global transformations don't change the inner structure of the components L_i^j, but reorganize them into a new shape. According to their reshaping behavior three **classes of transformations** are considered:

(1) **Shape-preserving** transformations leave the shape of a 2D-array unchanged. The data components L_i^j of the current 2D-array are moved to other places (i', j') in the resulting 2D-array.

(2) **Reshaping** transformations change the shape of the 2D-array in a prescribed way. The set of data $\{ L_i^j \mid i = 0, \dots, m - 1, j = 1, \dots, n \}$ of the current 2D-array remains the same but the items L_i^j are restructured into a new shape.

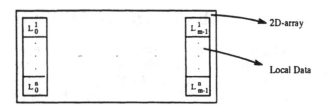

Figure2: *Data in a global state of shape (n,m)*

(3) **Array-creating** transformations change the number of the considered 2D-arrays. For the creation, the *LoDa* L_i of the current 2D-array are divided into disjoint subsets which form the new 2D-arrays. For the creation of one 2D-array from a set of 2D-arrays, the *LoDa* of the 2D-arrays are joined. In both cases, the internal compositions of the *LoDa*'s are unchanged. The use of array-creating transformations in a program is *block-structured*, i.e. a creation of several 2D-arrays is followed be a corresponding join operation. Different pairs of array-creating transformations are fully-nested.

Array-creating transformations provide the possibility to consider different 2D-arrays forming a partition of the local data. Local and global functions are applied to each single 2D-array as described for the entire set of local data. Those applications are performed independently and offer a second kind of parallelism, called **array parallelism** (see e.g. Fig.1, when 1a is performed in parallel with 1b).

The 2DT-paradigm includes arbitrary global transformation possessing one of the behaviors described above. Examples for each class of transformations are given in section 6. For each concrete (implemented) 2DT-language a fixed set of global transformations is provided. In this sense, 2DT describes a class of 2DT-languages.

The language 2DT-FP: The functional language FP [Bac78] is chosen to express local computations. Thus, the *LoDa* L_i and also the data components L_i^j of data in a global state are FP-objects. The local functions are FP-functions which are executed on each component L_i of a tuple of FP-objects $(L_0, \ldots, L_{m-1})$ in parallel in SPMD-ic fashion producing a new tuple of FP-objects.

The execution of a program $\mathcal{P}$ essentially consisting of a sequence of local FP functions and global transformations is done by consecutively applying the functions to the problem data L from the left to the right, i.e.

$$\mathcal{P} L = (T_k; \ldots; T_1) L = T_k (\ldots (T_1 (L)))$$

";" between local and global transformations also causes synchronization. For the exact syntax and semantics see [BRSW93a].

3   Virtual Processes

The local data L_i, $i = 1, \ldots, m$, are associated with **virtual processes** with process numbers i. More precisely, the association of data with virtual processes means that computations on LoDa L_i are performed by the corresponding process.

The global shape-preserving transformations, which move data across the LoDa of 2D-arrays, serve as the **communication** mechanism between the virtual processes.

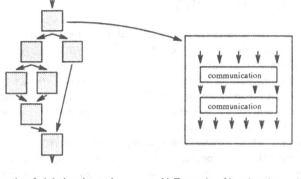

a) Example of global-task graph   b) Example of local-task graph

Figure3: *Two-level task graph*

Because of this special implicit description of communication, all virtual processes associated to one 2D-array take part in each communication phase. Synchronization has to ensure correct message passing for each transformation.

The creation of new 2D-array components via reshaping transformations extends the number of the current virtual processes for the next local computation. Thus, spawning and deletion of virtual processes is connected to these data-manipulations.

The array-creating transformations divide the processes into groups each performing different tasks, i.e. 2D-arrays are represented by **groups of virtual processes**. In each group, the virtual processes are numbered consecutively starting with 0.

Because of the alternation of local computations and global transformations, 2DT is appropriate for the formulation of loosely-synchronous algorithms consisting of consecutive segments (phases) of independent but similar computations separated by communication phases (coarse grain compute-communicate algorithm). In each phase, a process uses data received from other processes in the last communication phase. Changing the number of virtual processes by reshaping transformations allows to fully exploit the intrinsic parallelism of an algorithm on the virtual level.

The **task graph** is the conceptual structure representing the execution of a dynamically changing set of virtual processes. Within each single group, the **local-task graph** is structured into phases of computations and phases of communication with a variable dynamic number n_i of tasks due to reshaping. Due to array-creating transformations, those homogeneous **local-task graphs** are arranged in a **group-task graph** of more general unbalanced structure. Figure 3 shows an example of a group-task graph where the nodes are local-task graphs and the arrows symbolize array-creating transformations. We consider two alternatives to handle **group-parallelism**:

- Depth first, i.e. the group-task graph is traversed with a depth first strategy.
- Breadth first, i.e. the group-task graph is traversed with a breadth first strategy.

4   Abstract Machine

The next step from the idealized view of a variable number of virtual processes to an implementation on a processor-network with a fixed number of physical processors, i.e. from an infinite virtual parallelism to a finite one, is the mapping of a variable number of virtual processes to a fixed number of processors. To this end, we consider an **abstract machine model** consisting of a fixed number p of **abstract processors**.

An allocation from virtual processes to abstract processors is associated with the basic problems of distributed computing:

load balancing, virtual process migration, group management.

It is in the nature of this basic problems that the best strategy for one of the problems may contradict the best solution to the others, e.g. good load balancing may cause lots of virtual process migration between abstract processors, or cheap group management may entail bad load balancing and much virtual process migration. Thus, an acceptable allocation strategy has to be a compromise between the competing distribution problems. On the other side, the allocation decision influence and restrict the run-time functions:

scheduling, change of allocation, communication between abstract processors.

Thus, the allocation is the link between the conceptual strategy for solving the basic problems and the achievable run-time behavior. We provide an allocation mechanism representing the chosen allocation strategy in an appropriate data-structure VAPT which is used for the run-time functions. The abstract machine supports this separation between strategy and execution, and the abstract machine code contains the data structure VAPT. Several allocation strategies are discussed.

4.1   Processor Allocation

The abstract processors $P_0, \ldots, P_{p-1}$ are numbered consecutively but there is no constraint to a special topology of the network, in particular not to a processor-array. Each virtual process when created is allocated to an abstract processor. Because of the definition of virtual processes this comprises the distribution of both, the data and the respective computation work.

The allocation of all current virtual processes to abstract processors is described by an **allocation function**. Because of the varying number of virtual processes, the allocation mapping is not fixed but may change due to global transformations. Therefore, in the course of program execution, we will have a sequence of *allocation functions* $\mathcal{A}_t : \{0, \ldots, n_t - 1\} \longrightarrow \{0, \ldots, p - 1\}, \quad t = 1, 2, \ldots$
where n_t is the current number of virtual processes. The period in which one allocation function $\mathcal{A}_t$ holds is called **allocation phase** t and the change to a new allocation phase $t + 1$ (a new allocation function $\mathcal{A}_{t+1}$) is referred to as **reallocation**. The virtual process j existing in allocation phase t is executed on the abstract processor $\mathcal{A}_t(j), \ j = 0, \ldots, n_t - 1$. During a local computation the allocation function is fixed. The allocation may change after a global transformation. But, each allocation phase may cover several computation and communication phases.

The current allocation information is stored in a table, the **VAPT** (virtual-to-abstract-processor table) providing the correct allocation function $\mathcal{A}_t$ in the phases of local computation and in subsequent communications. As described before, several groups of virtual processes may exist at the same time. There is one $VAPT_g$ to describe the allocation information for each group g. Thus, in case of a set of groups we have a set of VAPT's each of which stores the allocation mapping for one group of virtual processes.

From the point of view of each abstract processor in a given allocation phase t, the set of virtual processes is divided into **internal** and **external** processes. The set
$$Internal_t = Internal_t(P_l) = \{ k \mid \mathcal{A}_t(k) = l \}, \quad (l = 0, \ldots, p - 1),$$
contains the process numbers of the internal virtual processes of P_l within phase t; all other currently existing virtual processes are external processors for P_l. There is a partition of internal virtual processes according to group membership.

We will experiment with several simple allocation strategies which avoid frequent reassignments of virtual processes to abstract processors (virtual process migration), while keeping a balanced distribution of virtual processes on the abstract ones.
The 2DT-paradigm offers the following simple allocation situation:

- Independent tasks are directly expressed in the 2DT-program due to 2DT- and group-parallelism.

- A homogenuous task graph is given because all local computation within the same group are of similar size. The execution time may still be different, because the programs may use process numbers. However, likelihood for this is small. Thus, we can rather safely work under the assumption that a balanced process distribution implies a balanced load distribution. A balanced process distribution can be established during the initial distribution phase and maintained by redistribution.

If the number of abstract processors is greater than the number of virtual processes the assignment is straightforward. However, we suppose that the number of virtual processes exceeds the number of abstract processors, i.e. many virtual processes will be executed by one abstract processor.

Allocation strategies:

(1) Random allocation:
    The local data are distributed over the abstract processors at random. [BSW89] shows that with high likelyhood a good distribution can be achieved. However, locality is not guaranteed.

(2) Multifit algorithm for nonpreemptive tasks [CGJ78]:
    The set of nonpreemptive tasks, as it is e.g. given for numerical algorithms, is distributed over the processors by an efficient approximation algorithm ([CGJ78]). The global execution time is at most by a factor 1,220 worse than the global execution time of an optimal allocation.

(3) $\lceil \frac{n}{p} \rceil$-consecutive allocation [BRSW93b]:
    The n local data of each 2D-array are evenly distributed over the abstract processors such that each holds at most $\lceil \frac{n}{p} \rceil$ -consecutive local data of the array.
    (CA) *The number of LoDa allocated to abstract processors differs at most by one* (New load-balancing is needed after log p resize operation (sec.6),see[BRSW93b])

(4) Group-oriented allocation:
    The allocation of virtual processes partitions the set of physical processors according to the group structure of the virtual processes, i.e. the following invariance is always guarantees the:
    (BF) *No virtual processes of different 2D-arrays execute on the same processor*
    This simplifies the communication implementing global transformations, since messages are exchanged only inside groups of virtual processes.

(5) History-sensitive allocation:
Depending on the current allocation situation stored in the VAPT, a new allocation is incrementally computed avoiding too many process migration.

4.2 Structure of Abstract Processors

Conceptually, all virtual processes have identical copies of the translated 2DT-FP program. They apply this code to their local data. The semantics of the different copies, however, differ, since the code contains process numbers.

In an implementation, all internal virtual processes of one abstract processor **share** the same copy of the code. The abstract processor schedules them with the right processor number and the right local data. In the same way, all other common information are factored out and are part of the abstract processor (**context sharing**). All scheduling strategies discussed will also allow the sharing of the runtime stacks for function calls. This leads to the following **structure of an abstract processor**:

- the program,
- VAPT's, one for each group containing at least one internal virtual process,
- allocation phase information: (number of internal virtual processes, total number of virtual processes, address of the first internal process, height of LoDa.)
- input- and output-buffers for communication with other abstract processors,
- a run-time system supporting scheduling, synchronization, updating VAPT's and communication (external and internal restoring)
- lists of virtual process descriptions of internal processes (one for each group involved).

Abstract processor

program
allocation information
group information
Lists of virtual processes

The concept of context sharing leaves small virtual process description. The **representation of a virtual process** is reduced to their individual components, especially to the local data and the virtual process number. Furthermore, information for local computations (e.g. size and address of local data) and information used for the scheduling by the abstract processor (e.g. program counter) are contained.

Group context sharing makes context sharing between processes of the same group cheap. This is essentially exploited by using the group-oriented allocation (4), where each abstract processor runs only virtual processes from one group. Thus, we have process migration in favour of cheap context switches.

4.3 Abstract Machine Code

The generated machine code has to perform both, the execution of virtual processes and the management of allocation. The following table contains 2DT-FP functions and the intended behavior of the translated program:

2DT-FP function in source program	Execution on the abstract processors
FP-function	Execution for internal processes
Shape-preserving transformation	Redistribution of data
Reshaping transformation	Updating the VAPT
	Redistribution of data
Array-creating transformation	Creation or deletion of VAPT's
	Updating of VAPT's
	Redistribution of data

An identical updating of the VAPT's is performed by all abstract processors, according to the same chosen global allocation strategy. Creation or deletion of VAPT's reflect the creation or deletion of groups due to array-creating transformations.

4.3.1 Communication

Shape-preserving global transformations are translated into appropriate communication code. Therefore, the virtual communication messages (which can be created directly from the global transformations) have to be converted to abstract messages. Abstract processors realizing virtual communication perform communication between internal virtual processes by reshuffling the data in place. Abstract communication redistribute data of external processes (**redistribution**).

Reshaping and array-creating transformations give rise to the **reallocation** of abstract processors (and to the updating of the VAPT), i.e. the whole data-structure describing a virtual process is forwarded to another abstract processor.

According to redistribution and reallocation, we have to distinguish differnet kinds of atomic messages for abstract communication, e.g.:

- Redistribution message (Dist) for 2D-array component L_i^j:

  $(Dist, processno, com, contents)$,

  where $contents$ is the value to be stored in the virtual process with number $processno$ in local data component com.

- Reallocation message (Allo) for virtual process description with local data L_i:

  $(Allo, processno, contents)$

  where $contents$ is the virtual process description to be stored as virtual process $processno$.

For the abstract communication, we provide an appropriate set of input-buffers and output-buffers, i.e. each abstract processor P_l possesses $p-1$ input-buffer $\mathcal{I}_k$ and $p-1$ output-buffers $\mathcal{O}_k$, $k \in \{0, \ldots, p-1\} - \{k\}$.

In order to realize the packing of large messages and to use efficient topology-dependent communication primitives, each abstract processor splits the communication phases into three separate steps (**communication bundling**):

(1) preparation of atomic messages,

(2) abstract communication and

(3) extracting and distributing of atomic messages.

In detail in each step the following is performed:

(1) Redistribution messages are prepared according to the generating transformation. The abstract destination is determined with the help of the VAPT. The destination for a reallocation messages is also given by the VAPT updated according to the considered transformation.

(2) After finishing the preparation step, the atomic messages in each output buffer $\mathcal{O}_k$, $k \in \{0, \ldots, p-1\} - \{k\}$ are combined to one large message. When all the local virtual processes have finished this, communication takes place. Because communication is caused by global transformations, every processor knows how many messages (at most $p-1$) it expects from this transformation.

If every abstract processor holds internal processors of each current groups, we have to perform a synchronous **total exchange** operation, see [BT89]. In case of group-oriented allocation, a synchronous *total exchange* operation is performed on subnets. The communication can also be expressed in terms of communication primitives, e.g. **non-blocking send** actions, **blocking receive** actions, cf. [And91] which are available on most topologies as offered e.g. by [BBD+87].

(3) The atomic messages of the received large messages are stored. Messages of type *Dist* are stored as the component *com* of the local data of virtual process *processno*. Messages of type *Allo* are inserted in a list of virtual processes of the same group as process number *processno*.

4.3.2 Scheduling – Group Management

According to the two-level task graph (see Fig.3), the abstract machine has to perform two different kinds of scheduling.

Scheduling in the small: Local computations for internal processes within the the same group are scheduled by the abstract processor. The same is done for the local parts of shape-preserving global transformations. Scheduling will switch between virtual processes after local computations and the set up phase of messages.

Scheduling in the large: On the level of groups of virtual processes, scheduling is performed according to the chosen depth-first or breadth-first strategy.

The depth-first strategy admits only one active 2D-array at a time performed by scheduling in the small. Depth first group scheduling may severely restrict the amount of parallelism. Computation and communication phases are strictly sequential, thus potentially leaving processors idle durnig communication phases and the network idle during computation phases.

Breadth-first group scheduling strategy has to solve the problem that messages caused by several transformations may coexist in the network. Using the processor allocation strategy (4), the abstract processors are grouped according to the grouping of the virtual processes, i.e. no processor runs virtual processes from more than one group, because of invariance (BF). Hence, message exchange for each application of a transformation is restricted to one subnet. This strategy may better exploit the network, but it still leaves the processors idle during group communication phases.

A more general breadth first group scheduling offers the greatest degree of parallelism. Local computations of one group may be performed overlapping with communication phases of another group for each processor. However, this will lead to the situation, that one processor may receive messages from different transformation applications at the same time.

4.3.3 Synchronization

Synchronization is needed in parallel systems, if the relative speed of processes may influence the result of computations. This is mainly due to competing accesses to shared resources. 2DT-FP does not have shared or global variables. Furthermore, synchronization ensures that local computations take place on the correct data transmitted in the last communication phase.

Because within a local-task graph communication phases are restricted by the special global transformations, **local synchronization** (see [BT89]) is used, i.e. a processor knows from which other processor it has to expect messages and thus it starts a new computation once it has received all these messages. Hence, explicit synchronization is eliminated.

There is only one problem potentially needing synchronization. This is the coexistence of messages from different global transformations without clear indication of what was the transformation application which generated it.

In case of depth-first group scheduling strategy which admits only one active 2D-array at any time local synchronization can be exploited and no extra communication is required.

The breadth-first group scheduling together with group-oriented allocation strategy with invariant (BF) restricts communication to a subnet. Hence, we also have local synchronization.

For breadth-first group management with general allocation, we have to solve the problem of identifying the right (virtual) receiver. A unique identification scheme for transformation applications is introduced which is described in detail in [BRSW93b]. This also leads to an implicit synchronization similar the one in the depth-first case. Every group member on one processor knows how many messages to expect. Again, no extra communication is required.

5 Code Generation

The code for the abstract machine is generated by the code-generating function $\mathcal{G}$. This function $\mathcal{G}$ translates a 2DT-FP programs into abstract machine code. The generated abstract code has to perform modifications on data-structures describing virtual processes. As mentioned before, all abstract processors execute identical copies of an abstract program. The semantics differ because of different internal processes *Internal* and different VAPT information. # denotes the number of the virtual process currently executed.

We restrict the presentation to the translation of the global transformations in the message creating phase. Some functions used in the target code are:

Function	Behavior
schedule	scheduling of internal processes
update	updating of the VAPT
store	storing data into the appropriate buffer or data-structure

(1) Let T be a global shape-preserving transformation

```
schedule for # ∈ Internalₜ :
{  For j = 1,...,n do
  msg =  create-msg (T,j);
  if ( VAPT (dest(msg)) =  own abstract processor number )
    then store(msg, dest(msg))
    else store(msg, O_VAPT(dest(msg)))
  endif   }
```

where create-msg(T,j) is a macro creating the destination of a message component j for Transformation T, e.g. for the transpose transformation $c2r$ (cf. sec.6) we have:

$$\text{create-msg} \ (\ c2r \ ,j) = (Dist \ , (\# * n + j - 1) \ \text{mod} \ m, (\# * n + j - 1) \ \text{div} + 1, L_\#^j)$$

(2) Let T be a global reshaping transformation (reallocation from t to $t+1$):

```
update(T) VAPT ;
rename virtual processes (T)
create (or delete) processes (T)
schedule for # ∈ Internal_t :
{  msg = create-msg (T,j);
   if (VAPT(dest(msg)) = own abstract processor number )
     then store(msg, dest(msg))
     else store(msg, O_VAPT(dest(msg)))
   endif  }
```

(3) Let T be a global array-creating transformation (for group oriented allocation):

```
create (or delete) VAPT's (T)
rename virtual processes (T)
schedule for # ∈ Internal_t :
{   if (A_t ≠ VAPT (#))
      then msg = create-msg (T,#);
    store(msg, O_VAPT(dest(msg)))
    endif   }
```

The application of a program to the problem data is performed by the **apply** command. Before running the program, the expected situation on the abstract processors has to be initialized:

(a) Each abstract processor builds up its internal structure with an empty list of virtual processes.

(b) The program is loaded into the program store.

(c) According to the problem data division, the first allocation function A_1 is determined and stored.

(d) The virtual processes are initialized according to the VAPT .

(e) The local data are stored in their corresponding virtual structure.

6 Examples of Global Transformations

In this chapter, we present transformations proposed in [BRSW93a] and illustrate their communication behavior on the virtual level.

6.1 A Shape-Preserving Transformations: Transpose

The transpose operation columns-to-rows (c2r) applied to a rectangular 2D-array changes the data storage in column-major order to row-major order. The transformation rows-to-columns (r2c) performs the opposite.

virtual process	0	1	...	$m-1$		virtual process	0	1	...	$m-1$
1	a_1	a_{n+1}	...	$a_{(m-1)n+1}$	$\xrightarrow{c2r}$ $\xleftarrow{r2c}$	1	a_1	a_2	...	a_m
$\vdots$	$\vdots$	$\vdots$		$\vdots$		$\vdots$	$\vdots$	$\vdots$		$\vdots$
n	a_n	a_{2n}	...	a_{mn}		n	$a_{(n-1)m+1}$	$a_{(n-1)m+2}$	...	a_{nm}

The transformation c2r re-distributes the contents a_{i*n+j} of LoDa L_i^j into the LoDa of the virtual processor with the number

$$(i * n + j - 1) \bmod m \quad \text{for } i = 0, \ldots, m - 1, \ j = 1, \ldots, n$$

as tuple component with number

$$(i * n + j - 1) \operatorname{div} m + 1 \quad \text{for } i = 0, \ldots, m - 1, \ j = 1, \ldots, n.$$

Thus, each virtual process $\# \in \{0, \ldots, m - 1\}$ has to send tuple component j to the virtual process $\#'$ with number

$$\#' = (\# * n + j - 1) \bmod m \quad \text{for } j = 1, \ldots, n$$

which depends on its own processor number $\#$. Therefore each abstract processor creates the messages

$$(Dist, \ (\# * n + j - 1) \bmod m, \ (\# * n + j - 1) \operatorname{div} + 1, \ L_\#^j)$$

of type $Dist$ which take part in a communication phase described in section 4.3.

The transformation r2c re-distribute the contents $a_{(j-1)*m+i+1}$ of LoDa L_i^j into the LoDa of the virtual processor with the number

$$(i + (j - 1) * m) \operatorname{div} n \quad \text{for } i = 0, \ldots, m - 1, \ j = 1, \ldots, n$$

as tuple component with number

$$(i + (j - 1) * m) \bmod m + 1 \quad \text{for } i = 0, \ldots, m - 1, \ j = 1, \ldots, n.$$

The atomic messages are formed analogously to the transformation c2r.

6.2 A Reshaping Transformations: Resize

Resize(2) or Resize(-2)-transformations "double" or "half" the number of virtual processes and re-distribute the data in the following way. For simplicity, let n and m be even.

virtual process	0	...	$m-1$		virtual process	0	1	...	$2m-2$	$2m-1$
				$\xrightarrow{resize(2)}$						
1	a_0^1	...	a_{m-1}^1	$\xleftarrow{resize(-2)}$	1	a_0^1	$a_0^{\lceil n/2 \rceil + 1}$	...	a_{m-1}^1	$a_{m-1}^{\lceil n/2 \rceil + 1}$
$\vdots$	$\vdots$		$\vdots$		$\vdots$	$\vdots$	$\vdots$		$\vdots$	$\vdots$
n	a_0^n	...	a_{m-1}^n		n	$a_0^{\lceil n/2 \rceil}$	a_0^n	...	$a_{m-1}^{\lceil n/2 \rceil}$	a_{m-1}^n

In order to perform a resize(2)-transformation, each abstract processor performs:

- The VAPT is extended and updated.
- The processor numbers of the existing virtual process $\#$ are renamed in $\#' = 2 * \#$, $\# = 0, \ldots, m - 1$.
- The virtual processes with number $\#' = 2 * l + 1$, $l = 0, \ldots, m - 1$ are created in the appropriate abstract processor determined in the VAPT.
- The contents $a_\#^{\lceil n/2 \rceil + 1}, \ldots, a_\#^n$ of the renamed virtual process $\#' = 2 * \#$, $\# = 0, \ldots, m - 1$ are sent to the virtual processors with the numbers $\#' + 1$ in order to be the contents of $L - \#' = L_{\#'=1}^1, \ldots, L - \#' + 1^{\lceil n/2 \rceil}$.
- The 'length of the LoDa' is updated. The 'number of processes' is updated.

6.3 An Array-Creating Transformations: Split&Glue

Split&Glue transformation splits the 2D-array into two son arrays. The operation of Split&Glue is determined by some arbitrary boolean condition that is applied to all columns: Those having the same result ($True$ or $False$) are grouped together in the same son array. A separate and parallel computation (supplied as an argument to the constructors) is performed on every son array. When both computations have terminated, their results (two new 2D-arrays) are joined back forming a **single** 2D-array.

virtual process	0	...	$m-1$
	a_0	...	a_{m-1}
	b_0	...	b_{m-1}

$\xrightarrow{split}$

virtual process	0	...	m_1-1
	a_{k_0}	...	$a_{k_{m_1-1}}$

virtual process	0	...	m_2-1
	a_{l_0}	...	$a_{l_{m_2-1}}$

where $b_i \in \{True, False\}$, $i = 0, \ldots, m-1$, $m_1 + m_2 = m$
and $b_{k_\kappa} = True$, $\kappa = 1, \ldots, m_1 - 1$ $b_{l_\nu} = False$, $\nu = 1, \ldots, m_2 - 1$.

virtual process		
	a_0 ... a_{m_1-1}	
virtual process	0 ... m_2-1	
	b_{l_0} ... b_{m_2-1}	

$\xrightarrow{glue}$

virtual process	0	...	m_1-1	m_1	...	m_1+m_2-1
1	a_0^1	...	$a_{m_1-1}^1$	b_0^1	...	$b_{m_2-1}^1$
$\vdots$	$\vdots$		$\vdots$	$\vdots$		$\vdots$
n'				$b_0^{n'}$	...	$b_{m_2-1}^{n'}$
$\vdots$	$\vdots$		$\vdots$	$\vdots$		$\vdots$
n	$a_{k_0}^n$	...	$a_{m_1-1}^n$	@	...	@

where $n \geq n'$ and @ is a null element (cf.[BRSW93a]). Depending on the allocation strategy, communication with messages of type *Allo* take place or not.

7 Conclusion

The 2DT paradigm provides a two-level parallelism of so-called apply-to-all parallelism and group parallelism. For the implementation we discussed several allocation strategies appropriate for the regular SPMD-mode of 2DT providing a course grain compute communicate scheme with regard to our design goals for distributed programming. Special emphasize was laid on group management handling group-parallelism. The design goals are achieved by the concepts of restricted dynamic allocation, packing of messages, context sharing and communication bundling.

The introduced implementation concept has an open structure concerning implementation decisions and also language design decisions. Thus, it allows the exchange of allocation strategies and communication concepts. As well, the implementer can add new 2D-transformation to an existing 2DT-implementation.

Currently, we are implementing 2DT-FP on the iPSC/860. We will experiment with the introduced allocation strategies using different kinds of test programs from e.g. numerical algorithms. This is connected with the design of distributed algorithms for (numerical) application and the study of usable 2D-transformation in the applications. Furthermore, the implementation concept will be applied to an imperative base language.

References

[And91] G.R.. Andrews. Paradigms for process interaction in distributed programs. *ACM Computing Surveys*, 23(1):49–90, 1991.

[Bac78]   J. Backus. Can programming be liberated from the von Neumann style? A functional style and its algebra of programs. *Communication of the ACM*, 21(8):613–641, 1978.

[BBD+87]   J. Boyle, R. Butler, T. Disz, B. Glickfeld, E. Lusk, R. Overbeek, J. Patterson, and R. Stevens. *Portable Programs for Parallel Processors*. Holt, Rinehart and Winston, New York NY, USA, 1987.

[BRSW93a]   Y. Ben-Asher, G. Rünger, A. Schuster, and R. Wilhelm. 2DT-FP: An FP based programming language for efficient parallel programming of multiprocessor networks. In *PARLE'93*, LNCS 694, pages 42–55. Springer Verlag, 1993.

[BRSW93b]   Y. Ben-Asher, G. Rünger, A. Schuster, and R. Wilhelm. Load balancing and communication for a parallel functional language. Submitted for publication, 1993.

[BSW89]   Y. Ben-Asher, H. Seidl, and R. Wilhelm. The TRANSPOSE machine: A global implementation of a parallel graph reducer. In *Proc. of Tencon'89*, Bombay, 1989.

[BT89]   D.P. Bertsekas and J.N. Tsitsiklis. *Parallel and Distributed Computing*. Prentice Hall, 1989.

[BW91]   D. Banerjee and C. Walinsky. An optimizing compiler for FP* – a data-parallel dialect of FP. *Parallel and Distr. Proc.*, pages 70–78, 1991.

[CGJ78]   E.G. Coffman, M.R. Garey, and D.S. Johnson. An Application of Bin-Packing to Multiprocessor Scheduling. *SIAM Journal of Computing*, 7(1):1–17, 1978.

[DP93]   M. Danelutto and S. Pelagatti. Parallel implementation of FP using a template-based approach. In M. van Eekelen R. Plasmeijer, editor, *Implementation of Functional Languages*, pages 7–22, Nijwegen, Sept. 1993.

[Hil93]   J. Hill. Vectorizing a non-strict functional language for a data-parallel "Spineless (not so) Tagless G-machine". In M. van Eekelen R. Plasmeijer, editor, *Implementation of Functional Languages*, pages 87–100, Nijwegen, Sept. 1993.

[Jou91]   G.K. Jouret. Compiling functional languages for SIMD architectures. *Parallel and Distributed Processing*, pages 79–86, 1991.

Global Code Selection for Directed Acyclic Graphs*

Andreas Fauth[1], Günter Hommel[1], Alois Knoll[2], Carsten Müller[1]
fauth@cs.tu-berlin.de

[1] Technische Universität Berlin, Institut für Technische Informatik,
Franklinstr. 28/29, D-10587 Berlin, Germany
[2] Universität Bielefeld, Technische Fakultät,
Postfach 10 01 31, D-33501 Bielefeld, Germany

Abstract. We describe a novel technique for code selection based on data-flow graphs, which arise naturally in the domain of digital signal processing. Code selection is the optimized mapping of abstract operations to partial machine instructions. The presented method performs an important task within the retargetable microcode generator CBC, which was designed to cope with the requirements arising in the context of custom digital signal processor (DSP) programming. The algorithm exploits a graph representation in which control-flow is modeled by scopes.

1 Introduction

In the domain of medium-throughput digital signal processing, micro-programmable processor cores are frequently chosen for system realization. By adding dedicated hardware (accelerator paths), these cores are tailored to the needs of new applications. Optimized processor modules can be reused, which is a major benefit compared to *high-level synthesis* [28] where a completely new design is developed for each application. Because of the application-specific add-ons and the rather short lifetimes of a specific design, there is a need for retargetable software development tools, especially code-generators.

1.1 Overview

In the next section we will shortly discuss several related approaches to code generation and point out some differences of our system. Section 3 introduces the overall architecture and functionality of the CBC code generator. Section 4 explains the code selection task and the basic techniques used. In section 5 our algorithm is presented. We conclude the paper with experimental results.

* Part of this research is supported by the ESPRIT 2260 ("SPRITE") project of the European Community and Siemens AG, München.

2 Related Work

Lansdkov et al. [27] present a machine model and methods for microcode generation. A subtask of code selection called *bundling* and a subset of scheduling called
compaction are described. Both methods have a local view on the subject program. The YC system [6] deals with code selection but does not provide detailed
scheduling. A phase called *combiner* only tries to concatenate adjacent operations. The work of Rimey [31, 32] describes a compiler for application-specific
DSPs. The main attention, however, is paid to scheduling and data-routing (i.e.
mainly register assignment and spilling). Code selection and scheduling are only
performed on straight-line code. Optimizations across branch boundaries are
not performed. The MARION system [2, 3] performs code generation for RISC
architectures. Here, a simple approach for code selection is chosen. A recursive-
descent brute-force tree pattern matcher neither considers graph structure of
the intermediate code nor global subexpressions. Our implementation is based
on the work of Fraser et al. [13, 14].

Points of major differences between our code selection approach and similar
tasks in "classic" code generation (CG) are:

- *Complexity of datapaths.* CBC has to deal with highly specialized and optimized datapaths. The hardware units make the efficient execution of frequently used operation sequences possible. Operation patterns for the functional units of these datapaths are much more complex than for standard
  microprocessors.
- *Type-handling.* DSP algorithms may employ a large variety of different word
  lengths and numerical types. The hardware operators are restricted to fixed
  word lengths. A correct mapping must always be found. In most CG work
  this topic is neglected because language definitions (and hence the compilers)
  are restricted to "implementation-dependent" types.
- *Evaluation order.* Approaches like [6, 7] dealing with code selection assume
  a fixed evaluation order, which is usually derived from the imperative source
  code. There is no explicit scheduling phase included in the back-ends. Commonly, register allocation is performed during code selection. Most of the
  time this is done by graph coloring [4] or "on-the-fly".
- *Parallelism of functional blocks.* Most DSP architectures contain several
  functional units that work in parallel. Therefore, the final code cannot be
  emitted during or immediately after the code selection phase because *partial*
  instructions must be "compacted" into *complete* instructions at a later stage
  of compilation exploiting the possible parallelism. Consequently, code selection must not specify the complete behavior of the machine for each cycle.
  It must only select code for each of the individual units.
- *Expressions are DAGs.* Intermediate programs formulated in *directed acyclic
  graphs* (DAGs) pose a problem to classic code selection approaches. "*We
  assume that the intermediate code and the target code are presented as trees
  or terms*" [8] is a typical statement. Tree matching methods [1] are popular.

– *Machine description.* In the compiler writer community machine descriptions are mainly intended to be used by the code generator only. Some detailed knowledge of the compiler is necessary to write good descriptions. By giving the semantics for each instruction as a transformation of the machine state, we describe the instruction set in a behavioral way. Out of this machine *description*, various machine *models* can be generated depending on the application (e.g. code generator, assembler or simulator).

– *Intermediate representation.* Our intermediate representation is based on a data- and control-flow graph description that differs from the representations used in many compilers.

3 Anatomy of the Compiler

In CBC, code generation is split into different tasks. Each of these is performed by a specific tool. The intermediate results are passed on in human-readable text files. Figure 1 shows the general layout of the code generator, the underlying data- and rule-base as well as the retargeting mechanism.

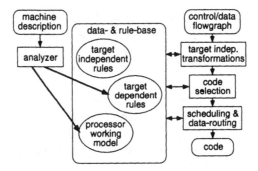

Fig. 1. System overview of CBC's code-generator and its retargeting process.

The primary goal is to generate highly optimized code from the description of the algorithm, which is specified graphically or textually in a signal flow graph. In principle, it is also possible to write the algorithm in other languages that are capable of modeling parallel behavior in an adequate way, e.g. the synchronous subset of the applicative real-time DSP language ALDiSP [16]. The intermediate representation can be easily obtained from a signal flow graph and will be described in section 3.3.

3.1 Retargeting

In our approach, the language nML [15] is used to describe the target architecture (see Fig. 2). Originally designed as a simple means for expressing programming models as found in the usual programmer's manuals, it has turned out to be powerful enough to describe current and future DSP cores – it may even serve as the basis for high-level hardware synthesis [12]. Its main advantage from the programmer's point of view, however, is its compactness combined with its readability. nML is intended for describing arbitrary *single instruction stream* architectures. Such architectures feature a single program counter, but can otherwise consist of an "unlimited" number of building blocks. Based on attribute grammars, nML is flexible and reasonably easy to use.

```
type word = int(14)
type addr = card(20)

mem REG[8,word]
mem RAM[2**20,word]
mem latch[3,word]

op instruction = jump | aluOp | ...
op alu(a:aluAction,s1:src,s2:src,d:dst)
  action = { latch[0]=s1; latch[1]=s2; a.action;  d=latch[2]; }
  syntax = format("%s %s,%s,%s",a.syntax,s1.syntax,...)
  image = ...

op aluAction = sub | add | ...
op sub()
  action = { latch[2] = latch[0] - latch [1]; }
  ...

mode src = reg | ...
mode reg(n:card(3)) = REG[n]
  syntax = format("R%d",n)
  image = format("01%b",n)
...
```

Fig. 2. Excerpt from an nML machine description.

When retargeting the compiler, the nML analyzer examines the instruction set and the memory description of the target processor and builds a *machine model*, i.e. a representation of the capabilities and constraints of the machine. The process of building this model is detailed in [10, 12]. The machine model, along with the datapath constraints and machine-independent transformation rules are given as input to the generic (parameterized) code generator. The transformation rules specify, for example, how to perform a 32-bit addition on a 16-bit machine. The phases of code generation and the construction of the generic compiler are outlined in [9, 11].

3.2 Code Generation Script

The main tasks of code generation are:

- *Signal flow graph translation.* This is the algorithmic design entry to the code generator. The specification of the application program is constructed using a schematic editor and a simulation tool. The resultant signal flow graph is translated by this front-end into the code generator's internal data format.
- *Control-flow transformations.* Transformations concerning the mutually exclusive execution of operations depending on certain conditions are performed to reduce the overall execution time. A pure data-driven representation is translated into a hybrid data/control-driven representation reflecting the requirements of branch controllers and conditional transfers used in programmable DSP systems [11, 26].[3]
- *Code selection.* Subsets of the algorithm are mapped to datapaths. First, high-level operations of the algorithmic input are expanded into machine-executable operations. Then, chains of expanded operations are merged to form more complex operations that are provided by the machine. This clustering reduces the complexity of the scheduling task and allows optimized code generation in reasonable time.
- *Scheduling and data-routing.* The operations in the graph are ordered in time. To produce high quality code, efficient scheduling is a necessity. The goal of scheduling is minimum execution time for a given algorithm on an architecture which is fixed at compile-time. Therefore, the assignment of registers to intermediate values, the generation of data-routes (including spill-code) and scheduling are performed in parallel [23, 32].

3.3 Intermediate Representation

The intermediate representation is a *control/data-flow graph* (CDFG). A CDFG is a program description based on a directed graph (N, E) consisting of two finite sets: the nodes $n_i \in N$ represent the operations of the program and the directed edges $e_i \in E$ which are ordered pairs of nodes $e_i = (n_j, n_k)$ display dependencies between the operations. An edge can either model a *data-flow dependency* (i.e. a data flow path) or an additional *control-flow constraint*.[4] The CDFG describes the body of the main execution loop of an application. Cycles in the graph result only from *algorithmic delay operations* which are used to refer to values from earlier incarnations of loops.

The *data-flow graph* models all data dependencies and operations. An operation node can be executed whenever input data is available.[5] Inputs and outputs of the program are represented as data sources and data sinks. Data is

---

[3] This task is actually split in two: One phase before and one phase after code selection. The first phase rewrites scope structures and the second inserts jump operations.

[4] Note that each data-flow edge implicitly models a control-flow constraint.

[5] All preceding control-flow constraints must also be satisfied.

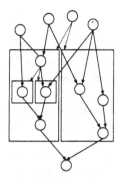

Fig. 3. A CDFG with nested conditional scopes. Each box represents one scope. The two large boxes represent top-level exclusive scopes. The two small boxes represent a pair of exclusive scopes local to the left top-level scope. The nodes represent operations and the arcs represent data-flow edges. The dashed arcs are flag edges from the condition to the true and the false case.

represented as *signals*. A signal represents an *infinite stream* of values. For *synchronous* data-flow, the amount of data produced and consumed for each node is specified a priori. Our data-flow model limits the amout of data produced and consumed in a single cycle to exactly one. The execution of an operation therefore consists mainly of the *use* of one signal at each incoming edge and the *definition* of one signal at each outgoing edge.[6]

The *control-flow graph* is basically a hierarchical structure of *macro nodes*. A macro node is a cluster of operations and other macro nodes. They are used to model loops and conditional *scopes*. All operations inside a specific conditional scope are related to a certain condition. Additionally, *control-flow edges* display precedence relations between operations. At the beginning of code generation there are few control-flow edges; later phases insert additional control-flow information modeling *in-place storage* of signals and the programming of the *branch controller*. The scheduler must find an explicit execution order for all operations, resulting in a sequentially executable microprogram.

For the different stages of code generation, three distinct sets of arithmetic and logic operations exist in a common library:

- *Abstract operations* (AOs). This is set of high-level operations that is available in the initial input-level graph.
- *Machine-executable operations* (MEOs). This set consists of operations which correspond to primitives of the **nML** description. All initial CDFG operations must be mapped to members of this set.
- *Datapath operations* (DOs). The third set comprises operations which occupy a full datapath. They are the basic entities for the scheduling process. These

---

[6] At this stage of the translation, all multi-rate segments of the program must be translated into loops or unrolled into straight-line code.

operations are formed out of the MEOs during chaining and represent the valid combinations of MEOs.

Besides these operations, some *canonical operations* identifying the action on dedicated hardware (such as accelerator paths) can also be included in the algorithm at each stage of the translation. Since they represent both abstract and datapath operations they are included in the CDFG upon entry to the script and need not be transformed during code selection. Two more groups exist:

- *Transfer operations.* These are used to describe assignments of data to memory locations and moves on buses. They are inserted into the description to route data between different storage locations and correspond to addressing modes and move operations.
- *Control-flow operations.* All conditional and unconditional jumps belong to this set.

4   The Problem of Code Selection

Prior to code selection, the algorithm consists of operations that are machine-independent and well-typed. After code selection, the algorithm must consist of operations that are equivalents for clusters of MEOs. These clusters are associated with datapaths and must not violate encoding restrictions. The first stage of code selection consists of two interleaved phases: *machine-parameterized macro expansion* and *mapping to machine-executable operations*. The second stage maps parts of the algorithm to datapaths.

4.1   The General Approach: Macro Expansion and Chaining

During *macro expansion*, operations in the CDFG are expanded into operations available on the machine. For example, multiplications are broken down to combinations of additions and shifts or into Booth-multiplication steps [24]. This process is controlled by rules, which are parameterized by the set of specific hardware operators offered by the target machine[7]. Therefore, the *rules* are machine-independent, but the *choice* between them is driven by the structure of the target machine.

When *mapping* to MEOs, limited word lengths are taken into account, i.e. the expanded execution of an operation on a smaller word length datapath is constructed. For example, an addition of two 32 bit values could be performed on a 16 bit datapath with two additions (assuming an addition with carry is possible). This task employs the CATHEDRAL-2ND tool for expansion [28]. However, it relies heavily on our own operation library [29], which is two-fold: A machine-independent part describes constant folding and other peephole optimizations; a machine-dependent part describes all MEOs as well as the corresponding expansion rules. The machine-dependent entries are either generated or instantiated

---

[7] This set is identified during the analysis of the nML machine description.

from templates during the retargeting process. Implementation alternatives are given from which the appropriate expansion can be chosen.

To allow the generation of optimized code within reasonable time, it is important to reduce the complexity of the scheduling task. Therefore, the second part of the code selection task maps subsets of the algorithm onto datapaths prior to scheduling. Once all high-level operations are refined to MEOs, clusters of direct data-dependent operations which can be performed on a datapath within a single cycle are identified. These *chains* of operations are merged and replaced by a single operation each, thus forming more complex operations that are provided by the machine. These *datapath operations* occupy a complete datapath. In Fig. 4 a CDFG is clustered to be executed on the depicted datapath. The shift operations (>>) are executed on the SHIFTER and the arithmetic operations (+ and -) are executed on the ALU CORE.

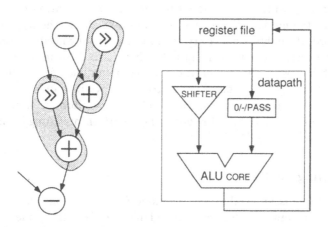

Fig. 4. A CDFG fragment and a datapath

Our chaining process resembles code selection in standard compilers since not all possible combinations of operations are legal chains. Restrictions which must not be violated result from the instruction set definition (see section 4.3).

4.2 Global Chaining

As outlined earlier, the goal of chaining is a "good" assignment of machine operations to datapaths. This implies that chaining *assists* the scheduler; it could indeed be integrated into the scheduling phase at the expense of increased complexity and run time. On the other hand, when chaining is done outside the context of scheduling, little information about resource usage is available. Especially in the presence of multiple *similar* datapaths[8] it is hard to estimate the

---

[8] Informally, two datapaths are called similar if they share many chaining patterns.

impact of a particular chaining decision on the quality of the resulting code: Operator assignment performed during chaining may result in schedules not fully exploiting potential parallelism of the machine. To decouple the two tasks, the chaining tool must annotate chains with implementation *alternatives*. In this paper we can thus neglect the problem of similar datapaths.

Since the architectures under consideration feature complex datapaths, we emphasize that whole *expressions* are assigned to a single datapath whenever possible. A chaining decision can affect the choices for distant operations, i.e., it has *global* effects. Therefore, large pieces of the CDFG must be considered when making a specific decision.

4.3 Encoding Restrictions

In general, the set of operation tuples executable on a datapath is not equal to all possible combinations of the hardware operators' functionalities; the designer may (and usually will) have imposed restrictions on operation chains. This is quite natural: the number of possible combinations affects the length of the instruction word. It might be necessary to omit some (rarely needed) combinations to reduce the instruction word length. Furthermore, there may be conflicts in the datapath hardware that prohibit certain combinations. As a result, code selection has to comply with encoding restrictions. As it is quite clear that the datapath structure alone is not sufficient to hold this information, we decided to represent legal chains as a set of rewrite rules. Pattern matching is employed to find legal chains in the CDFG.

4.4 Matching on Trees

Pattern matching is an established technique for instruction selection from expression trees in compilers for imperative languages [17, 21]. Code selection for stock microprocessors focuses mostly on a good exploitation of complex addressing modes. In the context of CBC, however, the emphasis is on good utilization of the complex datapaths. Nevertheless, similar tools can be used at the technical level. In the CBC environment, all legal patterns are generated by the nML front-end [9] and stored as a set of match-replace pairs (see Fig. 5 for an example). The match-replace database is intentionally held human-readable to allow an experienced user to modify some rules or add new rules by hand (e.g. for special optimizations). The depicted rule does not take commutativity of the add operation into account. This is not a serious problem; the nML front-end simply generates multiple patterns (in this case, s = add(t,i2) is replaced by s = add(i2,t)).

In the context of our compiler, the term rewrite system is not one monolithic unit; pattern matching and rewriting are separated phases. The tree parser generator we use, IBURG [14], is only concerned with the matching phase; the connection to the rewrite phase is made by match rule numbers. The tree grammar (from which the tree parser is generated) and the rewrite procedure are both generated by our chaining preprocessor, which takes the rewrite rules as

```
MATCH
   i1 = reg;
   i2 = reg;
   c  = const({-8..7});              /* A value constraint. */
   t  = shift(i1,c);
   s  = add(t,i2);
REPLACE COST=1
   s  = shiftadd(i1,i2,c);
ENDM
```

Fig. 5. A sample rewrite rule for the datapath of Fig. 4.

its input. The incorporated match algorithm is an extension to the BURS (Bottom Up Rewrite System) [30] theory and allows the computation of an optimal rewrite sequence for a tree (by matching the rewrite rules to subtrees), given a fixed set of rewrite rules with fixed costs. This computation takes time linearly proportional to the size of the tree. For the selection of the optimum match, tree parsing with dynamic programming is used [1]. The tree parser generator BURG [13] performs the dynamic programming at parser generation time and thus generates highly efficient pattern matchers. IBURG, a heavily simplified BURG version, still generates very efficient parsers, but their running time is no longer independent of the number, size, and structure of the patterns.[9] Because of its simplicity, IBURG can be modified quite easily. We extended it to accept certain match conditions in the rules; this way we can conveniently express type constraints or other operand constraints which are imposed by the hardware operators.

5   Code Selection on Graphs

Commonly, code selection is performed on expression trees. These are (partial) statements usually directly reflecting source language statements. The programs being compiled in our environment contain a large amount of decision making and common subexpressions. As mentioned above, cycles in the graph only result from values produced by delay operations. These are not considered during code selection.[10] Hence expressions in our CDFG model are DAGs. This means that intermediate results can have more than one use (Fig. 6a) which can also reside in different conditional scopes (Fig. 6b). Figure 6c shows a signal that has multiple definitions in different conditional scopes. In traditional compilers, conditions are at "borders" of basic blocks. The if-then-else statements themselves are also subject to code selection. In our approach, operation nodes of the CDFG

---

[9] However, informally speaking, for our purposes the generated parser have "nearly" linear behavior and are still fast enough.

[10] This is indeed a topic for future investigations.

have a *conditional context*. For each condition a *flag* is computed and connected to a macro node, i.e. a scope. Then, global data-flow is specified, i.e. signals "enter" and "leave" scopes. This representation facilitates code selection that transcends basic blocks.

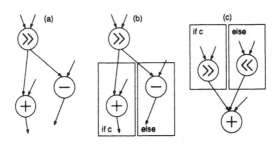

Fig. 6. Cases of interest to our global chaining approach: (a) multiple uses in the same scope, (b) multiple uses in different scopes and (c) multiple definitions.

Consider the architecture depicted in Fig. 4. A value produced by the SHIFTER is not immediately available for more than one operation. For that purpose an addition with zero must be performed to pass the value unchanged through the ALU CORE, i.e. the value is "spilled" to a register. We assume that the datapaths do not fork (and thus do not allow multiple uses within themselves). This implies that an operation defining a multiply used value can never be chained. The CDFG in Fig. 6a would be mapped to three operations (a **shift**, an **add** and a **sub**) instead of two in the optimal case (a **shift-add** and a **shift-sub**). The best results possible for the datapath of Fig. 4 are shown in Fig. 7.

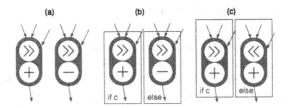

Fig. 7. The best solutions to the three different cases of Fig. 6.

5.1 The Simple Approach: "Undagging"

Earlier section were concerned with *tree* parsing and pattern matching in *trees*. On the other hand, it was unveiled that CDFGs are definitely not tree-like in the general case. The resulting problems have to be solved. Taking the previous section into account, it can be seen that some subgraphs indeed have a tree structure; namely those that lie between points of multiple uses and multiple definitions. Incidentally, the values which are defined or used more than once must be held in registers: multiple definitions require a proper modeling of control-flow which cannot (generally) be mapped onto the datapath; multiple uses map to different instructions.[11] This leads to a very simple chaining method: Cutting the DAG whenever a value is defined or used in multiple places yields a set of (usually small) trees. These trees are then individually processed by the rewrite system and reconnected afterwards to compose a chained version of the original DAG.

5.2 A More Sophisticated Approach: Heuristic Node Duplication

The advantage of the previous method is its simplicity. However, in a significant number of cases chaining possibilities are lost due to cuts at multiple uses or definitions. We seek a way to improve this situation. The key insight is that the CDFG must be modified in order to create more chaining possibilities.[12] Consider the cases where chaining possibilities may be missed. There are essentially four of them:

- *A signal has one definition and multiple uses in the same scope.* This implies that this signal must be made available to different DOs (since multiple uses in the datapath are not possible). By duplicating the definition once for each use, the multiple use has been resolved (while introducing a multiple use at each operand) and the desired chaining possibilities have been created.
- *A signal has one definition and multiple uses, at least one in another scope.* To generate a chaining possibility, the uses must be within the same scope as the definition. A further look reveals that this case resembles the previous one; it is solved in basically the same manner.
- *A signal has multiple definitions (in mutually exclusive scopes) and one use outside the scopes of the definitions.* A chaining possibility can be created by duplicating the use and nesting the copies into the scopes of the definitions. However, we must bear in mind that if the use has yet another operand multiply defined in different scopes, a particular evaluation order for the mentioned defining scopes would be enforced. This could be undesirable (see Fig. 8a).
- *A signal has multiple definitions (in mutually exclusive scopes) and multiple uses.* This case is not further considered since there are rarely any cases where duplication of operations could lead to shorter code. Consider a signal that has n uses and m definitions. If each of these operations is (trivially) chained to a single DO, we get $n + m$ operations. If all necessary copies of operations are generated to get more chaining possibilities and each of these would actually be chained, the result would be $n \times m$ DOs (see Fig. 8b).

---

[11] This is a consequence of the postulation that no multiple uses exist in the datapaths.

[12] More exactly, we do not want to create chaining possibilities *per se* but only in those places where this will lead to an improvement of the generated code.

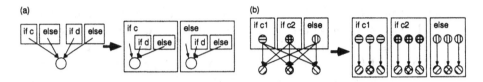

Fig. 8. Node duplication examples. Conditions c and d in case (a) are independent of each other. Conditions c1 and c2 in case (b) are exclusive to each other.

It can be seen that the creation of chaining possibilities is associated with duplication of nodes. When duplicating excessively, the graph might grow too large. This is overcome by first partitioning the graph, which yields (usually) small partitions, and then processing each partition in turn. The partitions are chosen so that no chains across partition boundaries are possible.

One problem not yet mentioned is the *identification* of chaining possibilities. A simple heuristic is employed: For all pairs of MEOs, the pattern base is looked up counting the occurrences of an edge between both operations. (This is quite informal, but should be intuitively justified.) This information is then used for partitioning; two operations are put into the same partition if a chaining possibility exists. Partitions including only one operation are *trivial cases.*

When duplicating into scopes (either at a multiple definition or at a multiple use), the code size might be increased but (usually) not the execution time because only one of the exclusive scopes is executed. To the case shown in Fig. 6a, however, this argument cannot be applied. Therefore, a *common subexpression elimination* (CSE) phase, which succeeds the pattern matcher, removes most of the unchained operation copies from the graph. This also works for duplications at scope boundaries. Since with duplication there is a danger that the number of operations (and thus program size) increases unduly, a cost function is used to resort to the simple undagging method in cases where the node duplication heuristic fails. The cost is computed for both the undagging and the node duplication method[13] as the weighted sum of the number of resulting DOs (a rough estimate of the code size) and the expected number of executed DOs on each execution path (a rough estimate of execution time). The better alternative is kept.

6 Results

The experimental results shown in Table 1 are taken from a "real-life" AD-PCM algorithm, which is incorporated into speech compression applications. The (exemplary) datapath from Fig. 4 served as target architecture. The tool was implemented and tested on a SPARC station IPX using C++. All CPU times including parsing and computation of statistics are less than one minute. Therefore, they are not explicitly given.

---

[13] This is not overly expensive, as the pattern matching and rewriting is quite fast.

Table 1. Experimental results

design	machine- ex. opns.	datapath operations	
		undagging	node dupl.
ENCODE	514	417 (-18.9%)	399 (-22.4%)
ADQUANT	55	51 (-7.3%)	51 (-7.3%)
IADQUANT	21	16 (-23.8%)	15 (-28.6%)
PREDICT	317	262 (-17.4%)	249 (-21.5%)
TONE_DET	25	17 (-32%)	17 (-32%)

7   Conclusion

We have presented an algorithm for code selection on control/data-flow graphs. The approach is based on a global view on the subject programs. The points of interest are multiple uses of values resulting from common subexpressions and multiple definitions of values resulting from conditional scopes. An implementation of the algorithm is incorporated into the CBC compiler and was successfully tested with the Siemens DECT (Digital European Cordless Telephone) design. One line of future research includes the coupling of code selection and scheduling as well as the adaption of our technique to loops.

References

1. A.V. Aho, M. Ganapathi, S.W. Tjiang: Code Generation Using Tree Matching and Dynamic Programming. ACM TOPLAS 11:4 (1989) 491–516
2. D.G. Bradlee, R.R. Henry, S.J. Eggers: The Marion System for Retargetable Instruction Scheduling. Proc. PDLI'91, SIGPLAN Notices 26:6 (1991) 229–240
3. D.G. Bradlee, S.J. Eggers, R.R. Henry: Integrating Register Allocation and Instruction Scheduling for RISCs. 4th Int. Conf. on Arch. Support for Prog. Lang. and Operating Systems (1991) 122–131
4. P. Briggs: Register Allocation via Graph Coloring. Ph. D. Thesis, Rice Univ., Houston, Texas (1992)
5. R.G.G. Cattell: Automatic Derivation of Code Generators from Machine Descriptions. ACM TOPLAS 2:2 (1980) 173–190
6. J.W. Davidson, C.W. Fraser: Code Selection through Object Code Optimization. ACM TOPLAS 6:4 (1984) 505-526
7. H. Emmelmann, F.-W. Schöer, R. Landwehr: BEG – a Generator for Efficient Back Ends. Proc. PLDI'89, SIGPLAN Notices 24:7 (1989) 227-237
8. H. Emmelmann: Code Selection by Regularly Controlled Term Rewriting. Code Generation – Concepts, Tools Techniques, Springer (1992) 3–29
9. A. Fauth, A. Knoll: Automated Generation of DSP Program Development Tools Utilizing a Machine Description Formalism. Technical Report 1992/31, Technische Universität Berlin, Fachbereich 20, Informatik, Berlin (1992)
10. A. Fauth, A. Knoll: Automatic Generation of DSP Program Development Tools Using a Machine Description Formalism. Proc. IEEE Int. Conf. on Acoustics, Speech and Signal Processing (1993) 457–460

11. A. Fauth, A. Knoll: Translating Signal Flowcharts into Microcode for Custom Digital Signal Processors. Proc. Int. Conf. on Signal Processing (1993) 65–72

12. A. Fauth, M. Freericks, A. Knoll: Generation of Hardware Machine Models from Instruction Set Descriptions. VLSI Signal Processing VI (1993) 242–250

13. C.W. Fraser, R.R. Henry, T.A. Proebsting: BURG – Fast Optimal Instruction Selection and Tree Parsing. ACM SIGPLAN Notices 27:4 (1992) 68–76

14. C.W. Fraser, D.R. Hanson, T.A. Proebsting: Engineering a Simple, Efficient Code Generator Generator. ACM Letters on Prog. Lang. and Systems 1:3 (1993) 213–226

15. M. Freericks: The nML Machine Description Formalism. Technical Report 1991/15, Technische Universität Berlin, Fachbereich 20, Informatik, Berlin (1991)

16. M. Freericks, A. Knoll: Formally Correct Translation of DSP Algorithms Specified in an Asynchronous Applicative Language. Proc. Int. Conf. on Acoustics, Speech and Signal Processing (1993) 417–420

17. M. Ganapathi, C.N. Fischer: Description-driven code generation using attribute grammars. Proc. of the 9th POPL (1982) 108–119

18. M. Ganapathi, C.N. Fischer, J.L. Hennessy: Retargetable Compiler Code Generation. Computing Surveys 14:4 (1982) 573–592

19. M. Ganapathi, C.N. Fischer: Affix Grammar Driven Code Generation. ACM TOPLAS 7:4 (1985) 560–599

20. M. Ganapathi, C.N. Fischer: Integrating Code Generation and Peephole Optimization. Acta Informatica 25 (1988) 85–109

21. R. Giegerich: Code selection by inversion of order-sorted derivors. Theoretical Computer Science 73 (1990) 177–211

22. R.S. Glanville, S.L. Graham: A new method for compiler code generation (Extended Abstract). Conf. Record of the 5th POPL (1978) 231–240

23. R. Hartmann: Combined scheduling and data routing for programmable ASIC systems. Proc. European Design Automation Conference EDAC'92 (1992)

24. J.L. Hennessy, D.A. Patterson: Computer architecture: a quantitative approach. Morgan Kaufmann Publishers (1990)

25. C.M. Hoffmann, M.J O'Donnell: Pattern Matching in Trees. JACM 29:1 (1982) 68–95

26. M. Rim, R. Jain: Representing Conditional Branches for High-Level Synthesis Applications. Proc. 29 Design Automation Conf. (1992) 106–111

27. D. Landskov, S. Davidson, B.D. Shriver, P.W. Mallet: Local microcode compaction techniques. Computing Surveys 12:9 (1980) 261–294

28. D. Lanneer, F. Catthoor, G. Goossens, M. Pauwels, J. Van Meerbergen, H. De Man: Open-ended System for High-Level Synthesis of Flexible Signal Processors. Proc. European Design Automation Conf. EDAC'90 (1990) 272–276

29. G. Meyer-Berg: The Library LIB for the Hardware Independent Compiler CBC. ESPRIT-II Project 2260 "SPRITE" Report CBC.b/Siemens/Y4m12/2 (1992)

30. T.A. Proebsting: Simple and efficient BURS table generation. Proc. PLDI'92, SIGPLAN Notices 27:6 (1992) 331–340

31. K. Rimey, P.N. Hilfinger: A Compiler for Application-Specific Signal Processors. VLSI Signal Processing III (1988) 341–351

32. K. Rimey, P.N. Hilfinger: Lazy data routing and greedy scheduling. 21st Annual Workshop on Microprogramming MICRO-21 (1988) 111–115

33. Discussion: Code Generator Specification Techniques. Led by Chris Fraser, Summarized by J. Boyland and H. Emmelmann, Code Generation – Concepts, Tools Techniques, Springer (1992) 66–69

Compiling Nested Loops for Limited Connectivity VLIWs

Adrian Slowik, Georg Piepenbrock, Peter Pfahler

Universität-GH Paderborn, Fachbereich Mathematik/Informatik
Warburger Str. 100, D-33098 Paderborn, Germany
Email: {adrian, gepi, peter}@uni-paderborn.de

Abstract. Instruction level parallelism (ILP) is a generally accepted means to speed up the execution of both scientific and non-scientific programs. Compilation techniques for ILP are in a sense "general-purpose" in that they do not depend on these source program characteristics. In this paper we investigate what can be gained by ILP techniques that are specialized for scientific code in the form of nested loop programs. This regular program form allows us to apply well-known techniques taken from the theory of loop transformation. We present a compilation algorithm based on both standard and non-standard transformations to increase fine-grained parallelism for software pipelining, to reduce communication overhead by integrated functional unit assignment and to minimize memory traffic by maximizing data reusability between adjacent computations. We present first results which show impressive speedups compared to conventionally software-pipelined code. Our investigations are based on the *limited connectivity VLIW* architectural model which is a realistic (= realizable) VLIW machine made up of multiple clusters with private register files.

1 Introduction

A VLIW (*Very Long Instruction Word*) architecture consists of several functional units which synchronously execute different operations in parallel. Application programs take advantage of such an architecture by specific compilation techniques which exploit fine-grained parallelism and apply scheduling techniques on the instruction level (*Instruction Level Parallelism, ILP*).

Ideally, the functional units (*FUs*) of a VLIW processor are connected to a common register memory that can supply two data operands and perform one write operation per functional unit in each cycle. Practically, there are technological restrictions: To the best of our knowledge, there are no technologies for building register banks with a large number of ports (e.g. > 16) that do not suffer a severe performance degradation compared to RAMs with a small number of ports. For this reason, all commercial VLIW-like machines (e.g. Multiflow TRACE, Intel i860, IBM System 6000) have been built using multiple register files with a limited number of ports. Each register file is connected only to a subset of the functional units. [CDN92] uses the term "Limited Connectivity VLIW (LC-VLIW)" to characterize these architectures. In the Multiflow TRACE [CNO+87] these register/FU partitions are called "clusters". Communication between the clusters is achieved by special communication busses. Fig. 1 shows a LC-VLIW consisting of 3 clusters that are connected by a cyclic communication bus (other topologies are possible).

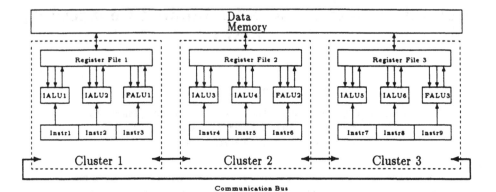

Fig. 1. LC–VLIW with 3 Clusters

In the past few years much work has been done in the field of compilation techniques for VLIW machines. The same is true for superscalar machines which from the compiler's point of view are very similar. Important research topics were local and global scheduling techniques, and the scheduling of cyclic control structures (*software pipelining*). Rau and Fisher give an excellent survey over this work [RF93]. Most publications put emphasis on the fact that the VLIW model does not require special source code characteristics. VLIW compilation can exploit instruction level parallelism for any source program whereas other parallel architecture models (e.g. vector machines) depend on certain source program forms (e.g. nested DO loops). In other words, VLIW architectures are suitable for the parallel execution of both scientific and non-scientific application programs. This fact lead to the development of compilation techniques for VLIW machines which are in a sense "general-purpose". Specific VLIW techniques for scientific code have received much less attention.

In this paper we investigate how VLIW compilation can benefit from scientific source code. We present VLIW code generation techniques for nested loop programs. This program form is frequently used in scientific code. Nested loop programs promise the following advantages for the VLIW compilation process:

- Data dependences can (to a great extend) be analyzed during compilation time. Hence, there is no need for pessimistic assumptions limiting the scheduling freedom.
- There is a well-understood transformation theory for nested loop programs. These transformations have been developed e.g. in the area of vectorization, for systolic array compilation, for massively parallel systems, and for the optimization of data locality and cache memory access. We propose to use these standard loop transformations to increase the instruction level parallelism for VLIW machines and to reduce the memory traffic (and code size) by replacing memory accesses (and address computations) by inter-cluster register communication.
- Regular data access patterns known at compile time offer new possibilities for functional unit assignment to minimize the costs of inter-cluster communication.

The rest of this paper is organized as follows: Sect. 2 introduces nested loop programs and the transformation theory developed for these programs. In Sect. 3 and 4 we propose a compilation technique for nested loop programs for VLIW machines. This technique will use a series of standard and non-standard loop transformation steps that convert the source program to a form that supports highly optimizing VLIW code generation:

- Transformation to a loop nest with a dependence free innermost loop.
- Cluster Assignment for whole iteration points. This avoids inter-cluster data communication in the code for the innermost loop body. If this assignment leads to an insufficient utilization of the cluster resources, a mapping from many iteration points to one cluster can be generated.
- Moving data dependences to the loop directly enclosing the innermost loop. This enables reuse of data kept in registers, thus reducing the amount of expensive memory access.
- Load balancing to compensate the different work load due to memory accesses in "outer" iteration points and register usage in "inner" points.

Sect. 5 shows the first results of our investigations by comparing the code produced by our transformation technique for some standard example programs to conventionally software pipelined code.

2 Transformation Theory for Nested Loop Programs

Much work has been done to exploit parallelism from nested loops [Ban93] [ZC90]. Loop transformations such as loop skewing, reversal, permutation (SRP) and loop tiling have been shown to be useful in extracting parallelism [WL91b] or in increasing data locality [WL91a]. The transformations can be used to construct modified loop nests where e.g. only outer loops carry dependences. These nests provide fine-grained parallelism which is useful for tightly coupled massively parallel systems.

Loop quantization [Nic88] applies skewing and tiling techniques to increase instruction level parallelism. Vectorizing compilers use skewing, reversal and loop permutation to enable an efficient utilization of vector units [AK87]. [Lam74] and [Dow90] apply similar techniques to extract hyperplanes in the iteration domain of nested loops which can be executed in parallel. [Kun88] and [MF86] derive efficient systolic arrays from transformed loop nests where data locality is utilized to pass computed values for subsequent use to neighboring processors.

The SRP loop transformations will be introduced by applying them to an ideal and normalized example loop nest. Loop bounds are constant or linear functions of outer loop variables. This property ensures a convex loop iteration domain. Each instance of the inner loop body can be identified with the iteration vector $\mathbf{iv} = (l_1, \cdots, l_n)$. l_i denotes the specific value of the loop variable belonging to loop L_i. Dependences between statements in different iterations can be characterized by distance vectors $\mathbf{d} = (d_1, \cdots, d_n) = \mathbf{iv}_2 - \mathbf{iv}_1$. In a loop nest all distance vectors $\mathbf{d}$ are lexicographically nonnegative and form the columns of the dependence matrix D. Dependent computations have to remain in the original sequential order. Therefore a transformation is legal only if all transformed distance vectors $\mathbf{d}_t \in D_t$ remain nonnegative.

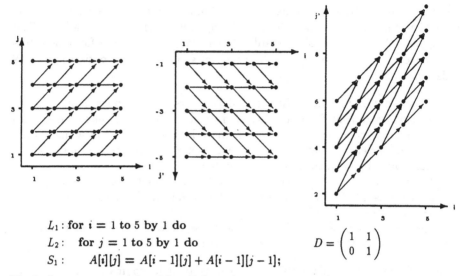

L_1: **for** $i = 1$ **to** 5 **by** 1 **do**

L_2:   **for** $j = 1$ **to** 5 **by** 1 **do**

S_1: $A[i][j] = A[i-1][j] + A[i-1][j-1];$

$$D = \begin{pmatrix} 1 & 1 \\ 0 & 1 \end{pmatrix}$$

Fig. 2. Loop nest example with self dependent statement and iteration domain of the original, reversed and skewed loop nest.

SRP-transformations can be modeled as linear transformations in the iteration space, represented by unimodular matrices. By applying the transformations any occurrence of loop variable l_i in the statement part is substituted by the i-th element of the transformed iteration vector $\mathbf{iv}_t = T \cdot \mathbf{iv}$. T denotes the possibly compound transformation matrix modifying the dependence matrix to $D_t = T \cdot D$. Recomputing new loop bounds after transformation can be done by Fourier Elimination in the integer domain [WL91b]. Skewing and reversal are commonly used to transform loop nests to a fully permutable form where all components of the transformed dependence vectors are nonnegative. This important property allows arbitrary permutation and tiling transformations. The SRP transformations will now be applied to the example loop nest in Fig. 2.

Reversal can be achieved by using the matrix T_r which is the identity matrix where the i-th element on the main diagonal is -1. This matrix reverses the i-th loop in the nest. The reversed loop runs from the negative upper bound $(-ub_i)$ to the negative lower bound $(-lb_i)$ of the former loop L_i. The transformed dependence matrix and the resulting loop nest are shown in Fig. 3.

L_1: **for** $i = 1$ **to** 5 **by** 1 **do**

L_2:   **for** $j' = -5$ **to** -1 **by** 1 **do**

S_0: $j = -j';$

S_1: $A[i][j] = A[i-1][j] + A[i-1][j-1];$

$$T_r = \begin{pmatrix} 1 & 0 \\ 0 & -1 \end{pmatrix}$$

$$D_{T_r} = T_r \cdot D = \begin{pmatrix} 1 & 1 \\ 0 & -1 \end{pmatrix}$$

Fig. 3. Program after reversal transformation

Skewing adds to an inner loop variable an multiple value of an outer loop variable. The transformation matrix is the identity matrix with a single constant value in the lower left triangle e.g. $t_{i,k}(i > k)$. Loop variable l_k is skewed by the value $t_{i,k} \cdot l_i$. In the transformed example loop nest(Fig. 4) there are no dependences between iterations with equal j' (cf. Fig. 2). Skewing doesn't change the execution order of the statement part, so this transformation is always legal.

$L_1:$ **for** $i = 1$ **to** 5 **by** 1 **do**
$L_2:$ **for** $j' = i+1$ **to** $i+5$ **by** 1 **do**
$S_0:$ $j = j' - i;$
$S_1:$ $A[i][j] = A[i-1][j] + A[i-1][j-1];$

$$T_s = \begin{pmatrix} 1 & 0 \\ 1 & 1 \end{pmatrix}$$

$$D_{T_s} = T_s \cdot D = \begin{pmatrix} 1 & 1 \\ 1 & 2 \end{pmatrix}$$

Fig. 4. Program after skewing the inner loop

Permutation exchanges loops in the nest. The transformation is performed by the identity matrix with permuted rows. When applying this transformation care has to be taken of computing the new loop bounds properly [WL91b] (Fig. 5).

$L_1:$ **for** $j = 2$ **to** 10 **by** 1 **do**
$L_2:$ **for** $i = \max(j-5,1)$ **to** $\min(j-1,5)$ **by** 1 **do**
$S_0:$ $j = j' - i;$
$S_1:$ $A[i][j] = A[i-1][j] + A[i-1][j-1];$

$$T_p = \begin{pmatrix} 0 & 1 \\ 1 & 0 \end{pmatrix}$$

$$D_{T_p} = T_p \cdot D = \begin{pmatrix} 0 & 1 \\ 1 & 1 \end{pmatrix}$$

Fig. 5. Program after permutation

3 Compiling Nested Loops for LC-VLIWs

In conventional VLIW-compilation source code is first translated to machine code and then scheduled for the given machine. The schedule is computed solely on the basis of the operation dependency graph. We exploit the regular structure of nested loop programs to map whole iteration points onto one cluster and then refine the assignment by mapping machine instructions to the functional units of the cluster. The quality of both mappings can be drastically enhanced by the application of well known loop transformations to the given loop nest. Thus the problem to determine a high quality mapping becomes a transformation selection problem.

Starting with a presentation of a model capturing properties of the loop nest, we proceed by giving descriptions of essential stepping-stones encountered during the selection process. We illustrate the transformations by incrementally applying them to a well known example loop nest. Data reuse, parallelism and resource utilization are discussed. The transformation will consist of a series of simple steps dedicated to the aspects mentioned above. Fig. 6 shows the sequence of transformation steps applied to a loop nest. The first four steps determine transformations represented by

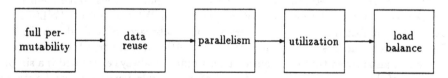

Fig. 6. The transformation steps

appropriate matrices and will be denoted by $T_{fp}, T_{loc}, T_{wave}$ and T_{util}, respectively. Due to the restriction to SRP-transformations matrices T_{fp} up to T_{wave} will be unimodular, whereas T_{util} may be not unimodular. Step 5 provides a row vector r_{rot} causing clusters to execute identical instruction sequences. The whole transformation is represented by the product $r_{rot} \cdot T_{util} \cdot T_{wave} \cdot T_{loc} \cdot T_{fp}$.

3.1 Assignment of Iterations to Clusters

Prior to the discussion of single selection steps we introduce the notion of a cluster assignment mapping whole loop iterations to clusters. Properties of this mapping will be fully exploited in Sect. 4 but they already impose restrictions on the transformation selection for data reuse. The assignment mapping provides the basis for reuse of operands in subsequent iterations. If both the generation and the use of one value take place on the same cluster, reuse is possible without any extra effort. If two different clusters are involved, a series of register-register transfers will be issued on clusters in-between source and destination. Due to small entries in dependence vectors, the distance to be covered is usually very small, most often a single hop is sufficient. Because all clusters are identical, only distances and directions are of interest here. This simplifies the piecewise linear function which captures the assignment resulting from the transformation phase and is given in (1).

$$C(\mathbf{i}) = (\mathbf{r}_{rot} \cdot T \cdot \mathbf{i}) \bmod c = (\mathbf{r}_{rot} \cdot T_{util} \cdot T_{wave} \cdot T_{loc} \cdot T_{fp} \ \mathbf{i}) \bmod c \qquad (1)$$

Function C maps each iteration $\mathbf{i}$ to exactly one of the c clusters of the machine.

3.2 Modeling dependences of the loop nest

We will use a straight-forward extension of the commonly used dependence matrix to guide the transformation selection phase tailored to instruction level parallelism. For a nest of n loops the extended dependence matrix $D \in M(\mathbb{Z}, n, m)$ is built of two submatrices D_W and D_R, arranged as $D = (D_W | D_R)$. Submatrix D_W includes dependence vectors imposing a certain execution order on iterations, submatrix D_R includes somewhat artificial dependences indicating a common read between iterations. Vectors from D_R do not impose any restrictions on the execution order of iterations but are crucial to the reuse optimization of read only operands.

3.3 Transformation selection

Transforming for full permutability: The task of the first phase is to provide a canonical form of the given loop nest, the fully permutable nest (fp-nest for short). The dependence matrix of a fp-nest does not contain any negative entries and hence allows to permute the nesting of loops arbitrarily. It is also the starting point for many transformation techniques presented in recent publications which stem from different areas of compilation as exploiting parallelism [WL91b], locality [WL91a], or partitioning iteration spaces of arbitrary size into subspaces of limited size [RS92]. The interested reader is referred to reference [WL91b] for more details on this topic. There it is also proven that the required transformation always exists and is a simple sequence of skewing transformations. Step 1 of the compilation process can be stated as follows: Find a transformation with matrix T_{fp} satisfying $\det(T_{fp}) \in \{-1, 1\}$ and

$$\forall \ i \in \{1, \ldots, n\}, j \in \{1, \ldots, m\} : \ d'_{ij} \geq 0 \qquad \text{where } (d'_{ij}) = T_{fp} \cdot D_W$$

Nonnegativity in D_R is of no importance, as each vector in D_R can be turned into a nonnegative vector multiplying it by -1. This is trivially legal, because there is no difference, whether a value is first used in a computation c_1 and then in a computation c_2 or vice versa. The restriction of $\det(T_{fp})$ to 1 or -1 is due to the use of SRP-transformations.

The example given in Fig. 7 will accompany all stages of compilation and is the well known Horner loop (cf. [Dow90]). Because there are no negative entries

L_1: **for** $I = 1$ **to** N **by** 1 **do**
L_2:   **for** $J = -N$ **to** $-I$ **by** 1 **do**
S_1: $B[I][-J] = B[I-1][-J] + X * B[I][-J+1];$

$$D = \begin{pmatrix} 1 \; 0 \mid 1 \; 0 \\ 0 \; 1 \mid 0 \; 1 \end{pmatrix}$$

Fig. 7. The untransformed Horner loop and its dependences

in D_W, there is no need to apply any transformation to gain full permutability. Hence $T_{fp} = I_2$, denoting the identity matrix of dimension 2. We now focus on transformations tailoring the loop nest to the specific machine model sketched in Fig. 1. The selection phase proceeds by searching for factors T_{loc}, T_{wave} and T_{util}, refining the overall linear-transformation.

Transforming for Data-Reuse: Load and store instructions belong to the most expensive instructions of architectures available nowadays. They involve peripheral memory operating at lower rates than the CPU. As the gap between memory access time and CPU cycle time widens, techniques minimizing memory access receive additional importance, even for architectures using fast cache-memories.

Values produced in one iteration and required during subsequent iterations can be reused without a memory fetch if involved iterations differ only in the parallel and the innermost sequential loop components. This observation is easily translated into properties of dependence vectors. For operands to be reused, there must be at most two nonzero entries in the components of dependence vectors describing the flow of data. Hence we are looking for a transformation matrix T_{loc} maximizing function $reuse(T_{loc}, D)$ in (2), capturing the reuse of operands:

$$reuse(T_{loc}, D) = |\{\mathbf{d}' \mid \mathbf{d}' = T_{loc} \cdot \mathbf{d} \wedge (d'_1, \ldots, d'_{n-2}) = \mathbf{0}\}| \qquad (2)$$

Due to the fact that nonzero components of dependence vectors have to appear in the same rows of the transformed dependence matrix, the problem to find an optimal reuse transformation becomes intractable.

The above observation leads to a simple heuristic algorithm. We want to gather nonzero components in a minimum number of rows. Therefore we apply a variant of the Gaussian-elimination algorithm, producing additional zero components in the dependence matrix and keeping the loop nest fully permutable. As it is well known from linear algebra, the number of nonzero rows in the resulting dependence matrix will be equal to the dimensionality of the vector space spanned by a maximal set of linear independent dependence vectors. Due to this property, we can not expect to reuse all data in the general case as long as we can not reduce the dimensionality. Preprocessing the loop nest with reorder and distribution transformations may yield this desired effect but is beyond the scope of this paper.

algorithm *Determine_T_{loc}*:

> $T_{loc} := I_n;$
> Apply elimination algorithm; $T_{loc} := T_{loc} \cdot T_{elim};$
> Permute zero rows outermost; $T_{loc} := T_{loc} \cdot T_{out};$
> Permute critical row innermost-1; $T_{loc} := T_{loc} \cdot T_{crit};$

end *Determine_T_{loc}*.

The algorithm is a straight-forward formulation of the given explanation. If the dependence vectors do not span the entire iteration space we move zero rows outermost, because they do not exhibit reuse. An explanation of substep 3 is postponed to the related Sect. 4. This algorithm was inspired by techniques presented in [Fea92], where the Gaussian elimination is applied to optimize data distribution for distributed memory computers, which obviously is a closely related problem.

$L_1:$ **for** $J = -N$ **to** -1 **by** 1 **do**
$L_2:$ **for** $I = 1$ **to** $-J$ **by** 1 **do** $\qquad D = \begin{pmatrix} 0 & 1 & | & 0 & 1 \\ 1 & 0 & | & 1 & 0 \end{pmatrix}$
$S_1:$ $B[I][-J] = B[I-1][-J] + X * B[I][-J+1];$

Fig. 8. The Horner loop after reuse transformation and its dependences

There is no reuse to gain in our example. As is easily seen, the dependence vectors in D_W are linear independent and no SRP transformation can exist, making them span a one dimensional space only. The innermost row is detected to be the critical one and therefore permuted into row $n - 1 = 1$. Thus T_{loc} is a simple permutation matrix, exchanging the two rows of the dependence matrix D.

Transforming for Parallelism: To operate clusters in parallel at least one loop must be a parallel one. From the viewpoint of data reuse one parallel loop is already enough. More levels of parallelism are equivalent to more loops without dependences (otherwise there would be no parallelism), thus inhibiting data reuse between neighboring iterations of parallel loops. The parallelism will be generated using a wavefront transformation comprising SRP-transformations only. The following observation provides the basis for this transformation:

> Loop i of a nest $(L_1, \ldots, L_n)$ with depth n can be executed in parallel
> $\Longleftrightarrow \forall j \in \{1, \ldots, m\}, \mathbf{d}_j = (d_1, \ldots, d_n) : (d_1, \ldots, d_{i-1}) > 0 \lor d_i = 0$ (3)

Condition (3) expresses that a dependence has to exist either in a level $j < i$ or in a level $j > i$, but there must be no dependence on the i-th level.

As we want to exploit the fine-grained parallelism at the instruction level by a VLIW-machine, the innermost loop of the nest must be a parallel one. Because we are interested in just one level of parallelism, we have to satisfy condition (3) for the case of $i = n$. Therefore we have to guarantee that all column vectors constituting the transformed dependence matrix satisfy the special case of (3) given in (4).

$$\forall j \in \{1, \ldots, m\}, \mathbf{d}_j = (d_1, \ldots, d_n) : (d_1, \ldots, d_{n-1}) > 0 \qquad (4)$$

Having the fp-nest, the parallelizing transformation is constructed as a sequence of less than n skewing transformations $T_{i,n}^S$ and one final permutation transformation

$T^P_{n-1,n}$. The matrix depicted in (5) represents a general transformation of this kind and assures condition (4) for an already fully permutable loop nest:

$$
T_{wave} = \begin{pmatrix}
1 & 0 & \cdots & 0 & 0 & 0 \\
0 & 1 & \cdots & 0 & 0 & 0 \\
\vdots & \vdots & \ddots & \vdots & \vdots & \vdots \\
0 & 0 & \cdots & 1 & 0 & 0 \\
1 & 1 & \cdots & 1 & 1 & 1 \\
0 & 0 & \cdots & 0 & 1 & 0
\end{pmatrix} = T^P_{n-1,n} \cdot T^S_{1,n} \cdot T^S_{2,n} \cdots T^S_{n-1,n} \tag{5}
$$

Applying T_{wave} to an arbitrary fp-nest yields a new fp-nest with at least one level of parallelism in the innermost loop. T_{wave} first makes the components of dependence vectors in the n-th level nonzero and than exchanges the two innermost loops. The property of full permutability assures $d_{i,j} \geq 0$ for all i, j. Also there always exists at least one i such that $d_{i,j} > 0$, otherwise the zero-vector representing a self-dependent computation would be included in the dependence matrix, contradicting the sequential computation order. Hence we have $(\sum_{i=1}^{n} d_{i,j}) > 0 \; \forall j \in \{1, \ldots, m\}$.

The above wavefront scheme is applicable to generate up to $n-1$ levels of parallelism, as is often the case for systolic array compilation [MF86] by adjusting the final permutation transformation appropriately. For $j < n$ levels of parallelism rows n and j must be exchanged. The matrix given in (5) works for all fp-nests but introduces redundancy for fp-nests with dense rows. In practice, we reduce the number of necessary skewing-transformations using the greedy-algorithm sketched below:

algorithm $Determine\_T_{wave}$:

> $T_{wave} = I_n$;
> **while** $\exists j \in \{1, \ldots, m\} : (d_{1,j}, \ldots, d_{n-2,j}, d_{n,j}) = 0$ **do**
> > choose any $i \in \{1, \ldots, n-1\} : \left\{ \begin{array}{l} \text{s. t. adding row } i \text{ to row } n \text{ of } D \text{ will elim-} \\ \text{inate a maximum number of zero entries} \end{array} \right.$
> > $t_n^{wave} := t_n^{wave} + t_i^{wave}$; $d_n := d_n + d_i$;
>
> **od**
> $swap(t_{n-1}^{wave}, t_n^{wave})$;

end $Determine\_T_{wave}$.

Fig. 9 shows our sample loop nest after transformation for parallelism. The innermost loop is now a parallel loop as is indicated by the keyword **parallel**.

L_1: **for** $I = 1 - N$ **to** 0 **by** 1 **do**
L_2:   **for** $J = -N$ **to** $I - 1$ **by** 1 **do parallel**
S_1: $B[I - J][-J] = B[I - J - 1][-J] + X * B[I - J][-J + 1]$;

$$D = \begin{pmatrix} 1 & 1 & | & 1 & 1 \\ 0 & 1 & | & 0 & 1 \end{pmatrix}$$

Fig. 9. The Horner loop after wavefront transformation and its dependences

3.4 Transforming for Resource-Utilization

The main problem we face here is to provide enough useful machine instructions to finish up with a stream of large instruction words that is as dense as possible.

Its execution makes the best possible use of the assumed machine. The transformation step for improved resource-utilization evaluates information provided by a preliminary schedule to derive further transformations increasing the code density.

We need to know the portion of the time slots for functional units not yet filled with useful instructions. A function provided by the scheduler module is aware of empty slots and provides the desired nonnegative value e. Unrolling adjacent iterations places them onto the same cluster, provides multiple instruction sequences to execute and promises to fill the empty slots. The number of empty slots e we can fill using this approach heavily depends on the dependences existing between unrolled iterations. If we unroll dependent iterations, we can not expect their machine instructions to result in dense, long instruction words, because they have to be placed in subsequent time slots obeying execution order restrictions. From the number e and the schedule length l we derive the parameter of the unroll-transformation by $u := \lceil \frac{l}{l-e} \rceil$. As we have already made the innermost loop a parallel loop that trivially is free of dependences, we unroll exactly u of its iterations and end up with multiple instruction sequences being independent. Two iterations $\mathbf{i} = (i_1, \ldots, i_n)$ and $\mathbf{j} = (j_1, \ldots, j_n)$ now belong to the same iteration if

$$\lfloor i_k / u_k \rfloor = \lfloor j_k / u_k \rfloor \quad \forall k \in \{1, \ldots, n\} \tag{6}$$

Using matrix notation, we arrange the numbers u_k on the diagonal of a square matrix and get the matrix T_{util} introduced in (1). For nontrivial unrolling at least one of the u_k is not 1 and therefore $\prod_{k=1}^{n} 1/u_{kk} = \det(T_{util})$ may not be 1. Here we leave the set of unimodular transformations. As we are interested in unrolling the innermost and parallel loop only, we immediately have $u_i = 1 \ \forall i \in \{1, \ldots, n-1\}$ and complete the construction of the factor T_{util} by setting $u_n = u$. Fig. 10 depicts

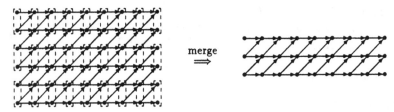

Fig. 10. Merging two adjacent iterations of the parallel loop

an unrolling of the innermost Horner loop by factor 2. Unrolling means merging adjacent iterations along the innermost parallel loop and reduces the iteration space by the unroll factor.

Our approach is a variant of loop quantization [Nic88] with the restriction to unroll the innermost loop only. Unrolling the innermost loop seems to be a severe restriction at first. But as loop nest of depth two are the most common ones, unrolling the parallelized loop onto clusters and software-pipeling the innermost loop of the remaining nest performs very well in the average case. (See Sect. 5 for early results).

4 Code Generation

This section deals with the problem of code generation for the transformed nest. The first task is to compute the source level code of the transformed nest. Computing bounds having applied SRP-transformations is easy and exhaustively treated in [WL91b], for example. The decomposition into convex subspaces is more difficult but possible using the algorithms presented in [AI91], which are more powerful than necessary here. Finally, problems specific to the machine code level are discussed and supplements necessary to make the final code work properly are presented.

Computing the transformed nest: To generate the transformed loop nest, algorithms generating a loop nest after tiling transformations and generating loop bounds from a set of inequalities are used. They are given in [AI91] and not discussed here. We have to extract the inequalities from the transformed loop bounds and additional inequalities bounding the rectangular subspaces for the cluster mapping. The latter ones can be computed, given the number of clusters utilized and the number of iterations merged to one node. As the final result on source level we get a loop nest of depth $n + 1$. The additional loop is used to cover the two dimensional iteration space with the rectangular tiles. The remaining loops control higher dimensions of the iteration space. Fig. 11 shows the final source code loop

L_1: **for** $t = 0$ **to** $N - 1$ **by** c **do**
L_2:   **for** $I = 1 - N + t$ **to** $c - N - 1$ **by** 1 **do**
L_3:   **for** $J = -N + t$ **to** $-N + t + 1$ **by** 1 **do parallel**
S_1: $B[I - J][-J] = B[I - J - 1][-J] + X * B[I - J][-J + 1];$
L_4:   **for** $I = c - N + t$ **to** 0 **by** 1 **do**
L_5:   **for** $J = -N + t$ **to** $-N + t + c - 1$ **by** 1 **do parallel**
S_2: $B[I - J][-J] = B[I - J - 1][-J] + X * B[I - J][-J + 1];$

Fig. 11. The horner-loop after final transformation

nest of the running example. Loop L_1 initiates the execution of tiles with height c, loop nest (L_2, L_3) covers triangles left by the rectangular subspaces covered by (L_4, L_5). Fig. 12 depicts the iteration spaces for the loop nests (L_2, L_3) and (L_4, L_5) and exactly one value of the outermost loop counter t.

Inserting startup and finalization code: The loop bounds of the transformed nest usually constitute a polytope of arbitrary shape. To cover the points in the polytope by an effective computation of our LC-VLIW, we need to isolate areas of rectangular shape and sufficient parallelism. Therefore, the iteration space of the loops has to be decomposed into disjoint subspaces which can be processed separately. This decomposition requires an additional precaution to run properly. Fig. 12 depicts a typical subspace-decomposition. Because the LC-VLIW model does not have any mechanism to disable some of its clusters for certain iterations, areas with varying parallelism have to be cut off. The resulting iteration space is of rectangular shape and therefore very well suited for the assumed machine. As

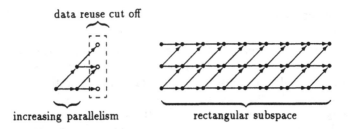

data reuse cut off

increasing parallelism

rectangular subspace

Fig. 12. Iteration space decomposition

the figure already indicates, additional instructions have to be inserted between separated iteration spaces. The sequence to be executed before any instruction of the rectangular space establishes our loop invariant. Reused operands are read from registers and kept in registers for reuse during subsequent iterations. Therefore, this sequence has to fetch operands used within but not generated by computations of the rectangular space.

Generating code for rectangular subspaces: To emit correct and efficient code for rectangular subspaces, the compiler has to obey several restrictions imposed by our technique. In general, data is reused in the parallel (spatial) as well as in the surrounding sequential (temporal) domain. Unfortunately, the cluster processing the lower border of the rectangular subspace not only has to perform the instructions resulting from operations belonging to the loop body, but also has to fetch operands from memory. Therefore, this cluster has to execute additional instructions for address calculation and fetching of reused operands. The remaining clusters do not issue load instructions, they receive these operands using more efficient communication instructions not involving the memory interface. Due to the difference in execution time, most clusters waste cycles waiting for few clusters driven by longer instruction sequences.

To solve this problem, we apply a technique of load balancing to the so far transformed nest and achieve an uniform load distribution. The idea is to move load instructions for operand fetching in a round-robin manner through available clusters. This is easily accomplished using the loop-rotation transformation described in [Wol90]. It is applicable without any inspection of dependence vectors, because the rotated loop is known to be free of dependences. Fig. 13 shows the application of rotation to our example. In each sequential iteration a different cluster now performs the additional load instructions. To generate code without any branches, we need

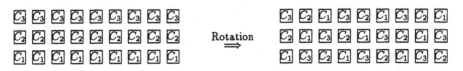

Rotation ⇒

Fig. 13. Rotating the cluster assignment for even load balance

to unroll $\mathrm{lcm}(c, |s|)$ sequential iterations, where $|s|$ denotes the shift of the rotation. If each cluster processes iterations belonging to the border, there is an optimal load balance between all clusters. Their instruction sequences do not differ, they just access different memory locations which leads to an overall shorter execution time for the sequential domain. Since rotation is possible for different directions and values, a procedure determining these values on the basis of the so far transformed loop nest is required.

Given the dependence matrix, we have to select the direction and step value for the rotation, i. e. we have to find a vector $r_{rot} \in \mathbf{Z}^n$ optimizing load balance and transport latency. Two aspects are of interest here: minimizing the number of values to move and minimizing the delay incurred by communication. The instruction reusing a value produced in a previous iteration will block and prevent all dependent instructions from execution as long as the desired value is not provided. Therefore we place the generation and use of the value having the least amount of time to travel from source to destination on the same cluster. Using this heuristic, we favour the localization of time critical communications over the minimization of inter cluster data exchange.

The product $r_{rot} \cdot d = s$ denotes the distance and direction a reused operand has to move to its destination. The generated value is the result of a root node in the DAG representing the assignment in question. We search for a vector r_{rot} placing the critical communication onto one cluster. Employing our assignment function (1), we have to assure $C(i) = C(j)$ for involved iterations. The critical communication satisfies $use(d_{crit}) - gen(d_{crit}) = min$. The difference $use - gen$ provides the level distance in the operation dependency graph resulting from expressions used within the loop body. Now vector r_{rot} must solve the equation $r_{rot} \cdot d_{crit} = 0$, obeying the restriction $r_{n-1} \neq 0 \wedge r_j = 0 \quad \forall j \in \{1, \ldots, n-2\}$. Fig. 14 illustrates the above

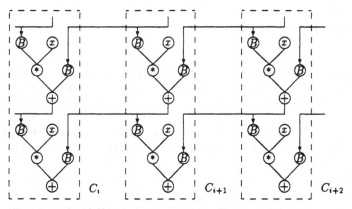

Fig. 14. Abstract operation dependency graph for the body of the horner-loop

reasoning. The rotation is chosen, such that the most time critical iteration reusing B is mapped onto the same cluster as the generating iteration. For this example we have $r_{rot} = (1, -1)$ and localize the generation of $B[I][J]$ and reuse in $B[I][J-1]$ from the original loop nest given in Fig. 7.

5   Preliminary Results and Conclusions

We have presented a loop transformation technique to optimize VLIW performance of nested loops. The result of these transformations is used as input to a conventional software pipelining VLIW code generator. We evaluated the proposed transformation technique using an experimental VLIW compilation environment [Pfa92]. The machine model we used is a 3-cluster VLIW architecture similar to the one depicted in Fig. 1. The input programs were "matrix" (a matrix * vector multiplication), "convolution" (a convolution loop), "horner" (polynomial evaluation), and "sor" (successive over-relaxation).

Fig. 15 shows our preliminary results. It compares the length of the initiation interval II determined by the software pipelining scheduler for both the original and the transformed program loops. If we neglect the execution time of the prologue and epilogue code of the software pipeline, this length is equivalent to the execution time (in machine cycles) for the loop body. In the original program this loop body covers exactly one iteration point. The transformed loop body covered 9 iteration points for each of our input programs.

Input	Original Loop		Transformed Loop	
	II	cycles/iteration point	II	cycles/iteration point
matrix	27	27	72	8
convolution	25	25	62	6.9
horner	26	26	62	6.9
sor	35	35	126	14

Fig. 15. Length of the initiation intervals

Due to the impressive speedups and the fact that the proposed techniques apply to a large subset of loop programs, we expect our algorithm to work very well in the average case. Nevertheless, several questions remain open for further research

- Can the VLIW performance be further increased by a more flexible functional unit assignment strategy, e.g. by spreading iteration points across clusters ("one-to-many mapping")?
- How do the proposed transformation techniques interact with other well-known loop techniques such as reordering and distribution?
- How can non-clustered VLIW and superscalar architectures benefit from the proposed or similar loop transformations?

References

[AI91]   C. Ancourt and F. Irigoin. Scanning polyhedra with DO loops. In *3rd ACM SIGPLAN Symposium on Principles and Practise of Parallel Programming*, pages 39–50, July 1991.

[AK87]   Randy Allen and Ken Kennedy. Automatic translation of FORTRAN programs
           to vector form. *ACM Transactions on Programming Languages and Systems*,
           9(4):491–542, October 1987.

[Ban93]   Utpal Banerjee. *Loop Transformations for Restructuring Compilers*. Kluwer
           Academic Publishers, 1993.

[CDN92]   A. Capitanio, N. Dutt, and A. Nicolau. Partitioned register files for VLIWs: A
           preliminary analysis of tradeoffs. In *Proc. 25th Annual Int'l Symp. on Microar-
           chitecture*, 1992.

[CNO+87]   R. P. Colwell, R. P. Nix, O'Donnel, J. J. Pappworth, and P. K. Rodman. A
           VLIW architecture for a trace scheduling compiler. In *2nd International Con-
           ference on Architectural Support for Programming Languages and Operating Sys-
           tems*, October 1987.

[Dow90]   Michael L. Dowling. Optimal code parallelization using unimodular transforma-
           tions. *Parallel Computing*, 16:157–171, 1990.

[Fea92]   Paul Feautrier. Toward automatic distribution. Technical Report 92.95,
           IBP/MASI, December 1992.

[Kun88]   Sun Yuan Kung. *VLSI Array Processors*. Information and system sciences se-
           ries. Prentice Hall, 1988.

[Lam74]   Leslie Lamport. The parallel execution of DO loops. *COMMUNICATIONS OF
           THE ACM*, 17(2):83–93, 1974.

[MF86]   Dan I. Moldovan and Jose A. B. Fortes. Partitioning and mapping algorithms
           into fixed size systolic arrays. *IEEE-TRANSACTIONS ON COMPUTERS*, c-
           35:1–12, January 1986.

[Nic88]   Alexandru Nicolau. Loop quantization: A generalized loop unwinding technique.
           Journal of Parallel and Distributed Computing, 5:568–586, 1988.

[Pfa92]   P. Pfahler. A code generation environment for fine-grained parallelization.
           In *Proc. 2nd PASA Workshop, GI/ITG Mitteilungen der Fachgruppe 3.1.2
           "Parallel-Algorithmen und Rechnerstrukturen (PARS)"*, February 1992.

[RF93]   B.R. Rau and J.A. Fisher. Instruction-level processing: History, overview, and
           perspective. *The Journal of Supercomputing*, 7(1/2), 1993.

[RS92]   J. Ramanujam and P. Sadayappan. Tiling multidimensional iteration spaces for
           multicomputers. *Journal of Parallel and Distributed Computing*, 16:108–120,
           1992.

[WL91a]   Michael E. Wolf and Monica S. Lam. A data locality optimizing algorithm. In
           *Proceedings of the ACM SIGPLAN 91 Conference on Programming Language
           Design and Implementation, Toronto, Ontario, Canada*, pages 30–44, June 1991.

[WL91b]   Michael E. Wolf and Monica S. Lam. A loop transformation theory and an
           algorithm to maximize parallelism. *IEEE TRANSACTIONS ON PARALLEL
           AND DISTRIBUTED SYSTEMS*, 2(4):452–471, October 1991.

[Wol90]   Michael Wolfe. Data dependence and programm restructuring. *The Journal of
           Supercomputing*, 4:321–344, 1990.

[ZC90]   Hans Zima and Barbara Chapman. *Supercompilers for Parallel and Vector Com-
           puters*. ACM Press Frontier Series. Addison Wesley, 1990.

Delayed Exceptions — Speculative Execution of Trapping Instructions

M. Anton Ertl   Andreas Krall

Institut für Computersprachen
Technische Universität Wien
Argentinierstraße 8, A-1040 Wien
{anton,andi}@mips.complang.tuwien.ac.at
Tel.: (+43-1) 58801 {4459,4462}
Fax.: (+43-1) 505 78 38

Abstract. Superscalar processors, which execute basic blocks sequentially, cannot use much instruction level parallelism. Speculative execution has been proposed to execute basic blocks in parallel. A pure software approach suffers from low performance, because exception-generating instructions cannot be executed speculatively. We propose delayed exceptions, a combination of hardware and compiler extensions that can provide high performance and correct exception handling in compiler-based speculative execution. Delayed exceptions exploit the fact that exceptions are rare. The compiler assumes the typical case (no exceptions), schedules the code accordingly, and inserts run-time checks and fix-up code that ensure correct execution when exceptions do happen.

Key Words: instruction-level parallelism, superscalar, speculative execution, exception, software pipelining

1 Introduction

Computer designers and computer architects have been striving to improve uniprocessor performance since the invention of computers[JW89, CMC+91]. The next step in this quest for higher performance is the exploitation of significant amounts of instruction-level parallelism. To this end superscalar, superpipelined, and VLIW processors[1] can execute several instructions in parallel. The obstacle to using these resources is the dependences between the instructions. Scheduling (code reordering) has been employed to reduce the impact of dependences. However, the average instruction-level parallelism available within basic blocks is less than two simultaneous instruction executions [JW89].

To circumvent this barrier several methods have been developed to execute basic blocks in parallel. They are based on speculative execution, i.e. the processor executes instructions from possible, but not certain future execution paths. This can be implemented in hardware through backup register files, history buffers or reservation

---

[1] For simplicity, we will use the term "superscalar" in the rest of the paper, but delayed exceptions can be used with any of the techniques for exploiting instruction-level parallelism.

stations [Tom67, HP87, SP88, Soh90]. A less expensive approach relies on compiler techniques for global instruction scheduling like trace scheduling, software pipelining and percolation scheduling [RG81, Fis81, Ell85, Nic85].

Exceptions pose serious problems to compiler-only approaches: The compiler must not move exception-generating instructions up across conditional branches (unless the instruction appears in all directions that the branch can take). E.g., a load that is moved up across its guardian NULL pointer test will trap wrongly. In addition, exception-generating instructions must not be reordered with respect to other exception-generating instructions, because the order of the exceptions would be changed. All these control dependences restrict the instruction-level parallelism to a low level: It is hardly higher than the level possible without speculative execution.

In this paper we propose *delayed exceptions*, a technique that combines low hardware cost, high performance and correct exception handling by putting most of the responsibility for exception handling on the compiler. Delayed exceptions can be implemented as a binary compatible extension of current architectures.

2   The Basic Idea

Delayed exceptions exploit the fact that exceptions are rare. The compiler assumes the typical case (no exceptions), schedules the code accordingly, and inserts run-time checks and fix-up code that ensure correct execution when exceptions do happen.

To implement this idea, every register is augmented with an exception bit; two versions of exception-generating instructions are needed: The trapping version is used in non-speculative execution and behaves traditionally. The trap-noting version is used for speculative execution; it does not trap, but notes in the trap bit of the result register whether the instruction would have trapped. This trap-noting instruction can be moved around as freely as other non-trapping instructions. Instructions dependent on that instruction can then also be moved up by speculating on the outcome to the exception-checking branch.

Finally a branch instruction checks trap-notes and branches to the fix-up code if necessary. The fix-up code triggers the trap and recalculates registers that received wrong values. The fix-up code is subject to the same control dependences that the exception-generating instruction was originally.

3   A Motivating Example

We will introduce the concept of delayed exceptions by a small example. Figure 1 shows the C function strlen which computes the length of a zero-terminated string. Figure 2 shows the assembly language output of a compiler for the MIPS R3000. We have changed the register names to make the program more readable.

The problem in software pipelining this loop is the lb (load byte) instruction, which can trap on illegal memory access. Assuming a two-cycle load latency and a one-cycle branch latency, each iteration needs three cycles even on a superscalar processor, unless delayed exceptions are used to enable speculative execution of the lb.

```
int strlen(char *s) {
  char *t = s;
  while (*s != '\0')
    s++;
  return s-t;
}
```

Fig. 1. The C function `strlen`

```
#   1      int strlen(char *s) {
strlen:
#   2      char *t = s;
          move    t,s          # t=s
#   3      while (*s != '\0')
          lb      t0,0(s)       # t0=*s
          beqz    t0,end        # while (t0 != '\0')
loop:
#   4      s++;
          addu    s,s,1         # s++
          lb      t0,0(s)       # t0=*s
          bnez    t0,loop       # while (t0 != '\0')
end:
#   5      return s-t;
          subu    v0,s,t        # return_value = s-t
          j       ra            # return
```

Fig. 2. MIPS R3000 assembly language source of function `strlen`

```
                     move t,s
         lbx0 t0,0(s)   addu0 s,s,1
         lbx1 t1,0(s)   addu1 s,s,1
loop0: lbxn t2,0(s)     addun s,s,1  bxn-2 t0,xcept0 beqzn-2 t0,ret0
loop1: lbxn+1 t0,0(s)   addun+1 s,s,1 bxn-1 t1,xcept1 beqzn-1 t1,ret0
loop2: lbxn+2 t1,0(s)   addun+2 s,s,1 bxn t2,xcept2  bnezn t2,loop0
ret0:                   subu s,s,3
ret1:                   subu v0,s,t               j ra
xcept0: lbn-2 t0,-3(s)
                                      bnezn-2 t0,loop1
         subu s,s,3                   b ret1
xcept1: lbn-1 t1,-3(s)
                                      bnezn-1 t1,loop2
         subu s,s,3                   b ret1
xcept2: lbn t2,-3(s)
                                      bnezn t2,loop0
         subu s,s,3                   b ret1
```

Fig. 3. Software pipelined version of Fig. 2 with delayed exceptions

We software pipelined this code using delayed exceptions (see Fig. 3). We unrolled the loop thrice and renamed registers to eliminate write-after-read (WAR) dependencies. The loop now executes in one cycle/iteration on a hypothetical superscalar processor[2], unless an exception occurs. We assume that the processor has enough resources to execute one line (of Fig. 3) per cycle.

A few words of explanation are necessary. lbx (load byte and note exception) is the trap-noting version of lb; It sets the exception bit of the result register if an exception occurs and clears it otherwise. If one of the earlier bytes was zero, the function will return without ever seeing the bx belonging to the lbx. I.e., exceptions caused by wrong speculations are ignored. However, if the speculation was right, the bx will be executed; If the exception bit is set, the bx (branch on exception bit) instruction branches to the fix-up code. In the present case, the fix-up code consists of a lb that accesses the same address as the lbx and thereby calls the trap handler.

The indices of the instructions indicate the iteration the instructions belong to. The addu is executed speculatively, too. We could have renamed registers to save the old value of s for the off-loop execution paths and for the fix-up code. Instead, our code repairs s by subtracting 3.

4 The Compiler Technique

4.1 The Percolation Scheduling Framework

Percolation scheduling is a general framework for global instruction scheduling [Nic85]. It contains a few *core transformations* for moving instructions. *Enabling transformations* (e.g. register renaming) give the core transformations greater freedom to move the code. *Guidance rules* decide when and where to apply the transformations.

In this framework, the exception delaying transformation described below is an enabling transformation.

Delayed exceptions can also be fitted into other global scheduling models. E.g., in the context of trace scheduling [Fis81, Ell85], exception-generating instructions would be moved around freely; the fix-up code is inserted by the book-keeping process.

4.2 The Exception Delaying Transformation

The basic transformation used in delayed exceptions is shown in Fig. 4. The trapping instruction is split into a trap-noting instruction and the exception-checking branch bx to the fix-up code.

The fix-up code must trigger the trap and set the registers to the correct values. Before applying other transformations, the only register to be recomputed is the result register of the instruction. These functions are performed by the trapping version of the instruction[3].

---

[2] We did not exploit more parallelism (e.g. by *combining*[NE89] the addus or by speculating in both directions) in order to keep the example simple.

[3] Of course, the transformation should not be reapplied to the trapping instruction in the fix-up code.

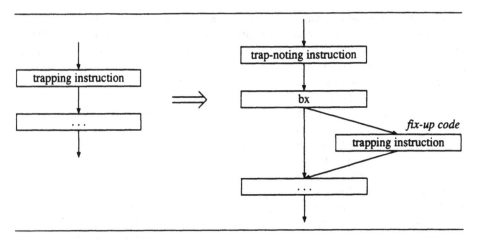

Fig. 4. The exception delaying transformation

The trapping version of the instruction in the fix-up code is still subject to the old control-dependences, i.e. it must not be moved across other trapping instructions (this preserves the order of exceptions) or up across branches.

This transformation may appear to be a bad deal, because it increases the number of executed instructions. However, on superscalar processors the execution time is determined mainly by dependences between instructions. Due to the dependences there are often idle resources (instruction bandwidth, functional units); these resources can be utilized for executing independent instructions without increasing execution time. Therefore, replacing dependences with additional instructions is often a win.

4.3 Enabled transformations

The exception delaying transformation is an enabling transformation. First of all, it enables the compiler to move the trap-noting version of the instruction up across branches (i.e. speculative execution of the instruction). More importantly, it also makes speculation on the outcome of the trap-check possible. I.e., instructions that depend on the exception-generating instruction can be moved up across the exception-checking branch and other branches.

How is this done? When moving the instructions up into the branches of the exception-checking conditional, both branches get a copy of the instruction. The copy in the fix-up code stays there, bound by the dependence on the trapping instruction, while the other copy can move further up until it reaches the trap-noting instruction. The code motions have to take the data dependences into account, so the source registers of the operations in the fix-up code are preserved, since they are live until the fix-up code. Transformations like register renaming or repairing [EK92] can be used to remove these dependences and enable further moves. The trap-notes have to be treated like normal registers, i.e. the trap-noting instruction is a definition and the trap-check is a use (see Section 5.3).

```
if (p != NULL) {
    i = j + p->info;
    p = q;
    ...
}
```

Fig. 5. A common C fragment

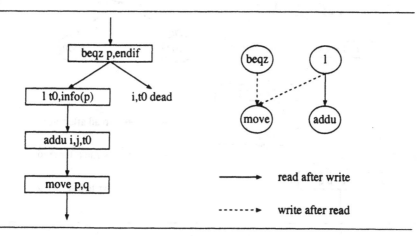

Fig. 6. Assembly version of Fig. 5

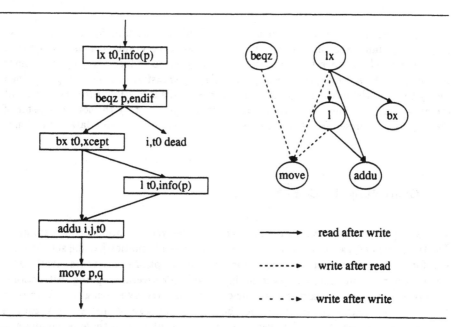

Fig. 7. Figure 6 after the exception delaying transformation

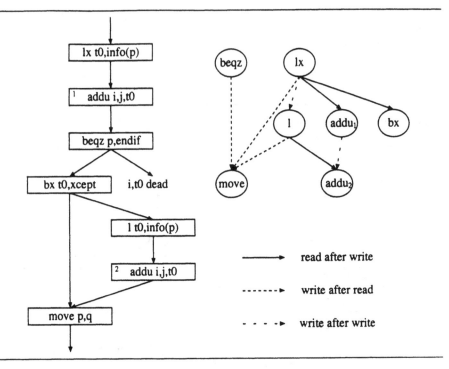

Fig. 8. Figure 7 after another code motion

As an example, we transform a typical C idiom (see Fig. 5). Figure 6 shows its assembly language version and the data dependence graph. Let us assume that there is a need to move the operations up in order to reduce the impact of later dependences. First we apply the exception delaying transformation (see Fig. 7). Then we try to move the other instructions (see Fig. 8). This is possible with the **addu**, but the **move** cannot be moved above the **bx**, since it would destroy the source register of the **l** (this is represented as a write-after-read dependence in the data dependence graph).

4.4 Controlling the Code Expansion

The example also shows a possible problem with delayed exceptions: code explosion. The two remedies used in the context of run-time disambiguation [Nic89] should work well for delayed exceptions, too: applying delayed exceptions only to frequently used program parts; and using one piece of fix-up code for several trapping instructions. Finally, the cache and paging behaviour can be improved by moving the fix-up code out-of-line into extra pages. An upper bound for the size of the recovery code is the original code size times the average depth of speculation, if there is one piece of recovery code per (non-**bx**) branch.

5 Architectural Considerations

5.1 Which Instructions are Affected

A program can trap on memory access exceptions, arithmetic exceptions (overflow and divide by zero) and explicit trap instructions.

Memory access exceptions can be generated by loads and stores. Loads can be easily executed speculatively using delayed exceptions. Stores alter memory, so they can hardly be undone. Therefore exceptions are not the only obstacle to speculative execution of stores. Fortunately there is no need to execute stores speculatively, since dependences on the store can be eliminated by run-time disambiguation [Nic89] and register renaming. Therefore a trap-noting store is neither necessary nor sensible.

Arithmetic exceptions can be generated by many floating-point and integer instructions. Trap-noting versions of these instructions are needed. Instructions that also have a non-trapping version (e.g. add (trapping) and addu (non-trapping)) are a special case. Instead of producing a third version, the non-trapping instruction could be changed into a trap-noting instruction in this case. However, this can affect register allocation, as explained in Section 5.3. The architect has to balance opcode waste against a (probably tiny) performance loss due to possible spilling.

Trap instructions are usually used for system calls, emulation of non-implemented hardware or bounds checks. Noting a trap early by speculation offers no advantages. Therefore trap-noting versions of trap instructions do not make sense.

5.2 Accessing the Exception bits

The exception bits have to be conserved across context switches. Therefore they can be read and written through (a) special control register(s). Before reading them they must be up-to-date. This can be achieved by waiting until all pipelines have run dry.

This possibility of access can prove useful for other situations, too: Interrupt handlers can use delayed exceptions, if they save and restore the exception bits. It could even be used for saving and restoring around procedure calls, enabling better scheduling across calls. Of course this would require user-level access to the exception bits and a faster method than letting the processor run dry.

5.3 Noting the Exception

In the examples above, the exception is noted by a bit associated with the result register of the trap-noting instruction. This provides for simple adressing, but restricts register allocation: The register may not be used as the result register of a trap-noting instruction until the note is dead, i.e. until it is checked or an execution path is chosen that does not contain the check (i.e. an execution path that would not have contained the trapping instruction in the first place).

As an alternative, the notes could be addressed explicitly and allocated separately. This would make register allocation easier, but trap-noting instructions would need extra bits in the instructions for addressing the note.

5.4 Precise Exceptions

Some instructions (e.g. memory access and floating point on the MC88100) can cause exceptions late in the pipeline, when other, later instructions have already modified the processor state. Therefore, the processor cannot be simply restarted from the faulting instructions. These imprecise exceptions have several disadvantages, e.g. they make exception handlers implementation-dependent. In order to implement precise interrupts, many expensive hardware schemes for restoring the processor state have been proposed [SP88, HP87].

Delayed exceptions open the road to precise exceptions without any backup hardware: The exception delaying transformation must be applied to every instruction in the program that can cause imprecise exceptions. In the fix-up code, a special instruction tx (trigger exception) is prepended to the trapping instruction. tx traps early and therefore precisely.

There's just one problem: The trap does not occur at the instruction that originally caused the exception, but at the tx. However, the compiler makes sure that the input registers have the right values for rerunning the exception-causing instruction.[4] In addition to the values of the registers, the exception handler usually wants to know the exception-causing instruction and the type of the exception. The latter can be stored in the exception note·(which has to be extended for this purpose), while the instruction resides just after the tx.

5.5 Page Faults

Like on any other processor, instruction fetch page faults are handled immediately. Data access page faults caused by a trap-noting instruction are noted like other exceptions and later handled in the fix-up code, if the processor executes the appropriate path. If a different path is executed, the note has no effect. This is an advantage over the approach proposed for general percolation [CMC+91], where speculative page faults are always serviced, even if they are not needed.

5.6 Instruction Issue Bandwidth

In the programs we measured (see Section 6) 16%–24% of the dynamically executed instructions can generate exceptions. Since this is nonnumerical code, most of these instructions will be executed speculatively on a high-degree superscalar machine. Each of these speculatively executed instructions would add a bx instruction to the instruction stream. Delayed exceptions increase the needed instruction issue bandwidth by up to 24% and need additional functional units for executing the bx instructions. These needs can be reduced by having bx instructions that test several notes and branch to a combined piece of fix-up code.

---

[4] These are the same compiler techniques that ensure correct processing of delayed exceptions (see Section 4.3).

6   Potential Speedup

To evaluate the potential benefit of delayed exceptions, we performed a trace-driven simulation [BYP+91, Wal91, LW92]. To get an upper bound, we assumed infinite resources (instruction bandwidth, functional units), perfect register renaming, perfect alias detection, and perfect branch prediction. To have a few machine models between the extremes, we restricted perfect branch prediction, to predict only the next n branches. Note that 0 predicted branches prevents speculative execution, but some global scheduling is still possible: instructions can be moved down.

In other words, for our perfect model, we considered only read-after-write (RAW) dependences, through both registers and memory, and dependences from branches to all later stores. For limited branch-prediction we added dependences between branches and all instructions that are more than n branches later in the trace. Without delayed exceptions, we also added dependences between branch instructions and all later exception-generating instructions.[5]

Throughout the simulations, we used the latencies of the R3000 processor (e.g. 2-cycle loads). The instruction level parallelism is computed by dividing the number of instructions by the critical path length of the dependence graph.

The benchmark programs used are: an abstract Prolog machine interpreter (Prolog), an instruction scheduler (sched), and compress 4.1 (compress). They were compiled on a DecStation 5000 with the manufacturer's C compiler and then run with typical input to produce traces. Due to limitations of our tracer we produced and analysed only short traces ($\approx 500,000$ instructions).

The results are shown in Fig. 9. Without delayed exceptions, even perfect branch prediction gives only speedups of 1.08–1.31 over having no speculation. This clearly shows that speculative execution is hardly worth bothering, if it cannot be applied to exception-generating instructions (another variation of Amdahl's Law). Even with only one-deep speculation delayed exceptions beat the perfect model without delayed exceptions. In other words: Every machine that has enough resources to profit from speculative execution will profit from delayed exceptions. The perfect models differ by a factor of 3.8 (sched), 7.4 (compress) and 9.5 (Prolog).

The improvement on a realistic machine with a real scheduling algorithm is of course somewhat lower, but still impressive: Mahlke et al. report a speedup of 18%–135% (average 57%) for sentinel scheduling (see Section 7) on non-numeric programs for a superscalar processor of degree 8 [MCH+92]. They report an average speedup of 32% for numeric benchmarks. Delayed exceptions should give similar results.

7   Related Work

Ignoring exceptions by using non-trapping instructions has been proposed for circumventing the problem [CMC+91]. Instead of trapping on e.g. an illegal memory

---

[5] A compiler could use control-dependence analysis to move instructions up across branches in a non-speculative way. If our simulation took this into account (i.e. did not count those branches), it would result in a somewhat higher instruction-level parallelism for all models but the perfect model. Due to the data given in [LW92] and Amdahl's Law we believe that the effect of this optimization would not be very large and would not change our conclusions.

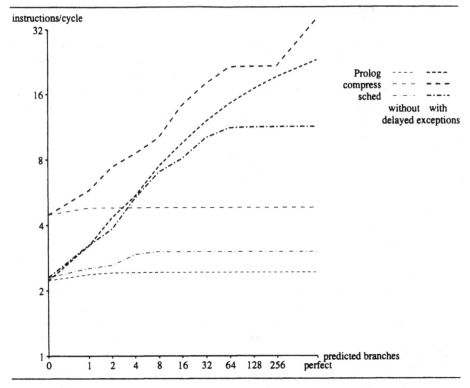

Fig. 9. Instruction-level parallelism with and without delayed exceptions

access, a garbage value is returned. The justification for this behaviour is that correct programs do not trap. Unfortunately this justification is wrong. Exceptions are used in many applications. [AL91] lists several applications of memory access exceptions. Besides, in our opinion the assumption of completely correct programs is unrealistic. Delayed exceptions solve the problem instead of ignoring it.

Speculative loads [RL92] note the exception in a bit associated with the result register. The first instruction that uses the result triggers the trap. This means that the load can be executed speculatively, but not its use. In contrast, delayed exceptions permit arbitrary chains of speculative operations.

The *TORCH* architecture [SLH90, SHL92, Smi92] uses programmer-visible shadow register files for compiler-based speculative execution. TORCH as described in [SLH90] can handle exceptions using a reexecution scheme implemented in hardware. In the meantime they have switched to using compiler-generated recovery code. In contrast to delayed exceptions, TORCH uses hardware to restore the state before the exception and then executes the recovery code. TORCHs recovery code contains all speculative instructions since the exception, while our fix-up code contains only instructions that dependent on the trap-noting instruction.

Sentinel scheduling [MCH+92] uses a bit in every instruction that says whether the instruction is executed speculatively. Speculative instructions set and propagate exception bits; the first non-speculative instruction triggers the trap (if the bit is set). Recovery is ·performed by reexecuting the whole code starting from the instruction that caused the exception. The bottom-line differences between delayed exceptions and sentinel scheduling are: Sentinel scheduling does not preserve the order of the exceptions; It doubles the number of opcodes, whereas delayed exceptions only double the exception-generating instructions. Sentinel scheduling needs special hardware for propagating the exception bits and the address of the exception-generating instruction; and it produces more register pressure (the source registers for all instructions between speculative instruction and sentinel have to be preserved, while our fix-up code needs only the source registers for instructions that depend on the trap-noting instruction); it cannot move exception-generating instructions beyond irreversible instructions like stores. Delayed exceptions use more instruction bandwidth (for exception-checking branches) and they produce more code (fix-up code).

Write-back suppression [BMH+93] is specific to superblock[6] scheduling. It uses hardware to suppress the register file updates by the excepting instruction and all subsequent instructions that have the same or higher speculation distance. If execution reaches the home basic block of the excepting instruction, these instructions are reexecuted by hardware with write-back and trapping enabled. This mechanism produces less register pressure than delayed exceptions, because the hardware ensures that instructions that will be reexecuted later will not write over registers needed during reexecution. The main disadvantage of write-back suppression is its restriction to superblock scheduling and unidirectional speculation.

8   Conclusion

Speculative execution is the key to making optimal use of superscalar processors. However, in a pure compiler-based approach exception-generating instructions must not be executed speculatively. This restriction virtually eliminates speculative execution and its advantages.

In the spirit of RISC technology, *delayed exceptions* combine a simple hardware extension with sophisticated compiler techniques to solve this problem. Speculative exception-generating instructions just note the exception in a bit associated with the result register. If the speculation was right, the bit is checked by a special branch instruction. If the bit is set (i.e. there was an exception), it branches to compiler-generated fix-up code. This code triggers the trap and ensures correct recovery. Delayed exceptions permit the compiler to move exception-generating instructions as freely as non-trapping instructions.

Trace-driven simulation shows that every processor that profits from speculative execution (e.g. most superscalar processors) would profit from delayed exceptions. The upper bound for speedups achievable by delayed exceptions for the studied traces is 3.8-9.4.

---

[6] A superblock can be entered only from the top, but can be left at several points.

Acknowledgements

The referees, Thomas Pietsch and Franz Puntigam provided valuable comments on earlier versions of this paper. Section 5.2 was inspired by the "Trapping speculative ops" discussion on the Usenet news group comp.arch, especially by Stanley Chow and Cliff Click.

References

[AL91]   Andrew W. Appel and Kai Li. Virtual memory primitives for user programs. In ASPLOS-IV [ASP91], pages 96–107.

[ASP91]   *Architectural Support for Programming Languages and Operating Systems (ASPLOS-IV)*, 1991.

[ASP92]   *Architectural Support for Programming Languages and Operating Systems (ASPLOS-V)*, 1992.

[BMH+93] Roger A. Bringman, Scott A. Mahlke, Richard E. Hank, John C. Gyllenhaal, and Wen-mei W. Hwu. Speculative execution exception recovery using write-back suppression. In *26th Annual International Symposium on Microarchitecture (MICRO-26)*, pages 214–223, 1993.

[BYP+91]   Michael Butler, Tse-Yu Yeh, Yale Patt, Mitch Alsup, Hunter Scales, and Michael Shebanow. Single instruction stream parallelism is greater than two. In ISCA-18 [ISC91], pages 276–286.

[CMC+91] Pohua P. Chang, Scott A. Mahlke, William Y. Chen, Nancy J. Warter, and Wen-mei W. Hwu. IMPACT: An architectural framework for multiple-instruction-issue processors. In ISCA-18 [ISC91], pages 266–275.

[EK92]   M. Anton Ertl and Andreas Krall. Removing antidependences by repairing. Bericht TR 1851-1992-9, Institut für Computersprachen, Technische Universität Wien, 1992.

[Ell85]   John R. Ellis. *Bulldog: A Compiler for VLIW Architectures*. MIT Press, 1985.

[Fis81]   Joseph A. Fisher. Trace scheduling: A technique for global microcode compaction. *IEEE Transactions on Computers*, 30(7):478–490, July 1981.

[HP87]   Wen-mei Hwu and Yale N. Patt. Checkpoint repair for high-performance out-of-order execution machines. *IEEE Transactions on Computers*, 36(12):1496–1514, December 1987.

[ISC91]   *The 18th Annual International Symposium on Computer Architecture (ISCA)*, Toronto, 1991.

[JW89]   Norman P. Jouppi and David W. Wall. Available instruction-level parallelism for superscalar and superpipelined machines. In *Architectural Support for Programming Languages and Operating Systems (ASPLOS-III)*, pages 272–282, 1989.

[LW92]   Monica S. Lam and Robert P. Wilson. Limits of control flow on parallelism. In *The 19th Annual International Symposium on Computer Architecture (ISCA)*, pages 46–57, 1992.

[MCH+92] Scott A. Mahlke, William Y. Chen, Wen-mei W. Hwu, B. Ramakrishna Rau, and Michael S. Schlansker. Sentinel scheduling for VLIW and superscalar processors. In ASPLOS-V [ASP92], pages 238–247.

[NE89]   Toshio Nakatani and Kemal Ebcioğlu. "Combining" as a compilation technique for VLIW architectures. In *22nd Annual International Workshop on Microprogramming and Microarchitecture (MICRO-22)*, pages 43–55, 1989.

[Nic85]   Alexandru Nicolau. Uniform parallelism exploitation in ordinary programs. In *1985 International Conference on Parallel Processing*, pages 614–618, 1985.

[Nic89]   Alexandru Nicolau. Run-time disambiguation: Coping with statically unpredictable dependencies. *IEEE Transactions on Computers*, 38(5):663–678, May 1989.

[RG81]   B. R. Rau and C. D. Glaeser. Some scheduling techgniques and an easily schedulable horizontal architecture for high performance scientific computing. In *14th Annual Microprogramming Workshop (MICRO-14)*, pages 183–198, 1981.

[RL92]   Anne Rogers and Kai Li. Software support for speculative loads. In ASPLOS-V [ASP92], pages 38–50.

[SHL92]   Michael D. Smith, Mark Horowitz, and Monica S. Lam. Efficient superscalar performance through boosting. In ASPLOS-V [ASP92], pages 248–259.

[SLH90]   Michael D. Smith, Monica S. Lam, and Mark A. Horowitz. Boosting beyond static scheduling in a superscalar processor. In *The 17th Annual International Symposium on Computer Architecture (ISCA)*, pages 344–354, 1990.

[Smi92]   Michael David Smith. *Support for Speculative Execution in High-Performance Processors*. PhD thesis, Stanford University, 1992.

[Soh90]   Gurindar S. Sohi. Instruction issue logic for high-performance, interruptable, multiple functional unit, pipelined processors. *IEEE Transactions on Computers*, 39(3):349–359, March 1990.

[SP88]   James E. Smith and Andrew R. Pleszkun. Implementing precise interrupts in pipelined processors. *IEEE Transactions on Computers*, 37(5):562–573, May 1988.

[Tom67]   R. M. Tomasulo. An efficient algorithm for exploiting multiple arithmetic units. *IBM Journal of Research and Development*, 11(1):25–33, 1967.

[Wal91]   David W. Wall. Limits of instruction-level parallelism. In ASPLOS-IV [ASP91], pages 176–188.

On the Implementation of Abstract Interpretation Systems for (Constraint) Logic Programs*

Gerda Janssens and Wim Simoens**

K.U. Leuven, Department of Computer Science
Celestijnenlaan 200A, B-3001 Heverlee, Belgium
{gerda,wims}@cs.kuleuven.ac.be

Abstract. We report on an experiment with two tools for global analysis of logic programs. Both systems implement a top-down framework for abstract interpretation. PLAI (Programming in Logic with Abstract Interpretation) developed by Hermenegildo and Muthukumar is written in Prolog. GAIA (Generic Abstract Interpretation Algorithm) developed by Le Charlier and Van Hentenryck is written in C. With each system we have developed two applications. As abstractions we used a domain mode for logic programming and a domain freeness for constraint logic programming over numerical and unification constraints.
Our results allow implementors to make a more knowledgeable choice between both systems and identify a number of practical issues (e.g. normalisation and optimisations) that arise in implementing abstract interpretation systems. The comparison of the results for modes and freeness illustrates the impact of the complexity of abstractions on the performance of the analysis. Moreover, as our experiments use state of the art technology, they give an idea of the feasibility of realising practical abstract interpretation tools based on these and similar abstractions. To our knowledge, this is the first paper that reports on coupling the same abstract domain with abstract interpretation algorithms that use C (GAIA) and Prolog (PLAI).

1 Introduction

Abstract interpretation [7] is widely used for the global analysis of logic programs and, more recently, also for Constraint Logic Programming [4, 5]. Frameworks have been developed, applications have been discussed and experimental results have been reported by many authors (see [8] for references). This work is motivated by the need for optimisation in LP compilers to close the gap

---

* This work was funded in part by ESPRIT project 5246 PRINCE and by Diensten voor de Programmatie van het Wetenschapsbeleid (project RFO-AI-02).

** The first author is a post-doctoral researcher of the Belgian National Fund for Scientific Research. Part of the research reported in this paper was performed while the second author was visiting Brown University.

with procedural languages. Recently two generic algorithms, GAIA (Generic Abstract Interpretation Algorithm) developed by Le Charlier and Van Hentenryck [13, 14], and PLAI (Programming in Logic with Abstract Interpretation) developed by Hermenegildo and Muthukumar [18, 19], became widely available. Both algorithms are fine tuned implementations inspired by the top-down framework of Bruynooghe [2][3]. While these systems differentiate regarding some design decisions, the most noticeable difference is that GAIA is written in C, while PLAI is in Prolog. Researchers interested in using these generic algorithms are confronted with the choice between both systems, between the relative ease of programming the application specific operations in Prolog and the more demanding task of programming them in C, with the expectation of obtaining a better performance.

In this paper we report on an experiment where two applications have been developed in both systems. We identify a number of practical issues that arise in designing and implementing abstract interpretation systems (e.g. normalisation and optimisations). Our results show that the real performance gap between both systems is much larger than the factor 5 – 10 which is reported by previous Prolog – C comparisons [17, 21], namely for small programs performing similar algorithms on similar data structures. An important reason is that C allows to use very different data structures for representing the elements of the abstract domain, and consequently also very different algorithms for realising the abstract operations upon these elements. This has a major impact on memory consumption and performance. The complexity of the abstraction has a serious impact on the performance of the analysis. Although much slower, it was no problem to do a simple analysis of quite large programs with PLAI. Experimenting with a complex analysis is also feasible, however the memory consumption and execution time of the abstract operations become dominating and may cause problems when analysing large programs. So one can state that PLAI is adequate for developing experimental prototypes but not for integration in a production compiler. For the latter task, GAIA is much better suited and one can expect the extra effort to be rewarded with substantial speedups (10 – 100). The results obtained for freeness give an idea of the feasibility of such complex domains in production compilers.

Our results dispute the claims of Tan and Lin [20], which report a performance improvement of 100 on a simple domain by compiling the abstract interpretation into the framework of the WAM, instead of the usual interpreter-based approach. Our experiments suggest that the difference is not only due to the effect of compilation, but also to the fact that their interpreter-based analysis is done in Prolog and the compiled analysis in C.

The rest of this paper is organised as follows. In the next section, we review the abstract interpretation systems GAIA and PLAI. Section 3 gives an overview of the abstract domains used in the experiments. Section 4 presents the benchmarks used. Section 5 describes our experiments and compares GAIA and PLAI on the two domains while Section 6 contains the conclusions of this research.

---

[3] GAIA can also be viewed as an instance of a universal fixpoint algorithm instantiated to a fixpoint semantics for logic programming.

2 The Abstract Interpretation Systems

This section discusses informally some algorithmic and implementation aspects of the abstract interpretation systems that we found relevant for our experiments. We assume some familiarity with top-down frameworks for abstract interpretation of logic programs, such as [2].

2.1 Overview of the Approach

As both GAIA and PLAI can be viewed as inspired by the abstract interpretation framework for logic programs of Bruynooghe [2], we briefly recall some basic ideas of this framework. It closely mimics the procedural semantics and gives detailed information about call and success substitutions of the predicates: it constructs an AND-OR graph for a given program and a given query specification. This information can be used for example for further optimisations of the analysed program [17, 21].

A generic abstract interpretation system consists mainly of two parts:

- The *domain-dependent operations* are the abstract operations that need to be implemented in order to instantiate the system to a specific domain.
- The *fixpoint algorithm* computes abstract substitutions for each program point in the analysed program. These abstract substitutions can be used to construct the AND-OR graph of Bruynooghe's framework.

The key ideas behind top-down abstract interpretation can be summarised as follows. To solve a query to a procedure p with an abstract substitution β, the algorithm considers each clause defining p and groups the result of the clause analyses using an abstract operation (this is the so-called OR-node of Bruynooghe's framework). The analysis of a clause considers each goal in turn applying the same algorithm to each goal with the abstract substitution obtained for the goal (this is the so-called AND-node of Bruynooghe's framework). Recursion is handled in a special way to guarantee correctness while preserving the safeness of this analysis. When a recursive call is encountered with the same abstract substitution, no new subcomputation is initiated. Rather a lower approximation of the result of this call is returned for the recursive call. The initial lower approximation can simply be the bottom element of the domain or can be computed in a more sophisticated way. The approximation may be updated when a call collects the results of its clauses. If the used approximation has been updated and if the call depends on itself recursively, a new analysis is required. The overall computation is thus an iterative process which terminates when none of the approximations used in the computation have been updated during the last iteration. This framework can be used both for logic programs and constraint logic programs. For CLP the notions of unification and substitutions are generalised to those of conjunction and constraints [9].

The efficient algorithms on which GAIA and PLAI are based aim at optimising the top-down computation of the AND-OR graph. Although the computation is organised around the AND-OR graph, it is not stored as such. Both algorithms gather call and success substitutions for the predicates in the program. They both optimise the computational cost of the fixpoint computation, e.g. by avoiding to use bottom as the first approximation of the success substitution of a recursive call, by reducing the computational effort which is performed during the successive iterations in computing the success substitution of a recursive call, and by using the already obtained results when it happens that a predicate is called several times with the same call substitution.

In the rest of this section we discuss differences between them that we found relevant for our experiments.

2.2 Interface

Normalisation. An important difference between them affects the domain dependent part and is related to *the approach towards normalisation*. A number of operations are simpler when the arguments of the heads and the calls are variables. For example, the normalisation of the append/3 program is as follows:

```
append(X,Y,Z) :- X = nil, Y=Z.
append(X,Y,Z) :- X = [E|X'], Z = [E|Z'], append(X',Y,Z').
```

The effect of normalisation is to make the unifications explicit, isolating them from the other abstract operations, and to introduce extra variables. How desirable normalisation is depends on the application. Isolating the unifications can make other operations substantially simpler, however, having the extra variables can substantially increase the size of the abstract substitutions in the program points (the size can be exponential in the number of clause variables for some domains). Note also that normalisation can decrease precision. With PLAI, users can decide whether to use normalisation or not, GAIA requires strong normalisation, unifications must be of the form $X = Y$ or $X = f(Y_1, \ldots, Y_n)$ with $X, Y, Y_1, \ldots Y_n$ distinct variables. The possible loss of precision due to the weakness of information regarding the dependencies between variables which is stored in the abstractions can be compensated by the reexecution strategy [2, 15]. However, the introduction of extra variables remains and can be a problem in some applications. Therefore, GAIA has been slightly modified to allow weaker forms of normalisation. The modified GAIA system assumes that the input programs fulfill some minimal normalisation requirements, namely atoms are of the form $p(X_1, \ldots, X_i)$ and the arguments are distinct variables. The unifications still have to be explicit, but the application decides about their actual form. In our experiments GAIA and PLAI analyse identical programs in weak normal form.

Representation of Variables. Another difference is the internal representation of the program, in particular the representation of the variables in the source program. In GAIA the program variables are represented by numbers i.e. 0,1, ..., while PLAI represents program variables by free Prolog variables. The difference is important for the choice of the data structure for the abstract substitutions. Note that abstract substitutions often contain sets of variables (see also the high level description of the two abstract domains in Section 3). In GAIA, this is a set of numbers (between 0 and n) for which a bit representation is a compact and reasonably efficient representation in C. In PLAI this is a set of free variables that can be represented by an ordered list in Prolog, but this representation consumes more memory and requires more time to process. The variable representation in PLAI allows the use of Prolog specific implementation techniques, e.g. using unification to rename abstract substitutions, but bit operations cannot be used with this free variable representation.

2.3 Fixpoint Algorithm

Avoiding Redundant Computation. In the treatment of a recursive predicate, the Original version of GAIA recomputes all clauses defining the predicate. PLAI does better: it recomputes only the clauses from which the predicate is reachable. Both systems redo the unifications, however they avoid to recompute calls to predicates for which the call pattern has not changed. They simply pick up the success substitution stored in the previous iteration. GAIA has a variant, the Prefix version which is theoretically more efficient, as it starts recomputation from the point where the recursive call receives a new success substitution (to allow this the abstract substitution in the program point prior to the recursive call is stored, the abstract substitution of other program points is not stored). For example, PLAI and the Original version of GAIA will reexecute the unifications in the recursive clause of append, while the Prefix version of GAIA will not. In practice, it is not always the case that the Prefix version is better as the extra cost of storing and fetching the full substitution in the point prior to the recursive call can be more substantial than the cost of recomputing the calls prior to the recursive call.

Granularity of the Analysis and Annotation. The analysis can derive different call patterns for a procedure, e.g. the same procedure can be called from different points in the program or recursive calls may have other call patterns than the original one. Both systems compute dynamically as many versions, i.e. call patterns, for a procedure as encountered during fixpoint computation. The systems have a different approach towards presenting the computed AND-OR graph to the user. GAIA outputs all versions explicitly, while PLAI gives one version – the most general one – for each predicate. A version is annotated with abstract substitutions in the program points. PLAI keeps the abstract substitution in every program point (so that it can be used directly to annotate the program), while GAIA only keeps the call and success patterns for the predicate calls. So that at the moment of annotation, the AND-OR graph has to be partly recomputed in GAIA. This post-processing step of GAIA is straightforward and linear in the size of the programs and has the advantage of reducing the storage of information which may not be relevant during the fixpoint computation. Apparently, the design decision of PLAI slows it down as there is the overhead of storing this information (i.e. copying these substitutions in Prolog's record database).

2.4 Implementation Language

In addition to the previous aspects, when one tries to compare GAIA and PLAI, one has to take into account the well known differences between the procedural programming paradigm and the logic programming paradigm. PLAI uses Prolog and this allows rapid prototyping. This is especially advantageous while one is still experimenting with the expressive power of the abstract domain. In the case of GAIA, one has to implement the abstract domain in C and this seems only worthwhile once a definite decision about the abstraction has been made. On the other hand, there remains the performance gap between Prolog and C for which a factor of at most 10 is put forward in [17, 21] for some small programs using similar data structures, but which can be much higher when the C version encodes the information in a different way and processes it with different algorithms (cf. different internal representation of variables).

3 The Abstract Domains

We have coupled GAIA and PLAI with two abstract domains. The abstract operations are defined for (weakly) normalised programs, although this is not required by PLAI. Each domain has been implemented in C and in Prolog. For each language we took an appropriate data structure that allowed to use the full power of the language. It is the intention of the authors that the implementation of the domains allows a fair comparison between the two systems.

These two domains are very different from a complexity viewpoint and enable us to study the impact of normalisation and sizes of the abstract substitutions on the systems. In addition, they give interesting data on the feasibility of other domains such as complex sharing domains.

The domain mode aims at deriving instantiation states of program variables in logic programs. The domain mode is also used in [13] and is a reformulation of the domain in [2]. An abstract substitution has three components: (1) the mode component associates the mode var, ground or any with each program variable, (2) the sval component defines an equivalence relation between program variables that definitely have the same value, and (3) the sharing component defines an equivalence relation between program variables that possibly share a variable. The abstraction of $\{X = f(Y_1, Y_2), Y_1 = T\}$ is the triplet: $(\{mode(X, any), mode(Y_1, var), mode(Y_2, var), mode(T, var)\}, \{\{X\}, \{Y_1, T\}, \{Y_2\}\}, \{\{X, Y_1, Y_2, T\}\})$. The set $\{Y_1, T\}$ in the sval component expresses that Y_1 and T have the same value. The set $\{X, Y_1, Y_2, T\}$ in the sharing component expresses that the four variables might have a common variable.

The freeness domain [11, 12] derives information about definite freeness of program variables in constraint systems. It deals with mixed constraint systems in CLP programs, namely systems containing numerical constraints, e.g. $Y_1 + T = 3$, and unification constraints, e.g. $X = f(Y_1, Y_2)$. The abstraction extends the notion of possible sharing in the context of LP towards possible dependencies established by constraint systems in CLP. In order to decide about definite freeness of a variable the abstraction must capture the dependencies that are created by the constraint system. Then we can safely compute which variables might get instantiated – and are possibly not free – when a particular variable gets a value. The abstraction has again a mode compo-

nent and a set of sets of variables describing a.o. possible dependencies. The constraint system $\{X = f(Y_1, Y_2), Y_1 + T = 3\}$ is abstracted by the tuple: $(\{mode(X, any), mode(Y1, var), mode(Y2, var), mode(T, var)\}, \{\{X\}, \{X, Y_1\},$ $\{X, Y_2\}, \{Y_1, T\}, \{X, T\}, \{X, Y_1, Y_2\}, \{X, Y_1, T\}, \{X, Y_2, T\}, \{X, Y_1, Y_2, T\}\})$.
A variable, e.g. T, has mode var as long as $\{T\}$ does not appear in the second component. The value of T depends on Y_1 and via Y_1 the value of T also depends on X. The sets $\{Y_1, T\}$ and $\{X, T\}$ express these (possible) dependencies. Note that the set of sets is closed under union. The technical reasons for this are beyond the scope of this paper (see [12]).

For this paper it is important to notice the difference in space requirements of the abstractions. mode requires quadratic space in the number of variables in the worst-case because of the sharing component on pairs of variables. freeness may require exponential space since it maintains sets of sets of variables to express sophisticated dependencies between variables. Hence its size is very sensitive to the introduction of extra variables by normalisation. Note that [10] describes two ways to reduce the size of the freeness domain (by combining it with definiteness information [9] and by using a more compact representation for the information).

4 Benchmarks

The programs we use for the simple mode domain are the same as in [13]. They are "pure" logic programs and used for various purposes from compiler writing to equation-solvers, combinatorial problems and theorem-proving. Hence they should be representative of a large class of programs.

For the freeness domain, we have chosen CLP specific examples. Due to the intrinsic size of the abstract substitutions, we had to restrict the size of the benchmark programs. Lengthlist and Sumlist compute resp. the length and the sum of the elements of a given list. Meal is a program to compute balanced meals. Vecadd is a program to compute the sum of two vectors (as lists). Matvec computes the multiplication of a matrix with a vector and Matmul is a program for the multiplication of two matrices. Another famous program is the mortgage program. We used it with two different call-patterns (mg1 and mg2 for short. The relevant difference between them is that mg2 gives rise to two call patterns, while mg1 only to one). Runge-kutta and trapezoid encode integration methods to solve first order ordinary differential equations. The programs are taken from the Prolog III example programs or programs shared by the PRINCE partners.

5 Experiments

This section reports upon our experience gained in using GAIA and PLAI when coupling them with two different abstract domains. Based on the experiments we draw some conclusions which can help developers to make a more knowledgeable choice between the two systems. First, we investigate the behaviour of GAIA when coupled with different domains. Then, we compare the abstract interpretation applications developed with GAIA and PLAI. Finally, an overview is given of points which our experiments showed to be important for the developer of abstract interpretation applications. The experiments are done on a SUN SPARC2 and the execution times (CPU times) are given in seconds. PLAI is compiled using SICStus 2.1 #3.

5.1 On Coupling GAIA with Different Domains

The GAIA-system implements two different algorithms of [13]: the Original version and the Prefix version. They differ in the kind of optimisations used during the successive iterations of the fixpoint computations as explained in Section 2.3.

Table 1. Execution time of GAIA coupled with the mode domain

Program	Or	Pr	Pr/Or%	
append	0.01	0.00	0.00	the append program
cs	5.86	3.02	51.53	cutting stock problem
disj	2.08	0.81	38.94	solve disjunctive scheduling problem
gabriel	0.77	0.36	46.75	browse program from gabriel benchmark
kalah	1.55	0.79	50.96	the game of kalah
peep	2.60	1.18	45.38	peephole optimisation in SB-prolog compiler
pg	0.33	0.14	42.42	specific mathematical problem by W. Older
plan	0.20	0.09	45.00	planning program from Sterling & Shapiro
press	3.66	1.73	47.26	equation solver program
qsort	0.22	0.09	40.90	the quicksort program
queens	0.10	0.05	50.00	the n-queens program
read	3.75	1.54	41.06	tokeniser/reader by O'Keefe and Warren
Average			45.47	

Our Starting Point. The behaviour of the Prefix version with respect to the Original version is very different for our abstract domains. The execution times for mode are given in Table 1: the first column (Or) gives the time of the Original version and the second column (Pr) the time of the Prefix version (we used the same mode domain and actually the same C-code as in [13]). For freeness the same information is given under the heading DS1Strong in Table 2. In case of the mode domain, the Prefix version needs on the average only 45% of the time of the Original version, while for the freeness domain this is 381%. This is partly due to the effect of the intrinsic size of the freeness domain on the fixpoint optimisations of the Prefix version, since freeness is no longer polynomial in the worst-case as mode is, but rather exponential. However, two other causes, namely the choice of the data structure for the freeness domain and the degree of normalisation, have been identified.

The Impact of Data Structures. We used the following data structures for the set of sets of variables in the freeness domain:

1. First, a red-black tree [1] (balanced binary tree), where each node was extended with a pointer to the next in-order element (DS1) has been chosen

Table 2. Execution times of GAIA coupled with the **freeness** domain: influence of the data structure on the behaviour of GAIA

Program	DS1Strong			DS2Strong		
	Or (1)	Pr (2)	(2)/(1)%	Or (3)	Pr (4)	(4)/(3)%
sumlist	0.11	0.14	127.27	0.14	0.13	92.86
lengthlist	0.05	0.05	100.00	0.05	0.05	100.00
meal	0.97	1.57	161.86	0.38	0.45	118.42
vecadd	6.23	15.73	252.49	6.43	5.75	89.42
matvec	4.81	9.85	204.78	4.93	4.41	89.45
mg1	38.70	364.54	941.96	38.77	36.45	94.02
mg2	187.37	1654.11	882.80	188.11	186.63	99.21
Average			381.60			97.63

because it allows fast and easy binary search for the set of sets and the red-black colouring convention keeps the tree balanced. The pointer was used to have an ordered list representation to speed-up the implementation of some of the abstract operations. Profiling both versions showed that the time needed in the Prefix version to store and fetch the information for the fix-point optimisation is bigger than the time needed by the Original version to do the whole computation. For example in the case of mg1, the time used for the Prefix optimisations is a factor 5.2 of the time to redo the computations shortcut by the optimisations. The Prefix optimisations require copying of abstract substitutions. In the case of freeness this is expensive because of the intrinsic exponential size of the abstract substitutions. Moreover, copying is complicated by the pointer to the next in-order element.

2. To speed-up the copy operation, we removed the pointer to the next in-order element and used just a red-black tree to represent the set of sets of variables (DS2). Now, the time needed to copy an abstract substitution dropped with more than 90% and the Prefix version is on the average 2.5% faster than the Original version (see part of Table 2 under heading DS2strong).

In the mode domain, the time needed to store (or fetch) an abstract substitution is almost negligible: the size of a substitution is polynomial and the used data structure allows a very fast copy, so here the performance of the Prefix version is much better than the Original version.

The Impact of Degree of Normalisation. By degree of normalisation we mean the kind of restrictions put on the allowed forms for unification and numeric constraints. The stronger the normalisation, the more extra variables are used: e.g. X = f(A,B), A = h(Y), B = 1 is the strongly normalised form of X = f(h(Y),1). The effect of the degree of normalisation can best be shown through some examples using the freeness domain: here the size of the abstract substitutions is exponential with respect to the number of variables in the clause: e.g. (1) for sumlist, introducing one extra variable causes the time to be doubled, and (2) if in both the first and second clause of mortgage five extra variables are introduced, the time needed in GAIA (and PLAI) was multiplied with at least a

Table 3. Execution times of GAIA coupled with the **freeness** domain: effect of normalisation on DS1

Program	DS1Strong		DS1Weak		(3)/(1)%	(4)/(2)%
	Or (1)	Pr (2)	Or (3)	Pr (4)		
sumlist	0.11	0.14	0.02	0.02	18.18	14.29
lengthlist	0.05	0.05	0.02	0.02	40.00	40.00
meal	0.97	1.57	0.01	0.01	1.03	0.64
vecadd	6.23	15.73	1.16	1.37	18.62	8.71
matvec	4.81	9.85	1.43	1.39	29.73	14.11
matmul	509.37	OOM	19.44	35.35	3.82	/
mg1	38.70	364.54	1.19	0.92	3.07	0.25
mg2	187.37	1654.11	3.65	4.24	1.95	0.26
runge-kutta	OOM	OOM	363.75	451.43	/	/
trapezoid	OOM	OOM	618.70	OOM	/	/
Average					14.55	11.18

Table 4. Execution times of GAIA coupled with the **freeness** domain: effect of normalisation on DS2

Program	DS2Strong		DS2Weak		(3)/(1)%	(4)/(2)%
	Or (1)	Pr (2)	Or (3)	Pr (4)		
sumlist	0.14	0.13	0.01	0.01	7.14	7.69
lengthlist	0.05	0.05	0.01	0.01	20.00	20.00
meal	0.38	0.45	0.02	0.02	5.26	4.44
vecadd	6.43	5.75	1.08	0.96	16.80	16.70
matvec	4.93	4.41	1.46	0.99	29.61	22.45
matmul	527.83	486.23	19.13	16.28	3.62	3.35
mg1	38.77	36.45	1.10	0.86	2.84	2.36
mg2	188.11	186.63	3.61	3.07	1.92	1.64
runge-kutta	OOM	OOM	357.69	367.72	/	/
trapezoid	OOM	OOM	610.92	536.58	/	/
Average					10.90	9.83

factor 60.

GAIA strongly normalised the programs internally in the system. This caused not only a very bad time performance on the **freeness** domain, but also memory problems: due to the exponential size of the abstract substitutions, the introduction of only a few extra variables causes a lot of extra memory needed (e.g. we were not able to compute the abstract interpretation of matmul, runge-kutta or trapezoid). Therefore, we modified the GAIA system: the normalisation was removed from the framework and the user can tune the degree of normalisation with respect to his abstract domain (e.g. for our applications the unifications must be of the form $X = t$ with t any term). For the **freeness** domain, the execution times for this weak normalisation are given in Tables 3 and 4 under the headings DS1Weak and DS2Weak, where OOM stands for *Out Of Memory*. The performance improves with respect to the strong normalisation for both data structures and both versions with at least 85%. For the mode domain, one can choose to have a strongly normalised input program, as the introduction of a few new variables does not cause time or memory problems.

Note that the best implementation of freeness with GAIA uses the red-black tree without extra pointer under weak normalisation i.e. DS2Weak in Table 4.

5.2 Comparison of GAIA and PLAI Based on the Developed Abstract Interpretation Applications

Table 5. Execution times of GAIA and PLAI coupled with the mode domain

Program	GAIA Pr	PLAI Anal	Garb_St	Total	Total/Pr	Anal/Pr
append	0.00	0.19	0.00	0.19	/	/
cs	3.02	104.99	25.34	130.33	43.15	34.76
disj	0.81	27.04	8.39	35.43	43.74	33.38
gabriel	0.36	14.62	3.96	18.58	51.61	40.61
peep	1.18	65.69	16.54	82.23	69.69	55.67
pg	0.14	5.20	1.60	6.80	48.57	37.14
plan	0.09	3.83	1.27	5.10	56.67	42.56
press	1.73	69.88	14.78	84.66	48.94	40.39
qsort	0.09	3.47	1.00	4.47	49.67	38.56
queens	0.05	1.57	0.90	2.47	49.40	31.40
read	1.54	174.97	37.99	212.96	138.28	113.62
Average					59.97	46.81

Table 6. Execution times of GAIA and PLAI coupled with the freeness domain

Program	GAIA Pr	PLAI Anal	Garb_St	Total	Total/Pr	Anal/Pr
sumlist	0.01	0.17	0.00	0.17	17.00	17.00
lengthlist	0.01	0.15	0.00	0.15	15.00	15.00
meal	0.02	0.21	0.00	0.21	10.50	10.50
vecadd	0.96	10.23	5.74	15.97	16.64	10.66
matvec	0.99	11.31	6.69	18.00	18.18	11.42
matmul	16.28	169.52	128.53	298.05	18.31	10.41
mg1	0.86	8.71	5.89	14.60	16.98	10.13
mg2	3.07	29.92	17.42	47.34	15.42	9.75
runge-kutta	367.72	/	/	OOM	/	/
trapezoid	536.58	/	/	OOM	/	/
Average					16.00	11.86

GAIA and PLAI are state of the art implementations. Fixpoint optimisations are incorporated in the Prefix version of GAIA and in PLAI. The data structures used to represent the elements of the abstract domain and the algorithms used to process them are very different due to the different nature of the programming languages Prolog and C and due to the internal representation of the program variables by the systems. What we compare is the performance of both analyses for the same source programs in the same normal form. For PLAI, we give the time needed for the analysis (Anal), for garbage collection and stack shifts (Garb_St) and the total time (Total).

For the mode domain, all benchmarks – including quite large programs – can be run by both systems. However, there is a performance difference of about a factor 60 on the average between GAIA and PLAI (cfr. Table 5). For the more complex **freeness** domain, only small programs can be run with PLAI due to memory problems. The average performance improvement for them is about a factor 16 (cfr. Table 6).

The difference between the systems is partly due to the different approaches towards avoidance of redundant computation, annotating programs and granularity of the analysis (as described in Section 2.3) and partly due to the performance gap between Prolog and C. However, we noticed that a substantial amount of the execution time goes into the abstract operations (e.g. about 98% for the **freeness** domain coupled to GAIA). So, the difference between GAIA and PLAI is mainly due to the abstract operations and it turns out that for this kind of applications the performance gap between Prolog and C is bigger than a factor 5 – 10 which was put forward for some small programs using similar data structures in [17, 21]. In our applications, the implementations of the abstract domains use quite different data structures in C than in Prolog. For the **freeness** domain – and to a lesser degree also for the mode domain – the abstract operations mainly manipulate the sets of sets of variables. They have a much more efficient implementation in C than in Prolog. A set of variables is represented in GAIA by a bit representation (1 memory cell represents a set of at most 32 variables), while in PLAI an ordered list is used (a simulation of the bit representation cannot be used because the variables in PLAI are represented internally by free variables). For example for a set of 5 elements, 10 times more memory cells are used in Prolog than in C. The abstract operations can be implemented more efficiently for the bit representation than for the ordered lists. The data structures in C can be updated destructively, while in Prolog parts of them have to be copied. Moreover, a program that uses more memory is likely to use more time due to non-locality.

Recently, Tan and Lin [20] have investigated the alternative of compiling abstract interpretation into the framework of the WAM. A prototype analyser based on this idea (written in C) is compared with the analyser in Aquarius [21] (written in Prolog) and gives a performance improvement of a factor of over 150 in the average. Unfortunately, both analysers were coupled to different abstract domains. If the same domain is used, their conservative estimate is a speedup of over 100 for relatively small programs. For mode we obtain a factor 60 as an average for a representative set of programs. However, this is obtained by a meta-interpreting approach for which [20] claims that the compilation into WAM is a promising alternative. Our results seem to contradict their conclusion in the sense that the performance gap between Prolog and C could be at least as significant as the difference between an interpreter-based and a compiler-based approach for abstract interpretation.

5.3   Important Issues for Abstract Interpretation Applications

When choosing a tool to develop an abstract interpretation system, the user should be aware of the following important points:

1. The approach towards normalisation has an effect on the abstract domain. If the abstract interpretation tool imposes normalisation, one should take this into account during the design of the abstract domain, because its expressive power must be strong enough to obtain the desired precision. If no normalisation is required, the user can choose the degree of normalisation for the application at hand.

   The abstract interpretation tool should leave enough freedom to the user w.r.t. normalisation: e.g. PLAI does not require any normalisation and in the version of GAIA we adapted the degree of normalisation is left to the user.

2. The internal representation of the variables affects the choice of the data structure for the abstract substitutions, in particular the data structure to represent a set of variables.

3. The inherent size of the abstract substitutions might interact with the systems approach towards fixpoint optimisations: the behaviour of the Prefix version with respect to the Original version of GAIA is quite different in the case of the freeness domain than in case of the mode domain.
   Moreover, the approach towards fixpoint optimisations affects the choice of the data structure for the abstract substitutions. Both abstract interpretation tools store extra information containing abstract substitutions. This involves storing/copying of the abstract substitutions into global data structures. Note that in Prolog this is typically done by using the record data base or using dynamic predicates that are asserted and retracted. Now, putting more (redundant) information in the data structure for the abstract substitutions (i.e. using a smart representation that trades space for time) speeds up the abstract operations, but might slow down the fixpoint optimisations due to their size. This phenomenon was observed during our experiments where the occurrence of a pointer in DS1 complicated the copying operation in GAIA and made the Prefix version slower than the Original one.

   The user should be careful when chosing a data structure for the abstract substitutions because the size and the internal organisation (cfr. internal pointers) may interact with the storing/copying of the information done by the fixpoint optimisations.

4. The user should have the option to tune the output of the system towards his needs, e.g. the desired number of versions and the way the results are presented to the user. The flexibility of both systems can be improved.

5. Each programming paradigm has its specific characteristics which are advantageous at different stages of the development of an abstract interpretation system, namely the prototyping phase and the production phase.

6. Neither of the systems offers extra facilities to debug the application under development. One has to rely on the debugging facilities for the underlying language.

6   Conclusions

The paper reports on our experiments of coupling two different abstract domains – modes and freeness – with GAIA and PLAI. An important motivation is the need of turning abstract interpretation into a practical compilation tool. GAIA (written in C) and PLAI (written in Prolog) are both fine tuned implementations of efficient abstract interpretation algorithms. Modes [13] is an instance of a well known application in the context of LP, whereas freeness [12] has recently been proposed in the context of CLP. The two domains are of a different complexity: the intrinsic size complexity of freeness is in the worst case exponential; that of modes polynomial. Freeness can be seen as a representative example of abstractions analysing complex dependencies between program variables.

The paper contains an overview of design decisions in GAIA and PLAI which our experiments showed to be relevant for developers of applications. They are based on different design decisions concerning the interface between the fixpoint algorithm and the abstract domain (normalisation and representation of variables) and concerning the fixpoint algorithm (avoiding redundant computation and annotating programs). Our experiments showed that the performance of the abstract interpretation systems is affected by the degree of normalisation and by the choice of the data structures. An inappropriate choice of the latter can destroy the effect of optimisations that aim at reducing the number of abstract operations, as shown by the experiments on coupling freeness with GAIA. Our experiments illustrate the impact of the complexity of the abstractions on the feasibility of integrating them – and also comparable abstractions – in practical compilation tools. As the performance for freeness is unacceptable for larger programs, the reduction of its size as proposed in [10] is essential to make it practical. Another important observation is that for our experiments most of the execution time is spent on the abstract operations. Therefore, the implementation of the abstract domain turns out to be crucial. In this context, the comparison between systems developed with GAIA and with PLAI boils down to a comparison between C and Prolog. PLAI has the advantage of supporting rapid prototyping which is interesting while experimenting with the abstract domain. Quite complex domains such as freeness can be run only on example programs. GAIA allows to make implementations of the abstract domains that obtain better performance and consume less memory. In production systems these factors are important to use the system for all kinds of programs. Tan and Lin [20] conclude that a compiler-based approach to abstract interpretation could be a factor 100 better than an interpreter-based one. This difference seems to be due to writing the compiler-based one in C and the interpreter-based one in Prolog, as our experiments reveal the impact of the performance difference between C and Prolog. Their conclusions hold for an abstract domain which extends the mode domain with type information. Recently, the paper [3] describes a bottom up Prolog implementation for groundness analysis by means of the domain Prop of propositional formulae, which is quite different from the above domains. For this particular domain, the efficiency of [3] is comparable with the C implementations described in [6, 16].

In order to implement an application with GAIA and PLAI, one has to know how the programs are represented internally in the systems. The main development effort has to be put in the abstract operations. For example, for the freeness domain the difference in development time (including experiments with different data structures) was about a factor 3.

Acknowledgement

We are indebted to Maria Garcia de la Banda and Francisco Bueno for making PLAI available and for providing us with the necessary information about the implementation details of PLAI, to Vincent Englebert for coupling the mode domain with PLAI and to Pascal Van Hentenryck and Maurice Bruynooghe for the many valuable comments on the draft versions of this paper.

References

1. R. Bayer. Symmetric binary B-trees : Data structure and maintenance. *Acta Informatica*, 1:290–306, 1972.
2. M. Bruynooghe. A practical framework for the abstract interpretation of logic programs. *Journal of Logic Programming*, 10(2):91–124, Feb. 1991.
3. M. Codish and B. Demoen. Analysing Logic Programs Using "Prop"-ositional Logic Programs and a Magic Wand. In D. Miller, editor, *Proceedings of the 1993 International Logic Programming Symposium*, pages 114–129, Vancouver, October 1993. MIT Press.
4. J. Cohen. Constraint logic programming languages. *Communications of the ACM*, 30(7):52–68, 1990.
5. A. Colmerauer. An introduction to PROLOGIII. *Communications of the ACM*, 30(7):69–96, 1990.
6. M.-M. Corsini, K. Musumbu, A. Rauzy, and B. Le Charlier. Efficient Bottom-up Abstract Interpretation of Prolog by means of Constraint Solving over Symbolic Finite Domains. In M. Bruynooghe and J. Penjam, editors, *Programming Language Implementation and Logic Programming*, Lecture Notes in Computer Science 714, pages 75–91, Tallinn, Estonia, 1993. Springer Verlag.
7. P. Cousot and R. Cousot. Abstract interpretation: A unified lattice model for static analysis of programs by construction or approximation of fixpoints. In *Proceedings of the Fourth ACM Symposium on Principles of Programming Languages*, pages 238–252, Los Angeles, 1977.
8. P. Cousot and R. Cousot. Abstract interpretation and application to logic programs. *The Journal of Logic Programming*, 13(2 and 3):103–179, 1992.
9. M. G. de la Banda and M. Hermenegildo. A Practical Approach to the Global Analysis of CLP Programs. In D. Miller, editor, *Proceedings of the 1993 International Logic Programming Symposium*, pages 437–455. MIT Press, October 1993.
10. V. Dumortier and G. Janssens. Towards a Practical Full Mode Inference System for CLP(H,N). Technical Report CW185, Department of Computer Science, Katholieke Universiteit Leuven, Dec. 1993.
11. V. Dumortier, G. Janssens, and M. Bruynooghe. Detection of Free Variables in the Presence of Numeric Constraints. In *Proceedings of JICSLP'92 Post-conference workshop on CLP*, pages 105–118, 1992.

12. V. Dumortier, G. Janssens, M. Bruynooghe, and M. Codish. Freeness Analysis in the Presence of Numerical Constraints. In D. S. Warren, editor, *Proceedings of the Tenth International Conference on Logic Programming*, pages 100–115. MIT Press, June 1993.

13. V. Englebert, B. Le Charlier, D. Roland, and P. Van Hentenryck. Generic Abstract Interpretation Algorithms for Prolog : Two Optimization Techniques and Their Experimental Evaluation. In M. Bruynooghe and M. Wirsing, editors, *Proceedings of the 4th International Symposium on Programming Language Implementation and Logic Programming (PLILP 92)*, pages 311–325, Leuven, 1992. LNCS, Springer Verlag. Also in *Software Practice and Experience, Volume 23 No. 4 pp. 419–460, 1993*.

14. B. Le Charlier, K. Musumbu, and P. Van Hentenryck. A generic abstract interpretation algorithm and its complexity analysis (extended abstract). In K. Furukawa, editor, *Proceedings of the Eighth International Conference on Logic Programming*, pages 64–78, Paris, 1991. MIT Press, Cambridge.

15. B. Le Charlier and P. Van Hentenryck. Reexecution in abstract interpretation of prolog (extended abstract). In K. Apt, editor, *Proceedings of the Joint International Conference and Symposium on Logic Programming*, pages 750–764, Washington, 1992. MIT Press, Cambridge.

16. B. Le Charlier and P. Van Hentenryck. Groundness Analysis for Prolog: Implementation and Evaluation of the Domain Prop. In D. Schmidt, editor, *ACM SIGPLAN Symposium on Partial Evaluation and Semantics-Based Program Manipulation, PEPMA'93*, pages 99–110, Copenhagen,Denmark, 1993. ACM Press.

17. A. Mariën, G. Janssens, A. Mulkers, and M. Bruynooghe. The impact of abstract interpretation: An experiment in code generation. In G. Levi and M. Martelli, editors, *Proceedings of the Sixth International Conference on Logic Programming*, pages 33–47, Lisbon, 1989. MIT Press, Cambridge.

18. K. Muthukumar and M. Hermenegildo. Deriving A Fixpoint Computation Algorithm for Top-Down Abstract Interpretation of Logic Programs. Technical Report ACT-DC-153-90, Microelectronics and Computer Technology Corporation (MCC), Austin, TX 78759, Apr. 1990.

19. K. Muthukumar and M. Hermenegildo. Compile-time Derivation of Variable Dependency Using Abstract Interpretation. *Journal of Logic Programming*, 13(2&3):315–347, July 1992.

20. J. Tan and I. Lin. Compiling Dataflow Analysis of Logic Programs. In *ACM SIGPLAN'92 PLDI*, pages 106–115, 1992.

21. P. Van Roy and A. M. Despain. High-Performance logic programming with the Aquarius Prolog compiler. *IEEE Computer*, pages 54–67, Jan. 1992.

A Suite of Analysis Tools Based on a General Purpose Abstract Interpreter

Thomas Cheatham, Haiming Gao, Dan Stefanescu

[1] Harvard University***
[2] Software Options, Inc.
Cambridge, Mass. 02138

1 Introduction

This paper reports on one aspect of an ongoing project that is developing and experimenting with new compiling technology. The overall system is called the *Kernel Based Compiler System*, reflecting the fact that the representation of a program used in much of the processing is that of *kernel terms*, essentially the Lambda Calculus augmented with constants.

While the compiling technology is applicable to a wide spectrum of programming languages as well as a wide spectrum of target machine architectures, we expect High Performance FORTRAN (HPF) and its extensions to be programming languages of particular concern because of their anticipated importance to the High Performance Computing Community.

The compiler being developed is "unbundled" in the sense that it consists of several components, $C_1, \cdots, C_N$, and compilation consists of applying component C_1 to program text and applying C_j, for $j = 2, \cdots, N$ to the result computed by component C_{j-1}.

One of the issues that we are using the compiler system to study is the suitability of various new linguistic constructs for particular application areas and techniques for the efficient realization of these constructs on a variety of High Performance Computers. Thus, we want it to be as straightforward as possible to extend each C_j, to deal with the new constructs. Ideally, we want each component to have a firm mathematical basis so that, for example, we can prove appropriate correctness results.

No compiler for a non-trivial language or target is ever really *simple* in one sense because it is inevitably a large program. However, we have strived to make each component, C_j, simple in the sense that it offers general purpose mechanisms that can be specialized to a particular tasks, so that we can separate the concerns regarding the mechanisms and those regarding the particular specializations in order to achieve simplicity.

This paper is concerned with a suite of *Analysis* components of the system that annotate a program with static estimates of certain aspects of the behavior

*** Work supported by ARPA Contract Nr. F19628-92-C-0113. Authors current address: Aiken Computation Laboratory, Harvard University, 33 Oxford St, Cambrige, MA 02138. E-mail: cheatham, gao, dan@das.harvard.edu

of that program. The point of this annotation is to prepare for annotation-enabled transformations that produce a more efficient program. Our approach is to develop a general purpose *Abstract Interpreter* that does the control flow analysis that is required by all analysis tasks and constructs a data structure called the *behavior graph* that relates the behaviors of various terms – herein called the *flows* of those terms — in such a way that doing a wide variety of analysis tasks is quite straightforwardand inexpensive.

In the next section we discuss some related work. We then define the kernel terms that are used and present an overview of the abstract interpreter that is followed by several examples of particular analysis tasks. Following this, we discuss the details of the abstract interpreter and close with a discussion of the current status of the project, and some future plans.

2 Related Work

Our method falls into the category of data-flow analyses based on abstract interpretations (see [4]). A seminal work by Cousot in this area is [3] which sets a rigorous framework for such analyses for the case of flowchart languages. It is not straightforward to extend Cousot's work to languages that permit higher order functions where there is no explicit "flowchart" available, that is, to situations where one aspect of the abstract interpretation is to determine the control flow. Any solution to this problem has to deal with the issue of abstracting functions. Basically, there are two approaches in this area.

A function can be abstracted denotationally, i.e. its concrete graph has to be transformed into an abstract graph. In general, this approach may encounter problems due to the size of the abstract graph even if one considers only the program imposed inputs as in [4].

The other option is to use a syntactic based approximation which computes only an approximation of the abstract graph of a function, but it does it using some fixed resources. Typically, (see [11], [9], [6] and [5]) one uses resources proportional with the number of different entities in the program.

A more elaborate solution to this problem was given by Shivers (see [7] and [8]) who introduced a technique for computing approximations to the control-flow graph at compile time. His method defines abstract semantic functions for CPS (continuation passing style) Scheme which are then used to implement an instrumented interpreter which returns the result of the required analysis. Two analyses (0CFA and 1CFA) are used to illustrate the approach.

The function abstraction methodology is clarified and generalized in [10] which presents a theory for general flow analysis which approximates values (both basic and functional) computed within a functional program according to a syntactic notion of equivalence. The analysis is presented in an equational setting in the style of Cousots' original paper (see [3]).

While in the spirit of [10], the method presented in this paper uses a different, but equivalent, system of constraints chosen to expose optimization opportunities which avoid the unnecessary fixpoint iterations inherent in Shivers approach and therefore its large running costs ([12]).

Finally, our work is similar to that reported in [13]. We differ by dealing with higher order functions and employing a call context mechanism that permits a finer grained analysis of behavioral differences that arise at different call sites.

3 Kernel Terms

The kernel terms that we consider are, essentially, terms in the Lambda Calculus that is augmented with constants (both data and function constants).

We assume there are disjoint sets $\mathcal{C}$, $\mathcal{N}$, and $\mathcal{F}$, where $\mathcal{C}$ is a set of data constants (like integers and reals), $\mathcal{N}$ is a set of parameter names, and $\mathcal{F}$ is a set of function constants, or *primitive functions*, like those for arithmetic operations on integers and reals or those for communicating data between different processors.

A kernel term, t, is:

- $t \sim c$ — a constant, $c \in \mathcal{C}$, or
- $t \sim p$ — a primitive, $p \in \mathcal{F}$, or
- $t \sim x$ — a parameter, $x \in \mathcal{N}$, or
- $t \sim \lambda x_1 \cdots x_k.B$ — an abstraction, where $k \geq 0$, the x_j are distinct parameter names, $x_j \in \mathcal{N}$, for $j = 1, \cdots, k$, and B is a term, or
- $t \sim {}_i(t_1 \cdots t_p)$ — an application, where i is a label identifying that application, $p \geq 1$, and the t_j are terms, for $j = 1, \cdots, p$.

We assume that the parameters of each abstraction are distinct, that the parameters of distinct abstractions are distinct, and that the labels of distinct applications are distinct. We also assume that the set $\mathcal{F}$ contains the primitive *cond* that takes three arguments — a predicate and two values — and returns the first value if the predicate is true and the second if it is false.

While the use of kernel terms as an "intermediate language" is not unusual in compilers for languages like ML and other functional languages, it may seem somewhat surprising when considering as a major application a language such as FORTRAN. The reason for choosing kernel terms is fourfold. First they provide the functionality necessary for any non-trivial programming language such as binding names and applying functions. The second reason is that they are sufficient in the sense that given an appropriate set of primitives, any programming language construct can be modeled as kernel terms. Thirdly, they are very simple — there are only five basic constructs — and this simplicity induces a corresponding simplicity in many of the compiler components and makes the task of proving various properties of these components tractable. Finally, the ability to deal with higher order functions makes the compiler applicable to all programming languages and permits higher order extensions to HPF to be considered.

With each kernel term, t, we associate Φ_t, the *flow* of t, an estimate of some aspect of the behavior of t. If t is an application, $t \sim {}_i(t_1 \cdots t_p)$, we use ϕ_i

as shorthand for $\Phi_{i(t_1 \cdots t_p)}$ and that is the reason for introducing labels for applications. The purpose of the abstract interpreter is to determine, for each term t, its flow, Φ_t.

4 An Overview of the Abstract Interpreter

An abstract interpreter seeks to determine certain aspects of the behavior of the terms of a program. One aspect of the behavior that is always of interest is the *control flow* of the program, that is, the set of functions that can be called from the operator position of each application. We follow [8] and define **nCFA** analysis to produce estimates of the inputs to and results of each function that depend on the call site and up to $\max(n-1, 0)$ previous call sites. In particular **0CFA** is the analysis determining a single estimate of the inputs to and results of each function independent of its call sites.

In this paper we actually use a slight variant of **0CFA** that might be denoted **0+1CFA** which combines **0CFA** estimates for λ-expressions with **1CFA** estimates for primitive functions.

Some of the analysis tasks, other than control flow analysis, that might be of interest are the following:

- What is the *type* of the value associated with each term, so that when the type can be determined statically we can eliminate certain run-time checks and/or dispatches.
- Which parameters are *useless*, in the sense that no result depends upon them, so that they can be removed from the program.
- What are the sets of *basic induction parameters*, that is, the sets $\pi_j = \{x_{j1}, \cdots, x_{jn_j}\}$, for $j = 1, \cdots, k$, such that x_{ji} is bound only to a constant or to x_{jq} plus or minus a constant for one or more q, $1 \leq q \leq n_j$, that may permit certain strength reduction transformations, like replacing array subscript computations with pointer incrementing operations.
- Which parameters of a function are *strict* and which are *lazy*, where a parameter that is strict is always used and one that is lazy may or may not be used, and thus its computation might be deferred until it is determined that it is actually used.

For each analysis task, we require an appropriate set of *abstract values* to describe the behaviors of terms for that analysis task. For control flow analysis, the appropriate set of abstract values is the set of all subsets of the primitives and abstractions that occur in a program term. For type analysis, it is the set of all subsets of the types of the terms in a program. We discuss several other sets when we introduce the examples later.

Whatever set of abstract values is appropriate for some analysis task, they form a lattice, $\mathcal{L}$. If we have two estimates, say φ_1 and φ_2, of the flow of some term, Φ_t, then the least upper bound, $\varphi_1 \sqcup \varphi_2$, where $\sqcup$ is the join defined on the lattice $\mathcal{L}$, is also an estimate of Φ_t. We sometimes denote "φ_1 is an estimate of Φ_t" by $\Phi_t \geq \varphi_1$, treating $\geq$ as the partial order operator in the lattice $\mathcal{L}$.

One novel aspect of our treatment of the various lattices appropriate for various analyses is that we do not represent the lattice elements directly, instead introducing a data structure that we call the *behavior graph*. The nodes of a behavior graph, $\mathcal{G}$, are flows of program terms and *surrogates* for various abstract values. The (directed) arcs of the behavior graph define the relationships between the flows of terms and the surrogates for abstract values. Given some particular analysis task, finding the abstract values that comprise the estimate of the behavior of some term, t, that is, Φ_t, with respect to that analysis task is done by *tracing* all non-cyclic paths in $\mathcal{G}$ from the node for Φ_t, mapping from nodes that represent surrogates to the particular abstract value appropriate for the analysis task at hand. We presently explore several examples.

Our method of abstract interpretation of some program term, p, involves two phases:

Phase I: Construct the *behavior graph* for p, where the nodes of the behavior graph are flows of program terms and *surrogates* for abstract values and the arcs of the behavior graph define the relationships between the flows of terms and the surrogates for abstract values. Phase I is independent of the particular analysis task(s) to be considered.

Phase II: Given the behavior graph, the behavior of some term with respect to some particular analysis task is determined by *tracing* the behavior graph in a way that depends on the analysis task and interpreting the surrogates in a fashion that also depends on that task.

We now consider several examples (for more examples see [1]).

5 Some Examples of Abstract Interpretation For Various Analysis Tasks

We here consider several examples of abstract interpretation for various analysis tasks.

5.1 Type Annotation

Consider the program (where the term p is ignored):

$$P_1 = {}_1(\lambda f._2(f\ 1)\ _3(cond\ p\ \lambda x._4(+\ x\ 1)\ \lambda y._5(*\ y\ 2)))$$

Here, P_1 binds f to one of two abstractions and then applies f to 1.

The first phase of abstract interpretation results in the behavior graph shown in Figure 1.

Some comments:

- The interpretation of the node $\beta(\Phi_f)$ is the set of flows of the bodies of those abstractions that f can be bound to. A β node has no arcs emanating and is dealt with in a manner discussed below.

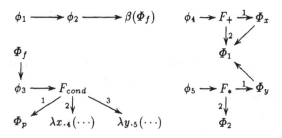

Fig. 1. Behavior Graph for P_1

- The interpretation of the fragment $\phi_1 \to \phi_2 \to \beta(\Phi_f)$ is that the flow of application $_1(\cdots)$ is at least the flow of application $_2(\cdots)$ and that is at least the flow of the body of whatever abstractions f can be bound to.
- The interpretation of the fragment $\Phi_x \to \Phi_1$ is that the flow Φ_x is at least Φ_1 and arises from the fact that x is a parameter of one of the abstractions bound to f and is thus bound to the constant 1.
- The interpretation of the fragment
$$\phi_4 \to F_+ \overset{1}{\to} \Phi_x$$
$$\downarrow 2$$
$$\Phi_1$$
is that the flow of $_4(\cdots)$

is at least the surrogate, $F_+(\Phi_x, \Phi_1)$, that represents the flow resulting from applying the primitive $+$ to x and 1. Note that this surrogate is represented in the behavior graph using three nodes with ordered arcs (as indicated by the numbers on the arcs) from the node for F_+ to the flows of the two arguments that $+$ is applied to.

Given the above behavior graph, consider the particular task of determining the types of the several terms of P_1. The abstract values appropriate for this task might be thought of as comprising the very simple lattice:

$$\{int, bool\} = \top$$
$$\{int\} \qquad \{bool\}$$
$$\{\} = \bot$$

Here, int and $bool$ are intended to suggest the types of integer and boolean values.

In order to do the analysis, we have to specify how to treat each of the surrogates, Φ_1, $F_+(\Phi_x, \Phi_1)$, and so on for this analysis task. For each primitive, p, we assume that there is a function F_p^{type} that, applied to the arguments of the surrogate node F_p, returns the type of that node. Additionally, we assume that for each constant surrogate, Φ_c, there is a map, $V^{type}(\Phi_c)$ that provides the type of that constant.

For this application, we assume that F_+^{type} and F_*^{type} return int (independent of their arguments) and that the map V^{type} for Φ_c returns int for c an integer. We further assume that $F_{cond}^{type}(\Phi_{N_1}, \Phi_{N_2}, \Phi_{N_3}) = \Phi_{N_2} \cup \Phi_{N_3}$.

We define the iterator $Trace^{type}(\varphi)$ that traces all non-cyclic paths from some node, φ, and does the following:

- For each F_p node with k (ordered) argument arcs to nodes $\varphi_1, \cdots, \varphi_k$ it returns $F_p^{type}(\varphi_1, \cdots, \varphi_k)$, as discussed above.
- For Φ_c it returns $V^{type}(\Phi_c)$.
- For a $\lambda x_1 \cdots x_k.B$ node it returns

$$\Phi_{x_1} \times \cdots \times \Phi_{x_k} \rightarrow \Phi_B$$

- For $\beta(\varphi)$ it returns the flows of the bodies of all abstractions in the flow φ.

We then use $Trace^{type}$ on the nodes of the value graph to find:

$$\phi_1 = \phi_2 = \beta(\Phi_f) = \phi_4 = \phi_5 = \Phi_x = \Phi_y = int$$

$$\Phi_f = \phi_3 = int \rightarrow int$$

5.2 Basic Induction Parameter Detection

The sets of *basic induction parameters* are the sets $\pi_j = \{x_{j1}, \cdots, x_{jn_j}\}$, for $j = 1, \cdots, k$, such that x_{ji}, for $i = 1, \cdots, n_j$, is bound only to a constant or to x_{jq} plus or minus a constant for one or more q, $1 \leq q \leq n_j$.

Consider the following example:

$$\boxed{P_2 = {}_1(f\ 0)}$$

where f and g are bound(via some mechanism akin to LETREC), respectively, to the following lambdas:

$$\lambda n.{}_2(cond\ p\ {}_3(f\ {}_4(g\ n))\ {}_5(\lambda m.{}_6(f\ {}_7(+\ m\ 2))\ {}_8(+\ n\ 3)))$$

$$\lambda x.{}_9(+\ x\ 1))$$

and p is ignored.

Here f is a function of n that either calls itself with the result of applying g to n or introduces m bound to $n + 3$ and calls itself with $m + 2$. The function g simply adds one to its argument. The behavior graph for P_2 is shown in Figure 2.

The first question that must be addressed is that of the appropriate set of abstract values to employ for this analysis task. Since we are interested only in parameters that are bound to integers or other parameters plus or minus integers, a natural lattice might be $\perp \cup \top \cup 2^{\{(\Phi_x, \Phi_c)\}} \cup 2^{\{\Phi_c\}}$, where Φ_x ranges over all parameter flows and Φ_c ranges over all the flows of integer constants that occur in P_2. Here, $\langle \Phi_x, \Phi_c \rangle$ is interpreted to mean the parameter x plus the constant c and Φ_c is interpreted to mean the constant c.

Now consider the following interpretation for F_+^{biv}, that is, F_+ for the task of basic induction variable detection. If F_+^{biv} has as arguments the flow of a parameter, say Φ_x, and the flow of an integer constant, say Φ_c, its flow is $\langle \Phi_x, \Phi_c \rangle$,

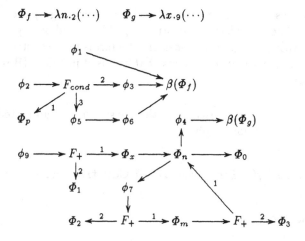

Fig. 2. Behavior Graph for P_2

and otherwise its flow is $\top$, and similarly for other primitives that can increment an argument.

The interpretation of F_{cond}^{biv} is that it returns the union of its second and third arguments, and for the remaining primitives, p, F_p^{biv} returns $\top$.

The interpretation of $V^{biv}(\Phi_c)$ is Φ_c for integers and $\top$ for anything else. Let $Trace^{biv}$ be an iterator that returns the result of tracing some node and returning all the abstract values it encounters, evaluating F_p^{biv} on its arguments if F_p nodes are encountered and V_C^{biv} if constants are encountered. Then for each parameter flow, Φ_x, we do the following:

1. Let Φ_x^{biv} be $\{\}$, the empty set.
2. For each φ in $Trace^{biv}(\Phi_x)$, if $\varphi = \top$ then set $\Phi_x^{biv} = \top$ and otherwise set $\Phi_x^{biv} = \Phi_x^{biv} \cup \{\varphi\}$.

For the above example we obtain:

$$\Phi_n^{biv} = \{\langle \Phi_x, \Phi_1\rangle, \Phi_0, \langle \Phi_m, \Phi_2\rangle\}$$

$$\Phi_x^{biv} = \{\langle \Phi_x, \Phi_1\rangle, \Phi_0, \langle \Phi_m, \Phi_2\rangle\}$$
$$\Phi_m^{biv} = \{\langle \Phi_n, \Phi_3\rangle\}$$

Thus, n, x, and m constitute a set of basic induction variables.

6 Phase I of Abstract Interpretation — Establishing the Behavior Graph

The construction of the behavior graph for some program term takes place in two phases:

Phase IA: Let p be some program term and $\mathcal{G}$ the behavior graph for p, initially the empty graph. The first phase in constructing $\mathcal{G}$ is carried out by the function γ that, starting with p, recursively considers the terms in p, constructing pieces of $\mathcal{G}$ and determining a set of constraints that are used in Phase IB to complete the behavior graph.

Phase IB: In this phase, we "discharge" the constraints accumulated in Phase IA to complete the behavior graph.

6.1 The Function $\gamma(t)$ for Phase IA of Constructing the Behavior Graph $\mathcal{G}$

$\gamma(t)$ for term t is as follows:

$\boxed{t = c}$ Install Φ_c in $\mathcal{G}$

$\boxed{t = \lambda x_1 \cdots x_k.B}$ Call $\gamma(x_1), \cdots, \gamma(x_k), \gamma(B)$ and install $\lambda x_1 \cdots x_k.B$ in $\mathcal{G}$

$\boxed{t = x}$ Install Φ_x in $\mathcal{G}$

$\boxed{t = {}_i(M\ N_1 \cdots N_k)}$ Call $\gamma(M), \gamma(N_1), \cdots, \gamma(N_k)$, and dispatch on M as follows:

$\qquad \boxed{M = \lambda x_1 \cdots x_k.B\text{:}}$ Install in $\mathcal{G}$:

$$\Phi_{x_j} \longrightarrow \Phi_{N_j}, \text{ for } j = 1, \cdots, k \text{ and}$$

$$\phi_i \longrightarrow \Phi_B$$

$\qquad \boxed{M = p, p \in \mathcal{F}\text{:}}$ Install in $\mathcal{G}$:

$$\phi_i \longrightarrow F_p \xrightarrow{1} \Phi_{N_1}$$
$$\downarrow k$$
$$\Phi_{N_k}$$

$\qquad \boxed{M = \phi_j \text{ or } M = \Phi_f\text{:}}$ Call

$$\textit{Unknown-operator}(i, \Phi_M, \langle \Phi_{N_1}, \cdots \Phi_{N_k} \rangle)$$

The non-trivial case for γ is that for dealing with an operator that is an application or a parameter and this is the case that establishes the constraints alluded to above. Consider the application term $t \sim {}_i(f\ t_1 \cdots t_k)$, where f is a parameter and the t_j are arbitrary terms. When we know what set of abstractions f can be bound to we can, for the j-th parameter, Φ_{y_j} of each of these abstractions, establish the arc $\Phi_{y_j} \longrightarrow \Phi_{N_j}$. However, as we traverse the program term using γ, we may encounter an application of f before we have determined the set of all the abstractions and primitives that f can be bound to and thus we need some sort of mechanism to defer construction of parts of the behavior graph until these sets can be determined. Such a mechanism is discussed in the next section.

6.2 α Sets, α Constraints, and β Flows

As noted above, we require some sort of mechanism to defer dealing with the flows of operators that are not explicit abstractions or primitives until such time as we can determine which abstractions might be contained in those flows. For this purpose, we introduce the set $\alpha_j(\Phi_M)$ that is a set of parameter flows that will, ultimately, contain the flow of the j-th explicit parameter of each abstraction that can be in the operator flow, Φ_M.

Additionally, we introduce the constraints $\alpha_j(\Phi_M) \succeq \varphi$ that specify, for each parameter flow, $\Phi_x \in \alpha_j(\Phi_M)$, that the fragment $\Phi_x \rightarrow \varphi$ belongs in $\mathcal{G}$. Thus, α constraints *package* fragments of $\mathcal{G}$ that have yet to be installed and will be installed when we determine the contents of the corresponding α sets.

In addition to the α sets and α constraints on flows, we introduce the β flows, where, if Φ_M is the flow of an operator, $\beta(\Phi_M)$ denotes the set of all the flows of the bodies of the abstractions that can be in Φ_M.

Now we can describe the effects of calling

$$Unknown\text{-}operator(i, \Phi_M, \langle \Phi_{N_1}, \cdots \Phi_{N_k} \rangle)$$

a call which is made when the flow variable Φ_M is in the operator position of application i and the flows of the arguments to Φ_M are $\Phi_{N_1}, \cdots, \Phi_{N_k}$. The result of such a call is to establish α constraints for Φ_M and to establish the flow ϕ_i as at least the β flow of Φ_M, that is, we establish the constraint $\alpha_j(\Phi_M) \succeq \Phi_{N_j}$ for $j = 1, \cdots, k$ and add the arc $\phi_i \longrightarrow \beta(\Phi_M)$ to $\mathcal{G}$.

7 Phase IB – Completing the Behavior Graph

When an explicit abstraction appears in the operator position of an application, the inequalities on the flows of its parameters are established directly by γ. However, when a flow variable (a parameter flow or application flow) appears in the operator position, constraints on the flows of its parameters are established indirectly via the constraints $\alpha_j(\Phi_M) \succeq \Phi_{N_j}$ that "package" what will eventually lead to arcs in the behavior graph, effectively deferring installing them until the members of the $\alpha_j(\Phi_M)$ sets are known. These members are discovered whenever there is some flow variable, Φ_M, that can be the flow of an operator and there is a abstraction, $\lambda x_1 \cdots x_k.B$ in the estimate of Φ_M, which implies that the j-th explicit parameter of that abstraction, Φ_{x_j}, is in $\alpha_j(\Phi_M)$, for $j = 1, \cdots, k$. The constraints on some parameter flow, Φ_y, are *revealed* when we realize that Φ_y is a member of some α_j set, $\Phi_y \in \alpha_j(\Phi_M)$, and thus for each constraint $\alpha_j(\Phi_M) \succeq \Phi_{N_j}$, we "unpackage" that $\succeq$ constraint by adding $\Phi_y \rightarrow \Phi_{N_j}$ to $\mathcal{G}$.

An algorithm for revealing constraints and completing the behavior graph $\mathcal{G}$ is:

1. For each flow Φ_M that has α constraints and each φ in $Trace^{c/a}(\Phi_M)$, if $\varphi = \lambda y_1 \cdots y_k.B$ then add Φ_{y_j} to the set $\alpha_j(\Phi_M)$, for $j = 1, \cdots, k$.

2. For each j, Φ_M, Φ_y, and φ such that $\Phi_y \in \alpha_j(\Phi_M)$ and $\alpha_j(\Phi_M) \succeq \varphi$, install $\Phi_y \rightarrow \varphi$ in $\mathcal{G}$ to *unpackage* a constraint.

3. If step 2 resulted in an increase in the estimate of any parameter flow, return to step 1 and otherwise terminate.

The iterator $Trace^{cfa}(\Phi_M)$ has the job of delivering all the abstractions in the (current) estimate of Φ_M and is discussed in the following section.

7.1 The $Trace^{cfa}$ Iterator

The iterator, $Trace^{cfa}(\Phi_M)$, has the task of delivering all the abstractions in the current estimate of some flow, Φ_M, that is the flow of an operator of some application that has α constraints. There are a couple of issues that must be dealt with. First, the behavior graph can have cycles that arise when $\Phi_x \geq \Phi_y$ and $\Phi_y \geq \Phi_x$ for two parameter flows, Φ_x and Φ_y, or when there are mutually recursive functions. The second issue is that of efficiency — we would like the cost of constructing the graph to be peoportional to the number of edges it contains. The "environment" global parameter, ν, is used to deal with breaking cycles in the behavior graph and is initially the empty environment, ϵ. In general, ν is a stack of frames where a frame is a set of flows that are being traced and it permits the detection of cycles.

The definition of $Trace^{cfa}(\Phi_M)$ is to initialize $\nu = \epsilon$ and then for each node φ on each path from Φ_M, to dispatch per case as follows:

$\varphi \sim \lambda x_1, \cdots, x_k.B$	$Deliver(\lambda x_1, \cdots, x_k.B)$

| $\varphi \sim \Phi_x$ **for a parameter,** x | Proceed as follows: |

1. If $\Phi_x \in Top(\nu)$, where $Top(\nu)$ is the topmost frame in ν then this parameter flow has already been traced and nothing is done.
2. Otherwise, add Φ_x to $Top(\nu)$ and trace the parameter flow.

| $\varphi \sim F_{cond}(\Phi_{N_1}, \Phi_{N_2}, \Phi_{N_3})$ | Proceed as follows: |

1. For each φ in $Trace^{cfa}(\Phi_{N_2})$, $Deliver(\varphi)$.
2. For each φ in $Trace^{cfa}(\Phi_{N_3})$, $Deliver(\varphi)$.
3. Continue the outer iteration.

| $\varphi = \beta(\varphi')$ | Proceed as follows: |

1. If $\beta(\varphi') \in \nu$, then this node has already been traced and we simply continue the iteration.
2. Otherwise, proceed as follows:
   (a) Push a new frame containing $\beta(\varphi')$ to ν.
   (b) For each φ in $Trace^{cfa}(\varphi')$ such that $\varphi = \lambda x_1 \cdots x_k.B$, deliver $Trace^{cfa}(B)$.
   (c) Pop ν and continue the outer iteration.

| $Otherwise$ | Continue the iteration. |

Here, "$Deliver(\varphi)$" means that φ is one of the values delivered by the iterator. Some comments:

1. If an abstraction is encountered, it is delivered.
2. If an application of the primitive *cond* is encountered, we recursively call $Trace^{cfa}$ on its second and third arguments and then continue the original iteration. This is, of course, paradigmatic, and each other primitive that might return an abstraction must also be traced in the appropriate fashion.
3. The node $\varphi = \beta(\varphi')$ has no arcs emanating from it and denotes the set of bodies of all the abstractions that are in the estimate of φ'.
4. If the node encountered is anything else (like a surrogate for a constant other than an abstraction, an application, and so on), we deliver nothing and continue following the path we are on.

Efficiency Considerations The issue of the efficiency of $Trace^{cfa}$ is to avoid tracing parts of the behavior graph that have already been traced. To deal with this we introduce, for each flow that has α constraints, a set of flows containing each flow that has already been traced. We then consult this set and stop tracing whenever we encounter a node already traced. As a result, the construction of the behavior graph involves traversing its edges only once. Once the behavior graph is constructed, computing the flows takes at most the time taken by the local transitive closure algorithm.

7.2   Correctness

The minimal solution to the system of immediate, α and β constraints described in section 6.2 corresponds to the least fixed of the following system of equations[4]:

– For each constant term $t = k$, include the equation

$$\phi_t = \{\overline{k}\};$$

where $\overline{k}$ is the abstraction of constant $k \in C$.
– For each lambda expression $t = \lambda x.B$ include the equation

$$\phi_t = \{t\};$$

– For each function parameter x of $f = \lambda x.B$ include the equation

$$\phi_x = \bigcup \{\phi_b \mid f \in \phi_a\};$$

where $_i(a\ b)$ is some application.
– For each application $_i(a\ b)$ include the equation:

$$\phi_i = \bigcup \{\phi_q \mid \lambda y._q B \in \phi_a\}$$

---

[4] For simplicity, we consider only one argument lambda expressions

The first two equation sets implement the immediate constraints. The last two equation sets have to do with the flow across function boundary. The third equation set corresponds to the α and shows that the flow of a parameter x is the collection of the arguments at all call sites of its function f. Finally, the last equation corresponds to the *beta* constraints and computes the flow of an application as the collection of all results returned by all functions applied there. The soundness of this system with respect to an operational semantics is proven in [10].

8   Status

We have developed a prototype implementation of the Abstract Interpreter described in this paper in Common Lisp and are in the process of experimenting with this prototype by applying it to various analyses, including approximative type recovery, strength reduction, basic induction parameters, and strictness analysis. Preliminary results are encouraging in that they show the efficiency of our approach to be much superior to that reported in [12]. With most practical programs the cost of constructing the behavior graph is linear in the number of terms in a program, becoming slightly non-linear only when some abstraction can be returned from many applications.

The abstract interpreter actually implemented deals with a number of complications that were omitted from this paper in the interests of readability and employs algorithms that are very incremental, doing, we believe, the minimum work required. The full details are presented in [1]. One difference is that the actual implementation deals with multiple values in the sense that it assumes that there is a primitive called *block* that returns whatever values are fed to it as arguments. Thus, (*block* 1 2) returns the two values 1 and 2 and the interpretation of $(f\ (g\ x)\ y)$ is that f is fed whatever values g returns plus that bound to y, and so on. The complication that this introduces is that when the γ function is traversing program terms and encounters the application $_i(t_1 \cdots t_p)$ it must determine the operator and the operands of the application. That is, it is possible that t_1 and t_2 produce no values and that the operator is the first value produced by t_3. To deal with this case the lattice used for control flow analysis is augmented with the two abstract values *value* and *void* indicating, respectively, a single value and no value. If, when γ is traversing the program terms, it cannot determine the operator and/or the operands of an application, that application is deferred until Phase IA when sufficient information has been developed that the operator and operands can be determined.

Another feature of the implementation is that it deals with "exit fuctions". We introduce another parameter name space, $\hat{\mathcal{N}}$ and generalize abstractions to have the form $\lambda \hat{f} x_1 \cdots x_k.B$ where the interpretation of $\hat{f} \in \hat{\mathcal{N}}$ is, in the body B when that abstraction is being applied, an *exit function* that will, when called, exit that application of the abstraction with whatever values are fed to $\hat{f}$ as results. Thus exit functions are similar to **catch** and **throw** in most LISPs. The complication introduced are minor and discussed in detail in [1].

Our implementation has also been extended to produce finer estimates in order to cater to what we believe is an important type of optimization, particularly when dealing with a variety of high performance computers as targets. Suppose that there is a library of functions for dealing with, for example, linear algebra computations. Then one sort of optimization we might want is to specialize the library functions when certain arguments are known at compile time by doing partial evaluation in order save run time costs. We believe that this application requires call site specific analysis. Using the theory described in [10] we have extended the abstract interpreter described here to handle flows of the form Φ_t^σ, where t is a term and $\sigma \in \Sigma$ is an abstract *call conctext* with the result that tracing in the behavior graph will become sensitive to the call context component of nodes.

9 Conclusions and Future Work

This paper presented an approach for constructing a suite of optimizers based on a general purpose abstract interpreter coupled with an optimization task specific analyzer followed by transformations enabled by annotations.

We believe that the work reported here has great potential for providing a sound basis for and an efficient implementation of a number of optimizers, ranging from such standards as strength reduction and common sub-expression elimination to such novel applications as static determination of data mapping for languages designed for massively parallel computing.

However, much remains to be done. One important concern is to prove the soundness of the proposed approach and the correctness of the algorithms presented and to develop complexity measures of those algorithms and [10] provides partial answers.

Another is the development of tools that support the customization of the general framework to particular optimization problems, that is the implementation of the functions F_p^τ and operations on the lattice over which they operate.

Finally, we are concerned with implementing a large inventory of optimizers for HPF and other parallel languages like BSP-L([2]), an intermediate parallel language for the BSP model of computation([14]) and gathering experimental data that will let us judge the efficacy of our approach.

References

1. Thomas Cheatham, Haiming Gao, and Dan Stefanescu *The Harvard Abstract Interpreter* Technical Report, Harvard University, April 1993.
2. Thomas Cheatham, Jr., Amr Fahmy and Dan Stefanescu *BSP-L — A Programming Language for the Bulk Synchronous Processing Model*, Center for Research in Computing Technology, Harvard University, December 1993
3. Patrick Cousot and Radhia Cousot *Abstract interpretation: a unified lattice model for static analysis of programs by construction of approximate fixpoints*, Conference Record of the Fourth ACM Symposium on Principles of Programming Languages, pages 238-252, 1977.

4. Neil Jones and Alan Mycroft *Data Flow Analysis of Applicative Programs Using Minimal Functions Graphs: Abridged Version*, Conference Record of the Thirteenth ACM Symposium on Principles of Programming Languages, pages 296-306, 1986.

5. Mike Karr and Steve Rosen *Dynamic Crossreference Analysis*, lecture notes, 1992.

6. Jens Palsberg and Michael I. Schwartzbach *Safety Analysis versus Type Inference*, Information and Computation, to appear.

7. Olin Shivers *Control Flow Analysis in Scheme* ACM SIGPLAN '88 Conference on Programming Language Design and Implementation, Atlanta GA, June 22-24, 1988.

8. Olin Shivers *Control-Flow Analysis of Higher Order Languages or Taming Lambda*, Technical Report CMU-CS-91-145, Carnegie Mellon University, May 1991.

9. Peter Sestoft *Replacing Function Parameters by Global Variables*, FPCA'89, pages 39-53, 1989.

10. Dan Stefanescu and Yuli Zhou *An Equational Framework for the Abstract Analysis of Functional Programs*, Proceedings of ACM Conference on Lisp and Functional Programming, Orlando, 1994.

11. Mitchell Wand and Paul Steckler *Selective and Lightweight Closure Conversion*, ACM Symposium on Principles of Programming Languages, Portland, 1994.

12. Atty Kanamori and Daniel Weise *An Empirical Study of an Abstract Interpretation of Scheme Programs* Technical Report CSL-TR-92-521, Computer Systems Laboratory, Stanford University, April 1992.

13. Mary Hall and Ken Kennedy, *Efficient Call Graph Analysis*, ACM Letters on Programming Languages and Systems, Vol. 1, No. 3, Sept. 1992, pp 227-242.

14. L. G. Valiant *A Bridging Model for Parallel Computation* Communications of the ACM, 33(8):103-111, 1990

Flow Grammars – a Flow Analysis Methodology

James S. Uhl and R. Nigel Horspool

Department of Computer Science
University of Victoria[1]

Abstract: Flow grammars provide a new mechanism for modeling control flow in flow analyzers and code optimizers. Existing methods for representing control flow are inadequate in terms of both their generality and their accuracy. Flow grammars overcome these deficiencies and are well-suited to the specification and solution of data flow analysis problems.

1 Introduction

Source programs must be subjected to sophisticated and extensive optimization to approach the full potential of modern computer architectures. Many powerful optimizations rely on *static analysis* of the source code. Examples of such static analysis include: live variable analysis [8], various forms of constant propagation [10,20], and aliasing analysis [4]. All of these static analyses may be realized as instances of *flow analysis problems*. They share the following general framework [10]:

1. A *model* of the program defines points where information is to be determined, as well as specifying how control may flow between those points at run-time.

2. A set of *abstract states* representing the desired static information is created. In the case of constant propagation, for example, each abstract state is a partial mapping from variable names to values. Generally this *information space* is a structured as a lattice or semi-lattice [5,10]. For some analyses, this set of states may even depend upon the structure of the model used to represent the program [17].

3. A set of *flow equations* relating the abstract state of the program at one point with the points that may immediately precede or follow it during execution.

The goal is to find a least fix point solution to the set of equations. The solution is then used to guide the optimization process.

This paper describes a new formalism which we call *flow grammars*, developed for use in the *Flow Analysis Compiler Tool* (FACT), an on-going research project at

---

1. P.O. Box 3055, Victoria, BC, Canada V8W 3P6. {juhl,nigelh}@csr.uvic.ca

the University of Victoria [19]. Specifically, we demonstrate how context-free flow grammars may be used to model both intra- and inter-procedural control flow; we subsequently show how to interpret a context free grammar as a set of data flow equations; and we give an approach for solving these equations. Finally, we demonstrate that programming language control constructs form a hierarchy which corresponds in a natural manner to a hierarchy of grammar classes.

2 Program Executions

This section motivates the use of grammars to model control flow. The essential idea is to represent each possible execution of a program as a string of symbols, called an *execution path*, where each symbol corresponds to a fixed run-time action that may be made by the program during execution (e.g., an assignment). Following the framework of denotational semantics, each run-time action may be viewed as a function transforming one program state into another. In a *concrete semantics*, the program state consists of the values of all variables, as well as the input and output streams; such states are called *concrete states*. Static analyses typically define an *abstract semantics* where program states contain only the information needed to infer facts about the concrete state at various points of execution; these states are called *abstract states*. Since these facts must be true regardless of which path is followed on a given run, static analyses must consider all possible executions of a program. A mechanism for representing a (potentially unbounded) number of execution paths is needed. Recursive set equations, where each set contains zero or more execution paths, satisfy this requirement. These equations correspond to grammars in formal language theory.

2.1 Execution Paths

An *execution path* represents a single execution path through part of a program. A *complete execution path* represents a single execution of an entire program. Consider the program in Fig. 1, where program points are indicated by numbers to the left of the code. Program point 4, for example, occurs between the assignments "$f := f * i$" and "$i := i - 1$". Each execution path may be viewed as a sequence of program point pairs. For this program there is one complete execution path (though a given static analysis may not be able to determine this fact):

$$(1,2) \ (2,3) \ (3,4) \ (4,5) \ (5,6) \ (6,3) \ (3,4) \ (4,5) \ (5,7) \ (7,8)$$

For better readability, we abbreviate the path description to:

$$t_1 \ t_2 \ t_3 \ t_4 \ t_{5/6} \ t_6 \ t_3 \ t_4 \ t_{5/7} \ t_7$$

The decision at the **if** statement is embodied in the symbols $t_{5/6}$ and $t_{5/7}$: when control proceeds from point 5 to point 6, the true branch has been taken; when control proceeds from point 5 to point 7, the false branch was taken. In this formulation, an execution path is simply a string of symbols, each of which represents one or more run-time actions.

```
        program ex(output);
        label 10;
        var i, f:integer;
        begin
1           i := 3;
2           f := 1;
3       10:     f := f * i;
4               i := i - 1;
5           if i>1 then
6               goto 10;
7           writeln(f)
8       end.
```

Fig. 1. Example Pascal program

2.2 Representation

To perform optimization, a compiler needs to know the (abstract) state of the program at each point p irrespective of which execution path was followed to reach p. Thus, a compiler must consider the *entire* set of possible execution paths to compute the abstract state at each point in the program.

Suppose S_i is the set of execution paths starting from point i in a program and ending at the end of the program. Then the control flow of the source program yields a set of relationships among these sets. For a backwards analysis of the example program, these relationships may be represented by the family of set equations, as shown in Fig. 2. The *least fixed point (lfp) solution* of these equations yields the set of execution paths from each point to the end of the program. Note that there is only one path from point 6 to the end of the program, "$t_6 t_7$", and, correspondingly, the lfp solution of $S_6 = \{ t_6 t_7 \}$ and $S_7 = \{t_7\}$. The loop in the program (points 3 through 6) implies that there are an infinite number of possible executions, and thus execution paths in the sets $S_1, S_2, ..., S_6$ each contain an infinite number of paths.

$$S_1 = \{t_1\} \bullet S_2$$
$$S_2 = \{t_2\} \bullet S_3$$
$$S_3 = \{t_3\} \bullet S_4$$
$$S_4 = \{t_4\} \bullet S_5$$

$$S_5 = \{t_{5/6}\} \bullet S_6 \cup \{t_{5/7}\} \bullet S_7$$
$$S_6 = \{t_6\} \bullet S_3$$
$$S_7 = \{t_7\}$$

$$\text{where } A \bullet B = \{\alpha\,\beta \mid \alpha \in A, \beta \in B\}$$

Fig. 2. Backward analysis execution path equations for the example program

In a forward analysis, information is known at the start of execution and must be propagated forward through the program. This is represented by equations that the "mirror" the backwards analysis equations, as shown in Fig.. Here, S_1 is the start of the program, and consequently its least fixed point solution contains only the empty execution path, ε. Similarly, S_2 contains only the execution path t_1, since there is only one path from the start of the program to point 2. The top of the loop, at point 3, introduces a union of paths, one entering the loop from outside (point 2) and the other from the bottom of the loop (point 6). Again the lfp solution to these equations has a structure defined by the equations that yields only execution paths representing possible executions.

$$S_1 = \{\varepsilon\}$$
$$S_2 = \{t_1\} \bullet S_1$$
$$S_3 = \{t_2\} \bullet S_2 \cup \{t_6\} \bullet S_6$$
$$S_4 = \{t_3\} \bullet S_3$$
$$S_5 = \{t_4\} \bullet S_4$$

$$S_6 = \{t_{5/6}\} \bullet S_5$$
$$S_7 = \{t_{5/7}\} \bullet S_5$$
$$S_8 = \{t_7\} \bullet S_7$$

Fig. 3. Forward analysis execution path equations for the example program

2.3 Generating Execution Paths with a Grammar

The equations in Fig. 2 correspond exactly to the regular grammar in Fig. 4. What have previously been called "symbols" are now terminals in a grammar. Similarly, the variables in Fig. 2 are now non-terminals.

The set of strings generated by each of the non-terminals in this grammar is equal to the lfp solution of the corresponding equation in Fig. 2. Note also that non-terminals at the end of each production act as *continuations*, indicating where execution is to proceed.

$$S_1 ::= t_1 S_2 \qquad\qquad S_5 ::= t_{5/7} S_7$$
$$S_2 ::= t_2 S_3 \qquad\qquad S_6 ::= t_6 S_3$$
$$S_3 ::= t_3 S_4 \qquad\qquad S_7 ::= t_7$$
$$S_4 ::= t_4 S_5$$
$$S_5 ::= t_{5/6} S_6$$

Fig. 4. Grammar generating execution paths for example program

2.4 Semantics

Given a set of equations describing execution paths, along with semantic functions for each symbol, it is possible to define a generalized program semantics that takes into account the behaviour of all possible executions. In this context, the run-time semantics of a program are known as *concrete semantics*, and the flow analysis semantics are called *abstract semantics*.

In a concrete semantics, the semantics of one statement is a function which maps one program state into another program state. For a given statement S, the semantic function is written as $[\![S]\!]$. The semantics of an execution path may be defined inductively. In the most basic instance, the semantics of the null statement (represented as the empty string) is the identity function, $I \equiv \lambda S.S$. For a sequence of statements along *one* execution path, the semantic functions associated with each symbol are composed, yielding:

$$[\![S_1 ; S_2 ; ... S_n]\!] \equiv [\![S_n]\!] \circ ... \circ [\![S_2]\!] \circ [\![S_1]\!]$$

In a flow analysis, the goal is to compute an *abstract state* for each point p in the program that summarizes the possible *concrete states* that may occur at p during execution. That is, the semantic functions map one abstract state to another and the semantics of *sets* of execution paths are defined. An abstract state is generally a member of a lattice, say L. Given two paths between point a and point b, P_1 and P_2, the desired abstract semantics is:

$$[\![P_1 \text{ or } P_2]\!] \equiv [\![\{P_1,P_2\}]\!] \equiv [\![\{P_1\}]\!] \wedge [\![\{P_2\}]\!]$$

where $\wedge$ is the *meet* operator used to ensure that the abstract state represents all possible concrete states that may occur, regardless of which path is taken. In practice, the precision implied in this equation can become arbitrarily expensive to compute and approximation must be used to limit the computation time.

For example, for S_1 in Fig. , we have:

$$[\![S_1]\!] \equiv [\![\{\varepsilon\}]\!] \equiv \lambda S.S$$

and, thus, $[\![S_1]\!] \equiv \lambda S.S$. For S_2, the semantic function for S_1 must be composed with the meaning of the set $\{t_1\}$:

$$[\![S_2]\!] = [\![\{t_1\}]\!] \circ [\![S_1]\!]$$
$$= [\![\{t_1\}]\!] \circ (\lambda S.S)$$
$$= [\![\{t_1\}]\!]$$

Here the semantics of the singleton set $\{t_1\}$ is composed with the identity function, which is just the semantics of the singleton set itself.

When two sets are merged in a union, as in the equation for S_3 above, the *meet* of the corresponding functions must be computed. This is typically the *point-wise meet*, $\wedge:(L{\rightarrow}L){\rightarrow}(L{\rightarrow}L)$, of the functions, defined as:

$$f_1 \wedge f_2 = \lambda S.f_1(S) \wedge f_2(S)$$

where $\wedge:L{\rightarrow}L$ is the meet operator of the underlying lattice. In the case of S_3, the equation is:

$$[\![S_3]\!] = ([\![\{t_2\}]\!] \circ [\![S_2]\!]) \wedge ([\![\{t_6\}]\!] \circ [\![S_6]\!])$$

Figure 5 shows the complete set of forward analysis equations for the example program. The goal of static analysis is to compute the portion of the least fixed point functionals for each of these equations needed to determine the abstract state at each point in the program.

$$[\![S_1]\!] = [\![\{\varepsilon\}]\!]$$
$$[\![S_2]\!] = [\![\{t_1\}]\!] \circ [\![S_1]\!]$$
$$[\![S_3]\!] = ([\![\{t_2\}]\!] \circ [\![S_2]\!]) \wedge ([\![\{t_6\}]\!] \circ [\![S_6]\!])$$
$$[\![S_4]\!] = [\![\{t_3\}]\!] \circ [\![S_3]\!]$$

$$[\![S_5]\!] = [\![\{t_4\}]\!] \circ [\![S_4]\!]$$
$$[\![S_6]\!] = [\![\{t_{5/6}\}]\!] \circ [\![S_5]\!]$$
$$[\![S_7]\!] = [\![\{t_{5/7}\}]\!] \circ [\![S_5]\!]$$
$$[\![S_8]\!] = [\![\{t_7\}]\!] \circ [\![S_7]\!]$$

Fig. 5. Semantic equations for forward analysis

3 Definition: Flow Grammar

A *flow grammar* is a quadruple $G=(\Sigma_N, \Sigma_T, P, S)$ where: Σ_N is the set of *flow non-ter-minals*, Σ_N, corresponding to the program points; Σ_T is the set of *flow terminals* corresponding to run-time actions such as assignments; P is a set of *flow productions* of the form $\alpha ::= \beta$, where $\alpha \in \Sigma_N^+$ and $\beta \in (\Sigma_T \cup \Sigma_N)^*$; and S is the *flow start symbol* and corresponds to the beginning of the program.[1]

3.1 Example: Interprocedural Control Flow

Interprocedural analysis requires a context-free flow grammar to model the matching of calls and returns. Figure 6 shows a small Pascal program which is used to demonstrate interprocedural data flow analysis in the next section. Flow productions modeling the example program are shown in Fig. 7. Of particular importance are the productions corresponding to the procedure calls, "$S_4 ::= t_{4/1} S_1 t_{6/5} S_5$" and "$S_8 ::= t_{8/1} S_1 t_{6/9} S_9$". Both of these productions have an embedded non-terminal, S_1, representing entry to the procedure being called. Terminals $t_{4/1}$ and $t_{8/1}$ represent the actions that occur on procedure entry from points 4 and 8, respectively. Similarly, $t_{6/5}$ and $t_{6/9}$ represent the actions that occur upon return to the respective call sites.

``
    program example(output);
    var f,i:integer;
    procedure nfact;
    begin
1   if i<=1 then
2   f := 1
        else begin
3   i := i-1;
4   nfact;
5   f := f*i
        end
6   end;
``
	``
	(* this is an incorrect
	     implementation of
	     factorial *)
	
	    begin
	7 i:=5;
	8 nfact;
	9 write(f)
	10 end.
	``

Fig. 6. Example Pascal program

$$S_1 ::= t_{1/2} S_2 \qquad\qquad S_7 ::= t_7 S_8$$
$$S_1 ::= t_{1/3} S_3 \qquad\qquad S_8 ::= t_{8/1} S_1 t_{6/9} S_9$$
$$S_2 ::= t_2 S_6 \qquad\qquad S_9 ::= t_9 S_{10}$$
$$S_3 ::= t_3 S_4 \qquad\qquad S_{10} ::= t_{10}$$
$$S_4 ::= t_{4/1} S_1 t_{6/5} S_5$$
$$S_5 ::= t_5 S_6$$
$$S_6 ::= t_6$$

Fig. 7. Flow grammar for program of Fig. 6

---

1. Σ^* is the set of all strings over Σ, including the empty string ε; Σ^+ is the set of all non-empty strings over Σ.

Note that procedure calls are handled naturally in the semantic equations, in the case of the call from the main program, we have:

$$[\![\, S_8 \,]\!] = [\![\, \{t_{8/1}\} \,]\!] \circ [\![\, S_1 \,]\!] \circ [\![\, \{t_{6/9}\} \,]\!] \circ [\![\, S_9 \,]\!]$$

3.2 Discussion

It is interesting to consider the relationship between the Chomsky hierarchy [7] and various programming language constructs. The boundary between the context-free (type 2 in the hierarchy) and context-sensitive (type 1) flow grammars is important because the former admit the straightforward translation to flow equations shown above, but the latter do not.

A regular flow grammar (type 3) corresponds directly to a flow graph, and is therefore capable of representing the same intraprocedural constructs, including if/then/else, loops, and gotos to (constant) labels. Label variables are somewhat anomalous. At the expense of increased size, a regular flow grammar can precisely (up to the usual assumption that all control flow choices are possible at any branch, and that any one branch is independent of any previous branch) model intraprocedural control flow containing only simple label variables. The idea is to encode the current state of all label variables into each non-terminal of the flow grammar. This results in a finite number of non-terminals, because there must be a finite number of simple label variables, each of which can assume a finite number of label values. When an assignment to a label variable occurs, the productions ensure the continuation non-terminal encodes the correct state. Note, however, that label variables in arrays and other dynamic structures cannot be precisely tracked in this manner using a regular flow grammar (although conservative approximate tracking that takes account of aliasing is possible).

Context-free flow grammars add the key capability of modeling procedure calls and returns, making them suitable for many interprocedural flow analysis problems. A finite number of simple procedure variables may be directly encoded into the non-terminals similar to the encoding of label variables above. A goto statement whose (constant) target is not local causes premature termination of one or more activation records, including their suspended continuations. Surprisingly, this can be modeled with a context-free flow grammar by creating productions that generate prefixes of execution paths that eventually end with a production representing the non-local goto. Ginsburg and Rose show that the language of all proper prefixes of a context-free language is itself context-free [6], validating the assertion that such control flow is still context-free; details relating this result to flow grammar construction may be found in [19].

We note several important aspects of the flow grammar methodology:

1. Interprocedural and intraprocedural control flow are unified into a single all-encompassing model.

2. Results from formal language theory are useful when projected into patterns of control flow. For example, in-line expansion may be effected by the elimination of a production.

3. The structure of regular and context-free flow grammars naturally reflects a set of flow equations; a data flow analysis simply interprets the terminals and non-terminals in appropriate domains.

3.3 Interprocedural Data Flow Analysis: an Example

Within a flow grammar, each non-terminal represents an execution point in the program. As shown above, each non-terminal may be interpreted as representing the *state* of the program at that point. The state should, of course, capture just the information that is relevant to the data flow problem that we are interested in. For the *live variables* problem, the state is usually described by the set of variables that are *live* at a program point (i.e., there exists a path from that point to a use of that variable without an intervening assignment to the variable).

Translating our example context-free flow grammar to a set of backwards flow equations (as would be needed for solving the live variables problem) yields the family of equations in Fig. 8.

As a concrete example of the general technique, we now consider the specific problem of determining variable liveness at a given point in the program. For *intraprocedural* live variables, the lattice $L = 2^V$, where $V = \{i, f\}$, suffices, so that each $S_i \in 2^{\{i, f\}}$. The meet operator $\wedge$ is set union. With this interpretation and for the particular problem of live variables, the effects of the terminals may be described by set equations corresponding to "gen" and "kill" sets [1]; for example, t_5 represents the execution of the statement "$f := f * i$" which kills f and then generates f and i, thus:

$$[\![\{t_5\}]\!] = \lambda x . ((x - \{f\}) \cup \{f, i\}) = \lambda x . (x \cup \{f, i\})$$

Figure 9 shows the abstract semantic functions for all the terminals in the example program.

As described above, a richer domain is required for a precise *interprocedural* analysis. In general, the effect of a statement inside a function depends on the environment

$$[\![S_1]\!] = [\![\{t_{1/2}\}]\!] \circ [\![S_2]\!] \wedge [\![\{t_{1/3}\}]\!] \circ [\![S_3]\!]$$
$$[\![S_2]\!] = [\![\{t_2\}]\!] \circ [\![S_6]\!]$$
$$[\![S_3]\!] = [\![\{t_3\}]\!] \circ [\![S_4]\!]$$
$$[\![S_4]\!] = [\![\{t_{4/1}\}]\!] \circ [\![S_1]\!] \circ [\![\{t_{6/5}\}]\!] \circ [\![S_5]\!]$$
$$[\![S_5]\!] = [\![\{t_5\}]\!] \circ [\![S_6]\!]$$
$$[\![S_6]\!] = [\![\{t_6\}]\!]$$
$$[\![S_7]\!] = [\![\{t_7\}]\!] \circ [\![S_8]\!]$$
$$[\![S_8]\!] = [\![\{t_{8/1}\}]\!] \circ [\![S_1]\!] \circ [\![\{t_{6/9}\}]\!] \circ [\![S_9]\!]$$
$$[\![S_9]\!] = [\![\{t_9\}]\!] \circ [\![S_{10}]\!]$$
$$[\![S_{10}]\!] = [\![\{t_{10}\}]\!]$$

Fig. 8. Backwards flow equations for program in Fig. 6

$$[\![\{t_{1/2}\}]\!] = \lambda x . (x \cup \{i\}) \qquad [\![\{t_{6/5}\}]\!] = \lambda x . x$$
$$[\![\{t_{1/3}\}]\!] = \lambda x . (x \cup \{i\}) \qquad [\![\{t_{6/9}\}]\!] = \lambda x . x$$
$$[\![\{t_2\}]\!] = \lambda x . (x - \{f\}) \qquad [\![\{t_7\}]\!] = \lambda x . (x - \{i\})$$
$$[\![\{t_3\}]\!] = \lambda x . (x \cup \{i\}) \qquad [\![\{t_{8/1}\}]\!] = \lambda x . x$$
$$[\![\{t_{4/1}\}]\!] = \lambda x . x \qquad [\![\{t_9\}]\!] = \lambda x . (x \cup \{f\})$$
$$[\![\{t_5\}]\!] = \lambda x . (x \cup \{f, i\}) \qquad [\![\{t_{10}\}]\!] = \lambda x . x$$

Fig. 9. Abstract semantic functions for terminal symbols

of the function call. Therefore, we use a domain whose elements have the form *environment* → *state* to provide the values associated with terminals and non-terminals of the flow grammar. For the live variables problem, both the state and the environment may be represented by a set of live variables. I.e., the environment of a function call is the state at the point of call. In this case, the set of variables that are live on return from the function. Thus all values, for both terminals and non-terminals, belong to the domain of functions, $2^V \rightarrow 2^V$. However, it is unnecessary to compute the function values fully. We only need to know the effects of statements inside a function for those invocation environments that actually occur. Thus, our iterative approach for finding a fixpoint is demand-driven and, in general, only partially computes the functions.

Our analysis uses the fact that no variable in the program is live at the point where the program terminates. (If a program sets a status variable that could be inspected by the operating system on return, such a variable would be deemed to be live at program point S_{10}). The iteration to compute the functions proceeds as follows. Each value shows what is known about the various functions at each iteration. Suppose that, in the course of an iteration, $[\![S_2]\!]$ currently has the value $\{ \{f\} \rightarrow \{\}, \{f, i\} \rightarrow \{i\} \}$. This would indicate that the function containing point S_2 is currently known to have two calling environments, $\{f\}$ and $\{f, i\}$. That is, in one set of calls to the enclosing function, f is the only live variable on exit and in another set of calls, both f and i are live on exit. When that function is invoked in the $\{f\}$ environment, the set of live variables at point S_2 is $\{\}$; similarly the calling environment $\{f, i\}$ gives $\{i\}$. If the value of $[\![S_2]\!]$ is shown as the empty set Φ, this corresponds to the bottom element of the enriched lattice and means that no invocations of the function containing point S_2 have been processed yet.

Initially, we want to know what is live at the beginning of the program, and this is represented by $[\![S_7]\!](\{\})$. That is, S_7 is contained in the main program and the environment for the main program is an empty set – no variables are live on exit. The demand for $[\![S_7]\!](\{\})$ triggers the addition of $\{\} \rightarrow \{\}$ to $[\![S_{10}]\!]$, and initiates the first iteration, which proceeds as follows:

1. $[\![S_9]\!](\{\})$ is computed from $[\![S_{10}]\!](\{\})$ yielding $\{f\}$, which is added to $[\![S_9]\!]$.

2. The computation of $[\![S_8]\!](\{\})$ requires the value of $[\![S_1]\!](\{f\})$. Since $[\![S_1]\!]$ is currently Φ, this triggers the addition of $\{f\} \rightarrow \{\}$ to $[\![S_6]\!]$, and the (optimistic) value $\{\}$ is used for $[\![S_1]\!](\{f\})$.

3. The iteration concludes with the empty set as the current value of $[\![S_7]\!](\{\})$.

Figure 10 shows the entire computation.

Within a given iteration, partial function values are computed in the order shown in the table. Note that this particular order leads to rapid convergence; other orders will yield the same solution but will usually require more iterations.

Reading from the final column of the table, we can deduce that there are no live variables at the beginning of the program, since $[\![S_7]\!](\{\}) = \{\}$. (That is, if there are no live variables at the end of execution, then there are no live variables at the start of execution.) This result is a simple application of live variable analysis which proves that all variables are initialized before being used. The final column also shows which variables are live at each program point. Given a function value F for some program point p, then the set of variables that are live at p is computed as $\bigcup_{X \rightarrow Y \in F} Y$. For example, the set of live variables at point S_2 is $\{i\}$; in one calling environment, the set is empty

State	Iteration Number			
	1	2	3	4
$[\![S_6]\!]$	Φ	{ {f}→{f} }	{ {f}→{f}, {f,i}→{f,i} }	{ {f}→{f}, {f,i}→{f,i} }
$[\![S_5]\!]$	Φ	{ {f}→{f,i} }	{ {f}→{f,i}, {f,i}→{f,i} }	{ {f}→{f,i}, {f,i}→{f,i} }
$[\![S_4]\!]$	Φ	{ {f}→{} }[b]	{ {f}→{}, {f,i}→{} }	{ {f}→{i}, {f,i}→{i} }
$[\![S_3]\!]$	Φ	{ {f}→{i} }	{ {f}→{i}, {f,i}→{i} }	{ {f}→{i}, {f,i}→{i} }
$[\![S_2]\!]$	Φ	{ {f}→{} }	{ {f}→{}, {f,i}→{i} }	{ {f}→{}, {f,i}→{i} }
$[\![S_1]\!]$	Φ	{ {f}→{i} }	{ {f}→{i}, {f,i}→{i} }	{ {f}→{i}, {f,i}→{i} }
$[\![S_{10}]\!]$	{ {}→{} }	{ {}→{} }	{ {}→{} }	{ {}→{} }
$[\![S_9]\!]$	{ {}→{f} }	{ {}→{f} }	{ {}→{f} }	{ {}→{f} }
$[\![S_8]\!]$	{ {}→{} }[a]	{ {}→{i} }	{ {}→{i} }	{ {}→{i} }
$[\![S_7]\!]$	{ {}→{} }	{ {}→{} }	{ {}→{} }	{ {}→{} }

[a.] And add element {f}→{} to set [S_6].

[b.] And add element {f, i}→{} to set [S_6].

Fig. 10. Example live variable computation

and in the only other environment, the set is {i}, taking their union yields the desired answer.

3.4 An Iteration Strategy

An obvious method for speeding convergence of the iteration is to ensure that whenever a computation is performed, as many as possible of its abstract inputs are already computed. This is precisely what the techniques of Jourdan and Parigot to solve "grammar flow analysis" problems [9] yield. Combining these methods with the algorithm of Sharir and Pnueli [17, pp. 207-209] results in an effective solution procedure. In essence, the flow grammar is partitioned into a set of sub-components that encapsulate recursion, resulting in a directed acyclic graph. Iteration is then performed by visiting the sub-components in reverse topological order.

3.5 Handling Arguments to Procedures

Arguments to procedures are, in general, handled by defining an appropriate lattice and mappings for the call/return/exit terminals. The bit-vector technique of Knoop and Steffen [13], for example, may be applied directly. As more than one flow analysis specification may be incorporated into the compiler, determination of aliasing may be performed before subsequent analysis to ensure conservative solutions.

4 Previous Work

Previous work on control flow analysis is limited; most effort has been devoted to various aspects of data flow analysis. As mentioned above, graphs are the most frequently discussed mechanism for representing control flow [5,10,12,14,17] and *graph grammars* [11] were considered for use in FACT. Graph grammars are effective for representing hierarchical control structures, but cannot handle the arbitrary control flow made possible by the **goto** statement, and also cannot effectively match calls with returns.

Languages with various flavours of procedure variables provide many challenges to effective flow analysis. Weihl's approach ignores local control flow effects to derive a conservative approximation of the possible values each procedure variable may have [21]. Shivers addresses the difficult task of determining a control flow model for a Scheme program where all functions are bound dynamically [18].

The task of specifying control flow in terms of syntax is addressed by Sethi's *plumb* project [16]. In essence, plumb allows a continuation passing style semantics to be specified for a programming language using a special function composition operator. Flow grammars can also be considered as representing control flow using continuations, but in a more direct manner.

Work on static analysis in the form of data flow analysis and abstract interpretation is extensive. Performing flow analysis at the source level ("high-level data flow analysis") for specific data flow problems has been considered by Rosen [15] and Babich and Jazayeri [2,3]. Generalization of various related flow analysis techniques into uniform frameworks includes the work of the Cousots [5], Kam and Ullman [10] and Kildall [12]. Marlowe and Ryder provide an excellent survey of data flow analysis problems and the computational cost of their solutions in [14].

Yi and Harrison describe a tool called Z1 [22] whose goals are similar to those of FACT. Static analyses in Z1 are specified by defining an (abstract) interpreter along with appropriate lattices.The abstract interpreter operates on an intermediate representation of the source program in which gotos have been eliminated. Z1's novel lattice definition mechanism is of particular interest: though somewhat restrictive, it allows the precision of the analysis to be controlled by projecting the analysis lattices. FACT differs from Z1 by not requiring the explicit writing of an abstract interpreter. Instead, the user specifies the construction of a flow grammar in terms of the abstract syntax of the source language and an analysis on the resulting grammar.

5 Discussion and Future Work

Our main achievement has been to integrate intraprocedural and interprocedural flow analysis in a seamless manner. Flow grammars not only represent control flow effectively, but are directly amenable to specifying data flow analysis problems as well. We argue that, in a general purpose tool such as FACT, it is appropriate to begin with an accurate control flow model and lose precision at the data flow analysis stage; rather than lose precision even prior to data flow analysis by constructing an inaccurate control flow model.

Flow grammars open up a variety of avenues for future research. Preliminary work on modeling programs containing more diverse language constructs, such as exception handlers and bounded numbers of procedure variables, is encouraging. Aside from unrestricted flow grammars, we are also considering the use of two-level grammars to model the dynamic nature of procedure variables. While not discussed in this paper, we have found examples of programs for which control flow is naturally modeled by Type 0 grammars.

Work is proceeding on the algorithm to solve the flow problems generated from flow grammars. Because FACT is intended to be general purpose, minimal assumptions are made about the data flow analysis framework: that the lattice is of finite height and that all functions are monotonic. Currently under investigation is an algorithm which computes the effect of a function call using iteration for up to k different elements in the input domain, and then uses conservative approximations when necessary for subsequent inputs. The use of the restricted lattices as found in Z1 is also under investigation.

References

[1] Aho, A., R. Sethi and J. Ullman. *Compilers, Principles, Techniques, and Tools*, Addison-Wesley Publishing, 1986.

[2] Babich, W. and M. Jazayeri. "The Method of Attributes for Data Flow Analysis Part I:Exhaustive Analysis," *Acta Informatica* 10, 1978, pp. 245-264.

[3] Babich, W. and M. Jazayeri. "The Method of Attributes for Data Flow Analysis Part II: Demand Analysis," *Acta Informatica* 10, 1978, pp. 265-272.

[4]   Cooper, K., K. Kennedy and L. Torczon. "The Impact of Interprocedural Analysis and Optimization in the $\mathbf{R}^n$ Programming Environment," *ACM TOPLAS* 8, 4, October 1986, pp. 491-523.

[5]   Cousot, P. and R. Cousot. "Abstract Interpretation: a Unified Lattice Model for Static Analysis of Programs by Construction or Approximation of Fixpoints," *4th POPL*, January 1977, pp. 238-252.

[6]   Ginsburg, S. and G. F. Rose. "Operations which preserve definability in languages," *JACM* 10(2), April 1963, pp. 175-195.

[7]   Hopcroft, J. E. and J. D. Ullman. *Introduction to Automata Theory, Languages, and Computation*, 1979, pp. 217-228.

[8]   Hecht, M. *Flow Analysis of Computer Programs*, Elsevier, 1977.

[9]   Jourdan, M. and D. Parigot. "Techniques for Improving Grammar Flow Analysis," *ESOP'90, LNCS 432*, pp. 240-255.

[10]   Kam, J. and J. Ullman. "Monotone Data Flow Analysis Frameworks," *Acta Informatica* 7, 1977, pp. 305-317.

[11]   Kennedy, K. and L. Zucconi. "Applications of a Graph Grammar for Program Control Flow Analysis," *4th POPL*, January 1977, pp. 72-85.

[12]   Kildall, G. "A Unified Approach to Global Program Optimization," *(1st) POPL*, October 1973, pp. 194-206.

[13]   Knoop, J. and B. Steffen. "The Interprocedural Coincidence Theorem," *4th Intl. Conf., CC'92*, October 1992, pp. 125-140.

[14]   Marlowe, T. and B. Ryder. "Properties of Data Flow Frameworks," *Acta Informatica* 28, 1990, pp. 121-163.

[15]   Rosen, B. "High-Level Data Flow Analysis," *CACM* 20, 10, October 1977, pp. 712-724.

[16]   Sethi, R. "Control Flow Aspects of Semantics-Directed Compiling," *ACM TOPLAS* 5, 4, October 1983, pp. 554-595.

[17]   Sharir, M. and A. Pnueli. "Two Approaches to Interprocedural Data Flow Analysis," in *Program Flow Analysis: Theory and Applications*, Muchnick S. and Jones N. (eds.), 1981, pp. 189-233.

[18]   Shivers, O. "Control Flow Analysis in Scheme," *PLDI'88*, June 1988, pp. 164-174.

[19]   Uhl, J. S. *FACT: A Flow Analysis Compiler Tool*. Ph.D. Dissertation, in preparation.

[20]   Wegman, M. and F. Zadeck. "Constant Propagation with Conditional Branches," *ACM TOPLAS* 13, 2, April, 1991, pp. 181-210.

[21]   Weihl, W. "Interprocedural Data Flow Analysis in the Presence of Pointer, Procedure Variables, and Label Variables," *7th POPL*, January 1980, pp. 83-94.

[22]   Yi, K. and Harrison, W. L. "Automatic generation and management of interprocedural program analyses," *20th POPL*, January 1993, pp. 246-259.

Provable Correctness
of Prototype Interpreters in LDL

Ralf Lämmel, Günter Riedewald
Universität Rostock, Fachbereich Informatik
18051 Rostock, Germany
E-mail: (rlaemmel I gri)@informatik.uni-rostock.de

Abstract. LDL is a system supporting the design of procedural programming languages and generating prototype interpreters directly from the language definition. A language definition is based on GSFs - a kind of attribute grammars - and the denotational semantics approach. It is shown how denotational semantics can be transformed into Prolog. It is also shown how the correctness of the prototype interpreters can be proved using a technique developed by Clark and extended by Deransart.

1 Introduction

A particularly important problem in software development is to guarantee the functional correctness of software. Because the theory of programming languages and their implementation is well-understood and there is a close relation between theory and practice, compilers and interpreters could be the first complex software systems developed in a manner guaranteeing correct products by automatizing as much steps as possible and by using suitable correct tools including preproduced correct components.

But what does it mean "a compiler (including interpreter) is correct" ? According to [KPy80], [Sch76] a translation is correct iff it is semantic-preserving, i.e. a source program and its corresponding target program have the same meaning. [KPy80] gives some minimal set of sufficient conditions guaranteeing the property of semantic-preserving and exploits a generalization of attribute grammars to define semantics, whereas in [Sch76] an algebraic approach is used where language constructs are elements of a typed word algebra. [TWW81], [M73] apply an algebraic approach based on syntactical algebras. Boot-strapping techniques as used in [PRO92] or in [To90] can support the development of correct compiler generators.

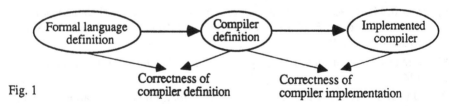

Fig. 1

To define compiler (including interpreter) correctness we will start with the language definition (Fig. 1). A formal language definition is the fundamental of a compiler definition. According to the compiler definition the compiler must be implemented. The question of correctness appears at the following points of the whole process:

- The language definition and the compiler definition define the same language (*correctness of compiler definition*): For any program p its input-output behaviour w.r.t. the language definition is identical with the input-output behaviour of the compiled program p w.r.t. the compiler definition.

- The compiler definition and the implemented compiler define the same language (*correctness of compiler implementation*): For any program p once compiled w.r.t. the compiler definition and once compiled using the implemented compiler the input-output behaviour is the same.

The concept used in our project LDL ([R91a], [R91b], [R92], [Lä93], [RL93]) is aimed at the development of correct prototype interpreters directly from the language definition thereby mixing both mentioned notions of compiler correctness. Our language definitions consist of
- a GSF (Grammar of Syntactical Functions - a kind of attribute grammars) describing the concrete syntax and the static semantics,
- a denotational semantics definition describing the dynamic semantics.

The derived prototype interpreters are written in Prolog. This language was selected, because:
- GSFs are closely related to Prolog programs and after some modifications a GSF can directly be used as a Prolog program offering the core of a prototype interpreter.
- If the syntax of the language can be defined by an LL(k)-grammar there is no need of a parser because the Prolog system itself can be exploited.
- It is well-known that in general in Prolog programs the same parameter positions can be used once for input and once for output if certain conditions are satisfied. In LDL this property is exploited to derive test program generators from the same language definition as it is used for prototype interpreters.
- The correctness of the prototype interpreter, especially of the implemented denotational semantics definition, w.r.t. the language definition can be proved applying the inductive proof method ([D90]).
- Other parts of LDL, that is to say the knowledge base and the tool for language design (see Section 2), are preferably to be implemented in a logic programming language. Therefore the fact that the prototype interpreters are implemented in Prolog contributes to the technical simplicity of LDL.

The rest of the paper is subdivided as follows. Section 2 describes the basic concepts of the LDL system. In Section 3 basic notions are mentioned. Section 4 describes our approach to correct prototype interpreters.

2 The LDL concept

2.1 Structure of LDL

Keeping in mind Koskimies' statement ([K91]) *"The concept of an attribute grammar is too primitive to be nothing but a basic framework, the 'machine language' of language implementation."* LDL offers a higher-level tool supporting the definition of procedural languages and their implementation in form of a prototype interpreter. For this purpose the LDL library contains predefined language constructs together with their denotational meaning expressed by Prolog clauses. These semantics components are correct w.r.t. the usual denotational definition (see Section 4). The knowledge base and the tool for language design ensure the derivation of correct prototype interpreters from these correct components. At present the library contains all usual Pascal constructs and some additional constructs.

The system LDL is based on the idea from [R91a] and exploits GSFs for the language definition. Moreover, in LDL there is a test program generator producing syntactically correct programs satisfying the context conditions of the defined language and possessing certain additional properties. For more exhaustive considerations of LDL and provable correct prototype interpreters within LDL the reader is refered to [RL93].

2.2 Prototype interpreters

The structure of a prototype interpreter can be seen from Fig. 2. The development of prototype interpreters is based on the following ideas:
- Because GSFs and Prolog programs are closely related a source language definition in form of a GSF may be the core of a prototype interpreter written in Prolog. The syntactical and semantical structure of the language is described by the GSF.
- The semantics definition can be a stepwise process. First, we could be interested only in the calling structure of the semantic functions of a given source program. Finally, we are interested in the computation of the source program. Thus our semantics definition consists of two levels:
  1. The meaning of a program is a term consisting of names of semantic functions in the GSF sense which can be considered as the abstract syntactical structure of the program. It can be defined using a GSF with special production rule patterns.
  2. Based on the denotational approach the interpretation of terms is defined by Prolog clauses.
- Before computing the meaning of a source program its context conditions are checked.

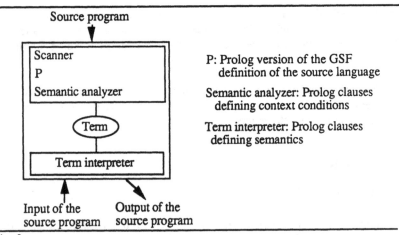

Fig. 2

The prototype interpreter operates as follows:
- A source program is read token by token from a text file.
- Each token is classified by a standard scanner. It is a part of LDL.
- The parsing and checking of context conditions is interconnected with scanning. If the context-free basic grammar of the GSF describing the source language is an LL(k)-grammar the Prolog system itself can be used straightforwardly for parsing, whereas LR(k)-grammars require to include a special parser.

- Recognizing a language construct its meaning in form of a term is constructed by connecting the meaning of its subconstructs.
- The term representing the meaning of the whole program is interpreted by associating the function names of the term with functions which e.g. transform program states.

3 Basic definitions

3.1 Denotational semantics

Our semantics descriptions are recursive function definitions describing the mapping of syntactical elements to their meanings. Syntactical domains are considered as sets of terms, whereas semantic domains are assumed to be complete partial orders (cpos). The reader is expected to be familiar with conventional denotational semantics ([St77]). Here, we will mention only some basic functions and notational conventions applied in this paper.

Let be BOOLEAN = {true,false} $\perp$, D, D_1, ..., D_n arbitrary semantic domains (cpos). The following basic functions are assumed to be available:

- projections $\underline{el}_i$ for product domains ($D_1 \times ... \times D_n$), the usual list operations <u>head</u>, <u>tail</u>, <u>cons</u>, <u>null</u> for domains of sequences D^*, operations $\underline{out}_i$ (mapping from sum to the i-th summand), $\underline{in}_i$ (vice versa), $\underline{is}_i$ or $\underline{isD}_i$ (test predicate for the i-th summand) for sum domains ($D_1 + ... + D_n$), <u>equal</u> as usual predicate for equality for any D
- <u>cond</u>: BOOLEAN $\times$ D $\times$ D -> D to express conditionals (the arrow notation b -> d_1,d_2 of <u>cond</u>(b,d_1,d_2) is sometimes prefered)
- functional operator for error propagation:
  $$... \otimes ... : (D + \{error\}\perp) \times (D \to (D + \{error\}\perp)) \to (D + \{error\}\perp)$$
  d $\otimes$ f = { error, if d = error
          { f($\underline{out}_1$(d)), else
- modification operator ... [... / ...], where f[y_0/x_0] returns a function f´ with f´(x_0) = y_0 and $\forall$ x $\neq$ x_0: f´(x) = f(x)

Elements of product domains and domains of sequences are enclosed in brackets < and >. Elements of sum domains are represented as pairs (d,i), where i refers to the summand of the operand which the element d was taken from. For sum domains we apply as usual some kind of simple unification, i.e. exp_1 = x -> exp_2, exp_3 (where x is meta-variable of summand domain D_i) is an abbreviation for $\underline{is}_i$(exp_1) -> (λx.exp_2) $\underline{out}_i$(exp_1), exp_3.

3.2 Logic programming and correctness

The reader is expected to be familiar with the basic notions of logic programming. Here we shall only include the main definitions needed for the inductive proof method ([D90]).
Let S be a set of sorts, F an *S-signature* (declaring the signature of function symbols over S), V an S-sorted set of variables. The *free F-algebra* T(F,V) is identified as the set of the well-formed and "well-typed" terms. The term algebra T(F) is identified with the set of all ground terms. For both algebras T(F,V) and T(F) the operations are interpreted as usual as term constructors. T(F,V)$_s$ (T(F)$_s$) denotes the set of all (ground) terms of sort s.

To write down specifications for logic programs describing the relations which should be defined by the clauses of a logic program we will use a logical language (first order) with a specific interpretation. A logical language L is a 4-tupel $<S,F,R,V>$, where S is a set of sorts containing the sort bool interpreted as BOOL = {true,false}, F an S-signature, R a set of many-sorted predicate symbols (every $p \in R$ is of sort bool) and V an S-sorted set of variables. L contains all formulae over V, F, R and applying connectives $\forall, \exists, <=>, =>,$ $\wedge, \vee, \sim$. By $\phi[t_1/v_1, ...,t_n/v_n]$ the result of the *substitution of variables* v_i by terms t_i in the formula ϕ is denoted. We denote by free(ϕ) the possibly empty set of the free variables of the formula ϕ of L.

To interprete formulae from L we need a so-called *L-structure* which declares the interpretation of the function and predicate symbols. An *L-structure* D is a structure of the form $< \{ D_s \}_{s \in S}, \{ f_D \}_{f \in F}, \{ r_D \}_{r \in R} >$, with S, F, R defined as above and where $< \{ D_s \}_{s \in S}, \{ f_D \}_{f \in F} >$ is a heterogeneous F-algebra and for each r in R r_D is a total mapping $r_D: D_{s1} \times ... \times D_{sn} \to BOOL$. A formula ϕ in L is *valid* in D ($\models_D \phi$), iff for all assignments v the interpretation of ϕ yields true.

In this paper logic programs are written down in Prolog notation (Edinburgh syntax), although we restrict ourselfs (for most parts) to definite clause programs (DCPs) neglecting their evaluation by a particular Prolog system. A *DCP* P is a 4-tupel $<PRED,FUNC,CLAUS,VAR>$, where PRED is a finite set of predicate symbols, FUNC a finite set of function symbols, FUNC $\cap$ PRED = $\varnothing$, VAR some set of variables, CLAUS a finite set of clauses defined as usual over PRED and TERM = T(FUNC,VAR). DEN(P) denotes the set of all atomic logic consequences of P.

Definition 1 (Specification S of P on L and D):
Let be L = $<S,F,R,V>$ a logical language, D an L-structure, P = $<PRED,FUNC,CLAUS,VAR>$ a DCP. A *specification* S of P on L and D is a family of formulae S = { S_P}$_{p \in PRED}$ such that $S_P \in L$, VAR $\subseteq$ V, FUNC $\subseteq$ F. For every p of PRED of arity n, varg(p) = {$p_1,...,p_n$} is the set of variable names denoting any possible term in place of the 1st, ..., n-th argument of p. It is imposed free(S_P) $\subseteq$ varg(p).

#

Definition 2 (Valid specification S of P):
A specification S of P on L and D is *valid* (or P is correct w.r.t. S) iff
$$\forall \ p(t_1,...,t_n) \in DEN(P) \models_D S_P [t_1/p_1, ..., t_n/p_n],$$
where n is the arity of p. The notation will be abbreviated by $S_P [t_1, ..., t_n]$.

#

Definition 3 (Inductive specification S for DCP P):
A specification S of P on L and D is *inductive* iff for every c in CLAUS,
$$c: r_0(t01,...,t0n_0) :- r_1(t11,...,t1n_1),...,r_m(tm1,...,tmn_m),$$
$$\models_D S^{r_1} [t11, ..., t1n_1] \wedge ... \wedge S^{r_m} [tm1, ..., tmn_m]$$
$$=> S^{r_0} [t01, ..., t0n_0]$$

#

Proposition:
If S of P is inductive then S is valid for P.

#

4 Correctness of prototype interpreters

4.1 Overview

Our aim is to prove the correctness of prototype interpreters constructed as described in subsection 2.2. As we have seen the meaning of a language construct is defined in two steps: first a term is constructed which can be considered as the abstract syntactical structure of the language construct, and second the term is interpreted by Prolog clauses. Because the term construction is described by a GSF (language definition), which then is transformed into a Prolog program, to prove the correctness of a prototype interpreter means to prove first the correctness of the GSF including its transformation and second the correctness of the Prolog clauses interpreting terms. Using a special form of production rule patterns of a GSF (see [RL93]) the first proof is trivial. Therefore, in the sequel we will focus only on the second proof.

There are two approaches how to realize this proof. The first one is an algebraic approach (see [RL93]). Here we will use another approach exploiting the inductive proof method for logic programs as described in [D90]. The idea of the method is the following. To prove the correctness of a logic program three kinds of semantics must be taken into consideration:
- The *intended semantics*: It describes the intentions of a programmer, e.g. in form of relations.
- The *specified semantics*: It describes the semantics really specified by the logic program. It can be identified with the set of all proof-tree roots of the program.
- The *operational semantics*: It takes into account the implementation of a logic program (computation of proof-trees).
To prove the correctness of a logic program means to prove that the intended and the specified semantics are equal and that the operational semantics "preserves as much as possible" the same semantics. In the following subsections we will focus our attention on the first problem neglecting the second one.

In our case the intended semantics will be the denotational semantics SD of a programming language and the specified semantics is given by the logic program SP intended to implement SD. Before transforming SD into SP and proving (in interconnection) the correctness of SP w.r.t. SD some modifications of SD are necessary. For clarity we will apply a simple imperative programming language VSPL (Very Simple Programming Language) as a running example. VSPL contains some simple language constructs of Pascal, namely:
- declarations of variables of type integer and boolean
- expressions built from constants and variables applying the usual arithmetic and relational operations on the domains of integer and boolean values
- empty statements, assignments, sequences, alternatives, iterations.

The general task to derive a logic program from a recursive function definition (see subsections 4.2, 4.3, 4.4) consists of the definition of the following representations:
- *Representations of elements from domains*: Elements of syntactical and non-functional semantic domains, are represented by ground terms. For functional domains we give transformation rules eliminating the necessity of these domains already within the

semantics description. This approach is sufficient at least for language descriptions of imperative languages we have considered (Pascal-like languages).

- *Representations of functional equations*: In general, named functions defined by equations are represented within a logic program as predicates. An equation is represented by a definite clause. The intention is that a logic program applied to the representation of a function argument "computes" an answer iff the corresponding function application returns a value and the computed answer is the representation of the function result (see subsection 4.4). Therefore parameter positions of the derived predicates are divided into input and output parameter positions.

4.2 Semantics description

First, the syntactical domains of the considered language will be defined in an algebraic way. Therefore a set S_{Syn} of sorts, an S_{Syn}-signature F_{Syn} and an S_{Syn}-sorted set V_{Syn} of variables will be introduced. The sorts from S_{Syn} correspond to the final syntactical domains which are sets of terms (e.g. the syntactical domain of expressions is identified with $T(F_{Syn})$expression). A term can be considered as a linear representation of the abstract syntactical structure of a language construct. F_{Syn} describes function symbols which can be applied to construct syntactical elements. V_{Syn} introduces meta-variables for the semantics description. Second, semantic domains and semantic functions will be defined.

Example 1 (Excerpt of the description of VSPL):

Syntactical domains:	idconst	... syntactical identifiers CV
	expression	... expressions E
	statement	... statements S
	. . .	
	var: idconst -> expression	... variable expression
	skip: -> statement	... empty statement
	concat: statement × statement -> statement	... statement sequence
	assign: idconst × expression -> statement	... assignment
	. . .	
Semantic domains:	ID = . . .	... identifiers V
	INTEGER = {0,1,-1,2,-2,...}$_\perp$	... integer values I
	VALUE = (BOOLEAN + INTEGER)	... values VAL at all
	MEMORY = ID -> (VALUE + {undef}$_\perp$)	... memories M
	. . .	

Semantic functions BDCV, IE and IC describing meanings of resp. syntactical identifiers, expressions and statements:

$$BDCV: T(F_{Syn})idconst \to ID$$
$$IE: T(F_{Syn})expression \to MEMORY \to (VALUE + \{error\}_\perp)$$
$$IC: T(F_{Syn})statement \to MEMORY \to (MEMORY + \{error\}_\perp)$$

(SD.1)	IE (var(CV)) (M)	=	M(BDCV(CV)) = VAL -> VAL, error
(SD.2)	IC (skip) (M)	=	M
(SD.3)	IC (concat(S1,S2)) (M)	=	IC (S1) (M) ⊗ λM'.IC (S2) (M')
(SD.4)	IC (assign(CV,E)) (M)	=	IE (E) (M) ⊗ λVAL.M[VAL/BDCV(CV)]

. . .

#

4.3 Transformation of the semantics description

The derivation of the logic program SP from the denotational semantics SD requires some modifications of SD. Especially functional domains must be flattened.

Representing functions by sequences

The fact that finite functions can be considered as finite sequences of ordered pairs may be exploited to avoid some functional domains, e.g. a function $f: D_1 \rightarrow (D_2 + D')$, where D_1, D_2 are arbitrary (non-functional) semantic domains and $D' = \{undef\}_\perp$ and f maps nearly all $d \in D_1$ to undef, can be represented as an element f' of $(D_1 \times D_2)^*$ consisting of all pairs $<x_i,y_i>$, $x_i \in D_1$, $y_i \in D_2$ with $y_i = f(x_i) \neq undef$. f' can be applied as f by an auxiliary function (see Example 2). The important substitution operator (at least for such functions) can also be redefined very easy.

Example 2 (Representing memories of VSPL by sequences):
In SD of VSPL elements of MEMORY are either the uninitialized memory or they are obtained by the application of the substitution operator. Now MEMORY is defined by MEMORY = $(ID \times VALUE)^*$. The operators for application and substitution

    APPLY: $(ID \times VALUE)^* \times ID \rightarrow (VALUE + \{undef\}_\perp)$

    UPDATE: $(ID \times VALUE)^* \times ID \times VALUE \rightarrow (ID \times VALUE)^*$

can be defined following the style of recursive function definition, e.g. for APPLY:
    APPLY(M,V) = <u>null</u>(M) -> undef,

                              <u>el</u>$_1$(<u>head</u>(M)) <u>equal</u> V -> <u>el</u>$_2$(<u>head</u>(M)),APPLY(<u>tail</u>(M),V)

Because of this new definition of MEMORY, modifications within SD are necessary, e.g. the right hand side of (SD.1) would become to:
    APPLY(M,BDCV(CV)) = VAL -> VAL, error

                                                                     #

Freezing computation of meanings

If we include e.g. procedures, semantic functions work over functional domains modelling meanings of program fragments. The environment must hold meanings of procedures beeing functional entities. To eliminate such functional domains we can exploit that concrete functions of such domains are usually only instantiated by the application of some semantic function to a syntactical object. Therefore it is possible to copy this syntactical element through the semantics description instead of its meaning (obtained by the application of the semantic function to this syntactical element) and to apply the corresponding semantic function if all arguments are known. E.g. for the procedure construct, the syntactical term beeing a procedure declaration can be bound in the environment. When the procedure is called, this syntactical term can be interpreted, since the actual parameters and the state are known. This approach was successfully applied for the implementation of the language constructs procedures, functions, escapes (exits) and gotos in a Pascal-like language. Especially continuation semantics can be implemented applying this approach.

Eliminating higher-order operators

Denotational descriptions apply generic operators with a signature often based on functional domains (e.g. the introduced $\otimes$) or on domains not further restricted. Such operators are intended to shorten descriptions by figuring out often used parts of descriptions. Functional domains arising from such operators can often be eliminated by substituting the application of the operator by the application of the definition of the operator itself (e.g. the right hand side of (SD.3) applying ⊗ would become to IC (S1) (M) = M' -> IC (S2) (M'), error).

Assuming uncurried and named functions

First we assume that for any curried function (e.g. for IE and IC of VSPL) a new uncurried version is applied in the sequel. Any application of a curried function has to be substituted by the application of the corresponding uncurried version. Second we can assume the absence of lambda abstractions, since we don't represent functional domains at all.

4.4 Derivation of correct logic programs

We are going to describe the derivation of a logic program $SP = <PRED,FUNC,CLAUS,VAR>$ from the denotational semantics SD. Therefore a term representation of elements of any domain applied within SD is given. Furthermore the implementation of the functional equations by definite clauses is described. For that purpose a set of sorts S_{DCP}, an S_{DCP}-signature F_{DCP} and an S_{DCP}-sorted set of variables V_{DCP} (all together describing the set of terms which can be applied within SP) will be constructed. We assume, that SP is "well-typed", i.e. any p є PRED can be considered as many-sorted predicate symbol (w.r.t. S_{DCP}), F_{DCP} declares the signatures of the function symbols of FUNC; VAR can be partitioned as in V_{DCP} (which corresponds to the meta-variables of SD) and the terms and atoms of CLAUS are "well-typed". Moreover we need a logical language $L_{SP} = <S_{DCP}, F_{SP},R_{SP},V_{SP}>$, which will be applied to write down the specification S_{SP} of SP and which is interpreted by an L_{SP}-structure D_{SP} mirroring suitable components of the denotational semantics SD. The components of L_{SP} are defined as follows:
- V_{SP} is an S_{DCP}-sorted set of variables beeing an extension of V_{DCP} and containing the variables from varg(p) for any p є PRED (see 3.2, Definition 1).
- F_{SP} is an S_{DCP}-signature beeing an extension of F_{DCP}. Additional function symbols beeing place holders for the functions from SD are included, where we use as function symbol the same name as for the corresponding function in SD, but quoted, e.g. cond' is a function symbol which is interpreted by the function cond in D_{SP}.
- R_{SP} offers predicate symbols for usual equality (=) for any domain.

The specification S_{SP} of SP will assign to any predicate from SP a formula from L_{SP} stating that the parameters of the predicate are in relation as defined by the corresponding function from SD.

We will construct an injective function φ assigning to any domain of SD the corresponding sort from S_{DCP}. For bottom elements of the semantic domains no representation is defined. Such a representation is not needed, since we use semantics definitions which do not apply ⊥, especially not for error handling. The latter is done by including additional error elements. We introduce the notion >D< for any domain D refering to the set of all representable values from D. >D< is different from D only for semantic domains, where >D< contains any element from D, but the bottom element and (for domains of products, sequences and sums) such containing bottom elements. For any domain D we will construct a function π_D: $>D<$ $->$ $T(F_{DCP})\phi(D)$ defining the representation of elements of $>D<$ as ground terms of the corresponding sort. For any function symbol f included into F_{DCP} an interpretation within D_{SP} will be defined by $\Psi(f)$.

Syntactical domains

The representation of elements from syntactical domains is straightforward. A syntactical element, which is a term per definition, is represented within the logic program as the same term. The function symbols of F_{Syn} are interpreted as term constructors by Ψ.

Elementary domains

Elements from finite elementary semantic domains (e.g. BOOLEAN) are represented by constant symbols. Thus we include for any element from a finite elementary domain a constant symbol (with the same notation) into F_{DCP} to be interpreted as the corresponding element in D_{SP}. For infinite elementary semantic domains (e.g. INTEGER, ID) a finite number of function symbols of appropriate signature must be applied allowing the construction of an infinite set of (ground) terms where each term represents one element from the domain, e.g. the natural numbers could be represented as usual by zero: $->$ nat, succ: nat $->$ nat, where zero is interpreted as 0 and succ as successor function. Within a concrete Prolog implementation offered data types can be exploited.

Domains of sequences

Let be D an arbitrary domain for which a representation is already defined. In order to represent elements from D^* in SP we include a new sort s_{D^*} in S_{DCP} and two new function symbols [ ]$_D$ and [...|...]$_D$ in F_{DCP} (to represent the empty list and non-empty lists resp.), where: $\phi(D^*) = s_{D^*}$

$$[ ]_D: \; -> s_{D^*}$$
$$[...|...]_D: \phi(D) \times s_{D^*} \; -> s_{D^*}$$

$\pi_{D^*}(<>) = [ ]_D$. Let be $n > 0$, $\forall d_i \in D$, $i=1,...,n$:

$$\pi_{D^*}(<d_1,...,d_n>) = [\; \pi_D(d_1) \; | \; \pi_{D^*}(<d_2,...,d_n>) \;]_D.$$

The interpretation of [ ]$_D$ is the empty list and of [...|...]$_D$ is a list constructor, i.e. $\Psi([ ]_D) = <>$ and $\Psi([...|...]_D) = \underline{cons}$.

Whenever the index D in [ ]$_D$ and [...|...]$_D$ is uniquely defined by the context we will omit D. The representation of tupels from product domains is similar to that of sequences.

Sum domains

For every summand of sum domains a unique constructor will be used to build the representation by surrounding the representation of the element from the summand domain. Let D_1, ..., D_n be arbitrary domains for which a representation is already defined, $D = (D_1 + ... + D_n)$. In order to represent elements from D in SP we include a new sort s_D in S_{DCP}, new function symbols f_1, ..., f_n in F_{DCP}, where $f_i \neq f_j$ if $i \neq j$, and a bijective function α_D: $\{1,...,n\} \; -> \{f_1,...,f_n\}$ assigning to any summand a certain function symbol, i.e. $\alpha_D(i) = f_i$, where $i=1,...,n$. Furthermore we define:

$$\phi(D) = s_D$$
$$f_1: \phi(D_1) \; -> s_D, \; ..., \; f_n: \phi(D_n) \; -> s_D.$$

Let be $1 \leq i \leq n$, $\forall d_i \in D_i$: $\pi_D((d_i,i)) = f_i(\pi_{D_i}(d_i))$, $\Psi(f_i) = \underline{in}_i$. To simplify the representation we declare a special case, if D_j with $1 \leq j \leq n$ is an elementary semantic domain of the form $\{\omega\}_\perp$, then: $f_j: \rightarrow s_D$, $\pi_D((\omega,j)) = f_j$, $\Psi(f_j) = \underline{in}_j(\omega)$.

It can be proved, that for any domain D π_D is a bijective function ([Lä93]), i.e. different elements from a domain D have different images in $T(F_{DCP})_\phi(D)$ and π_D^{-1} is defined.

Implementing recursive function definitions

Let $D_1, ..., D_k, D_{k+1}, ..., D_m$ be arbitrary domains, where $m \geq 1$ and $k < m$. If $f: D_1 \times ... \times D_k \rightarrow D_{k+1} \times ... \times D_m$ is the function from SD to be implemented within SP, the predicate p is considered as a correct implementation of f if:

(*) $\forall x_1 \in >D_1<, ..., \forall x_m \in >D_m<:$

   $p(\pi_{D_1}(x_1),...,\pi_{D_m}(x_m)) \in DEN(SP)$ iff $f(x_1,...,x_k) = <x_{k+1},...,x_m>$

Since we have not defined representations of the bottom elements of any semantic domain in (*) only representable assignments are taken into consideration. The predicates are not intended to "process" or "return" bottom elements or elements containing bottom elements. Including bottom elements in our considerations would unnecessarily blow up our implementation. In the sequel we always assume assignments restricted to representable values as explicitly stated in (*). To prove (*) two steps have to be processed:

(=>) Any computed answer (by p) is correct w.r.t. f. Below we consider the implementation of particular functions and prove (=>) in interconnection using the inductive proof method (see 3.2).

(<=) Any pair of argument and result of f builds an answer of p. This problem is sketched at the end of this subsection following [DF89] (so-called completeness).

Predicates implementing basic functions

For some basic functions one could assume ad hoc implementations.

Example 3 (Implementation of $\underline{is}_i$):

Let be $D = (D_1 + ... + D_n)$, $1 \leq i \leq n$. The function $\underline{is}_i$ is implemented by the predicate p_{is_i} described by the following clauses: $p_{is_i}(f_i(X_i),\text{true})$.
                                         $p_{is_i}(f_j(X_j),\text{false})$.

where $j = 1,...,n$ and $j \neq i$ and $f_k = \alpha_D(k)$ for $k=1,...,n$. If f_k is a constant symbol - as mentioned for the special case of summands built from a set with one element - the first parameter position of p_{is_i} has not the form $f_k(X_k)$ but the form f_k.

This implementation method for $\underline{is}_i$ will be applied to a particular sum domain and the implementation will be proved to be correct. Let be $D = (\text{VALUE} + \{\text{error}\}_\perp)$, $\alpha_D(1) = \text{eok}$, $\alpha_D(2) = \text{eerror}$. Then the implementation of $\underline{is}_1$ (i.e. $\underline{is}\text{VALUE}$) is defined by the predicate isev: isev(eok(VAL),true).
                              isev(eerror,false).

The specification $\mathbf{S}^{isev}$ (following the notation as introduced in 3.2) for isev describing the relationship between its second and first parameters is: $isev_2 = \underline{is}_1'(isev_1)$. To prove the correctness of isev w.r.t. $\mathbf{S}^{isev}$ it remains to show that the following formulae are valid (applying $\mathbf{D}_{SP}$ as interpretation):   (I)   true $= \underline{is}_1'(\text{eok}(VAL))$
                                         (II)   false $= \underline{is}_1'(\text{eerror})$

In $\mathcal{D}$SP eok and eerror will be interpreted as $\underline{in}_1$ and $\underline{in}_2$(error) resp. (see definition of Ψ for constructors of elements of sum domains). Concerning (I): $\underline{is}_1(\underline{in}_1(\text{VAL}')) = \underline{is}_1((\text{VAL}',1)) = $ true for all VAL' ϵ >VALUE<, thus (I) is valid. Concerning (II): $\underline{is}_1(\underline{in}_2(\text{error})) = \underline{is}_1((\text{error},2)) = $ false and thereby (II) is valid.

#

Basic functions implemented by term construction

Basic functions need not always to be implemented by special predicates. For example it is sometimes possible to implement them by term construction on parameter positions where their result is needed, e.g. the representation of the result of an application of $\underline{in}_i$ w.r.t. a sum domain D is always obtained from the representation of the argument of $\underline{in}_i$ by surrounding it with $\alpha_D(i)$.

Composition operator

The most important tool to derive predicates from recursive function definitions is the rule how to handle the composition operator $^\circ$. If the function f is defined as a composition $f_n {}^\circ \dots {}^\circ f_1$ of the functions $f_1, \dots, f_n$ (i.e. $f(x) = f_n(\dots(f_1(x))\dots))$ and $p_1, \dots, p_n$ are implementations of $f_1,\dots,f_n$ resp. in the sense of (*), then the predicate p defined by the definite clause $p(X_1,X_{n+1}) :- p_1(X_1,X_2),\dots,p_n(X_n,X_{n+1})$ is certainly a correct implementation of f in the sense of (*).

Special implementation of conditionals

For reasons of the implementational behaviour we suggest to figure out every application of <u>cond</u> in an additional predicate as follows. Let be D_1, D_2 arbitrary domains, $l,r: D_1 \to D_2$, p_l and p_r are implementations of l and r resp., then f: BOOLEAN $\times D_1 \to D_2$ with $f(b,d) = \underline{cond}(b,l(d),r(d))$ can be implemented by the following predicate p:

$$p(\text{true},X,Y) :- p_l(X,Y).$$
$$p(\text{false},X,Y) :- p_r(X,Y).$$

Clearly, this implementation is correct. Implementing an f': $D_1 \to D_2$ with $f'(x) = \underline{cond}(e(x),l'(x),r'(x))$, e: $D_1 \to$ BOOLEAN, l',r': $D_1 \to D_2$, one can often avoid an explicit implementation of e if the result of $e(x)$ (true or false) corresponds to a certain term structure of $\pi_{D_1}(x)$. The clauses implementing f' can then ensure their applicability by ensuring the certain term structure of the input parameter.

Example 4 (Special handling of <u>cond</u>):

We give an implementation for the auxiliary function APPLY introduced in Example 2. Therefore we define the constructors for the sum domain D = (VALUE+{undef}$\perp$) as follows: $\alpha_D(1)$ = mok, $\alpha_D(2)$ = merror. The predicate apply implements APPLY using the following clauses, where these clauses implement directly the three possible paths through APPLY as controlled by the two applications of <u>cond</u> within APPLY:

(A1)   apply([],V,merror).
(A2)   apply([(V,VAL)|M],V,mok(VAL)).
(A3)   apply([(V1,VAL)|M],V,MR) :- V1 \== V,apply(M,V,MR).

As it can be seen for the functions <u>null, head, tail, el</u>$_i$ applied to define APPLY no special implementation is required. For the predicates applied in (A1) - (A3) the specifications are:

S^{apply} : $apply_3 = APPLY'(apply_1,apply_2)$

$S^{\backslash==}$: $\sim\backslash==_1 = \backslash==_2$

To prove S^{apply} the validness of the formulae (I) - (III) has to be considered:

(I) $merror = APPLY'([\ ],V)$

(II) $mok(VAL) = APPLY'([(V,VAL)|M],V)$

(III) $\sim V1 = V \wedge MR = APPLY'(M,V) => MR = APPLY'([(V1,VAL)|M],V)$

Concerning (I): Obviously valid, since $APPLY(<>,V') = in_2(undef)$ for any $V' \in >ID<$.

Concerning (II): $APPLY(\underline{cons}(<V',VAL'>,M'),V') = \underline{in}_1(VAL')$ for all representable V',VAL',M', since (see definition of APPLY) $\underline{null}(\underline{cons}(...)) = false$ and $\underline{el}_1(\underline{head}(\underline{cons}(<V',VAL'>,M'))) = V'$ and $\underline{el}_2(\underline{head}(\underline{cons}(<V',VAL'>,M'))) = VAL'$.

Concerning (III): $APPLY(\underline{cons}(<V1',VAL'>,M'),V') = APPLY(M',V')$ for all representable $V',V1',VAL',M'$ with $V1' \neq V'$, since $\underline{null}(\underline{cons}(...)) = false$ and $\underline{tail}(\underline{cons}(<V1',VAL'>,M')) = M'$.

#

Equations of semantic functions

Semantic functions are usually described in such a way, that for any alternative for constructing elements from the domain to which meanings are assigned to (i.e. for any function symbol of the considered sort) a separate equation is given. The reflection within the derived logic program is straightforward: for every equation of a semantic function one definite clause has to be included.

Example 5 (Implementing equations of semantic functions):
The semantic function IC will be implemented by the predicate com. E.g. the following two clauses correspond to the semantic clauses (SD.2) and (SD.3).

(C1)   com(skip,M,cok(M)).

(C2)   com(concat(S1,S2),M,CR) :- com(S1,M,CR1),concat1(S2,CR1,CR).

The application of $\underline{cond}$ in (SD.3) (changed as above: IC (concat(S1,S2),M) = IC (S1,M) = M' -> IC (S2,M'), error) was figured out as described above, where the resulting predicate is concat1. Therefore (C2) implementing (SD.3) refers to concat1 with the following specification:

$S^{concat1}$: $concat1_3 = \underline{cond}'(\underline{is}_2'(concat1_2), \underline{in}_2'(error), IC'(concat1_1,\underline{out}_1(concat1_2)))$

If $D=(MEMORY+\{error\}\bot)$, $\alpha_D(1) = cok$, $\alpha_D(2) = cerror$, the specification S^{com}: $com_3 = IC'(com_1,com_2)$ can easily be proved to be valid.

#

Now we want to sketch how to prove (<=). The main idea for proving that the predicate p is complete w.r.t. the specification SP (i.e. w.r.t. a certain function) is to ensure that for any possible assignment v satisfying SP (in our case for any pair of function argument and corresponding function result) it is possible to find an instance of a clause for p such that the parameters in the head instance are equal to $v(p_1),...,v(p_n)$ (starting the "construction") and the parameters in the instances of the atoms in the body are assignments satisfying S_{SP} (ensuring the possibility to continue the "construction"). More roughly spoken, if p is the predicate implementing the function f, we have to prove that for any pair of argument and result for f there is a clause of p which is applicable on the representations of this pair and where the body implements at least f restricted to this case.

Example 6 (Completeness of apply, see also Example 4):
As specifications of the clauses (A1) - (A3) we take the parts of the definition of APPLY which we intended to implement by the clauses (as demanded by the conditionals).

S^{apply1}: $\underline{null}'(apply_1) = true \wedge apply_3 = \underline{in_2}'(undef)$
S^{apply2}: $\underline{null}'(apply_1) = false \wedge \underline{el_1}'(\underline{head}'(apply_1)) = apply_2$
$\qquad \wedge apply_3 = \underline{in_1}'(\underline{el_2}'(\underline{head}'(apply_1)))$
S^{apply3}: $\underline{null}'(apply_1) = false \wedge \sim \underline{el_1}'(\underline{head}'(apply_1)) = apply_2$
$\qquad \wedge apply_3 = APPLY'(\underline{tail}'(apply_1), apply_2)$

The completeness follows from the construction.

#

Proving the completeness of predicate p w.r.t. S^P possible "recursive calls" have to be considered to be finite. For denotational functions another property is important, that is to say the "construction" should terminate iff the corresponding computation terminates (e.g. an infinite loop will never terminate and thereby the corresponding recursion could not be proved to be finite). To prove the recursion for a predicate p to be finite, we must give a function μ_p mapping all assignments for parameters of p into a set in which "<" denotes a well-founded relation. During the "construction" as sketched above for any instance $q(a'_1,...,a'_m)$ in the body of a clause of p which could correspond to a recursive call of p one has to check that $\mu_q(a'_1,...,a'_m) < \mu_p(a_1,...,a_n)$, where $p(a_1,...,a_n)$ is the instance of the head.

Example 7 (Proving the finite recursion of apply):
We assume $\mu_{apply}(M,...,...)$ as length of list M. There is direct recursion in (A3). Thus we have to check the assignments for S^{apply3}. With < as usual for N_0, it is observable that $\mu_{apply}([...|\pi MEMORY(M')],...,...) < \mu_{apply}(\pi MEMORY(M'),...,...)$.

#

5 Conclusions and future work

We have presented an approach for deriving a provable correct prototype interpreter (as a Prolog program) directly from a language definition consisting of a special kind of attribute grammars and a semantics definition in the denotational style. The described approach is used in the Language Development System (LDL).

The main advantages of our approach are the following (see also the Introduction):
- It contains a method *how* to derive the Prolog program offering a prototype interpreter from the language definition.
- Our language definitions avoid some disadvantages (e.g. mixing of static and dynamic semantics or unsufficient description of static semantics) of other well-known forms.
- The obtained prototype interpreter can easily be shown to be correct w.r.t. the language definition and can be extended by new components preserving correctness.

- In difference to us other approaches using Prolog for the implementation of denotational semantics, usually apply the lambda notation and/or execute the semantics description on a lambda machine, which for instance introduces remarkable inefficiency.

There are the following points for further investigation:
- The described implementation method for the denotational semantics should be proved to be semantics preserving in general. Afterwards - assuming a correct implementation of the method itself - prototype interpreters could be derived automatically.
- The approach for proving the correctness of the derived prototype interpreter exploiting the inductive proof method (as applied in this paper) should be compared with the algebraic approach as considered e.g. in [Ma79], [RL93].
- There are other logic programming languages which seem to be more useful as implementation language of the prototype interpreters and for LDL at all, e.g. Gödel with its facilities for meta-programming and modules and its many-sorted type system.
- The operational semantics of our prototype interpreters should be considered more completly and formally. Moreover we are looking for ways to get more realistic prototype interpreters (e.g. as in [L89]).

References

[AM91]   Alblas,H., Melichar,B. (Eds.) : Attribute grammars, Applications and Systems, Proc. of the International Summer School SAGA, Prague, Czechoslowakia, June 1991, LNCS # 545, Springer-Verlag

[D90]   Deransart, P.: Proof Methods of Declarative Properties of Definite Programs, Rapports de Recherche No 1248, INRIA, Juni 1990

[DF89]   Deransart, P.; Ferrand, G.: A methodological view of logic programming with negation, In: O.M. Tammepuu (Ed.), Informatics '89, Proc. of the Soviet-French Symposium, Tallinn, May 29 - June 2, 1989, Estonian Academy of Sciences, Institute of Cybernetics, 76 - 91

[K91]   Koskimies,K.: Object-orientation in attribute grammars, In: [AM 91], 297-329

[KP92]   Kastens,U., Pfahler,P. (Eds.): Compiler Construction, 4th International Conference, CC '92, Paderborn, FRG, Oct. 1992, Proc., LNCS # 641, Springer-Verlag

[KPy80] Krishnaswamy,R., Pyster,A.B.: On the correctness of semantic-syntax-directed translations, JACM, Vol. 27, No. 2, April 1980, 338-355

[L89]   Lee,P.: Realistic compiler generation, The MIT Press 1989

[Lä93]   Lämmel,R.: Prolog-Implementation denotationaler Semantikbeschreibungen, Diplomarbeit, Universität Rostock, FB Informatik, Jan. 1993

[M73]   Morris,F.L.: Advice on structuring compilers and proving them correct, Proc. ACM Symposium on Principles of Programming Languages, Boston, 1973, 144-152

[Ma79]   Majster,M.E.: A unified view of semantics, Technical Report 79-394, Cornell University, Ithace, New York, Dep. of Computer Science, 1979

[PRO92] Buth,B. et al.: Provably correct compiler development and implementation, In: [KP92], 141-155

[R91a]   Riedewald,G.: Prototyping by using an attribute grammar as a logic program, In: [AM91], 401-437

[R91b]   Riedewald,G.: The LDL - Language Development Laboratory, Preprint CS-1-91, Dec. '91, Universität Rostock, FB Informatik

[R92]   Riedewald,G.: The LDL - Language Development Laboratory, In: [KP92], 88-94

[RL93]   Riedewald,G.;Lämmel,R.: Provable Correctness of Prototype Interpreters in LDL, Preprint CS-9-93, Sept. '93, Universität Rostock, FB Informatik

[Sch76] Schmeck,H.: Ein algebraischer Ansatz für Kompilerkorrektheitsbeweise, In: Informatik-Fachberichte 1, 1976, Springer-Verlag, 33-42

[St77]   Stoy,J.E.: Denotational Semantics: The Scott-Strachey Approach to Programming Language Theory, MIT-Press, 1977

[To90]   Tofte,M.: Compiler Generators, EATCS Monographs on Theoretical Computer Science, Vol. 19, Springer-Verlag, 1990

[TWW81] Thatcher,J.W., Wagner,E.G., Wright,J.B.: More on advice on structuring compilers and proving them correct, Theoretical Computer Science 15 (1981), 223-249

Developing Efficient Interpreters Based on Formal Language Specifications

Arnd Poetzsch–Heffter [1]

Institut für Informatik
Technische Universität
D–80290 München
poetzsch@informatik.tu-muenchen.de

Abstract

The paper reports on extensions to the MAX system enabling the generation and re-finement of interpreters based on formal language specifications. In these specifications, static semantics is defined by an attribution mechanism that allows to enrich syntax trees by control flow graphs. The dynamic semantics is defined by evolving algebras, a framework that has been successfully used to specify realistic programming languages.

We apply the combined framework to a non–trivial example language and show how the resulting language specification can be refined in order to improve the efficiency of the generated interpreters. The framework provides enough modularity and flexibility so that such refinements can be carried out by local changes within the framework. Finally, we explain the implementation of the extensions to MAX.

1 Introduction

Motivation Certainly, many agree with Tofte that "... a realistic language definition is a very delicate object" ([Tof90], p. 109). Nevertheless, different tasks and levels in language design and implementation are til now solved and supported based on different, often unrelated frameworks; consequently, for each task a specification has to be produced from scratch. E.g. there are frameworks for providing very high–level, readable, and formal language specifications (e.g. [Mos92]); and frameworks to specify compilation tasks focussing on efficiency: attribute grammars to express identification, typing, and context checking; control flow based specifications for data flow analyses to support optimizations; and pattern driven code generators.

Our ideal picture to relate the different specifications is a tree the root of which is the high–level language specification; a step to a child represents refinements or enrichments eventually leading to implementations of specific language–dependent tools. And a child should use as much as possible from the parent specification. The framework we present in this paper should be understood as a step towards this picture, even though we focus here on a specific example, the development of interpreters.

Approach In [PH93b], we showed how first–order recursive functions defined on occurrence structures can be used like attributes in an attribute grammar specification. In fact, recursive functions on occurrence structures provide a more expressive framework than attribute grammars in that they allow to formally specify an enrichment of the syntax tree by non–local edges. (On the other hand, attribute grammars allow in general for more efficient implementations; cf. relation to other work.) Here, we use a slightly extended version of occurrence structures to specify control flow and use evolving algebras developed by Gurevich to specify the dynamic semantics of programming languages.

Figure 1 shows the control flow graph for the expression $7 + f(a, 0)$ as syntax tree enrichment. The evolving algebra specifies how to interpret these graphs; in particular it

---

[1]Supported by DFG grant Po 432/2-1.

specifies the semantics of the graph nodes — called *tasks*. These tasks may have parameters (omitted in the figure); e.g. the BinOp-task has the operator Add, the argument expressions "Int" and "CallExp" and the result expression "BinExp" as parameters (cf. section 3). The graph nodes denoted by "o" are called *program points*; they are an auxiliary device enabling to specify the task graph locally for each tree production.

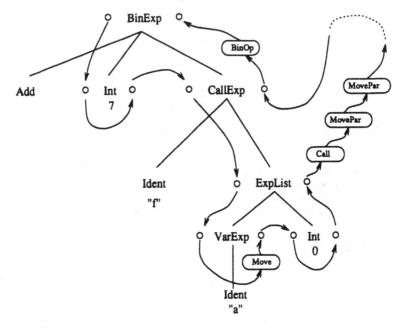

Figure 1: Control flow for expression $7 + f(a, 0)$

After providing the formal background, we illustrate the framework by specifying a non-trivial example language. In section 4, we refine this language specification to an interpreter specification. Section 5 explains how the MAX system ([PH93b]) was extended.

Relation to other Work Our work should be understood as a step towards filling the gap between very high–level language specification frameworks that are optimized versus readability and formality and specification frameworks that are designed to generate tools that can compete in efficiency with hand–writen tools.

To illustrate one of the differences between language specification frameworks like denotational, natural, or action semantics and our framework, let us consider a standard specification of an imperative language with loops and local blocks. If we interpret the shown program fragment according to such a specification, the environment has to be changed each time the loop is entered or exited (the binding for "a" has to be changed). In an interpreter one would like to avoid this overhead. As our specifications can be based on the occurrences of the syntax tree, we could refine such a specification by using a static function from used identifier occurrences to their declaration occurrences and a global environment mapping variable declarations to values. I.e. we seperate a static aspect (namely identifier binding) from

```
int a = 2;
int b = 10
    ...
while( b > 9 ){
    int a;
    ...
    a = a+1 ;
}
```

the dynamic semantics and globalize the environment. In a similar way, we can specify a static function yielding for each jump statement the corresponding target statement, thereby refining control flow.

The goal of the presented work is not to substitute higher–level frameworks that are more convenient to use, trimmed versus readability, or have specific theoretical properties (all this is true e.g. for action semantics; see [Mos92]). The goal is to provide a system supported formal framework that allows to express stepwise refinement of specifications; in particular it should be flexible enough to express globalizing transformations (cf. [Sch85]), seperation of static from dynamic aspects, improvements on the control flow, and refinements based on data types.

Compared to attribute grammar based system, our system supports the specification of dynamic semantics and is more expressive as far as the formal part of specifications is concerned. On the other hand, if e.g. the flow graphs are encapsulated in semantic actions, attribute grammar specifications can be understood as refining our specifications towards efficiency. In addition to that, our work is related to systems enabling the implementation of data flow analyses ([Wil81]) and allows to bring data flow analysis and language semantics together (see [PH93a]; for a denotational approach cf. [Ven89]).

Another very important relation is to works using programming language specifications to define the semantics of programming logics. In particular, it is related to positional semantics as defined in [CO78]. In deed, our framework can be understood as a generalization of positional semantics in that it provides very flexible formal methods to define positions and the transition relation. Thereby it makes the logic approach of [CO78] applicable to realistic programming languages.

2 Formal Background

This section introduces the formal concepts our specifications are based on. First, we define occurrence algebras, an extension of term algebras. Occurrence algebras provide occurrence sorts (e.g. the sort of the variable declaration occurrences in a syntax tree). Having the occurrences as elements in the formal framework allows to specify graphs and thereby enables very rich program representations. Then, we give a short introduction to evolving algebras that are used to specify the dynamic semantics. Both concepts use the notion of "algebras": An *algebra* is given by a set U, called the universe of the algebra, and a set of functions that take their arguments in U^n and yield values in U.

2.1 Occurrence Algebras

Occurrence algebras extend order–sorted term algebras by providing sorts for the occurrences of terms. They simplify and generalize the concept of occurrence structures as presented in [PH93b]. Before the formal definition, we give an informal introduction. Consider the abstract syntax for the expressions of our example language:

```
Exp       = Int | VarExp | CallExp | BinExp
VarExp    ( Ident )
CallExp   ( Ident ExpList )
ExpList   * Exp
BinExp    ( Operator Exp Exp )
Operator  = Add | ...
Add       ()
```

i.e. an expression is in integer constant, a variable occurrence, a function call, or a binary expression; and e.g. a call has two components: the identifier of the called function and the actual parameter list. To define control flow graphs as shown in the introduction, we must be able to refer to a "father" of a term. But in term algebras there is no "father" of a term. That is why we consider occurrences in terms. Occurrences are represented as usual by a pair (t, l), where t is a term and and l a list of positive integers $i_1, \ldots, i_n$ describing the path from the root of t to the subterm occurrence. We use the notation $@(t; i_1, \ldots, i_n)$ and write $@(t; \epsilon)$ for the root occurrence of t. E.g. $@(\text{CallExp}("f", \text{ExpList}(\text{VarExp}(\underline{"x"}), \text{VarExp}("x")))$; 2,1,1) represents the first occurrence of identifier x in the abstract syntax term for $f(x, x)$. The father of this occurrence is the first occurrence of the corresponding variable expression: $@(\text{CallExp}("f", \text{ExpList}(\underline{\text{VarExp}("x")}, \text{VarExp}("x")))$; 2,1).

It is useful to extend the sorting on terms to occurrences: An occurrence of a subterm s of sort S is said to be of sort S@; e.g. the occurrences given above are of sort Ident@ and VarExp@ respectively. Using occurrence sorts, we can define new sorts. For example the program points before and after expression occurrences as shown in figure 1 can be defined by the productions:

```
ExpPoint  =  Before  |  After
Before    (  Exp@  )
After     (  Exp@  )
```

In the following, we define what the occurrence algebra for a set of productions is.

Definition 2.1 Let PRODSORTS and PRIMSORTS be two disjunct sets of symbols called production and primitive[2] sort symbols. A *sort symbol* is a production or primitive sort symbol followed by a possibly empty sequence of @-symbols, i.e. has the form S@*, where S ∈ PRODSORTS ∪ PRIMSORTS. The set of sort symbols is denoted by SORTS.

- A *production* has one of the following forms: $S(S_1 \ldots S_m)$ (called *tuple production*), or $S * T$ (called *list production*), or $S = S_0 | \ldots | S_n$ (called *class production*), where S ∈ PRODSORTS, S_i, T ∈ SORTS, and m, n are natural numbers; S is called the *left hand side* of the respective production.

- Let Π be a finite set of productions such that for each S ∈ PRODSORTS there is exactly one production with left hand side S. For each sort in SORTS\PRIMSORTS we inductively define a set of *elements* assuming that the sets for the primitive sorts are given:

  - $S(t_1, \ldots, t_n)$ is an element of sort S if $S(S_1 \ldots S_n) \in \Pi$ and each t_i is of sort S_i;
  - $S(t_1, \ldots, t_n)$ is of sort S if $S * T \in \Pi$ and each t_i is of sort T;
  - t is of sort S if $S = S_0 | \ldots | S_n \in \Pi$ and t is of sort S_i for one i, $0 \le i \le n$;
  - $@(t; \epsilon)$ is of sort S@ if t is of sort S;
  - $@(t; i_1, \ldots, i_m)$ is of sort S@ if $t \equiv T(t_1, .., t_{i_1}, .., t_n)$ is of sort T and $@(t_{i_1}; i_2, \ldots, i_m)$ is of sort S@.

  Elements generated by the first two rules are called *terms*; elements generated by the last two rules are called *occurrences*.

- The universe of the *occurrence algebra* defined by Π consists of the elements as defined above, the elements of the primitive sorts, and the extra element *nil*; the functions of the occurrence algebra defined by Π are:

---

[2]Throughout this paper, we assume the primitive sorts Ident, Int, and Bool

- functions defined on occurrences: $fath(x)$, $lbroth(x)$, $rbroth(x)$, $son(i, x)$, the father, left/right brother, i-th son of occurrence x; $term(x)$, the subterm that corresponds to occurrence x.

- functions defined on terms: $subterm(i, t)$, the i-th subterm of t; $append(e, l)$, $first(l)$, $rest(l)$ with the usual meaning on list terms; for each list production S * T the empty list constructor $S()$; and for each tuple production S * T the constructor $S(t_1, \ldots, t_n)$. (For convenience, we use the same name for the sort (roman font) and the corresponding constructor (italic).)

- for each sort S a boolean function $isS(x)$ testing whether x is of sort S.

- the functions defined on the primitive sorts.

Whenever a function is applied to elements where the meaning as described[3] above is not defined, it yields the extra element nil.

□

2.2 Evolving Algebras

Evolving algebras are a powerful framework for specifying programming language semantics. They have been used to specify the semantics of many different programming languages including C ([GH92]), PROLOG ([BR92]), and Occam ([GM89]). Here, we summarize the definition of evolving algebras given in [Gur91].

In an evolving algebra specification, the computation states are described by algebras. The evolving algebra specifies how the states are related to their successor states; i.e. it specifies a successor relation on algebras: Given an algebra A, it describes how the functions of A may be "updated" to get a successor algebra — reflecting the intuition that in a computation step only a small part of the state is changed.

As an introductory example let us specify the semantics of lists of assignments of the form $\langle variable \rangle := \langle variable \rangle$. We assume the list functions $isempty$, $first$, and $rest$, and the selector functions lhs, rhs yielding the left/right hand sides of assignments. The state information that changes during execution is represented by the unary function VAL mapping variables to values and the "0-ary function" AL holding the rest of the assignment list. In the following, we call functions that may change during execution $dynamic$; and dynamic 0-ary functions are called $dynamic\ variables$. Here is an evolving algebra specifying the semantics of assignment lists:

```
IF ¬isempty(AL) THEN   AL := rest(AL)                          FI
IF ¬isempty(AL) THEN   VAL(lhs(first(AL))) := VAL(rhs(first(AL)))  FI
```

The evolving algebra has two rules. Rules are executed in parallel: Given an algebra A, evaluate the guards, the right hand side expressions of the updates, and the arguments on the left hand sides of the updates (here `lhs(first(AL))`). Then, perform those updates with a true guard. The following definition makes this more precise:

Definition 2.2 An *evolving algebra* EA is given by a finite set of rules of the form **IF** $guard$ **THEN** $f(arg_1, \ldots, arg_n) := rhsexp$ **FI**, where $guard$, arg_i, and $rhsexp$ are variable free expressions and n is the arity of f.

---

[3] A technical report spelling this out in more rigorous terms by algebraic laws is in preparation.

- Let A be an algebra containing the boolean values and a function for all function symbols occurring in EA. An algebra A' is an *EA–successor* of A if updating the functions of A according to the following procedure yields A': Let *UPDATES* be the set of updates of those rules the guard of which evaluate to true in A. Evaluate all arguments and right hand side expressions occurring in *UPDATES* and replace them by their values. The resulting set may contain subsets of contradicting updates, e.g. $g(b_1,\ldots,b_n) := r$ and $g(b_1,\ldots,b_n) := q$ with $r \neq q$. From these subsets of contradicting updates eliminate non–deterministically all updates but one, resulting in a set of non–contradicting updates. Change the functions of A according to this set of updates, i.e. change the value of function f at point $a_1,\ldots,a_n$ to r if there is an update $f(a_1,\ldots,a_n) := r$.

- A sequence $(A_i)_{i \in \mathbb{N}}$ of algebras such that A_{i+1} is an EA–successor of A_i for all i is called a *computation* of EA with initial algebra A_0.

□

For practical purposes, the restricted syntax of evolving algebras as defined above is rather inconvenient. Assuming that the considered algebras always contain a binary function $\wedge$ yielding *true* exactly if both arguments are *true* and a unary function $\neg$ yielding true for the argument *false*, we can introduce the following four syntactical extensions — the associated rules show how to transform the extended syntax into the restricted syntax above:

- unguarded assignments as rules: $f(\vec{a}) := rhsexp$
  ⇒ IF *true* THEN $f(\vec{a}) := rhsexp$ FI;

- nested if-rules: IF *guard1* THEN IF *guard2* THEN *body* FI FI
  ⇒ IF *guard1* $\wedge$ *guard2* THEN *body* FI

- rule lists in the body of if-rules: IF *guard* THEN $R_1 \ldots R_n$ FI
  ⇒ IF *guard* THEN R_1 FI ... IF *guard* THEN R_n FI

- if-then-else-rules: IF *guard* THEN *body1* ELSE *body2* FI
  ⇒ IF *guard* THEN *body1* FI IF $\neg$ *guard* THEN *body2* FI

It goes without saying that any combination of these extensions is allowed.

3 Specifying Control Flow and Dynamic Semantics

In this section, we apply occurrence algebras and evolving algebras to specify the semantics of an imperative example language called TOY in the following. Even though necessarily small, TOY contains some features that are difficult to handle in many other language specification frameworks, namely return statements (showing how to handle jumps or exceptions) and recursive function procedures with side effects (showing how to handle such procedure calls in expressions). The TOY specification demonstrates how to enrich syntax trees by control flow information and how to use this information to specify dynamic semantics. This modularization of the dynamic semantics specification into two parts may seem complicated at first sight. However, its advantages become clear when applying it to realistic size languages (cf. the discussion in section 5) or to the implementation of efficient interpreters (cf. section 4). In addition to this, the flow information or similar enrichments of the syntax tree can be used for data flow analysis and code generation in compilers.

The semantics specification in the following two subsections proceeds as follows: First, we specify the state space of TOY programs. Then, we introduce a set of atomic actions —

so-called *tasks* — and give an evolving algebra semantics for them. Finally, we specify the control flow of TOY in terms of program points and tasks. But before that, we have to give the missing productions of the abstract syntax of TOY (the expression syntax was given in section 2):

```
Program         ( DeclList  )
DeclList        * Decl
Decl            = Var | Proc
Var             ( Ident  )
Proc            ( Ident ParamList.params Body  )
Body            ( StatList  )
ParamList       * Param
Param           ( Ident  )

StatList        * Stat
Stat            = WhileStat | IfStat | AssignStat | ReturnStat
WhileStat       ( Exp StatList  )
IfStat          ( Exp StatList StatList  )
AssignStat      ( Ident Exp  )
ReturnStat      ( Exp  )
```

As shown in the production for Proc, we allow to define selectors for tuple components; i.e. if P is of sort Proc, the expressions "P.params" and "subterm(2,P)" are equivalent.

3.1 The Dynamic Semantics of Tasks

This section has three parts: The first defines objects and locations; the second provides the sort definitions for tasks; and the third gives the evolving algebra for TOY.

Objects and Locations TOY has global objects and objects that are local to a procedure incarnation. Global objects need exactly one location to store the corresponding value; local objects need a location for each procedure incarnation. The global objects of TOY are the variables and integer constants[4]. Parameters are local objects. Are there other local objects? As we have to deal with procedure calls in expressions, we must keep track of those parts of expressions that are evaluated before a call. The easiest way to do this is to consider expression occurrences as local objects (this is called a store semantics in [MS76] and reflects the notion of temporary objects in compiler construction). Beside this, it is convenient to consider procedures as local objects for passing their return values. These considerations are formally expressed by the following productions:

```
Object          = GlobalObject | LocalObject
GlobalObject     = Var@    | Int@
LocalObject     = VarExp@ | CallExp@ | BinExp@ | Param@ | Proc@
Location        = GlobalObject | Automatic
Automatic       ( LocalObject Incar  )
Incar           = Nat
```

The relation between locations and values is captured by the function VAL,

```
DYN VAL( Location L ) Int: IF Int@ L: term(L)    ELSE    ??
```

where the keyword DYN indicates that VAL is a dynamic function. The body of a dynamic function defines its values in the initial state: VAL yields for an integer node the corresponding value and an arbitrary value of sort Int (the result sort) for all other locations.

---

[4]Treating constants as objects simplifies the specification.

Tasks and Control Information   The atomic actions the TOY semantics is based on are the tasks defined by the following productions. A branch task has three components: the expression node of the corresponding condition and the two possible successors. A return task has the returning procedure as component. A call task the expression where it is called. A move task its source and destination etc. The precise usage of the tasks is specified in section 3.2 — in particular the successors of tasks.

```
Task        =  Branch | Return | SinglSucc | Start | End | Point
SinglSucc   =  Move | MovePar | BinOp | Call
Branch      (  Exp@.cond    Task.ttsucc   Task.ffsucc )
Return      (  Proc@.rproc  )
Call        (  CallExp@.cexp      Task.succ )
Move        (  Object@.src        Object@.dst      Task.succ )
MovePar     (  LocalObject@.src LocalObject@.dst  Task.succ )
BinOp       (  Operator.op Exp@.left Exp@.right  Exp@.dst Task.succ )
Start       ()
End         ()
TaskStack   *  Task
IncarStack  *  Incar
```

The control information in a state consists of the current task CT, the control stack CTR_S recording the return points of the active procedures, the current incarnation CI, the stack of active incarnations INCAR_S, and an incarnation counter NEXTINCAR:

```
DYN  CT        () Task:          Start()
DYN  CTR_S     () TaskStack:     push( End(), TaskStack() )
DYN  CI        () Incar:         0
DYN  INCAR_S   () IncarStack:    IncarStack()
DYN  NEXTINCAR() Incar:          1
```

As explained above, the bodies of these dynamic variables specify their initial values.

Evolving Algebra for TOY   The evolving algebra for TOY essentially contains for each task sort one rule. The first rule specifies the semantics of a branch:

```
IF  isBranch(CT) THEN
    IF VAL(loc(CT.cond,CI)) = 0  THEN  CT := CT.ffsucc ELSE  CT := CT.ttsucc FI
FI
```

As in C, the value *false* is represented by 0 in TOY. The function *loc* yields for each object its current location:

```
FCT  loc( Object@ OBJ, Incar IC ) Location:
    IF  LocalObject@ OBJ  :  Automatic( OBJ, IC )  ELSE  OBJ
```

The start task initializes CT to the point before the main procedure and the parameter of the main procedure to the input value (the specification of mproc and the declaration of the dynamic variables PROGRAM and INPUT are given in the appendix):

```
IF  isStart(CT)  THEN
    CT    := Before(mproc(PROGRAM))
    VAL( loc( son(1,mproc(PROGRAM).params), CI ) ) := INPUT
FI
```

The rules for the tasks with a single successor are rather straightforward. The function *eval* evaluates a binary operator on two arguments (cf. appendix). In order to understand the rule for the return task below, one should notice here that a call task pushes the point after the call expression on the control stack:

```
IF isSinglSucc(CT) THEN
  CT := CT.succ
  IF isMove(CT)    THEN  VAL(loc(CT.dst,CI)) := VAL( loc(CT.src,CI) )          FI
  IF isMovePar(CT) THEN  VAL(loc(CT.dst,CI)) := VAL( loc(CT.src,top(INCAR_S))) FI
  IF isBinOp(CT)   THEN  VAL(loc(CT.dst,CI)) :=
                         eval( CT.op, VAL(loc(CT.left,CI)), VAL(loc(CT.right,CI)) )
  FI
  IF isCall(CT)    THEN
    CTR_S     := push( After(CT.cexp), CTR_S)
    INCAR_S   := push( CI, INCAR_S )
    CI        := NEXTINCAR
    NEXTINCAR := NEXTINCAR + 1
  FI
FI
```

On return of a procedure: If the end task is on top of the control stack, then the return value
of the procedure is copied to the dynamic variable OUTPUT. Otherwise the return value
is copied to the expression node corresponding to the continuation point of the returning
procedure:

```
IF isReturn(CT) THEN
  CT    := top(CTR_S)
  CTR_S := pop(CTR_S)
  IF top(CTR_S) = End()
    THEN  OUTPUT := VAL( loc(CT.rproc,CI) )
    ELSE  VAL( loc( top(CTR_S).node, top(INCAR_S)) ) :=  VAL( loc(CT.rproc,CI) )
          CI        := top(INCAR_S)
          INCAR_S := pop(INCAR_S)
  FI
FI
IF isEnd(CT)   THEN  skip        FI
IF isPoint(CT) THEN  CT := succ(CT)  FI
```

The specification of the successor function for program points (used in the last line) is the
topic of the next section.

3.2 Control Flow

As illustrated in the introduction, control flow can be understood as an enrichment of the
syntax trees. Such enrichments are specified in two steps: First, we specify the set of program
points; then, we specify by an attribution process how the syntax trees are enriched. To
describe control flow for TOY, we introduce program points before and after statements,
statement lists, expressions, expression lists, and procedures:

```
ExecNode   = Exp© | ExpList© | Stat© | StatList© | Proc©
Before     ( ExecNode.node )
After      ( ExecNode.node )
Point      = Before | After
```

We specify the control flow as a function *succ* that returns for each program point the
successor task. For reasons that become clear when we discuss implementation aspects
(cf. section 5), we consider *succ* to be an attribute of the points, i.e. a function the values of
which are computed once for a given program and stored for use during program execution.
From a formal point of view, an attribute is just a unary function. The successor of a point
depends on the context of the node to which the point belongs. We use the pattern notation
of the MAX system to refer to the different contexts in which such a node may occur.
E.g. let P be the point after a node N and N be the node representing the condition of a
while statement; then the successor of P is the branch task that has N as first component, the

point before the body of the loop as *tt*-successor, and the point after the loop as *ff*-successor; this is expressed as follows (for conditional expressions in the specification language, we use a colon to seperate conditions from then–branches in order to distinguish it from EA-rules):

```
IF  WhileStat@<N,BD>  W :  Branch( N, Before(BD), After(W) )
```

The following specification shows the other cases for points after nodes (the cases for points before nodes are trivial and given in the appendix). The function *decl* maps every identifier to its declaration and the function *proc* maps each element of sort ExecNode to the enclosing procedure (cf. appendix). The function *next* yields the next program point in a left to right tree traversal (cf. section 5). The most interesting case is a call with parameters, because

```
ATT  succ( Point P ) Task:
  LET  N == P.node :
  IF  P = After(N) :
    IF  Proc@ N             :  Return( N )
      | WhileStat@<N,BD>  W :  Branch( N, Before(BD), After(W) )
      | WhileStat@<E,N>    :  Before( E )
      | IfStat@<N,TB,EB>   :  Branch( N, Before(TB), Before(EB) )
      | IfStat@<_,N,_> IS  :  After( IS )
      | AssignStat@<ID,N> A :  Move( N, decl(ID), After(A) )
      | ReturnStat@<E> N   :  Move( E, proc(N), After(proc(N)) )
      | BinExp@<O,L,N> E   :  BinOp( term(O), L, N, E, After(E))
      | CallExp@<ID,<>N> C :  Call( C, Before(decl(ID)) )
      | CallExp@<ID,<PAR,*> N> C:
          Call( C, parcopy( PAR, son(1,decl(ID).params), Before(decl(ID)) ) )
    ELSE  next(P)
    | P = Before(N) :
      .... // see appendix
  ELSE  nil()
```

it demonstrates how to construct task structures that are not directly related to the syntax tree (cf. the picture in the introduction): In the case here, we build up the sequence of parameter moves using the function *parcopy*:

```
FCT  parcopy( Exp@ APAR, Param@ FPAR, Task SUCC ) Task:
  IF  rbroth(APAR) = nil() :  MovePar(APAR,FPAR,SUCC)
  ELSE  MovePar( APAR, FPAR, parcopy(rbroth(APAR),rbroth(FPAR),SUCC) )
```

4   Towards Specification of Efficient Interpreters

If we add a concrete syntax to the TOY specification given in the previous section and the appendix ([PHE93] shows how to do that), we can execute TOY programs using the prototype system described in section 5. However, the stepping from program point to program point would make these executions slow and the storage consumption would make them almost unfeasible, because we would need storage proportional to the total number of procedure incarnations occurring in an execution (and not proportional to the maximal number of simultaneously active incarnations). In this section, we refine the language specification of TOY to a specification of a reasonably efficient interpreter by eliminating unnecessary stepping and by switching to a stack organisation for the automatic storage. The point we want to make here is that both refinements can be achieved by small and local modifications of the TOY specification and that these modifications can be carried out within the presented framework.

Avoiding Unnecessary Stepping The stepping from program point to program point without executing a "real" task can be avoided by using the attribute *tasksucc* instead of *succ* in the evolving algebra rule for points: *tasksucc* yields for each point the next task to be

```
ATT tasksucc( Point P ) Task:
  IF isPoint( succ(P) ) :  tasksucc(succ(P))  ELSE  succ(P)
```

executed. We could even do a little better by avoiding all program points except those that break up loops; in TOY, these are the points before conditions of while statements and before procedures (because of recursion). To do this, we essentially have to make *tasksucc* and *succ* mutually recursive.

Stacks for Automatic Storage This paragraph shows how the TOY specification can be refined to implement automatic storage by a standard stack organization (cf. e.g. [AU77]). Locations will be simply natural numbers (i.e. the dynamic function VAL can be considered as an array). We assume the two attributes *size* and *addr* with the following signature:

```
ATT size( Proc© ) Nat
ATT addr( Object© ) Nat
```

size(P) is the number of locations needed for an incarnation of procedure P; *addr* yields for a global object its location, for a local object its relative address, i.e. the offset from the first location in a procedure incarnation. (It should be clear that the well–known algorithms to compute *size* and *addr* can be expressed in our framework.)

Using the dynamic variable CI as first location in a procedure incarnation (i.e. as "stack pointer"), we need the following changes to the TOY specification:

- replace the definition for Location by "Location = Nat" and the definition for Incar by "Incar = Location";

- change the body of the function *loc* to

```
IF LocalObject© OBJ :  IC + addr(OBJ)  ELSE  addr(OBJ)
```

- replace the updates of CI in the rules for the start and call task by:

```
CI  :=  numberofvars(PROGRAM)        // for the start task
CI  :=  size( decl( son(1,CT.cexp) ) )   // for the call task
```

where the function *numberofvars* yields the number of variable declarations.

After these changes all occurrences of NEXTINCAR can be removed. (And a renaming of Incar, etc. is advisable for mnemonic reasons.)

Further Improvements Of course, further improvements are possible — approximating more and more what a compiler does. To mention only one[5], the costly calls to *loc* can be eliminated by splitting the move task into three tasks reflecting the "addressing modes": MoveGlobToLoc, MoveLocToLoc, and MoveLocToGlob. After a replacement of all occurrences of the move task, the calls to *loc* can be replaced either by the global address or by the relative address plus CI.

The focus of this section was to demonstrate how systematic refinements can be carried out in the presented formal framework. It goes without saying that the illustrated method apply to compiler construction as well.

---

[5] According to our performance analysis, the most profitable one.

5 Implementation Aspects and Experiences

We implemented a prototype on top of the MAX system that generates interpreters from specifications based on occurrence algebras, attribute and function specifications, and evolving algebras. This section summarizes the implementation aspects of this prototype and discusses the experiences we made so far.

5.1 Implementation Aspects

This section sketches the extensions to the MAX system and the prototype implementation used for executing evolving algebras. For the following it is helpful to consider the run of a generated interpreter as a three step process:

1. Reading: includes parsing and encoding of the nodes; see below.

2. Attribution: includes attribute evaluation (and context checking).

3. Interpretation: execute the input program according to the evolving algebra.

Extensions to MAX The efficiency of our occurrence algebra implementation stems from the fact that during the attribution and interpretation phase for a program PROG we only have to deal with occurrences of one term or a very small number of terms, namely the syntax tree of PROG and possibly some intermediate representations. This allows us to work with efficient encodings[6] for these occurrences (instead of using a direct implementation of the term-natlist-pairs). Let us call this set of occurrences the *nodes*[7] of a program. Encodings of nodes were already exploited in the MAX implementation (see [PH93b] p. 144). As program points showed up to be helpful for many purposes (cf. section 5.2), we implemented program points as well by encodings. Essentially, the system provides a predefined sort PredefPoint and functions *before(n)*, *after(n)* yielding the point before and after a node n as well as the functions *node(p)*, *next(p)* yielding the node corresponding to a point p and the next point according to a left to right tree traversal. The encoding allows us to implement *before*, *after*, and *node* by an array access and *next* by an addition. User-defined program points are then treated as subsorts of sort PredefPoint.

In the specifications, we distinguished functions and attributes (e.g. *succ* was specified as an attribute). As mentioned earlier, the semantics of attributes and unary functions are the same. But the implementation is different. The relevant values of the attributes, i.e. the attribute values for the nodes and points, are computed once and cached for later use. One of the main advantages of encodings is that caching becomes simple: As the encodings of all elements of one sort form an integer interval, the attribute values can be stored in an array having this interval as range. In particular, we can handle attributes on points in an efficient way, in particular control flow information as given by *succ*.

Executing Evolving Algebras The implementation of evolving algebras has two aspects: the representation of the dynamic functions and the stepwise execution of the rules. In our prototype, we only allow dynamic variables and unary[8] dynamic functions. Dynamic functions are implemented by arrays. If the parameter sort has an encoding, this is done the same simple way as for the attributes. If the parameter sort is Int or Nat, the needed parts of the array are dynamically allocated in blocks; the mapping from indices to blocks is recorded by a binary tree. For all other parameter sorts, we hash the term representation of

---

[6]Our implementation uses a four byte integer for all codings mentioned in the following.

[7]This definition is consistent with the informal use of "node" in the previous sections.

[8]Functions with greater arity can be handled by defining a tuple sort for their parameter sort tuple.

the parameters. Of course, this can drastically slow down reads and updates (and by that the interpretation): E.g. an update to VAL in the version of section 3 can be more than 50 times slower than an update to VAL in the version of section 4 with parameters of sort Location = Nat.

As all rules of an evolving algebra have to be executed in parallel, we divide each computation step in two substeps: Compute all arguments and right hand sides of updates with true guard and then perform the updates in some order. To avoid testing the guards twice, we keep track of the updates that have to be performed in a list of pointers to parameterless procedures; each of these procedures performs the set of updates corresponding to one node in the tree of conditionals that reflects the nesting of rules in the evolving algebra. As a small optimization, we use case statements to implement branching according to sort tests.

5.2 Generation of Language–Specific Programming Tools

The experiences we made so far are very promising. We generated some tools for small languages like TOY and miniML, and developed a specification for a C subset that includes the entire expression and statement syntax. The control flow graphs based on tasks are not only a good technique for closing the gap between formal language specifications and interpreter specifications, but provide as well a flexible basis for the development of other language specific programming tools. E.g. it showed to be fairly simple to enrich interpreter specifications to get source level debuggers; and for them program points are a very natural way to specify the stepping. In another application we built a (hand–coded) data flow analysis on top of control flow graphs; and again we could reuse almost the whole static part of the language/interpreter specification. Last but not least, some aspects of code generation become simpler in our approach; in particular the generation of jumps and instruction labels is simplified.

6   Conclusions

We proposed a combination of occurrence algebras, recursive first–order functions, and evolving algebras as a programming specification framework. Even though its formal foundations are comparably simple, the framework is sufficiently expressive to specify all kinds of programming languages including parallel ones (cf. [GM89]). Its flexibility makes it attractive for stepwise refinements of specifications. We attempted to demonstrate this by refining a non–trivial language specification. Finally, we described a prototype implementation that generates interpreters or other language–dependent programming tools from specifications.

As described in the introduction, one of the motivations for this research was to fill the gap between high–level language specifications and efficiency oriented specification techniques and to learn how to refine the former towards the latter. Whereas we consider the relation between high–level specifications and our framework a topic for future research, the refinements needed to acheive more efficient language implementations are much better understood. E.g. to develop a production quality compiler from the refined TOY specification of section 4, add optimization techniques, refine the set of tasks w.r.t. a suitable intermediate representation for code generators and then adapt this refined specification to more specialized and more efficient compiler construction tools. The refinement approach not only helps to systematize compiler development and allows for early prototyping, but should eventually provide the techniques to prove realistic compilers correct.

The development of the MAX system is still in progress. Currently, we improve the efficiency of the attribute evaluation ([Mer93]). The next envisaged extension is a fixpoint evaluator to prototype high–level data flow analyses based on control flow graphs.

References

[AU77]   A. V. Aho and J. D. Ullman. *Principles of Compiler Design.* Addison–Wesley, 1977.

[BR92]   E. Börger and D. Rosenzweig. A simple mathematical model for full Prolog. Technical Report TR–33/92, Dipartimento di Informatica, Universita di Pisa, 1992.

[CO78]   R. L. Constable and M. J. O'Donnell. *A Programming Logic: With an Introduction to the PL/CV Verifier.* Winthrop Publishers, 1978.

[GH92]   Y. Gurevich and J. Huggins. The semantics of the C programming language. In E. Börger et al., editor, *Computer Science Logic*, pages 274–308, 1992. LNCS 702.

[GM89]   Y. Gurevich and L. Moss. Algebraic operational semantics and Occam. In E. Börger et al., editor, *Computer Science Logic*, pages 176–192, 1989. LNCS 440.

[Gur91] Y. Gurevich. *Evolving Algebras*, volume 43, pages 264–284. EATCS Bulletin, 1991.

[Mer93] R. Merk. Generierung von MAX–Attributauswertern. Master's thesis, Technische Universität München, 1993.

[Mos92] P. Mosses. *Action Semantics.* Cambridge University Press, 1992. "Tracts in Theoretical Computer Science".

[MS76]   R. Milner and C. Stratchey. *A Theory of Programming Language Semantics.* Chapman and Hall, 1976.

[PH93a] A. Poetzsch-Heffter. Interprocedural data flow analysis based on temporal specifications. Technical Report 93-1397, Cornell University, 1993.

[PH93b] A. Poetzsch-Heffter. Programming language specification and prototyping using the MAX system. In J. Penjam M. Bruynooghe, editor, *Programming Language Implementation and Logic Programming*, 1993. LNCS 714.

[PHE93] A. Poetzsch-Heffter and T. Eisenbarth. The MAX system: A tutorial introduction. Technical Report TUM-I9307, TU, April 1993.

[Sch85] D. A. Schmidt. Detecting global variables in denotational specifications. *Transactions on Programming Languages and Systems*, 7:299–310, 1985.

[Tof90] M. Tofte. *Compiler Generators.* Springer–Verlag, 1990.

[Ven89] G. A. Venkatesh. A framework for construction and evaluation of high–level specification of program analysis techniques. *ACM Conference on Progamming Language Design and Implementation*, 1989.

[Wil81] R. Wilhelm. Global flow analysis and optimization in the MUG2 compiler generating system. In S. Muchnick and N. D. Jones, editors, *Program Flow Analysis: Theory and Applications*, pages 132–159. Prentice–Hall, 1981.

A Completing the TOY Specification

The following parts of the TOY specification describe the identification and complete the specification given in section 3:

```
DeclOrParam      = Decl | Param
EnvSite          = DeclOrParam | Body
DeclOrParamList  * DeclOrParam@


FCT  idstr( DeclOrParam@ D ) String:  idtos( term(son(1,D)) )

ATT  env( EnvSite@ ES ) DeclOrParamList :
    IF  Program@< <ES,*> >       :  append( ES, DeclOrParamList() )
    |  Proc@<_,<ES,*>,_> FD      :  append( ES, env(FD) )
    |  Proc@<_,<>,ES> FD         :  env(FD)
    |  Proc@<_,<*,PD>,ES>        :  env(PD)
    |  DeclList@<*,DC,ES,*>      :  append( ES, env(DC) )
    ELSE                            nil()

FCT  corr_env( ExecNode N ) DeclOrParamList:
    IF  Body@<N> :  env(N) ELSE  corr_env( fath(N) )

FCT  lookup( String ID, DeclOrParamList ENV ) DeclOrParam@:
    IF  ENV = DeclOrParamList() :  nil()
    |  ID = idstr(first(ENV)) :   first(ENV)
                         ELSE  lookup( ID, rest(ENV) )

ATT  decl( Ident@ IDN ) DeclOrParam@:
    IF  DeclOrParam@<IDN,*> D   :   D
    ELSE   lookup( idtos(term(IDN)), corr_env(fath(IDN)) )


ATT  proc( ExecNode N ) Proc@ :   IF  Body@<N> B:  B  ELSE  proc( fath(N) )
FCT  mproc( Program@ P ) Proc@ :  lookup( "main", env(son(-1,son(1,P))) )

ATT  succ( Point P ) Task:
   LET  N == P.node :
   IF  P = After(N) :
     // see section 3
   |  P = Before(N) :
     IF  Proc@<_,_,<SL>> N   :  Before(SL)
       |  AssignStat@<ID,E> N :  Before(E)
       |  VarExp@<ID> N       :  Move( decl(ID), N, After(N) )
       |  CallExp@<ID,EL> N   :  Before(EL)
       |  BinExp@<_,LO,_> N   :  Before(LO)
     ELSE  next(P)
   ELSE  nil()

FCT  eval( Operator OP, Int L, Int R ) Int:
   IF  OP = Add()  :  L + R
   |  ...
   ELSE  nil()

DYN  INPUT  () Int :       ??
DYN  OUTPUT () Int :       ??
DYN  PROGRAM() Program@:   ??
```

Generating an Efficient Compiler for a Data Parallel Language from a Denotational Specification

Johan Ringström, Peter Fritzson, Mikael Pettersson

Email: {johri,petfr,mikpe}@ida.liu.se
Phone: +46 13 281000, Fax: +46 13 282666

Abstract. There are very few examples of the generation of efficient compilers from denotational specifications. Usually such compilers generate code which is orders of magnitude slower than from hand-written ones. However, as has been demonstrated by our DML (Denotational Meta Language) compiler generation system, through appropriate single-threading analysis it is possible to obtain code of comparable quality to hand-written compilers. Another problem with denotational specifications is, because of their denotational nature, the need to introduce complicated power domains to model non-determinism and parallelism. In this work we have used a more practical two-level approach: use denotational specifications to model the meaning of the source language in terms of an abstract machine of low-level operations, including data-parallel operations. Then use operational semantics for the specification of this abstract machine.

This paper reports experience from building a prototype compiler for a small Algol-like parallel language using a version of the DML system called DML-P, which has been extended to support data-parallel operations. The final code contains calls to a portable data-parallel vector code library (VCODE CVL). The speed of generated compilers are within a factor of three from handwritten ones. Extensive benchmarks of a DML-P generated compiler are presented.

1 Introduction

The high abstraction level of denotational semantics makes it attractive as a language specification formalism. However, many efforts to generate compilers from denotational semantics specifications, starting with the SIS system by Peter Mosses 1979 [12], have resulted in compilers and code that run very slowly - often 100 to 1000 times slower compared to commercial compilers, and that also do not interface to commercial product-quality parsers or code generators. The situation has gradually improved through the work of several researchers, e.g. Sethi [25], Paulson [15], Raskovsky [20], Wand [30], Appel[1], Jouvelot[9], and later work by Mosses [13], until Lee [11] and Petterson [16] demonstrated the first practical compiler generation systems accepting denotational specifications.

In comparison with the MESS [11] system, the DML system goes several steps further. It interfaces well with standard tools and it automatically generates a code generator that emits intermediate quadruple code. DML can handle denotational specifications in continuation-passing style, which is well suited for specifying arbitrary control structures. The high code quality obtained using DML-generated compilers for Algol-like languages is possible due to escape-analysis of the intermediate representation, which removes all closures that would otherwise be present at run-time.

However, languages with non-determinism or parallelism are awkward and complicated to specify using denotational semantics since power domains have to be introduced. In order to cope with such languages in a practical way, we have instead turned to a two-level approach: use a denotational specification to model the meaning of the source language in terms of an abstract machine of low-level operations including data-parallel operations, then use operational semantics to specify the abstract machine. In this paper we report some experience of using this approach, including benchmarks obtained from generated compilers. The DML-P (P for parallel) compiler generator system provides a prototyping environment for the design of efficient compilers for data parallel computers. This system has been developed from an early version of the original DML-S (S for Sequential) system. This system implements the SML core language plus structures and signatures. It also includes constructs that make the implementation of a denotational specification easier. The development is done by adding support for data parallel operations as well as a more complete set of primitive operators and types in the target intermediate language.

First we briefly describe data parallel languages using a Predula Nouveau example, which is the subject language in this report. Then follows a brief introduction to denotational semantics including some excerpts of the Predula Nouveau denotational specification, after which we discuss two target data-parallel abstract machines. We continue by giving a description of the implementation of the DML-P compiler generator and the CPS-graph module. This graph is the internal representation for compiled programs. Finally we present benchmarks for generated compilers followed by conclusions and future work.

2 Data Parallel Languages

The data-parallel programming paradigm [6] has become popular in recent years since it exploits massive parallelism while preserving a simple deterministic programming style. Many algorithms can be expressed as operations on collections of similar data objects. Therefore languages containing data parallel programming constructs are called *collection-oriented languages* [2]. In this paper we use a small data-parallel Algol-like language called Predula Nouveau (a successor to Predula, PaRallel EDUcational LAnguage [21]) as a test case in our work on compiler generation for data parallel languages. This language includes a number of constructs operating on arrays, allowing the utilization of parallelism when operating in parallel on elements of such arrays.

Figure 1 shows a small Predula Nouveau program that calculates the inner product. The

```
main() is
    a, b : array 0..5 of integer;
    c : integer;
begin
    for i in 0..5 loop
        a(i) := i;      (* a := (0, 1, 2, 3, 4, 5) *)
        b(i) := 5-i;    (* b := (5, 4, 3, 2, 1, 0) *)
    end;
    (* First perform elementwise multiplication. Then add the
       products together into the c variable. *)
    c := reduce(op +, each(op *, a, b));
    write(c,"\n");
end;
```

Fig. 1. Inner product - a small Predula Nouveau example of data-parallelism.

arrays a and b contain source vectors which are used when calculating the inner product. This is done by applying the reduce function on the elementwise products of the elements in the two arrays. This intermediate array is calculated by the each function using the multiplication operator. The each and reduce operators are data parallel in that they apply their operator argument to all array elements at the same time.

2.1 Data-Parallel Operators

One of the earliest programming languages which included collection oriented programming capabilities is APL [8], which is centered around a vector-like data type. Numerous modern data parallel languages have followed this style of a collection data type together with a set of associated operations. Predula Nouveau includes a parallel version of the array data type found in the Algol family of languages. The *reduce, scan, each*, and *enumerate* operators are used in Predula Nouveau.

For example, the *reduce* operator takes an operator and an array as arguments. The intuitive meaning is to put the argument operator between the array elements and then to evaluate the resulting expression. This operator must be associative in order not to give a result that depends on the topology of the evaluation tree. It also must have an identity element. This value is returned if an empty array is supplied to *reduce*. Denotational definitions of *reduce* and some other data-parallel operators like *scan, each*, and *enumerate* can be found in [22].

3 Denotational Semantics

In a denotational specification, the meaning of a program is a mapping from an abstract syntax to denotations. Domains that form the source of this mapping are called *syntactic domains*. Domains that form the denotations are called *semantic domains*. For a detailed discussion of the foundations of this area, see [26,28]. A more practically oriented introduction is found in [4].

We want to describe a computer language including the operational behaviour of parallel programs while avoiding unnecessary detail, but we also want to be able to automatically generate a compiler for the language. Our approach is to describe the static semantics and part of the dynamic semantics of a programming language using a denotational semantics and to describe the remaining dynamic semantics using an operational semantics. These two parts are from now on named *high-level* and *low-level* semantics. We name the operational part low-level, since it is closer to the target machine. The most well-known example of a language specified by a denotational specification is Scheme [19]. Another example is OCCAM, which uses a combination of a denotational specification for the sequential part of the language and a CSP-based method for the parallel part [7].

3.1 Compiler Generation from Denotational Semantics

Figure 2 illustrates the compiler generation process. The specification of the low level intermediate language could be formally defined using some operational semantics formalism, see e.g. [18]. However, here we adopt a more pragmatic approach by mapping the intermediate representation directly to quadruples which are emitted in the form of calls to the VCODE [3] library together with simple C statements.

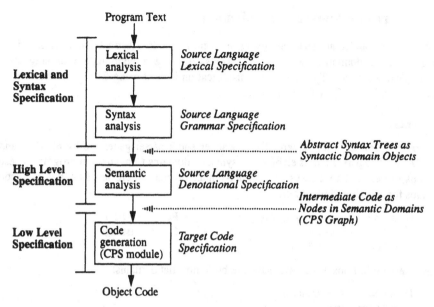

Program Text

Fig. 2. The translation of a source program to object code by a compiler generated by the DML system. The kinds of specification formalism are shown for the modules.

The DML system encapsulates the mapping to target code in a *Continuation Passing Style (CPS) graph*. The nodes in this graph are lambda calculus expressions. By the way the continuation is constructed, lambda abstractions can be stack allocated [18]. This makes it easier for the backend to generate efficient code.

When generating a compiler, e.g. for a tiny subset of C, the original CPS-graph [16] module from the DML-S system can be used, but for Predula Nouveau it is necessary to add extensions for the parallel part of the language, as will be shown later.

3.2 A Comment on the Denotational Specification Notation

Most work on denotational semantics use the Oxford School notation. A very concise notation using one letter identifiers in the greek alphabet is usually used. This is nice for articles and short examples, but not practical for large machine-processable language specifications. Therefore we have adopted Standard ML [5] syntax. Examples of transformations between Oxford School notation and SML are given below.

Oxford School notation	SML notation	
ρ_1	env1	(*variable ref.*)
$\varepsilon_3 \rightarrow \varepsilon_1 \mid \varepsilon_2$	if pred then exp1 else exp2	(*conditional*)
$\chi\rho$	dcont env	(*application*)
$\lambda\alpha.\alpha$	fn x => x	(*lambda*)
(α,β)	(a,b)	(*tuple formation*)
$\langle\alpha,\beta,\gamma\rangle$	[a,b,c]	(*sequences*)
let x ≡ y in z	let val x = y in z end	(*local binding*)
$1 \in Int$	(*expressed by SML pattern matching*)	(*membership check*)
$1\ in\ C$	(*expressed by SML constructors*)	(*injection*)
$\alpha \mid D$	(*expressed by SML pattern matching*)	(*projection*)

4 The Predula Nouveau Specification

Syntax and semantics are specified using different methods. Abstract syntax is described using syntactic domains. Semantics is expressed using a continuation passing style denotational semantics. This part of the specification is built using CPS primitives which are expressed in a CPS back end module.

4.1 Syntax

The concrete syntax is implemented as a scanner and a parser generated by ML-Lex and ML-YACC. The parser builds elements in syntactic domains from an input program. These domains correspond to classes of abstract-syntax objects. There are five flat syntactic domains for literals and identifiers.

$L_n \in$ Nml	(integer numerals)		$L_r \in$ Real	(reals)
$L_c \in$ Char	(characters)		$L_s \in$ Str	(strings)
$I \in$ Ide	(identifiers)			

Using these definitions it is now possible to build non-flat domains:

D	$\in$ Decl	(declarations)
T	$\in$ TExpr	(types)
F	$\in$ Param	(item in function prototype parameter list)
E	$\in$ Expr	(expressions)
C	$\in$ Cmd	(statements)

At the top level a Predula Nouveau program is a D value. Abstract syntax are equations on syntactic domains. Let us define some equations:

$$D ::= \text{null} \mid \text{type I T} \mid \text{var I T} \mid \text{vari I T E} \mid \text{varic I T E} \mid \text{fun I P T C} \mid D_1 D_2$$
$$P ::= \text{var I T M} \mid \text{varc I T M} \mid P*$$
$$M ::= \text{no} \mid \text{var}$$
$$T ::= \text{tvar I} \mid \text{arr } T_1 T_2 \mid T*$$
$$E ::= L_c \mid L_n \mid L_r \mid L_s \mid I \mid \text{un } E_1 E_2 \mid \text{bin } E_1 E_2 E_3 \mid \text{app E} \mid E*$$
$$C ::= \text{skip} \mid \text{loopi C} \mid \text{loopd D E C} \mid \text{break} \mid \text{cont} \mid \text{return E}$$
$$\mid \text{decl E} \mid \text{expr E} \mid \text{cond E G} \mid C_1 C_2$$
$$G ::= E C \mid G*$$

Variable declarations have three summands: uninitialized, initialized, and constant initialized declarations. Arrays are composed of two types. The first type is the index type and the second is the element type. Definite loops are composed of an induction-variable declaration (including the loop range), a count step expression, and the loop body.

4.2 Semantics

In the semantics specification function domains are used in addition to sum, product, and sequence domains that build the syntactic domains. We concentrate on the part of the predefined environment that specifies data-parallel operators.

The *DVal* domain contains values that can be denoted in a Predula Nouveau program. Predefined value and type environments are defined by the following domain equations:

$$VEnv \equiv Ide \rightarrow DVal \times Type \qquad TEnv \equiv Ide \rightarrow Type \qquad Env \equiv VEnv \times TEnv$$

Denotable values are bound to names in *VEnv* and denotable types are bound to names in *TEnv*. This defines two separate name spaces for Predula value and type identifiers in a natural way. For the pairs in *VEnv* the *Type* domain component is the type of the denotable value. The following function builds *TEnv* values when partially applied:

$$mktyp\ (ide,t)\ tenv\ ide2 \equiv if\ ide=ide2\ then\ t\ else\ tenv\ ide2$$

For example, *mktyp* ([["integer"]], *IntType*) produces a value in the *TEnv* → *TEnv* domain. Larger environment segments are built by function composition on such values. Compare this to symbol tables in traditional compilers.

4.2.1 Definition of the Data-Parallel Functions in Predula Nouveau

We are now ready to define the Predula Nouveau data-parallel operators in the predefined environment. In order to do this we use the *mkopr* function in analogy to the *mktyp* function above to build the value environment. One important observation is that the parallel operational semantics does not have to be specified anywhere in the denotational semantics. The second argument position of *mkopr* in the definition below contains a type checking function for the operator. The third and fourth positions define parameter and result modes. The last position maps to operators in the CPS graph. The Predula Nouveau scan, reduce, and each functions are overloaded: they come in integer, real, and boolean versions. The integer versions, including enumerate, are shown below:

$$
\begin{aligned}
iparoprs \equiv\ &mkopr\ ([["enumerate"]], enumtc \quad intT,\ I\_ENUM)\ o \\
&mkopr\ ([["each"]], \qquad\quad eachtc\ 1 \quad intT,\ I\_EACH1)\ o \\
&mkopr\ ([["each"]], \qquad\quad eachtc\ 2 \quad intT,\ I\_EACH2)\ o \\
&mkopr\ ([["scan"]], \qquad\quad scandtc \quad\ intT,\ I\_SCAND)\ o \\
&mkopr\ ([["scan"]], \qquad\quad scansdtc\ intT,\ I\_SCANSD)\ o \\
&mkopr\ ([["scan"]], \qquad\quad scanstc \quad\ intT,\ I\_SCANS)\ o \\
&mkopr\ ([["reduce"]], \qquad reduceutc\ intT,\ I\_REDUCE)\ o \\
&mkopr\ ([["reduce"]], \qquad reducestc\ intT,\ I\_REDUCES)
\end{aligned}
$$

For a definition of the binding of real and boolean data parallel functions (together a total of 22) and a more detailed discussion of the type checking functions that are used in the composition, see [22].

4.3 Data-Parallel Extensions in Predula Nouveau

Most of the extensions are introduced to support data parallelism. These extensions consist of the addition of a number of data-parallel functions, like *enum, scan, reduce,* and *each,* that work on the array type.

Currently only one-dimensional arrays of scalar or real values are possible. Still, we feel that this set, which however probably is too small to be used in real-life data-parallel programming, is large enough to demonstrate the feasibility of compiler generation for data-parallel programming languages from denotational specifications.

5 Data Parallel Target Codes

5.1 VCODE and Paris

The VCODE system [3] implements an abstract machine of data-parallel vector operations. It is portable between several parallel architectures including the CRAY and CM-2, but also sequential architectures, such as the Sun workstation. The VCODE operations are implemented on top of a library of C routines, the C Vector Library (CVL).VCODE is a single assignment stack-based language where all instructions operate on arrays. There are no free scalars, not even on the stack. The data-parallel functions are limited to arrays of scalars and floating-point numbers: it is not possible to directly build nested arrays or multidimensional arrays. Instead the VCODE data-parallel functions can handle segmented arrays.

Both VCODE and the CM-2 Paris library [29] are cumbersome to use due to the many implementation details that need to be incorporated in such programs. This applies especially to Paris. VCODE, on the other hand, is limited due to its single-assignment vector-stack, i.e. vectors on the stack cannot be destructively updated. There also is no way to store scalars except as unit vectors, and there are no global or heap stores to complement the stack. Also, to manage multidimensional or nested arrays it is necessary to keep the array topology in a separate segment array. Array decomposition for massively-parallel computers is an active research area: see for example [10].

6 Implementation of the Compiler Generator

The SML/NJ system is used to generate implementations from denotational semantics specifications. Specifications can almost be transformed verbatim to SML/NJ: very few transformations are necessary.

6.1 The module design

The specification is partitioned into three groups of modules, as is shown in Figure 3. The figure also shows the generation of a compiler from specification modules. The language specification part contains language specific modules. The general functions part consists of a module that contains definitions which are independent of both the specified language and the target platform. This module includes the definition of some auxiliary functions in the denotational definition. The lower right part contains implementation dependent specification modules.

All these modules together generate the lower left part in Figure 3 which shows the modules in the generated compiler. The generated Front module transforms the input program to an abstract syntax tree. Mid transforms the abstract syntax tree to a CPS graph through the M semantic function. Back transforms the graph to target code (in our case ANSI C quadruples and calls to the CVL library). Currently the SML/NJ module system is used to implement the module composition.

We claim that this way of building the system offers two important benefits. First, the division between the denotational part and the operational part of the language specification is expressed in a natural and flexible way that makes automatic generation of a compiler

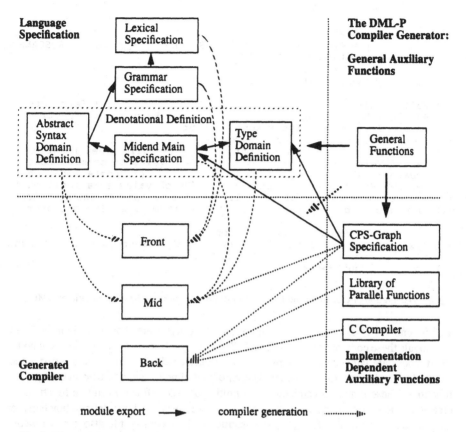

Fig. 3. The module structure of typical language specifications, the DML-P compiler generator, and the generated compiler.

practical. Second, the strong modularisation makes it possible to reuse parts of the specification between different languages. Currently, only the CPS-graph module has been used for more than one language since it also has been used to specify the Tiny-C language in the DML-S system.

6.2 The Predula Nouveau Language Specification

The Predula Nouveau abstract syntax domain definition, midend main specification, and type domain definition (the modules in the dashed box in Figure 3) are written in denotational semantics. The abstract syntax definition is used by both the grammar specification and by the midend. The type domain definitions module contains denotational definitions of the type system. The midend main specification module contains most of the Predula Nouveau semantics including the M (as in meaning) semantic function.

6.3 The CPS-Graph Specification

The CPS-graph specification module generates part of the Back part of the generated compiler in Figure 3. The module interface includes a number of constructors which builds

```
datatype Opr = ...
            | I_ENUM
            | R_EACH1   | R_EACH2   | R_SCAN  | R_SCANS  | R_SCANSD
            | R_REDUCE  | R_REDUCES

val Lambda : Typ * (Val -> Cont) -> Kont

val Halt : unit -> Cont                              (* Terminate *)
val Return : Val -> Cont                    (* Return from function *)
val Call : Func * Val list * Kont -> Cont
val Cond : Val * Cont * Cont -> Cont
val New : bool * Typ * Kont -> Cont          (* Build a new location *)
val Send : Val * Kont -> Cont          (* Send value to command cont *)
val Update : Val * Val * Cont -> Cont          (* Update location *)
val Fetch : Val * Kont -> Cont          (* Fetch value in a location *)
val VIndex : Val * Val list * Val list * Kont -> Cont (* Get arr loc *)
val PrimFunc : Opr -> Func          (* Func from primitive operator *)

val fix_cont : (Cont -> Cont) -> Cont
val fix_func : Typ * bool list * (Val list -> Func -> Cont) -> Func

val codgen : Cont -> unit
```

Fig. 4. Declaration of Operators and Basic Term Building Blocks of the CPS module of DML-P

a CPS lambda expression. The most important constructors are shown in Figure 4. Inside the module these constructors build a graph. The CPS graph consists of three kinds of nodes. Cont nodes are lambda expressions that do not bind a value to a new name. Kont nodes are used to bind values to new names. The third kind of node, named Func in the figure, is functions. These functions can be either primitive or user-defined. Primitive functions are created by the PrimFunc constructor from primitive operators. User-defined functions can only be defined via the fix_func constructor. This constructor also binds function parameters.

The module also exports the codgen function which generates object code from the CPS lambda expression. Presently, this code is an ANSI-C program that together with the VCODE CVL is sent to the C compiler for compilation to object code. Section 7 gives a more detailed discussion of the code generation module concentrating on the data-parallel extensions compared to the CPS-graph module in the DML-S system. A discussion of the technical detail of the interface and implementation of the module is also found in Appendix A of [18].

6.4 Using the CPS Module Constructors

Let us illustrate using the I_ENUM integer data-parallel enumeration operator. Assume we want to apply this operator to its arguments. This is done using the Call constructor:

```
Call(PrimFunc I_ENUM,args,kont)
```

The first argument to Call is the function to be applied. This is the I_ENUM operator injected into the Func domain. The second argument arg is a sequence of evaluated left or right value arguments to Call. The last argument is the expression continuation that receives the result of the application. For a user-defined function, the call constructor instead uses a value in the Func domain defined by the fix_func constructor.

The `fix_cont` constructor is used to express fixpoints of loops. The `fix_cont` and `fix_func` constructors are the only ones that can be used to express recursion. The `Fetch` constructor fetches an atomic value from a location. The `VIndex` operation sends a location in an array to an expression continuation. Combining these two it is possible to fetch an element from an array location:

```
VIndex(arr,[offset],[index],Lambda(x,Fetch(x,kont)))
```

`VIndex` sends its location result to `Fetch` using a `Lambda` binding. Work is ongoing to generalise `VIndex` to multidimensional and nested arrays.

7 The New Code Generation Module for Data-Parallel Operations

Here we shortly talk about the internals of the code generation module and the modifications that were necessary to make to the original DML-S system CPS module able to generate data-parallel code [18].

First, new primitive operators have been added. The original module contained 11 operators. These operators were created with the goal of compiling a small subset of the C language. The extended module in DML-P contains a total of 83 operators. This larger amount is partly due to the increased number of types that is supported by the module, but also because the operator domain includes 22 new data-parallel operators, counting different types. The truncated definition of the operator semantic domain in Figure 4 includes some of these data-parallel operators.

Second, the new module can handle a greater range of types than the original module. This includes characters, strings, and floating point numbers. This also made it necessary to add new constructors for literals.

Third, the data-parallel extensions make it necessary to implement arrays more carefully. Currently only fixed size arrays are supported, but work is ongoing to support arrays with dynamically determined size.

Fourth, the most important extension is the addition of the VCODE CVL. This is done as external C calls to the library operations. This library is linked with the generated object code.

From a code generation point of view, the CPS-graph module linearizes the graph into a sequence of instructions. In the original module this is done in two phases. First the graph nodes are marked. This includes counting of references. If a `Cont` node is referenced by more than one other node, it is assigned a label. In the new DML-P module a new phase is added that scans types. This is done to make it possible to declare all necessary types in the beginning of the generated C code. In the next phase, C functions are generated from the function denotations in the graph. This includes the generation of quadruple style C statements from the command continuations in the graph.

7.1 Code Generation Aspects

The program in Figure 1 compiles to the code shown in Figure 5. Arrays are currently implemented as C structs, illustrated by the `ttl` type in the figure, with a single component, the array elements. This makes arrays first-class C objects. Work is under way to make it possible to delay determination of array size until array creation time and to include

```
#include <stdio.h>
#include <math.h>
#include "datapar.h"

typedef struct{long body[6];
} ttl;

void t1(){
long t23;
long t29;
long t32;
long  *t31;
long  *t34;
char t27;
long  *t18;
long t38;
long  *t17;
long t39;
long t41;
long  *t40;
long t42;
ttl  *t16;
ttl t43;
long t45;
long  *t44;
long t46;
ttl  *t11;
ttl t47;
long t49;
long  *t48;
long t50;
ttl  *t6;
ttl t51;
t6=&t51;
t48=&t50;
 *(t48)=0;
t49=6;
{long t52;
for(t52=0;t52<t49;t52++){
t6->body[t52]= *t48;
}}
t11=&t47;

t44=&t46;
 *(t44)=0;
t45=6;
{long t53;
for(t53=0;t53<t45;t53++){
t11->body[t53]= *t44;
}}
t16=&t43;
t40=&t42;
 *(t40)=0;
t41=6;
{long t54;
for(t54=0;t54<t41;t54++){
t16->body[t54]= *t40;
}}
t17=&t39;
 *(t17)=0;
t18=&t38;
 *(t18)=0;
L36:t27= *t18<=5;
if(!t27) goto L35;
t34=t6->body+( *t18-0)*1;
 *(t34)= *(t18);
t31=t11->body+( *t18-0)*1;
t32=5- *t18;
 *(t31)=t32;
t29= *t18+1;
 *(t18)=t29;
goto L36;
L35:(each_i_mul(t16,6,t6,t11),t16);
t23=reduce_i_add(t16,6);
 *(t17)=t23;
printf("%ld", *t17);
printf("%s","\n");
return ;
}

int main(){
(void)t1();
exit(0);
}
```

Fig. 5. Inner product - generated C code.

segmentation information into arrays. This will result in the addition of more fields to this struct including a size field. For segmented arrays a segmentation descriptor will also be added.

The each and reduce calls are shown near the end of the generated code. The each call generates a C comma expression where the last component gives a valid return value. The each_i_mul call is the result of the integer elementwise multiplication in the CVL.

As is illustrated by Figure 5 there is much a compiler can do to improve the code. This includes constant and variable propagation optimizations. The current experience is that the C compiler does a good job on scalar values, but that there is room for improvement for arrays.

8 Benchmarks of a DML-S Generated Compiler for a Sequential C Subset

In order to make a rough comparison between the quality of stand-alone C-based compilers generated by the original DML-S system and the quality of commercial compilers, we prepared a 1000-line program example in a small C subset called Tiny-C, for which a compiler was generated. This program contains function calls, integer and integer array arithmetic in addition to control structures such as if-statements, loops, etc. This example is measured on a Sparcstation ELC workstation (rated at approximately 20 MIPS). Measured time is elapsed time. Code size is measured on the linked executable file. The generated compiler frontend is in C, and produces low-level quadruples expressed in C syntax, which are fed through the standard SunOS 4.1 CC backend.

The generated compiler was approximately three times slower in compilation speed than the Sun C++ compiler (version 2.1) (the generated compiler processing 1954 lines/minute versus 7100 lines/minute for Sun C++ when generating un-optimized code, or 1036 lines/minute versus 2600 lines/minute when generating optimized code). However, the execution speed of the generated code was approximately the same, 7.8 seconds for the optimized code from the generated compiler versus 7.4 seconds when executing the optimized code from Sun's C++ compiler. However, when using the Gnu C compiler as the backend instead of the Sun C compiler, the Tiny-C compiler generated code which was about 2.5 time slower than code from the Gnu C compiler (3.4 seconds versus 1.4 seconds). Apparently the structure of the intermediate code from the Tiny-C compiler precludes some optimizations.

	Without back-end optimization			With optimization (-O2)		
	Code size (kb)	Compila-tion time (seconds)	Execution time (seconds)	Code size (kb)	Compila-tion time (seconds)	Execution time (seconds)
Gen. Tiny-C compiler with Sun CC backend	40 kb	30.7	30.9	24 kb	57.9	7.8
Sun C++ only	24 kb	8.4	26.5	16 kb	23.1	7.4
Gen Tiny-C compiler + Gnu C	40 kb	33.6	8.7	16 kb	33.5	3.4
Gnu C compiler only	24 kb	8.9	4.6	16 kb	13.4	1.4

9 Benchmarks of a DML-P Generated Compiler for Predula Nouveau

The original DML compiler generation system is implemented in Scheme. It produces compilers in Scheme which are translated to C using Bartlett's Scheme-to-C compiler. Thus stand alone compilers in C, accepting source programs and producing quadruples, are obtained.

The DML-P system has been developed from the original DML system by porting the DML backend to SML/NJ, and by extending the set of low-level operations in the target language to include data-parallel vector operations and scalar operations for a larger range of primitive types (integers, floating point numbers, strings, characters), and arrays built from the mentioned scalar or real types. DML-S only included support for integers and arrays of integers.

The generated compiler frontend which is implemented in SML/NJ, accepts Predula Nouveau source text, and produces low level quadruple code in C, which is then further compiled and linked using the GCC (version 2.4.5) compiler and linker.

9.1 Compiling performance

In the first benchmark, the generated compiler is compared to GCC for speed and maximal heap size on a Quicksort program. The recursive sorting function in Quicksort is unrolled between 0 and 1000 times. 52 logarithmically distributed samples are taken from this range resulting in program sizes varying between 10 and 17000 lines of Predula code. Data for the benchmark was produced on a Sparc1 IPC workstation with 36Mb of primary memory. A similar Quicksort program implemented in C is also measured in this way. Measured time is user+system time.

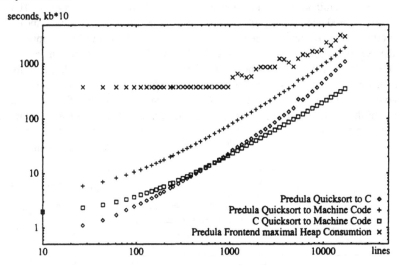

The maximal heap size for the Predula frontend during compilation is about 3.7 Mb up to about 1000 lines of source code, where the size starts to grow stepwise up to about 30 Mb. The Predula frontend alone is about as fast on smaller Predula Quicksort programs as the Gnu compiler is on smaller C Quicksort programs, but the frontend is slower on larger programs. Considering the entire Predula compiler, most of the time is spent in GCC. This is due to the voluminous code that is currently generated by the Predula frontend.

	Code size (kb)	Compilation time (seconds)	Execution time (seconds)
Predula Nouveau frontend only	---	18.3	---
Predula Nouveau frontend with Gnu C -O2 backend	24	94	22.4
Hand-written C program compiled with Gnu C -O2	24	39	11.8

9.2 Run time performance

The second benchmark compares a 1000 line unrolled Predula Quicksort program to a 1000 line unrolled C Quicksort program. Both programs initialize and sort a 1000 element array 1000 times. The table is measured on a Sparcstation ELC. Measured time is elapsed time and code size is measured on the linked executable file. Compilation speed is about 640 lines/minute for the Predula compiler and about 1540 lines/minute for the Gnu C compiler on 1000 line programs.

10 Conclusions and Future Work

The presented system, DML-P, is to our knowledge one of the first denotational semantics based compiler generators that automatically generates practical compilers for data parallel languages. The system uses a continuation passing style internal representation. This is a graph that includes data-parallel operators. One important goal is to arrive at a sufficiently general set of operators in the intermediate representation to be useful as a target for compilers for a wide range of data-parallel languages. However, despite of being prototypes, compilers generated by DML-S or DML-P has demonstrated surprisingly good performance. Some directions for future work are shown below:

- Include multi-dimensional and nested/segmented arrays in the Predula Nouveau language to evaluate whether DML-P needs any extensions for this.
- Include a Forall construct.
- Code generation for a wider range of parallel architectures.
- Further development of the low-level operational semantics and the CPS graph so it can handle data-parallel operations with multi-dimensional and nested/segmented arrays.

Substantial work still needs to be done on the use of optimization techniques in order to generate better data-parallel object code. This includes further work on using and developing the CPS graph as a formally defined intermediate representation in which data-parallel operations can be expressed.

11 References

[1] Andrew W. Appel. *Compiling with Continuations.* Cambridge University Press, 1991.

[2] Guy Blelloch. *Vector Models for Data-Parallel Computing.* MIT press, 1990.

[3] Guy Blelloch, Siddhartha Chatterjee, Fritzs Knabe, Jay Sipelstein, Marco Zagha. *VCODE Reference Manual (Version 1.3)* Department of Computer Science, Carnegie-Mellon University, Pittsburgh, PA 15213, Jul 1992.

[4] Michael J. C Gordon. *The Denotational Description of Programming Languages.* Springer-Verlag, 1979.

[5] Robert Harper, Robin Milner, Mads Tofte. *The Definition of Standard ML, Version 4.* The MIT Press, 1990.

[6] W. Daniel Hillis, Guy L. Steele, Jr. *Data Parallel Algorithms,* Communications of the ACM, Dec 1986, Vol.29, No.12, pp. 1170-1183.

[7] C. A. R. Hoare. *Communicating Sequential Processes,* Prentice-Hall, 1985, ISBN-0-13-0153289-8.

[8] Kenneth E. Iverson *A Programming Language,* John Wiley & Sons, Inc., 1962.

[9] Pierre Jouvelot. *Designing new languages or new language manipulation systems using ML.* SIGPLAN Notices, 21:40–52, Aug 1986.

[10] Kathleen Knobe, J. D. Lucas, Guy L. Steele. *Data Optimization: Allocation of arrays to reduce communication on SIMD machines.* Journal of Parallel and Distributed Computing, 8:102–118, Feb 1990.

[11] Peter Lee. *Realistic Compiler Generation.* PhD thesis, University of Michigan, 1987. Ph.D. thesis published by MIT press 1989.

[12] Peter D. Mosses. *SIS - Semantic Implementation System.* PhD thesis, Aarhus University, 1979. TR DAIMI MD-30.

[13] Peter Mosses. *Unified Algebras and Action Semantics.* In Proc. Symp. of Theor. Sci. (STACS'89), LNCS-349, 1989.

[14] Edwin, M. Paalvast, A. J. Gemund, Henk J. Sips. *A method for parallel program generation with an application to the Booster language.* In Proceedings of the 1990 ACM Fourth International Conference on Supercomputing in Amsterdam, 11-15 Jun 1990.

[15] L. Paulson. *A semantics-directed compiler generator.* In Proceedings of the 9th ACM Conference on Principles of Programming Languages, pages 224–233, 1982.

[16] Mikael Pettersson. *Generating efficient code from continuation semantics.* In Proceedings of the 1990 Workshop on Compiler-Compilers, LNCS-477, Schwerin, Germany, 1990. Springer-Verlag.

[17] Mikael Pettersson, Peter Fritzson. *DML - A Meta-Language and System for the Generation of Practical and Efficient Compilers from Denotational Specifications.* In Proc. of the IEEE International Conference on Computer Languages, San Francisco, Apr 27-30, 1992.

[18] Mikael Pettersson. *DML - A Language and System for the Generation of Efficient Compilers from Denotational Specifications.* Licentiate thesis No 319. Department of Computer and Information Science, Linköping University, May 1992.

[19] H. Abelson, N. I. Adams IV, D. H. Bartley, G. Brooks, R. K. Dybvig, D. P. Friedman, R. Halstead, C. Hanson, C. T. Haynes, E. Kohlbecker, D. Oxley, K. M. Pitman, G. J. Rozas, G. L. Steele jr., G. J. Sussman, Mitchell Wand. *Revised⁴ Report on the Algorithmic Language Scheme.* Nov 1991.

[20] Martin R. Raskovsky. *Denotational semantics as a specification of code generators.* In Proceedings of the ACM SIGPLAN 82 Conference on Compiler Construction, pages 230–244, 1982.

[21] Johan Ringström, Peter Fritzson, Johan Fagerström. *Predula, A Multiparadigm Parallel Programming and Debugging Environment,* In Proceedings of EUROMICRO'91 conference in Vienna, short note session, IEEE Sep 1991.

[22] Johan Ringström *Compiler Generation for Parallel Languages from Denotational Definitions.* Licentiate thesis, spring 1993. Thesis No. 380.

[23] J.R. Rose and Guy L. Steele, Jr. *C*: An extended C language for data parallel programming,* Technical Report PL 87-5, Thinking Machines Corporation, 1986.

[24] Gary W. Sabot: *Paralation Lisp - Architecture Independent Parallel Programming,* MIT Press, 1988.

[25] Ravi Sethi. *Control flow aspects of semantics directed compiling.* Technical Report CSTR-98, Bell Labs, 1981.

[26] David A. Schmidt. *Denotational Semantics, A Methodology For Language Development.* Allyn and Bacon Inc., 1986.

[27] Richard M. Stallman. *Using and Porting GNU CC.* 1989.

[28] Joseph E. Stoy. *Denotational Semantics.* MIT Press, 1977.

[29] Thinking Machines Corporation. *Introduction to Programming in C/Paris (Version 5).* Thinking Machines Corporation, Cambridge, Massachusetts, Jun 1989.

[30] Mitchell Wand. *A semantic prototyping system.* In Proc of the ACM SIGPLAN'84 Compiler Construction Conference, pages 213–222, 1984.

Adding Semantic and Syntactic Predicates To $LL(k)$: $pred\text{-}LL(k)$

Terence J. Parr[1] * and Russell W. Quong[2]

[1] University of Minnesota
Army High Performance Computing Research Center
parrt@acm.org
[2] Purdue University
School of Electrical Engineering
quong@ecn.purdue.edu

Abstract. Most language translation problems can be solved with existing $LALR(1)$ or $LL(k)$ language tools; e.g., YACC [Joh78] or ANTLR [PDC92]. However, there are language constructs that defy almost all parsing strategy commonly in use. Some of these constructs cannot be parsed without semantics, such as symbol table information, and some cannot be properly recognized without first examining the entire construct, that is we need "infinite lookahead."

In this paper, we introduce a new $LL(k)$ parser strategy, $pred\text{-}LL(k)$, that uses semantic or syntactic predicates to recognize language constructs when normal deterministic $LL(k)$ parsing breaks down. Semantic predicates indicate the semantic validity of applying a production; syntactic predicates are grammar fragments that describe a syntactic context that must be satisfied before application of an associated production is authorized. Throughout, we discuss the implementation of predicates in ANTLR—the parser generator of The Purdue Compiler-Construction Tool Set.

1 Introduction

Although in theory, parsing is widely held to be a sufficiently solved problem, in practice, writing a grammar with embedded translation actions remains a non-trivial task. Ignoring arguments concerning the use of $LL(k)$ versus $LR(k)$ parsing strategies, it is often the case that semantic information (such as symbol table information) is required to parse a particular language correctly and naturally. While $LR(k)$-based parsers can be augmented with run time tests that alter the parse, bottom-up strategies have convenient access to much less semantic and context information than a top-down $LL(k)$ parser; hence, we have chosen to augment $LL(k)$ with predicates.

* Partial support for this work has come from the Army Research Office contract number DAAL03-89-C-0038 with the Army High Performance Computing Research Center at the U of MN.

In this paper, we present *pred-LL(k)*, the class of languages recognized by conventional *LL(k)* parsers augmented with semantic and syntactic predicates, which can specify the semantic and syntactic applicability of any given grammar production. *Semantic predicates* are run time tests that can resolve finite lookahead conflicts and syntactic ambiguities with semantic information. *Syntactic predicates* resolve finite lookahead conflicts by specifying a possibly infinite, possibly nonregular, lookahead language. Syntactic predicates are a form of selective backtracking that allow the recognition of constructs beyond the capabilities of conventional parsing; this capability is becoming necessary, e.g., [ES90] indicates that unbounded lookahead is required to correctly parse C++. We have implemented *pred-LL(k)* using an existing *LL(k)* parser generator called ANTLR (the parser generator used in PCCTS—the Purdue Compiler-Construction Tool Set) [PCD93]. ANTLR is widely used tool; there are over 1000 registered users in over 37 countries and numerous universities are using it in compiler classes.

Our paper is organized as follows. Section 2 describes the previous work in this area and Section 3 provides numerous examples illustrating the utility of semantic and syntactic predicates. Section 4 describes the behavior of semantic and syntactic predicates more formally and how their introduction affects normal *LL(k)* grammar analysis and parsing.

2   Previous Work

Attribute grammars have received attention in the literature since their introduction [Knu68] because they allow the specification of the grammar and the translation semantics in one description. Unfortunately translations implemented in this manner can be slow and many translations are difficult to express purely as functions of attributes; according to [Wai90], pure attribute grammars have had little impact on compiler construction.

[LRS74] considered the practical application of attribute grammars to compilers by characterizing the types of attribute grammars that could be efficiently handled via *LR(k)* "bottom-up" and *LL(k)* "top-down" parsing methods. They showed that *LL(k)* has an advantage over *LR(k)* in semantic flexibility (e.g., *LL(k)* parsers may inherit attributes from invoking productions); despite this advantage of *LL(k)*, some researchers have argued that augmenting *LR(k)* with predicates is more suitable than augmenting *LL(k)* due to concerns over recognition strength (see LADE[3], YACC++[4], and [Gan89], [McK90]). However, with the addition of syntactic and semantic predicates, *pred-LL(k)* parsers can potentially recognize all context-free[5] and many context-sensitive languages beyond the ability of existing *LR(k)* systems.

---

[3] LADE is a registered trademark of Xorian Technologies

[4] YACC++ is a registered trademark of Compiler Resources, Inc.

[5] ANTLR-generated parsers can be coerced into backtracking at all lookahead decisions to accomplish this, however, general backtracking is well known to be exponentially slow.

Other researchers have developed similar notions of predicated $LL(k)$ parsing. For example, [MF79] introduced the class of $ALL(k)$ grammars that could specify two types of semantic predicates, disambiguating and contextual, that were used to handle the context-sensitive portions of programming languages; the authors implemented an $ALL(1)$ parser generator [MKR79] based upon their $ALL(k)$ definition. Our approach differs from [MF79] in a number of ways. Whereas they allow exactly one disambiguating predicate per production, we allow multiple predicates and do not distinguish between disambiguating and contextual predicates, as this differentiation can be automatically determined (the grammar analysis phase knows when a lookahead decision is nondeterministic and can search for semantic predicates that potentially resolve the conflict). Our predicate definition permits the placement of predicates anywhere within a production and, more importantly, specifies the desired evaluation time by the location of the predicate. Further, the disambiguating predicates of [MF79] require that the user specify the set of lookahead k-tuples over which the predicate is valid. Our predicates are automatically evaluated only when the lookahead buffer is consistent with the context surrounding the predicate's position (ANTLR grammar analysis can compute the k-tuples). Although in theory, the predicates of [MF79] and the predicates described herein are equivalent in recognition strength, in practice our predicates allow for more concise and more natural language descriptions; additionally, our predicate scheme has been implemented in an $LL(k)$ parser generator rather than in an $LL(1)$ parser generator, which dramatically increases the recognition strength of the underlying parsers.

Another top-down parser generator and language, S/SL [HCW82], allows parsing to be a function of semantics. This method was accomplished by allowing rule return values to predict future productions. Unfortunately, their system had a number of weaknesses that rendered it impractical for large applications; e.g. it appears that parsers could only see one token of lookahead and the user had to compute prediction lookahead sets by hand.

3 Examples of Using Predicates

Programmers routinely handle many context-sensitive language constructs with context-free grammars through a variety of ah hoc "tricks" taught in most compilers courses. For example, when a syntactic structure is ambiguous, semantic information is often used by the lexical analyzer to return different token types for the same input symbol. In addition, grammars are often twisted (into an unreadable condition) in an effort to remove parser nondeterminisms and syntactic ambiguities. In this section, we provide two examples that illustrate the benefits of using semantic information in the parser rather than the lexical analyzer and we provide an example that illustrates how syntactic predicates can be used to resolve finite $LL(k)$ lookahead problems. In this paper, we use the terminology shown in the following table.

What	Example	Description
nonterminal	a, varName	starts with lower case
terminal	ID, FOR	starts with upper case
raw input	"int" "for"	regular expr in a string
action	<< i++; >>	enclosed in << ...>>
predicate	<< i==0 >>?	construct followed by a ?
semantic pred	<< i==0 >>?	enclosed in << ...>>?
syntactic pred	(declaration)?	enclosed in (...)?
i^{th} lookahead symbol	LA(3)	LA(i), $1 \leq i \leq k$
text of ith lookahead symbol	LATEXT(1)	LATEXT(i), $1 \leq i \leq k$

We now present some examples motivating the need for predicates during parsing. Consider FORTRAN array references and function calls, which are syntactically identical, but semantically very different:

```
expr : ID "\(" exprlist "\)" <<arrayref_action>>
     | ID "\(" exprlist "\)" <<fncall_action>>
     ;
```

There are two common approachs to resolving this ambiguity. First, one may merge the two alternatives and then examine the symbol table entry for the ID to determine which action to execute:

```
expr : ID "\(" exprlist "\)"
       <<if ( isvar($1) ) arrayref_action else fncall_action;>>
     ;
```

where the $1 is the attribute (of type character string here) of ID.

In the second approach, the lexical analyzer modifies the token type according to whether the input ID is a variable or a function by examining the symbol table. The grammar then becomes context-free:

```
expr : VAR  "\(" exprlist "\)" <<arrayref_action>>
     | FUNC "\(" exprlist "\)" <<fncall_action>>
     ;
```

while these methods are adequate, they quickly become unmanageable as the complexity of the grammar increases. The lexical analyzer would be required to know more and more about the grammatical context in order to make decisions; in essence, the user has to hand code a significant part of the parser in the lexical analyzer. A more elegant solution is possible via semantic predicates, in which all code fragments pertaining to context-sensitivity are constrained to the grammar specification. The same expression that would normally be used to differentiate the two actions or to return different token types may be used to alter the normal $LL(k)$ parsing strategy by annotating the grammar, thereby, allowing array references and function calls to be treated as grammatically different constructs, which was the original, fundamental goal:

```
expr : <<isvar(LATEXT(1))>>? ID "\(" exprlist "\)" <<arrayref_action>>
     | <<isfunc(LATEXT(1))>>? ID "\(" exprlist "\)" <<fncall_action>>
     ;
```

where LATEXT(1) is the text of the first symbol of lookahead and the "?" suffix operator indicates that the preceding grammar element is a predicate. In this case, the predicates are semantic predicates that are to be used in the production prediction mechanism to differentiate the alternative productions.

As a more complicated example, consider the definition of classes in C++. Identifiers (IDs) are used as the class name, member function names and the constructor name. (In C++, a constructor is a special member function that has the same name as the class itself and does not have a return type.) For example,

```
class Box {
    Box() { /* constructor for class Box */ }
    draw() { /* member function */ }
    some_user_type val;  /* member variable */
};
```

A simplified grammar fragment for C++ class definitions such as:

```
class_def
    :   "class" ID "\{" ( member )+ "\}" ";"
    ;


member
    :   ID "\(" args "\)" func_body      /* constructor */
    |   ID "\(" args "\)" func_body      /* normal member function */
    |   ID declarator                    /* member variable */
    ;
```

is syntactically ambiguous (like the previous FORTRAN example), but the constructor requires special handling. The conventional method would be to have the lexical analyzer return different token types for the various ID references. There are numerous problems with this solution, but we will give only two here. First, because C++ class definitions can be nested, the lexical analyzer would need access to a stack of terminals that represent the enclosing class names. Only in this way can it decide between a normal function name and the class constructor. But, what is the purpose of the parser if the lexical analyzer is tracking the grammatical structure? Second, if the parser has lookahead depth greater than one, having the lexer return tokens based on semantic context would be problematic as symbols may not have been added to the symbol table before the lexical analyzer had to tokenize its input. E.g., when the lexer tokenizes ID, the symbol table must be up to date otherwise the lexer might incorrectly categorize ID. In the previous example, if k, the lookahead depth, equals 3, immediately after seeing **"class"**, the lexer would have to tokenize **"Box"**, **"{"**, and **"Box"**. The second **"Box"** would not be recognized as the current class name, as we have not yet entered the class definition.

Semantic predicates, in contrast, would not be evaluated until the correct context—after the parser had passed the class header and had entered the class name into the symbol table—and could easily be added to **member** to resolve the ambiguity.

```
member[char *curclass]
    :   <<strcmp(curclass,LATEXT(1))==0>>?
        ID "\(" args "\)" func_body         /* constructor */
    |   <<!istypename(LATEXT(1) && strcmp(curclass,LATEXT(1))!=0>>?
        ID "\(" args "\)" func_body         /* normal member function */
    |   <<istypename(LATEXT(1))>>?
        ID declarator                        /* member variable */
    ;
```

where **istypename(LATEXT(1))** returns true if the text of the first symbol of lookahead is listed in the symbol table as a type name else it returns false; lookahead of $k = 2$ is used to differentiate between alternatives 1 and 3. Note that the current class can be passed into **member** because of the nature of top-down $LL(k)$ parsing and is used to determine whether a member function is the constructor. The predicates would be incorporated into the production prediction expressions and, hence, would resolve the syntactic ambiguity.

Occasionally a grammar developer is faced with a situation that is not syntactically ambiguous, but cannot be parsed with a normal $LL(k)$ parser. For the most part, these situations are finite lookahead nondeterminisms; i.e., with a finite lookahead buffer, the parser is unable to determine which of a set of alternative productions to predict. We again turn to C++ for a nasty parsing example. Quoting from Ellis and Stroustrup [ES90],

> "There is an ambiguity in the grammar involving *expression-statements* and *declarations*... The general cases cannot be resolved without backtracking... In particular, the lookahead needed to disambiguate this case is not limited."

The authors use the following examples to make their point, where **T** represents a type:

```
T(*a)->m=7;     // expression-statement with type cast to T
T(*a)(int);     // pointer to function declaration
```

Clearly, the two types of statements are not distinguishable from the left as an arbitrary number of symbols may be seen before a decision can be made; here, the **"->"** symbol is the first indication that the first example is a statement. Quoting Ellis and Stroustrup further,

> "In a parser with backtracking the disambiguating rule can be stated very simply:

1. If it looks like a *declaration*, it is; otherwise
2. if it looks like an *expression*, it is; otherwise
3. it is a syntax error."

The solution in ANTLR using syntactic predicates is simply to do exactly what Ellis and Stroustrup indicate:

```
stat:   (declaration)? declaration
    |   expression
    ;
```

The meaning of rule **stat** is exactly that of the last quote. Rule **stat** indicates that a **declaration** is the syntactic context that must be present for the rest of that production to succeed. As a shorthand, ANTLR allows the following alternative:

```
stat:   (declaration)?
    |   expression
    ;
```

which may be interpreted in a slightly different manner—"I am not sure if **declaration** will match; simply try it out and if it does not match try the next alternative." In either notation, **declaration** will be recognized twice upon a valid declaration, once as syntactic context and once during the actual parse. If an expression is found instead, the declaration rule will be attempted only once.

At this point, some readers may argue that syntactic predicates can render the parser non-linear in efficiency. While true, the speed reduction is small in most cases as the parser is mostly deterministic and, hence, near-linear in complexity. Naturally, care must be taken to avoid excess use of syntactic predicates. Further, it is better to have a capability that is slightly inefficient than not to have the capability at all. I.e., just because the use of syntactic predicates can be abused does not mean they should be omitted. In the following section, we formalize and generalize the notion of a predicate and discuss their implementation in ANTLR.

4   Predicated $LL(k)$ Parsing

We denote $LL(k)$ grammars that have been augmented with information concerning the semantic and syntactic context of lookahead decisions as $pred\text{-}LL(k)$. The semantic context of a parsing decision is the run time state consisting of attributes or other user-defined objects computed up until that moment; the syntactic context of a decision is a run time state referring to the string of symbols remaining on the input stream. As demonstrated in the previous section, $pred\text{-}LL(k)$ parsers can easily resolve many syntactic ambiguities and finite-lookahead insufficiencies. In this section, we discuss the behavior of semantic and syntactic predicates and describe the necessary modifications to the usual $LL(k)$ parsing.

4.1 Semantic Predicates

A semantic predicate is a user-defined action that evaluates to either true (success) or false (failure) and, broadly speaking, indicates the semantic validity of continuing with the parse beyond the predicate. Semantic predicates are specified via "<<*predicate*>>?" and may be interspersed among the grammar elements on the right hand side of productions like normal actions. For example,

```
typename
    : <<istype(LATEXT(1))>>?  ID
    ;
```

defines a rule that recognizes an identifier (ID) in a specific semantic context, namely ID must be a type name. We have assumed that **istype()** is a function defined by the user that returns true *iff* its argument is a type name determined by examining the symbol table. If rule **typename** were attempted with input ID, but that ID was not listed as a type name in the symbol table, a run-time parsing error would be reported; the user may specify an error action if the default error reporting is unsatisfactory. The predicate in this role performs *semantic validation*, but the very same predicate can take on a different role depending on the how **typename** is referenced. Consider the following C++ fragment, in which we need to distinguish between a variable declaration and a function prototype:

```
typedef int T;
const int i=3;
int f(i);      // same as int f = i;   initialize f with i
int g(T);      // function prototype; same as "int g(int);"
```

The third declaration defines **f** to be an integer variable initialized to 3 whereas the last declaration indicates **g** is a function taking an argument of type **T** and returning an integer. The unpleasant fact is that there is no syntactic difference between the declarations of **f** and **g**; there is only a semantic difference, which is the type of the object enclosed in parentheses. Fortunately, a *pred-LL(k)* grammar for this small piece of C++ (i.e. for the last two declarations) can be written easily as follows,

```
def :    "int" ID ( var        <<var_decl_action>>
                  | typename <<fn_proto_action>>
                  )
         ";"
    ;

var :    <<isvar(LATEXT(1))>>?  ID
    ;

typename
    :    <<istype(LATEXT(1))>>?  ID
    ;
```

As before with **typename**, we define the rule **var** to describe the syntax and semantics of a variable. While **var** and **typename** are completed specified, the subrule in **def** appears syntactically ambiguous because in both cases the token stream (for the whole rule) would be "int", ID, "(", ID, ")", ";", because ID would match both alternatives **var** and **typename** of the subrule. However, the subrule in **def** has referenced rules containing predicates that indicate their semantic validity. This information is available to resolve the subrule's ambiguous decision. Thus, the same predicates that validate **var** and **typename** can be used as *disambiguating predicates* in rule **def**. The action of copying a predicate upward to a pending production to disambiguate a decision is called *hoisting*. E.g., we must hoist the <<isvar()>>? predicate from the rule **var** upwards into rule **def**. Essentially, disambiguating predicates "filter" alternative productions in and out depending on their semantic "applicability." Productions without predicates have an implied predicate of <<TRUE>>?; i.e., they are always assumed to be valid semantically. Predicates are all considered validation predicates as they must always evaluate to true for parsing of the enclosing production to continue, but occasionally they are hoisted to aid in the parsing process. When ANTLR's grammar analysis phase detects a syntactic ambiguity (actually, any non-$LL(k)$ construct), it searches for *visible* semantic predicates that could be hoisted to resolve the ambiguous decision; the exact definition of visible is provided in a future section. In this way, ANTLR automatically determines which role each predicate should assume.

An important feature is that the hoisting of semantic predicates cannot result in nonlinear parsing complexity—the parser is only charged for the time to initiate execution of a predicate. There are a finite number of hoisted semantic predicates known at analysis time; the user actions within do not count just as normal actions executed from within the parser are not considered to effect fundamental parser complexity. In the following subsections, we describe more precisely the notions of *pred-$LL(k)$* grammar analysis, predicate hoisting, and predicate context.

pred-$LL(k)$ **Parsing Strategy.** Semantic predicates, both validation and disambiguating, are easily added to the normal $LL(k)$ parsing strategy. Validation predicates are used as simple tests to determine whether the input is semantically correct and do not alter the $LL(k)$ parse. The predicate <<π>>? is functionally equivalent to the following normal action embedded in a grammar:

<<if (!π) { *call standard predicate failure routine*}>>

Disambiguating predicates, namely those which are hoisted to resolve a syntactic ambiguity, are incorporated into the normal production prediction expression. For example, in the previous case regarding the C++ variable versus function prototype, ANTLR would generate the following C code for the the syntactically ambiguous subrule contained in rule **def**:

```
if ( LA(1)==ID && isvar(LATEXT(1)) ) {
    var();
} else if ( LA(1)==ID && istype(LATEXT(1)) ) {
    typename();
} else
    parse error;
```

Note that ANTLR-generated parsers attempt productions in the order specified. Parsing in this new environment can be conveniently viewed in the following manner:

1. *Disable invalid productions.* An *invalid* production is a production whose disambiguating predicate(s) evaluates to false.
2. *Parse as normal subrule.* Once a list of *valid* productions has been found, parse them according to normal $LL(k)$ rules.

In general, predicates must follow the following three rules for parsing to behave as we have described:

1. A predicate referenced in rule **a** can be a function only of its left context and tokens of its right context that will be within the lookahead buffer available at the left edge of **a**. When syntactic predicates are used, this lookahead buffer may be arbitrarily large.
2. Predicates may not have side-effects.
3. Disambiguating predicates may not be a function of semantic actions situated between themselves and the syntactically ambiguous decision. E.g., a predicate cannot depend on an action over which it will be hoisted; an action provides an easy way to prevent a predicate from being hoisted.

pred-LL(k) **Grammar Analysis and Hoisting.** Semantic predicates are incorporated into the parsing process (hoisted) when grammar analysis indicates that normal $LL(k)$ is insufficient to differentiate alternative productions. This section provides a glimpse into how $LL(k)$ analysis is augmented to automatically determine predicate roles.

$LL(k)$ grammars can be reduced to a set of parsing decisions of the form

```
a   :   α
    |   β
    ;
```

It is well known that **a** is non-$LL(k)$ *iff* α and β generate phrases with at least one common k-symbol prefix; i.e., for $\mathbf{s} \Rightarrow^*_{lm} w a \delta$, $T = FIRST_k(\alpha\delta) \cap FIRST_k(\beta\delta) \neq \emptyset$ where T represents the set of k-tuples that predict both productions, w is a terminal string, δ is a terminal and nonterminal string, $\mathbf{s}$ is the start symbol, and $\Rightarrow^*_{lm}$ is the closure of the usual leftmost derivation operator. In order to define *pred-LL(k)*, the set of predicates that are candidates for hoisting into a prediction expression must be described. Consider the following grammar fragment.

```
a   :   b β | γ ;
b   :   <<π>>? α
```

A predicate is *visible* from a decision, such as that in **a**, if it can be evaluated without consuming a symbol of lookahead[6] and without executing a user action; i.e., all visible predicates appear on the left edge of productions derivable from **b** and γ, but predicates at the left edge of β would not be visible if α derives at least one token.

Rule **a** is *pred-LL(k)* *iff* it is *LL(k)* (T is empty) or the set of visible predicates for each production *covers* T. A predicate, π, covers a tuple, t, *iff* $t \in$ context(π) where context(π) is the set of lookahead k-tuples that predict the production from which π was hoisted; e.g., context(π) above is $FIRST_k(\alpha\beta\delta)$ where $s \Rightarrow_{lm}^* wa\delta$ and **s** is the start symbol. Only those predicates that cover a tuple in T are used for disambiguation and if T is incompletely covered for a production (there exists a k-tuple t with no covering predicate), the enclosing decision is non-*pred-LL(k)* and an ambiguity warning is given to the grammar developer. Further, to yield a deterministic *pred-LL(k)* parser, exactly one syntactically viable production must be semantically valid (its visible predicates all evaluate to true); the predicates for any other syntactically viable productions must not succeed. Turning again to our ambiguous subrule in **def**, T is {ID}, both predicates are visible, their context is {ID}, and we note that, in that simplified grammar, we assume an ID can never be both a variable and a typename.

Hoisting a predicate, π, into a prediction expression in another rule is not as simple as copying the predicate. The predicate should only be evaluated under the syntactic context in which it was found—the current lookahead buffer must be a member of the context computed for π; for an example illustrating why predicate context is necessary see the ANTLR 1.10 release notes [PCD93].

Using our complete terminology, we can now summarize our *pred-LL(k)* analysis approach: When a non-*LL(k)* decision is encountered, all visible, covering predicates are hoisted, along with their context, into the prediction expressions for that decision; such predicates assume the role of disambiguating semantic predicate.

4.2 Syntactic Predicates

We saw in previous sections how disambiguating semantic predicates can be used to resolve many syntactic ambiguities. However, there are a number of non-*LL(k)*, unambiguous, grammatical constructs that semantic information cannot

---

[6] A generalization of this simple definition, allows hoisting of predicates up to k symbols ahead. We define the *hoisting distance* to be how many terminal symbols exist between the ambiguous decision and the predicate; in this terminology, our discussion in this paper is limited to hoisting distances of 0.

resolve. The most obvious example would be left-recursion, but left-recursion can be removed by well-known algorithms. The nastiest grammar construct is one in which two alternative productions cannot be distinguished without examining all or most of the production. While left-factoring can handle many of these cases, some cannot be handled due to action placement, non-identical left-factors, or alternatives productions that cannot be reorganized into the same rule. The $pred$-$LL(k)$ solution to the problem of arbitrarily-large common left-factors is simply to use arbitrary lookahead; i.e., as much lookahead as necessary to uniquely determine which production to apply. In this section we introduce *syntactic* predicates that, like disambiguating semantic predicates, indicate when a production is a candidate for recognition; the difference lies in the type of information used to predict alternative productions—syntactic predicates employ structural information rather than information about the "meaning" of the input.

Syntactic predicates are specified via "(α)?" and may appear on the left edge of any production of a rule or subrule. The required syntactic condition, α, may be any valid context-free grammar fragment except that new rules may not be defined. Consider how one might write a grammar to differentiate between multiple-assignment statements and simple lists such as:

```
(a,b) = (3,4);
(apple, orange);
```

One obvious grammar is the following:
```
stat:   list "=" list ";"
    |   list ";"
    ;
```

where `list` is a rule, defined elsewhere, that recognizes an arbitrarily long list of expressions. The grammar is not $LL(k)$ for any finite k, unfortunately, due to the common left-factor. E.g., upon seeing "(red, green, blue, ...," an $LL(k)$ parser does not know which alternative to choose. Left-factoring would resolve this problem, but would result in a less readable grammar. We have found that having to constantly manually left factor rules leads to confusing and non-natural grammars. Furthermore, if we assume that the grammar cannot be factored because actions are needed on the left edge of the productions, nothing can be done to resolve the lookahead decision with normal $LL(k)$. In contrast, the nondeterministic decision is easily resolved through the use of a single syntactic predicate:

```
stat:   ( list "=" )?  <<action₁>>  list "=" list ";"
    |                  <<action₂>>  list ";"
    ;
```

The predicate specifies that the first production is only valid if "list "="" is consistent with (matches) an arbitrarily large portion of the infinite lookahead buffer. ANTLR assumes that the production prediction expressions are evaluated in the order specified and, hence, the second production is the default case to attempt if the syntactic predicate (`list "="`)? fails. A short form of the syntactic predicate exists that would allow a functionally equivalent, but less efficient, formalization of `stat`:

```
stat:    ( list "=" list ";" )?
    |    list ";"
    ;
```

This can be interpreted in a slightly different manner—that the first production may not match the input, but rather than reporting a parsing error, try the next viable production (here, the second production is also predicted by the next k symbols of lookahead and is, therefore, considered viable).

While syntactic predicates are an elegant means of extending the recognition strength of conventional $LL(k)$ through selective backtracking, one might argue that a $LALR(k)$ parser automatically left-factors alternative productions obviating the need for the previous syntactic predicates. However, recall that we assumed actions were inserted on the left edge of the two productions to inhibit left-factoring. After only a few moments thought, rule `stat` (with actions) is seen to be non-$LALR(1)$ because rule "cracking" forces actions to production right edges—producing a reduce-reduce conflict.

Because syntactic predicates are, by definition, not guaranteed to match the current input, they have an effect on user actions, semantic predicate evaluation, and normal $LL(k)$ grammar analysis. The following subsections briefly describe the issues in these areas.

Syntactic Predicates effect upon Actions and Semantic Predicates.
While evaluating a syntactic predicate, user actions, such as adding symbol table entries, are not executed because in general, they cannot be "undone;" this conservative approach avoids affecting the parser state in an irreversible manner. Upon successful evaluation of a syntactic predicate, actions are once again enabled—unless the parser was in the process of evaluating another syntactic predicate (syntactic predicates may invoke rules that themselves evaluate syntactic predicates).

Because semantic predicates are restricted to side-effect-free expressions, they are always evaluated when encountered. However, during syntactic predicate evaluation, the semantic predicates that are evaluated must be functions of values computed when actions were enabled. For example, if your grammar has semantic predicates that examine the symbol table, all symbols needed to direct the parse during syntactic predicate evaluation must be entered into the table before this backtracking phase has begun.

Syntactic Predicates effect upon Grammar Analysis. ANTLR constructs normal $LL(k)$ decisions throughout predicated parsers, only resorting to arbitrary lookahead predictors when necessary. Calculating the lookahead sets for a full $LL(k)$ parsers can be quite expensive, so that, by default, ANTLR uses a linear approximation to the lookahead, called $LL^1(k)$ and only uses full $LL(k)$ analysis when required[7]. When ANTLR encounters a syntactic predicate, it generates the instructions for selective backtracking as you would expect, but also generates an $LL^1(k)$ decision. Although no finite lookahead decision is actually required (the arbitrary lookahead mechanism will accurately predict the production without it) the $LL^1(k)$ portion of the decision reduces the number of times backtracking is attempted without hope of a successful match. For example, referring to the C++ declaration versus expression grammar example in Section 3, if the current input token were "42", rule **stat** would immediately attempt the second production—**expression**. On the other hand, if the current input token were "abc", then the **declaration** rule would be attempted before attempting **expression**. If neither productions successfully matched the input, a syntax error would occur.

An unexpected, but important benefit of syntactic predicates is that they provide a convenient method for preventing ANTLR from attempting full $LL(k)$ analysis when doing so would cause unacceptable analysis delays.

5 Implementation

We have implemented a *pred-LL(k)* parser generator in the latest version of ANTLR, which is part of the Purdue Compiler Construction Tool Set (PC-CTS). Due to space constrains, we will discuss the ANTLR implementation of *pred-LL(k)* in a future paper.

ANTLR is not just a research tool; many industrial and academic sites are currently using ANTLR for everyday use. Readers interested in obtaining ANTLR and other the other tools in PCCTS may contact the email server at **pccts@ecn.purdue.edu**.

6 Conclusion

In this paper, we have introduced a new predicated $LL(k)$ parser strategy, *pred-LL(k)*, that uses semantic and syntactic predicates to resolve syntactic ambiguities and parsing conflicts due to the limitations of finite lookahead. In theory, *pred-LL(k)* can recognize all context-free languages (albeit, expensively) as well as many context-sensitive languages. Moreover, these methods have been cleanly integrated into ANTLR—a widely used public-domain $LL(k)$ parser generator. We believe that *pred-LL(k)* represents a significant advance toward the development of natural, easy to read, grammars for difficult languages like C++.

---

[7] Polynomial approximation of higher degree, $LL^m(k)$, are also possible [Par93], but $LL^1(k)$ is sufficient in practice.

7 Acknowledgements

We would like to thank Ariel Tamches, Dana Hoggatt, Ed Harfmann, and Hank Dietz, who all helped shape the definition of semantic predicates.

References

[ES90]   Margaret A. Ellis and Bjarne Stroustrup. *The Annotated C++ Reference Manual.* Addison Wesley Publishing Company, Reading, Massachusetts, 1990.

[Gan89] Mahadevan Ganapathi. Semantic Predicates in Parser Generators. *Computer Language,* 14(1):25–33, 1989.

[HCW82] R. C. Holt, J. R. Cordy, and D. B. Wortman. An Introduction to S/SL: Syntax/Semantic Language. *ACM TOPLAS,* 4(2):149–178, April 1982.

[Joh78] S. C. Johnson. *Yacc: Yet Another Compiler-Compiler.* Bell Laboratories; Murray Hill, NJ, 1978.

[Knu68] Donald E. Knuth. Semantics of Context-Free Languages. *Mathematical Systems Theory,* 2(2):127–145, 1968.

[LRS74] P. M. Lewis, D. J. Rosenkrantz, and R. E. Stearns. Attributed Translations. *Journal of Computer and System Sciences,* 9:279–307, 1974.

[McK90] B. J. McKenzie. LR parsing of CFGs with restrictions. *Software–Practice & Experience,* 20(8):823–832, 1990.

[MF79]   D.R. Milton and C.N. Fischer. $LL(k)$ Parsing for Attributed Grammars. In *Proceedings of Automata, Languages and Programming, Sixth Colloquium,* pages 422–430, 1979.

[MKR79] D.R. Milton, L.W. Kirchhoff, and B.R. Rowland. An $ALL(1)$ Compiler Generator. In *Conference Record of SIGPLAN Symposium on Compiler Construction,* 1979.

[Par93] Terence John Parr. *Obtaining Practical Variants of $LL(k)$ and $LR(k)$ for $k > 1$ by Splitting the Atomic k-Tuple.* PhD thesis, Purdue University, West Lafayette, Indiana, August 1993.

[PCD93] Terence Parr, Will Cohen, and Hank Dietz. The Purdue Compiler Construction Tool Set: Version 1.10 Release Notes. Technical Report Preprint No. 93-088, Army High Performance Computing Research Center, August 1993.

[PDC92] T.J. Parr, H.G. Dietz, and W.E. Cohen. PCCTS 1.00: The Purdue Compiler Construction Tool Set. *SIGPLAN Notices,* 1992.

[Wai90] W. M. Waite. Use of Attribute Grammars in Compiler Construction. In *Attribute Grammars and their Applications; Lecture Notes in Computer Science,* volume 461, pages 254–265. Springer-Verlag, 1990.

Cosy Compiler Phase Embedding
with the CoSy Compiler Model[*]

Martin Alt[1]   Uwe Aßmann[2]   Hans van Someren[3]

[1] Universität des Saarlandes, alt@cs.uni-sb.de
[2] Universität Karlsruhe IPD, assmann@ira.uka.de
[3] ACE Associated Computer Experts bv, Amsterdam, hvs@ace.nl

Abstract. In this article we introduce a novel model for compilation
and compiler construction, the CoSy(COmpiler SYstem) model. CoSy
provides a framework for flexible combination and embedding of compiler phases — called engines in the sequel — such that the construction
of parallel and (inter-procedural) optimizing compilers is facilitated. In
CoSy a compiler writer may program some phase in a target language
and embed it transparently — without source code changes — into different compiler contexts, such as with alternative phase order, speculative
evaluation[4], parallel evaluation, and generate-and-test evaluation. Compilers constructed with CoSy can be tuned for different host systems
(the system the compiler runs on, not the system it produces code for)
and are transparently scalable for (shared memory) multiprocessor host
configurations.
To achieve this, CoSy provides an engine description language (EDL)
which allows to describe the control flow and interaction of compiler
engines. A novel structure definition language (fSDL) is introduced for
the specification of data, access side effects, and visibility control. A
configuration description (CCL) is used to tune the embedding of the
engines to the host system characteristics and limitations.
In order to guarantee transparent embedding, CoSy introduces for each
engine a logical view on the common intermediate representation. CoSy
generates code that maps these views onto the physical representation,
code that helps the programmer to manipulate it, as well as code that
schedules the interaction of the engines.
The proposed model of compilation does not depend on source language,
programming language, or host architecture. It is not restricted to compiler construction and may have applications in a wide area of software
engineering.

1   Motivation for CoSy

One of the major aims in compiler construction is to improve the efficiency
of the generated code by extensive optimization. While this has become more

---

[*] This work was supported in part by ESPRIT project No. 5399 COMPARE
[4] the concurrent evaluation according to different strategies with subsequent selection
of the best one

and more important since modern processors (RISC, superscalar, multi-pipeline) have appeared, which is the best (or even a good) strategy for optimization, is still unclear.

An optimizer writer has to choose between three strategies. The first is to use an optimal implementation of the optimization method. This strategy is unrealistic because most optimizations are known to be NP-hard, and thus can be applied only for very small parts of code (compare the superoptimizer approach [GK92] or the work on peephole optimizer generation).

Therefore, usually the second possibility is chosen, which is to use heuristics. An additional reason for this is that not all information may be available at a certain point in the compilation; we may have to make weak approximations about the effects of subsequent compiler phases. This may result in an algorithm with very unpleasant results in certain situations. Instead of making assumptions about effects of some phases, one would like to inspect the effects by letting those phases run, i.e. one would like to weaken the classical sequential phase ordering.

The third possibility is to apply several heuristics or a heuristic with several settings concurrently, evaluate their results and choose the best result for further processing. In essence this means that competition between different algorithms or different parameterizations is performed. This becomes more and more applicable because shared memory multiprocessors become common, and one would like to make use of their parallel processing capability. However, the use of this technique causes a lot of implementation overhead. Not only the comparison and assessment of the results have to be implemented but also specialized data structures and algorithms which take the speculative evaluations into account.

The CoSy model of compilation has been developed: to weaken the sequential phase ordering and to enable parallel competitive evaluation. Its aim is to facilitate the development of fast compilers generating efficient code. It provides means to embed handwritten or generated compiler phases as black boxes into different compiler contexts without source code changes. It can be seen as a compiler construction toolbox, that gives us the possibility to test compiler structures and select the best one. And it will also enable us to utilize optimization by speculative evaluation, generate-and-test evaluation, parallel evaluation, and alternative orderings.

1.1 Potential of CoSy

A lot of optimization problems benefit from the capabilities of CoSy; in the following we will give some examples.

Several problems can exploit speculative evaluation. Register allocation can be performed with different numbers of registers for parameter passing, global registers, and basic block local registers. Because register allocation and instruction scheduling influence each other, speculative evaluation can be used to find a better code ordering [Bra91]. Different register allocation methods can be applied competitively, and a machine simulator or a performance prediction tool engine can be used to select the best version (this also means that the simulator or performance prediction engine is part of the compiler context). Currently there are a number of different algorithms for pointer alias analysis; such analysis is the basis for optimization on programs with pointers. Because it is difficult to judge in advance which of them yields the best result they can be run competitively and by combining their results better information can be obtained. There are many more examples, but the central issue is: how can we avoid reprogramming engines when we embed them in a different context? How can we experiment with different parameterizations of the algorithms and make use of competitive evaluation?

With speculative evaluation there are alternative algorithms to produce the competing versions. We can also use the generate-and-test method, employing one algorithm which generates several alternative versions, one after the other. Generate-and-test is applicable when the range of the parameters we want to manipulate is intractably large. As an example regard the register allocation algorithm of Chaitin [Cha82]. It has about two parameters we can tune, the first is which registers are deleted from the interference graph in a round and the second is which registers must be spilled if the graph cannot be colored. We can easily imagine a register allocator that generates several of these allocations and have again a selector engine that measures register life times to select the best version. We may stop the production of new versions if we think we have reached a local optimum. Generate-and-test, however, needs special prerequisites in the engines. Is it possible to avoid reprogramming of engines and embed them transparently into such a context?

Another parameter that influences the optimization results is how the optimization engines are ordered. Because certain optimizations enable or disable others (see [WS90]), the optimizer writer should be given a means to embed an engine into several ordering contexts, e.g. into loops that run until no optimization can be applied anymore (exhaustive transformation); or into loops whose iteration number is configured by the machine. Of course exhaustive transformation can be implemented with support of the algorithm to indicate what changed, but this may slow down an engine when it is embedded in a non-loop context. How can we automate the detection of such changes and achieve transparent embedding of engines into alterable orderings?

One method to speed up an algorithm is making a parallel version for it. It is often argued that this is of no use in a compiler because there are a lot of dependencies among the engines. While this is true in general there are certain optimizations which don't have internal dependencies, e.g. when some analyses are done on procedures in a data parallel way [LR92]. For these cases we would like to give the programmer an easy method to embed his engine into a parallel context. However, this normally requires rewriting of a large amount of code because synchronization primitives have to be inserted. How can the transparent embedding of an engine into a parallel context be achieved?

Besides that CoSy answers all these questions a further advantage is that it uses a clear specification methodology for interfaces between the engines to enhance the modularity and the maintainability of the generated systems. We are able to replace engines by new releases with a small amount of time and system resources. Because side effects of engines are known precisely, the effects of such an exchange can be estimated and lead at most to a regeneration of the system. This also enhances reusability and interoperability between several compilation systems. It is easy to reuse some engine from an other system, also in object format. The clear specification allows to generate efficient sequential compilers for uni-processor systems.

The aim of this overview article is to explain how CoSy solves flexible engine embedding transparently. In essence this is achieved by a separation of interaction of engines, the engines themselves, and the access of the engines to the common data. While engines are user-provided (hand-written or generated), interaction of engines and access of the engines to data are generated by CoSy and depend on the embedding of the engine. For this CoSy introduces three languages that work together. EDL (engine description language) describes the interaction of the engines and is used for generation of control flow embedding, i.e. supervising code. fSDL (full structure definition language) is used to describe the view of an engine including its side effects so that the access functions to the data can be generated according to the embedding as well as the data structure definitions. And CCL (CoSy configuration language) makes it possible to adapt the configuration of the generated compiler to the particular characteristics and limitations of the host system for efficiency reasons.

2 Mechanisms for flexible engine embedding

In CoSy we use the following compilation model. A set of engines work in parallel on global data (common data pool, CDP) so that exchange of information is easy. Engines are synchronized under the control of (generated) supervisor code. Access to the data is — and this is (programming) convention — done using access routines from a generated library and macro package, the data manipulation and control package (DMCP).

In order to achieve flexible and transparent engine embedding CoSy uses the following mechanisms. The interaction of engines and the embedding context of an engine is described by a fixed set of *interaction schemes* from which the supervisor code can be generated. With knowledge of the interaction definition, the DMCP library is generated which guarantees synchronized access. This means that the actual (physical) access method of an engine to its data is determined by the context it runs in. Engines can be clustered together to processes and this information can be used to optimize synchronization for these combined engines.

This may be necessary to tailor a CoSy system to the host on which it runs, i.e. to adapt it to a limited number of processors, processes, semaphores or some amount of shared memory. The following sections will explain these mechanisms in more detail.

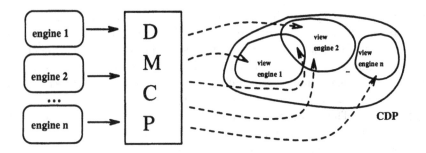

Fig. 1. The CoSy model, engines and the common data pool

2.1 Context specification by interaction schemes

We identified several useful interaction schemes for compilation systems: It is possible to embed an engine into sequence, loop, pipeline, data parallel, speculative, server and generate-and-test contexts.

Sequence and loop interaction model sequential evaluation and iteration over a set of engines. When there are no data dependencies between the activities of some engines, CoSy aims to set up a parallel evaluation of these. Engines in a *loop* may be reactivated for another loop incarnation if a special loop termination engine decides to start the engine sequence again. Such repeated execution normally occurs in a transformation engine which depends on information it modifies (e.g. dead-code elimination together with constant propagation).

Engines which are embedded in a *pipeline* receive an arbitrary number of work units one after the other and overlap their successive operations on them in time. For example, intraprocedural optimization can often be pipelined with the code generator. With *data parallel interaction* as many engines are created as there are work units. Most of the intraprocedural dataflow analysis settings can be mapped to this scheme. Synchronization code for accessing global information can be generated automatically.

A *speculative interaction scheme* embeds a fixed number of engines such that these engines may work without disturbing each other. Each engine gets its own version of the data in which those parts are replicated that would cause dependencies (shadowing). After the run of these engines, a selector engine investigates the results and selects the best. A very interesting application is the concurrent execution of code selectors followed by an assessment engine that chooses the best result.

A *server interaction scheme* allows an engine to call another engine from its algorithmic part, e.g. a constant propagation engine may call an interpreter engine for evaluating constant expressions.

In *optimistic (generate-and-test) interaction* a producer is combined with an experimental engine in such a way, that the producer can create new versions arbitrarily often, and submit them to an experimental engine which can try them out for feasibility. These versions are tested in parallel, each by a new experimental engine. The results of these experiments are collected and the best one is chosen by a special selector engine. This means that here an arbitrary number of versions can be investigated. Optimistic register allocation with several parameters is a nice example of this.

All interaction scheme specifications are block structured, i.e. an interaction scheme combines some *component engines* to a new one, a *composite engine*, which can be combined again. This results in a hierarchical specification of interaction schemes, the *engine hierarchy*.

This also means that the generation of the supervisor code can be done in a hierarchical way: each interaction scheme results in an *engine stub* that supervises the component engines, and *engine envelopes*, for each component engine one, which provide a standard interface between the stub and the component engines. (See figure 2)

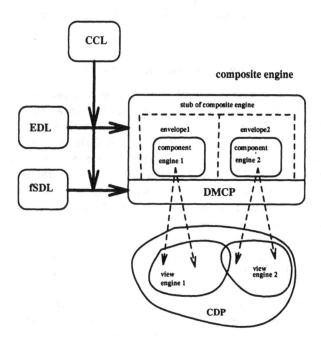

Fig. 2. What CoSy generates and how engines are embedded into the generated code

2.2 Data Structure Definition

We developed a language (fSDL) for the specification of the data structures the engines work on. An engine works on typed memory pieces, called *operators* in fSDL. Each operator has a fixed number of fields that can be divided into two sets, the annotations and the structure carrying fields that point to other operators. Sets of operators, their fields and properties (about which more below) are collected in so-called *domains*, forming the types in the system. Structural objects consist of operators from a domain with their internal edges. The edges are implicitly drawn by the structural fields. From this data structure specification a variety of functions can be generated, e.g. equality predicates, copy functions etc. The allowed types of fields may be extended by externally defined data structures, called *opaques*; they are the black boxes in the specification. Their use requires that some interfaces have to be explicitly defined such as the equality predicate.

The language has a mechanism for specifying data structures with generic or non-standard functionality, the *functor*. It is a parametrized specification, the parameters are *domains* on which the new structure is based. The result of the instantiation is a data structure (a domain in fSDL) with the added functionality. We will see in the examples through the paper that we import the integer of the machine with its usual operations as *opaque* and the functionality of a list by applying a *functor*.

2.3 Access specification by views and side effects

If we specify engine interactions (control flow) we can not yet guarantee that the system runs correctly, because of the side effects and data dependencies of the engines on the CDP. They can be approximated, if we are able to specify as exactly as possible what an engine does with the CDP. fSDL includes constructs to specify an engine's *logical view*. We are interested in two aspects: which data is touched, and how is it touched. The allowed kind of access of operators and fields can be specified by properties (read, write, new, destroy). Sets of these entities are called *domains*, as mentioned above. The touched data must be reachable from the parameters, that are given to the engine (no global variables). The parameters of engines and fields in operators are typed with *domains*; therefore, domains exactly describe which parts of the CDP are actually touched and how they are touched. The transitive closure over all domains of an engine's parameters make up the *logical view* of the engine.

The following example may illuminate this. Suppose the CDP includes structures of the following form. A module has a procedure list and a procedure has a list of instruction trees. The instructions contain virtual and real register numbers as well as their operands and operations. Figure 3 describes the physical layout of the operators **module**, **procedure**, and **instruction** in the CDP.

For a register allocator this view has to be modified slightly. A register allocator may work only on one procedure, reads the virtual register number, sets the real register number, and modifies the instruction list because it may insert spill code. It never changes existing instruction trees and often only works on one procedure. This set of effects on our example CDP can be described by the domain description from figure 4. The identifiers enclosed in [] denote the access properties which are imposed on the fields in these domains. The logical

```
domain MODULE: {
   module <
      procedure:   LIST(PROC)      // procedure list
   >}
domain PROC : {
   procedure <
      instructions: LIST(INSTR),  // the instruction list
      loops        : LIST(LOOP)    // list of loops, not further specified
   >}
domain INSTR : {
   instruction <
      virtual_register: INT,       // virtual register numbers
      real_register  : INT,        // real register numbers
      operation      : INT,        // enum of operation
      operands       : INSTR       // operands
   >}
```

Fig. 3. Physical layout of data structures

view of the register allocator of our example is also depicted in figure 5. Fields enclosed in the dotted region are visible and read-only while fields in the dashed region are also writable. Other fields are not visible.

```
domain RegisterAlloc: {
   procedure <
      instructions: LIST [WRITE] (RegisterInstruction) [READONLY]
   > }
domain RegisterInstruction: {
   instruction <
      virtual_register: INT [READONLY],
      real_register  : INT [WRITE],
      operation      : INT [READONLY],
      operands       : RegisterInstruction [READONLY]
   >}
```

Fig. 4. Domains of register allocator

The fSDL-compiler (fSDC) only produces those access functions in the DMCP whose fields and effects have been specified in an engine's logical view. This guarantees that engines can neither modify nor read other parts of the CDP. In our example the fSDC produces read and write functions for the fields which implement the list internally and for **real_register**. For the field **loops** no function is generated, for the others only read functions are generated. It is

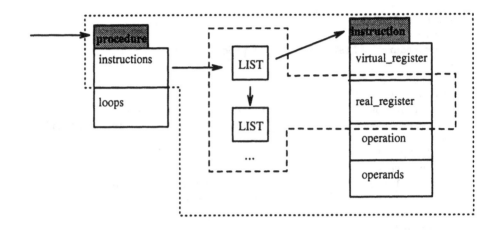

Fig. 5. Domains serve to specify the logical view of an engine

clear that an engine using these domains may not write `virtual_register`, nor replace the list by an other. list.

In order to facilitate the definitions of new domains from existing one, fSDL provides a powerful *calculus* over domains that provides inheritance and restrictive operations such that each engine parameter has a related domain which describes exactly the effect of that engine. In essence the following access methods for DMCP functions can be generated.

- Depending on whether the engine reads or writes a field, or allocates or destroys a node, read, write, allocation and free functions are generated.
- If the access to a field does not suffer from a data dependency which may be introduced by the interaction schemes, straight forward access is provided (direct access).
- If there is a data dependency, an access using a serializing protocol is used (serializing access).
- The user may weaken the kind of dependency such that only a locking protocol is used (locking access).
- If the engine is embedded into a speculative or optimistic interaction scheme, the field is replicated (shadowed) and access to the engine's shadow is yielded (shadowed access).

These functions have the same interface but map the engine's logical view to a physical data access which is dependent on the engine embedding (*view mapping*).

All these accesses can either be access functions which are linked-in (linked DMCP) or they can be inlined (inlined DMCP), so that more efficient access is provided. The former approach is more flexible because engines need not be recompiled when they are embedded into other compilers; they just can be linked with different DMCPs. The latter, an inlined DMCP, provides more efficient access so that more efficient compilers can be built.

2.4 Configuration

Another specification influences the generation of engine stubs (the synchronization code that is generated from interaction schemes) and DMCP access functions. This is the description in CCL, the CoSy configuration language. Despite that logically all engines work in parallel it is possible to reduce the number of parallel units by clustering engines. This has the effect that process invocations to engines collapse to normal procedure calls and synchronization can be optimized or even omitted.

Clustering even serves to achieve a totally sequential compiler if all engines are clustered, or a compiler that consists only of few processes, if a few engines are left non-clustered. Reasonably fast compilers on sequential machines can be configured.

3 Interaction schemes

In this section we will present some examples and show how transparent engine embedding can be used for optimization We will assume that the CDP contains structures as specified in figures 3 and 4. The engine parameters of the interaction schemes that are used to access the physical view of the engine are typed with domain names and with one annotations out of the set IN, INOUT, OUT. The semantics is as follows; an IN handle can not be changed by the engine, an INOUT may, and an OUT handle has to be changed. IN and INOUT handles are initialized, OUT handles not.

3.1 Embedding into parallel context

Suppose we have an intraprocedural register allocator which uses Chaitin's method [Cha82]. How do we organize the process for a list of procedures in a module? There are several possibilities, the easiest one is to run the job in parallel on the procedural level, because there are no dependencies between the register allocations for the procedures. In EDL this would be specified as follows. Note that the parameter of the engine is typed with a domain expression in fSDL which we explained above. If a domains contains exactly one operator or every operator has the same field, we may use the *dot* notation for referencing the fields of that operator.

```
ENGINE CLASS allocate_all(IN m: MODULE) {
   p{} <= m.OPERATOR procedure    // decomposition into work units for
DATAPARALLEL                      // data parallel execution
   registeralloc(p) }
```

This specification declares that so for each procedure an engine `registeralloc` is started in parallel. Of course some mechanism has to be provided that each engine gets its work unit. This is done by a decomposer function which walks the list of procedures and hands over each element (each work unit) to an instance of the `registeralloc` engine. This decomposer can be generated automatically from this specification because the mapping of a list to this set is straightforward or in more complex cases, it can be hand-written. The {} notation denotes the set of work units.

If we don't use clustering this may lead to an enormous amount of scheduling of parallel engines. Instead the register allocator may be embedded into a pipeline, and then only one engine is created which receives the work units one after the other:

```
ENGINE CLASS allocate_all(IN m: MODULE) {
    p<> <= m.OPERATOR procedure    // decomposition into work units
PIPELINE                          // for pipelining
    registeralloc (p) }
```

Note that this does not require the change of a single source code line in the engine. All that is necessary, the generation of work units, the decomposition of the procedure list, the generation of engines and the waiting for completion is generated automatically in the engine stubs, envelopes and access methods.

Of course clustering can be used to coalesce all work into one process if we specify additionally in CCL " `CLUSTER allocate_all` ". This means that `registeralloc` is generated as a sequential subroutine of `allocate_all`, and that the decomposition is just a simple loop over the list of all procedures.

3.2 Embedding into speculative context

In the following we show an example how engines can be embedded into a speculative context. We use as an example competitive register allocation. Suppose the compiler writer has three register allocators working with the three methods [Cha82] [CH84] [HGAM92]. We reuse the view specification from figure 4 for each of these register allocators and also for the speculative composite engine.

```
ENGINE CLASS registeralloc (IN p:RegisterAlloc) {
SPECULATIVE
    chaitin(p)
    chow_henessy(p)
    hendren(p)
SELECT  registeralloc_selector(p) }
```

At runtime the speculative interaction scheme behaves as follows: First the values of the original fields which are to be modified as well as all objects that are reachable from them are copied into shadows (special memory, not accessible from every engine). This means in our case that the field `real_register` is copied into its shadows as well as that the whole instruction list is replicated twice. The replication for any engine-parameter pair can be done in parallel.

Each register allocator works in parallel on its private copy because its generated access functions provide *shadow access*. When all engines are finished the selector determines the best version and copies it back to the original fields, i.e. an unique instruction list is determined again. Then the interaction scheme ends and all other engines can run as if no speculative interaction had taken place.

Of course the selector engine `registeralloc_selector` needs special access functions which give access to all data shadows. If the selection process can be expressed by a mapping of the shadowed structure to the natural numbers and a cost function then the selection can be generated automatically.

Note that `registeralloc` can be substituted in any context by each of the three register allocators without source code change. It is no problem to embed this speculative interaction in the pipelined or data parallel interaction schemes above; the engine hierarchy allows us to do this orthogonally.

3.3 Embedding into alterable engine orderings

In this section we leave the field of register allocation and turn to complex optimization orderings. We show how a simple linear optimization engine can be reconfigured into a complex one with a sophisticated ordering. This is exemplified by the proposal [WS90] which takes several dependencies between the used optimizations into account. First we show how a simple optimizer may be specified in EDL just by concatenating some simple engines. For simplicity we ignore the side effect description here.

```
ENGINE CLASS optimizer (IN p:PROC) {
SEQUENCE
    constant_propagation(p.instructions)
    dead_code_elimination(p.instructions)
    invariant_code_motion(p)
    loop_interchange(p)
    loop_unrolling(p.loops)
    loop_fusion(p.loops)
    strip_mining(p.loops) }
```

In this simple optimizer we perform one optimization after the other. We do not care about a good ordering, i.e. about repetition of engines that are mutually recursively dependent. Such a simple optimizer may be advantageous when we have a sequential machine or when we need quick compilation.

However it is possible to embed the engines in a much more sophisticated way. This following scheme is coded after the engine dependency graph of figure 6 [WS90].

```
ENGINE CLASS optimizer (IN p:PROC) {
SEQUENCE
    constant_propagation(p.instructions)
    complex_opt(p)
    strip_mining(p.loops) }
```

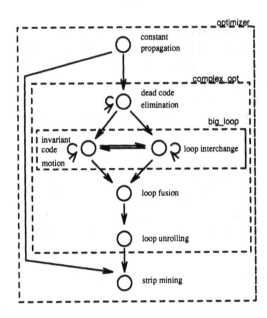

Fig. 6. Dependency graph of optimizations after Whitfield

At the beginning of the optimizer a constant propagator and in the end a strip miner runs. The complex optimizations in the middle are modeled in a sequence interaction scheme:

```
ENGINE CLASS complex_opt (IN p:PROC) {
SEQUENCE
    dead_code_elimination_loop(p.instructions)
    big_loop(p)
    loop_fusion(p.loops)
    loop_unrolling(p.loops) }
```

We only show the complex loop of code motion and loop interchange. This engine is a loop which runs until no further changes occur. Its components are loops over **invariant_code_motion** and **loop_interchange**, respectively.

```
ENGINE CLASS big_loop(IN p:PROC) {
LOOP
EXIT change_detector(p)
    invariant_code_motion_loop(p.instructions)
    loop_interchange_loop(p.loops)}
```

We now embed the engines from the simple optimizer in the complex ordering without source code change. We have to detect transparently whether an engine changes something. Within CoSy the *exit engine* of a loop can be used for this. Initially the **change_detector** engine makes a copy of the data; when it is called after a loop incarnation, it compares the copy with the new data and, if nothing has changed, terminates the loop.

All used data of the engines is known from the specification of their logical views, so the copying and comparison in the exit engine can be generated automatically from the domain specifications (state tracking). Thus even the exit engine need not be programmed by the user.

3.4 Embedding into generate-and-test context

In this section we show an embedding of the engines `invariant_code_motion` and `loop_interchange` from the previous example in a generate-and-test (optimistic) context. This means that we let a selector decide between an arbitrary number of versions.

Actually in optimistic interaction two selection strategies are combined. First it is decided whether a version is worthwhile by investigating the version alone. Then all versions which have survived are compared and the best one is selected. The semantics of the optimistic interaction scheme can be described by the following pseudo code.

```
do { PRODUCE();  ·
       if (PRESELECT())  TRY();
} while (PRODUCEMORE());
FINALSELECT();
```

This means that a producer engine (PRODUCE) produces new versions of certain optimizations, one after the other, each on separate copies. A second engine (PRESELECT) decides whether the version is worthwhile (pre-selection). TRY is given the version as a shadow and forked off so that it may experiment with the version. In the meanwhile, it is checked by PRODUCEMORE whether PRODUCE should be given another try to produce a version. If so, a next version will be generated and the whole process is repeated. Note that PRESELECT and PRODUCEMORE can run in parallel because they only look at versions and do not modify them. Otherwise, the production stops. The results of the experiment on each version are collected by FINALSELECT which performs the final global selection. This scheme seems to be rather complicated; however, some of these engines may do nothing, in fact. For example, if no pre-selection method is known, there need not be a PRESELECT engine.

```
ENGINE CLASS code_motion_and_loop_interchange(IN p:PROC) {
OPTIMISTIC
   PRODUCE      invariant_code_motion(p)
   PRESELECT    estimate_register_lifetimes(p)
   PRODUCEMORE  threshold(p)
   TRY          loop_interchange(p)
   FINALSELECT  static_code_analysis(p) }
```

Our example performs as follows. First invariant code motion is done in the PRODUCE engine. As pre-selection criterion we take the amount of register lifetimes which results from the code motion. Thus we may withdraw already in `estimate_register_lifetimes` some useless versions. Then the TRY engine `loop_interchange` needs to work only on "better" versions. To decide whether the production should be stopped, engine `threshold` could just contain a counter which is increased and compared to a threshold number. In the end, engine `static_code_analysis` evaluates the information of a frequency analysis and estimates the cost of the resulting code versions.

Again the embedding of the engines does not require to change them. Because the side effects are known precisely a lot of work can be done in parallel.

4 Related work

The attempts to parallelize compilers can be divided into two main directions. One tries to parallelize algorithms like scanning or parsing and is language independent. The other others parallelize existing compilers and are therefore source– and target language dependent. In contrast, CoSy will give a very general mechanism (programming languages) for compiler construction.

There have not been many attempts to design languages neither for module re-embedding nor for side effect descriptions. FX [JG90] and JADE [LR91] contain basic principles for side effect description but fSDL goes further because it allows the convenient combination of these descriptions via its domain calculus. JADE also provides a mechanism to synchronize tasks over a shared memory, however its side effect descriptions are mixed with source code so that the re-embedding of a part of the system may not be as easy as with CoSy. CoSy also allows much more kinds of embedding than JADE, and allows flexible configuration and non-deterministic execution.

In early works of [Tic79] and [DK76], they define the concepts of a Module Interconnection Language. This specification language consists of simple input-output specification but is dependent on the implementation language of the modules, because it includes its type concept.

In many aspects CoSy has inherited from IDL [NNGS89]. However, IDL has a somewhat different compilation model: processes communicate via channels and not via a shared common data pool. Therefore IDL requires processes to communicate via external instances like files. Also processes execute sequentially. CoSy allows for much faster communication among engines and still allows correct, also parallel evaluation, because of its powerful data and side effect description mechanism. Furthermore, CoSy allows speculative and optimistic interaction. Therefore the CoSy model will be a major step forward in the reuse of compiler engines and flexible compiler construction.

5 Conclusion

We have shown how the CoSy compiler model can be used to embed compiler engines flexibly into a lot of different compilation and optimization contexts.

CoSy enables the compiler writer to reuse engines, write scalable, parallel, and portable compilers, and tune the performance of his system by exchanging interaction schemes or manipulating the configuration of the system. This all is possible because CoSy provides novel description mechanisms for data structures, side effect descriptions, as well as engine interactions.

For the first time speculative, optimistic, parallel evaluation as well as alterable engines orderings are provided in an orthogonal and unified way for compiler construction. CoSy enables cosy engine embedding: this will facilitate construction of parallel and (inter-procedural) optimizing compilers.

References

[Bra91]   D. G. Bradlee. *Retargetable Instruction Scheduling for Pipelined Processors*. PhD thesis, University of Washington, 1991.

[CH84]   F.C. Chow and J.L. Hennessy. Register allocation by priority based coloring. In *Proceedings of the ACM SIGPLAN Symp. on Compiler Construction*, June 1984.

[Cha82]   G.J. Chaitin. Register allocation and spilling via graph coloring. In *SIGPLAN Conference on Programming Language Design and Implementation*, June 1982.

[DK76]   Frank DeRemer and Hans Kron. Programming-in-the-large versus Programming-in-the-small. *IEEE*, Nov 1976.

[GK92]   T. Granlund and R. Kenner. Eliminating branches using a superoptimizer and the GNU C compiler. In *ACM SIGPLAN Conference on Programming Language Design and Implementation*, pages 341–352. ACM, June 1992.

[HGAM92] L. J. Hendren, G. R. Gao, E. R. Altman, and C. Mukerji. A register allocation framework based on hierrchical cyclic interval graphs. In U. Kastens and P. Pfahler, editors, *CC 92, 4th International Conference on Compiler Construction, LNCS 641*, pages 176–191, 1992.

[JG90]   Pierre Jouvelot and David K. Gifford. Algebraic reconstruction of types and effects. In *ACM Conference on Principles of Programming Languages (POPL)*, 1990.

[LR91]   M. S. Lam and M. C. Rinard. Coarse-grain parallel programming in Jade. In *ACM Conference on Principles and Practice of Parallel Processing (PPOPP)*, pages 94–105. Computer Systems Laboratory, Stanford University, 1991.

[LR92]   Y-f. Lee and B. Ryder. A comprehensive approach to parallel data flow analysis. In H. Zima, editor, *Workshop on compilers for parallel computers*. Austrian Center for Parallel Computation, 1992.

[NNGS89] J.R. Nestor, J.M. Newcomer, P. Giannini, and D.L. Stone. *IDL:The Language and its Implementation*. Prentice Hall, Englewood Cliffs, 1989.

[Tic79]   Walter F. Tichy. Software Development Control Based on Module Interconnection. In *Proc. of the 4th International Conference on Software Engineering*, Sep 1979.

[WS90]   D. Whitfield and M. L. Soffa. An approach to ordering optimizing transformations. In *ACM Conference on Principles and Practice of Parallel Programming (PPOPP)*, 1990.

Towards Provably Correct Code Generation for a Hard Real-Time Programming Language

Martin Fränzle and Markus Müller-Olm [*]

Institut für Informatik und Praktische Mathematik
Christian-Albrechts-Universität Kiel
Preußerstr. 1–9, D-24105 Kiel, Germany
E-Mail: {mf|mmo}@informatik.uni-kiel.d400.de

Abstract. This paper sketches a hard real-time programming language featuring operators for expressing timeliness requirements in an abstract, implementation-independent way and presents parts of the design and verification of a provably correct code generator for that language. The notion of implementation correctness used as an implicit specification of the code generator pays attention to timeliness requirements. Hence, formal verification of the code generator design is a guarantee of meeting all deadlines when executing generated code.

1 Introduction

For an increasing number of applications, software failures may be very costly in terms of economic loss or even human suffering. This is particularly true for hard real-time control programs, where correctness does not only depend on logical correctness of results, but also on timely delivery of services.

Testability of such software is poor, as timing constraints add an additional dimension to the behaviour to be examined and, furthermore, dictate the speed of the testing process. Traditionally, this problem has lead to a purely pragmatic separation of concerns: Algorithmic correctness is dealt with by using programming notation, which — whenever reliability is required — is subject to thorough or sometimes even formal investigation, whereas timing properties are dealt with a posteriori by inspection of the machine code generated by a compiler.

Unfortunately, this approach leaves two different problems unresolved: On one hand, investigation of the algorithmic properties stops too early in the development process, as due to the absence of verified development software, particularly compilers, improper target code may still result. On the other hand, inspection of timing properties starts too late in the development process, possibly leading to expensive iterations in development.

Both problems could be resolved by a programming language supplying means to express the relevant patterns of timeliness, together with a highly

---

[*] This report reflects work that has been partially funded by the Commission of the European Communities under ESPRIT Basic Research Action 7071 "ProCoS II" (Provably Correct Systems II) and by the Deutsche Forschungsgemeinschaft under contract DFG La 426/13-1.

dependable, i.e. correctness-preserving, compiler. Firstly, a dependable compiler would give certainty about the correctness of machine code whenever the same is true for the source program, making backcompilation, machine code inspection, and similar costly target code analysis techniques superfluous. Secondly, implementation-independent means of expressing timing constraints at the source level could make timing subject to the same paradigm of stepwise development currently successfully applied to algorithmic development.

The traditional approach to achieving reliability of compilers is validation by running test suites, i.e. by compiling a number of test programs and testing their executables. It is questionable whether this can give sufficient confidence to replace target code inspection in safety-critical software development, as test programs normally exhibit rather simple behaviour to allow detection of errors. As stated earlier, this is especially true with respect to timing. Hence, highly dependable compilers for real-time programming languages cannot be constructed without formal verification of their vital parts, particularly code generators.

The aim of the ESPRIT project "Provably Correct Systems II" (abbreviated ProCoS II) is to contribute to the state of the art in development of correct software-hardware systems for embedded, safety-critical real-time control by elaborating an experimental framework for the stepwise, correctness-preserving development of such systems. In this framework, the programming language plays the role of an interface between high levels of abstraction, where system development requires human ingenuity, and low levels of abstraction, where correctness preserving transformations can be applied fully automatic by compilers.

Thus, one of the immediate goals of ProCoS II is to provide a prototype of a real-time programming language designed to solve the interfacing problem between system specification and system implementation and to develop a verified prototype compiler for this language. On one hand, the programming language has to provide sufficiently expressive timing operators to make program correctness arguments without recurrence to a particular implementation possible. On the other hand, it must be implementable on realistic hardware by avoiding overly idealized timing properties.

A prototype compiler might be taken as a pragmatic proof of the latter claim. But far beyond this, its existence will be a demonstration of the feasibility of high-dependability compiler development, opening the perspective for banning target-level work from safety-critical system development.

This paper gives an overview on the work undertaken thus far in ProCoS II towards this goal. Section 2 gives an introduction to ProCoS's real-time programming language TimedPL, and section 3 shows how to extend it to a larger real-time process language used to embedd TimedPL and the target machine language into a common framework in section 6. In section 4, a general notion of one process implementing another is sketched, which is exploited in section 7 to define the detailed correctness predicates for code to be generated for the different syntactic categories of TimedPL. In section 8, these correctness predicates are put to use by stating concrete target code patterns for some source code patterns and by exploiting the algebra of the process language to show implementation correctness.

2   The Real-Time Programming Language TimedPL

ProCoS's real-time programming language TimedPL [FvK93] features concepts to describe both the desired logical and temporal behaviour of programs. Using this basic distinction, TimedPL may be understood as being composed of

1. a simple imperative kernel for describing logical behaviour via imperative sequential algorithms,
2. timing operators for decoration of sequential algorithms, assigning execution times to their logical behaviour, and
3. parallel composition of timed sequential algorithms, introducing concurrency for the sake of both expressivity and efficiency.

TimedPL is closely related to occam [inm88a], albeit dropping some features from occam for scientific treatability, but seriously adding to its expressivity in ProCoS's central field of research, namely real-time software development.

Like in occam, a program is a set of sequential processes executing in parallel and communicating with each other and with the environment solely via unidirectional, synchronous channels. Synchronicity means that whenever a process wants to communicate on a channel it has to wait until the partner residing at the other end of that channel is also willing to communicate. By disallowing shared variables, there is a clear syntactic distinction between effects that might affect parallel partners, namely communications on channels, and those that are completely encapsulated in a sequential process and may be optimized by a compiler, namely state transformations.

Table 1: Outline of TimedPL's syntax

$\langle program \rangle ::= \langle chandecl \rangle^* \, \text{par} \, (\langle parallel \ component \rangle^+)$

$\langle chandecl \rangle ::= \text{chan} \, \langle channel \rangle \, \text{latency} \, \langle time \rangle :$

$\langle time \rangle ::= \langle non - negative \ real \rangle$

$\langle parallel \ component \rangle ::= \langle inaccuray \ spec \rangle \langle sequential \ program \rangle$

$\langle inaccuray \ spec \rangle ::= \text{drift} \, \langle real \ larger \ 1 \rangle : \text{granularity} \, \langle time \rangle :$

$\langle sequential \ program \rangle ::= \langle variable \ declaration \rangle^* \langle sequential \ process \rangle$

$\langle variable \ declaration \rangle ::= \text{var} \, \langle variable \rangle^* :$

$\langle sequential \ process \rangle ::= \text{skip} \, | \, \text{stop} \, | \, \langle variable \rangle := \langle expression \rangle \, |$
$\langle channel \rangle ? \langle variable \rangle \, | \, \langle channel \rangle ! \langle variable \rangle \, |$
$\langle sequential \ process \rangle ; \langle sequential \ process \rangle \, |$
$\text{if} \, \langle bool \ exp. \rangle \, \text{then} \, \langle seq. \ proc. \rangle \, \text{else} \, \langle seq. \ proc. \rangle \, |$
$\text{while} \, \langle bool \ expression \rangle \, \text{do} \, \langle sequential \ process \rangle \, |$
$\langle upper \ bound \rangle \, | \, \langle alternative \ statement \rangle$

$\langle upper \ bound \rangle ::= [\langle sequential \ process \rangle] \leq \langle time \rangle$

$\langle alternative \ statement \rangle ::= \text{alt} \, (\langle timed \ alternative \rangle^*)$

$\langle timed \ alternative \rangle ::= \text{wait} \, \langle time \rangle : \langle channel \rangle ? \langle variable \rangle \, \rightarrow \, \langle seq. \ proc. \rangle$

2.1   The Imperative Kernel

The imperative kernel of TimedPL is essentially the language of while programs, extended by input and output commands to unidirectional, synchronous channels, and by input-guarded alternatives providing a means to conditionally react upon different external stimuli arriving via channels.

More specificly, untimed sequential processes are composed from the atomic processes skip (representing the identical state transformation), stop (meaning deadlock, i.e. idling forever), assignments, input commands $c?x$ (waiting for communication on channel c and, if communication proceeds, assigning the communicated value to variable x), and output commands $c!e$ (waiting for communication on channel c and, if communication proceeds, sending the value of the expression e along the channel). Atomic processes can be composed by sequential composition, conditionals, while-loops, and input guarded alternatives to form more complicated sequential algorithms.

The imperative kernel of TimedPL is intended for describing the logical behaviour of sequential algorithms. Consequently, unless restricted by addition of timing operators (as described in the next section), execution speed of sequential processes is completely unspecified. This means that any implementation yielding correct logical behaviour, i.e. input-output sequences, is acceptable regardless of its speed.

More specificly, only runtime of TimedPL's *atomic* processes is unspecified, whereas composition operators, even those involving evaluation of control constructs, do *not* take extra execution time beyond that taken by the component processes. The latter convention significantly enhances the expressive power of composition operators when dealing with timed component processes.

2.2 Timing Operators

The intended field of application of TimedPL is hard real-time programming, i.e. construction of programs where correctness does not only depend on algorithmic well-behavedness, but also on never missing any deadline, be it a lower or an upper bound for the time of delivering a certain service. Therefore, we need mechanisms to constrain the runtime consumption of parts of sequential algorithms. TimedPL offers three such mechanisms:

1. upper bounds on the time spent by sequential processes for state transformations,
2. delayed readiness of guarding communications in alternatives, and
3. upper bounds on the time-to-communication taken by a communication command when its communication partner is ready, called the communication's *latency*.

Upper bound timing. Upper bounds can be placed anywhere inside a sequential process for bounding execution time of the enclosed part, which is itself a sequential process. The upper bound timing operator

$$\langle upper\ bound \rangle ::= [\langle sequential\ process \rangle] \leq \langle time \rangle$$

confines the enclosed sequential process to spend at most the amount allowed by the upper bound of time controlled by itself, i.e. not spent waiting for communication partners, until termination. If this contradicts with timing conditions imposed by inner timed alternatives, the semantics is miraculous, meaning that the process is not implementable and has to be rejected by the compiler.

Timed alternatives. Lower bounds on reactivity can be achieved by using the delayed readiness of guarding communications offered by timed alternatives

⟨*timed alternative*⟩ ::= **wait** ⟨*time*⟩ : ⟨*channel*⟩?⟨*variable*⟩ → ⟨*sequential process*⟩ .

An alternative statement consists of processes guarded by input guards, where the readiness of the guarding communications is established when the delay time stated in the guard has elapsed. In contrast to occam, timing is hard, i.e. readiness is established *at* the moment the delay elapses, not arbitrarily thereafter. The latter condition might seem unimplementable due to the impossibility of *absolutely* exact hardware clocks, but TimedPL's semantics features a distinction between local clocks (which may be inaccurate) and global time. This distinction is part of the definition of TimedPL's parallel composition operator, cf. section 2.3.

Communication latencies. Often systems communicating through synchronous channels are understood under the *maximum progress assumption*, where a communication has to take place as soon as both communication partners are simultaneously ready for a communication. This gives nice timing properties, but is unrealistic even for systems with an own processor for each parallel component, as hardware and protocol delays in detecting readiness of a communication partner do not only limit reactivity, but may even blurr the temporal order of events.

In TimedPL programs, a *lower bound on progress* of each communication is explicitly stated. I.e. if communication partners are simultaneously ready for a communication, communication of that or another competing event need not happen unless both communication partners have been simultaneously ready for the event for a specified amount of time, called the latency associated to that event. Communication latencies are assigned at a per-channel basis by making latency specifications part of the channel declaration.

2.3 Parallel Composition

A real-time programming language not offering parallelism would be incomplete with respect to both efficiency of progams and expressibility of control algorithms requiring concurrent actions. Hence, TimedPL programs are systems of timed communicating sequential processes combined by outermost parallelism.

In any implementation, timing properties can be guaranteed only with respect to hardware timers, which, unfortunately, do not accurately reflect real-world time due to clock drift and discretization. The consequences of identification of both timing regimes on the behaviour of synchronous systems can be drastic, as independent subsystems may loose synchronicity due to the imperfection of technical clock devices. Thus, we have to model the effects of timer inaccuracies in the semantics of TimedPL to achieve reliable designs.

The concept of coping with these implementation dependencies offered by TimedPL is straightforward: The programmer has to state acceptable clock tolerances for the individual parallel components. Each parallel component is prefixed by an inaccuracy specification stating the maximum allowed drift and discreteness of its local clock. Semantically, these inaccuracy specifications can be taken as a guarantee by the programmer that the correctness of his control algorithm will not be affected by local clocks being imprecise in the stated range. Similarly to the mathematical treatment of component tolerances by the calculus of accidental error in, e.g., electrical engineering, a calculus of nondeterminism caused by clock inaccuracy and of its propagation through different programming operators can be elaborated, providing a mathematically sound basis for mostly separating the problem of dealing with implementation tolerances from the design of a real-time control system as such. Work undertaken in ProCoS II on the semantic basis of such a calculus of timing inaccuracy can be found in [FMO93].

3 Extending TimedPL Towards a Process Calculus

TimedPL's syntax, as outlined in table 1, defines different syntactic layers, namely programs, parallel components, sequential programs, and sequential processes, representing implementation concepts and thus making sense for a compilable language. But when reasoning about real-time control processes, that syntactic variety can be a burden. A more homogeneous process language TimedProc used in the remainder of this article as a framework for reasoning can be derived from TimedPL by dropping syntactic restrictions. In TimedProc, all the syntactic productions defining TimedPL's syntactic classes ⟨program⟩, ⟨parallel component⟩, ⟨sequential program⟩, and ⟨sequential process⟩ are put together to define the single syntactic class ⟨process⟩, allowing for parallelism, inaccuracy specifications, and variable declarations inside subprocesses. Furthermore, a generalized bound construct

$$\langle general\ bound \rangle ::= [\langle process \rangle] \in \langle set\ of\ times \rangle$$

and an assertion statement

$$\langle assertion \rangle ::= \texttt{assert}\ \langle bool\ expression \rangle$$

are added to the process constructions.

A general bound $[\pi] \in T$ confines the enclosed process π to spend a runtime in the bounding set T of times until termination, where — as with upper bound timing — time spent waiting for a communication partner does not count. In the remainder of this article, the notation **wait** T , where T is a set of times, will be used as a convenient abbreviation for the process $[\texttt{skip}] \in T$ that idles for a time in T.

An assertion **assert** b does nothing (not even consume time) whenever the Boolean expression b is true in the current state. But whenever b evaluates to false, **assert** b behaves completely unreliable, implying that *any* implementation is correct under these circumstances. Thus, prefixing a process by an assertion **assert** b means that an implementation need only be well-behaved whenever b evaluates to true.

We obtain a common framework for reasoning about source and target programs by defining the semantics of the machine language by an interpreter expressed in TimedProc in section 6, since TimedProc is a superset of our source language TimedPL.

4 Implementation Correctness

When dealing with correctness of code generation we need a rigorous notion of whether one process implements another one or not. As we are dealing with embedded systems, there is a very natural notion directly at hand:

A process ψ implements or refines a process π, denoted $\psi \sqsupseteq \pi$, iff π can be safely replaced by ψ in any context.

I.e., ψ *may* only engage in interactions with its environment that π may also engage in, and ψ *must* engage in any interaction π must engage in. This has to apply with respect to both the logical behaviour and timing, i.e. an implementing process will in particular respect all the deadlines that the implemented process meets.

Using this kind of reasoning, which can be formalized by associating each process with the set of trajectories over its state space it may engage in [vK93], algebraic laws of refinement between processes (or implementation correctness, respectively) can be established, equipping TimedProc with a calculus of process refinement. Table 2 gives examples of TimedProc's refinement rules.

Table 2: Some refinement laws of TimedProc

$x := e\,;x := f \doteq x := f[e/x]$	{Assignment merge}
$[\pi] \leq t \sqsupseteq [\pi] \leq t'$, if $t \leq t'$	{Tightening Bounds}
$[x := e] \in T \doteq [x := e] \in \{0\}\,;\text{wait } T$	{Assignment-Bound}
$\text{wait } T\,;[x := e] \in T' \doteq [x := e] \in T'\,;\text{wait } T$	{Assignment-Wait}
$\text{wait } T \sqsupseteq \text{wait } T'$, if $T \subseteq T'$	{Wait-Refinement}

where $\doteq$ is semantic equivalence, i.e. $\pi \doteq \psi$ iff $\pi \sqsupseteq \psi$ and $\psi \sqsupseteq \pi$, and $f[e/x]$ denotes expression f with every occurence of variable x being replaced by expression e.

---

5 Conceptual Framework of Code Generator Verification

In software engineering it is largely accepted that the formulation of specifications must preceede the construction of programs. Often even a derivation of programs out of specifications by formal or informal transformations is recommended instead of a-posteriori verification. Similarly the design of provably correct machine code to be generated by a compiler should be preceeded by the formulation of the appropriate correctness predicate. The construction of a verified code generator described in this paper is inspired by some ideas of [Hoa91]. One of them is to base correctness of code on the notion of source language refinement consistently extending the chain of refinement steps that led to the source program down to the level of the machine program. A definition in terms of refinement formulae is enabled by defining the machine language semantics by an interpreter $\mathcal{I}$ in source language-like notation.

After the correctness relation has been fixed, correct code can be described by means of theorems about this relation. Typically for compound constructs $op(\pi_1, \ldots, \pi_n)$ these theorems take the form of an implication that under certain syntactic conditions on the surrounding code establishes the correctness of code for the compound construct provided correct code for the components $\pi_1, \ldots, \pi_n$ is supplied. The collection of these theorems allows to define a compiling relation syntactically in a compositional way that is guaranteed to be a subrelation of the correctness relation, i.e. a (syntactic) specification of a correct code generator. In this way the collection of theorems specifies the code generator.

In simple situations (and in particular for entire programs) the correctness predicate can be defined directly as refinement between the source program π and the interpretation of an implementing machine program m:

$$\pi \sqsubseteq \mathcal{I}m .$$

But in more sophisticated situations further parameters are necessary. If for example the data spaces of the source and the target program are different then a retrieve-mapping Ψ that describes their relationship could be used as an additional parameter of the correctness predicate:[2]

$$\Psi ; \pi \sqsubseteq \mathcal{I}m ; \Psi .$$

6 Machine Language

The work reported in this article aims at the design of a provably correct code generator that translates TimedPL to transputer code [inm88b]. Of main interest here are the timing aspects, in particular the guarantee that time bounds requested in source programs are met by the generated machine code. The assumption of TimedPL that control structures do not consume time by themselves largely simplifies the reasoning about programs. But clearly, code running on a conventional processor needs time for the evaluation of the Boolean guards that steer the control flow and for the execution of the jump instructions that move the program counter to appropriate places.

The solution to this problem is based on the observation that only the preservation of the timing of external communications and of the communicated values is important for correctness. Internal computation can be moved arbitrarily as long as this does not affect communications. Therefore a compiler for TimedPL can shift the computation time overhead for the implementation of control structures to sequentially neighboured processes.

This section introduces a simple abstract machine language. It has been designed in order to allow a treatment of the timing aspects in isolation and to illustrate how the timing of machine instructions can be formally captured in a process algebraic setting. A number of other translation tasks for a compiler to transputer code and for code for conventional processors in general are not discussed in this paper as solutions are well-known. Examples are the assignment of storage locations to variables, the translation of mnemonic assembler

---

[2] We assume that Ψ can be written inside the language of processes into which the source language is embedded.

instructions to sequences of bytes, and the generation of code for the evaluation of expressions.

The model machine has the following components: a program counter P, two accumulators A and B for integer resp. Boolean values, a storage that is addressed directly by variable names (avoiding the compiler task of assigning integer addressed storage locations to program variable names), and channels that are addressed directly by channel names (avoiding the need to assign links to channels when translating TimedPL to the machine language). Its instruction set is given by the following grammar, where i ranges over instructions.[3]

$$i ::= \mathtt{stopp} \mid \mathtt{eval}(e) \mid \mathtt{eval}(b) \mid \mathtt{stl}(x) \mid \mathtt{out}(c) \mid \mathtt{in}(c) \mid \mathtt{j}(l) \mid \mathtt{cj}(l) \;.$$

A *machine program* m is a sequence of instructions. We use the notation $\#m$ for the length of m and $m_1 \frown m_2$ for the concatenation of m_1 and m_2.

Informally, the logical behaviour of the instructions is as follows: $\mathtt{stopp}$ stops the machine, $\mathtt{eval}(e)$ evaluates the integer expression e leaving the result in register A, $\mathtt{eval}(b)$ evaluates the boolean expression b leaving the result in register B, $\mathtt{stl}(x)$ stores the contents of register A to the memory location x, $\mathtt{out}(c)$ communicates the contents of register A synchronously on channel c, $\mathtt{in}(c)$ reads an integer value synchronously from channel c and writes it to register A, $\mathtt{j}(l)$ performs a relative jump by l, and $\mathtt{cj}(l)$ acts like $\mathtt{j}(l)$ if the register B contains the value false, otherwise it transfers control to the following instruction.

One of the ideas of the chosen approach to code generator verification is to define the machine language semantics via an interpreter written in a process language into which the source language is embedded. Typically such an interpreter consists of one loop essentially. The loop's body consists of a conditional that branches to appropriate actions for each of the machine instructions. The action describing the *untimed* meaning of the instruction $\mathtt{eval}(e)$, for example, is given by the process $\mathtt{A}, \mathtt{P} := e, \mathtt{P} + 1$.

An interpreter defining the *instruction timing* in addition to the logical behaviour can be obtained by using time bounds at appropriate places in the interpreter. The property of the process language that the composition operators do not take time themselves simplifies this. Therefore time is spent only by the actions that describe the logical behaviour of the single instructions. The idea is to define for each instruction i a set $\mathcal{T}(i)$ of possible execution times and to use $\mathcal{T}(i)$ as time bound for the corresponding action. The process defining the *timed* meaning of $\mathtt{eval}(e)$, for example, is $[\mathtt{A}, \mathtt{P} := e, \mathtt{P} + 1] \in \mathcal{T}(\mathtt{eval}(e))$.

Processor manuals state the number of machine cycles $n(i)$ that are necessary for evaluation of an instruction i. On a machine with clock rate r, execution time of i therefore is $\frac{n(i)}{r}$. But this calculation is oversimplified since the clock generator of the machine cannot be assumed to be accurate. We assume that the imprecision of the clock can be quantified by a *drift constant* $d_M \geq 1$ in the following way: If the machine clock advances by t then the time t' that has actually passed satisfies $\frac{t}{d_M} \leq t' \leq d_M * t$. There are two possibilities for incorporation of clock

---

[3] At the time being the model machine does not contain instructions for the implementation of alternatives. We are not yet able to handle them appropriately in a way that generalizes to transputer code.

drift into the semantics description by an interpreter: It can either be specified locally for each instruction by using $T_{\text{drift}}(i) = \{t \mid \frac{1}{d_M} * \frac{n(i)}{r} \le t \le d_M * \frac{n(i)}{r}\}$ instead of $T(i)$ or globally for the entire machine by applying the drift operator **drift** d_M at the outermost level. Local drift specification more directly captures the intuition that the execution time of single instructions is not accurately determined but that only certain intervals can be guaranteed. Global drift specification on the other hand can be more conveniently used in compiler proofs. A compiler must only check that the globally specified drift d_M of the machine is smaller than or equal to the drift allowed by the source program. Fortunately, one can show that it is immaterial whether drift is specified locally or globally, because the drift operator distributes over all sequential operators and only weakens the time bounds of a sequential process if time bounds are not nested.

Table 3 contains the timed semantics of the machine language. $\mathcal{M} m$ describes the possible timed behaviours arising from interpreting machine program m. The assertion **assert** $P = \#m + 1$ at the end of the definition of $\mathcal{I}$ ensures that every terminating execution actually ends at address $\#m + 1$. Otherwise the interpreter behaves arbitrary and the machine program can not be a refinement of a reasonable program. In this way the obligation is posed on the compiler constructor to use only code sequences of this kind.

Table 3: Machine Language Semantics

$\mathcal{M} m \stackrel{\text{def}}{=} \textbf{drift } d_M : \mathcal{I} m$

$\mathcal{I} m \stackrel{\text{def}}{=} \textbf{var } \text{P}, \text{A}, \text{B}:$
$\qquad [\text{P}:=1] \in \{0\} \; ; \; \textbf{while } 1 \le \text{P} \wedge \text{P} \le \#m \textbf{ do } Step \; ; \; \textbf{assert } P = \#m + 1$

$Step \stackrel{\text{def}}{=} \textbf{if } m[\text{P}] = \textbf{stopp then stop}$
$\qquad\quad \textbf{else if } m[\text{P}] = \textbf{eval}(e) \textbf{ then } [\text{A}, \text{P}:=e, \text{P}+1] \in T(\textbf{eval}(e))$
$\qquad\quad \textbf{else if } m[\text{P}] = \textbf{eval}(b) \textbf{ then } [\text{B}, \text{P}:=b, \text{P}+1] \in T(\textbf{eval}(b))$
$\qquad\quad \textbf{else if } m[\text{P}] = \textbf{stl}(x) \textbf{ then } [x, \text{P}:=\text{A}, \text{P}+1] \in T(\textbf{stl}(x))$
$\qquad\quad \textbf{else if } m[\text{P}] = \textbf{j}(l) \textbf{ then } [\text{P}:=\text{P}+1+l] \in T(\textbf{j}(l))$
$\qquad\quad \textbf{else if } m[\text{P}] = \textbf{cj}(l) \textbf{ then } [\text{P}:= \textbf{if } \text{B} \textbf{ then } \text{P}+1 \textbf{ else } \text{P}+1+l] \in T(\textbf{cj}(l))$
$\qquad\quad \textbf{else if } m[\text{P}] = \textbf{out}(c) \textbf{ then } [c!\text{A} \; ; \; \text{P}:=\text{P}+1] \in T(\textbf{out}(c))$
$\qquad\quad \textbf{else if } m[\text{P}] = \textbf{in}(c) \textbf{ then } [c?\text{A} \; ; \; \text{P}:=\text{P}+1] \in T(\textbf{in}(c))$
$\qquad\quad \textbf{else chaos}$

The generation of correct code employs some properties of the interpreter I that can be proved by application of refinement laws. For example an empty code sequence does not change anything and needs no time for execution:

$$\mathcal{I} <> \doteq \textbf{wait } 0 \; .$$

This indicates one way of implementing **skip**. A somewhat more elaborate property shows how to implement an assignment statement:

$$\mathcal{I} < \textbf{eval}(e), \textbf{stl}(x) > \; \doteq \; [x := e] \in T(\textbf{eval}(e)) + T(\textbf{stl}(x)) \; . \qquad (1)$$

Evaluating an expression e first and storing the result to x afterwards, behaves like the assignment $x := e$. It terminates in a time in $\mathcal{T}(\mathbf{eval}(e)) + \mathcal{T}(stl(x))$. Note that the additional assignment of the value of e to the register $\mathbf{A}$ is not observable since $\mathbf{A}$ is a local variable of $\mathcal{I}$.

7 Correctness Predicates

This section describes the correctness predicates for code to be generated for the different syntactic categories of TimedPL. We start with the correctness predicate for sequential processes.

According to the translation theorem about parallel components sketched in the next section only for entire parallel components it must be checked whether the drift of the machine clock is tolerable. Sequential processes can be implemented with the idealized assumption that the clock is accurate. Therefore the machine language interpreter $\mathcal{I}$ with idealized instruction timing can be used in the correctness predicate rather than the drifting one $\mathcal{M}$. Thus an obvious candidate for a correctness predicate for implementation of a sequential process sp by a machine program m is the predicate defined by the formula

$$sp \sqsubseteq \mathcal{I} m .$$

Although this is a nice predicate for passing implementation correctness from sequential processes to parallel components, it is not well-suited as a predicate for inheriting it from sub-processes since a number of phenomena must be handled.

(i) It must be decided whether time bounds are satisfied by the machine code. Since we are heading for a compositional code generator specification the correctness predicate must give information about the execution time of the code or – what turns out to be more convenient – about bounds that can be guaranteed for the source process.

(ii) The time needed for evaluation of Boolean guards and jumping to appropriate parts of code when evaluating conditionals or loops must be transferred to sub-processes or sequential predecessor or successors due to the assumption that evaluation of control structures does not take extra time. Therefore the correctness predicate must also give information about spare time of the code.

(iii) Execution of code cannot be arbitrarily moved in time if it contains communication instructions, since the communications are visible to the environment. There is a rather complex dependency of inner bounds and shift of spare time. Consider for example the processes

$$\pi_1 = [\mathbf{skip} ; c!1 ; \mathbf{skip}] \in [0,3] \text{ and}$$
$$\pi_2 = [\mathbf{skip}] \in [0,1] ; [c!1] \in \{0\} ; [\mathbf{skip}] \in [0,2] .$$

Both of them can be implemented by $\pi' = \mathbf{wait}\ 1 ; [c!1] \in \{0\} ; \mathbf{wait}\ 1$. Execution time of π' is 2 and spare time in both cases is 1. But in case of π_2 the spare time may only be used for initial (internal) actions of the sequential successor and must not be used for executing final (internal) actions of the sequential predecessor. On the other hand when implementing π_1 by π' the spare time can be transferred to either the predecessor or the successor or even split between them.

(iv) In contrast, internal computation can be arbitrarily moved in time. If e.g. $\pi_3 = [x := 7] \in [0, 3]$ is implemented by $\pi_3' = [x := 7] \in \{2\}$, then an arbitrary amount of spare time t is available to the sequential predecessor if $t - 1$ time units are transferred to the sequential successor and vice versa.

(v) Sometimes a bound requested for the source process is more narrow than the bound immediately guaranteed for the target code, for example if $\pi_4 = [c!\,1] \in \{0\}$ is implemented by $\pi_4' = [c!\,1] \in [0, 1]$. Then the uncertainty about the termination time of the target program must be transferred to the sequential successor.

To handle these phenomena we use a triple of time sets as additional parameters of the correctness predicate. This triple describes one possible use of the code in a sequential environment. It consists of

- a lower bounded non-empty set $u \subseteq \mathbf{R}$, describing a starting time shift and a starting uncertainty accepted by the code,
- a lower bounded non-empty set $u' \subseteq \mathbf{R}$ describing a resulting termination time shift and termination time uncertainty that must be transferred to the sequential successor,
- a time bound $T \subseteq \mathbf{R}_{\geq 0} \cup \{\infty\}$ that can be guaranteed for the source process.

The predicate S defined below holds if a sequential process π is implemented by the machine program m accepting a start shift and uncertainty u that results in a termination shift and uncertainty u' such that the bound T can be guaranteed for π.

$$S \, \pi \, m \, u \, u' \, T \quad \text{iff for all } \tau, \tau' \in \mathbf{R}_{\geq 0} \text{ such that } \tau + u \geq 0 \text{ and } \tau' + u' \geq 0:$$

$$\text{wait } \tau \; ; \; [\pi] \in T \; ; \; \text{wait } \tau' + u' \sqsubseteq \text{wait } \tau + u \; ; \; \mathcal{I} \, m \; ; \; \text{wait } \tau' \; ,$$

where $\tau + u$ is the set $\{\tau + t \mid t \in u\}$ and $\tau + u \geq 0$ is written instead of $t \geq 0$ for all $t \in \tau + u$, and similarly for $\tau' + u'$.

Note that for a fixed source process π and implementing machine code m different values for u, u', T are possible. In particular often a narrower bound T can be guaranteed by transferring a wider termination time uncertainty to the sequential successor via u'. Consider, for example, $\pi = \text{skip} \; ; \; c!\,x \; ; \; \text{skip}$ and m such that $\mathcal{I} \, m = \text{wait } 1 \; ; \; [c!\,x] \in \{0\} \; ; \; \text{wait } [0, 1]$. We can choose $u = u' = \{0\}$ and $T = [1, 2]$. Alternatively we could choose $u = \{0\}$, $u' = [0, 1]$, $T = \{1\}$. Many other values for the triple u, u', T are also acceptable.

Translation of the remaining syntactic categories programs, parallel components, and sequential programs employs the assumption that each of the parallel components of a program has its own processor for execution and that the parallel interaction of processors is correctly described by the parallel operator of the process language. A further assumption is that the maximal latency $\delta_M(c)$ of a channel c on a network of processors can be determined. Then the correctness predicates for the translation of these categories are given by straightforward refinement formulae. A formal statement is omitted due to lack of space.

8 Translation Theorems

This section presents a few of the theorems about the code correctness predicates that form the specification of a code generator. The proofs for these theorems are based on the laws of TimedProc. Due to lack of space we do not give the complete collection of theorems here. Furthermore we will only give one of the proofs. The theorems that allow to infer implementation correctness of programs and parallel components from implementation correctness of their constituent parts are quoted here in a textual form only. For some of the constructs building sequential processes formal statements of the correctness theorems are given. A more complete collection of theorems together with their proofs can be found in [MO93].

A program pr is correctly implemented if each of its constituent parallel components is correctly implemented and if $l \geq \delta_M(c)$ for each channel c that is declared in pr with latency l. This follows immediately from monotonicity of parallel composition with respect to refinement.

A parallel component pc is correctly implemented if its constituent sequential process sp is correctly implemented (more precisely if $S\,sp\,m\,\{0\}\,\{0\}\,T$ for an arbitrarily chosen $T \subseteq Time_\infty$) and the maximum allowed drift specified in pc is greater than or equal to the drift d_M of the machine clock.

Theorem 1 (Translation of assignments). *An assignment statement $x := e$ can be implemented by evaluating the expression e first and then storing the result value to the location x with an appropriate timing condition:*

If $m = <\mathtt{eval}(e), \mathtt{stl}(x)>$ and $u + T(\mathtt{eval}(e)) + T(\mathtt{stl}(x)) \subseteq u' + T$
then $S(x := e)\,m\,u\,u'\,T$.

Proof.

$\qquad$ wait $\tau + u$; $\mathcal{I}\,m$; wait τ'
$\quad \sqsupseteq$ {Formula (1)}
$\qquad$ wait $\tau + u$; $[x := e] \in T(\mathtt{eval}(e)) + T(\mathtt{stl}(x))$; wait τ'
$\quad \sqsupseteq$ {Assignment-Bound law, Assignment-Wait law, Wait-Additivity}
$\qquad$ wait τ ; $[x := e] \in \{0\}$; wait $\tau' + u + T(\mathtt{eval}(e)) + T(\mathtt{stl}(x))$
$\quad \sqsupseteq$ {Wait-Refinement law, $u + T(\mathtt{eval}(e)) + T(\mathtt{stl}(x)) \subseteq u' + T$}
$\qquad$ wait τ ; $[x := e] \in \{0\}$; wait $\tau' + u' + T$
$\quad \sqsupseteq$ {Wait-Additivity, Assignment-Bound law}
$\qquad$ wait τ ; $[x := e] \in T$; wait $\tau' + u'$

$\hfill \square$

Theorem 2 (Translation of inputs). *An input statement $c\,?\,x$ can be implemented by first reading a value from channel c and then storing it to location x, with an appropriate timing condition:*

If $m = <\mathtt{in}(c), \mathtt{stl}(x)>$, $u = \{0\}$ and $T(\mathtt{in}(c)) + T(\mathtt{stl}(x)) \subseteq u' + T$
then $S(c\,?\,x)\,m\,u\,u'\,T$.

The difference in the timing conditions of the above two theorems mirrors that internal actions can be shifted arbitrarily in contrast to externally visible communications. For the implementing code of an assignment statement any starting shift set u is acceptable as long as it is compensated by the termination shift set u'. Possible starting and termination shift sets for the code of an input statement however are more precisely determined.

Theorem 3 (Translation of sequential composition). *Concatenating code for two processes π_1 and π_2 yields code for their sequential composition π_1 ; π_2. The sum of bounds of the components provide a guaranteeable bound. The termination uncertainty of the first component must be acceptable as a starting uncertainty for the second component:*

$$\text{If } S\,\pi_1\,m_1\,u_1\,u_1'\,T_1,\; S\,\pi_2\,m_2\,u_2\,u_2'\,T_2,\text{ and } u_1' \subseteq u_2$$
$$\text{then } S\,(\pi_1\,;\,\pi_2)\,(m_1\,{}^\frown m_2)\,u_1\,u_2'\,(T_1 + T_2)\ .$$

Theorem 4 (Translation of upper-bounds). *An upper-bound t can be asserted for a source program π if a subset of $[0, t]$ is guaranteeable:*

$$\text{If } S\,\pi\,m\,u\,u'\,T \text{ and } T \subseteq [0, t] \text{ then } S\,([\pi] \leq t)\,m\,u\,u'\,T\ .$$

These theorems together with theorems for the remaining constructs induce syntactically defined subrelations of the correctness predicates. The remaining task of compiler construction is to implement these relations. We intend to build a prototype implementation in a functional language like Miranda or ML [Tur86, Wik87]. Thus we must construct functions corresponding to the induced relations. The problem is that the timing parameters u, u' and T can be neither parameters nor parts of the result as in both cases there is a large freedom of choice for them. But the choice is not arbitrary. Only some of the possible values can succesfully be used. Our idea is to use a finite characterization of the set of all possible triples (u, u', T) or of a useful subset.

9   Discussion

This paper has given an overview on current work done in the ProCoS II project concerning the construction of a provably correct compiler for a hard real-time language. The construction has been split into a number of tasks:

(i) A precise definition of the source language has been given. In particular its semantics has been formalized. Work towards this goal is documented in [FMO93, FvK93, vK93]. Furthermore to allow algebraic reasoning about programs, refinement laws have been established. Section 2 to 4 gave an informal account on this work.

(ii) Similarly, a precise definition of the target language is required. Up-to-now a model machine language has been considered (see section 6 and [MO93]). Clearly, to obtain a compiler that translates to machine code of an actual processor its machine language must be formalized. This has been done in the predecessor project ProCoS I for the transputer [inm88b], but without considering timing [Pro93]. We plan to extend this work towards timing.

(iii) The code to be generated by the compiler has been specified (see sections 7 and 8 and [MO93]).

(iv) This code generator specification will be transformed to a fully constructive version.

(v) The compiler will be implemented in a functional language. This comprises construction of a frontend and the implementation of the code generator.

(vi) For a dependable compiler, also a reliable execution mechanism for the implementation language of the compiler is necessary. [BBF92] shows how this can be achieved by application of bootstrapping. A more detailed account can be found in [Pro93].

References

[BBF92] Bettina Buth, Karl-Heinz Buth, Martin Fränzle, Burghard v. Karger, Yassine Lakhneche, Hans Langmaack, and Markus Müller-Olm. Provably correct compiler development and implementation. In U. Kastens and P. Pfahler, editors, *Compiler Construction*, pages 141–155. Springer, 1992. LNCS 641.

[FMO93] Martin Fränzle and Markus Müller-Olm. *Drift and Granularity of Time in Real-Time System Implementation*. ProCoS II project document [Kiel MF 10/2], Christian-Albrechts-Universität Kiel, Germany, August 1993.

[FvK93] Martin Fränzle and Burghard von Karger. *Proposal for a Programming Language Core for ProCoS II*. ProCoS II project document [Kiel MF 11/3], Christian-Albrechts-Universität Kiel, Germany, August 1993.

[vK93] Burghard von Karger. *A simple wide-spectrum model for real time systems*. ProCoS II project document [OU BvK 9/6], Oxford University Programming Research Group, UK, August 1993.

[MO93] Markus Müller-Olm. *On Translation of TimedPL and Capture of Machine Instruction Timing*. ProCoS II project document [Kiel MMO 6/2], Christian-Albrechts-Universität Kiel, Germany, August 1993.

[Hoa85] C.A.R. Hoare. *Communicating Sequential Processes*. Prentice Hall International, 1985.

[Hoa91] C.A.R. Hoare. Refinement algebra proves correctness of compiling specifications. In C.C. Morgan and J.C.P. Woodcock, editors, *3rd Refinement Workshop*, Workshops in Computing, pages 33–48. Springer-Verlag, 1991.

[inm88a] INMOS ltd. *occam 2 Reference Manual*. Prentice Hall International, 1988.

[inm88b] INMOS ltd. *Transputer Instruction Set – A Compiler Writer's Guide*. Prentice Hall International, 1988.

[Pro93] Dines Bjørner, C.A.R. Hoare, Hans Langmaack (Eds.). *Provably correct systems*. ProCoS I final deliverable, 1993. Available from the Department of Computer Science, Technical University of Denmark, Building 3440, DK-2800 Lyngby.

[Tur86] David Turner. An overview of miranda. *SIGPLAN Notices*, 1986.

[Wik87] Åke Wikström. *Functional Programming Using Standard ML*. Series in Computer Science. Prentice-Hall, 1987.

Supporting Array Dependence Testing for an Optimizing/Parallelizing C Compiler

Justiani and Laurie J. Hendren

McGill University, Montréal, Québec, Canada

Abstract. The effectiveness of parallelizing and optimizing compilers depends on the ability to do accurate dependence analysis. In the case of programs that use arrays, array dependence analysis methods are critical, and powerful methods for dependence testing have been widely established. In order to collect the input required to actually apply the dependence tester, one must first apply the following *support phases*: (1) locate all admissible loop nests, (2) collect the normalized index expressions for each array reference, and (3) determine which pairs of array references must be tested. When implementing a dependence testing framework in C, each of these support phases must deal with complexities such as the presence of pointers and complicated control flow due to complex loop structures. Furthermore, each phase must be performed as accurately as possible so as to maximize the number of admissible loop nests and minimize the number of dependence pairs requiring testing.

This paper describes the design and implementation of the support phases as developed in the dependence testing framework for the McCAT (McGill Compiler Architecture Testbed) optimizing/parallelizing C compiler. By taking advantage of the simplified and structured intermediate representation, and the advanced points-to (alias) and reaching definition analyses available in the McCAT compiler, we provide a unified framework for implementing all of the support analyses required for array dependence testing. As part of this framework we demonstrate scalar backward analysis, generalized induction variable detection, canonical subscript analysis, symbolic manipulation, and demand-driven constant propagation in the presence of complex C features.

1 Introduction and Motivation

Accurate and efficient data dependency analysis is an important cornerstone of any parallelizing compiler. For programs using arrays and nested loops, various powerful dependence analysis methods have been widely established [3, 5, 6, 11, 12, 13, 17]. The basic dependence problem is to decide whether two subscripted references to the same array in a loopnest access the same memory location under certain constraints imposed by the boundaries of the loop iteration space. In general, the dependence problem reduces to solving a system of linear diophantine equations subject to a set of linear inequality constraints. This is a two-step process. The first phase is to set up a system of dependence equations and inequalities. In the second phase, a decision algorithm determines if the system has integer solution [17]. The goal of the dependence testing is to disprove dependence of as many array subscripted pairs as possible and as early as possible.

This mathematically well-defined problem of dependence testing requires, as input, a set of equations and equalities derived from the application program under analysis. These equations and equalities must be collected in as precise a manner as possible, even for complicated programs that use complex loops and/or pointer data structures. Thus, one requires a complete framework of *support analyses* that can be used to collect accurate inputs for dependence testers. Without such a framework, even the most powerful dependence testers are useless.

Unlike typical scientific programs written in Fortran, which often have regular loop nests and simple forms of aliasing (due to call-by-reference), the more general features found in C tend to promote more complex loops and the use of data structure abstractions that often involve pointers. Making overly conservative assumptions about loops and/or aliasing due to pointers can significantly reduce the quality of the dependence testing result. Thus, the development of *support analyses* in the context of C parallelizing compilers must effectively handle these additional complexities.

1.1 Motivating Examples

All dependence testing methods are usually built upon the following assumptions: (1) admissible loopnests have a nice, regular behaviour expressed by the behaviour of loop variables, (2) all the array subscripts and loop limits have been represented in canonical forms or affine functions of loop indices, (3) subscript-pairs are collected from pairs of references to the same array name.

However, real C programs often do not fit nicely into these patterns, and the support analyses must deal with several complications. From the examples in Figure 1, we can demonstrate that the following points need to be addressed before any dependence tests can be applied:

Example 1: This program illustrates the problem of detecting whether or not the loop is admissible. In general, admissible loops should not update the loop variable. The presence of pointer assignment in statement S1 means that an *admissible loopnest detector* should check that the assignment to *s does not update the loop variable i. Without precise alias or points-to analysis, one must conservatively assume that *s might refer to i. In our compiler context, we can use the results of our *points-to* (alias) analysis to decide whether or not s can point-to i [1, 2].

Example 2: This program illustrates the case where the programmer has not provided the array subscripts in terms of the loop variables. Thus, we need automatic methods to convert the array subscripts ind1 and ind2 into a canonical form relative to the loop variables. This involves scalar backward analysis, induction variable analysis, demand-driven constant propagation, canonical subscript analysis, and possible involvement of symbolic manipulation of the canonical subscript expressions. Furthermore, these methods must all be able to handle expressions using pointer variables.

Example 3: This program illustrates the problem of determining if two array names refer to the same array. In order to be safe, the dependence testers must be used in all cases where the array names *may* refer to the same array. In this program we need to detect whether or not the array names v and w refer to the same array.

1.2 Our Support Analysis Framework

In this paper we present a framework for *support analyses* to support array dependence testing that has been designed and implemented for the McCAT optimizing/parallelizing C compiler. [1] This framework has been designed to handle the full

---

[1] The McGill Compiler/Architecture Testbed is being developed in order to study the interaction between compiler techniques and advanced architectural features [8].

Example 1 :
main()
{ int w[100];
    int i,p;
    int *s;
    s = &i;
    ...
    for (i=1;i<=99;++i)
    {
S1 :   *s= 2 * p;
          w[i] = w[i+1];
    }
}
	Example 2 :
	main()
	{ int w[10];
	    int i,p,q,a,ind1,ind2;
	    int *s,*r;
	    s = &i;
	    r = &q;
	    q = 2;
	    for(i=1; i<=9; i++)
	    { p = q + 3;
	       *r = p - 4;
	       a = p - i;
	       ind1=a-2*((*s)+3*i);
	       ind2=p+2*i;
	       w[ind1]=w[ind2];
	    }
	}
		Example 3 :
		main()
		{ int v[10];
		    int i,j;
		    int *w;
		    w=v;
		    ...
		    for(i=1;i<10;++i)
		    {
		S1 : v[i-2] = w[i+1];
		    }
		}

Fig. 1. Motivating Example C Programs

complexities of the C language that affect array dependence analysis, while at the same time supporting complete information and compact representation for applying various dependence testing methods.

The rest of this paper is organized as follows. First we discuss the overall structure and foundations of our approach in section 2. Section 3 presents the introduction of our *support analysis* framework, while sections 4, 5, 6 and 7 provides the details of the framework and illustrate them with some simple examples. Finally, we cover related work in section 8 and draw conclusions in section 9.

2 Foundations

Although powerful features of C language make the *support analyses* nontrivial, the McCAT compiler provides an environment which provides the necessary founda-tions: (1) SIMPLE, a *compositional* structured intermediate representation that was designed to handle various complications in C in a standard, simple and structured manner, (2) precise interprocedural alias information as computed by *points-to* anal-ysis, and (3) reaching definition analysis that includes reaching definitions for pointer variables.

Figure 2 illustrates these important parts of the McCAT environment. Note that the first phase takes a collection of C program files, and produces a simpli-fied and compositional structured representation called SIMPLE. Then, points-to analysis and reaching-definition analysis take as input the simplified representation and provides as output SIMPLE decorated with points-to information and reaching-definition information. The important points relevant for our topic are briefly de-scribed in Sections 2.1 and 2.2. A complete presentation of the points-to analysis and reaching-definition analysis is discussed elsewhere [1, 2, 9, 14]. Given the deco-rated SIMPLE representation, the next step is the support analysis for dependence testing, which is the main topic of this paper. This support analysis takes advan-tage of *the simplification phase, the reaching-definition information* and *the points-to information.*

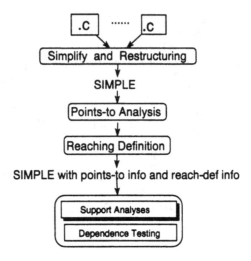

Fig. 2. Overview of the McCAT Environment

2.1 SIMPLE Intermediate Representation

The first foundation of our approach is that McCAT provides a compositional structured intermediate representation called SIMPLE that can represent all the complexities of C in a simple, standard and structured fashion. The *simplify* phase includes: breaking down complex statements into a series of basic statements, simplifying complex expressions and control structures into simple ones, simplifying function arguments to constants or variables, and moving initializations in the declarations into statements in the body. Even though simplified, SIMPLE retains the array and structure references for various analyses that need high-level variable references and type information. Therefore, this representation has been designed to be most suitable for compositional (structured) analysis framework [8].

In Figure 3, we present a simplification of an example program that we use throughout this paper. On the left is the original program, and on the right is the SIMPLE version.

2.2 Points-to and Reaching Definition Analysis

The compositional nature of SIMPLE allows regular and explicit control flow in the program representation that is suitable for compositional analyses. One of the most important analyses is *points-to* analysis which is an interprocedural analysis that computes all possible *points-to* relationships for each program point. We say that p *definitely points-to* x if p definitely contains the address of x. Similarly, we say that p *possibly points-to* x if p possibly contains the address of x. Unlike traditional alias analysis which computes alias pairs of the form (p,*x) and (*p,**y), our points-to analysis gives every important stack location a name, and encodes only the relationships between these names. In most cases the stack location names are just the variable names. The only special case is that we generate special names for stack locations corresponding to function parameters with pointer types. For example, a parameter a with type **int would have three stack locations a, a(1), and a(2) where the names a(1) and a(2) are abstract names corresponding to locations accessible via *a and **a. This naming scheme and associated points-

```
                              main()
                              { int w[11],i,k,p,q,a;
main()                          int *r,*y;
{ int  w[11];                   int temp_3,temp_2,temp_1,temp_0,temp_4;
  int i,k,p,q,a;                r = &q;
  int *r,*y;                    if (1) y = &p; else y = &i;
  r = &q;                       p = 4;
  if(1) y = &p;                 for (i=1;i<=10;i=i+1)
  else y = &i;                  { q = p + 2;
  p = 4;                          k = q + 2;
  for (i = 1; i <= 10; ++i)       temp_2 = *r;
  { q = p + 2;                    temp_3 = *y;
    k = q + 2;                    temp_1 = temp_2+temp_3;
    a = w[p-(*r+*y)];             temp_0 = p - temp_1;
    p = *r - 5;                   a = w[temp_0];
    w[k] = p;                     temp_4 = *r;
  }                               p = temp_4 - 5;
}                                 w[k] = p;
                                }
                              }
```

Fig. 3. Example of SIMPLE

to abstraction provides a compact representation that can be used directly in our support analyses.

Based on the points-to analysis, the reaching-definition analysis provides a list of all definitions for uses at each program point. For the case of a use of the form x, the reaching definitions for x include all direct definitions of the form x = a op b as well as any definite or possible indirect definitions of the form *p = a op b where p points-to x. In the case of a use of the form *p, we include all reaching definitions (both direct and indirect) for all variables pointed to by p.

3 Overview of the Support Analysis Framework

The goal of the support analysis is to provide a suitable environment for the application of dependence testing methods. Such a support analysis framework consists of three phases as given below and each of these phases are described more fully in subsequent sections.

Admissible loopnest detection: The first phase is a mechanism to filter only certain types of loopnests that are amenable for analysis with dependence testers. This filter should find as many admissible loopnests as possible.

Subscript Normalization: Once the admissible loopnests have been detected, each array subscript must be expressed in a normalized form (most often in terms of the enclosing loop variables and loop bounds). In general this requires a variety of subscript normalizations such as: scalar backward analysis, generalized induction variable detection, canonical analysis, demand-driven constant propagation, and symbolic manipulation.

Array-pair collection: Given that each array subscript is expressed in a canonical form, the next phase must determine which array reference pairs must be tested. In general, two array references a[exp1] and b[exp2] must be tested if a might refer to the same array as b.

4 Admissible Loopnest Detection

Loopnest detection selects certain loopnests that are amenable to be analyzed. The idea behind this selection is to guarantee that the loopnest behaviour can be expressed by the regular behaviour of the loop indices. In dealing with loops, one must address the following potential problems with loopnests that make them inadmissible. Note that some of the problems are made more complex by the general form of loops in C, and the presence of pointers.

Problem 1: Each loop should be defined with the initialization, increment and test on exactly one loop variable. If a pointer variable of the form *p is used as the loop variable, then p should point-to exactly one variable.

Problem 2: Many dependence testers assume that the increment to the loop variable is 1. If the loop provided by the programmer has a different increment, then loop normalization must be applied [3, 5, 13, 19].

Problem 3: The body of the loop should be free from irregular control flow such as **break** and **continue**. The loop body should not call functions that update the loop variables.

Problem 4: The loopnest body should not modify the loop variables (either directly, or indirectly through a pointer).

Problem 5: The loopnest body should not modify the value of the increment or loop bound. There may exist some programs where there is an assignment to the increment or loop bound, but this assignment does not change the value.

Problems 1, 2 and 3 are very obvious. We choose to illustrate problems 4 and 5 using the two examples in Figure 4. In example 1, at program point S1, the points-to information says that s *definitely points-to* i. Since $*s$, which is exactly i, is modified in S1, we can not express any array subscripts in term of linear function of loop variable i anymore, because i is not regularly incremented by 1. Thus, the loopnest in example 1 is not admissible. Suppose if in S1 we have information saying that s *definitely points-to* some variable other than i, then the loopnest is admissible. Therefore, in an environment with pointers, without any points-to information, in order to be *safe*, the analysis may result in the worst assumption. In example 2, at program point S1, loop-bound variable $tem0$ is being modified in the loopnest scope. Yet, the redefinition does not really change the value of $tem0$ as recognized in the loop header since the modifiers are both defined outside the loopnest scope. Thus, this loopnest can be categorized as admissible.

```
Example 1 : Bad-loop            Example 2:
main()                          m = 5; n = 9;
{ int w[100],i,p,*s;            for(i=0;i<m;i=i+1)
  s = &i;                       {    tem1 = n + m;
  for (i = 1; i <= 99; ++i)          tem0 = tem1 + n;
  {                                  for(j=0;j<tem0;j=j+1)
S1 :      *s= 2 * p;                 { c[i][j]=c[i][j];
          w[i] = w[i+1];                 tem1 = n + m;
  }                             S1: tem0 = tem1 + n;
}                                    }
                                }
```

Fig. 4. Example Loopnests

5 Subscript Normalization

Having filtered all admissible loopnests in the program, the next step is subscript normalization for every array reference appearing in the admissible loopnests. When designing and implementing the subscript analysis for C, the following three major problems may arise:

Problem 1: The first problem is that programmers often reduce the number of redundant computations using a scalar variable as temporary variable to store the value of a common subexpression [19]. Then this temporary scalar variable is used as the array subscripts such that the array indices are not in the form of linear function of loop variables. In the case of our SIMPLE intermediate representation, each complex array reference is broken down into a series of three address statements. This causes a similar problem.

Problem 2: The second problem is that there may exist some *induction variables* whose values are systematically incremented or decremented by a certain value in a loop. The use of such induction variables may *hide* the linearity and admissibility conditions of array subscripts. However, often the induction variables may be rewritten relative to the loop variables, thus making more subscripts admissible.

Problem 3: The final major problem is that it is unlikely that all array subscript expressions are written in the standard canonical form $a_0 + a_1 * i_1 + \cdots + a_n * i_n$, where $a_0, a_1, \cdots, a_n$ are integer coefficients and $i_1, i_2, \cdots, i_n$ are loop variables, such that the dependence testing methods can not be applied directly. Thus, each index expression must be rewritten to conform to the standard canonical form.

The goal of the subscript normalization is essentially to capture the canonical forms of array subscripts in order to apply dependence testing. This normalization is achieved through a three-step process: (1) build a *general expression tree* which captures all possible index expressions and induction variables (uses points-to and reaching definition analysis), (2) given the general expression tree, build a list of possible *subscript expression trees*, and (3) express each subscript expression in canonical form.

5.1 Phase 1 : Building a General Expression Tree

In our SIMPLE intermediate form, each complex array subscript expression has been simplified to either a constant or a variable name. In order to collect all possible expressions corresponding to a variable name index, we perform a backward demand-driven analysis at the loopnest level using reaching definition and points-to information to build a general expression tree.

To illustrate our approach, consider the previous example in Figure 5(a). Consider that we want to build a general expression tree for index tem0 of array w in statement S1 as shown in Figure 5(b). The basic idea is that we trace back through all reaching definitions of tem0 building a general expression tree. In this case the index tem0 has definition tem0 = p-tem1 that reaches S1, so we build the expression p-tem1 under the index tem0. Similarly, we continue this process for p and tem1 recursively. When an indirect reference is reached, we use the points-to information to expand the indirection with all variables that the indirect reference points-to. For example, *r is expanded to q and *y is expanded to p and i. Moreover, there is a possibility that *an induction pattern* is detected during the backward process. This is when the same variables with the same reaching-definitions are repeated in the backward process, such as variable p inside the dashed box that shows induction pattern in the example in Figure 5(b). If this is the case, after the induction pattern tree is completely built, an *induction processing function* is called to calculate the induction formula for all the induction variables existing in the pattern. From our example, the induction calculation is done for variables p, tem4 and q. If later there is a *use* of an induction variable that already has a calculated formula, such as variables p and q under *r and *y in Figure 5(b), the backward analysis stops for that particular path, and keeps the pointer to the calculated formula for later use.

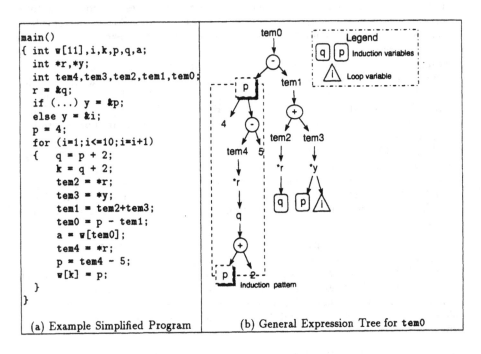

```
main()
{ int w[11],i,k,p,q,a;
  int *r,*y;
  int tem4,tem3,tem2,tem1,tem0;
  r = &q;
  if (...) y = &p;
  else y = &i;
  p = 4;
  for (i=1;i<=10;i=i+1)
  {   q = p + 2;
      k = q + 2;
      tem2 = *r;
      tem3 = *y;
      tem1 = tem2+tem3;
      tem0 = p - tem1;
      a = w[tem0];
      tem4 = *r;
      p = tem4 - 5;
      w[k] = p;
  }
}
```

(a) Example Simplified Program   (b) General Expression Tree for tem0

Fig. 5. Building General Expression Tree

To summarize, a general expression tree is represented with the original variable at the root, and leaves of the following form: (a) a constant, (b) a loop variable, (c) an induction variable, or (d) a loop invariant variable (i.e. a variable with a definition outside of the loopnest). Interior nodes in the expression tree are of the following form: (a) a variable (has children representing all binary or unary expressions that could define the variable), or (b) an indirect reference (has children representing all variables pointed to by the reference).

In some respects, this general expression tree form is similar to SSA-form [4, 18] in the sense that it captures an induction pattern. The major difference is that our technique builds a structure specific for particular indices. Furthermore, our structure captures all possible expressions due to both control flow (multiple possible reaching expressions) and indirect pointer references (multiple possible pointed-to variables).

5.2 Phase 2 : Building a List of Expression Trees

The next step of subscript normalization is the process of building a list of *alternative expression trees* for an array index from the general expression tree built in the previous phase.

We use the previous example to illustrate this phase. If we look at the root and the leaves of the general expression tree in figure 5, we can derive that there are two possible canonical forms for array index $tem0$ that comes from expression $tem0 = p - (q + p)$ or the expression $tem0 = p - (q + i)$. Furthermore, p and q are induction variables where p is equivalent to $-3 * i + 7$, and q is equivalent to $-3 * i + 9$. Therefore, the array index $tem0$ has two possible canonical values, which are $3 * i - 9$ and $-1 * i - 2$. The list of subscript expression trees for $tem0$ built in this phase is shown in Figure 6 (left). The list of expression trees is built by traversing the general expression tree bottom up, building a list of possible expression trees for each sub-tree. In addition, all induction variables are expanded to their appropriate expressions.

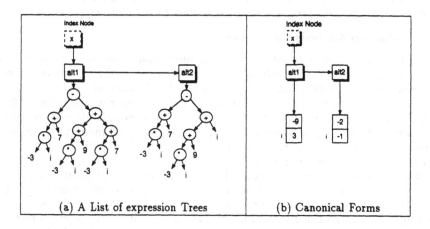

| (a) A List of expression Trees | (b) Canonical Forms |

Fig. 6. Canonical Analysis

5.3 Phase 3 : Canonical Analysis

After creating the list of expression trees of indices, the next step is canonical analysis. This phase is a recursive traversal on the subscript expression tree of each index which applies rewriting rules to get the canonical form $a_0 + a_1 * i_1 + \cdots + a_n * i_n$ where $i_1, i_2, \cdots, i_n$ are loop indices, and $a_0, a_1, \cdots, a_n$ can be either integer coefficients or unresolved symbolic coefficients. For example, expression trees for index $tem0$ in Figure 6(a) will generate arrays of integer coefficients (canonical form) as shown in Figure 6(b). The following rules are incorporated to get the canonical form :

Rule 1 Constant Distribution: This is the case when we have an expression of the form $c*(a_0 + a_1 * i_1 + \cdots + a_n * i_n)$ where $a_0, a_1, \cdots, a_n$ are integer coefficients and c is integer constant, then we transform it into $(c*a_0) + (c*a_1) * i_1 + \cdots + (c*a_n) * i_n$.

Rule 2 Negative Propagation: This is the case when there are some *additive terms* scoped by a negative sign, we distribute the negative sign down to the coefficient level. For example expression $a_0 - (a_1 * i_1 + a_2 * i_2) + \cdots + a_n * i_n$ will be transformed into $a_0 + (-a_1) * i_1 + (-a_2) * i_2 + \cdots + a_n * i_n$.

Rule 3 Coefficient Grouping: This is the case when there is more than one coefficient of the same index expressed in some *additive terms*, such as $a_0 + a_1 * i_1 + \cdots + a_n * i_n + p * i_1 - q * i_n$. We transform it into $a_0 + (a_1 + p) * i_1 + \cdots + (a_n - q) * i_n$.

Rule 4 Symbolic Coefficient Resuming: This is the case where some coefficients are not integer. The above three rules are applied, but the remaining symbolic coefficients are expressed in *symbolic expression subtrees*.

When the above rules do not resolve the canonical forms totally (all integer coefficients are formed) or partially (some symbolic coefficients left), we then apply partial symbolic elimination/execution on the expression trees, which can result in canonical forms.

6 Collecting Array-Pairs

The final phase of the support analysis is to determine which array reference pairs must be tested. When dealing with C this can be relatively complicated since the arrays are often referenced via pointers. Thus, we must use the points-to information to determine when two array references may refer to the same actual array.

6.1 Points-to Analysis for Arrays

When calculating points-to information, the most straight-forward approach is to approximate an entire array with one stack location. Thus, the information that a definitely points to b means that a points to the first location of array b.

Example 1 in Figure 7 gives an example of points-to information collected for a simple program. After the statement c = a we have the information the c definitely points-to a. This means that direct references to array a and indirect references to array c might interfere, and they must be tested.[2] After the conditional we have the information that d possibly points-to a or d possibly points-to b.

We may also get points-to relationships via parameters that point to arrays. In Example 2, Figure 7, we see that in the function g, we have the information that parameter x definitely points-to an invisible location x(1), while y definitely points-to a *different* invisible location y(1).[3] This means that indirect references to array x and array y are guaranteed to be distinct, and there is no need to do dependence tests on such pairs. However, in function f we have the situation where x definitely points-to x(1) and y definitely points-to x(1) as well. Thus, the indirect references to x and y in function f may interfere, and the dependence tester must be applied to such pairs.

If we also consider the possibility of pointer arithmetic and the ability to capture the address of interior elements of arrays, a better approach for points-to analysis is to abstract the entire array as two stack locations: one stack location stands for the location of the first element of the array, and the other stack location stands for the rest of the array. Thus, for each array a, we have information about a_head and a_tail. In Example 3, Figure 7, after the statement b = a we have the information that b definitely points-to a_head, while after the statement c = &a[exp] we have

---

[2] Note that in C one must look at the *type* of the array to determine if it is a direct reference or an indirect reference. In Example 1 there will be *direct* references to a and b, and *indirect* references to c and d.

[3] These invisible location names are generated by the points-to analysis, and are used as anonymous names for variables that are not visible in the scope of the procedure under analysis.

the information that c possibly points-to a_head or c possibly points-to a_tail (assuming that exp could be any valid index into a, including 0.). The final statement, d = b++ illustrates that after incrementing b, d definitely points-to a_tail.

Example 1	Example 2	Example 3
| ```
main()
{ int a[100], b[100], *c, *d;
  c = a;  /* c = &a[0] */
  /* (c -> a) */
  ...
  if (exp)
    d = a;
  else
    d = b;
  /* (d -> a)?  (d -> b)? */
  ...
}
``` | ```
main()
{ int a[100], b[100];
  g(a,b);
  f(a,a);
}
g(int *x, int *y)
{ /* (x -> x(1))
     (y -> y(1)) */
  ...
  x[i] = y[i+1];
  ...
}
f(int *x, int *y)
{ /* (x -> x(1))
     (y -> x(1)) */
  ...
  x[i] = y[i+1];
  ...
}
``` | ```
main()
{ int a[100], *b, *c, *d;
  b = a; /* &a[0] */
  /* (b -> a_head) */
  ...
  c = &a[exp];
  /* (c -> a_head)?
     (c -> a_tail)? */
  ...
  d = b++;
  /* (d -> a_tail) */
}
``` |

Fig. 7. Examples of Points-to analysis for arrays

6.2 Using Points-to Analysis

Given the points-to information as outlined in the previous section, the problem of collecting array pairs for dependence testing is vastly simplified. If one array reference is a write, and the other array reference is a read or write, then dependence testing must be performed if it is possible that the array references refer to the same actual array. Given points-to analysis, there are three ways in which two array references refer to the same array:

1. if both are *direct* references, and they refer to the same array name; *or*
2. if one is a *direct* reference to some array a, and the other is an *indirect* reference to some array b, and b points-to a; *or*
3. if both are *indirect* references via some names a and b, and there exists a third abstract stack name c such that a points-to c and b points-to c.

Thus, to collect all array pairs to be tested, one just considers all read/write and write/write pairs, and determines if one of these three cases applies. If so, the pair must be tested.

7 Advanced Features

7.1 Symbolic Manipulation

The symbolic manipulation and execution of expressions is extremely useful for solving symbolic dependence analysis. As a result of our support analysis, the canonical forms for index expressions are expressed as an array of either integer coefficients or symbolic expression subtrees. This representation allows us to perform several symbolic manipulations in a straightforward manner.
```

First, when a pair of subscript expressions contain the same symbolic term, we have to make sure that the same definitions reach the pair of variables involved in both expressions. This is to guarantee that there is no update to the variables involved in the symbolic comparison along the control flow paths between the two references. If the above condition is satisfied, then we can apply symbolic inequality and symbolic elimination when forming the dependence equation for the dependence testers.

To illustrate this, consider the examples in Figure 8. In example 1, after applying the subscript normalization phase, we get the canonical form $(1)i + (2)j + (x - y)$ as the index of array w in statement S1 and $(1)i + (1)j + (2 + x - y)$ as the canonical index of statement S2. Since there are no updates to variables x and y along the control flow paths between statements S1 and S2, *symbolic elimination* can be applied in order to get the subscript dependence equation $i_1 + 2j_1 - i_2 - j_2 - 2 = 0$. Similarly, in example 2, the symbolic elimination on the indirect addressing can be applied, since there are no updates of variable x or array b along the control flow path between S1 and S2.

```
Example 1 :                         Example 2 :
main()                              main()
{ int  w[100];                      { int  w[100];
  int i,j,x,y;                        int b[10];
  x = ...;                            int i,j,k,x;
  y = ...;                            x = ...;
  ...                                 ...
  for (i=1;i<=9;++i)                  for (i=1;i<=9;++i)
    for (j=1;j<=9;++j)                  for (j=1;j<=9;++j)
    {                                   {
S1 : w[i+2j+x-y] = ...;             S1 : w[i+2j+x-b[k]]= ...;
S2 :        ... = w[i+j+2+x-y];     S2 :        ... =w[i+j+2+x-b[k]-2]
    }                                   }
}                                   }
```

Fig. 8. Symbolic Elimination

7.2 Extended Backward Analysis

Currently, the backward analysis for subscript normalization is done in the scope of loopnests, since it is used to reveal the subscript expressions in terms of loop variables. The method used in this backward analysis is a solid foundation for more general uses of backward demand-driven analysis. For example, we can extend the backward analysis to handle complete function bodies, or even to handle interprocedural reaching definitions. The extension of the backward analysis to the function level would be useful for *loop invariant* variables and it can improve the power of symbolic manipulation and constant propagation.

Figure 9 shows us some examples of how the extended backward analysis gives some advantages in symbolic manipulation and constant propagation. In example 1, if we apply backward analysis at the loopnest level, we get the canonical pair $(1)i + (2)j + (y - 6)$ and $(1)i + (1)j + (x + 2)$. Whereas, the extended backward analysis can capture the definition for y in terms of x so that the canonical pair will be $(1)i + (2)j + (x - 11)$ and $(1)i + (1)j + (x + 2)$. Applying symbolic elimination to this pair will result in $i_1 + 2j_1 - i_2 - j_2 - 13 = 0$ for the dependence equation. In example 2, the extended backward analysis captures the intraprocedural constant propagation. The backward analysis at the loopnest level produces the canonical pair $(1)i + (2)j + (y - 6)$ and $(1)i + (1)j + (x + 2)$. Whereas, the extended backward analysis can capture definitions for $y = x - 4$ and $x = 8$ such that the canonical pair will be $(1)i + (2)j + (-2)$ and $(1)i + (1)j + (10)$.

```
Example 1 :                        Example 2 :
main()                             main()
{ int w[100];                      { int w[100];
  int i,j,x,y;                       int i,j,x,y;
  x = ...;                           x = 8;
  y = x-5;                           y = x-4;
  ...                                ...
  for (i=1;i<=9;++i)                 for (i=1;i<=9;++i)
    for (j=1;j<=9;++j)                 for (j=1;j<=9;++j)
    {                                 {
s1 :    w[i+2j+y-6] = ...;          S1 :    w[i+2j+y-6] = ...;
S2 :            ... = w[i+j+2+x];   S2 :            ... = w[i+j+2+x];
    }                                 }
}                                  }
```

Fig. 9. Extended Backward Analysis

8 Related Work

The traditional treatment of support analyses usually consists of several phases such as scalar forward substitution, induction variable substitution, canonical transformation and constant propagation, where each phase is a transformation of program code segments [19]. Since subscript normalization is the inverse of *redundant expression elimination*, applying the sequences of subscript transformations will result in *some new code segments* which require *dead code elimination* and *redundant expression elimination* to be reapplied, which is inefficient.

Recently, an implementation based on SSA using use-def chains has been described [15]. Instead of using def-use chains for each definition, as in [10, 16], which supports forward-flow analysis due to consistency of direction between flow analysis and def-use chains, the SSA-based method offers a demand-driven data-flow analysis which typically requests information at a program point from its data-flow predecessors. In some respects, the SSA-based approach is similar to our approach - our reaching definition information is basically use-def chains which enable the demand-driven analysis. The key difference is that we base our analysis on tree-based compositional intermediate representation and structured analysis, while the SSA-based approach is built on graph-based analysis.

Detecting induction variables using the SSA form has also been discussed [4, 18]. The proposed technique is based on SSA graphs and a modified Tarjan's algorithm for recognizing SCRs (Strongly Connected Regions) of CFG. This technique is then expanded to recognize other types of IVs such as Wrap-Around Variables (WAV), Flip-Flop and Periodic variables (FPV), Non-Linear Induction Variables (NLIV) and Monotonic Variables (MV). In addition, the algorithm can also identify Nested Induction Variables (NIV) in the presence of determinable trip counts of the loop. Currently, our induction processing (based on the patterns collected during the backwards demand-driven analysis) can handle basic, multiply-defined, mutually-updated and nested induction variables properly, and can detect periodic and monotonic induction variables, but does not calculate the formulas. Non-linear and geometric induction variables are currently being incorporated without any serious problems.

A framework to solve the dependence problem in the presence of unknown symbolic expressions has also been introduced [6, 7]. This approach uses forward flow analysis in order to do symbolic constant propagation, partial symbolic execution and approximate semantic analysis in the program, before applying classical data dependence testers. The symbolic constant flow analysis is applied on multi-level linked list representing symbolic expressions. These symbolic manipulations are also available in our support analysis using a different approach. Instead of going forward, our approach is demand-driven backward analysis at the loopnest level, which is currently extended to backward analysis the top of the functions for the loop invariant variables. This extension exposes more opportunities for symbolic manipulation and will allow for demand-driven constant propagation in the presence of points-to information.

A major difference in our approach is that we fully incorporate points-to information in detecting loopnests, collecting array-pairs and replacing any occurrences of indirect reference and indirect component reference along the backward path in the demand-driven subscript analysis. This allows us to get more precise canonical expressions and thus more precise dependence results.

9 Conclusions and Further Work

This paper has discussed the design and implementation of the support analyses required for precise array dependence testing in our optimizing/parallelizing McCAT C compiler. We have presented this support analysis as three phases: (1) admissible loopnest detection, (2) the collection of normalized index expressions (subscript normalization), and (3) the determination of array-reference pairs that must be tested.

Our approach builds on the structured intermediate representation (SIMPLE), and the results of points-to and reaching-definition analysis. The SIMPLE representation provides a good environment for detecting admissible loop nests, while the points-to analysis and reaching-definition analysis enables our subscript normalization. The points-to analysis is also a key factor in detecting admissible loops and determining the array-pairs that must be tested. Without such analyses, overly conservative assumptions would have to be made, and spurious dependence tests would be required.

We have implemented this support analysis and connected it to a practical dependence testing framework based on a wide variety of dependence testers [5, 11, 12, 17]. We plan to continue this work by incorporating more advanced features in the support analysis, and by experimenting with the effect of precise points-to analysis on the accuracy of the dependence testing.

References

1. M. Emami, L. J. Hendren, and R Ghiya. Context-Sensitive Interprocedural Points-to Analysis in the Presence of Function Pointers. *Proceedings of the SIGPLAN'94 Conference on Programming Language Design and Implementation (to appear)*, June 20-24, 1994.
2. Maryam Emami. A Practical Interprocedural Alias Analysis for An Optimizing C Compiler. *Master's thesis, McGill University*, July 1993.

3. Paul Feautrier. Dataflow Analysis of Array and Scalar References. *In the series, Research Monographs in Laboratoire MASI, Universite Paris et Marie Curie, Paris,France*, September 1991.

4. Michael P. Gerlek. Detecting Induction Variables using SSA-form. *OGI-CSE Technical Report 93-014, Oregon Graduate Institute*, June 7, 1993.

5. Gina Goff, Ken Kennedy, and Chau-Wen Tseng. Practical Dependence Testing. *Proceedings of the SIGPLAN'91 Conference on Programming Language Design and Implementation*, pages 15–29, June 26-28, 1991.

6. M. Haghighat and C. Polychronopoulos. *Symbolic Dependence Analysis for High-Performance Parallelizing Compilers*. Pitman, London and MIT Press, Cambridge, MA, 1991.

7. M. Haghighat and C. Polychronopoulos. Symbolic Analysis: A Basis for Parallelization, Optimization and Scheduling of Programs. *Sixth Annual Workshop on Languages and Compilers for Parallel Computing, Portland, Oregon*, pages dd1–dd23, August 12-14, 1993.

8. L. J. Hendren, C. Donawa, M. Emami, G. Gao, Justiani., and B Sridharan. Designing the McCAT Compiler based on a Family of Structured Intermediate Representations. *Fifth Workshop on Languages and Compilers for Parallel Computing. Also to appear in LNCS*, August 1992.

9. L.J. Hendren, M. Emami, C. Verbrugge, and R. Ghiya. A Practical Context-sensitive Interprocedural Analysis Framework for C Compilers. *ACAPS Technical Memo 72, School of Computer Science, McGill University*, July 1993.

10. Richard Johnson and Keshav Pingali. Dependence-based Program Analysis. *Proceedings of the SIGPLAN'93 Conference on Programming Language Design and Implementation*, pages 78–89, June 23-25, 1993.

11. Xiangyun Kong, David Klappholz, and Kleanthis Psarris. The I Test : An Improved Dependence Test for Automatic Parallelization and Vectorization. *IEEE Transactions on Parallel and Distributed systems*, 2(3):342–349, July 1991.

12. Vadim Maslov. Delinearization : An Efficient Way to Break Multiloop Dependence Equations. *Proceedings of the SIGPLAN'92 Conference on Programming Language Design and Implementation*, pages 152–161, June 17-19, 1992.

13. Dror E. Maydan, J.L.Hennessy, and Monica S. Lam. Efficient and Exact Data Dependence Analysis. *Proceedings of the SIGPLAN'91 Conference on Programming Language Design and Implementation*, pages 1–14, June 26-28, 1991.

14. Bhama Sridharan. An Analysis Framework for the McCat Compiler. *Master's thesis, McGill University*, December 1992.

15. Eric Stoltz, Michael P. Gerlek, and Michael Wolfe. Extended SSA with Factored Use-Def Chains to support Optimization and Parallelization. *OGI-CSE Technical Report 93-013, Oregon Graduate Institute*, June 7, 1993.

16. Mark N. Wegman and F. Kenneth Zadeck. Constant Propagation with Conditional Branches. *ACM Transactions on Programming Languages and Systems*, 13(2):181–210, April 1991.

17. Michael Wolfe. *Optimizing Supercompilers for Supercomputers*. The MIT Press, Cambrigde, Massachusetts, 1989.

18. Michael Wolfe. Beyond Induction Variables. *Proceedings of the SIGPLAN'92 Conference on Programming Language Design and Implementation*, pages 162–174, June 17-19, 1992.

19. Hanz Zima and Barbara Chapman. *Supercompilers for Parallel and Vector Computers*. ACM Press, Addison-Wesley Pub. Co., New York, 1990.

Processing Array Statements and Procedure Interfaces in the PREPARE High Performance Fortran Compiler *

Siegfried Benkner, Peter Brezany and Hans Zima

Institute for Software Technology and Parallel Systems, University of Vienna,
Brünnerstrasse 72, A-1210 Vienna, Austria

Abstract. Recently, a standard set of extensions for Fortran 90, called High Performance Fortran (HPF), has been developed which would provide a portable interface to a wide variety of parallel architectures. HPF focuses mainly on issues of distributing data across the memories of a distributed memory multiprocessor. This paper proposes techniques for processing HPF data distribution and data alignment specifications, array statements and procedure interfaces in the HPF compiler which is being developed in the ESPRIT project Prepare.

1 Introduction

A significant amount of software research for developing programming environments for distributed memory multiprocessors is currently underway both in academia as well as industry. The research effort can be broadly categorized into three classes, namely parallelizing compilers, languages, and support tools. Recently, a standard set of extensions for Fortran 90, called **High Performance Fortran (HPF)** [8], has been developed which would provide a portable interface to a wide variety of parallel architectures.

The ESPRIT-3 project Prepare ([16]) aims to develop a High Performance Fortran compiler within an integrated programming environment.

This paper proposes techniques for processing HPF data distribution and data alignment specifications, array statements and procedure interfaces in the Prepare HPF Compiler in the basic stage which deals with the subset HPF. In the next section we describe the model underlying the compiler, and introduce the basic terminology used in the remaining sections. Section 3 introduces techniques for the basic restructuring of array statements. Processing procedure calls is discussed in Section 4. The rest of the paper briefly deals with compiler optimizations (Section 5), and an overview of related work (Section 6), followed by the conclusion. The complete compiler specification can be found in [2].

---

* The work described in this paper was carried out as part of the ESPRIT research project P 6516 PREPARE, and funded by the Austrian Research Foundation (FWF) and the Austrian Ministry for Science and Research (BMWF).

2 Basic Model and Terminology

The parallelization process as described in this paper is based on the so-called *SPMD* (Single Program Multiple Data) [11], or data parallel model of computation. Starting from the user specified data alignment and data distribution directives the compiler has to determine the layout of the data on the set virtual of processors and to determine how to spread the work among the processors available. Work distribution is achieved by applying the *owner computes* rule, so that each processor only computes those data elements that are allocated in its local memory. Access to non-local data is handled via explicit message passing.

2.1 Basic Concepts

In the following we assume that all declarations of objects (i.e. arrays, processor arrays, templates) are normalized such that the lower bound in each dimension is 1. Figure 1 summarizes the notation used in this paper.

A, B, T	names of arrays	I^A	index domain of array A
N	size of array dimension	i	global index, $1 \leq i \leq N$
N_T	size of align target dimension	$f(i)$	function, mapping indices of
M	parameter for *BLOCK(M)* or		*lhs* array to corresponding
	CYCLIC(M) distributions		indices of *rhs* array
P	total number of processors	$e(i)$	alignment function
	in dimension		$e(i) = i * k + d$
p	individual processor, $1 \leq p \leq P$	$[l : u : s]$	regular array section
$\delta(i)$	distribution function	Δ^A	distribution descriptor

Fig. 1. Table of symbols used in this paper.

2.1.1 Processors. The set of processors, W is represented in a program by one or more **processor arrays**. Any two processors in W communicate by exchanging messages. Our model abstracts from the machine topology.

2.1.2 Data Distribution. A distribution of an array is defined by three components: the array index domain, the processor array index domain, and a distribution function. An **index domain** of rank n, denoted by $\mathbf{I}$, can be represented in the form $\mathbf{I} = \mathbf{X}_{i=1}^{n} D_i$, where the so-called index dimension D_i is a non-empty, linearly order set of consecutive integers and $\mathbf{X}$ denotes the cartesian product.

Let in the following $\mathbf{I}_i^A$ and $\mathbf{J}_j^R$ denote the i-th index dimension of an array A and j-th index dimension of a processor array R, respectively. A **dimensional distribution function** of dimension i of A to dimension j of R can be described by a total function from the array index domain $\mathbf{I}_i^A$ to the processors index domain $\mathbf{J}_j^R$, denoted by $\delta_{R_j}^{A_i} : \mathbf{I}_i^A \rightarrow \mathcal{P}(\mathbf{J}_j^R) - \phi$, where $\mathcal{P}(\mathbf{J}_j^R)$ denotes the power set of $\mathbf{J}_j^R$.

$BLOCK(M)$	$CYCLIC(M)$	Replication
$\delta(i) = \left\{ \left\lceil \frac{i}{M} \right\rceil \right\}, M \geq \left\lceil \frac{N}{P} \right\rceil$	$\delta(i) = \left\{ 1 + \left(\left\lceil \frac{i}{M} \right\rceil - 1 \right) \bmod P \right\}$	$\delta(i) = \{ p \mid 1 \leq p \leq P \}$

Fig. 2. HPF Distribution Functions.

The distribution functions provided by HPF are $BLOCK(M)$, $CYCLIC(M)$ and replication which is denoted by a '*'. They are summarized in Figure 2. A distribution for a multi-dimensional array is specified by describing the distribution of each array dimension separately, without any interaction of dimensions.

2.1.3 Alignment. Let A denote a n-dimensional alignee and let T denote a m-dimensional alignment target. An alignment for dimension i of alignee A with respect to dimension j of the alignment target (or template) T is defined by a so-called **dimensional alignment function** which is a total function $\alpha_{T_j}^{A_i} : \mathbf{I}_i^A \rightarrow \mathcal{P}(\mathbf{J}_j^T) - \phi$. The distribution function for alignee A with respect to target T can be constructed from the dimensional distribution functions.

2.2 Data Layout

The set of local elements of a distributed array A (or template) on a particular processor p, denoted by $local^A(p)$ contains all those elements of A that are *owned* by p and therefore are stored in p's local memory.

$$local^A(p) = \{ i \mid \delta(i) = p \wedge i \in \mathbf{I}^A \}$$

The local element set of an array is the basis for the computation of execution sets and communication sets and is also needed for the transformation of array declarations. The set of local template elements is needed for the computation of the local element sets for arrays that are aligned with that template. In the following local element sets are specified via closed form expressions, analog to Fortran 90 section notation.

2.2.1 Local Elements of a Distributee. Due to the nature of the HPF distributions ($BLOCK(M)$ and $CYCLIC(M)$), the local element set of an array (template) dimension can be represented as a section by means of triplet notation. For $BLOCK$, $CYCLIC(1)$ and $BLOCK(M)$ distributed dimensions the local element set can be described by a single triplet. This, however, might be not the case for $CYCLIC(M)$ distributions, where the local element set of a processor may consist of more than one triplet, which complicates the handling of these sets at compile- and/or at runtime. The set of elements of a distributee A owned by a particular processor p (in global indices) is given by $local^A(p)$ as defined in Figure 3.

In the case of a $CYCLIC(M)$ distribution with $M < \left\lceil \frac{N}{P} \right\rceil$ some processors will get more than one section of array elements. The total number of sections on a particular processor p is given by n_p.

$BLOCK(M)$ **Distribution:**	$CYCLIC$ **Distribution:**
$local^A(p) = [(p-1) * M + 1 : min(p * M, N) : 1]$	$local^A(p) = [p : N : P]$

$CYCLIC(M)$ **Distribution:**

$$local^A(p) = \bigcup_{i=1}^{n_p} \sigma_i(p) = [\mathcal{L}_i(p) : \mathcal{U}_i(p) : 1]$$

$$\sigma_i(p) = [\mathcal{L}_i(p) : \mathcal{U}_i(p) : 1], \quad n_p = \left\lceil \frac{N - (p-1) * M}{P * M} \right\rceil$$

$$\mathcal{L}_i(p) = (p-1) * M + 1 + (i-1) * P * M, \quad \mathcal{U}_i(p) = min(\mathcal{L}_i(p) + M - 1, N)$$

Fig. 3. Local Elements of a Distributee A.

2.2.2 Local Elements of an Alignee. The alignment functions included in subset HPF are restricted to linear functions of the alignment dummy. We assume that immediate alignment functions have been normalized into ultimate alignment functions. The set of local elements on processor p of an array $A(1 : N)$, denoted by $local_T^A(p)$, which is aligned with an alignment target T by the alignment function $e(I) = k * I + d$ is determined by:

$$local_T^A(p) = e^{-1}(local^T(p) \cap e([1 : N])) = e^{-1}(local^T(p)) \cap [1 : N]$$

The resulting formulas are presented in Figure 4. Note that for $BLOCK(M)$ distributions n_p, the total number of sections, is always 1.

$$local_T^A(p) = \bigcup_{i=1}^{n_p} \sigma_i = \bigcup_{i=1}^{n_p} ([\mathcal{L}_{iT}^A(p) : \mathcal{U}_{iT}^A(p) : 1])$$

For $k > 0$,

$$\mathcal{L}_{iT}^A(p) = max \left(1, \left\lceil \frac{\mathcal{L}_i^T(p) - d}{k} \right\rceil \right), \quad \mathcal{U}_{iT}^A(p) = min \left(N, \left\lfloor \frac{\mathcal{U}_i^T(p) - d}{k} \right\rfloor \right)$$

and for $k < 0$,

$$\mathcal{L}_{iT}^A(p) = max \left(1, \left\lceil \frac{\mathcal{U}_i^T(p) - d}{k} \right\rceil \right), \quad \mathcal{U}_{iT}^A(p) = min \left(N, \left\lfloor \frac{\mathcal{L}_i^T(p) - d}{k} \right\rfloor \right)$$

where, $\mathcal{L}_i^T(p)$ and $\mathcal{U}_i^T(p)$ denote the lower and upper bound of $local_i^T(p)$.

Fig. 4. Local Elements of an Alignee.

2.3 Index Conversion

In this section we define functions which convert global indices to local indices.

$BLOCK(M)$ Distribution	$CYCLIC(M)$ Distribution
$g2l(i) = 1 + (i-1) \bmod M$	$g2l(i) = (i-1) \bmod M + M * \left\lfloor \frac{i-1}{M*P} \right\rfloor + 1$
$p = \left\lceil \frac{i}{M} \right\rceil,\ 1 \le i \le N,\ M \ge \left\lceil \frac{N}{P} \right\rceil$	$p = 1 + \left(\left\lceil \frac{i}{M} \right\rceil - 1 \right) \bmod P,\ 1 \le i \le N$

Fig. 5. Index Conversion for Distributees.

2.3.1 Index Conversion for Distributees. Given an array $A(1:N)$ with a $BLOCK(M)$ or $CYCLIC(M)$ distribution onto P processors, $1 \le p \le P$, and a global index i of A, then the corresponding local index l on processor p is determined as shown in Figure 5.

$$BLOCK(M)$$

$$g2l(i) = i - \mathcal{L}_T^A(p) + 1$$
$$p = \left\lceil \frac{i*k+d}{M} \right\rceil$$
where $\mathcal{L}_T^A(p)$ is the lower bound of $local_T^A(p)$ as in Figure 3.

$$CYCLIC(M)$$

$$g2l(i) = \left\lfloor \frac{n(i)-s_p}{abs(k)} \right\rfloor * \Sigma_p + SP_p[(n(i)-s_p) \bmod abs(k)] + o(i) - o_p + 1$$
$$p = 1 + \left\lfloor \frac{i*k+d-1}{M} \right\rfloor \bmod P$$

with

$n(i)$ ... section number of index i, $i \in \sigma_{n(i)}(p)$

$o(i)$ ... the offset of index i in section $\sigma_{n(i)}(p)$

s_p ... the number of the first non-empty section,
$|\sigma_{s_p}(p)| > 0 \ \wedge \ |\sigma_j(p)| = 0,\ 1 \le j \le s_p - 1$

o_p ... if $k > 0$: the offset of the first element in section $\sigma_{s_p}(p)$
if $k < 0$: the offset of the last element in section $\sigma_{s_p}(p)$

$SP_p[0:t_p]$ ... the so-called section-period table, with
$t_p = min(n_p - s_p + 1, abs(k))$
$SP_p[0] = 0,\ SP_p[1] = o_p + |\sigma_{s_p}|,$
$SP_p[j] = SP_p[j-1] + |\sigma_{s_p+j}|,\ 2 \le j \le t_p$

where $\Sigma_p = SP_p[t_p]$, $n(i) = \left\lfloor \frac{i*k+d-1}{M*P} \right\rfloor + 1$, $o(i) = \left\lfloor \frac{(i*k+d-1)\ \bmod\ M}{k} \right\rfloor$, and n_p as in Figure 3.

Fig. 6. Index Conversion for Alignees.

2.3.2 Index Conversion for Alignees. Let A denote an array that is ultimately aligned with an alignment target T by means of the alignment function $e(i) = i * k + d$. Let T be distributed by $BLOCK(M)$ over P processors. Given a global index i of A the corresponding local index l on processor p, $1 \le p \le P$

can be determined as shown in the left part of Figure 6. For alignees with a $CYCLIC(M)$ distributed target the index conversion is more complex.

Layout of T

Processor 1

σ_1	1	2	3	4	5	6	7
σ_2	36	37	38	39	40	41	42
σ_3	71	72	73	74	75	76	77
σ_4	106	107	108	109	110	111	112
σ_5	141	142	143	144	145	146	147
σ_6	176	177	178	179	180	181	182
σ_7	211	212	213	214	215	216	217
σ_8	246	247	248	249	250		

(local indices 1–7, 8–14, 15–21, 22–28, 29–35, 36–42, 43–49, 50–54)

Processor 2

σ_1	8	9	10	11	12	13	14
σ_2	43	44	45	46	47	48	49
σ_3	78	79	80	81	82	83	84
σ_4	113	114	115	116	117	118	119
σ_5	148	149	150	151	152	153	154
σ_6	183	184	185	186	187	188	189
σ_7	218	219	220	221	222	223	224

local index / global index (e.g. local 27, global 111); member of A(1::5)

Layout of A

Processor 1

σ_1			
σ_2	10	11	
σ_3	21	22	23
σ_4	33	34	
σ_5	45	46	
σ_6	56	57	58
σ_7	68	69	
σ_8	80		

$s_1 = 2$
$o_1 = 0$
$SP_1 = [0, 2, 5, 7]$

Processor 2

σ_1	1	2	
σ_2	12	13	
σ_3	24	25	
σ_4	35	36	37
σ_5	47	48	
σ_6	59	60	
σ_7	70	71	72

$s_2 = 1$
$o_2 = 1$
$SP_2 = [0, 3, 5, 7]$

```
      REAL A(80),T(250)
!HPF$ PROCESSORS R(5)
!HPF$ ALIGN A(I) WITH T(3*I+8)
!HPF$ DISTRIBUTE T(CYCLIC(7)) ONTO R

      A(1::5) = 0
```

Fig. 7. Layout of an Alignee with $CYCLIC(M)$ Distributed Target

The set of local elements (in global indices) can be described by a union of sections $\sigma_i(p)$ as shown in Figure 4. However, depending on the alignment parameters, some sections at the beginning or at the end may be empty. In the following the number of the first non-empty section on a particular processor p is denoted by s_p. The number of elements in each section may differ at most by 1 (except empty sections, the first non-empty section and the last nonempty section), with the maximum number of elements per section given by $\lceil \frac{M}{k} \rceil$ and the minimum number of elements per section given by $\lfloor \frac{M}{k} \rfloor$. The size of consecutive sections varies with a cycle of period length $k + 1$. The fact that the length of the individual sections on a particular processor differ, complicates local address calculation. An additional problem is that the first sections might be smaller than $\lfloor \frac{M}{k} \rfloor$. We, therefore take the approach to determine the period of section lengthes, and the number of the first non-empty section on each processor, and incorporate this information in the formula for global to local index conversion which is depicted in Figure 6. The SP_p table and the values for Σ_p, s_p and o_p

have to be determined for each processor once and can be used for local address generation as well as for the representation of local element sets and the parallelization of array assignment statements.

In Figure 7 the layout of the arrays A, T of the shown HPF code fragment and the corresponding SP_p tables are visualized for the first two processors.

2.4 Work Distribution

As already mentioned, work distribution is derived on basis of the *owner computes* paradigm. The set of elements of the *lhs* variable which have to be computed on a particular processor p is referred to as *execution set*, denoted by $exec(p)$. If the *lhs* variable of the assignment statement is a regular array section, the execution set can be represented using Fortran 90 triplet notation.

Let f denote the global index of the first element of the execution set on processor p, with $exec(p) \neq \phi$. Let $\Lambda(p) \subseteq local_T^A(p)$ denote the set of ϵ consecutive elements of $local_T^A(p)$ starting from element with index f.

$$\Lambda(p) \subseteq local_T^A(p) \quad |\Lambda(p)| = \epsilon, \quad \epsilon = SP \left\lceil \frac{k}{gcd(P,k)} \right\rceil * \left\lceil \frac{s}{gcd(P,s)} \right\rceil$$

Let $\Xi(p)$ denote the set of the first ξ elements ($1 \leq \xi \leq M$) of the execution set on processor p:

$$\Xi(p) = \{x_i \mid x_i \in (\Lambda(p) \cap [l : u : s]), 1 \leq i \leq \xi\}.$$

The execution set on processor p in *global indices* can then be represented as follows:

$$exec(p) = \bigcup_{i=1}^{\xi} \left[x_i : u_i : \frac{s * M * P}{gcd(P,k) * gcd(P,s)} \right]$$

By using the function $g2l()$, Σ_p and the SP table from Figure 6 the execution set in *local indices* is given by:

$$exec\_l(p) = \bigcup_{i=1}^{\xi} \left[g2l(x_i) : g2l(u_i) : \frac{s * \Sigma_p}{gcd(P,k) * gcd(P,s)} \right]$$

Fig. 8. Execution Sets for Array Assignments.

Let for an array assignment statement of the form $A(l : u : s) = ...$, $\mathbf{L} = [l : u : s]$ denote the so-called *lhs reference space* of array A. The execution set according to a an assignment to a regular array section $A(l : u : s)$ on a particular processor p can be determined by the intersection of the *lhs* reference space $\mathbf{L}$ with the local element set on this processor.

$$exec_{\mathbf{L}}^A(p) = local^A(p) \cap [l : u : s]$$

For $BLOCK(M)$ distributions the execution set can always be described via a single section whereas for $CYCLIC(M)$ distributions this might not be the case. The summary of closed form expressions for $exec(p)$ can be found in [2].

In the following we discuss in more detail the execution set generation for sections of alignees with a $CYCLIC(M)$ distributed target. As it will be seen the execution set corresponding to an assignment to a regular array section $A(l : u : s)$ can be represented by means of at most M array sections. To generate the execution set for an array section it is not necessary to determine the whole set $exec(p)$, but it suffices to compute at most the first M elements of $exec(p)$, denoted by $\Xi(p)$. Note that for the computation of $\Xi(p)$ the intersection of the reference space $(l : u : s)$ with at most $k * s + 1$ sections $\sigma_i(p)$, $s_p \le i \le s_p + k * s$, has to be determined. In Figure 8 this method for the generation of execution sets for regular array sections is summarized. As can be seen from Figure 7 the execution set for the array section $A(1 :: 5)$ for processor 1 is given in global indices by $[11 :: 35] \cup [21 :: 35]$ and in local indices by $[2 :: 7] \cup [3 :: 7]$. For processor 2 the execution set consists of only 1 section: in global indices $[1 :: 35]$ and in local indices $[1 :: 7]$.

2.5 Communication Sets

For the parallelization of assignment statements that reference distributed arrays, each processor has to determine the set of non-local elements it must receive from other processors in order to perform all the computations defined by its execution set. Furthermore it also has to determine which elements of its local element set have to be sent to other processors. Communication sets determine those elements a particular processor p must send (or receive) to (from) another processor q, in order to compute the elements of its execution set.

Consider an assignment statement of the form $A(l_1 : u_1 : s_1) = B(\tilde{l}_1 : \tilde{u}_1 : \tilde{s}_1)$. The set of elements a processor p must send to a processor q is called $send\_set(p, q)$. It comprises those elements of B that are in p's local memory and that are needed by another processor q. The set of non-local elements a processor p needs from a processor q is called $recv\_set(p, q)$. Note that $recv\_set(p, q)$ is given by $send\_set(q, p)$

---

for each processor q, $q \ne p$

1. generate the execution set for processor q, $exec_{\mathbf{L}}^A(q)$
2. determine $f(exec_{\mathbf{L}}^A(q))$, where $f(i) = \frac{(i - l_1)}{s_1} * \tilde{s}_1 + \tilde{l}_1$
3. compute the intersection $f(exec_{\mathbf{L}}^A(q)) \cap local^B(p)$ which corresponds to $send\_set^B(p, q)$

where $\mathbf{L} = [l_1 : u_1 : s_1]$.

Fig. 9. Communication Sets for Array Assignments.

In the case of array assignment statements computation of communication sets is based on regular section intersection. Computation of communication sets for an array assignment statement of the form shown above is summarized in Figure 9.

3 Processing Array Statements

There are two main steps in the initial parallelization of an HPF program:
(1) *Masking.* Executable statements are masked (guarded) to ensure that all variable updates are exclusively in the local memory of the executing processor.
(2) *Communication Insertion.* Possible data movements between processors are specified by means of so-called *communication descriptors COMMs* which are generated and inserted into the program instead of concrete communication statements to enable later optimizations.

Send Part

Receive Part

if $local^B(p) \cap$ rhs $\neq \phi$
 $\wedge$ p = MASTER($local^B(p)$)) then
 for each $q \in P$, $q \neq p$ do
  if $send\_set^B(p, q) \neq \phi$) then
   M = B($send\_set^B(p, q)$)
   send M to q
  endif
 endfor
endif

if $local^A(p) \cap$ lhs $\neq \phi$ then
 for each $q \in P$, $q \neq p$,
  p = MASTER($local^B(q)$) do
  if ($recv\_set^B(p, q) \neq \phi$) then
   receive M from q
  endif
 endfor
endif

Fig. 10. Specification of the COMM Descriptor.

3.1 High Level Communication Descriptor COMM

A communication descriptor contains all information that is needed for the calculation of execution sets and communication sets using the formulas derived in Sections 2.4 and 2.5. Communication descriptors are flexible enough to allow for: recognizing and removing redundant communication descriptors, movement of descriptors (i.e. extraction from loops, movement across procedure boundaries), fusion of communication descriptors, splitting into the sending and receiving components. Moreover, there enable a uniform treatment of references to scalars, array elements, and array sections. So optimization of communication is performed entirely on the level of communication descriptors. In the final phase which adapts the SPMD program for the target machine, communication descriptors are transformed into the explicit message passing form.

 Let lhs, rhs denote section subscripts and let Δ^A, Δ^B denote distribution descriptors of arrays A and B, respectively (each distributed array declared is represented by a descriptor). Let M denote a temporary buffer, and let P denote the set of available processors, with arbitrary processors $p, q \in P$. An array communication descriptor of the form COMM(Δ^A,< lhs >,Δ^B,< rhs >,M), which for example is generated in case of an array assignment statement $A(\text{lhs}) = B(\text{rhs})$, has the semantics introduced in the left part of Figure 10 when evaluated on a particular processor p. In this figure, *MASTER(s)* is a function which returns a uniquely defined processor m which ownes the array element set s. This processor is responsible for sending the data. The choice of m is system dependent.

In many cases the overlap area communication approach can be used. Then M will denote the overlap area description and the COMM will have the same semantics as the EXSR statement specified, for example, in [5, 6, 17].

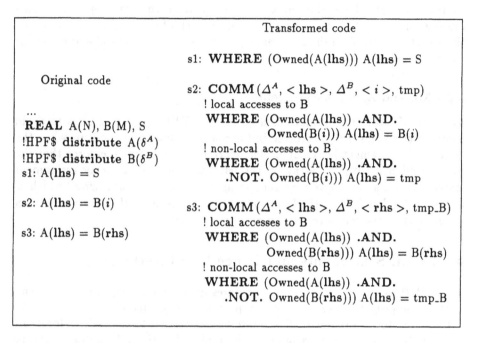

Fig. 11. Transformation of Array Assignment Statements.

3.2 Transformation of Array Assignments

The first step is *masking* which replaces each array assignment statement S of the program by the associated masked statement

$$\text{WHERE } (mask(S)) \ S$$

where *mask(S)* is expressed by a high level intrinsic function *Owned(ref)* which is also used for masking scalar assignments. The *ref* denotes the *rhs* reference which may be scalar or array valued of type logical. If *ref* is scalar valued the function returns the value *.TRUE.* if the array element denoted by *ref* is owned by the processor which is calling this function. If *ref* is array valued the function result is a logical array with the same shape as *ref*. Potential movement of non-local data is expressed by inserting the high level communication descriptor for the reference to a distributed array in the *rhs*.

If the *rhs* contains a distributed array the execution set of the statement is split into the local part that uses only data that is local on the executing processor, and the non-local part which uses some non-local data stored in the communication buffer (see transformation of statements *s2* and *s3* in Figure 11). Splitting also enables the subsequent optimizing transformation to achieve overlapping communication and computation (see Section 5).

Communication descriptors contain all the information that is needed for the calculation of execution sets and communication sets using the formulas derived in Sections 2.4 and 2.5. All possible cases that may arise during basic parallelization of array assignment statements are shown in Figure 11.

If on the right hand side more than one distributed array appears, a communication descriptor has to be generated for each of those arrays. However, in this case the splitting of the array assignment statement into local and non-local parts is more complex.

3.3 Masked Array Assignment

The goal of basic transformations applied to WHERE statements[2] is to avoid communication for arrays involved in the mask evaluation at the time when the assignment statement is executed. Therefore it is necessary to enforce that the mask is aligned with the array on the left hand side of the array assignment statement. This is achieved by generating a temporary mask array, which is aligned with the array on the left hand side. Prior to the WHERE statement an assignment to the temporary mask array is inserted.

4 CALL Statements and Procedure Interfaces

The *SPMD paradigm* is applied to procedures in an obvious way: a procedure call in the node program is executed by all processors allocated to the program. We assume that for every procedure the interface is explicit to the caller. Moreover, if the INHERIT directive is used the user provides an explicit descriptive or prescriptive distribution for the dummy argument in question.

Different transformation techniques are applied depending on whether the dummy arrays are of *assumed shape* or *explicit shape*. In the following sections this is described in greater detail.

4.1 Argument Passing via Assumed Shape Arrays

The actual argument has to be redistributed, if necessary, to match the corresponding dummy argument distributed. In this case argument passing can no longer be call by reference, and a *copy-in/copy-out* semantics must be adopted. In order to allow for later optimization based on communication descriptor movement, redistribution is performed by the caller before and after the call to the procedure.

A temporary array with the same size and shape as the actual array (section) is allocated with the desired distribution and the actual array (section) is

---

[2] We assume that WHERE constructs are transformed into a series of WHERE statements during the program normalization phase.

assigned to that temporary. Since this assignment may result in communication a high level communication descriptor is generated. In the CALL statement the original actual argument is replaced by the temporary. After the CALL statement the temporary array has to be reassigned to the original array, provided the INTENT(IN) attribute has not been specified for the corresponding dummy argument. This again may cause insertion of a communication descriptor.

4.2 Argument Passing via Explicit Shape Arrays

Argument passing using explicit shape dummy arrays is more complex than via assumed shape arrays because the restriction that the rank and shape of actual and formal array must be the same is absent. Therefore we must be able to handle cases where an n-dimensional actual array is associated with an m-dimensional formal array. Explicit shape dummies imply contiguous storage and rely on storage association between actual and formal array. Because the actual argument can be an array section we are forced to adopt in the basic parallelization phase the *copy-in/copy-out* argument transfer mechanism.

Original code	Transformed code

REAL A($N_1,...,N_n$)
 !HPF\$ **distribute** δ^A :: A
 ...
 CALL Sub(A(sec),...)
 ...
 	
 CONTAINS
   SUBROUTINE Sub(X,...)
   REAL X($M_1, ... ,M_m$)
   !HPF\$ **distribute** X(δ^X)
   ...
 END SUBROUTINE Sub
 	
 END PROGRAM
	REAL A($N_1, ... ,N_n$)
	 !HPF\$ **distribute** δ^A :: A
	 REAL, **ALLOCATABLE** :: T($:_1, ... ,:_m$)
	 ...
	 ! allocate T with distribution δ^X,
	 ALLOCATE (T($M_1, ... ,M_m$))
	 T = **RESHAPE** (A, **SHAPE** (T))
	 CALL Sub(T, ...)
	 A(sec) = **RESHAPE** (T, **SHAPE** (A(sec)))
	 DEALLOCATE (T)
	 ...
	 CONTAINS
	   ! procedure interface stays unchanged
	   ...
	 END PROGRAM

Fig. 12. Explicit Shape Dummy Arrays with Explicit Distribution.

Generally, if an array section is passed to an explicit shape dummy the array section has to be copied into a contiguous temporary array (Figure 12). This temporary is then passed to the procedure and assigned back to the original array section on exit form the procedure if necessary. If the distribution of a dummy argument array is specified explicitly, then the actual argument has to be redistributed, if necessary, to match it. Redistribution is achieved by allocating and assigning a temporary with the desired distribution. However, size and shape of this temporary are now determined by the dummy array rather than by the transferred section. Before each CALL statement to such a procedure an assignment of the original argument to the temporary array has to be generated. For those cases where the rank of the actual and formal argument differ this assignment is realized using the Fortran 90 *RESHAPE* function. The call to this intrinsic is later transformed into the call to a runtime library procedure.

The CALL statement has to be adjusted accordingly, and after the CALL statement the temporary array has to be assigned back to the original argument, provided the INTENT(IN) attribute has not been specified.

5   Optimizations

In this phase, the compiler applies transformations to improve performance of the resulting SPMD program. The program analysis must capture sufficient information to enable sophisticated optimizations. Data flow analysis information, for example, enables to decide whether execution and communication sets computed for an array statement can be reused for some of the following ones.

Original code

   A(lhs) = $\mathcal{F}$(B(rhs)) ! $\mathcal{F}$ denotes operations on elements of B

Transformed code

  COMMS (Δ^A, < lhs >, Δ^B, < rhs >, tmp_B)
  ! computations accessing only local elements of B - this hides the latency
  WHERE (Owned(A(lhs)) **.AND.** Owned(B(rhs))) A(lhs) = $\mathcal{F}$(B(rhs))
  COMMR (Δ^A, < lhs >, Δ^B, < rhs >, tmp_B)
  ! computations accessing non-local elements of B
  WHERE (Owned(A(lhs)) **.AND..NOT.** Owned(B(rhs))) A(lhs) = $\mathcal{F}$(tmp_B)

Fig. 13. Hiding latency by local computation.

There are several compiler optimizations which can reduce or hide the communication latency overhead. One of the approaches is called the *latency tolerance* [10]. The aim is to *hide* the message transmission time, by overlapping communication with parallel computation. The execution set for each processor is split into local and nonlocal parts in the way which was discussed in Section 3.2. Each processor executes separately parts of expressions which access only local data and those which access nonlocal data as expressed in Figure 13. COMM statements are split into send (COMMS) and receive (COMMR) parts whose semantics is clear from the specification introduced in Figure 10. COMMS is moved before the part performing local computations, and COMMR between this part and the one performing computations in which remote accesses are needed.

6 Related Work

In this paper we propose the systematic solution for general *BLOCK(M)* and *CYCLIC(M)* distributions allowing arbitrary HPF alignment functions. Solutions of many special cases of the problems discussed in this paper appeared in the literature. Li and Chen specified interprocessor communication by the descriptor called *communication pattern*. They used this descriptor in communication optimization. Koelbel [12] treats special communication set generation cases for data-parallel loops where arrays are distributed using a *BLOCK* or a *CYCLIC* distribution without considering any alignment aspects. Gupta et al. [7] extend Koelbel's techniques to *CYCLIC(M)* distributions and introduce a procedure for performing index conversion. Chatterjee at al. [4] also allow an arbitrary HPF alignment function. They construct a finite state machine to convert global indices of a regular array section to local ones. Unlike our approach, they do not preserve array sections after the index conversion. Moreover this kind of conversion cannot be applied to vector subscripted accesses. Stichnoth's approach [15] only allows alignment strides to be 0 or 1. Compiler communication optimizations are discussed in [9, 13]. Optimization techniques based on the runtime processing were developed by Saltz et al. [14], and the paper [3] describes their implementation in the SUPERB System.

7 Concluding Remarks

The techniques described in this paper are developed within the context of our research whose results have been documented in [2]. In the paper, we showed how data alignment and data distribution specifications are translated into mathematical functions that determine the ownership and adressing of local data. We introduced the methodology for derivation of execution sets applying the owner computes rule and derivation of communication sets. All the above terms create the basis for the implementation of masks and communication descriptors. The techniques described are now being implemented within the Prepare project and within the Vienna Fortran 90 ([1]) compiler.

Acknowledgment

The authors would like to thank the Prepare Project partners from ACE Amsterdam, TNO Delft and IRISA Rennes for useful discussions and comments on the document [2].

References

1. S.Benkner, B.Chapman, H.P.Zima. *Vienna Fortran90*. In Proceedings of the Scalable High Performance Computing Conference, Williamsburg, USA, pp. 51-59, April 1992.

2. S. Benkner, P. Brezany, H.P. Zima. *Functional Specification of the Prepare Parallelization Engine*. Internal Report of the Prepare Project, June 1993.

3. P.Brezany, M.Gerndt, V.Sipkova, H.P.Zima. *SUPERB Support for Irregular Scientific Computations*. In Proceedings of the Scalable High Performance Computing Conference, Williamsburg, USA, pp. 314-321, April 1992.

4. S. Chatterjee, J.R. Gilbert, F.J. Long, R. Schreiber, S-H. Teng. *Generating Local Addresses and Communication Sets for Data-Parallel Programs*. In Proceedings of the Fourth ACM SIGPLAN Symposium on Principles & Practice of Parallel Programming (PPOPP), 149–158, San Diego, May 19-22, 1993.

5. H.M. Gerndt, *Updating Distributed Variables in Local Computations*, Concurrency: Practice and Experience, Vol. 2(3), 171-193 (September 1990)

6. H.M. Gerndt. *Program Analysis and Transformations for Message-Passing Programs*. Proceedings of the Scalable High Performance Computing Conference, Williamsburg, Virginia, 60–67, April 26-29, 1992

7. S. K. S. Gupta et al. *Compiling Array Expressions for Efficient Execution on Distributed-Memory Machines*. Proceedings of ICPP'93.

8. High Performance FORTRAN Forum. *High Performance FORTRAN Language Specification*, Version 1.0, Rice University, Houston, TX, May 1993.

9. S. Hiranandani, K. Kennedy, C. Tseng. *Compiler Optimizations for Fortran D on MIMD distributed-memory machines*. In Proc. of Supercomputing'91, Albuquerque, NM, November 1991.

10. H. F. Jordan. *Scalability of Data Transport*. Proceedings of the Scalable High Performance Computing Conference, Williamsburg, Virginia, 1–8, April 26-29, 1992.

11. A.H. Karp. *Programming for Parallelism*. Computer 20(5), 43–57, May 1987

12. C. Koelbel. *Compiling Programs for Nonshared Memory Machines*. Ph.D. Dissertation, Purdue University, West Lafayette, IN, November 1990.

13. J. Li and M. Chen. *Compiling Communication-Efficient Programs for Massively Parallel Machines*. IEEE Transactions on Parallel and Distributed Systems, Vol.2(3), 361-376, July 1991.

14. J. Saltz, K. Crowley, R. Mirchandaney, and H. Berryman. *Run-time scheduling and execution of loops on message passing machines*. Journal of Parallel and Distributed Computing, 8(2):303–312, 1990.

15. J.M. Stichnoth. *Efficient Compilation of Array Statements for Private Memory Multicomputers*. Research Report CMU-CS-93-109, Carnegie Mellon University, Pittsburgh, February, 1993.

16. A. Veen, M. de Lange. *Overview of the Prepare Project*. In Proceedings of the Fourth Workshop on Compilers for Parallel Computers, Delft, Holland, December 1993.

17. H. Zima, B. Chapman. *Compiling for Distributed-Memory Systems*. Proc. of the IEEE, vol 81, n. 2, February 1993.

A Practical Approach to the Symbolic Debugging of Parallelized Code[1]

Patricia Pineo[*]

ppineo@alleg.edu

(814) 332-2883

Mary Lou Soffa

soffa@cs.pitt.edu

(412) 624-8425

Computer Science Department
University of Pittsburgh
Pittsburgh, PA   15260
Fax: (412) 624-5299

abstract -- A practical technique is presented that supports the debugging of parallelized code through global renaming and name reclamation. Global renaming creates single assignment code for programs destined to be parallelized. After parallelization, a reclamation of names not useful for either the execution or debugging of the code is performed. During execution non-current values can then be tracked and reported to the debugger. Results of experimentation indicate the enlargement of the name space is reasonable and that virtually all non-current values are reportable. The technique is independent of the transformations chosen to parallelize the code.

1. Introduction

The importance of renaming as a program transformation is growing with the increased recognition of its value in program analysis [CyFe87,Wolf89]. The two forms of renaming that have emerged as particularly useful are single assignment and static single assignment. In **single assignment** each assignment is made into a unique variable, and once computed, a variable will never be altered. **Static single assignment** differs in that although only one assignment statement may appear in the code for each variable, that statement can be repeatedly executed (as in a loop).

The usefulness of **static single assignment** has been demonstrated as a pre-processing stage to simplify dataflow analysis during the application of optimizing transformations [CFRWZ91]. It has also been shown useful in applying optimizations such as induction variable elimination [Wolf92]. Under the assumption of **single assignment** code, the problem of partitioning sequential code for a parallel environment is "drastically simplified" [BiNaRo89]. Single assignment is also shown useful in register allocation optimizations [BoDa91].

---

[1] Partially supported by National Science Foundation Grant CCR-91090809 to the University of Pittsburgh.
[*] Presenting Author

Although these single assignment forms have been shown to be useful for program analysis, their use during program execution has been restricted due to the impracticality of storage enlargement. In this paper we develop a technique that enables the use of renamed code during program execution. This is made possible by selectively reclaiming names prior to code execution.

This technique developed is another application of single assignment code - that of symbolic debugging of code that has been transformed by either traditional optimizations or parallelizing transformations. Because of code modification, deletion, reorganization and parallelization, the actual values of variables seen at breakpoints during runtime will often be different from the values expected by the programmer viewing the sequential, untransformed code. One approach to the problem of non-current variables is to force the programmer to directly view and debug the transformed code, but this approach requires that the user have familiarity with the parallel constructs available, the architecture and the mapping from the source to transformed code. A preferable approach is to allow the user to execute the transformed code on the parallel system but to debug the code from the viewpoint of the sequential code.

This approach to the problem of debugging transformed code has been visited for code transformed for traditional optimizations [Hen82,Zel83,CoMeRu88,PoSo88]. These techniques all create a history of specific optimizations performed with the objective of unwinding the optimizations selectively during debugging in order to recover non-current variables. These techniques work with a subset of 3-4 specific optimizations and must be expanded if other optimizations are applied. They are more successful when optimizations are local, becoming complex and expensive when code is moved across basic blocks. The present work differs in that expansive code motion does not increase the complexity, the work is not transformation dependent and the code is not modified during debugging. This last point is significant because code that is modified for debugging may execute during debugging runs, and then fail when debugging is not invoked.

This problem has also been considered by Gupta[Gupt88] in relation to debugging code reorganized by a trace scheduler. Gupta's technique enables expected values in reordered VLIW code to be reported. It requires debugging requests to be made in advance, and the recompilation of selected traces. The present work differs in that it allows inspection of all variables at any breakpoint without recompilation, and it is not architecture specific.

Each of these methods employs ad hoc techniques for saving and recovering non-current values in newly defined storage locations. By contrast, Global Renaming allows values to be stored and recovered in a unified way, without consideration of any code transformation. Because each value is carried in a unique name, renamed code can be transformed by unrestricted parallelizing transformations, and still be successfully debugged.

Unlike using renaming as a purely analytical technique, renaming in debugging has a problem in the explosion of the storage associated with single assignment programs. This problem is resolved in this work by the application of a second stage that reclaims names not needed for either parallel execution or debugging before execution occurs.

Thus, this paper presents a practical approach to the use of renaming in debugging of parallelized code. The techniques have been implemented and experimental results are presented. Through these experimental results, we demonstrate that after name reclamation, the storage expansion caused by the renaming is reasonable and virtually all non-current names can be reported.

There are several additional advantages of using the renaming approach for debugging transformed code. First, the renaming allows the exploitation of additional parallelism in program code by reducing data dependencies. Further, this same analysis can be used to simplify the application of several standard parallelizing transformations. Finally the technique imposes no restrictions on the number or type of parallelizing transformations applied. This allows the approach to interface easily with a variety of transformational packages aimed at diverse target architectures.

In this extended summary, we first present an overview of the technique. We then present the two analysis techniques, focusing on the reclamation of names. Experimental results are presented, showing that this approach is indeed a practical approach.

2. Overview of Debugging with Global Renaming

Practical high-level debugging with global renaming is accomplished in five stages. An overview of our technique is given in the algorithm of Figure 1. Two stages (numbered one and three) are introduced to bracket the application of parallelizing transformations. The primary purpose of the first stage is the renaming of the code and the production of AVAIL sets, which are sets that retain the current names of variables that should be reportable after the execution of the associated statement number in the original program. These sets provide the value tracking capability used by the debugger at execution time.

Algorithm -- High-level debugging of parallelized code

1. Globally rename code (IN: original code, OUT: single assignment code, AVAIL sets)
2. Apply user chosen parallelization transformations(IN: SA code, OUT:parallelized code)
3. Reclaim unneeded names (IN: parallelized SA code,
             OUT: reduced name parallelized code, INOUT: AVAIL)
4. Compile (IN: reduced name parallelized code, OUT: executable code)
5. Execute code through debugger modified to access AVAIL sets when values are requested

Figure 1 — Overview of the debugging technique

A simple program is shown passing through the stages of the system in Figure 2. Initially the code is globally renamed. This first stage produces a semantically equivalent version of the program in single assignment form, which assigns each (potentially non-current) value a unique storage name. The current names at each statement are retained in the AVAIL sets. The reduction of undesirable data dependencies by the renaming can also be observed in the example. Antidependencies (e.g., statement S1 δ^{-1} S3), and output dependencies (S6 d^{o} S7) are removed in the renamed code. The resulting code has been freed

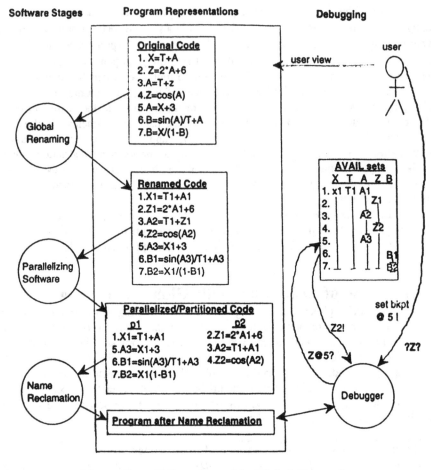

Figure 2 — Debugging with Global Renaming

from about half of the original data dependencies and thus allows a more aggressive exploitation of parallelism.

The single assignment code can now be parallelized by software targeted for any desired architecture. The choice of transformations applied in this process are not important to the debugging system. Regardless of where variables are moved, their version names carry the tag required by the debugger for later inquiries.

Once the parallelized code has been finalized, it may be that not all the names introduced through renaming are necessary. Some variables must be retained because they enable the reporting of a non-current value at debug time. In this example, the programmer (debugging from the viewpoint of the sequential code) may insert a breakpoint after statement 5 and request the value of Z. This breakpoint maps to statement of the parallelized code and the associated AVAIL set indicates that Z2 is the proper version of Z to report from the transformed code. Since Z2 must be reported (and not Z1) it is necessary to distinguish between the Zs and therefore the Z2 name must be maintained.

The other reason for not reclaiming names is to allow multiple copies of a variable to be live on different concurrent tasks, thereby enabling the exploitation of parallelism. In this example, A3 cannot share storage with A1, because A1 is simultaneously live on a concurrent process. Similarly A2 cannot share storage with A1 or A3.

The B2 variable is reclaimable because neither B1 nor B2 needs to be available on a concurrent task, nor is B1 live on any concurrent task. The decision to reclaim B2 will result in a change in statement 7 of the parallelized code where B2 becomes B1, and an accompanying update to the database in the B entry of the AVAIL set associated with statement 7.

This parallelized program with names reclaimed (which is no longer single-valued) can now be compiled and executed. The programmer, debugging from the viewpoint of the sequential code, places a breakpoint in the sequential code. This breakpoint maps through to the transformed code. When the breakpoint is encountered, a request for a value made by the programmer traps into the runtime interface. This module in turn replaces the variable name requested with the version name associated with the breakpoint position which is stored in the AVAIL data set. The debugger then proceeds to fill the revised request in the ordinary way. In this example, if the programmer places a breakpoint after statement 3, a request for X, T, A or Z will be replaced with requests for X1, T1, A2, or Z1 respectively and the new requests filled by the debugger. The global renaming and name reclamation processes are presented in greater detail in the following sections.

3. Global Renaming

The task of global renaming requires the creation of a new variable name at each variable definition, and also at each program location where divergent execution paths may join. This resolves ambiguity after the join point that may occur in trying to determine which of multiple names (values) should be used. Figure 3 shows this case.

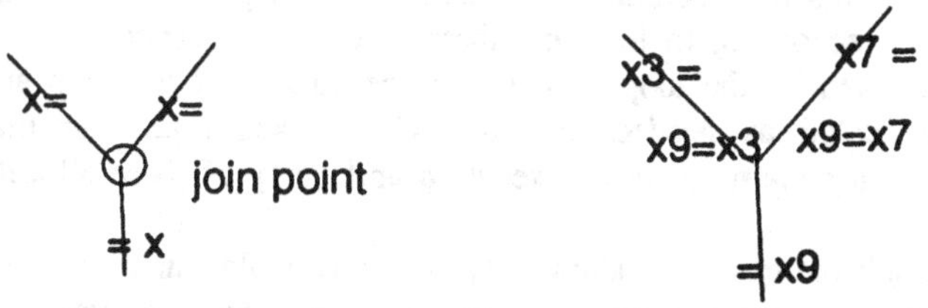

a) before renaming   b) after renaming
Figure 3 — Renaming at join points in program flow.

In addition, global renaming must find blocks of code that may be reentered (loops) and ensure that scalars within such blocks are expanded to vectors. This results in variables with altered types as well as altered names. Figure 4 shows this case.

a) before renaming   b) after renaming

Figure 4 — Renaming repeated code

In structured code, these join points and loops coincide with structure boundaries. In unstructured code, they are generally discovered by analysis on a Control Flow Graph (CFG). The variety of these approaches has resulted in the development of three distinct global renaming algorithms. The first is an algorithm for structured FORTRAN 77 code [PiSo91,Piaso93]. This algorithm produces optimal quality code in linear time and recognizes all high-level constructs. It is thus appropriate for use on a large subclass of FORTRAN programs. The second algorithm models unstructured code as a sequence of simple commands in a linear code space, infused with arbitrary GOTO's [Piaso93]. It is able to assert join points without production of the CFG, and so although it is very general, it still operates in linear time. However this algorithm inserts some unnecessary assignment statements. The most general of the algorithms (and the most expensive) is an extension of the dominance frontier algorithm of Cytron, Ferrante, Rosen, Wegman and Zadeck[CFRWZ91] which in its original form produces Static Single Assignment (SSA) code from unstructured code in $O(n^3)$ [Piaso93].

The extension necessary to tailor this algorithm to create single assignment code occurs in the discovery and renaming of loops. Each loop discovered in the CFG is assigned a unique looping subscript (analogous to the LS of Figure 4). Individual statements may belong to any number of loops. Variables defined have subscripts added according to loop membership of the statement. The size of the arrays is determined by the loop bounds. If the bounds of the loop are unknown, vectors are allocated as needed in "chunks" of fixed size. In practice these variables are often reclaimed before execution and many of these allocations do not occur.

Although the examples show only scalar variables, array variables are also renamed using analogous techniques. Any time an array is altered it is renamed, initiating a copy into a new array object. The expansion of array objects thus creates arrays of arrays.

While the renaming of arrays continues to remove all anti and output dependencies, it also has the effect of increasing the number of flow dependencies. These come about because the copying of an array object is dependent on the expression defining the new element *as well as* the last current array object. The array assignment A[7]=X is renamed as A2=copy[A1,7,X1]. The renamed code explicitly shows the dependency of the statement on both X1 and A1. The global renaming stage removes these introduced flow dependencies when it can be determined that they are unnecessary. These approaches and a more detailed discussion of global renaming are described in [Pineo93].

4. Name Reclamation

After the globally renamed program has been partitioned and parallelized, it is the task of name reclamation to eliminate the unnecessary names. This is accomplished in three steps by first computing the maintenance ranges of the values, then reclaiming the unnecessary names, and finally updating the AVAIL sets to reflect the changed names.

4.1 Computing Maintenance Ranges

As seen previously, there are two reasons for maintaining a name: 1) it is still **live**, 2) it still needs to be **available** for debugging. This requires the computation of a maintenance range for each value that includes the entire live range of the value and also its Available range. Symbolically,

$$MR_v = R_{Av} \cup R_{Lv}$$

where R_{Av} is the *available* range of the value computed *in the sequential code* and mapped into the transformed code, and R_{Lv} is the *live* range of the value *in the transformed code*.

It is straightforward to calculate R_{Av} by standard live range analysis with extensions to include statements up through the value redefinition. This is computed by the global renaming stage and stored in the AVAIL data set. However it is then incumbent upon the name reclamation stage to map these availability ranges into the transformed code. In this stage it is necessary to view both the AVAIL sets and the transformed code to determine when specific variables must be available to serve debugging requests in the transformed program. Discrete locales of availability are combined into one contiguous availability range, since variables are assigned only once and can therefore become available only once.

In the computation of R_{Lv}, it is assumed that the transformed program may be modified for some form of parallel execution. A live range for a value may end on a certain processor, but if the value is also live on a parallel task, it cannot be considered dead until there is a synchronization point between the tasks. Therefore live range analysis in a parallel environment requires an inspection of all subtasks that will be in concurrent execution. If a variable is live in only one subtask P1, then the variable dies when the last use is past. However, if the variable is also live on another task P2, then the variable is not dead until the P1-P2 synchronization following the last use. Furthermore, the variable is not completely dead until dead on all subtasks.

To illustrate these computations using the code of Figure 2, the A1 variable is available at statements S1-S2, and must be live at S1-S2. However, since S1 and S2 are on concurrent tasks the live range is extended to the synchronization point. Therefore MR_{A1}=S1-S7. Variable Z1 has an Avail range of S2-S3 and live range of S2-S3, giving MR_{Z1}=S2-S3. For variable Z2 the Avail range, S4-S7, and live range, S4, cross parallel tasks giving a giving a maintenance range MR_{Z2}=S1-S7.

Two variables are said to have overlapping maintenance ranges if they must both be maintained at the same time, as in the case of Z1 and Z2 above. When the two variables have the same root name, eg., X1 and X3, and non-overlapping ranges, it is always safe to reuse the address. Symbolically,

$$\text{if } MR_{v1} \cap MR_{v2} = \varnothing$$
$$\text{and } \text{Root } (V_1) = \text{Root } (V_2)$$
$$\text{then } @V_2 = @V_1.$$

The availability of a value can be seen as a further use in generating maintenance ranges. If viewed in this way, the maintenance range within a basic block can be simply defined as beginning at the first position of use of the variable and extending to the last.

In name reclamation, maintenance ranges are computed for each variable in each basic block. These "per block" maintenance ranges are used to create summary maintenance information, such that at each statement it is known whether the maintenance of a particular variable is required *at any time* prior to this statement, or *at any time* beyond this statement. This information is derived from the Control Flow Graph of the program. Backedges are removed from this graph since the reaching definitions of loop variables are handled by explicit mechanisms in renaming. In addition, irreducible flow graph constructs are resolved by removing edges representing backward branches in the written code. The resulting acyclic CFG is used to determine predecessor and successor blocks. Since there may also be concurrent blocks in the CFG, a block X that is concurrent to a block Y is considered both a predecessor and successor to Y.

This graph is then used to create three maintenance sets per block. A Maintenance Range$_i$ set is computed, which holds a minimum and maximum program location for each variable used or available in Basic Block$_i$. The computation of availability makes use of original statement line numbers that have been appended to the statement during renaming. These numbers indicate the original statement locations of lines of program code. After the application of program transformations, these numbers will normally be unordered and, in addition, may contain duplicated or missing numbers. However, these numbers provide crucial mapping information. Each time a statement line number is encountered, the associated AVAIL set is queried and any variable available at this line has its maintenance range updated with the present program location (in the transformed program).

After the MR$_i$ sets are computed for the blocks, they are used to compute boolean sets, Pre$_i$ and Post$_i$ for each block. Pre$_i$ contains a bit for each variable indicating whether the variable has a maintenance range in any predecessor of BB$_i$ (including concurrent blocks). Pre$_i$ is calculated from the immediate predecessors of BB$_i$ by

$$Pre_1 = \varnothing$$
$$Pre_i = \bigcup_{\substack{j \text{ an imm pred} \\ \text{of BB}_i \text{ or concurrent}}} (Pre_j \cup MR_j) \qquad \text{where a non-zero entry in } MR_j.min_k \\ \text{defines a true state}$$

Post$_i$ similarly indicates variables that have maintenance ranges in any successor to BB$_i$. Post$_i$ is calculated in inverse program order from immediate successors and concurrent blocks by

$$Post_{last} = \varnothing$$
$$Post_i = \bigcup_{\substack{j \text{ an imm succ} \\ \text{of BB}_i \text{ or concurrent}}} (Post_j \cup MR_j)$$

4.2 Reclaiming the Names

After the maintenance sets have been computed, names can be reclaimed from the code. The injunction against values sharing a variable name when they have overlapping maintenance ranges allows name reclamation to be modelled as a graph coloring problem. The graph consists of vertices v_i corresponding to each value generated. There is an edge from v_i to v_j whenever v_i and v_j may not share a variable name. Specifically this results when any of the following is true:

    1) the variables have different root names,
    2) the variables have differing dimensionality, or
    3) the variables have intersecting maintenance ranges.

At the beginning of the name reclamation process, this graph contains n vertices and is colored in n colors, where n is the number of variables in the globally renamed program. Name reclamation seeks to *recolor* this graph, using fewer colors. The reclaimed colors represent names that will not appear in the final executable program.

The graph is traversed starting from any arbitrary node. A color pool is maintained which represents the set of names that have been evaluated and will be retained. This set corresponds to the set of names finally held by the *visited* nodes. As the graph is traversed, an attempt is made to recolor each new node encountered with a color already in the color pool. Each candidate color is tried until one is found that has no conflict with the new node, or the list is exhausted. If the node cannot be recolored (the name cannot be reclaimed) then the node's original color is retained and added to the color pool.

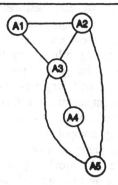

Figure 5 -- Name Reclamation by Recoloring

Figure 5 shows a globally renamed program containing five names, with maintenance range intersections (conflicts) shown as edges. The algorithm starts with an empty color pool and immediately adds A1 to the color set. A2 and A3 are also added because conflicts in the graph do not allow any of these names to share storage. In processing node A4, all colors in the pool (in *last-added* order) will be tested until one is found that does not conflict with A4. If no such color were found, A4 would be retained. However, in this case, after A3 is rejected, A2 is selected to replace A4. In the processing of the A5 node, A3 and A2 are rejected but A1 is selected. The resultant graph contains three names.

The algorithm presented does not compute a minimal name space, as the computation of a minimal name space is an NP-complete problem by a trivial polytransformation from graph coloring. Figure 5 shows that extra names may occasionally be allowed by this algorithm. A4 can be reclaimed by choosing to subsume A4 into either A1 or A2. The choice of A2 as described above will allow A5 to be reclaimed as well (subsumed by A1). However, had the A2 and A1 names been encountered in reverse order, causing A1 to be tried first and chosen, the choice of A1 for A4 forces A5 to be unnecessarily retained. The algorithm tries all active names starting with the last retained and the arbitrariness of this ordering allows nonoptimal name choices to be made in transformed programs. In practice extra names occur infrequently because conflict graphs tend to be characterized by many nodes and few edges.

Computing the maximal degree in the graph allows an upper bound to be placed on the number of colors required = maxdegree + 1. In the graph of Figure 5 the maximum degree is four, and the graph is recolored using three colors. To observe that maxdegree+1 represents an upper bound on retained names in name reclamation, consider the recoloring of the ith node where the degree of $node_i <=$ maxdegree. Assume also that the pool of available colors contains $<=$ maxdegree+1 colors. There are $<=$ maxcolors adjacent to $node_i$. If the color pool contains maxdegree+1 colors, then there exists at least one color not represented on nodes adjacent to $node_i$. This color can be chosen for $node_i$. If the color pool contains $<$ maxdegree+1 colors, then $node_i$'s color can be retained and added to the pool. After the coloring of $node_i$, the color pool still contains $<=$ maxdegree+1 colors.

In untransformed programs, each new definition kills the range behind it and thus there are no maintenance range intersections. As there are therefore no edges, all names are reclaimed except one (i.e., X=>X1).

A criticism of coloring algorithms may be that implementation becomes prohibitively expensive because the graphs involved get quite large. This is especially true for graphs created with single assignment programs. In practice the reclamation algorithm may be implemented without building the graph, using the pre, post and MR sets described above. Collectively they allow the existence of a conflict edge to be efficiently computed.

At each statement the name of a defined variable, V2 may be reclaimed if there exists another variable, V1, previously unreclaimed, such that V1 has the same root name and dimensionality as V2 and the two variables possess nonintersecting maintenance ranges. This last condition is computed by checking that $MR_{v_1} \cap MR_{v_2} = \emptyset$ within the block, that V2 has no maintenance range in a predecessor block and that V1 has no maintenance range in a successor block.

If the maintenance ranges are disjoint then the active name replaces the new name and the new name is reclaimed. This also causes maintenance sets for the active variable to be updated. If no active name can be found, the new name is retained and added to the active set.

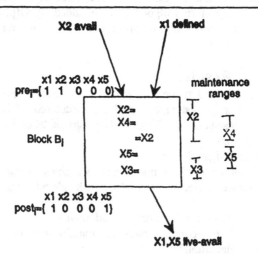

Figure 6 — Name reclamation in a basic block

Figure 6 illustrates the action of name reclamation. The example is simplified by showing only a single root name. The basic block shown is associated with a pre and post set. These indicate that X1 and X2 have maintenance ranges prior to B and that X1 and X5 have maintenance ranges after B. Beside the block the (contiguous) maintenance ranges are displayed. Active names that reach the block are {X1}. During the processing of the block, X2 will not be reclaimed by X1 because X2 has a previous maintenance range, and also because X1 has a later maintenance range. X2 is then added to the active set. X4 is also retained because it has a nonempty intersection with X2 and X1 has a post maintenance range. X5 will be subsumed by X4 because pre (X5) is false, post (X4) is false and X4 and X5 have an empty intersection. This reclamation causes updates to Pre(X4) and Post(X4) such that

$$Pre(X4) = Pre(X4) \mid Pre(X5)$$
$$Post(X4) = Post(X4) \mid Post(X5).$$

The inblock maintenance ranges of X4 and X5 are also merged and information is retained that X5 is henceforth known as X4 in the *ref-pointer* set. Now X3 cannot be subsumed by X4 because X4 has inherited post(X5). However, X3 can be subsumed by X2, and similar set updates are initiated. The block will finally contain only X2 and X4.

Another form of name reclamation occurs within loops. The algorithm will recover the expansion of objects when the loop in question was not chosen for parallelization. In the case of nested loops, each loop is associated with a unique looping subscript. Those associated with parallelized loops are retained while the others are reclaimed. The reconstruction of the looping subscript portion of each name is done whenever the name is added to the active set.

At the end of a block's processing, the exiting active set is saved for use by successor blocks. After all blocks are processed, the AVAIL database is updated with the name changes and rewritten for later use by the debugger.

A more detailed view of the name reclamation algorithm is given in the Appendix. The efficiency of this algorithm is bounded by O(plen x |var|) where plen is the length of the transformed program, and |var| is the number of variables in the transformed program.

5. Experimental Results

Global renaming and name reclamation have been implemented in about 3500 lines of C code in a system designed for structured FORTRAN 77. The experimental testbed consists of ten FORTRAN programs taken from the EISPACK and FFTPACK collections.

The issues investigated are:

1) Are there significant numbers of non-current variables in parallelized code?

2) What is the storage increase associated with global renaming, and name reclamation?

3) What factors are responsible for unreclaimed names?

4) What percentage of non-current variables remain unreportable using global renaming and name reclamation?

Table 1 shows the storage expansion measured in the testbed programs as they pass through the stages of the system. Storage is measured in words and is recorded for the original program, after global renaming, and after parallelization and name reclamation have been applied. For the purposes of measuring the storage implied by expanded variables in loops, any loop with uncertain bounds is assumed to execute 10 times[2]. For example, BAKVEC's original 153 memory words grows to 11937 after global renaming, representing an increase of 78 times the original. After parallelization and reclamation, the final storage requirement of BAKVEC is 283 words, or 1.84 times the original.

The degree to which storage is reclaimed varies inversely with the amount or parallelism inherent in the program. Highly parallel programs reclaim fewer names, while programs that undergo no parallelizing transformations have virtually all their introduced names reclaimed. The increases range from 1.1 to 7.3 times. The unusually high enlargement figures associated with BQR come from a program with deeply nested loops and several large parallelizable loops. The average storage enlargement measured in these programs was over 3900 times after global renaming. Excluding the anomalistic BQR, the average enlargement was still a discouraging 1368 times. However, after name reclamation the average program size was a more reasonable 2.5 times the original.

---

[2] This figure is derived from measurements taken by Knuth [Knu71] who reports the code and execution characteristics of 495 FORTRAN programs.

program	(words) original stor	renamed stor	times incr	after reclamation	times incr
1. BAKVEC	153	11,937	78	283	1.84
2. BALANC	252	33,401	129	392	1.08
3. BALBAK	127	32,721	257	257	2.02
4. BANDV	277	735,021	2653	348	1.25
5. BISECT	150	45,293	300	190	1.27
6. BQR	160	4,283,868	26768	1170	7.31
7. EZFFTI	39	5,880	150	171	4.38
8. EZFFTF	6150	23,967,981	3897	7060	1.15
9. EZFFTB	6148	28,055,204	4563	13848	2.25
10.DCHDC	60	14,560	242	164	2.73
average			3903		2.53

(without BQR 1368)

Table 1 — Storage Enlargement

In these tests the renamed code was parallelized by Parafrase-2, an automatic parallelizing package licensed through the University of Illinois[PGHL890]. It was noted that the parallelization of globally renamed code was significantly more successful than when the code was not renamed. Many more (and larger loops) were found parallelizable, an effect that was directly attributable to the reduction of data dependencies. More than six times as many program lines were found in parallelized loops using this technique.

program	names unreclaimed	due to parall	%	due to debugging	%
1. BAKVEC	130	20	15	110	85
2. BALANC	140	120	86	20	14
3. BALBAK	130	120	92	10	8
4. BANDV	71	64	90	7	10
5. BISECT	40	36	90	4	10
6. BQR	1010	1003	99	7	1
7. EZFFTI	132	130	98	2	2
8. EZFFTF	910	644	71	266	29
9. EZFFTB	7700	6506	84	1194	16
10.DCHDC	104	92	88	12	12
average				82	18

Table 2 -- Analysis of Unreclaimed Names

Table 2 shows the analysis of unreclaimed names. Names that are retained because the multiple versions of a variable need to be simultaneously live (as in a parallel loop) were charged to the parallelism column. Conversely, names retained for the purpose of tracking non-current variables were charged to debugging. Where code is reordered aggressively this number of variables charged to debugging can be high (as in the case of BAKVEC), but normally this number is eclipsed by the variables enabling additional parallelism. Over the group of programs, about 82% of the introduced variables enabled parallelization. The remaining 18% were required for value tracking non-current variables.

Program	Total VI	Non-current VI untreated code	%Total	Unreportable using technique	%Total
1. BAKVEC	288	72	25	1	0.3
2. BALANC	2,499	29	1	0	0
3. BALBAK	432	38	9	0	0
4. BANDV	11,160	318	3	1	0.0
5. BISECT	5,565	57	1	0	0
6. BQR	10,332	361	3.5	0	0
7. EZFFTI	1,960	420	21	15	0.8
8. EZFFTF	12,470	1967	16	0	0
9. EZFFTB	12,335	2070	17	0	0
10.DCHDC	4,225	96	2	0	0
averages			9.8%		0.01%

Table 3 — Variable Unreportability at Debug Time

Table 3 shows the measurement of the degree of non-currentness that exists in the parallelized programs. The number of variable instances was computed as the number of program variables times the number of program lines (only lines past the initial declarations and comments were counted). After transformations were applied the number of non-current variable instances (VI) was counted by counting the number of lines at which each variable is non-current (unreportable at debug time) and summing them over the variable set. The percentage of non-current variable instances was computed and averaged. Finally the number of unreportable variable instances using the proposed debugging technique was counted. These are places where, if a variable value were requested during debugging, the software would report the value is unavailable due to transformations applied. The last column shows this figure as a percentage of the total variable instances.

Some interesting results emerge from these tests. First the ballooning of storage after global renaming is quite large. From a low of 78 times expansion to a high of 26,000 times expansion (average 3800 times), clearly globally renamed code is far too unwieldy to be used directly. The large variation in this expansion depends (exponentially) on the depth of nesting in the program and (linearly) on the program length.

However, name reclamation succeeds in reducing the required storage to a manageable increase of 2.5 times the original. Of these unreclaimed names, a large majority are instrumental in increasing the parallelism in the program. The contribution of these 82% is clearly seen in the improved parallelism figures. The number of lines of code residing in parallelized loops increases an average of 6.4 times.

The experiments show that the existence of non-current variables in parallelized code is a problem. An average of 9.8% of all variable instances are found in non-current ranges in these programs. This figure was unexpectedly high. Without the debugging technique these would be unreportable at debug time. But using these methods only 0.01% of variable instances were still unreportable (due to eliminated code or code moved forward).

These results demonstrate the viability of the method. Not only do they show that the rather invasive nature of parallelizing transformations produces a large percentage of non-current variables, but they also seem to indicate that the cost of debugging such code is small. One could argue that only 18% of the 2.5x storage increase is due to debugging. Since

$$18\% * 1.5\text{x (new unreclaimed names)} = .27$$

it can be concluded that the storage enlargement cost of debugging transformed code is about one quarter of the original storage.

6. Conclusions

As compilers become increasingly autonomous with respect to the restructuring of code, the problem of debugging such transformed code grows in importance. The approach presented in this paper offers significant advantages to the user. It can be used with any transformational package without placing requirements or limitations on the transformations chosen. While the benefits of modular systems design are well-known, this characteristic is particularly useful with parallelizing packages, since the rapid evolution of defined transformations cripples a transformation-dependent approach.

The formation of single assignment code conveys advantages to later stages of code analysis as well. Parallelization is far more successful and all transformations requiring data dependence analysis are simplified. Code partitions are also computed easily. This work suggests that single assignment code captures properties of flow dependence that are so fundamental to the further manipulation of code, especially in a parallel environment, that it is a very appropriate first step to create this form from the input code via global renaming.

Name reclamation makes this a practical and workable approach by removing the unnecessary name allocations. Using this technique, parallelized programs are constructed in modestly expanded spaces, with far more parallelized code. And, most importantly, these programs can be successfully debugged.

APPENDIX — The Name Reclamation Algorithm

<u>Algorithm Reclaim Names(P:Procedure)</u>

1. *Compute Maintenance Sets (MR$_i$, Pre$_i$, Post$_i$)*
2. *Process Program Blocks Reclaiming the names*
3. *Update AVAIL data set with changed names*
end Reclaim Names

<u>Compute Maintenance Sets</u>

1. *Create Program Dependence Graph - Basic Blocks, with concurrency indicated.*
   Mark loop heads and delete backedges. Original statements are marked with original statement numbers.

2. *Read AVAIL Set associated with original sequential program.*

3. *For each Basic Block BB$_i$ do (in any order)*
   Mark the beginning and end of the maintenance range MR$_i$ of each variable used or defined in BB$_i$:
   For each program line of transformed program
   For each USE or DEF var$_k$
   if MR$_i$(k).min undefined then MR$_i$(k).min = program location
   MR$_i$(k).max = program location
   For each line number read on input {pointing to original statement location}
   for each var$_k$ in AVAIL(line number)
   if present loc < MR$_i$(k).min or undefined then
   MR$_i$(k).min = present location
   if present loc > MR$_i$(k).max then
   MR$_i$(k).max = present location

4. *Calculate Pre$_i$ for each BB$_i$ in program order. {Pre is a boolean set indicating which variables have maintenance ranges prior to BB$_i$}*
   $$Pre_i = \varnothing$$
   $$Pre_i = \underset{\substack{j \text{ an imm pred} \\ \text{of } BB_i \text{ or concurrent}}}{\cup} (Pre_j \cup MR_j) \text{ where a non-zero entry in } MR_i.min_k$$
   defines a true state

5. *Calculate Post$_i$ for each BB$_i$ in inverse program order. {Post indicates which variables have maintenance ranges after BB$_i$}*
   $$Post_{last} = \varnothing$$
   $$Post_i = \underset{\substack{j \text{ an imm succ} \\ \text{of } BB_i \text{ or concurrent}}}{\cup} (Post_j \cup MR_j)$$
end Compute Maintenance

Process Program Blocks

1. *Initialize*
    Active_set $_i$ = Ø   {set of active variable names}
    *For each variable k, ref_pointer(k)= 0 {ref_pointer points to new
        name if variable is renamed}*
2. *Rename*
    For each Basic Block BB_i (in program order)
    2.1 Update maintenance sets
        for all var_k do
            if (j = $ref\_pointer_k$) != 0 {var_j is new name of var_k}
            then $Pre_i(j)$ = $Pre_i(k)$ or $Pre_i(j)$
                $Post_i(j)$ = $Post_i(k)$ or $Post_i(j)$
                $MR_i(j).min$ = minimum($MR_i(k).min, MR_i(j).min$)
                $MR_i(j).max$ = maximum($MR_i(k).max, MR_i(j).max$)

    2.2 Compute Active_set$_i$ = $\bigcup\limits_{j=imm\ pred\ BB_i}$ Active_set$_j$

    2.3 Reclaim names in BB_i
        for each USE (var_k)
            if $ref\_pointer_k$ = j (>0) then
                replace var_k with var_j
        *for each DEF (var_k), try to reclaim name(until reclaimed
            or list exhausted):*
            if $ref\_pointer_k$ = j (>0) {variable already reclaimed}
            then replace var_k with var_j
            else
                for each var_A in active_set$_i$ with rootname matching var_k
                    determine whether maintenance ranges are disjoint:
                    *if not $Pre_i(k)$ {no previous maintenance range
                        var_k}*
                    and $MR_i(k).min$ >= present program location
                    *and not $Post_i(A)$ {no later maintenance range for
                        var_A}*
                    and $MR_i(A).max$ <= present program location
                    then {reclaim var_k, replace with var_A}
                    $ref\_pointer_k$ = A
                    $Post_i(A)$ = $Post_i(k)$
                    $MR_i(A).max$ = $MR_i(k).max$
        if var_k not reclaimed
            then {add var_k to active_set$_i$}
            *recompute looping subscript, retaining only those
                associated with parallelized loops*

    2.4 Save active_set$_i$ {to be used by immediate successor blocks}
end Process Blocks

Rewrite AVAIL Sets

For each line$_i$
    For each root name r
        let var_k = AVAIL (i,r)
        if $ref\_pointer_k$ = j then AVAIL (i,r) = var_j
    Rewrite AVAIL set to disk
end Rewrite AVAIL sets

References

[BeDa91] M. Benitez and J. Davidson, "Code Generation for Streaming: an Access/Execute Mechanism", *4th ASPLOS Conference*, Santa Cruz, April 1991, pp. 132-141.

[BiNaRo89] L. Bic, M. Nagel, and J. Roy, "Automatic Data/Program Partitioning Using the Single Assignment Principle", *Supercomputing 89*, pp. 551-556, Aug 1989.

[CoMeRu88] D. Coutant, S. Meloy and M. Ruscetta, "DOC: A Practical Approach to Source-Level Debugging of Globally Optimized Code", *SIGPLAN '88 Conf on Prog Lang Design and Impl*, Atlanta, GA, June 1988, pp. 125-134.

[CyFe87] R. Cytron and J. Ferrante, "What's in a Name? -or- The Value of Renaming for Parallelism Detection and Storage Allocation", *Proceedings of ACM Conference on Parallel Programming*. pp 19-27. 1987.

[CFRWZ91] R. Cytron, J. Ferrante, B. Rosen, M. Wegman and K. Zadeck, "Efficiently Computing Static Single Assignment Form and the Control Dependence Graph", *ACM Trans on Programming Lang and Systems*, October 1991, pp. 451-490.

[Gupt88] R. Gupta, "Debugging Code Reorganized by a Trace Scheduling Compiler," *Proceedings of Supercomputing 88 Conference*, 1988.

[Henn82] J. Hennessy, "Symbolic Debugging of Optimized Code", *ACM Transactions on Programming Languages and Systems*, Vol. 4 No. 3, July 1982. pp. 323-344.

[Knut71] D. Knuth, "An Empirical Study of FORTRAN Programs", *Software Practice and Experience* 1:2, 1971, pp. 105-133.

[PGHLS90] Polychronopoulos, Girkar, Haghighat, Leung, Schouten, "Parafrase-2 User's Newsletter", Center for Supercomputing R&D, University of Illinois, Urbana Illinois. Fall 1990.

[Pineo93] P.P. Pineo, "The High-level Debugging of Parallelized Code using Code Liberation", Ph.D. Thesis, Department of Computer Science, University of Pittsburgh, April 1993.

[PiSo91] P.P. Pineo and M. L. Soffa, "Debugging Parallelized Code using Code Liberation Techniques", *Proceedings of the ACM/ONR Workshop on Parallel and Distributed Debugging*, May 20-21, 1991, pp. 102-114.

[PoSo88] L. Pollock and M. L. Soffa, "High-Level Debugging with the Aid of an Incremental Optimizer", *Proceedings of the 21st Hawaii Intl Conference on System Sciences*, January 1988.

[Wolf89] M. Wolfe, Optimizing Supercompilers for Supercomputers, MIT Press, 1989.

[Wolf92] M. Wolfe, "Beyond Induction Variables", *SIGPLAN '92 conf on Prog Lang Design and Impl*, San Francisco, CA, pp. 162-174.

[Zell83] P. Zellweger, "An Interactive High-Level Debugger for Control-Flow Optimized Programs", *Proceedings of the ACM Sigsoft/Sigplan Soft. Eng. Symp on High-Level Debugging*, March 1983, pp 159-171.

Reducing the Cost of Data Flow Analysis By Congruence Partitioning [†]

Evelyn Duesterwald, Rajiv Gupta, Mary Lou Soffa

Department of Computer Science, University of Pittsburgh, Pittsburgh, PA 15260

Abstract. Data flow analysis expresses the solution of an information gathering problem as the fixed point of a system of monotone equations. This paper presents a technique to improve the performance of data flow analysis by systematically reducing the size of the equation system in any monotone data flow problem. Reductions result from partitioning the equations in the system according to congruence relations. We present a fast $O(n \log n)$ partitioning algorithm, where n is the size of the program, that exploits known algebraic properties in equation systems. From the resulting partition a reduced equation system is constructed that is minimized with respect to the computed congruence relation while still providing the data flow solution at all program points.

1 Introduction

Along with the growing importance of static data flow analysis in current optimizing and parallelizing compilers comes an increased concern about the high time and space requirements of solving data flow problems. Experimental studies show that performing sophisticated analyses over even small to medium-sized programs can take several hours [Lan92]. Phrased in the traditional data flow framework [KU77], the solution of a data flow problem is the greatest fixed point of a system of monotone equations. Each equation expresses the solution at one program point in terms of the solutions at immediately preceding (or succeeding) points. This formulation may result in overly large equation systems, limiting both the time and space efficiency of even the fastest fixed point evaluation algorithm.

A closer inspection of equation systems reveals that their sizes are unnecessarily enlarged due to the inherent inclusion of redundant equations. The structure of data flow equation systems requires the propagation of intermediate results throughout the program, including the propagation to program points where these results are of no relevance. As a consequence, multiple equations in the system carry identical information. Equations that duplicate information already expressed by other equations are redundant and their repeated evaluation during the fixed point iteration is clearly undesirable. If equivalent but smaller equation

---

[†] Partially supported by National Science Foundation Presidential Young Investigator Award CCR-9157371 and Grant CCR-9109089 to the University of Pittsburgh.

systems without redundancies were constructed, fixed point computations would be faster, independent of the evaluation algorithm used.

We present in this paper a systematic approach to minimize data flow equation systems by discovering congruence relationships among equations. Two equations are congruent only if their fixed points are equal. Thus, at least one of two congruent equations is redundant and can therefore be eliminated. Given a congruence relation an equivalent but reduced equation system is constructed by including only a single equation from each class of congruent equations. Our approach is general in that it is applicable to all monotone data flow analysis problems.

Previous approaches to avoid unnecessary evaluations of data flow equations include the methods based on *static single assignment form* [WZ85, AWZ88, RWZ88, CLZ86], *sparse evaluation graphs* [CCF90] and *dependence flow graphs* [JP93]. The idea behind these approaches is to by-pass some of the unnecessary equation evaluations by manipulating the underlying graphical program representation. We show that, by viewing the problem as an algebraic problem of congruence relations, our approach allows for conceptually simple algorithms that are both more general and powerful than previous graph-oriented methods.

The results of this paper are summarized as follows. We define a *congruence relation* among data flow equations that is based on exploiting the known idempotence property of the *meet* operator in the system. No assumptions are made on the sequence of intermediate values an equation may take during the fixed point iteration. These sequences of intermediate values are highly dependent on the particular iteration strategy that is used to compute the fixed point, but the notion of congruence is a valid relation for any such strategy. A fast partitioning algorithm is presented to compute the idempotence congruence relation in $O(n \log n)$ time and $O(n)$ space, where n is the size of the program. Using the computed congruence relation, a reduced equation system is constructed that only contains a single equation from each congruence class. By the definition of congruence, it is sufficient to compute the fixed point over only the reduced system using any of the standard evaluation strategies.

The approach of reducing equation systems by computing congruence relations can easily be extended to include other notions of congruence. The congruence relations discussed in [DST80, NO80] are based on common subexpressions. Alpern et al. [AWZ88] used a fast $O(n \log n)$ algorithm due to Hopcroft for minimizing finite automata to compute congruences by common subexpression for program optimization. We show that Hopcroft's algorithm can equally well be applied to disover common subexpression in data flow equations systems in order to enable further reductions.

The asymptotic performance of congruence partitioning to reduce a data flow equation system only depends on the size of the equation system. The complexity of the data flow problem, i.e., the cost of actually evaluating the equations, does not impact on the performance of the partitioning algorithm. The complexity of data flow problems varies dramatically, ranging from simple problems, such as live variable analysis, that can be implemented efficiently using bit vectors, to sophisticated time- and space-intensive analyses, such as alias analysis. Naturally, the benefits of congruence partitioning increase with the complexity of the data flow problem.

We present the pertinent background in data flow analysis in Section 2. Section 3 introduces congruence relations among data flow equations. The idempotence congruence relation along with our fast partitioning algorithm is presented in Section 4. Section 5 discusses congruence computations based on common subexpressions. We compare congruence partitioning with previous work and discuss other related work in Section 6. Conclusions are given in Section 7.

2 Data Flow Equation Systems

A data flow analysis is defined over a graphical representation of a program, usually the control flow graph $G = (N, E, n_0)$. The nodes N represent basic blocks [ASU86] in the program with a unique entry node n_0. The edges E represent transfer of control among basic blocks. We assume that $|E| = O(|N|)$. Given a node $n \in N$, $pred(n)$ ($succ(n)$) denotes the set of immediate predecessors (successors) of node n in G.

Data flow analyses are modeled in a *data flow framework* $D = (L, F, G, m)$, where:

- $(L, \leq, \bot, \top, \wedge)$ is a semi-lattice with a set L, a partial order $\leq$, a least element $\bot$ (bottom), a greatest element $\top$ (top) and a meet operator $\wedge$, such that for all $x, y, z \in L$: $x \wedge x = x$ (idempotence), $x \wedge y = y \wedge x$ (commutativity), and $x \wedge (y \wedge z) = (x \wedge y) \wedge z$ (associativity).
- $F \subseteq \{f : L \mapsto L\}$ is a space of monotone flow functions over L.
- $G = (N, E, n_0)$ is a control flow graph
- $m : N \mapsto F$ is a mapping of program nodes to functions in F.

The function $m(n)$ mapped to a node n (also denoted f_n) models the data flow when execution passes through node n. If $x \in L$ holds on entry of a node n then $f_n(x) \in L$ holds on exit from node n. [2].

A data flow framework induces a *system of data flow equations* parameterized by the nodes in the control flow graph:

$$x[n_0] = f_{n_0}(\bot)$$
$$x[n] = f_n(\bigwedge_{p \in pred(n)} x[p]) \text{ for } n \neq n_0$$

The solution of a data flow framework is the *greatest fixed point* assignment gfp : $N \mapsto L$ of the equation system based on the initial value $\top$. The monotonicity of F ensures that the greatest fixed point $gfp(n)$ of each equation $x[n]$ exists and is unique. For each node $n \in N$, $gfp(n)$ describes the data flow solution that holds on exit of node n.

---

[2] The framework models both forward and backward analyses by assuming that in a backward analysis the transposed control flow graph $G^t = (N, E^t)$ is used, where $E^t = \{(n, m) \mid (m, n) \in G\}$.

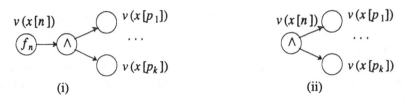

Fig. 1. The translation of equations into graphs.

The equation system X can be represented by a labeled directed graph $G = (V, E)$. The vertices in V represent equation variables and the operations of the right hand side of equations. An edge (v, w) in E describes that the expression represented by vertex v depends on the input represented by vertex w. We refer to this graph as an *equation graph*.

An equation $x[n] = f_n(\bigwedge_{p \in pred(n)} x[p])$ is translated into the graph shown in Fig. 1 (i). Corresponding to the function symbol f_n is a vertex $v(x[n])$ with $label(v(x[n])) = f_n$ that has a single successor vertex with label $\wedge$. The vertex labeled $\wedge$ has successors $v(x[p])$ for each predecessor p of node n. If the function f_n is the identity function, the equation reduces to $x[n] = \bigwedge_{p \in pred(n)} x[p]$. In this case no vertex for the function symbol is created, and the vertex $v(x[n])$ is the vertex labeled $\wedge$ as shown in Fig. 1 (ii). We partition the vertex set V into a set $V_\wedge$ of vertices labeled $\wedge$ (meet vertices) and a set V_f of vertices with a label denoting any other function symbol (function vertices).

Due to the direct correspondence between the graphical and textual representations of an equation system we will not always explicitly distinguish between the two. In discussing equation systems we assume that their graphs are transformed into graphs whose vertices have an indegree and outdegree of at most 2. This transformation is analogous to transforming the textual representation of the equation system into some form of three-address-code. The associativity of the meet operator ensures that a graph can always be transformed into this form by adding some additional vertices for each vertex whose indegree or outdegree is greater than 2. At most a constant number of vertices is added per edge in this process and the number of vertices remains $O(n)$ [DST80], where $n = |N|$ is the number of nodes in the control flow graph.

As the running example in this paper we consider alias analysis performed over procedure Insert, shown below. Alias analysis computes pairs of aliased variables. To simplify the representation, we consider a simple alias analysis that assumes that if a variable q is aliased to a variable p then any variable that q points to is aliased by any variable p points to. The lattice elements are collections of alias relations. A collection could be simply a set of alias pairs or, alternatively, a partition of the variables into sets of aliased variables. We omit showing the control flow graph for procedure Insert. The relevant program points at which data flow information is computed are numbered in curly braces in procedure Insert.

```
procedure Insert(x, val) /* insert a value val in a binary tree x */
begin
    val:=h(val); { 1 }
    repeat { 2 }
        p:=x; { 3 }
        if (val < x->key) then x=x->left; { 4 }
                          else x=x->right; { 5 }
    ;{ 6 }
    until (x = NULL); { 7 }
    new(x); x->key:=val; x->left:=NULL; x->right:=NULL; { 8 }
    if (val < p->key) then p->left:=x{ 9 }
        else p->right:=x; { 10 }
    ;{ 11 }
end
```

The equation system that expresses the analysis over procedure Insert is shown in Fig 2(i) along with its equation graph in Fig. 2 (ii). Each equation $x[n]$ refers to the alias information that holds at the program point n marked in procedure Insert. The meet operator $\wedge$ represents the union of two collections of alias relations into a single collection. The data flow equations are also based on a function $kill[y]$ that takes as an argument a collection of alias relations C and eliminates all alias relations for variable y from C. For more details of the analysis we refer the reader to [CC77]. With respect to congruence partitioning, the meet $\wedge$ and other functions like $kill[y]$ are merely uninterpreted symbols.

3   Congruence Relations

Given an equation system, our objective is to minimize the size of the system without evaluating any equation. Unfortunately, even the following restricted version of this minimization problem is NP-complete [GJ79]: Given a set of expressions constructed from uninterpreted constants and only the single commutative and associative operator, determine the minimum number of operations needed to evaluate all expressions. Thus, in general, we cannot expect an efficient algorithm to be able to eliminate all redundancies from X. However, we show that it is possible to minimize X with respect to certain well-defined classes of redundancies using a fast algorithm.

Redundancies are eliminated by discovering congruence relationships among equations. We only consider relationships among the final fixed point values of equations; two equations $x[n]$ and $x[m]$ in a system X are called *congruent* only if $gfp(n) = gfp(m)$.

Congruence is an equivalence relation (symmetric, reflexive and transitive) and therefore induces a partition π of the equations into *congruence classes*. All equations that are contained in the same congruence class in π have an identical fixed point. Given π we can reduce the original equation system by eliminating all but one equation from each congruence class. By the definition of congruence, the resulting reduced system is guaranteed to provide the same fixed point solution as the original system, independent of the particular evaluation strategy used. If

$x[1] = init$

$x[2] = x[1] \wedge x[7]$

$x[3] = kill[p](x[2]) \wedge (p, x)$

$x[4] = x[3]$

$x[5] = x[3]$

$x[6] = x[4] \wedge x[5]$

$x[7] = x[6]$

$x[8] = kill[x](x[7])$

$x[9] = (p, x) \wedge X[8]$

$x[10] = x[8] \wedge (p, x)$

$x[11] = x[9] \wedge x[10]$

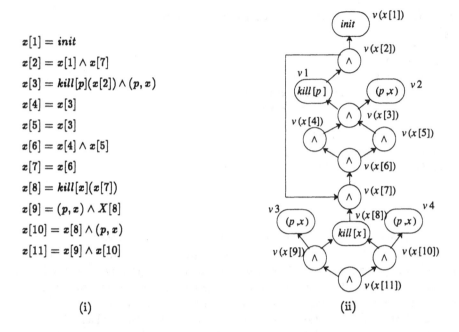

(i)   (ii)

Fig. 2. The data flow equation system (i) for a simple alias analysis over procedure Insert and its graphical representation (ii).

needed, the solution of the reduced system can later be expanded to the solution of all original equations using the computed partition π.

The following sections discuss how congruence relationships among the equations can be discovered by exploiting properties in the equation graph. We first present a partitioning algorithm that discovers congruence based on the idempotence property of the meet operator. We then show how an algorithm due to Hopcroft for minimizing finite automata can be adapted to discover additional congruences that result from common subexpressions. Fig. 3 shows the reductions in the equation system for the alias analysis of procedure Insert that are achieved by congruence partitioning explained in the next sections.

4   Congruence by Idempotence

This section describe the detection of congruences among data flow equations that result from the idempotence of the meet operator $\wedge$. Recall that a data flow equation is of the form:

$$x[n] = f_n\left(\bigwedge_{p \in pred(n)} x[p]\right)$$

Trivial congruences result from a special case of equations, where the function f_n is the identity function and node n has only a single predecessor p. In this

$$x[1] = init$$
$$x[2] = x[1] \wedge x[7]$$
$$x[3] = kill[p](x[2]) \wedge (p, x)$$
$$x[4] = x[3]$$
$$x[5] = x[3]$$
$$x[6] = x[4] \wedge x[5]$$
$$x[7] = x[6]$$
$$x[8] = kill[x](x[7])$$
$$x[9] = x[8] \wedge (p, x)$$
$$x[10] = x[8] \wedge (p, x)$$
$$x[11] = x[9] \wedge x[10]$$

(i)

$$x[1] = init$$
$$x[2] = x[1] \wedge x[3]$$
$$x[3] = kill[p](x[2]) \wedge (p, x)$$
$$x[8] = kill[x](x[3])$$
$$x[9] = x[8] \wedge (p, x)$$
$$x[10] = x[8] \wedge (p, x)$$
$$x[11] = x[9] \wedge x[10]$$

(ii)

$$x[1] = init$$
$$x[2] = x[1] \wedge x[3]$$
$$x[3] = kill[p](x[2]) \wedge (p, x)$$
$$x[8] = kill[x](x[3])$$
$$x[9] = x[8] \wedge (p, x)$$

(iii)

Fig. 3. The original equation system for the alias analysis of procedure Insert (i), the reduced system after partitioning by idempotence (ii), and the reduced system after a combined partitioning by common subexpression and idempotence and (iii).

case the equation reduces to a simple copy equation $x[n] = x[p]$. Clearly, the fixed points of $x[n]$ and $x[p]$ are identical and $x[n]$ and $x[p]$ are congruent.

The congruence relation based on copies can easily be computed in a single pass over the equation system. Initially, we assume each equation $x[n]$ is in a separate congruence class. For each copy equation $x[n] = x[m]$ that is encountered, the congruence class of $x[m]$ is merged into class of $x[n]$ creating a single class. A reduced equation system without copies is constructed by including from each congruence class only a single representative equation. Each operand that occurs in an included equation is replaced by the representative of its congruence class.

Idempotence congruence extends this trivial notion of copy congruences by also covering *hidden copies*. A hidden copy is an equation of the form $x = y \wedge z$ such that y and z are congruent. By the idempotence of the meet operator, the congruence of y and z implies that $gfp(y) \wedge gfp(z)$ reduces to $gfp(y)$ and equation x is essentially a copy. Thus, it can be determined that all three variables x, y, and z are congruent. Over an equation graph G, we obtain the following definition with respect to the idempotent meet operation $\wedge$ in G.

Definition 1 (Congruence by idempotence). *Let $G = (V, E)$ be an equation graph. A relation C on V is called an idempotence congruence relation, if $(v, w) \in C$ implies one of the following conditions:*
(1) $v = w$ (the vertices v and w are identical), or
(2) one of the vertices, say v, is labeled $\wedge$ and $(v, u) \in E$ implies $(u, w) \in C$

To verify that C is indeed a congruence relation we have to ensure that the base case of the recursive rule (2) as well as the application of rule (2) can only yield congruent pairs of vertices. The base case of rule (2) declares $(v, w) \in C$ if w is the sole destination of edges leaving v. In this case v represents a copy equation and v and w are congruent. If all destinations of edges leaving v are congruent to a vertex w then v reduces to w by idempotence and v and w are congruent (application of rule 2).

By its recursive definition, the idempotence congruence relation is not unique if G contains cycles. Consider the equations in (a):

$$
\begin{array}{lll}
x[1] = f(x[0]) & \qquad x[1] = f(x[0]) & \qquad x[1] = f(x[0]) \\
x[2] = x[1] \wedge x[3] & \qquad x[2] = x[1] \wedge x[2] & \\
x[3] = x[2] & & \\
\qquad \text{(a)} & \qquad \text{(b)} & \qquad \text{(c)}
\end{array}
$$

The partition $\pi_1 = \{c_1 = \{x[1]\}, c_2 = \{x[2], x[3]\}\}$ with the corresponding system (b) describes an idempotence congruence relation. However, the partition $\pi_2 = \{c_1 = \{x[1], x[2], x[3]\}\}$ also describes an idempotence congruence relation that provides the reduced system (c)[3]. We are interested in the maximal idempotence congruence relation (fewest number of congruence classes) for an equation graph. For the remainder of this paper, we use the symbol $C^\star$ to refer to the maximal idempotence congruence relation according to Definition 1. The relation $C^\star$ provides the *coarsest* partition $\pi^\star$ of the vertices in an equation graph such that two vertices are in the same partition only if they are congruent according to Definition 1.

We present a fast partitioning algorithm to compute $\pi^\star$ that starts with an initial partition π that places all possibly congruent pairs of equations in the same class. The partition π is iteratively refined until a stable partition $\pi^\star$ is reached that is consistent with the definition of $C^\star$. Given partition $\pi^\star$ we construct the equation system that is minimized with respect to idempotence congruence in the same way as previously described. That is, from each congruence class in $\pi^\star$ only one representative equation is included. The resulting equation system contains no copy equations and no hidden copies due to idempotence.

4.1 The Partitioning Algorithm

Computing the partition $\pi^\star$ by iterative refinement requires first determining an appropriate initial partition. If two vertices are initially placed in different congruence classes they can never discovered to be congruent. Thus, the initial partition must *overestimate* the congruence relation $C^\star$. A partition π overestimates $C^\star$, if $(v, w) \in C^\star$ implies that the vertices v and w are placed in the same congruence class in π. In order to enable the partitioning algorithm to converge quickly to $\pi^\star$, we are interested in finding the *finest* initial partition that overestimates $C^\star$.

Standard graph partitioning algorithms [AHU74] are based on an initial partition of the vertices by their label. Unfortunately, we cannot follow this approach for computing $C^\star$. Although function vertices with a different label cannot be congruent by idempotence, meet vertices may be congruent to any function ver-

---

[3] Note that the congruence between $x[1]$ and $x[2]$ only holds with respect to the *greatest* fixed point defined with the initial value $\top$ at each equation.

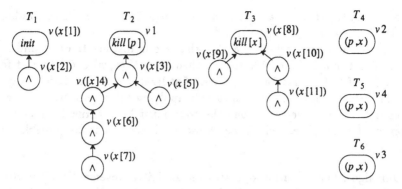

Fig. 4. A reverse DFST partition $\pi = T_1, \ldots T_6$ of the equation graph from Fig. 2(ii).

tex. We present a new partitioning algorithm and show how an overestimating initial partition of the vertices can be constructed in a canonical way.

Congruence classes in a partition are represented as *reverse trees* of vertices in an equation graph G. A reverse tree is a tree in which edges are directed from children to parent vertices. Thus, $\pi = T_1, \ldots, T_k$ is a collection of disjoint reverse trees and each tree T_i is a subgraph of the equation graph G. We will often refer to the reverse trees in a partition simply as trees and use the following notation for a given partition forest π. The root vertex of a tree T in π is denoted $root(T)$. For a given vertex v in a tree T, $parent(v)$ is the unique predecessor of v in G that is contained in T.

We construct an initial partition of the vertices in an equation graph G during a single reverse depth-first traversal of G, i.e., a depth-first traversal of the transposed graph of G. The resulting partition contains one tree (congruence class) for each function vertex in G. The tree T_v for a function vertex v is constructed by traversing each reachable edge in reverse direction, such that T_v is a reverse depth-first spanning tree (DFST) that is rooted at v and that does not include any other function vertex. The resulting forest of reverse DFSTs is called a *reverse DFST partition*. A reverse DFST partition for the equation graph from Fig. 2(ii) is shown in Fig. 4.

A reverse DFST partition for an equation graph is not unique since selections among multiple candidates to visit next are made arbitrarily. We show in the following lemma that any reverse DFST partition π safely overestimates C^*.

Lemma 1 *Let π be a reverse DFST partition for a graph G and let v and w be vertices in G. If $(v, w) \in C^*$ then v and w are in the same tree in π.*

Proof. For a vertex v in a tree T in π we use the notation $level(v)$ to denote the length of the path from v to $root(T)$. Given two distinct trees T_1 and T_2 in π, we first show that if v is a vertex in T_1 then $(v, root(T_2)) \notin C^*$ by induction on $l = level(v)$. (Basis $l = 0$) Clearly, $(root(T_1), root(T_2)) \notin C^*$ since two distinct function vertices cannot be congruent by idempotence. (Ind. $l > 0$) By hypothesis $(w, root(T_2)) \notin C^*$ if $level(w) < l$. Assume $(v, root(T_2)) \in C^*$ and $level(v) = l$.

Then by rule (2) of Def. 1 also $(parent(v), root(T_1)) \in C^\star$ which contradicts the hypothesis since $level(parent(v)) < l$.

Consider now two vertices v and w that are in distinct trees T_1 and T_2 and neither v nor w are the root vertex in their tree. If $(v, w) \in C^\star$ then it follows by rule (2) of Def. 1 that for the parent of at least one of the vertices, say v, we obtain $(parent(v), w) \in C^\star$. By repeatedly applying this argument, we eventually derive that the root vertex of one the trees must be congruent under $C^\star$ to a vertex in the other tree, which was however shown not to be possible. Hence, $(v, w) \notin C^\star$. $\qquad\qquad\qquad\qquad\qquad\qquad\qquad\qquad\qquad\qquad\qquad\qquad\qquad\square$

Our algorithm *Partition* operates on an initial reverse DFST partition π by subsequently refining π until the current partition is consistent with the definition of $C^\star$. In the resulting partition $\pi^\star$ two vertices v and w are left in the same tree only if $(v, w) \in C^\star$.

Algorithm *Partition*, shown below, maintains two lists of vertices, *worklist* and *splitlist*. *Worklist* is a list of current partition trees to be examined. Each tree T in *worklist* is examined in line (5) to determine whether it contains an interior vertex v that has a successor not in T. In this case, the vertices v and $parent(v)$ in T cannot be congruent under idempotence. To ensure that the two vertices do not remain in the same tree, vertex v is placed in *splitlist*. During the inner loop the tree of each vertex u in *splitlist* is split by disconnecting the subtree rooted at u. After the split one of the two resulting subtrees is placed in *worklist* to ensure that vertices that may trigger a subsequent split will be examined. *Partition* terminates when *worklist* is exhausted with the final partition $\pi^\star$.

Algorithm *Partition* performs the following operation on partition trees:
split(v): disconnects and returns the subtree rooted at v of the tree containing vertex v.

Algorithm *Partition* (Partitioning by idempotence)
Input: Equation graph $G = (V = V_f \cup V_\wedge, E)$
Output: Partition $\pi^\star = T_1, \ldots, T_k$ of V according to $C^\star$
Method:
1. create an initial reverse DFST partition $\pi = T_1, \ldots, T_l$ of the vertices in V;
2. *worklist* $\leftarrow \{T_1, \ldots, T_l\}$;
3. **while** *worklist* $\neq \emptyset$ **do**
4.   select and remove a tree T from *worklist*;
5.   *splitlist* $\leftarrow \{v \in V_\wedge \mid v$ has one successor in T and one successor not in $T\}$;
6.   **for each** $u \in$ *splitlist* such that u is not a root vertex in π **do**
7.   let T_1 be the tree containing vertex u;
8.   add $T_2 \leftarrow split(u)$ as a new tree to π;
9.   **if** $T_1 \in$ *worklist* **then** add T_2 to *worklist*
10.   **else** add the smaller of T_1 and T_2 to *worklist*;
11.   **endfor**;
12. **endwhile**;

We apply *Partition* to the initial reverse DFST partition from Fig. 4. The initial partition π corresponding to Fig. 4 and the final partition $\pi^\star$ after algorithm

Partition terminates are shown below, where congruence classes are displayed in columns. The original complete equation system was shown in Fig. 3 (i). The final partition $\pi^\star$ describes the congruences in that system that result from the copy equations $x[4], x[5], x[7]$ and from the hidden copy equation $x[6]$. Specifically, all equations in the column for $x[3]$ in $\pi^\star$ are found to have the same fixed point as equation $x[3]$. The reduced equation systems in which the four redundant (hidden) copy equations are eliminated is shown in Fig. 3 (ii).

	π									
$x[1]$	$x[3]$	$x[8]$								
$x[2]$	$x[4]$	$x[9]$								
	$x[5]$	$x[10]$								
	$x[6]$	$x[11]$								
	$x[7]$									

			$\pi^\star$					
$x[1]$	$x[2]$	$x[3]$	$x[8]$	$x[9]$	$x[10]$	$x[11]$
		$x[4]$				
		$x[5]$				
		$x[6]$				
		$x[7]$				

4.2 Analysis

We show that algorithm *Partition* computes the congruence relation $C^\star$, that is, the output partition $\pi^\star$ is the coarsest partition, such two vertices v and w are contained in the same tree in $\pi^\star$ only if $(v, w) \in C^\star$. We proceed with the proof by first showing in Lemma 2 that $\pi^\star$ is consistent with the definition of $C^\star$, that is, $\pi^\star$ is not too coarse. We then show in Lemma 3 that algorithm *Partition* is optimal in that $\pi^\star$ is the coarsest consistent partition.

Lemma 2 (Consistency). *Partition $\pi^\star$ is consistent with the definition of $C^\star$, for if v is a vertex in a tree T in $\pi^\star$ and v is not the root vertex of T then all successors of v are also in T.*

Proof. Assume v is a vertex in a tree T in $\pi^\star$ that is not the root vertex of T. Then v has one successor *parent*(v) in T. Assume on the contrary to the claim that v has another successor w not in T. In the initial partition π, vertex v is in some tree $T_1 \supseteq T$ and all trees are initially placed in *worklist*. The construction of *splitlist* in line (5) implies that w must also be in T_1 since otherwise a split during the first iteration would have separated vertex v from *parent*(v) contradicting the assumptions. Now, consider the point during the algorithm at which vertex w is separated from the vertices v and *parent*(v) and the vertices are placed in two different trees $T_2 \subseteq T_1$ containing w and $T_2' \subseteq T_1$ containing v and *parent*(v). After this separation at least one of T_2 and T_2' will be in *worklist*, which implies that vertex v will be separated from *parent*(v) after the new contents of *worklist* are exhausted, which again contradicts the assumptions. Hence, all successors of v must be in T. □

Lemma 3 (Optimality). *Partition $\pi^\star$ is as coarse as possible, that is, if $(v, w) \in C^\star$ then v and w are in the same tree in partition $\pi^\star$.*

Proof. We show by induction on the number i of *split* operations performed in algorithm *Partition* that two vertices v and w are in two distinct trees only if $(v, w) \notin C^\star$. (Basis $i = 0$) The claims holds for the initial partition by Lemma

1. (Ind. $i > 0$) Let π be the partition resulting after $i - 1$ split operations. The i-th split operation splits an edge (v, w) in some tree T only if v has another successor u in a different tree and by induction hypothesis: $(u, w) \notin C^\star$ and $(u, root(T)) \notin C^\star$. Hence, by rule (2) of Definition 1: $(v, w) \notin C^\star$ and also $(v, root(T)) \notin C^\star$. Let T_1 be the subtree of T rooted at v and let T_2 be the remaining portion of T after disconnecting T_1. Since the root vertices of the two trees, v and $root(T)$, are not congruent under $C^\star$, an analogous induction argument to the one in the proof of Lemma 1 shows that no vertex in T_1 can be congruent to a vertex in T_2 under $C^\star$. Thus, two vertices are in different trees in the new partition only if they are not congruent under $C^\star$. $\qquad\square$

Corollary 1. *Algorithm Partition correctly computes the idempotence congruence relation $C^\star$ (by lemmas 2 and 3).*

Theorem 1 (Complexity). *Algorithm Partition can be implemented in $O(n \log n)$ time and $O(n)$ space, where n is the number of vertices in the equation graph G.*

Proof. Constructing the initial partition takes $O(n)$ time. To calculate the total time spent in the while loop, we consider the number of times the tree of each vertex can be placed in *worklist*. Each time the current tree of a vertex w is added to *worklist* the tree's size is at most half the size of the previous tree containing w. Hence, a vertex' tree can be at most $\log n + 1$ times in *worklist*. *Splitlist* is constructed by a scan of the vertices whose tree was removed from *worklist* and the total number of vertices scanned is $O(n \log n)$. Operation *split* is executed at most n times, since there can be at most n partitions. Each call to *split* is implemented in $O(1)$ time by maintaining for each vertex a pointer to its position in the partition forest. To find the smaller of the two subtrees after a split in time proportional to the smaller tree (i.e., in total time $O(n \log n)$), the vertices in the two trees are counted by alternating between the trees after each vertex. The algorithm also requires a pointer for each vertex to its current partition tree, which is updated after each split only for the vertices of the smaller resulting tree. In summary, the total time spent in executing algorithm *Partition* is $O(n \log n)$. The size of no auxiliary data structure is more than $O(n)$ and $O(n)$ space is used to store the partition. $\qquad\square$

If the equation graph is constructed as described in Section 2, the size n of the graph is linear in the size of the program. In data flow problems that are based on a product lattice L^V, such as constant propagation, the equation at each program point is a vector $x = (x_1, \ldots, x_V)$. In constant propagation there is a component x_i for each of V program variables. In general, it will be beneficial to break the vector equation x into a set of V components equations $x_1, \ldots, x_V$ in order to expose additional congruences. In this granularity, the size of the equation graph increases to $V \times n$.

5 Congruence by Common Subexpression

Additional reductions in an equation system can be achieved by extending our definition of congruence to capture redundancies that result from sources other than idempotence. In [DST80, NO80] congruence relations are defined based on common subexpressions. For example, in Fig. 3 (ii), the term $x[8] \wedge (p, x)$ is a common subexpression in equations $x[9]$ and $x[10]$. The congruence relation by common subexpression is defined below by observing the commutativity of the meet operator.

Definition 2 (Congruence by common subexpression). *Let $G = (V, E)$ be an equation graph. A relation S on V is called common subexpression congruence relation if for vertices v and w with successors $v_1, \ldots, v_k$ and $w_1, \ldots, w_k$, $(v, w) \in S$ implies $label(v) = label(w)$ and $\forall\, 1 \le i \le k$:*

$$\begin{cases} (v_i, w_{p(i)}) \in S \text{ for some permutation } p \text{ on } \{1, \ldots k\} & \text{if } label(v) = \wedge \\ (v_i, w_i) \in S & \text{otherwise} \end{cases}$$

Partitioning a graph by common subexpression is a well known problem and a fast $O(n \log n)$ algorithm is due to Hopcroft's algorithm for minimizing finite automata [Hop71]. Among other applications, Hopcroft's algorithm was used to eliminate common subexpression in program optimization [AWZ88]. We present a different application by employing the algorithm to reduce data flow equation systems.

Hopcroft's algorithm starts with an initial partition π in which all vertices with an identical label are placed in the same congruence class in π. The algorithm iterates over the congruence classes to subsequently refine the current partition until it is consistent with Definition 2. The algorithm terminates with the coarsest partition in which two equations are in the same class only if they are congruent under S. An adaptation of Hopcroft's partitioning algorithm to partition equation graphs is shown below.

Algorithm *An adaptation of Hopcroft's partitioning algorithm*
Input: Equation graph $G = (V = V_f \cup V_\wedge, E)$
Output: Partition $\pi^* = C_1, \ldots, C_k$, where C_i is a collection of vertices in G
1. create an initial partition $\pi = C_1, \ldots, C_l$ of the vertices in V by their label;
2. $worklist \leftarrow \{C_1, \ldots, C_l\}$;
3. **while** $worklist \neq \emptyset$ **do**
4.   select and remove C_i from $worklist$;
5.   **for** $n \leftarrow 1$ **to** 2 **do**
6. $splitlist \leftarrow \{v \in V_f \mid$ the n-th succ. of v is in $C_i\}$
7. $\cup \; \{v \in V_\wedge \mid v$ has exactly n succ. in $C_i\}$; /* commut. of $\wedge$ */
8.   **for each** C_j such that $(splitlist \cap C_j) \neq \emptyset$ **and** $(C_j \not\subseteq splitlist)$ **do**
9.   create a new tree collection C in π;
10.   move each $u \in (splitlist \cap C_j)$ to C;
12.   **if** $C_j \in worklist$ **then** add C to $worklist$
13.   **else** add the smaller of C_j and C to $worklist$;
14.   **endfor; endfor;**
15. **endwhile**

If Hopcroft's algorithm is applied over the equation graph for the alias analysis of procedure Insert, the two equations $x[9] = (p, x) \wedge x[8]$ and $x[10] = x[8] \wedge (p, x)$ in Fig. 3 (i) are discovered to be congruent. The discovery of congruences due to common subexpressions may enable the detection of additional congruences by idempotence. For example, once we know that the two equations $x[9]$ and $x[10]$ are congruent, it can in turn be determined that equation $x[11] = x[9] \wedge x[10]$ is actually a hidden copy and in fact all three equations $x[9]$, $x[10]$ and $x[11]$ are congruent. To enable these second order effects, we can incorporate the results of common subexpression partitioning into the initial partition for idempotence partitioning. This is achieved by applying algorithm *Partition* to the equation graph that results if all vertices that were already found to be congruent are merged into a single vertex. The reductions in the equation system from Fig. 3 (i) that are enabled in this process are shown in Fig. 3 (iii). The additional improvements over the equations system that results from only partitioning by idempotence (Fig. 3 (ii)) are due to the discovery of the congruence among equations $x[9]$, $x[10]$ and $x[11]$.

Unfortunately, applying each partitioning algorithm once may not provide optimal results. In general, congruences that are found based on idempotence may enable the discovery of additional common subexpressions and vice versa. Thus, to find the maximal number of congruences requires computing the transitive closure of the union of the two congruence relations. This closure can be computed by iterating over the two partitioning algorithms until no more congruence can be discovered. Each time a new iteration is started the size of the equation graph is reduced resulting in a bound of $O(n^2 \log n)$. In practice, the number of common subexpressions in an equation graph may be small, in which case, it may be sufficient to compute each congruence partitioning only once. While this may sacrifice optimality, equation system reduction remains fast. Experimentation is needed to determine the benefits of computing the iterated congruence closure.

6 Related Work

A number of previous methods has focused on suppressing some of the unnecessary equation evaluations by manipulating the underlying graphical program representation. The sparse evaluation graph (SEG) approach [CCF90], achieves reductions in data flow equation systems indirectly by specializing a program's control flow graph G with respect to each analysis problem such that smaller equation systems will be generated. The SEG is obtained from a control flow graph G by eliminating some of the nodes in G that have an identity flow function. The construction of a SEG requires $O(e+n^2)$ time using dominance frontiers [CCF90] and $O(e \times \alpha(e))$ time using a recent more complicated algorithm [CF93], where e is the number of edges in a program's control flow graph G and n is the number of nodes in G. The SEG approach compares directly with our idempotence congruence partitioning algorithm in that the removal of control flow graph nodes with identity flow functions results in the elimination of redundant (hidden) copy equations. However, there are important problems for which the SEG approach fails to eliminate all (hidden) copies and algorithm *Partition* would construct strictly smaller equation systems. Constant propagation is an example of such a problem. It is likely in constant propagation that no flow graph nodes have an identity flow function, in which case the SEG would be identical to the original flow graph graph. However, even flow graph nodes with a non-identity flow function generate copy and hidden copy equations for all program variables that are not assigned a new value within that node. As our partitioning approach operates on the level of individual equation operations, these redundancies are exposed and can therefore be eliminated. In addition, congruence partitioning is, unlike the SEG approach, extensible to discover redundancies due to common subexpressions enabling further reductions in an equation system.

Other methods that improve data flow analysis by building specialized program graphs are applicable to only certain data flow problems. The *partitioned variable technique* [Zad84] constructs for each variable a simplified flow graph that enables a fast evaluation of the solution. However, this method is restricted to *partitionable* data flow problems that permit the analysis of each variable partition in isolation. The *global value graph* [RL77, RT82], *static single assignment form* (SSA) [SS70] and *dependence flow graphs* [JP93] are graphical representations that provide connections between definitions and uses of program variables. SSA form is constructed in $O(e + n^2)$ time based on dominance frontiers [CFR+91] and in $O(e \times \alpha(e))$ time based on a recent algorithm [CF93]. The benefits of using SSA for data flow analysis are limited to problems that are based on definition-use connections, such as constant propagation [WZ85]. A problem like available expressions does not benefit from SSA. The same limitation applies to the related *dependence flow graphs* that are constructed in $O(V \times e)$ time, where V is the number of program variables.

Computing congruence relations based on common subexpressions is a well known problem and efficient algorithms have been developed [NO80, DST80, Hop71]. Hopcroft's partitioning algorithm for minimizing finite automata was used in program optimization to detect equalities among variables based on common subexpressions over an extended SSA form of the program [AWZ88]. The authors describe a strategy to manipulate the SSA representation in order to combine congruent (equal) variables values from different branches of a structured if-statement. This treatment can be viewed as handling a special case of detecting idempotence congruences. Other methods to eliminate redundant program computations include value numbering [CS70], global value numbering based on SSA form [RWZ88] and methods based on the global value graph [RT82].

7 Conclusion

We presented a new and efficient approach to improve the performance of any monotone data flow analysis by reducing the size of data flow equation systems through congruence partitioning. The presented partitioning algorithms discover congruences among data flow equations by exploiting the algebraic properties of idempotence and commutativity of the meet operator. A remaining property of the meet that we have not discussed is associativity. Unfortunately, discovering congruences that are due to associativity is a much harder problem. The difficulty of discovering congruences by associativity results from the fact that an exponential number of different sequences of meet operations can yield congruent values by associativity. This problem with associative operators also arises in program optimizations, where *reassociation* techniques have been used as a heuristic to discover certain equalities by associativity [CM80]. We are currently considering whether reassociation would be a suitable approach to enable further reductions in data flow equation systems.

Our approach of congruence partitioning demonstrates the feasibility of applying principles of program optimization and analysis, such as common subexpression elimination, to optimize the analyzers themselves. We expect to investigate this issue further as part of our future work.

References

[AHU74] A.V. Aho, J.E. Hopcroft, and J.D. Ullman. *The Design and Analysis of Computer Algorithms*. Addison-Wesley, 1974.

[ASU86] A.V. Aho, R. Sethi, and J.D. Ullman. *Compilers, principles, techniques, and tools*. Addison-Wesley Publishing Company, Massachusetts, 1986.

[AWZ88] B. Alpern, M. Wegman, and F.K. Zadeck. Detecting equality of values in programs. In *Proc. 15th Annual ACM Symp. on Principles of Programming Languages*, pages 1–11, San Diego, California, January 1988.

[CC77] P. Cousot and R. Cousot. Static determination of dynamic properties of generalized type unions. In *Proc. ACM Conf. on Language Design for Reliable Software*, pages 77–93, Raleigh, North Carolina, March 1977.

[CCF90] J.D. Choi, R.K. Cytron, and J. Ferrante. Automatic construction of sparse data flow evaluation graphs. In *Conf. Rec. 18th Annual ACM Symp. on Principles of Programming Languages*, pages 55–66, Orlando, Florida, January 1990.

[CF93] R.K. Cytron and J. Ferrante. Efficiently computing ϕ-nodes on-the-fly. *Proc. 1993 Workshop on Languages and Compilers for Parallelism*, 1993.

[CFR+91] R.K. Cytron, J. Ferrante, B. Rosen, M. Wegman, and F.K. Zadeck. Efficiently computing static single assignment form and the control dependence graph. *ACM Transactions of Programming Languages and Systems*, 13(4):451–490, October 1991.

[CLZ86] R.K. Cytron, A. Lowry, and F.K. Zadeck. Code motion of control structures in high-level languages. In *Conf. Rec. 13th Annual ACM Symp. on Principles of Programming Languages*, pages 70–85, St. Petersburg Beach, Florida, January 1986.

[CM80] J. Cocke and P.W. Markstein. Measurement of program improvement algorithms. In *Proc. Information Processing 80*. North Holland Publishing Company, 1980.

[CS70]   J. Cocke and J.T. Schwartz. Programming languages and their compilers;
          preliminary notes. Courant Institute of Mathematical Sciences, New York
          University, April 1970.

[DST80]   P.J. Downey, R. Sethi, and R.E. Tarjan. Variations on the common subex-
          pression problem. *Journal of the ACM*, 27(4):758–771, October 1980.

[GJ79]   M.R. Garey and D.S. Johnson. *Computers and Intractability*. Freeman and
          Company, New York, 1979.

[Hop71]   J.E. Hopcroft. An n log n algorithm for minimizing states in finite automata.
          In *Theory of Machines and Computations*. Academic Press, New York, 1971.

[JP93]   R. Johnson and K. Pingali. Dependence-based program analysis. In *Proc.
          ACM SIGPLAN '93 Conf. on Programming Language Design and Imple-
          mentation*, pages 78–89, Albuquerque, New Mexico, June 1993.

[KU77]   J.B. Kam and J.D. Ullman. Monotone data flow analysis frameworks. *Acta
          Informatica*, 7(3):305–317, July 1977.

[Lan92]   W.A. Landi. *Interprocedural aliasing in the presence of pointers*. PhD thesis,
          Rutgers University, New Brunswick, New Jersey, 1992.

[NO80]   G. Nelson and D.C. Oppen. Fast decision procedures based on congruence
          closures. *Journal of the ACM*, 27(2), April 1980.

[RL77]   J. Reif and J. Lewis. Symbolic evaluation and the global value graph. In
          *Conf. Rec. 4th Annual ACM Symp. on Principles of Programming Lan-
          guages*, pages 104–118, January 1977.

[RT82]   J. Reif and R.E. Tarjan. Symbolic program analysis in almost linear time.
          SIAM Journal of Computing, 11(1):81–93, February 1982.

[RWZ88]   B. Rosen, M. Wegman, and F.K. Zadeck. Global value numbers and redun-
          dant computations. In *Conf. Rec. 15th Annual ACM Symp. on Principles of
          Programming Languages*, pages 12–27, San Diego, California, January 1988.

[SS70]   R.M. Shapiro and H. Saint. The representation of algorithms. Technical
          Report CA-7002-1432, Massachusetts Computer Associates, 1970.

[WZ85]   M. Wegman and F.K. Zadeck. Constant propagation with conditional
          branches. In *Conf. Rec. 12th Annual ACM Symp. on Principles of Program-
          ming Languages*, pages 291–299, New Orleans, Louisiana, January 1985.

[Zad84]   F.K. Zadeck. Incremental data flow analysis in a structured program editor.
          In *Proc. ACM SIGPLAN Symp. on Compiler Construction*, pages 132–143,
          June 1984.

Interprocedural Constant Propagation using Dependence Graphs and a Data-Flow Model

David Binkley
Loyola College in Maryland
4501 North Charles Street, Baltimore Maryland 21210-2699, USA.
binkley@cs.loyola.edu

Abstract. Aggressive compilers employ a larger number of well understood optimizations in the hope of improving compiled code quality. Unfortunately, these optimizations require a variety of intermediate program representations. A first step towards unifying these optimizations to a common intermediate representation is described. The representation chosen is the program dependence graph, which captures both control-flow and data-flow information from a program.

The optimization of (interprocedural) constant propagation is studied. The algorithm developed combines a program dependence graph called the system dependence graph (SDG) with the ideas of data-flow computing and graph rewriting. The algorithm safely finds the classes of constants found by other intraprocedural and intraprocedural constant propagation algorithms. In addition, the SDG allows constants to propagate *through* procedures. This enables the algorithm to discover constants in a calling procedure even thought no constants exist in the called procedure.

1. Introduction

Optimizing compilers employ a larger number of well understood optimizations in the hope of improving object code quality. These include, for example, code motion, call inlining, constant propagation, dead code elimination, loop interchanging, and register allocation [1, 2]. Unfortunately, these optimizations often require different intermediate representations of the program.

This paper describes the first step toward reducing the number of intermediate representations by unifying optimizations onto a common intermediate representation. The representation chosen is a variation of the program dependence graph [12, 17] called the *system dependence graph* (SDG) [15]. Program dependence graphs have been successfully used as an intermediate representation in parallelizing and vectorizing compilers to perform loop interchanging, strip mining, loop skewing, and other optimizations [2, 17]. A key feature of the SDG is its representation for programs with procedures and procedure calls. Recent trends toward programs with small procedures and a high proportion of procedure calls (typical of object oriented programs) have intensified the need for better interprocedural optimizations.

The optimization considered in this paper is interprocedural constant propagation [8, 19]. The goal of any constant propagation algorithm is to identify variables whose values are constant throughout all possible executions of the program. If a compiler can identify such variables it can improve the quality of the object code by replacing the variable with the constant and by propagating this constant to other expressions in the program. *Interprocedural* constant propagation concerns the propagating of constants to, from, and *through* called procedures.

The interprocedural constant propagation algorithm developed in this paper uses a *data-flow interpretation* of the SDG, incorporates *symbolic execution*, and uses *live code analysis*. The algorithm *safely* finds the same classes of constants found by traditional interprocedural and intraprocedural constant propagation algorithms [16, 19].

(A safe algorithm may miss some constants but all the variables it determines to be constant are guaranteed to be constant on all possible executions of the program.)

The data-flow interpretation of the SDG treats the SDG as a data-flow graph in which values "flow" on the dependence edges of the graph. This makes (constant) values available at uses as soon as they are determined (they do not have to propagate through unrelated nodes as in a control-flow-graph based algorithm).

The algorithm also employs symbolic execution of the SDG. This idea is a modification of the graph rewriting semantics for program dependence graphs given by Selke in [18]. It allows, for example, the optimization of a while-loop that sums the numbers from 1 to 10: while constant propagation alone would determine that a non-constant value is produced by the statement "$sum = sum + i$" in the body of the loop (because sum is assigned the values values $1, 3, 6, \cdots, 55$), symbolic execution replaces the loop with the assignment statement "$sum = 55$."

Live-code analysis is used to increase the number of constants found. Non-live (*i.e.*, dead) code includes unreachable code and useless code. Unreachable code is never executed on any execution of the program, while useless code has no effect on the output of the program. Removing unreachable code may improve constant propagation by reducing the number of definitions that reach a use. For example, if a constant and a non-constant value reach a use of x, then x's value is non-constant. If, however, the source of the non-constant value reaching the use of x is determined to be dead code and eliminated, then x's value is constant. Removing useless code does not improve constant propagation, but does reduce the size of the optimized code.

The remainder of this paper is organized as follows: Section 2 reviews the system dependence graph, Selke's graph rewriting semantics, and the constant propagation lattice. Section 3 presents the interprocedural constant propagation algorithm based on the SDG as an intermediate representation. Section 4 compares this algorithm with existing constant propagation algorithms and Section 5 presents conclusions.

2. Background

2.1. The System Dependence Graph

This section summarizes a minor extension to the definition of the SDG presented in [15]. The SDG models a language with the following properties:
1. A complete system is a single main procedure and a set of auxiliary procedures.
2. Parameters are passed by value-result.[1]
3. Input and output are modeled as streams; thus, for example, *print* (x) is treated as the assignment statement "$output\_stream = concatenate\ (output\_stream, x)$."

We make the further assumption that there are no calls of the form $P(x, x)$ or of the form $P(g)$ for global variable g. The former restriction sidesteps potential copy-back conflicts. The latter restriction permits global variables to be treated as additional parameters to each procedure; thus, we do not discuss global variables explicitly.

The SDG for system S contains one procedure dependence graph (PDG) for each procedure in S connected by interprocedural control- and flow-dependence edges. The PDG for procedure P contains vertices, which represent the components of P, and edges, which represent the dependence between these components. With the

---

[1] Techniques for handling reference parameter passing and aliasing are discussed in [15] and [6].

exception of call statements, a single vertex represents the predicates of if and while statements, assignment statements, input statements, and output statements of P; in addition, there is a distinguished vertex called the *entry vertex*, and an *initial-definition vertex* for each variable that may be used before being defined. Initial-definition vertices represent the assignment of the value 0 to these variables.

A call statement is represented using a *call* vertex and four kinds of *parameter vertices* that represent value-result parameter passing: on the calling side, parameter passing is represented by *actual-in* and *actual-out* vertices, which are control dependent (see below) on the call-site vertex; in the called procedure parameter passing is represented by *formal-in* and *formal-out* vertices, which are control dependent on the procedure's entry vertex. Actual-in and formal-in vertices are included for every parameter and global variable that may be used or modified as a result of the call; formal-out and actual-out vertices are included for every parameter and global variable that may be modified as a result of the call. (Interprocedural data-flow analysis is used to determine which parameters and globals may be used and/or modified as a result of a procedure call [3, 4].)

PDGs include three kinds of intraprocedural edges: *control dependence edges*, *data dependence edges*, and *summary edges*. The source of a control dependence edge is either the entry vertex, a predicate vertex, or a call-site vertex. Each edge is labeled either **true** or **false**. A control dependence edge $v \rightarrow_c u$ from vertex v to vertex u means that during execution, whenever the predicate represented by v is evaluated and its value matches the label on the edge to u, then the program component represented by u will eventually be executed provided the program terminates normally (edges from entry and call-site vertices are always labeled **true**; these vertices are assumed to always evaluate to **true**). Note that for the block structured language studied here each vertex has a single incoming control edge.

There are two kinds of data dependence edges, *flow dependence edges* and *def-order dependence edges*. Flow dependence edge $v \rightarrow_f w$ runs from a vertex v that represents an assignment to a variable x to vertex a w that represents a use of x reached by that assignment. The set of flow dependence edges is divided into two subsets: *loop-independent* and *loop-dependent*: loop-dependent edges represent values passed from one loop iteration to another; all other flow dependence edges are loop-independent. A def-order edge $v \rightarrow_{do(u)} w$ runs between vertices v and w, where both v and w represent assignments to x, the definitions at v and w reach a common use at u, and v lexically precedes w (*i.e.*, v is to the left of w in the system's abstract syntax tree).

Summary edges represent transitive dependences due to calls. A summary edge $v \rightarrow_s u$ connects actual-in vertex v at a call-site to actual-out vertex u at the same call site if there is a path in the SDG from v to u that *respects calling context* by matching calls with returns.

Connecting PDGs to form the SDG is involves, the addition of three kinds of interprocedural edges: (1) a *call* edge connects each call vertex to the corresponding procedure-entry vertex; (2) a *parameter-in* edge connects each actual-in vertex to the corresponding formal-in vertex in the called procedure; (3) a *parameter-out* edge connects each formal-out vertex to the corresponding actual-out vertex at all call sites. (A call edge is an interprocedural control edge; parameter-in and -out edges are interprocedural data dependence edges.)

Example. Figure 1 shows the PDG of a system without call statements. Figure 3(b) shows part of the SDG for a system with a call statement. In Fig. 3(b) at the call-site, the actual-in vertex for a is labeled "$x_{in} = a$" and the actual-out vertex "$a = x_{out}$." In procedure P, the formal-in vertex for x is labeled "$x = x_{in}$" and the formal-out vertex "$x_{out} = x$." In these figures as well as the remaining figures in the paper, actual-in, actual-out, formal-in, and formal-out vertices for the variables *output_stream* and *input_stream* are omitted for clarity.

2.2. A Graph Rewriting Semantics for the SDG

This section first overviews Selke's graph rewriting semantics for (single procedure) program dependence graphs and then extends this to a graph rewriting semantics for the SDG. Graph rewriting first chooses a vertex that has no incoming control or loop-independent dependence edges. It then fires the vertex: the vertex is removed along with its outgoing edges. In addition, it may add, remove, or update other vertices and edges in the graph. These additional actions for each kind of vertex are given informally in the following table; formal definitions are given in [18].

Vertex Kind	Rule
Enter:	No additional actions.
Assignment:	For an assignment vertex labeled "$x = exp$", modify the targets of all outgoing edges as follows: replace x with c *tagged* by x, written c^x, where c is the constant value of exp (exp's value is constant because the assignment vertex has no incoming data dependence edges). Tags allow subsequent rewritings to overwrite previous ones. Their need is illustrated in Fig. 2.
If-predicate:	Assume the predicate's value is **true** (the **false** case is symmetric). Remove all vertices representing statements in the **false** branch of the if statement along with their incoming and outgoing edges.
While-predicate:	If the predicate evaluates to **false** then all vertices representing the loop are removed along with their incoming and outgoing edges. Otherwise, if the predicate evaluates to **true** then copies of the vertices that represent the body of the loop are added to the graph. Copies are added as if one iteration of the loop had been unrolled and place before the original while-loop. (The difficult part of this rewriting is correctly determining the dependence edges associated with the new vertices).

In addition to modifying the graph, the rewriting of an input or output vertex effects the global input or output stream: input statements consume values from the head of the input stream, while output statements append values to the output stream.

Example. For the program in Fig. 1, Fig. 2(a) shows the graph after rewriting the entry vertex and then the vertices labeled "$x = 0$" and "$y = 1$" (in either order). The rewriting of "$x = 2$" illustrates the need for tags: because 0^x in the output vertex has the tag x, its value is replaced as a result of rewriting "$x = 2$" (Fig. 2(c)). Without tags, there is no way of knowing that the 0 was a rewritten x. Finally, rewriting the output vertex produces a 2 on the output stream (the tag is stripped when the value is output) and leaves the empty graph; thus, the evaluation terminates.

Rewriting the SDG

Rewriting the SDG requires adding a rule for call-site vertices. An information statement of this rule is given below, a formalization can be found in [5], which also indirectly extends Selke's semantics to the SDG. Like the while-loop rule, the call-site rule introduces copies of vertices. These new vertices are copies of the vertices

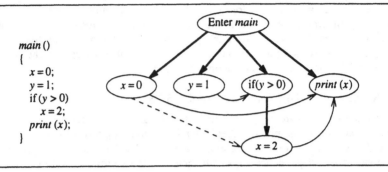

```
main ()
{
    x = 0;
    y = 1;
    if (y > 0)
        x = 2;
    print (x);
}
```

Figure 1. An example program and its program dependence graph. Bold arrows represent control edges, arcs represent flow-dependence edges, and dashed lines represent def-order edges. (In all the figures in this paper, unlabeled control edges are assumed to be labeled **true**.)

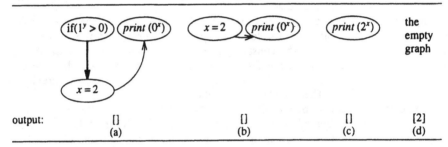

output:

[]	[]	[]	[2]
(a)	(b)	(c)	(d)

Figure 2. The rewriting of the program dependence graph from Fig. 1.

from the called procedure. Unlike the while-loop rule, computing the edges for the copies is trivial because of the interface (parameter vertices and edges) between a call site and the called procedure.

Vertex Kind	Rule
Call-site	Replace the call-site vertex with copies of the vertices for the called procedure (except its entry vertex). Change the interprocedural data dependence edges into (intraprocedural) flow dependence edges and the parameter vertices into assignment vertices.

Example. Figure 3 shows a program with a call and part of its rewriting. Figure 3(b) shows the SDG for the program shown in Fig. 3(a) after rewriting the enter vertex. Figure 3(c) shows the result of rewriting the call-site vertex "*call P*" where the flow dependence edges from "$x_{in} = a$" to "$x = x_{in}$" and from "$x_{out} = x$" to "$a = x_{out}$" have replaced the two interprocedural data dependence edges in Fig. 3(b).

2.3. The Constant Propagation Lattice

This section, based largely on [19], discusses the lattice used for constant propagation and introduces the notion of constant *confidence*. As shown in Fig. 4, the constant-propagation lattice is composed of a top element $\top$, an infinite collection of constants c_i, and a bottom element $\bot$. The value $\top$ represents "no information" or

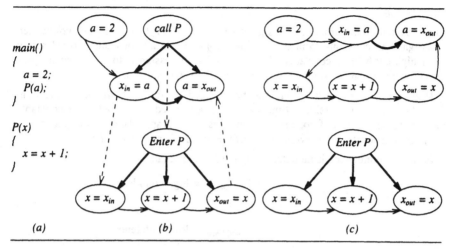

main()
{
  a = 2;
  P(a);
}

P(x)
{
  x = x + 1;
}

(a)   (b)   (c)

Figure 3. The call-site rewrite rule.

optimistically some yet undetermined constant. The value $\perp$ represents "non-constant", and is used, for example, in the case of a read statement.

Following the data-flow model, each flow dependence edge in the SDG is labeled by a lattice element, which represents the current best approximation to the value "flowing" down the edge (*i.e.*, the value produced by the assignment statement at the source of the edge). Initially, all edges are labeled $\top$, which represents the optimistic assumption that they will be labeled by some constant.

When a use of a variable is reached by multiple definitions, the definitions are combined by the lattice *meet* operator $\sqcap$ defined by the following table:

Rules for $\sqcap$	
$x \sqcap \top = x$	$c_i \sqcap c_j = c_i$ if $i = j$
$x \sqcap \perp = \perp$	$c_i \sqcap c_j = \perp$ if $i \neq j$
where x represents any of $\top$, $\perp$, or c_i	

The evaluation of expressions is strict: if any of the variables in the expression has the value $\perp$, then the expression has value $\perp$. (In some cases, this can be softened by taking special attributes of certain operators into account. For example, 0 times anything, including $\perp$, is 0.)

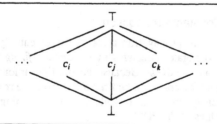

Figure 4. The three-level constant propagation lattice.

Confidence

Each constant in the program is assigned a confidence: *high* or *low*. High confidence is assigned to constants from the original program and all constants derived solely from high-confidence constants. Low confidence is assigned to all constants produced by operations involving low-confidence constants and $\top$).

High confidence constants will not be changed by further constant propagation. This allows more aggressive optimization to be performed. Low confidence constants may change as a result of updates in other parts of the graph. Thus, low confidence is assigned to a constant to prevent the unsafe removal of graph components.

Formally, confidence is modeled using the following lattice

$$\top_{confidence} = \text{high confidence}$$
$$|$$
$$\bot_{confidence} = \text{low confidence}$$

where the meet operation $\sqcap_{confidence}$ is defined as follows:

$$\top_{confidence} \sqcap_{confidence} \bot_{confidence} = \bot_{confidence}$$

In what follows, we omit the subscript *confidence*, when it is clear from context.

3. Interprocedural Constant Propagation

This section describes the interprocedural constant propagation algorithm based on the SDG in which constants "flow" through the SDG. The algorithm is enhanced by concurrently performing symbolic execution and live code analysis. Symbolic execution is accomplished using a variation of the rules from Sect. 2.2. Live-code analysis is performed by initially labeling all vertices as non-live and then marking vertices as live only as they are encountered during constant propagation. When the algorithm terminates remaining non-live vertices represent dead code that can be removed from the SDG.

Before presenting the interprocedural constant propagation algorithm in Sect. 3.2, Sect. 3.1 presents a data-flow based intraprocedural constant propagation algorithm. The algorithm in Sect. 3.2 will work with this or any other intraprocedural constant propagation algorithm. Both the intraprocedural and interprocedural algorithms have three steps: first the program's dependence graph is constructed. The graph is then rewritten according to a set of rewrite rules. Finally, the rewritten graph is used as an intermediate form for code generation, or, as discussed in Sect. 3.3, to produce optimized source.

3.1. Intraprocedural Constant Propagation

The intraprocedural constant propagation algorithm is essentially a data-flow interpreter. The interpreter propagates constants by continually *firing* (rewriting) vertices and propagating values along edges. Because no run-time information is available, the conditions under which a vertex can be fired *differ* from the rewriting discussed in Sect. 2.2. These differences are given in Rule 1. The remaining rewrite rules push information along the edges of the PDG.

1. The rewriting rules from Sect. 2.2 are modified as follows:

   (a) A vertex representing an action with a side effect (*e.g.*, printing) is never fired and is therefore removed from the graph only if it represents dead code.

(b) Since the rewriting of a while loop increases code size, two limits are placed on the number of such rewritings. These limits are controlled by the constants: *size_increase* and *max_times*. *Size_increase* limits the final code size of the loop (after optimization) to some multiple of the original loop code size. Thus, the number of unrollings is dependent on the effectiveness of optimization on the copy of the loop body. Since optimization may remove the entire body, *max_times* is used to limit the maximum number of times a loop can be unrolled. For example, *max_times* is needed to stop the optimization of "*while* $(n > 0)$ $n = 1$."

2. A def-order edge $a \rightarrow_{do(u)} b$ in which a and b have the same control predecessor implies the previously conditional assignment at b has been made unconditional with respect to the definition at b by an application of Rule 5. In this case, only the second definition at b actually reaches u, so the edges $a \rightarrow_{do(u)} b$ and $a \rightarrow_f u$ are removed from the graph.

3. If all incoming flow dependence edges for variable v have the same constant value c on them and these constants have high confidence then, the edges are removed and v is replaced by c^v. (If a previous rewrite has replaced v with c^v then all remaining incoming flow dependence edges must have c on them.) Any vertex left with no outgoing edges represents dead code and can be removed.

4. For an assignment vertex labeled "$x = e$", the expression e is evaluated by first using the meet operation to determine a value for each variable v used in e, then computing the value for e. Finally, this value is placed on all outgoing flow dependence edges of the assignment vertex. The confidence of this value is the meet of the confidences of all the input values. (Edges from non-live vertices contain the value of $\top$ with low confidence.)

5. A predicate vertex p, labeled with expression e is evaluated in the same manner as an assignment vertex. The resulting value v may cause certain control successors of p to become live: if v is $\top$ then *none* of the control successors become live; if v is **true** then the **true** successors become live; if v is **false** then the **false** successors become live; finally, if v is $\bot$ then *all* successors become live. Furthermore, if v is **true** or **false** with high confidence then all targets of outgoing control edges from p whose labels match v are made control dependent on the p's control predecessor. All remaining control successors of p along with their (transitive) control successors and p are removed from the graph.

Example. Figure 5(a) shows the graph before the rewriting of the vertex labeled "$a = 2$." The subsequent rewriting of the if vertex produces Fig. 5(b). After rewriting the remaining assignment vertex, the graph cannot be further rewritten because printing represents an operation with a side-effect. (As example of dead-code removal, if the if-predicate vertex had an incoming control edge and thus could not have been re-written, the read vertex would still have been removed as unreachable-code.)

Example. Figure 6 illustrates the propagating of values along data-flow edges. Figure 6(a) shows a sample PDG (in the figure $\bot$ represents a value previously determined to be non-constant). Figure 6(b) shows the effect of Rule (4) on the statement "$x = 2$" from the body of the if statement. Figure 6(c) shows the result of firing the other vertex labeled "$x = 2$" using the assignment-vertex rewrite rule from Sect. 2.2. Finally, Fig. 6(d) shows the result of firing Rule 3: all the incoming edges of the vertex labeled "*print* (2^x)" have the constant 2 with high confidence on them.

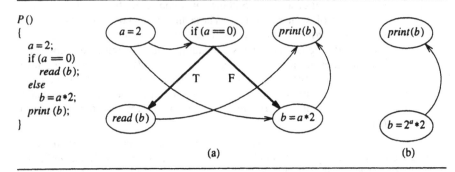

```
P ()
{
    a = 2;
    if (a == 0)
        read (b);
    else
        b = a*2;
    print (b);
}
```

Figure 5. An intraprocedure constant propagation example.

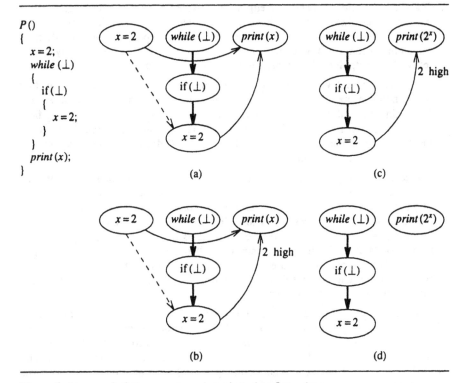

```
P ()
{
    x = 2;
    while (⊥)
    {
        if (⊥)
        {
            x = 2;
        }
    }
    print (x);
}
```

Figure 6. An example that propagates values along data-flow edges.

3.2. Interprocedural Constant Propagation

An interprocedural constant propagation algorithm can be obtained by adding the call-site rewrite rule from Sect. 2.2 to the intraprocedural algorithm developed in Sect. 3.1. However, this algorithm fails to take advantage of opportunities to partially propagate constants to, from, and through procedures when only some of the parameters are constants. For example, Rule 3 (see below) makes use of the fact that the incoming summary edges of an actual-out vertex indicate which actual-parameter's initial values must be constants in order to propagate constants through the called procedure to the actual-out vertex.

The following rules augment the intraprocedural constant propagation rules from Sect. 3.1 to perform interprocedural constant propagation:

1. Actual-in and formal-out vertices are treated as assignment vertices and parameter-in and parameter-out edges are treated as flow dependence edges.
2. Parallel to while-loop unrolling, application of the call-site rewrite rule of Sect. 2.2 is limited by the constants $call\_size\_increase$ and $call\_max\_times$.
3. If all the incoming summary edges of an actual-out vertex v labeled "$a = x_{out}$" have constants of high confidence on them, then a new assignment vertex labeled "$a = c$" is added to the SDG. Constant c is the value produced for x by the called procedure (see below). The new vertex has an incoming control edge from the control predecessor of the call-site vertex and all outgoing data dependence edges of the actual-out vertex are moved to the new vertex. Finally, the actual-out vertex is marked *useless* (see Rule 6).
4. If the incoming parameter-out edge of an actual-out vertex labeled "$a = x_{out}$" has the constant c of high confidence on it then the actual-out vertex is replaced, as in Rule 3, by a vertex labeled "$a = c$."
5. If all incoming parameter-in edges to formal-in vertex labeled "$x = x_{in}$" have the same constant c on them and these constants have high confidence, then a new vertex labeled "$x = c$" is added. This vertex is control dependent on the called procedure's entry vertex and the flow edges of the formal-in vertex are moved to the new vertex. At all call-sites the corresponding actual-in vertices are marked as useless (see Rule 6).
6. If, at all call-sites on P, the actual-in and actual-out vertices for a parameter are marked as useless, then these vertices are removed from the SDG along with the corresponding formal-in and formal-out vertices. This rule uniformly removes one of P's parameters.
7. A call-site vertex with only useless actual-out vertices is removed. Recall that there are actual-out vertices for input and output streams. Thus, a call with no actual-out vertices returns no values and produces no side-effects.

Computing the value of an actual parameter in Rule (3) requires executing some part of the called procedure. A program that contains the necessary statements to compute this value can be obtained from the SDG using program slicing [15]. In particular, a "b2" slice contains the necessary program components. Once this slice has been computed there are two ways of determining the final value of x. First, the constant propagation algorithm could be run on a copy of the the slice. The second, more efficient, option is to produce execute object code from the slice and then execute this object code [7]. (Because of the possibility of non-terminating computations, some limit must be placed on the resources devoted to computing x's value.)

Example. (In the following two examples, Rule 2 is ignored; thus, no in-lining is performed.) For the system shown in Fig. 7, Fig. 8 shows the PDG for procedure P after using Rule 3 to rewrite both actual-out vertices of the first call-site on Q and Rule 7 to subsequently remove the call-site. The actual-out vertex for y, for example, was the target of two summary edges, which had the constants 2 and 8 on them. Rule 3 replaced this actual-out vertex with an assignment vertex labeled "$y = 12$" (12 is the value computed by Q using the input values 2 and 8). The final SDG and its corresponding program (see Sect. 3.3) are shown in Fig. 9.

```
    main()              P(x, y)             Q(a, b)
    {                   {                   {
      i = 2;              Q(x, y);            a = a * 2;
      j = 8;              x = x - 2;          b = b + a;
      P(i, j);            Q(x, y);          }
      print(j);          print (x);
    }                   }
```

Figure 7. An interprocedural constant propagation example.

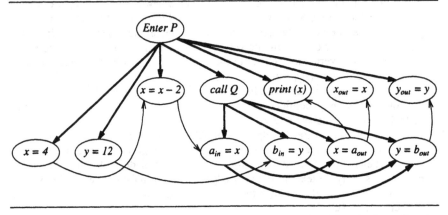

Figure 8. The PDG for procedure P of Fig. 7 after applying Rules 3 and 7 to the first call on Q.

Example. In the preceding example constant propagation removed procedure Q entirely. This example illustrates the removing of one of Q's parameters. Consider the optimization of the program in Fig. 7 if the initial value of j is non-constant (*i.e.*, replace "$j = 8$" with "*read* (j)"). In this case, the call-sites on procedure Q cannot be removed from P; however, propagating constants *through* call-sites, the incoming parameter-in edges of the formal-in vertex for parameter x in procedure Q both have the constant 2 with high confidence on them. Rule 5 rewrites the graph by replacing this formal-in vertex with the assignment vertex "$x = 2$." This produces a version of P without actual parameter x and a version of Q without formal parameter a. The resulting optimized version of the system is shown below:

```
    main ()             P (y)               Q (b)
    {                   {                   {
      read (j);           Q (y);              b = b + 4;
      P (j);              Q (y);            }
      print (j);         print (4);
    }                   }
```

3.3. Producing Source Code After Optimization

This section discusses how optimized source code is produced from the optimized SDG. Three uses of this source code include illustrating the effects of optimization to students and others unfamiliar with optimization, debugging optimized code, and producing optimized object code (although using the SDG as an intermediate form and directly producing optimized object code would be more efficient). For example, in debugging, making a programmer aware of optimization's effect allows the programmer to better understand the output from a debugger when debugging optimized code. This avoids the need to only debug unoptimized code or use a debugger that attempts the difficult and often impossible task of reversing optimization in an attempt to recover the state of the unoptimized program [10].

Producing source code from the optimized SDG is a two step process. Step one "backs up" optimization in order to allow step two to reconstitute a system from the SDG. The reasons this backup is necessary is that the data-flow interpretation of the SDG allows partial evaluation of statements. For some statement types (*e.g.*, call statements) partially evaluated statements cannot be part of a source program.

The backing up of optimization is necessary in two cases. First, when a constant has been propagated to an actual-in vertex but the actual-out vertex has not been removed from the graph. This is illustrated in Fig. 10(a) where the actual-in vertex labeled "$x_{in} = 1^a$" requires the call statement "*call P*(1)", while the actual-out vertex labeled "$a = x_{out}$" requires the call statement "*call P*(a)." The second case occurs

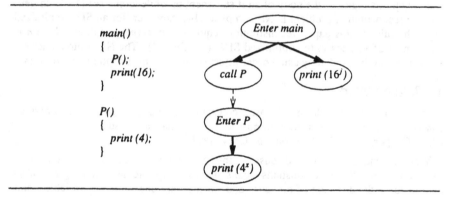

Figure 9. The result of optimizing the program from Fig. 7.

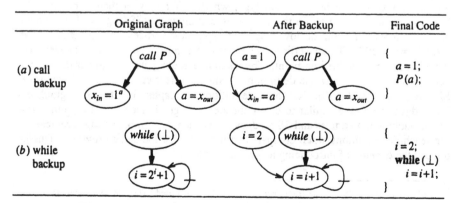

Figure 10. Examples of the two cases in which optimization backup is necessary.

when c^v has replaced v but there remains a reaching definition of v. This is illustrated in Fig. 10(b) where the use of i in the while loop shown in Fig. 10(b) has an incoming loop-carried flow dependence edge.

In both cases, backup of the optimization that replaced v with c^v at vertex x involves three steps: (1) potentially adding a new assignment vertex, labeled "$v = c$," (2) adding a flow dependence edge from this new vertex to x, and (3) replacing c^v with v in the label of x. Step (1) adds an assignment vertex only if a previous backup has not already added an assignment to the same variable at the same *location*. The *location* of this vertex is that of an assignment statement not nested within any other control structure[2] and immediately before the statement representing x and all statements representing vertices that have flow dependence edges to x.

Example. Figure 10(a) shows a partial SDG before and after applying the call-site backup step and (part of) the final reconstituted program. Figure 10(b) shows a partial SDG before and after applying the second backup step along with (part of) the final reconstituted program.

After all necessary backups, the final step in the constant propagation algorithm reconstitutes optimized source code from the optimized SDG. The difficult problem in reconstitution is finding a total order for the vertices in each *region* of each PDG (roughly put, a region is the body of an if statement or while loop—see [14]). In general the reconstitution problem is NP-complete [14]; however, for an SDG optimized using the rules in this paper, reconstitution requires only $O(n \log n)$ time, where n is the number of vertices in the optimized SDG (see Sect. 4). The NP-complete aspect of the problem is avoided by using order information from the unoptimized program.

4. Related Work

This section compares the SDG based constant propagation algorithm to previous constant propagation algorithms discussed by Wegman and Zadeck [19] and Callahan, Cooper, Kennedy, Torczon, and Grove [8, 13].

Wegman and Zadeck [19] discuss an intraprocedural constant propagation algorithm that finds all simple constants—constant that can be found assuming no information about the direction of branches and storing only one value per variable—and one that finds all *conditional constants*—those constants that can be determined by including tests for constants in the conditional branches. (Wegman and Zadeck actually discuss two algorithms of each type, which differ only in their complexity.) These algorithms are based on the static single assignment (SSA) graph [11], which augments a standard control-flow graph with special ϕ vertices—assignments of the form "$x = \phi(x, x)$." These vertices are placed at control join-points whenever two definitions of x reach the join-point. The result is that every use of x (other than at a ϕ vertex) is reached by a single definition. A similar effect can be obtained using the SDG and valve nodes [9]. Reaching definitions are captured in the SSA graph by SSA-edges, which are similar to data dependence edges in an SDG. For some programs, including ϕ vertices and SSA-edges can reduce the number of edges representing reaching definitions when compared to the SDG for the same program. This is done at the expense of introducing additional vertices.

---

[2] For c^v to replace v a rewrite rule from Sect. 2.2 must have been used. Therefore, no incoming control edge should be present for the vertex (*i.e.*, it should not be nested within any other control structure).

The algorithm discussed in Sect. 3.1, which finds all conditional constants, is essentially equivalent to the intraprocedural constant propagation algorithms given by Wegman and Zadeck. For interprocedural constant propagation, which Wegman and Zadeck also discuss, the algorithm developed in Sect. 3.2 has some advantages. These include, the use of summary edges in Interprocedural Rule (3) to determine that a procedure returns a constant value at a particular call-site even through other call-sites on the same procedure may pass non-constant values to the procedure. Rewriting an actual-out vertex using Rule (3) can "decouple" the body of the called procedure from the computation of the return value for the actual parameter. For example, consider a procedure with two parameters, a counter and some other variable. If the counter's return value can be determined to be constant using Rule (3) then the computation of the called procedure that involves the other variable can proceed in parallel with subsequent computations of the calling procedure that involve the counter.

Callahan et. al. discuss several interprocedural constant propagation algorithms centered around the constructions of *jump* and *return* functions. These functions describe how constants flow from procedure to procedure. The summary edges in the SDG and program slices taken with respect to actual-out vertices can be used to compute jump and return functions analogous to those discussed in [8]. A comparison of this approach to those suggested in [8] is the topic of future research.

5. Conclusion

Using dependence graphs and a data-flow model provides an efficient algorithm for interprocedural constant propagation. In many cases graph transformations are easier to visualize, create, and understand than transformations involving sets of variables and program text. One reason for this is that dependence graphs allow the program components involved in the optimization to be more easily isolated from other program components regardless of their textual location in the source code.

A key feature of the SDG is its inclusion of summary edges. These edges allow constants to propagate through called procedures, which increases the number of constants found by the algorithm. Summary edges have also proved useful in other operations involving the SDG, for example the two step program slicing algorithm presented in [15].

Finally, the adequacy of the SDG for representing programs [5] and the use of semantics preserving graph transformations [18] provides safety. Because each rewriting step is guaranteed to preserve the semantics of the original program, the program produced as a result of constant propagation is guaranteed to preserve the semantics of the original unoptimized program. The algorithm inherits its correctness proof from the correctness of the semantics based transformations. Thus, it successfully combines the rather theoretical results involving the adequacy and semantics of the SDG with the production of a practical algorithm. The result is a provably correct algorithm for interprocedural constant propagation.

References

1. Aho, A.V., Sethi, R., and Ullman, J.D., *Compilers: Principles, Techniques, and Tools,* Addison-Wesley, Reading, MA (1986).

2. Allen, R. and Kennedy, K., "Automatic translation of FORTRAN programs to vector form," *ACM Transactions on Programming Languages and Systems* 9(4) pp. 491-542 (October 1987).

3. Banning, J.P., "An efficient way to find the side effects of procedure calls and the aliases of variables," pp. 29-41 in *Conference Record of the Sixth ACM Symposium on Principles of Programming Languages,* (San Antonio, TX, Jan. 29-31, 1979), ACM, New York, NY (1979).

4. Barth, J.M., "A practical interprocedural data flow analysis algorithm," *Commun. of the ACM* 21(9) pp. 724-736 (September 1978).

5. Binkley, D., Horwitz, S., and Reps, T., "The multi-procedure equivalence theorem," TR-890, Computer Sciences Department, University of Wisconsin, Madison, WI (November 1989).

6. Binkley, D., "Slicing in the presence of parameter aliasing," pp. 261-268 in *1993 Software Engineering Research Forum,* (Orlando, FL, Nov, 1993), (1993).

7. Binkley, D., "Precise executable interprocedural slices," *to appear in ACM Letters on Programming Languages and Systems,* (1994).

8. Callahan, D., Cooper, K.D., Kennedy, K., and Torczon, L., "Interprocedural constant propagation," *Proceedings of the SIGPLAN 86 Symposium on Compiler Construction,* (Palo Alto, CA, June 25-27, 1986), *ACM SIGPLAN Notices* 21(7) pp. 152-161 (July 1986).

9. Cartwright, R. and Felleisen, M., "The semantics of program dependence," *Proceedings of the ACM SIGPLAN 89 Conference on Programming Language Design and Implementation,* (Portland, OR, June 21-23, 1989), *ACM SIGPLAN Notices,* (1989).

10. Chambers, C., Hözle, U., and Ungar, D., "Debugging optimized code with dynamic deoptimization," *Proceedings of the ACM SIGPLAN 92 Conference on Programming Language Design and Implementation,* (San Francisco, CA, June 17-19, 1992), *ACM SIGPLAN Notices* 27(7) pp. 32-42 (June 1992).

11. Cytron, R., Ferrante, J., Rosen, B.K., Wegman, M.N., and Zadeck, K., "An efficient method of computing static single assignment form," pp. 25-35 in *Conference Record of the Sixteenth ACM Symposium on Principles of Programming Languages,* (Austin, TX, Jan. 11-13, 1989), ACM, New York, NY (1989).

12. Ferrante, J., Ottenstein, K., and Warren, J., "The program dependence graph and its use in optimization," *ACM Transactions on Programming Languages and Systems* 9(3) pp. 319-349 (July 1987).

13. Grove, D. and Torczon, L., "Interprocedural constant propagation: A study of jump function implementations," *Proceedings of the ACM SIGPLAN 93 Conference on Programming Language Design and Implementation,* (Albuquerque, NM, June 23-25, 1993), pp. 90-99 ACM, (1993).

14. Horwitz, S., Prins, J., and Reps, T., "Integrating non-interfering versions of programs," *ACM Trans. Program. Lang. Syst.* 11(3) pp. 345-387 (July 1989).

15. Horwitz, S., Reps, T., and Binkley, D., "Interprocedural slicing using dependence graphs," *ACM Trans. Program. Lang. Syst.* 12(1) pp. 26-60 (January 1990).

16. Kildall, G.A., "A unified approach to global program optimization," pp. 194-206 in *Conference Record of the First ACM Symposium on Principles of Programming Languages,* (October 1973), ACM, New York, NY (1973).

17. Kuck, D.J., Kuhn, R.H., Leasure, B., Padua, D.A., and Wolfe, M., "Dependence graphs and compiler optimizations," pp. 207-218 in *Conference Record of the Eighth ACM Symposium on Principles of Programming Languages,* (Williamsburg, VA, January 26-28, 1981), ACM, New York, NY (1981).

18. Selke, R, "A graph semantics for program dependence graphs," pp. 12-24 in *Conference Record of the Sixteenth ACM Symposium on Principles of Programming Languages,* (Austin, TX, January 11-13, 1989), ACM, New York, NY (1989).

19. Wegman, M.N. and Zadeck, F.K., "Constant propagation and conditional branches," *ACM Transactions on Programming Languages and Systems* 13(2) pp. 181-210 ACM, (April, 1991).

Solving Demand Versions of Interprocedural Analysis Problems

Thomas Reps[1]

Datalogisk Institut, University of Copenhagen
Universitetsparken 1
DK-2100 Copenhagen East
Denmark

Abstract

This paper concerns the solution of demand versions of interprocedural analysis problems. In a demand version of a program-analysis problem, some piece of summary information (*e.g.*, the dataflow facts holding at a given point) is to be reported only for a single program element of interest (or a small number of elements of interest). Because the summary information at one program point typically depends on summary information from other points, an important issue is to minimize the number of other points for which (transient) summary information is computed and/or the amount of information computed at those points. The paper describes how algorithms for demand versions of program-analysis problems can be obtained from their exhaustive counterparts essentially for free, by applying the so-called "magic-sets" transformation that was developed in the logic-programming and deductive-database communities.

1. Introduction

Interprocedural analysis concerns the static examination of a program that consists of multiple procedures. Its purpose is to determine certain kinds of summary information associated with the elements of a program (such as reaching definitions, available expressions, live variables, *etc.*). Most treatments of interprocedural analysis address the *exhaustive* version of the problem: summary information is to be reported for *all* elements of the program. This paper concerns the solution of *demand* versions of interprocedural analysis problems: summary information is to be reported only for a single program element of interest (or a small number of elements of interest). Because the summary information at one program point typically depends on summary information from other points, an important issue is to minimize the number of *other* points for which (transient) summary information is computed and/or the amount of information computed at those points.

One of the novel aspects of our work is that establishes a connection between the ideas and concerns from two different research areas. This connection can be summarized as follows:

> Methods for solving demand versions of interprocedural analysis problems—and in particular interprocedural analysis problems of interest to the community that studies *imperative* programs—can be obtained from their exhaustive counterparts essentially for free, by applying a transformation that was developed in the *logic-programming* and *deductive-database* communities for optimizing the evaluation of recursive queries in deductive databases (the so-called magic-sets transformation [22,3,7]).

---

[1]On sabbatical leave from the University of Wisconsin–Madison.

This work was supported in part by a David and Lucile Packard Fellowship for Science and Engineering, by the National Science Foundation under grant CCR-9100424, and by the Defense Advanced Research Projects Agency under ARPA Order No. 8856 (monitored by the Office of Naval Research under contract N00014-92-J-1937).

This paper describes how the above approach can be used to obtain a demand algorithm for the interprocedural "gen-kill problems" (*i.e.*, problems in which the dataflow functions are all of the form $\lambda x . (x - kill) \cup gen$).

There are several reasons why it is desirable to solve the demand versions of interprocedural analysis problems (and, in particular, to solve them using the approach presented in this paper).

- *Narrowing the focus to specific points of interest.* In program optimization, most of the gains are obtained from making improvements at a program's "hot spots"—in particular, its innermost loops. Although the optimization phases during which transformations are applied can be organized to concentrate on hot spots, there is typically an earlier phase to determine dataflow facts during which an exhaustive algorithm for interprocedural dataflow analysis is used. A demand algorithm can greatly reduce the amount of extraneous information that is computed.

  With the approach presented in this paper, answers and intermediate results computed in the course of answering one query can be cached—that is, accumulated and used to compute the answers to later queries. (This can go on until such time as the program is modified, whereupon previous results—which may no longer be safe—must be discarded.) The use of cached information can further reduce the cost of responding to demands when there is a sequence of demands in between program modifications.

- *Reducing the amount of work spent in preprocessing or other auxiliary phases of a program analysis.* Consider a problem such as flow-insensitive side-effect analysis (*e.g.* MayMod, MayUse, *etc.*), which has a decomposition that includes two subsidiary phases: computing alias information and computing side effects due to reference formal parameters [5,11,10]. In problems that are decomposed into separate phases, not all of the information from subsidiary phases is required in order to answer an "outer-level" query. Given a demand at the outermost level (*e.g.*, "What is the MayMod set for a given call site c on procedure p?"), a demand algorithm for program analysis has the potential to reduce drastically the amount of work spent in preprocessing or other auxiliary phases by propagating only appropriate demands into earlier phases (*e.g.*, "What are the alias pairs that can hold on entry to p?").

  With the approach presented in this paper, this capability is obtained for free, as a by-product of the way the composition of two computations is treated by the magic-sets transformation.

- *Sidestepping incremental-updating problems.* An optimizing transformation performed at one point in the program can invalidate previously computed dataflow information at other points in the program. In some cases, the old information at such points is not a "safe" summary of the possible execution states that can arise there; the dataflow information needs to be updated before it is possible to perform optimizing transformations at such points. However, no good incremental algorithms for interprocedural dataflow analysis are currently known.

  An alternative is to use an algorithm for the demand version of the dataflow problem and have the optimizer place appropriate demands. With each demand, the algorithm would be invoked on the *current* program. (As indicated above, any information cached from previous queries would be discarded whenever the program is modified.)

- *Demand analysis as a user-level operation.* It is desirable to have program-development tools in which the user can interactively ask questions about various aspects of a program [19,26,18,13]. Such tools are particularly useful when debugging, when trying to understand complicated code, or when trying to transform a program to execute efficiently on a parallel machine.

When interprocedural-analysis problems are encoded in Coral [21] (or some other logic-programming language with a bottom-up evaluation strategy), demand algorithms can be obtained totally automatically. In principle, however, the approach described in the paper is not just restricted to interprocedural-analysis problems encoded in logic-programming languages. That is, the techniques can be carried over—as a hand-applied transformation—to program-analysis implementations written in other languages (such as C).

The remainder of the paper is organized as follows: Section 2 discusses background and assumptions. Section 3 summarizes our methodology for obtaining algorithms that solve the demand versions of interprocedural analysis problems. It also presents two examples that illustrate the capabilities of the magic-sets transformation. Section 4 shows how to obtain demand algorithms for the interprocedural gen-kill problems. Section 5 discusses related work. An excerpt from the transformed program that is the result of applying the magic-sets transformation to the program presented in Section 4 is attached as an Appendix.

2. Background and Assumptions

Interprocedural analysis is typically carried out using a graph data structure to represent the program: the graph used represents both *intra*procedural information—information about the individual procedures of the program—and *inter*procedural information—*e.g.*, the call/return linkages, the binding changes associated with entering a new scope in the called procedure, *etc.* For example, in interprocedural dataflow analysis, analysis is carried out on a structure that consists of a control-flow graph for each procedure, plus some additional procedure-linkage information [1,6,23,10].

In interprocedural analysis problems, not all of the paths in the graph that represents the program correspond to possible execution paths. In general, the question of whether a given path is a possible execution path is undecidable, but certain paths can be identified as being infeasible because they would correspond to execution paths with infeasible call/return linkages. For example, if procedure *Main* calls P twice—say at c_1 and c_2—one infeasible path would start at the entry point of *Main*, travel through the graph for *Main* to c_1, enter P, travel through the graph for P to the return point, and return to *Main* at c_2 (rather than c_1). Such paths fail to account correctly for the calling context (*e.g.*, c_1 in *Main*) of a called procedure (*e.g.*, P). Thus, in many interprocedural analysis problems an important issue is to carry out the analysis so that only *interprocedurally valid paths* are considered [23,20,8,14,17] (see Definition 4.3). With the approach taken in this paper, if the exhaustive algorithm considers only interprocedurally valid paths, then the demand algorithm obtained will also consider only interprocedurally valid paths.

To streamline the presentation, the dataflow analysis problems discussed in Section 4 have been simplified in certain ways. In particular, following Sharir and Pnueli [23] we assume that (i) all variables are global variables, (ii) procedures are parameterless, (iii) the programs being analyzed do not contain aliasing, and (iv) the programs being analyzed do not use procedure-valued variables. A few words about each is in order: Simplifications (i) and (ii) prevent the Sharir-Pnueli framework from being able to handle local variables and formal parameters of procedures in the presence of recursion; however, Knoop and Steffen have presented a generalization of the Sharir-Pnueli framework that lifts this restriction [15]. It is possible to generalize the approach described in Section 4 to implement the more general Knoop-Steffen framework. The interaction between interprocedural dataflow analysis and the computation of aliasing information has already been mentioned in the Introduction: with the approach presented in this paper only appropriate demands for aliasing information would be generated, which might greatly reduce the amount of work required for alias analysis. Finally, G. Rosay and the author have been able to develop a method for constructing call multigraphs in the presence of procedure-valued variables that is compatible with the dataflow-analysis method described in the paper; this work combines and extends the methods described by Lakhotia [16] and Callahan *et al.* [9]. (Because of space limitations, it is not possible to discuss these issues in more detail.)

In the logic programs given in the paper, we follow the standard naming convention used in Prolog: identifiers that begin with lower-case letters denote ground atoms; those that begin with upper-case letters denote variables. In Section 4, we also make use of a notation from Coral for manipulating relations with set-valued fields; this notation will be explained at the place it is first used.

3. Using the Magic-Sets Transformation to Obtain Demand Algorithms

Our methodology for obtaining algorithms that solve the demand versions of interprocedural analysis problems has two phases: (1) encode the algorithm for the exhaustive version of the problem as a logic program; (2) convert the algorithm for the exhaustive version to a demand algorithm by applying a transformation—known as the Alexander method [22] or the magic-sets transformation [3,7]—that was developed in the logic-programming and deductive-database communities for optimizing the evaluation of recursive queries in deductive databases. In principle, the second step is completely automatic; in practice—at least with the Coral system—to obtain the most efficient program, the user may need to rewrite certain recursive rules and reorder literals in some rules. (Such concerns are outside the scope of this paper.)

We now present two examples that illustrate the capabilities of the magic-sets transformation. (Readers already familiar with the magic-sets transformation should skip to the next section.)

The magic-sets transformation attempts to combine the advantages of a top-down, goal-directed evaluation strategy with those of a bottom-up evaluation strategy. One disadvantage with top-down, goal-directed search (at least the depth-first one employed in Prolog) is that it is incomplete—it may loop endlessly, failing to find any answer at all, even when answers do exist. Another disadvantage of top-down, goal-directed search is that it may take exponential time on examples that a bottom-up evaluation strategy handles in polynomial time.

A bottom-up strategy starts from the base relations and iteratively applies an "immediate-consequence" operator until a fixed point is reached. One advantage of a bottom-up evaluation strategy is that it is complete. It can be thought of as essentially a dynamic-programming strategy: the values for all smaller subproblems are tabulated, then the answer for the item of interest is selected. However, bottom-up evaluation strategies also have the main drawbacks of dynamic programming, namely that (i) much effort may be expended to solve subproblems that are completely irrelevant to the final answer and (ii) a great deal of space may be used storing solutions to such subproblems.

The magic-sets approach is based on bottom-up evaluation; however, the program evaluated is a *transformed* version of the original program, specialized for answering queries of a given form. In the transformed program, each (transformed) rule has attached to it an additional literal that represents a condition characterizing when the rule is relevant to answering queries of the given form. The additional literal narrows the range of applicability of the rule and hence causes it to "fire" less often.

Example. The gains that can be obtained via the magic-sets transformation can be illustrated by the example of answering reachability queries in directed graphs. Let "edge(v, w)" be a given base relation that represents the edges of a directed graph.

A dynamic-programming algorithm for the reachability problem computes the transitive closure of the entire graph—this information answers *all* possible reachability queries— then selects out the edges in the transitively closed graph that emanate from the point of interest. In a logic-programming system that uses a bottom-up evaluation strategy, the dynamic-programming algorithm can be specified by writing the following program for computing transitive closure:

```
tc(V, W) :- tc(V, X),  edge(X, W).
tc(V, W) :- edge(V, W).
```

In the Coral system, which supports the magic-sets transformation, the additional declaration

```
export tc(bf).
```

directs the system to transform the program to a form that is specialized for answering queries in which the first argument is bound and the second is free (*i.e.*, queries of the form "?tc(a, W)"). The transformed program that results is

```
tc_bf(V,W) :- magic_tc_bf(V),  tc_bf(V,X),  edge(X,W).
tc_bf(V,W) :- magic_tc_bf(V),  edge(V,W).
```

Given a query "?tc(a, W)", the additional fact "magic_tc_bf(a)" is adjoined to the above set of transformed rules. These are then evaluated bottom up to produce (as answers to the query) the tuples of the relation tc_bf.

A magic fact, such as "magic_tc_bf(a)", should be read as an assertion that "The problem of finding tuples of the form tc(a, _) arises in answering the query". In this example there are no rules of the form

```
magic_tc_bf(X) :- . . .
```

Consequently, during evaluation no additional facts are ever added to the magic_tc_bf relation; that is, the only "magic fact" ever generated is the initial one, magic_tc_bf(a). (Our next example will illustrate the more general situation.) Because all of the rules in the transformed program are guarded by a literal "magic_tc_bf(V)", the bottom-up evaluation of the transformed program only visits vertices that are reachable from vertex a. In effect, the original "dynamic-programming" algorithm—perform transitive closure on the entire graph, then select out the tuples of interest—has been transformed into a reachability algorithm that searches only vertices reachable from vertex a.
End of Example.

Example. Suppose we have a base relation that records parenthood relationships (*e.g.*, a tuple "parent(x, x1)" means that x1 is a parent of x), and we would like to be able to find all cousins of a given person who are of the same generation. (In this example, a person is considered to be a "same-generation cousin" of himself.)

In a logic-programming system that uses a bottom-up evaluation strategy, a dynamic-programming algorithm can be specified by writing the following program:

```
same_generation(X, X).
same_generation(X, Y) :- parent(X, X1),
                         same_generation(X1, Y1),
                         parent(Y, Y1).
```

The directive

```
export same_generation(bf).
```

directs the Coral system to transform the program to a form specialized for answering queries of the form "?same_generation(a, Y)", which causes the program to be transformed into:

```
magic_same_generation_bf(U)  :- magic_same_generation_bf(V),
                                 parent(V, U).
same_generation_bf(X, X)  :- magic_same_generation_bf(X).
same_generation_bf(X, Y)  :- magic_same_generation_bf(X),
                             parent(X, X1),
                             same_generation_bf(X1, Y1),
                             parent(Y, Y1).
```

Given a query "?same_generation(a, Y)", the additional fact "magic_same_generation_bf(a)." is adjoined to the above set of rules, which are then evaluated bottom up.

Unlike the previous example, the transformed program produced in this example *does* have a rule with "magic_same_generation_bf(U)" in the head.

```
magic_same_generation_bf(U)  :- magic_same_generation_bf(V),
                                 parent(V, U).
```

The presence of this rule will cause "magic facts" other than the original one to be generated during evaluation. Note that the members of relation magic_same_generation_bf will be exactly the ancestors of a (the so-called "cone of a" [3]). During bottom-up evaluation of the transformed rules, the effect of the magic_same_generation_bf predicate is that attention is restricted to just same-generation cousins of ancestors of a.
End of Example.

Note that in a bottom-up evaluation, the transformed program (the demand algorithm) will never perform more work than the untransformed program (the exhaustive algorithm) would—modulo a small amount of overhead for computing magic facts, which are reported to be only a small fraction of the generated facts [4]. In practice, the demand algorithm usually performs far less work than the exhaustive algorithm.

Beeri and Ramakrishnan have shown that the bottom-up evaluation of the magic-sets-transformed version of a logic program is optimal with respect to a given "sideways-information-passing strategy (sip)"—a strategy for deciding how information gained about tuples in some of a rule's literals is to be used in evaluating other literals in the rule. For a given sip, any evaluator that uses the same sip must generate at least as many facts as are generated during a bottom-up evaluation of the magic-sets-transformed version [7].

In our context, this result relates to the question of minimizing the number of program points for which "transient" dataflow-analysis information is computed and/or the amount of information computed at those points when a given demand is placed for dataflow information. Unfortunately, the Beeri-Ramakrishnan result is only a "relative-optimality" result—it only compares top-down and bottom-up evaluations that use the *same* sip. Consequently, the amount of "transient" summary information that a demand program-analysis algorithm computes will depend on the sip that is employed. Throughout the paper, we follow Coral and assume that the sip involves working left-to-right in a rule, exploiting at a given literal all information gained from evaluating the literals to its left. (This is also the same sip that Prolog's top-down evaluator uses.) Thus, the amount of "transient" summary information computed by the demand program-analysis algorithms we obtain depends on the order in which the literals appear in the rules.

In the subsequent sections of the paper, we do not actually discuss the programs that result from the magic-sets transformation—the transformed programs are quite complicated and presenting them would not aid the reader's understanding. (To convince the reader that this is the case, the Appendix presents an excerpt from the transformed program produced by the Coral system from the program discussed in Section 4.)

4. Interprocedural Dataflow Analysis Problems

This section describes how we can obtain demand algorithms for the interprocedural gen-kill problems by encoding an exhaustive dataflow-analysis algorithm as a logic program and applying the magic-sets transformation. The basis for the exhaustive algorithm is Sharir and Pnueli's "functional approach" to interprocedural dataflow analysis, which, for distributive dataflow functions, yields the *meet-over-all-valid-paths* solution to certain classes of flow-sensitive interprocedural dataflow analysis problems [23].

We assume that $(L, \sqcap)$ is a meet semilattice of dataflow facts with a smallest element $\bot$ and a largest element $\top$. We also assume that dataflow functions are members of a space of monotonic (or distributive) functions $F \subseteq L \to L$ and that F contains the identity function.

Sharir and Pnueli make use of two different graph representations of programs, which are defined below.

Definition 4.1. (Sharir and Pnueli [23]). Define $G = \cup \{ G_p \mid p$ is a procedure in the program $\}$, where, for each p, $G_p = (N_p, E_p, r_p)$. Vertex r_p is the entry block of p; N_p is the set of basic blocks in p; $E_p = E_p^0 \cup E_p^1$ is the set of edges of G_p. An edge $(m, n) \in E_p^0$ is an ordinary control-flow edge; it represents a direct transfer of control from one block to another via a goto or an if statement. An edge $(m, n) \in E_p^1$ iff m is a call block and n is the return-site block in p for that call. Observe that vertex n is *within* p as well; it is important to understand that an edge in E_p^1 does *not* run from p to the called procedure, or vice versa.

Without loss of generality, we assume that (i) a return-site block in any G_p graph has exactly one incoming edge: the E_p^1 edge from the corresponding call block; (ii) the entry block r_p in any G_p graph is never the target of an E_p^0 edge.

This first representation, in which the flow graphs of individual procedures are kept separate from each other, is the one used by the exhaustive and demand interprocedural dataflow analysis algorithms. The second graph representation, in which the flow graphs of the different procedures are connected together, is used to define the notion of interprocedurally valid paths.

Definition 4.2. (Sharir and Pnueli [23]). Define $G^* = (N^*, E^*, r_{main})$, where $N^* = \cup_p N_p$ and $E^* = E^0 \cup E^2$, where $E^0 = \cup_p E_p^0$ is the collection of all ordinary control-flow edges, and an edge $(m, n) \in E^2$ represents either a *call* or *return* edge. Edge $(m, n) \in E^2$ is a call edge iff m is a call block and n is the entry block of the called procedure; edge $(m, n) \in E^2$ is a return edge iff m is an exit block of some procedure p and n is a return-site block for a call on p. A call edge (m, r_p) and return edge (e_q, n) *correspond* to each other if $p = q$ and $(m, n) \in E_s^1$ for some procedure s.

The notion of interprocedurally valid paths captures the idea that not all paths through G^* represent potentially valid execution paths:

Definition 4.3. (Sharir and Pnueli [23]). For each $n \in N$, we define IVP(r_{main}, n) as the set of all *interprocedurally valid paths* in G^* that lead from r_{main} to n. A path

$q \in \text{path}_{G^*}(r_{main}, n)$ is in $\text{IVP}(r_{main}, n)$ iff the sequence of all edges in q that are in E^2, which we will denote by q_2, is **proper** in the following recursive sense:

(i) A sequence q_2 that contains no return edges is proper.

(ii) If q_2 contains return edges, and i is the smallest index in q_2 such that $q_2(i)$ is a return edge, then q_2 is proper if $i > 1$ and $q_2(i-1)$ is a call edge corresponding to the return edge $q_2(i)$, and after deleting those two components from q_2, the remaining sequence is also proper.

Definition 4.4. (Sharir and Pnueli [23]). If q is a path in G^*, let f_q denote the (path) function obtained by composing the functions associated with q's edges (in the order that they appear in path q). The **meet-over-all-valid-paths** solution to the dataflow problem consists of the collection of values y_n defined by the following set of equations:

$$\Phi_n = \bigsqcap_{q \in \text{IVP}(r_{main}, n)} f_q \qquad \text{for each } n \in N^*$$

$$y_n = \Phi_n(\perp) \qquad \text{for each } n \in N^*$$

The solution to the dataflow analysis problem is not actually obtained from these equations, but from two other systems of equations, which are solved in two phases. In Phase I, the equations deal with *summary dataflow functions*, which are defined in terms of dataflow functions and other summary dataflow functions. In Phase II, the equations deal with actual dataflow *values*.

Phase I of the analysis computes summary functions $\phi_{(r_p, n)}(x)$ that map a set of dataflow facts at r_p—the entry point of procedure p—to the set of dataflow facts at point n within p. These functions are defined as the greatest solution to the following set of equations (computed over a (bounded) meet semilattice of functions):

$$\phi_{(r_p, r_p)} = \lambda x . x \qquad \text{for each procedure } p$$

$$\phi_{(r_p, n)} = \bigsqcap_{(m, n) \in E_p} (f_{(m, n)} \circ \phi_{(r_p, m)}) \qquad \text{for each } n \in N_p \text{ not representing a return-site block}$$

$$\phi_{(r_p, n)} = \phi_{(r_q, e_q)} \circ \phi_{(r_p, m)} \qquad \begin{array}{l} \text{for each } n \in N_p \text{ representing a return-site block,} \\ \text{where } (m, n) \in E_p^1 \text{ and } m \text{ calls procedure } q \end{array}$$

Phase II of the analysis uses the summary functions from Phase I to obtain a solution to the dataflow analysis problem. This solution is obtained from the greatest solution to the following set of equations:

$$x_{r_{main}} = \perp$$

$$x_{r_p} = \bigsqcap \{ \phi_{(r_q, c)}(x_{r_q}) \mid c \text{ is a call to } p \text{ in procedure } q \} \qquad \text{for each procedure } p$$

$$x_n = \phi_{(r_p, n)}(x_{r_p}) \qquad \begin{array}{l} \text{for each procedure } p \\ \text{and } n \in (N_p - \{ r_p \}) \end{array}$$

Sharir and Pnueli showed that if the edge functions are distributive, the greatest solution to the above set of equations is equal to the meet-over-all-valid-paths solution (i.e., for all n, $x_n = y_n$) [23].

4.1. Representing an Interprocedural Dataflow Analysis Problem

To make use of the Sharir-Pnueli formulation for our purposes, it is necessary to find an appropriate way to use Horn clauses to express (i) the dataflow functions on the edges of the control-flow graph, (ii) the application of a function to an argument, (iii) the composition of two functions, and (iv) the meet of two functions.

In this paper, we restrict our attention to the class of problems that can be posed in terms of functions of the form $\lambda x . (x - kill) \cup gen$, with $\cup$ as the meet operator. (Examples of such problems are reaching definitions and live variables.) To encode the dataflow functions, we use *nkill* sets instead of *kill* sets; that is, each dataflow function is rewritten in the form $\lambda x.(x \cap nkill) \cup gen$. Such a function can be represented as a pair $(nkill, gen)$. Given this representation of edge functions, it is easy to verify that the rules for performing the composition and meet of two functions are as follows:

$$(nkill_2, gen_2) \circ (nkill_1, gen_1) = (nkill_1 \cap nkill_2, (gen_1 \cap nkill_2) \cup gen_2) \qquad (\dagger)$$
$$(nkill_2, gen_2) \sqcap (nkill_1, gen_1) = (nkill_1 \cup nkill_2, gen_1 \cup gen_2) \qquad (\ddagger)$$

An instance of a dataflow analysis problem is represented in terms of five base relations, which represent the following pieces of information:

e0(p, m, n)
> Edge $(m, n) \in E_p^0$; that is (m, n) is an ordinary (intraprocedural) control-flow edge in procedure p.

e1(p, m, n)
> Edge $(m, n) \in E_p^1$. Bear in mind that both endpoints of an e1 edge are in p; an e1 edge does *not* run from p to the called procedure, or vice versa.

f(p, m, n, nk_set, g_set)
> A tuple f(p, m, n, nk_set, g_set) represents the function on edge $(m, n) \in E_p^0$. (The set-valued fields nk_set and g_set represent the *nkill* set and the *gen* set, respectively.)

call_site(p, q, m)
> Vertex m in procedure p represents a call on procedure q.

universe(u)
> u is a set-valued field that consists of the universe of dataflow facts.

4.2. The Encoding of Phase I

We now show how to encode Phase I of the Sharir-Pnueli functional approach to dataflow analysis. There are two derived relations, phi_nk(p, n, x) and phi_g(p, n, x), which together represent $\phi_{(r_p, n)}$, the summary function for vertex n of procedure p. (Recall that each dataflow function corresponds to a pair $(nkill, gen)$.)

phi_nk(p, n, x)
> A tuple phi_nk(p, n, x) represents the fact that x is a member of the nkill component of $\phi_{(r_p, n)}$.

phi_g(p, n, x)
> A tuple phi_g(p, n, x) represents the fact that x is a member of the gen component of $\phi_{(r_p, n)}$.

The rules that encode Phase I perform compositions and meets of (representations of) dataflow functions according to equations ($\dagger$) and ($\ddagger$) (although the way in which this is accomplished is somewhat disguised).

Initialization Rule

```
phi_nk(P, start_vertex, X) :- universe(U), member(U,X).
```

In Coral, a literal of the form member(S, X), where S is a set, causes X to be bound successively to each of the different members of S. (If X is already bound, then X is checked for membership in S.) Thus, for each procedure p the *nkill* component of the function $\phi_{(r_p, r_p)}$ consists of the universe of dataflow facts (*i.e.*, nothing is killed along the 0-length path from the start vertex to itself).

Intraprocedural Summary Functions

The rules for *intra*procedural summary functions correspond to the equation

$$\phi_{(r_p, n)} = \prod_{(m, n) \in E_p} (f_{(m, n)} \circ \phi_{(r_p, m)}) \qquad \text{for each } n \in N_p \text{ not representing a return-site block}$$

Note from equation (†) that the composition $f_{(m, n)} \circ \phi_{(r_p, m)}$ is implemented as

$$(nkill_{f_{(m, n)}}, gen_{f_{(m, n)}}) \circ (nkill_{\phi_{(r_p, m)}}, gen_{\phi_{(r_p, m)}}) = (\ nkill_{\phi_{(r_p, m)}} \cap nkill_{f_{(m, n)}},$$
$$(gen_{\phi_{(r_p, m)}} \cap nkill_{f_{(m, n)}}) \cup gen_{f_{(m, n)}}\ ).$$

The three rules given below create the intraprocedural summary functions.

```
phi_nk(P, N, X) :- e0(P, M, N),
                   f(P, M, N, NK_set, _),
                   member(NK_set, X),
                   phi_nk(P, M, X).
phi_g(P, N, X)  :- e0(P, M, N),
                   f(P, M, N, NK_set, _),
                   member(NK_set, X),
                   phi_g(P, M, X).
phi_g(P, N, X)  :- e0(P, M, N),
                   f(P, M, N, _, G_set),
                   member(G_set, X).
```

For example, the first rule specifies the following:

> Given an intraprocedural edge in procedure P from M to N, where edge-function
> f's *nkill* component is NK_set, add $X \in$ NK_set to the *nkill* component of
> $\phi_{(r_p, N)}$ only if X is in the *nkill* component of $\phi_{(r_p, M)}$.

This is another way of saying "Take the intersection of the *nkill* components of $f_{(M, N)}$ and
$\phi_{(r_p, M)}$", which is exactly what is required for the *nkill* component of the composition
$f_{(M, N)} \circ \phi_{(r_p, M)}$.

Interprocedural Summary Functions

The rules for *inter*procedural summary functions correspond to the equation

$$\phi_{(r_p, n)} = \phi_{(r_q, e_q)} \circ \phi_{(r_p, m)} \qquad \begin{array}{l} \text{for each } n \in N_p \text{ representing a return-site block,} \\ \text{where } (m, n) \in E_p^1 \text{ and } m \text{ calls procedure } q \end{array}$$

From equation (†), the composition $\phi_{(r_q, e_q)} \circ \phi_{(r_p, m)}$ is implemented as

$$(nkill_{\phi_{(r_q, e_q)}}, gen_{\phi_{(r_q, e_q)}}) \circ (nkill_{\phi_{(r_p, m)}}, gen_{\phi_{(r_p, m)}}) = (\ nkill_{\phi_{(r_p, m)}} \cap nkill_{\phi_{(r_q, e_q)}},$$
$$(gen_{\phi_{(r_p, m)}} \cap nkill_{\phi_{(r_q, e_q)}}) \cup gen_{\phi_{(r_q, e_q)}}\ ).$$

Thus, the following additional rules account for the propagation of summary information
between procedures:

```
phi_nk(P, N, X) :- el(P, M, N),
                    call_site(P, Q, M),
                    phi_nk(P, M, X),
                    phi_nk(Q, return_vertex, X).
phi_g(P, N, X) :- el(P, M, N),
                    call_site(P, Q, M),
                    phi_g(P, M, X),
                    phi_nk(Q, return_vertex, X).
phi_g(P, N, X) :- el(P, M, N),
                    call_site(P, Q, M),
                    phi_g(Q, return_vertex, X).
```

For instance, the first rule specifies the following:

> Given an edge from M to N in P, where M is a call site on procedure Q, the *nkill* component of $\phi_{(r_p, n)}$ consists of the X's such that X is in both the *nkill* component of $\phi_{(r_P, M)}$ and the *nkill* component of $\phi_{(r_Q, \epsilon_Q)}$.

Again, this takes the intersection of the two *nkill* components, which is exactly what is required for the *nkill* component of the composition $\phi_{(r_Q, \epsilon_Q)} \circ \phi_{(r_P, M)}$.

Note that there are two rules—one intraprocedural, one interprocedural—whose head is phi_nk(P, N, X), each of which can contribute tuples to the relation phi_nk. In the flow graph, a given vertex N either has one el predecessor or a number of e0 predecessors. Thus, the rule for phi_nk in the intraprocedural group can cause tuples to be added to phi_nk because of different predecessors M of N. This gives the correct implementation because what is required is the meet (pointwise $\cup$) of the ϕ functions obtained from all predecessors, and the rule for the meet of two functions involves the union of *nkill* sets (see equation (‡)). Similar reasoning applies in the case of relation phi_g, which is defined using four different rules.

It should also be noted that the reason we chose our function representations to be *nkill/gen* pairs rather than *kill/gen* pairs was so that the meet of two functions could be handled by the union implicit in having multiple rules that define phi_nk and phi_g, as well as the fact that rules have multiple solutions. If *kill* sets had been used instead, then to implement the function-meet operation we would have needed a way to perform an intersection over the *kill* sets generated from all predecessors of N. (With the *nkill/gen* representation of functions, the only intersections needed are for implementing the *composition* of functions. For example, the first component on the right-hand side of rule (†) is $nkill_1 \cap nkill_2$. However, we never have to perform an explicit composition of an *arbitrary* number of functions: every composition involves exactly *two* functions, and hence requires taking the intersection of exactly *two* nkill sets. These (binary) intersection operations are implemented in the Coral program by having two literals—either f and phi_nk or two phi_nk's—in the *same* rule.) If we were to represent functions as *kill/gen* pairs, the (binary) meet of two functions would involve the operation $kill_1 \cap kill_2$. This would cause a problem because we need to perform meets over functions created from an *arbitrary* number of predecessors. That is, it would be necessary to perform the *k*-ary operation $\bigcap_{i=1}^{k} kill_i$; however, this cannot be captured statically in a single rule.

Remark. For similar reasons, a certain amount of finessing is required to handle interprocedural dataflow problems for which the meet operation in the semilattice of dataflow facts is $\cap$. (An example of such a problem is the available-expressions problem.) Such problems are dual to the problems for which meet is $\cup$ in the following sense: if the edge functions are of the form $\lambda x.(x \cap nkill) \cup gen$ they can be put into the form

$\lambda x . (x \cup gen) \cap (nkill \cup gen)$. If we define the pair $[a, b]$ to represent the function $\lambda x . (x \cup a) \cap b$, then all flow functions are of the form $[gen, nkill \cup gen]$. Composition and meet of $[\bullet, \bullet]$ pairs for an $\cap$-semilattice of dataflow facts are dual to composition and meet of $(\bullet, \bullet)$ pairs for a $\cup$-semilattice of dataflow facts. However, the meet (pointwise $\cap$) of k functions represented as $[\bullet, \bullet]$ pairs would require performing the k-ary operation $\overset{k}{\underset{i=1}{\cap}} gen_i$. Again, the problem is that this cannot be captured statically in a single rule.

To sidestep this difficulty, for intersection problems we would represent functions with $kill$ and $ngen$ sets: a pair $< kill, ngen >$ would represent the function $\lambda x . (x \cap \overline{kill}) \cup \overline{ngen}$. It can be shown that the meet (pointwise $\cap$) of two functions represented as $< \bullet, \bullet >$ pairs has the following implementation:

$$< kill_2, ngen_2 > \sqcap < kill_1, ngen_1 > = < (kill_1 \cap ngen_1) \cup (kill_2 \cap ngen_2), ngen_1 \cup ngen_2 >.$$

Consequently, the meet of k such functions represented as $< \bullet, \bullet >$ pairs is

$$\overset{k}{\underset{i=1}{\sqcap}} < kill_i, ngen_i > = < \overset{k}{\underset{i=1}{\cup}} (kill_i \cap ngen_i), \overset{k}{\underset{i=1}{\cup}} ngen_i >.$$

This avoids the need to perform an intersection of a collection of sets generated from a vertex's predecessors. The only intersections that need to be performed involve information that is generated along an *individual* edge (*i.e.*, $kill_i \cap ngen_i$); such binary intersections can be captured statically in a single rule. Combining the information from the set of *all* incoming edges involves only unions, and this can be handled using multiple rules (with multiple solutions).
End of Remark.

4.3. The Encoding of Phase II

In Phase II, (the representations of) dataflow functions are applied to dataflow facts. Given a set of dataflow facts x and a dataflow function represented as a pair $(nkill, gen)$, we need to create the set $(x \cap nkill) \cup gen$.

Phase II involves one derived relation, df_fact(p, n, x), which represents the fact that x is a member of the dataflow-fact set for vertex n of procedure p.

```
df_fact(P, start_vertex, X)  :- call_site(Q, P, C),
                                df_fact(Q, start_vertex, X),
                                phi_nk(Q, C, X).
df_fact(P, start_vertex, X)  :- call_site(Q, P, C),
                                phi_g(Q, C, X).
df_fact(P, N, X)  :- N <> start_vertex,
                     df_fact(P, start_vertex, X),
                     phi_nk(P, N, X).
df_fact(P, N, X)  :- N <> start_vertex,
                     phi_g(P, N, X).
```

The first and second rules propagate facts *inter*procedurally—from the start vertex of one procedure (Q) to the start vertex of a called procedure (P). The first rule specifies that

> X is a fact at the start vertex of P if (i) P is called by Q at C, (ii) X is a fact at the start vertex of Q, and (iii) X is not killed along the path in Q from the start vertex to C.

The second rule specifies that

> X is a fact at the start vertex of P if (i) P is called by Q at C and (ii) X is generated along the path in Q from the start vertex of Q to C.

As in Phase I, the meet ($\cup$) over all predecessors is handled by the disjunction implicit in having multiple rules that define df_fact(P, start_vertex, X), as well as the fact that rules have multiple solutions.

Rules three and four are similar to rules one and two, but propagate facts *intra*procedurally, *i.e.*, from the start vertex of P to other vertices of P.

4.4. Creating the Demand Version

The directive

```
export df_fact(bbf).
```

directs the Coral system to apply the magic-sets transformation to transform the program to a form that is specialized for answering queries of the form "?df_fact(p, n, X)". The transformed program (when evaluated bottom up) is an algorithm for the demand version of the interprocedural dataflow analysis problem: the set of dataflow facts for vertex n of procedure p is the collection of all bindings returned for X. During the evaluation of a query "?df_fact(p, n, X)", the algorithm computes phi_nk and phi_g tuples for all vertices on valid paths to vertex n, df_fact tuples for all start vertices that occur on valid paths to n, and df_fact tuples for vertex n itself; finally, it selects the bindings for X from the df_fact tuples for n.

5. Related Work

Previous work on demand-driven dataflow analysis has dealt only with the *intra*procedural case [2,27]. The work that has been reported in the present paper complements previous work on the intraprocedural case in the sense that our approach to obtaining algorithms for demand-driven dataflow analysis problems applies equally well to intraprocedural dataflow analysis. However, in intraprocedural dataflow analysis all paths in the control-flow graph are (statically) valid paths; for this reason, previous work on demand-driven *intra*procedural dataflow analysis does not extend well to the *inter*procedural case, where the notion of *valid paths* is important.

A recent paper by Duesterwald, Gupta, and Soffa discusses a very different approach to obtaining demand versions of (intraprocedural) dataflow analysis algorithms [12]. For each query of the form "Is fact f in the solution set at vertex v?", a set of dataflow equations are set up on the flow graph (but as if all edges were reversed). The flow functions on the reverse graph are the (approximate) inverses of the original forward functions. (A special function—derived from the query—is used for the reversed flow function of vertex v.) These equations are then solved using a demand-driven fixed-point finding procedure to obtain a value for the entry vertex. The answer to the query (true or false) is determined from the value so obtained. Some of the differences between their work and ours are as follows:

- Their method can only answer *ground queries* of the form "?df_fact(p, n, x)". With the approach used in this paper *any combination of bound and free arguments* in a query are possible (*e.g.*, "?df_fact(p, n, X)", "?df_fact(p, N, X)", "?df_fact(P, N, x)", *etc.*).
- Their method does not appear to permit information to be accumulated over successive queries. The equations for a given query are tailored to that particular query and are slightly different from the equations for all other queries. Consequently, answers (and intermediate values) previously computed for other queries cannot be reused.
- It is not clear from the extensions they outline for interprocedural dataflow analysis whether the algorithm obtained will properly account for valid paths.

Previous work on *inter*procedural data flow analysis has dealt only with the exhaustive case [23,15]. This paper has described how to obtain algorithms for solving demand versions of interprocedural analysis problems from their exhaustive counterparts, essentially for free. Section 4 describes how to use Horn clauses to specify an algorithm for the interprocedural gen-kill dataflow-analysis problems. Recently, M. Sagiv, S. Horwitz, and the author have devised a way to extend the techniques described in the paper to a much larger class of dataflow problems—in particular, those in which the dataflow functions are drawn from the collection of distributive functions in $2^D \rightarrow 2^D$, where D is any finite set.

After the work reported in this paper was completed, the work by D.S. Warren and others concerning the use of tabulation techniques in top-down evaluation of logic programs [24] was brought to my attention. These techniques provide an alternative method for obtaining demand algorithms for program-analysis problems. Rather than applying the magic-sets transformation to a Horn-clause encoding of the (exhaustive) dataflow-analysis algorithm and then using a bottom-up evaluator, the original (untransformed) Horn-clause encoding can simply be evaluated by an OLDT (top-down, tabulating) evaluator. Thus, another way to obtain an implementation of a demand algorithm for the interprocedural gen-kill dataflow-analysis problems would be to use the program from Section 4 in conjunction with the SUNY-Stony Brook XSB system [25].

Acknowledgements

Alan Demers, Fritz Henglein, Susan Horwitz, Neil Jones, Bernard Lang, Raghu Ramakrishnan, Genevieve Rosay, Mooly Sagiv, Marvin Solomon, Divesh Srivastava, and Tim Teitelbaum provided comments and helpful suggestions about the work.

Appendix: The Demand Interprocedural Dataflow Analysis Algorithm

The following is an excerpt from the transformed program produced by Coral from the interprocedural dataflow-analysis program presented in Section 4:

```
sup_1_1(Q,P,C) :-                    df_fact_bbf(P,start_vertex,X) :-
  m_df_fact_bbf(P,start_vertex),       sup_1_2(Q,X,P,C),
  call_site(Q,P,C).                     phi_nk_bbb(Q,C,X).
m_df_fact_bbf(Q,start_vertex) :-     sup_2_1(Q,P,C) :-
  sup_1_1(Q,P,C).                      m_df_fact_bbf(P,start_vertex),
sup_1_2(Q,X,P,C) :-                    call_site(Q,P,C).
  sup_1_1(Q,P,C),                    m_phi_g_bbf(Q,C) :-
  df_fact_bbf(Q,start_vertex,X).       sup_2_1(Q,P,C).
m_phi_nk_bbb(Q,C,X) :-
  sup_1_2(Q,X,P,C).                   ... and so on for 128 more lines
```

References

1. Allen, F.E., "Interprocedural data flow analysis," pp. 398-408 in *Information Processing 74: Proceedings of the IFIP Congress 74*, ed. J.L. Rosenfield, North-Holland, Amsterdam (1974).

2. Babich, W.A. and Jazayeri, M., "The method of attributes for data flow analysis: Part II. Demand analysis," *Acta Informatica* 10(3) pp. 265-272 (October 1978).

3. Bancilhon, F., Maier, D., Sagiv, Y., and Ullman, J., "Magic sets and other strange ways to implement logic programs," in *Proceedings of the Fifth ACM Symposium on Principles of Database Systems*, (1986).

4. Bancilhon, F. and Ramakrishnan, R., "Performance evaluation of data intensive logic programs," pp. 439-517 in *Foundations of Deductive Databases and Logic Programming*, ed. J. Minker, Morgan-Kaufmann (1988).

5. Banning, J.P., "An efficient way to find the side effects of procedure calls and the aliases of variables," pp. 29-41 in *Conference Record of the Sixth ACM Symposium on Principles of Programming Languages*, (San Antonio, TX, Jan. 29-31, 1979), ACM, New York, NY (1979).

6. Barth, J.M., "A practical interprocedural data flow analysis algorithm," *Commun. of the ACM* **21**(9) pp. 724-736 (September 1978).

7. Beeri, C. and Ramakrishnan, R., "On the power of magic," pp. 269-293 in *Proceedings of the Sixth ACM Symposium on Principles of Database Systems*, (San Diego, CA, March 1987), (1987).

8. Callahan, D., "The program summary graph and flow-sensitive interprocedural data flow analysis," *Proceedings of the ACM SIGPLAN 88 Conference on Programming Language Design and Implementation*, (Atlanta, GA, June 22-24, 1988), *ACM SIGPLAN Notices* **23**(7) pp. 47-56 (July 1988).

9. Callahan, D., Carle, A., Hall, M.W., and Kennedy, K., "Constructing the procedure call multigraph," *IEEE Transactions on Software Engineering* **SE-16**(4) pp. 483-487 (April 1990).

10. Cooper, K.D. and Kennedy, K., "Interprocedural side-effect analysis in linear time," *Proceedings of the ACM SIGPLAN 88 Conference on Programming Language Design and Implementation*, (Atlanta, GA, June 22-24, 1988), *ACM SIGPLAN Notices* **23**(7) pp. 57-66 (July 1988).

11. Cooper, K.D. and Kennedy, K., "Fast interprocedural alias analysis," pp. 49-59 in *Conference Record of the Sixteenth ACM Symposium on Principles of Programming Languages*, (Austin, TX, Jan. 11-13, 1989), ACM, New York, NY (1989).

12. Duesterwald, E., Gupta, R., and Soffa, M.L., "Demand-driven program analysis," Technical Report TR-93-15, Department of Computer Science, University of Pittsburgh, Pittsburgh, PA (October 1993).

13. Horwitz, S. and Teitelbaum, T., "Generating editing environments based on relations and attributes," *ACM Trans. Program. Lang. Syst.* **8**(4) pp. 577-608 (October 1986).

14. Horwitz, S., Reps, T., and Binkley, D., "Interprocedural slicing using dependence graphs," *ACM Trans. Program. Lang. Syst.* **12**(1) pp. 26-60 (January 1990).

15. Knoop, J. and Steffen, B., "The interprocedural coincidence theorem," pp. 125-140 in *Proceedings of the Fourth International Conference on Compiler Construction*, (Paderborn, FRG, October 5-7, 1992), *Lecture Notes in Computer Science*, Vol. 641, ed. U. Kastens and P. Pfahler, Springer-Verlag, New York, NY (1992).

16. Lakhotia, A., "Constructing call multigraphs using dependence graphs," pp. 273-284 in *Conference Record of the Twentieth ACM Symposium on Principles of Programming Languages*,(Charleston, SC, Jan. 11-13, 1993), ACM, New York, NY (1993).

17. Landi, W. and Ryder, B.G., "Pointer-induced aliasing: A problem classification," pp. 93-103 in *Conference Record of the Eighteenth ACM Symposium on Principles of Programming Languages*, (Orlando, FL, January 1991), ACM, New York, NY (1991).

18. Linton, M.A., "Implementing relational views of programs," *Proceedings of the ACM SIGSOFT/SIGPLAN Software Engineering Symposium on Practical Software Development Environments*, (Pittsburgh, PA, Apr. 23-25, 1984), *ACM SIGPLAN Notices* **19**(5) pp. 132-140 (May 1984).

19. Masinter, L.M., "Global program analysis in an interactive environment," Tech. Rep. SSL-80-1, Xerox Palo Alto Research Center, Palo Alto, CA (January 1980).

20. Myers, E., "A precise inter-procedural data flow algorithm," pp. 219-230 in *Conference Record of the Eighth ACM Symposium on Principles of Programming Languages*, (Williamsburg, VA, January 26-28, 1981), ACM, New York, NY (1981).

21. Ramakrishnan, R., Seshadri, P., Srivastava, D., and Sudarshan, S., "Coral pre-Release 1.0," Software system, Computer Sciences Department, University of Wisconsin, Madison, WI (1993). (Available via ftp from ftp.cs.wisc.edu.)

22. Rohmer, R., Lescoeur, R., and Kersit, J.-M., "The Alexander method, a technique for the processing of recursive axioms in deductive databases," *New Generation Computing* **4**(3) pp. 273-285 (1986).

23. Sharir, M. and Pnueli, A., "Two approaches to interprocedural data flow analysis," pp. 189-233 in *Program Flow Analysis: Theory and Applications*, ed. S.S. Muchnick and N.D. Jones, Prentice-Hall, Englewood Cliffs, NJ (1981).

24. Warren, D.S., "Memoing for logic programs," *Commun. of the ACM* **35**(3) pp. 93-111 (March 1992).

25. Warren, D.S., "XSB Logic Programming System," Software system, Computer Science Department, State University of New York, Stony Brook, NY (1993). (Available via ftp from sbcs.sunysb.edu.)

26. Weiser, M., "Program slicing," *IEEE Transactions on Software Engineering* **SE-10**(4) pp. 352-357 (July 1984).

27. Zadeck, F.K., "Incremental data flow analysis in a structured program editor," *Proceedings of the SIGPLAN 84 Symposium on Compiler Construction*, (Montreal, Can., June 20-22, 1984), *ACM SIGPLAN Notices* **19**(6) pp. 132-143 (June 1984).

Compile Time Instruction Cache Optimizations

Abraham Mendlson[1], Shlomit S. Pinter[1] and Ruth Shtokhamer[2]

[1] Dept. of Electrical Engineering
Technion, Haifa Israel
[2] Dept. of Computer and Information Sciences
University of Delaware, Delaware U.S.A

Abstract. This paper presents a new approach for improving performance of instruction cache based systems. The idea is to prevent cache misses caused when different segments of code, which are executed in the same loop, are mapped onto the same cache area. The new approach uses static information only and does not rely on any special hardware mechanisms such as support of non-cachable addresses. The technique can be applied at compile time or as part of object modules optimization. The technique is based on replication of code together with algorithms for code placement. We introduce the notion of abstract caches and present simulation results of the new technique. The results show that in certain cases, the number of cache misses is reduced by two orders of magnitude.

1 Introduction

As the speed of a processor increases, the penalties for cache misses become more severe. In order to improve performance, modern computers use a fast clock rate, long pipelines and cache memories, but their access time to the main memory remains relatively slow. Reducing instruction cache misses can improve the overall CPI (clocks per instruction) rate [6] that the processor can achieve. Recently, some widely used benchmarks revealed that there is an important class of programs which show a significant amount of instruction cache misses [8, 9, 2]. Hennessy and Patterson [5] distinguish between three sources for cache misses: (1) *Compulsory* (footprint [13]) – a miss caused when a processor accesses a cache block for the first time. (2) *Capacity* – a miss caused when the cache is too small to hold all the required data and (3) *Conflict* – a miss caused in set associative architecture when the replacement algorithm removes a line and soon fetches it again. According to [8] most of the instruction cache misses are of the conflict type and occur when different code segments within a loop are mapped onto the same cache set.

This paper presents a new approach for reducing instruction cache misses. It uses code replication together with replacement optimization in order to decrease conflict misses, and is based on static information only (information that can be derived at compile time). Conflict cache misses inside loops can be totally eliminated if the loop is small enough to fit in the cache and the code is mapped into the cache without an overlap; such a mapping is achieved by replicating instructions and properly mapping the copies to different sets of the cache. However, the replication increases the size of the code and the number of compulsory misses. On the other hand, the misses optimization problem based on the placement paradigm alone is an NP-complete problem and in practice it was found to be ineffective in many cases.

Most instruction cache optimization techniques use dynamic information; i.e., profiling information, which is gathered from executing the code on a selected set of input data. The Pixie [3] tools [11] and [10] use profiling information to find better placements for code segments. Information gathered dynamically is also used in [3, 8] for avoiding fetching into the cache instructions either when they are used only once before being purged from the cache, or because they might conflict with other code in the loop. Such instructions are left in the main memory (non-cachable). The effect of inlining procedures on the performance is discussed [9]. In [4], code fragments are repositions so that the cache line will not be polluted (will not contain instructions that are never referenced). All of these techniques were found to be successful mostly for small caches.

Our algorithm works in two phases. In the first one, instructions executed in a loop are arranged relative to each other so that no conflict misses occur if the cache can hold all of them. At this stage, it is assumed that the code is replicated when needed (e.g. a procedure could be replicated if it will be needed in two loops in different relative locations). In the next phase, the expended program (with its replications) is partitioned into parts that fit the cache size (termed abstract caches); during this process, the replications of a code assigned to a single abstract cache are merged. Our experiments show that the total increase in code size is around 5% to 10%. This is followed by heuristics for placing the code of each abstract cache (selecting its address in main memory) and globally trying to merge replications that can each be mapped to the same set in their relative abstract caches.

The new method improves the performance of most small and medium caches as long as the size of inner loops are smaller then the size of the cache. Several of our experiments show an improvement of two orders of magnitude in the number of instruction cache misses. Thus, it seems that the saving of conflict misses when a loop is executed outperforms the addition of compulsory misses due to the extra copies. Note that the new cache optimization can be applied at compile time or as part of object modules optimization (for example in the OM system [12]).

The rest of this paper is organized as follows: in Section 2, we provide a rigorous framework for instruction cache optimization algorithms by formulating the general problem and the optimization criteria. The first algorithm that partitions the flow graph into cache sized program parts (abstract caches) is presented in Section 3. In Section 4, we describe how program segments of different abstract caches are placed in the program address space. Performance benchmark results are presented in Section 5 and conclusions in Section 6.

---

[3] Pixie is a trademark of MIPS Computer Systems, Inc.

2   Definitions and the Cache Mapping Problem

In this section, we define the general setting of the problem.

2.1   The Cache

For simplicity, we consider in our framework a direct mapped instruction cache. The cache memory is partitioned into *lines* (sometimes called *blocks*) that can each hold a few memory words. The entire block is fetched or replaced in any cache operation that involves the memory. When using a direct mapped cache, any physical address has exactly a single cache line that can hold it. We discuss later on the adaptation of our method to different cache organizations as well.

2.2   The Cache Mapping Problem

The number of misses caused by a program depends on the input data, but since the placement of code segments in the virtual address space is fixed for all possible inputs, it may happen that a code mapping may be optimal for one execution and non-optimal for another. Thus, the mapping problem is defined with respect to a *typical set of executions* determined by some set of input data. The question of what is a good typical execution set depends on what information is available and whether we are looking to optimize the most frequently used execution, an average occurring execution or the worst possible case (i.e. choose the mapping for which the worst execution is the best). Note that many different executions of a single mapping can still be optimal. For example, whenever a conditional branch (which does not close a loop) occurs, the code segments on the true branch can be mapped in such a way that they will fall on the same cache lines as the code on the false branch owing to the fact that they never execute together.

The Cache Mapping Problem: *Given a set of cache parameters, a program, and a typical execution set, find a placement of the program parts (in the memory address space) that minimizes the total number of misses for the typical execution set.*

2.3   Program Structures and Intervals

To simplify our analysis of the program behavior, the input programs are assumed to be well-structured. Thus, loops are properly nested and every loop has a single exit point; a procedure call is always returned to the instruction immediately following the call (see [1] for justifications of the assumption). We present such a program by the Nested Flow Graph (NFG), which is a flow graph [1] augmented with information about the nesting structures of loops and the calls for procedures.

   In the flow graph, every node represents a basic block, and an edge from node v to node u indicates that the execution of u must follow that of v. In the NFG, there is another type of node called a *level node*; such a node represents a loop (its level) or a procedure call (when its body is not inline). In addition, we use *nesting edges* to indicate a change in the nesting level. The NFG is generated from the flow graph by replacing each loop closing back edge with a level node and directing such an edge to point into that level node (see Figure 1). The flow edges that enter the loop are now pointing to the level node and the flow edge leaving the loop is now drawn from the loop level node. Similar construction is applied to procedure calls. A nesting edge is drawn from a level node to the node that represents the beginning of the loop's (or procedure) body. For recursive (direct or indirect) procedure calls, we stop generating level nodes when there is a path from a previous call to the current call and the path contains a nesting edge.

The code fragment in Figure 1 has three loops and three procedure calls. Note that procedure B appears twice in the NFG, once when it is called from `loop2` and the second time when it is called from `loop3`.

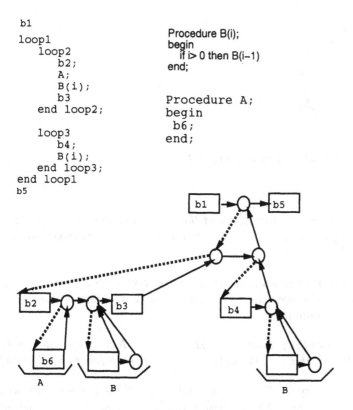

```
b1
loop1
    loop2
        b2;
        A;
        B(i);
        b3
    end loop2;

    loop3
        b4;
        B(i);
    end loop3;
end loop1
b5
```

```
Procedure B(i);
begin
    if i > 0 then B(i–1)
end;


Procedure A;
begin
    b6;
end;
```

Fig. 1. A code fragment and its NFG

Our two basic concepts – intervals and nesting interval trees – can now be defined based on the NFG of a program.

408

Definition 1 *An* **interval** *is a maximal connected sub-graph of the NFG that may not include parts nested under its level nodes. A* **segment** *is a connected sub-graph of an interval.*

Blocks **b1** and **b5** together with the level node between them are an example for an interval.

Definition 2 *A* **Nesting Interval Tree (NIT)** *of a nested flow graph is an ordered tree (order on the edges leaving a node) whose nodes are the intervals of the NFG and its edges are the nesting edges connecting the intervals.*

The nesting interval tree of the NFG in Figure 1 is presented in Figure 2.

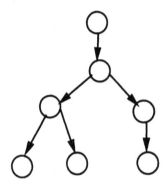

Fig. 2. The NIT of the code fragment in Figure 1

Definition 3 *Two intervals that represent the same expanded code (e.g. copies of a procedure's body replacing its calls) are called* **matching intervals** *(similar definition is used for segments).*

Note that matching intervals may appear in different places of the NFG. In particular, the body of a procedure which is called from different intervals is presented by different embodiments.

Definition 4 *The* **locality tree** *of a node, v, of the NIT is the sub-tree derived from the NIT by taking all the nodes reachable from v (on directed paths).*

Due to the redundancy (replication) of a code in the NFG a locality tree with a root v contains all the basic blocks (within the intervals nodes) for executing the program fragment represented by v. This redundancy will be used later as a powerful optimization technique.

Every mapping algorithm must place all the intervals (their basic blocks) that cover the program in the program address space so that: (1) intervals (other than matching intervals) do not overlap in memory; (2) matching intervals (e.g. those that were generated due to procedure calls) can be mapped onto the same address or onto different addresses (their names must then be modified).

The basic elements mapped by our algorithms are the intervals and segments of the program's NFG. Segments of an interval are used only when it is too large to be mapped entirely onto the cache. If the system can bypass the cache, it can be assumed that all the basic blocks that are not part of any loop are marked as non-cachable and are not part of any interval.

3 Partitioning the NFG Into Abstract Caches

The optimization algorithms use the NFG representation and the locality trees in order to map the program onto the main memory. The replications of code in the NFG are now used for generating a map that fits loop bodies (presented by the locality trees) within a single cache as long as possible. This local optimization uses abstract caches which are next presented together with some of their properties. In Section 3.2, we present a global optimization for mapping the instructions of the abstract caches into memory.

3.1 Abstract Caches

Definition 5 *An* **abstract cache** *is a connected subgraph of the NFG whose size (the total space taken by its basic blocks when its matching intervals are counted only once) is not greater than the size of the instruction cache divided by its associativity. A partition of a graph into abstract caches is an* **abstract cache cover (or cover)** *of the graph.*

Two important properties of abstract cache covers are summarized in the following lemmas:

Lemma 1. *Let C be an abstract cache cover of a nested flow graph G such that no two matching intervals are in different abstract caches. Then, all the basic blocks of G can be mapped onto a cache, whose size is at most the sum of all the abstract caches of C, without causing any conflict miss.*

Proof: In each of the abstract caches, all the basic blocks can be mapped sequentially. The total sum of the caches will be large enough to keep each program's line in a different cache line. Therefore, only footprint misses can occur.

Definition 6 *Two abstract caches can be* **mapped independently** *onto memory if their joint cover has no matching intervals.*

Lemma 2. *Given a program NFG with an abstract cache cover. If no loop is partitioned among different abstract caches and every abstract cache can be mapped independently of other abstract caches, then only compulsory cache misses can occur.*

Proof: Since no loop is partitioned between abstract caches, the program at the top level can be viewed as a sequence of abstract caches (phases of the program execution). As soon as the execution inside an abstract cache is terminated, the program will never access that code again (since the caches can be mapped independently). Since no abstract cache is larger than the physical cache, with Lemma 1, only compulsory cache misses can occur.

When replication is used, matching intervals of different abstract caches become distinct by a proper renaming. Thus, the number of footprint misses may still increase. To further reduce the additional footprint misses, global minimization of replicated code is needed. Such an optimization is employed during the final placement.

3.2 An Algorithm for Creating an Abstract Cache Cover

Since optimal mapping is defined with respect to a typical set of executions, we next discuss the set assumed by our algorithms. As we do not use profiling or run-time information, only the program structure can be used in our algorithms. We assume that the branches of a conditional are equally taken and the number of iterations in all loops are the same; thus the instructions in a loop which is nested within another loop will be executed many times more as the number of iterations per loop. Lastly, we assume that when the first instruction of a loop or a procedure is accessed its entire interval will be accessed next. In the discussion section, we consider a different set of assumptions and their effect on the mapping.

Selecting a cover for the NFG is done by traversing the nested interval tree starting from the leaves; in this way we try to keep locality trees in the same abstract cache as long as they fit. Each leaf interval is assigned to a different abstract cache. When traversing up the levels of the tree, abstract caches are merged as long as their total size (matching intervals are considered only once) is less than the cache size.

Abstract Cache Partitioning Algorithm

- Input: The NFG representation of the program, its nested interval tree $T = (V, E)$ of height H, and a cache size C.
- Output: A partition (cache cover) of the intervals into abstract caches each of size not greater than C.
- Step-1
  Assign each leaf interval of the NIT to a different abstract cache. If the size of an interval is larger than C, repeatedly extract from the interval a set of continuous basic blocks (segments) of size no greater than C and assign it to a new abstract cache.
- Step-2
  for i= H-1 **down to** 0 **do**
  * for every level node in level (height) i, make a cache cover list from the abstract caches of its descendent nodes; during this process merge

abstract caches whenever possible and leave only a single copy when several matching intervals are assigned to the same abstract cache.

* merge the cover lists of level i in a way similar to the above

- Step-3
  The cache cover list of the root is the cache cover of the program

Note that similar (matching) basic blocks, like those of called procedures, can appear in more than one abstract cache but will appear at most once in each abstract cache. Abstract caches preserve the locality of memory references generated by the processor since the graph is partitioned along the nesting levels of the NFG.

4 From Abstract Caches to the Process Address Space

In the last phase of our optimization the blocks in each abstract cache are positioned in the program address space (global optimization). The placement algorithm is based on *the basic placement algorithm* which is valid for the cases described in Lemma 2: In Section 4.2, we extend it to handle the general case. The extended algorithm applies heuristic methods for the global optimization.

4.1 The Basic Placement Algorithm

The basic placement algorithm assumes that no loop is divided among different abstract caches, and matching program intervals that reside in different abstract caches are renamed.

- Input: A list of abstract caches (ACs) covering the NFG.
- Output: A placement (address) for locating the intervals in the memory space.
- Data structures:
  Unplaced_list : A list of all ACs which have not been placed.
  Placed_list : A list of all ACs which have already been placed.
  Active_AC : The AC currently being placed.
  Program_address_space : An image of the program address space. There is an indication of each location whether it has already been placed or not.
  LPC : Points to the highest address in the program address space that has been used.
  Temp_cache : An array whose size is the same as the system cache. Used for placing the intervals of each AC.
- Initialization conditions: All the ACs are in the Unplaced_list, and LPC is 0.
- while Unplaced_list is not empty do
  1. Choose an AC from Unplaced_list to be the Active_AC.
  2. Place all intervals (their basic blocks) of Active_AC in Temp_cache continuously. This can always be done under the current assumptions (Lemma 2).

3. Copy **Temp_cache** to the program address space, starting at address LPC+1, and update LPC.
4. Put the **Active_AC** in **Placed_list**.

For mapping in the general case, there are two aspects to consider. The first one is when a replication is worthy (which affects the AC cover) and the second is the order in which to select the **Active_AC** in Step 1.

4.2 Extended Placement Algorithm — a Heuristic Approach

Since only static information is used, we assume that the entire cache is flushed when the processor exits an abstract cache. The basic algorithm is extended by checking how the placement of a replicated interval in one abstract cache can affect its placement when it appears in another abstract cache.

Consider the two calls in the inner loops of Figure 3. If the two copies of B are located in the same place relative to their abstract caches then no duplication is needed; otherwise extra footprint misses are generated in each iteration of **loop1**. Note that in both cases no conflict misses are generated for the inner loops. The exact number of misses depends on the number of iterations and the size of B. In the static case, where no information is provided on the number of times each loop is executed, we observe that preventing misses at innermost nesting loops is highly desirable.

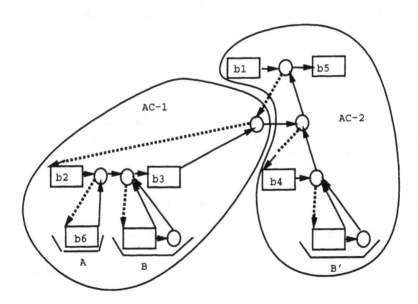

Fig. 3. Partition to abstract caches

Our extended placement algorithm is based on the basic algorithm. Its input is an abstract cache cover and the NFG in which matching intervals were not yet renamed. It uses an extra data structure `Placed_interval` to hold all the intervals which have already been placed in the program address space. Initially, `Placed_interval` is empty.

In Step 1, the policy for choosing the `Active_AC` is changed to follow a heuristic from the set H1 that is described later.

Step 2 becomes:

1. Try to place in `Temp_cache` all the intervals that belong to the `Active_AC` and which their replications appear in the `Placed_interval` list. The place in `Temp_cache` should coincide with the mapping onto the cache of the copy (one of them). If an interval cannot be placed in such a way, use a duplication policy from the set H2 which we describe later.
2. Place all the remaining intervals of the `Active_AC` in `Temp_cache`. If an interval cannot be placed, (not enough space), then it will be placed with the next abstract cache.

In Step 3, we must add the update of the `Placed_interval` list. Step 4 remains as in the basic algorithm.

In the algorithm, two sets of heuristics are used. The first, H1, determines the order in which abstract caches are chosen to be placed, and the second, H2, is used for deciding whether or not to duplicate an interval.

The order in which abstract caches are selected can be one of the following: *deep first* — choose the innermost interval to be the `Active_AC`, or a *sequential* selection which chooses some order of abstract caches which the program is most likely to visit, or lastly, a *random* choice can be made.

Each time an abstract cache is chosen, all of its intervals are mapped onto the process address space. But an interval that has a copy which is already placed in memory sometimes cannot be put in the temporary cache in the place to which its copy is mapped (the place is taken). In such a case, three policies for replications (H2) are suggested. The first is to *always replicate* — take a copy of the interval and rename it. The new interval is free of all other constraints and so can be mapped. The second is *never replicate* — use only a single version of the interval (the first one that was mapped). The last one is *sometimes replicate* — if a fraction of the desired space is occupied (overlapped), then a threshold limit is used to decide upon replication.

5 Simulation Results

This section presents simulation results of the UNZIP program which is used to uncompress and open '.ZIP' programs. A comparison is made between the program running with our optimization technique and without it. In our implementation, only procedures were replicated whenever the corresponding place in the cache was occupied by other parts of the blocks of the active abstract cache. The abstract caches were selected using a preorder search of the NFG.

First we describe the methodology being used for generating the traces and then we present and discuss the results.

5.1 Generating the Traces

We use the AE tool [7] to relocate and replicate basic blocks of programs in the main memory. This enables us to implement our algorithm independently of the compiler being used.

AE is a tool used for generating traces. It has three major phases: (1) generating static information about the program. This includes the control flow graph, a list of basic blocks with their respected addresses in memory, procedure calls, nesting of loops etc.; (2) gathering dynamic information on a particular run (using some input); (3) generating the trace by combining the program source file with the information from 1,2.

We modify the addresses of basic blocks generated in phase 1 of the AE tool in order to relocate and duplicate them according to our technique. The relocation is implemented by changing the starting point of a basic block, while replication is implemented by duplicating the description of the basic block and changing its ID and starting point. Note that by using this technique, the program keeps the same flow of control, but the addresses being generated may be shifted.

The flexibility of the AE tool is well suited to our purposes. On the other hand, the AE does not generate traces for library routines so we could not present the full capability of our technique. The instruction traces being generated were fed into the Dinero cache simulator [5].

5.2 The Simulation Results

The UNZIP program was chosen as an example for a medium size program. Its object code is 82K-bytes long, it contains 32 procedures and 22 untraced library procedures, 41 loops and 580 basic blocks. All the traces we used were 5.4M instructions long.

The cache performance is measured in terms of miss ratio for different cache and block sizes. Similar to other relevant works, we choose the cache organization to be direct mapped.

Table 1 presents the results for a cache size of 512 bytes. For such a small cache, our algorithm improves the cache miss ratio from 6% for a block size of 32 bytes to 12% for a block size of 4 bytes. The results indicate that the abstract caches were too small to hold significant loops, e.g. loops containing procedure calls. Note that a loop which does not call any procedure can be assumed to be sequentially placed for both cases.

For a cache size of 1024 bytes, our algorithm reduces the cache miss ratio compared to the C compiler by 30-35% depending on block size (see Table 2).

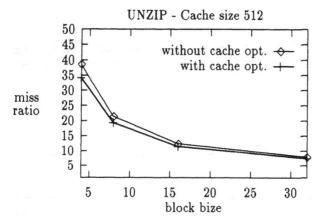

Table 1. UNZIP: Cache size 512 - 5,400,000 instructions

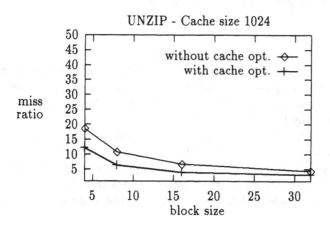

Table 2. UNZIP: Cache size 1024 - 5,400,000 instructions

Improvement of a few orders of magnitude in the cache misses is achieved with a cache size of 2048 bytes. Table 3 presents the miss ratio for this case. Due to the difference in magnitude, we present the graph in logarithmic scale.

The improvement presented in Table 3 is explained by the behavior of the program execution. Logically, the UNZIP program runs in phases. Each phase is typically composed of nested loops with procedure calls. Since the cache was large enough, our replication and relocation technique managed to place the called procedures of each phase in a conflict free manner. Thus, the total amount of misses is relatively close to the footprint of the execution and is not dependent

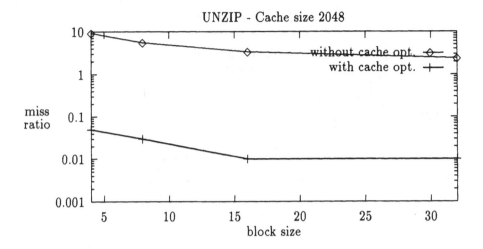

Table 3. UNZIP: Cache size 2048 - 5,400,000 instructions

on the number of times that the loops are executed.

Without replications, it is not possible to eliminate the conflicts caused by procedures called in different phases. In such a case, as soon as a cache conflict occurs in a loop, the number of cache misses depends on the dynamic nature of the program, i.e. how many times the loop is executed.

To support these conclusions we compared the footprint of our run (using a huge cache size) against the actual number of cache misses (using a cache size of 2048 bytes) with and without the cache optimizations. The results for block size of 32 bytes are 242 cache misses (footprint) compared with 474 cache misses using the cache optimizations and 130095 cache misses in the original placement generated by the compiler.

It is very likely that the above results would improve with a pre-fetch mechanism, since the replicated code is executed sequentially.

6 Conclusions and Future Work

We presented a new approach for optimizing instruction cache systems that can be applied during both compilation time and object modules optimization. The main idea in this approach is to prevent segments of codes that are executed in the same loop to be mapped onto the same cache area. Our approach differs from other techniques that use only compile time information and is based on two basic techniques: duplication of code and sophisticated placement algorithms.

We integrated our algorithm into a version of the AE tool which is based on the gcc compiler. The use of indirect methodology to examine our algorithm gives us a great deal of flexibility and the ability to get meaningful results in a reasonable amount of time. However, this approach has some limitations. In particular, it limits us to use relatively small input programs. Since a small program has a small footprint, the efficiency of our approach can be exemplified for small and medium caches only. We believe that our methodology can be even more effective when applied to larger programs.

For simplicity, we choose to use direct mapped cache memories. Nevertheless, the same algorithm can be easily extended to other cache organizations. If cache associative organization is used, the size of the abstract cache is reduced to the size of the cache divided by the associativity of the cache. Thus, more intervals can be mapped onto the same cache set before a miss occurs.

The algorithm presented here can be improved by further taking the program structure into account when placing the basic blocks. For example, the different paths of an if then else structure can be mapped onto the same cache area so that the cache will be used more efficiently to benefit smaller caches. Another possible extension can consider non-well structured programs as input.

The compilation technique presented in this paper was found to be effective for small and medium cache size and for inner loops of size smaller than the cache size. Note that we can use this information to optimize the amount of loop unrolling; i.e., the total size of the unrolled loop should not exceed the size of the cache.

Currently, we are investigating new improvements that include: the effect of different architecture mechanisms such as branch prediction, and instruction prefetching. The effect of different cache organization and parameters, and the effect of different application structures on the overall performance of our method.

References

1. A. V. Aho, R. Sethi, and J. D. Ullman. *Compilers — Principles, Techniques, and Tools*. Addison-Wesley, Reading, MA, 1986.
2. D. Bernstein, D. Cohen, Y. Lavon, and V. Rainish. Performance evaluation of instruction scheduling on the IBM RISC system/6000. In *25th Annual International Symposium on Microarchitecture*, pages 226–235, Portland, Oregon, December 1992.
3. C. Chi-Hung and H. Dietz. Improving cache performance by selective cache bypass. *Hawaii International Conference on System Science*, pages 277–285, 1989.
4. R. Gupta and C. Chi-Hung. Improving instruction cache behavior by reducing cache pollution. In *Proc. of Supercomputing '90*, pages 82–91, New-York, November 1990.
5. J. L. Hennessy and D. A. Patterson. *Computer Architecture: A Quantitative Approach*. Kaufman, 1990.
6. W. W. Hwu and P. H. Chang. Achieving high instruction cache performance with an optimizing compiler. In *The 16th International Symposium on Computer Architecture*, pages 242 – 251, Jerusalem Israel, May 1989.
7. J. R. Larus. Abstract execution: A technique for efficiently tracing programs. *Software Practice & Experience*, 20(12):1241–1258, 1990.

8. S. McFarling. On optimizations for instruction caches. In *The 3rd International Conference on Architectural Support for Programming Languages and Operating Systems*, pages 183–192, 1989.

9. S. McFarling. Cache replacement with dynamic exclusion. In *The 19th Annual International Symposium on Computer Architecture*, pages 191 – 200, Gold Coast, Australia, May 1992.

10. K. Pettis and R. C. Hansen. Profile guided code positioning. In *ACM SIGPLAN Conf. on Programming Language Design and Implementation*, pages 16 – 27, 1990.

11. M. D. Smith. Tracing with pixie. CSL-TR-91-497 91-497, Stanford University, Stanford, CA 94305-4055, November 1991.

12. A. Srivastava and D. W. Wall. A practical system for intermodule code optimization at link-time. *Journal of Programming Languages*, 1(1):1–18, 1993.

13. D. Thiébaut and H. S. Stone. Footprints in the cache. *ACM Transaction on Computer Systems*, 5(4):305–329, November 1987.

Instruction Scheduling over Regions:
A Framework for Scheduling Across Basic Blocks

Uma Mahadevan   *Sridhar Ramakrishnan*

email: uma@cup.hp.com   sridhar@cup.hp.com

California Language Laboratory

Hewlett Packard

Abstract

Global instruction scheduling is important for superscalar, superpipelined and VLIW machines. Instruction scheduling issues for scopes extending beyond a basic block are significantly different from those for scheduling within a basic block. This paper presents a general framework for performing scheduling across basic blocks. The method presented here identifies control flow sub-graphs termed *regions*, within which basic blocks are scheduled in forward topological order while hoisting instructions from basic blocks lower in the flow graph. Within each basic block, a directed acyclic graph represents the dependence information, while a *definition matrix* in conjunction with a *path matrix* represents the overall control and data dependence information within a region. These data structures are consulted prior to the global motion of an instruction and incrementally updated when necessary. In addition, precautions are taken to guarantee safe execution of speculative instructions. Limited renaming and code duplication is performed to overcome dependency constraints. Profile information is used when available to guide the choice of instructions. An optimizing compiler using this technique was implemented and evaluated using a set of standard performance benchmarks on real and hypothetical target machines.

1.0 Introduction

With the advent of superfast multi-issue and LIW machines the effects of traditional instruction scheduling within basic blocks have been dampened by the lack of useful instructions for hiding pipeline delays and cache latencies. On one hand, increased complexity in the hardware and higher clock speeds have had the virtual effect of lengthening pipeline delays, while on the other, the average size of basic blocks in integer programs have continued to remain small. In the absence of sophisticated dynamic scheduling hardware, the static scheduler is challenged by the difficult task of finding useful instructions to execute in the shadow of delays. Under such circumstances, it is critically important to expand the scope of instruction scheduling beyond the basic block. However, in moving instructions across basic blocks one has to be mindful of side-effects imposed by the control flow structure of the program. Allowing maximum freedom of movement of instructions while satisfying program dependency constraints is an interesting problem faced by all global schedulers. As with any scheduling problem, heuristics play a crucial role in determining whether it is beneficial from the point of view of application performance to move an instruction under a given circumstance.

In this paper we discuss a general framework to support the movement of instructions across basic blocks within a defined *region* or control flow sub-graph. We have proved the feasibility of our approach to the global scheduling problem by implementing it in the HP PA-RISC optimizing compiler. Not only is this a practical framework, but it is also extensible since it lends itself easily to various levels of aggressiveness in a product implementation. This paper also presents performance data for a few exemplary routines taken from the SPEC92 benchmark suite, using our enhanced compiler. We have tried to measure the effectiveness of our technique and the potential improvements attainable by conducting experiments with various values of key parameters influencing global scheduling.

The technique described in this paper is a logical extension of the commonly used list scheduling technique for scheduling within basic blocks. Within a region, each basic block is visited in control flow order and within each block top-down cycle scheduling is performed as in the traditional list scheduling case. The main difference stems from the fact that the candidate instructions can now come from other basic blocks. For instructions which belong to the block being scheduled, a local DAG lays down the data dependencies. When considering an instruction for movement from another block, some additional data structures such as the *definition matrix*, *path matrix* and the *virtual address* information are used to establish the *legality* and *safety* of scheduling the instruction in a foreign block. Additionally, some local and global heuristics are used to determine the *desirability* of scheduling the non-local instruction. Both speculative and control-equivalent blocks feed instructions to the list of available candidates[1].

In Section 2, this technique is compared with other known global scheduling methods. Section 3 and 4 provide a general description of the problem and its solution. In Section 5 we present actual performance results using this scheduling technique on an HP 735 as well as estimated results for some hypothetical multi-issue hardware models.

2.0 Other Global Scheduling Techniques

Scheduling across basic blocks is an inherent part of the trace scheduling technique used by the Multiflow compilers [1]. This technique uses profile information to select a trace through the program. It views all basic blocks in the trace as if they form a single block and then uses conventional techniques for scheduling instructions within the block. Special care is taken to generate compensation code when moving instructions above join points and until recently very little information has been reported in the area of reducing compensation code in off-trace paths [2]. Superblock scheduling [3] is similar to trace scheduling except for the fact that superblocks are single entry sub-graphs with no join points because the compensation code is generated a priori during superblock formation time. Once again profile information is used to guide the formation of superblocks. Bernstein and Rodeh discuss another technique which involves using a *program dependence graph* (PDG)[11], containing both control flow and data dependence information, as a framework for performing cross-block scheduling. Their paper [4] mentions that their implementation works on acyclic sub-graphs corresponding to innermost loops, alone. Another technique which works primarily on loops is the *software pipelining* algorithm described by Moon and Ebcioglu [5]. Their technique combines circular scheduling across backedges and cross basic block scheduling within the body of loops with control flow in them. So far all the techniques mentioned above assume no hardware support for correct execution of scheduled code. Lam and Smith [6] take a slightly different approach where the compiler aggressively schedules code across blocks with little or no analysis for safe execution of speculative instructions and then implement *boosting* in the hardware to guarantee safety. Another approach which uses a combination of architectural features and compile-time

---

1. The data structures and terms mentioned in this paragraph are described in detail in Section 3 of this paper.

scheduling support to accurately detect and report all exceptions, is *sentinel scheduling*[12].

In comparison with these techniques, region scheduling is performed on any arbitrary single entry control flow sub-graph, in the presence or absence of profile information. It assumes no hardware support to guarantee safe execution of the application program. Instead of forming a trace and generating compensation code a priori, we decided to integrate code duplication with the scheduling framework itself. By taking this approach, we felt that we could gain better control over code expansion, a significant concern for the traditional trace scheduling techniques. We wanted this technique to provide reasonable benefits even in the absence of profile information, but capable of taking advantage of execution frequency information when it is available. We also felt that, given sufficient parallelism in the hardware, the compiler can afford to schedule operations from infrequently executed paths in the otherwise unused issue slots. Further more, we did not wish to limit the scope of this technique to acyclic subgraphs or loops alone. Finally, we wanted a technique which is easy to implement within the framework of an optimizing compiler product.

3.0 Regions and freedom of motion

The terms *region scheduling* and *regions* have been used before in a much wider context. Rajiv Gupta and Mary Lou Soffa have described a three phase approach to performing global optimizations over an extended PDG [7] consisting of a conglomerate of regions. In their context, a region contains statements requiring the same control conditions. The regions as described in this paper are used as a framework strictly for instruction scheduling alone. For our purpose, any control flow sub-graph which has a single entry point can form a region and the largest such sub-graph becomes the scope of the global instruction scheduler. In a compiler product, one may wish to curtail the size of a region in the interest of saving compile time, but otherwise the regions can be arbitrarily large, and the scheduling algorithm does not depend on their size or shape. Regions can be nested if necessary and motion of instructions across region boundaries is not allowed[1]. We do allow movement of instructions in an outer region across the boundaries of an inner region such as a nested loop. A basic block can belong to only one region for any given program.

Within an acyclic region, such as the one given in Fig. 3.1, the basic blocks are scheduled in forward topological order i.e. A is scheduled before B, C and D; B and C are scheduled before D. The instructions move only in the direction opposite to the flow of control both within and across basic blocks. The arrows indicate the flow of control in Fig. 3.1. When we consider an instruction for movement from B to A, B becomes the source block for the instruction and A becomes the target block. For each basic block there are a set of partner basic blocks from which the candidate instructions are chosen. The partner basic blocks consists of the set of blocks dominated by the block being scheduled. For example, in the given figure the partner basic blocks for

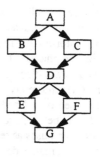

Fig. 3.1

---

1. As an exception, when code duplication is performed as described in Section 5, we do see movement of instructions across nested regions.

A are B,C,D,E,F and G, and the partners for D are E,F and G. In the current implementation, the other basic blocks have no partners. Once we implement the elaborate code duplication scheme described in Section 4 (last paragraph), each of B and C will have D,E,F,G as partners and each of E and F will have G as a partner.

Regions that have other regions nested within them are scheduled in the order inner to outer. After an inner region is scheduled, it is left unperturbed, that is, it becomes a single "opaque" node in the outer region. We can therefore, move instructions across nested loops.

There are three fundamental factors which affect the freedom of movement of instructions across basic blocks; i.e., legality, safety and desirability.

3.1 Legality

Legality of movement refers to the preservation of correct program behavior by ensuring that all data and control dependencies are honored by the transformations on the program graph associated with global scheduling. We propose that data dependency information within basic blocks be provided by individual DAGs constructed once before scheduling and incrementally updated during the scheduling process. In addition, this section prescribes a set of rules which when applied guarantee that the original data dependences across basic blocks are not violated. In considering an instruction I for movement from a source block D to a target block A:

    (i) the target operands for I must not be live-out[1] at A.

    (ii) the target operands must not be defined in intervening blocks in the paths between A and D.

    (iii) the target operands must not be defined by any instruction local to A which has not been scheduled yet.

    (iv) the source operands of I must not be defined in the intervening blocks.

    (v) the source operands must not be defined by any unscheduled local instruction in A.

    (vi) the target operands must not be used by any unscheduled instruction in A.

These rules apply not only to the register operands but also to the memory locations affected by the instruction. We assume that all register operands are pseudo registers which have been allocated using a value-numbering scheme by some earlier phase of the compiler.

In the current implementation, the basic block DAGs are built once before scheduling the region and then updated only for instructions which get moved out of a given block. The live-out information required for rule (i) is consulted and maintained over various optimization phases. The scheduler does an incremental update after every instruction that is moved across blocks, followed by a final full update over the entire region. Rules (iii), (v) and (vi) require last-use and last-def[2] information for each register and each memory operand used or defined within a given region. They are computed on a per-block basis immediately before, and maintained over the course of, scheduling the block. Intervening definitions and uses as required by rules (ii) and (iv) are obtained from the path matrix and the definition matrix data structures described in the following section.

---

1. By "live-out" we mean that the target register for I is used in some path from A to exit which does not include I. Therefore, if I were to move to A, the wrong value would reach that use of the register.

2. For each register number, the last instruction using the register and the last instruction defining the register within a basic block are recorded.

3.1.1 Path and Definition Matrices

The path matrix captures the control flow information within a region. For each pair of basic blocks T and S in a region, the matrix consists of the union of the set of all basic blocks which lie in all paths from T to S. The path matrix is computed using reachability information of basic blocks. A basic block B is said to lie in a path from T to S if B is reachable from T and S is reachable from B. For nested regions, the path matrix is computed just once for the outermost region, consisting of its constituent basic blocks and those of regions nested within.

The definition matrix captures the data dependence information within a region. It is an N x M matrix where N is the number of basic blocks in the region and M is the number of unique *resources* defined within the region. A resource in this context refers to either a register operand or a memory location referred to by an instruction. For each basic block B and resource R pair the definition matrix records the following pieces of information:
- a) the number of definitions of R in B,
- b) the path length[1] of R at the bottom of B, and
- c) whether the path length was set by a use or a definition of R.

The number of definitions is sufficient for applying the legality rules (ii) and (iv), while the path length information is used in the priority function for selecting instructions.

In conjunction with the path matrix and information about live-out registers, the definition matrix encapsulates dependencies which could otherwise be available from a PDG. However, the definition and path matrices are simpler to construct and *dynamically* update because they don't store dependency information between pairs of instructions. The live-out information has to be maintained anyway for other compiler optimizations. Also, using a PDG, it becomes difficult to represent situations such as the following: In Fig. 3.1, if two instructions, one in B and one in C were to both define the same register, it is legal to move either instruction to A but not both. By updating the live-out information for A after moving one instruction, we are able to prevent movement of the second instruction by rule (i).

In our product compiler, we don't let the size of regions grow beyond a thousand instructions in the interest of saving compile time. Under such circumstances, the size of matrices and their computation time forms an insignificant fraction of the overall time and memory usage of the optimizer.

3.2 Safety

A desired effect of global scheduling is to increase the distance between loads and their uses, possibly by hoisting the loads to basic blocks which appear earlier in control flow order, thereby overcoming both potential cache miss penalties and also load-use interlocks which exist on many hardware implementations today. Also, scheduling loads early can free up dependent high latency operations which can also benefit from cross block scheduling. However, under certain circumstances this motion of memory references could have the dangerous side-effect of raising access violation traps. Memory operations whose movement does not result in address violation are termed "safe" operations. The movement of a memory operation M from a source block S to a target block T can be unsafe if (a) the motion is *speculative*, i.e. execution of block T does not imply execution of block S, and

---

1. The region path length contribution for each resource computed as described in Section 3.3.

(b) M is a reference to a non-scalar variable such as an array or a pointer to a structure, henceforth referred to as an *aggregate* memory reference[1]. Memory references to scalar variables will be termed *singleton* references. Assuming that we are dealing with correct programs and the user does not reference memory locations which have not been allocated, singleton references, speculative or otherwise, can never raise an address violation trap. Therefore, only aggregate memory references need to be considered when performing safety analysis[2].

3.2.1 Compile-time analysis

One can establish the safety of moving memory references at compile time by stipulating a set of conditions. The underlying premise for all these conditions is the same: if one can ascertain that the same virtual address (VA) accessed by the candidate instruction, or some valid, constant offset off of it, is definitely referenced when the target basic block is executed then it is safe to move the speculative reference into the target block. Bernstein et. al. [8] have taken a similar approach in their path analysis algorithm to prove the safe movement of speculative memory references. They have gone further to state that if every path from the target block to the exit contains a reference to the VA under consideration, it is then safe to move the candidate instruction. In the case of applications which have infinite loops it may be incorrect to use the post-domination condition; therefore, we chose the less aggressive approach of using the domination criteria alone in our implementation.

We implemented a subset of such conditions and measured the effect on a set of benchmarks extracted from the SPEC92 suite. For each of the benchmarks, we considered a set of key routines in which the benchmarks spend most of their time. We targeted the code for a hypothetical *uniform*[3] machine with 2 issue slots. In this experiment we counted the total number of *Ready* instructions which refers to the sum of all candidate instructions available at the bottom of each basic block after scheduling the block. An instruction becomes a candidate as soon as all its predecessors in its DAG have been scheduled. Therefore, the set of candidates at the end of scheduling each block represents global instructions which were data ready but would have been scheduled in the block only if they met all three criteria governing the movement of instructions across blocks. We also counted the total number of *Unsafe* instructions which refer to the number of *Ready* instructions which were found to be unsafe for movement. We first computed the number of unsafe instructions assuming that ALL speculative aggregate memory references are unsafe, as a percentage of the Ready instructions ($Unsafe_1$). We then computed the percentage of unsafe instructions after implementing the safety assertion techniques mentioned earlier ($Unsafe_2$). In order to keep the total number of *Ready* instructions constant between the two cases, we suppressed the actual motion of instructions across blocks.

As expected, the results showed an overall decrease in the percentage of unsafe instructions

---

1. Note that speculative floating point operations that can trap may also be unsafe to move. However, we took the approach of providing a user defined option to prevent speculative movement of floating point operations which can raise a trap.

2. Aside from the correctness aspect, there may be performance implications of moving memory references across basic blocks such as cache/TLB misses, non-useful prefetches etc. However, this section will not address issues related to performance, instead it will concentrate on the correctness of moving aggregate memory references speculatively.

3. The term "uniform", as used in this context and also later in this paper, alludes to the assumption that there are no bundling constraints for multiple instruction issue. If the machine has 2 issue slots any two instruction types can be issued in the same cycle.

from *Unsafe₁* to *Unsafe₂* for some of the benchmarks. Analysis of these results revealed that, out of the chosen benchmarks, *li* and *eqntott* benefited the most by the enhanced safety checks. *Espresso* and *compress* were marginally affected, whereas the other benchmarks were not affected at all. Further analysis of the Fortran benchmarks indicated that using the remaining unimplemented conditions for proving safety could expose more opportunities for instruction movement across blocks. In general the percentage of *Unsafe* instructions we computed was conservative because in our compiler we consider branches and calls as unsafe instructions as well. Some of the integer benchmarks considered, such as *espresso*, have a very high percentage of branch instructions in their code. If we were to discount these instructions the percentage improvement due to safety assertion would become more pronounced for some of the routines.

3.3 Desirability

Although it might be legal and safe to move an instruction from the program correctness point of view, it may still be undesirable to move because of performance effects. There are two aspects of desirability, one of which is *absolute* and the other *relative*. An *absolute* desirability factor is used to determine whether a particular instruction is fit for movement or not independent of other available candidates, whereas a *relative* desirability factor is a priority function which helps us select one instruction over another. Register pressure is an absolute desirability factor. Often, the movement of instructions across blocks has the effect of increasing register live ranges. In our implementation, global scheduling is performed before register allocation to avoid constraints due to false dependencies. Under these circumstances it becomes essential for the scheduler to closely track register pressure effects within a region and ensure that aggressive movement of instructions does not cause an increase in the amount of spill code generated.

Another absolute desirability factor is the degree of speculation of the instruction being moved. In the absence of profile information, it is very hard to justify the movement of speculative instructions after all the local instructions in the target block have been scheduled. As a result, subsequent to scheduling all local instructions, our scheduler allows only control-equivalent instructions which do not increase the register pressure over a given limit to be scheduled in the target block.

As with the list scheduling technique, the priority function for instruction selection takes into account the critical path length, the critical resource usage, the register pressure effect local to the basic block and other machine dependent heuristics. The critical resource usage and local register pressure information are calculated on the fly but the critical path length is computed prior to scheduling. There are two components to the path length information, one the local (basic block) component and the other, the region component. Each instruction's local component is determined by starting at the leaf nodes of the local DAG and propagating the path length information upward. The region component is computed by taking the maximum of the region path lengths due to individual operand resources of the instruction. The region path length for each resource R at the "bottom" of a basic block B is available in the definition matrix cell [B,R] before scheduling and then propagated over the local DAG just like the local path length. The region path length for each resource in the definition matrix is initialized to zero at the time we construct the defintion matrix. It is then calculated in a separate pass as shown by the following algorithm.

Algorithm 1.1

```
Propagate_Region_Path_Length (region)
    Mark all basic blocks in region as not visited;
    For each bb B in region, in reverse control flow order {
        For each successor S of B in region  that has been visited {
            For each resource R defined in S {              /* obtain the contribution of S towards R */
                def_matrix[B,R].path_length =
                    MAX(def_matrix[S,R].path_length + local_path_length[S,R],
                    def_matrix[B,R].path_length);          /* do a max over all successor's contribution */
            }
            For each resource R in the def_matrix row for B {   /* obtain contribution of R not defined in S,
                def_matrix[B,R].path_length =                       but defined in some successor of S */
                    MAX(def_matrix[S,R].path_length, def_matrix[B,R].path_length);
                def_matrix[B,R].set_by_def  l= def_matrix[S,R].set_by_def;
            }
        }
        Mark B as visited;
    }
```

During the selection process the critical path length of each instruction is weighted by the basic block execution frequency[1]. This has the effects of a) preferring an instruction with the higher critical path length between two instructions with equal execution frequencies and b) preferring the instruction with the higher execution frequency (control-equivalent over speculative), unless the path length of the other is significantly higher, in which case it should be preferred.

Once again the desirability factor is largely determined by an appropriate set of heuristics for selecting an instruction and is greatly affected by the hardware model and the nature of the application program.

4.0 Renaming and code duplication

Since the scheduler sees instruction operands which are pseudo register resources, it is highly probable that false dependencies will introduce constraints in the movement of instructions across basic blocks. In order to overcome this problem our scheduler does some limited renaming in the case of anti and output dependencies preventing movement of candidates. The figures shown below illustrate the different situations under which renaming is done. Fig. 4.1 has an anti-dependency on r2 and renaming it to r2' allows us to move its definition across the use. The movement of this operation would prove beneficial if it is a long latency operation such as a load. Fig. 4.2 shows renaming in the presence of an output dependence (on r3) and in Fig. 4.3 we rename the source of a flow dependence (r2).

We could take one step further and propagate the copies to the uses of their target registers and thereby make the copy instructions redundant. This technique, known as *combining*, as well as renaming have been shown by Moon et. al. [5] to be effective in aiding global scheduling.

We conducted an experiment similar to the one used to assess the effectiveness of the safety

---

1. This frequency information is available either from dynamic profile data or is computed statically based on some heuristics. For example, static execution costs for basic blocks within a loop are higher than for those outside the loop.

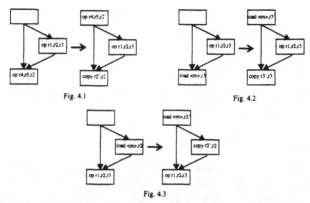

Fig. 4.1   Fig. 4.2

Fig. 4.3

assertion conditions. In this experiment, $Unsafe_1$ and $Unsafe_2$ were replaced by $Illegal_1$ and $Illegal_2$ respectively. $Illegal_1$ corresponds to the compiler which does not perform renaming and $Illegal_2$ corresponds to the compiler which does renaming. As in the safety case, the two values were computed by taking the $Illegal$ instructions as a percentage of the $Ready$ instructions. Also, the movement of instructions across blocks was suppressed to maintain the same set of $Ready$ instructions both with and without renaming. In this case, we found that *espresso* provides the maximum opportunity for renaming, *compress* and *mdljdp2* provide a few and all the others show insignificant improvements. Currently, our compiler does not attempt to rename floating point operations nor does it *combine* the copy operations resulting from renaming. Under the circumstances, integer loads are the primary targets for renaming and this was the cause for the reduction in illegal instructions for *espresso* and other benchmarks.

Another technique which has been proposed in the literature to increase the freedom of movement is code duplication [9]. This becomes particularly attractive in the presence of profile information. Although, our current implementation does not yet make extensive use of this technique, it does perform limited movement of instructions across backedges of loops. This is done specially

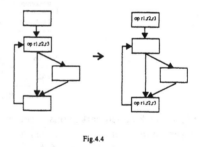

Fig.4.4

when an instruction causes an interlock in the home basic block and there are no global or local instructions available to schedule in the interlock cycle. This instruction is then pushed over the backedge of the loop within which it resides and is also duplicated in the header as illustrated in Fig. 4.4. The movement of instructions continues to be against the flow of control and our framework is flexible enough to handle both movement of instructions into predecessors and from successors with respect to a given basic block. A more general scheme would attempt to pipeline the entire loop by peeling off iterations into the header as outlined by the *software pipelining* algorithm described by Moon and Ebcioglu [5].

Another situation which warrants code duplication is the movement of an instruction across a join point to a speculative block. For example, in Fig. 3.1, if we were to move an instruction from block D to block C, the instruction has to be duplicated in block B to preserve correctness of the program. This is equivalent to the generation of compensation code in traditional trace scheduling compilers.

5.0 Performance Characteristics

In this section we present results of our global scheduling experiments targeted for the HP 735 and for some hypothetical machine models.

5.1 Performance on an HP 735

Table 1 shows the runtime improvements attained due to global scheduling on a select set of benchmarks taken from the SPEC92 suite, over and above optimized code performance. Column A gives the optimized code execution time in seconds without global scheduling, column B gives the time with global scheduling and column C shows the percentage improvement. These measurements were made on an HP model 735 machine based on the PA-RISC 7100 processor, running at 99 MHZ. This machine has two issue slots, whereby in each cycle one can issue one floating point and one integer operation simultaneously. It has 32 general purpose registers and 32 double precision floating point registers, also accessible as 64 single precision ones..

Benchmark	A	B	C%
023.eqntott	8.4	7.8	7.14
034.mdljdp2	36.2	34.2	5.52
022.li	69.3	67.7	2.30
026.compress	38.5	37.7	2.07
047.tomcatv	17.8	18.1	1.66
015.doduc	14.7	14.5	1.36
048.ora	27.1	26.8	1.11
008.espresso	24.3	24.2	0.41

Table 1: Region scheduling on an HP 735

Out of the 8 benchmarks considered, the largest improvement from region scheduling was observed for *eqntott*. Most of the improvement was obtained by moving loads across basic blocks away from the uses of the target registers, thereby reducing load-use interlocks present in the original code. We were able to achieve this by applying some of the safety assertion techniques discussed earlier. Aside from this reason, code duplication as described in Section 4.0 also provided some additional improvements, especially in the case of *li*. For the *mdljdp2* benchmark, region scheduling helped by moving high latency operations such as floating point divides across basic blocks and in *tomcatv* moving floating point operations helped reduce interlocks in the program. By scheduling them as early as possible within their region, it allowed these computations to happen in parallel with other, less expensive operations within the same region. The renaming technique helped overcome anti-dependencies in the *compress* benchmark. In the case of *espresso*, the scheduler was able to move several instructions across basic blocks but this movement did not contribute towards any significant performance improvements. Most of the instructions moved were simple integer operations. Since the HP 735 does not allow dual issue of integer instructions, this movement did not provide any new opportunities for reducing program execution time. Several other candidate instructions were able to meet the legality and safety requirements but failed to pass the desirability test due to increase in register pressure.

5.2 Performance on hypothetical machines

We felt that the performance improvements attainable by using our global scheduling algorithms were limited by currently available machine resources on the HP 735. Therefore, we decided to measure the potential performance gains due to region scheduling on wider issue hypothetical machines with larger number of functional units.

5.2.1 Dynamic Cycle Counts

We used a cycle counting mechanism to measure performance on the hypothetical machines described in the following sub-section.The cycle counter walks the instructions within a given procedure and estimates the number of cycles taken to execute all the instructions in each basic block. It then weights the number of cycles by the execution frequencies of the individual basic blocks and adds them to come up with a cumulative weighted cycle count for the entire procedure. The cycle counter is aware of the target hardware model in terms of issue slots, functional units and latencies. In addition, it tries to mimic dynamic branch behavior by using actual basic block execution frequencies from profile data when available and also by accounting for lingering latencies across basic blocks.

5.2.2 Speedup Measurements

We chose 5 different machine models for conducting our experiments, however we have shown the speedup measurements for only a couple of them. The following paragraphs describe the assumptions made for each with regards to issue slots, functional units and latencies.

A --> 1 issue slot
B --> 2 issue slots; max. of 1 floating-point, 2 fixed-point, 1 memory and 1 branch inst. per bundle[1].
C --> 4 issue slots; max. of 2 floating-point, 2 fixed-point, 1 memory and 1 branch inst. per bundle.
D --> 6 issue slots; max. of 2 floating-point, 2 fixed-point, 2 memory and 1 branch inst. per bundle.
E --> 8 issue slots; max. of 3 floating-point, 3 fixed-point, 2 memory and 1 branch inst. per bundle.

All machines from A to E assume a 1 cycle latency between the definition and use of the same register for integer ones, a 2 cycle load-use latency and a 2 cycle latency between a floating-point definition and use of the same register. Floating point divide and square-root operations, on the other hand, have an 8 cycle latency for single precision and a 15 cycle latency for double precision operands. Figure 5.1 shows the performance speedup attained with respect to Machine A with no region scheduling for 8 important routines, extracted from 8 different benchmarks from the SPEC92 suite. The routine *main* was taken from the floating point benchmark *tomcatv*. We calculated this speedup by dividing the dynamic cycle count for each routine on Machine A with no region scheduling by the dynamic cycle count on the other machines with and without region scheduling. In each figure, *Base* refers to the speedup with compiler optimization but without global scheduling and *Region* refers

---

1. A bundle refers to the instructions which are issued in the same cycle. The issue slots determine the maximum number of instructions which can be issued in a bundle.

to the speedup with compiler optimization but without global scheduling and *Region* refers to the speedup with global scheduling. For these experiments we assumed that the target machine had 32 general egisters and 32 double precision floating point registers (also accessible as 64 single-precision registers).

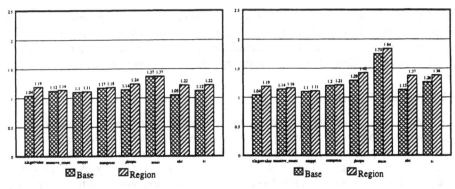

Fig. 5.1.1 Speedup on Machine B   Fig. 5.1.2 Speedup on Machine C

Fig. 5.1 Speedup on non uniform machine models

We find that region scheduling provides improvements ranging from 1% to 20% over the base optimizing compiler depending on the target machine and the application routine. In general, the improvements increased with higher number of issue slots except for *cmppt* and *massive_count*. When we investigated these two routines we discovered that in the case of *cmppt*, the scheduler was doing its best with the current level of unrolling of the time critical loop and that there is not enough parallelism within a single iteration to exploit the availability of more issue slots. Further unrolling can expose more opportunities for the scheduler. Alternatively, software pipelining this loop can yield as much benefit or more. On the other hand, in the case of *massive_count*, the scheduler was limited by high register pressure and going from 6 to 8 issue slots reduced performance gain over the base compiler.

At this point, we wondered whether the choice of non-uniform machine models, although realistic, was dampening the potential performance gains attainable by global scheduling. Therefore, we conducted the same experiment on a set of uniform machine models with the same number of issue slots. Fig. 5.2 shows the results of this experiment.

We found that increasing the number of available functional units caused less than 5% difference in the integer benchmarks performance with the Base as well as the Region compilers. Functional unit resources were not the constraining factor here. However, with the floating point routines, depending on the application, the speedup is either insignificant as in the case of *abc*, or as large as 30% as in the case of the *main* routine in *tomcatv*. Therefore, having more functional units is useful for some of the floating point applications but does not make a significant difference for the integer applications chosen here. In fact, we noticed a performance degradation with region scheduling on *cmppt* on uniform machine models going from 2 to 8 issue slots. On investigating this behavior, we discovered that our register pressure heuristics are not tuned to generate optimal code for higher issue slot machines. Generation of spill code with region scheduling was causing a degradation in performance as the number of issue slots increased.

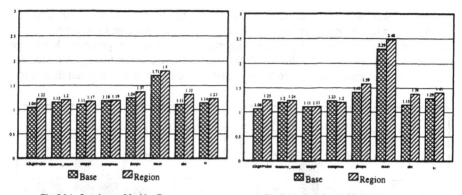

Fig. 5.2.1 Speedup on Machine B   Fig. 5.2.2 Speedup on Machine C

Fig. 5.2 Speedup on uniform machine models

In an attempt to understand the factors inhibiting global scheduling performance on the integer benchmarks given here, we decided to study their behavior assuming that an infinite number of registers were available for our use. Fig. 5.3 shows the results of this experiment.

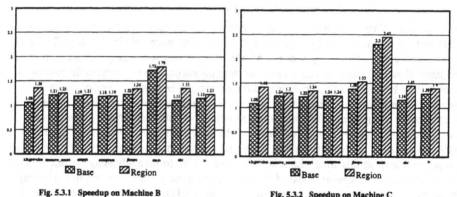

Fig. 5.3.1 Speedup on Machine B   Fig. 5.3.2 Speedup on Machine C

Fig. 5.3 Speedup on uniform machine models with unlimited number of registers

This time we found that the improvement due to region scheduling over the Base compiler increased anywhere from 5 to 25% with the exception of *compress*. However, there are no performance degradations due to region scheduling in this case. The contribution of region scheduling seemed to increase for some of the floating point routines as well, although not by a significant amount.

We conducted one last experiment by disabling all safety checks and allowing unconstrained movement of all memory operations barring the legality and desirabilty checks. Fig. 5.4 shows the results of this experiment.

Initially, we were a little surprised by the results because, on the average, the improvements seemed to be less than those on the vanilla uniform machine models. On closer investigation, we discovered that it is again the number of real registers and the inaccuracy of register pressure heuristics limiting the overall performance gain. Relaxing

432

the safety constraint had the same effect as increasing the number of issue slots and functional units in the target machine. Both caused more instructions to be moved across basic blocks, thereby increasing overall register pressure in the program. Since the heuristics used by the scheduler did not closely match those used by the register allocator for generating spill code, the final code generated turned out to be less optimal than in the

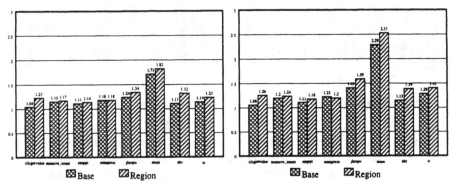

Fig. 5.4.1 Speedup on Machine B   Fig. 5.4.2 Speedup on Machine C

Fig. 5.4 Speedup on uniform machine models with unsafe movement

vanilla case. When we tried the same experiment with infinite number of registers we obtained the results shown by Fig. 5.5. We noticed improvements in the range 3% to 7% for both *xlxgetvalue* and *cmppt* over and above what was seen using infinite number of registers alone. In *jloopu* we moved several more instructions than we did in the case of safe movement. However, this movement did not materialize into a performance benefit because these instructions came from a frequently executed large basic block, where they were already being successfully multi-issued without causing interlocks. In the case of *abc* no additional movement occurred because the instructions that were unconstrained by safety now failed the legality check. Since our implementation does not rename floating point operations at this time, the scheduler was unable to take advantage of the relaxed safety constraint. In *tomcatv* most of the aggregate memory references are found in single basic block loops and therefore the scheduler did not find any new opportunities for moving instructions.

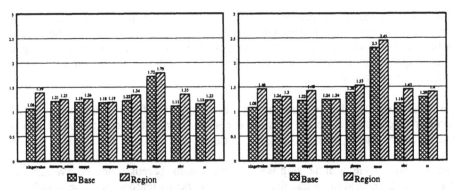

Fig. 5.5.1 Speedup on Machine B   Fig. 5.5.2 Speedup on Machine C

Fig. 5.5 Speedup on uniform machine models with unlimited number of registers and unsafe movement

This set of experiments form a good example to illustrate the fact that it is not enough to address any one of the three fundamental factors that affect movement of instructions across basic blocks. It is essential to provide a well balanced solution which would address all three issues simultaneously in order to attain a significant performance gain using cross-block scheduling.

6.0 Conclusions and Future Work

This paper describes a *practical* and *extensible* framework for global instruction scheduling, which has been incorporated into a compiler product. Using an implementation based on this framework, we have shown the performance impact of global scheduling on a set of benchmarks extracted from the SPEC92 suite. We conducted a set of experiments on a variety of hypothetical target machine models and studied the behavior of the chosen applications under the different circumstances. We observed that, depending on the amount of parallelism available in the application and the resources available in the target machine, this global scheduling technique can yield anywhere from modest to large performance improvements over traditional optimizations. Our analysis also exposes pitfalls in retargeting an existing compiler product to more advanced machines with larger number of available resources. We have also shown that it is desirable (and possible) for compilers to statically perform safety analysis of speculative aggregate memory references by reducing it to a dataflow problem (as in [8]).

Some of the areas in which we would like to enhance our implementation to further our understanding of these subjects are general code duplication, global scheduling under an SSA form of the application program, and interactions between the global scheduler and other optimization components such as the software pipeliner and the register allocator. Currently, we perform limited, context specific, code duplication in our implementation. We would like to extend it to a general solution for moving instructions across join points in the flow graph. Under this framework, we would also like to understand the implications of moving instructions across PHI functions when the program is in SSA form. We realize that, sometimes, movement of instructions across basic blocks can open up opportunities for removing branches, thereby eliminating the penalties associated with them. Furthermore, this can help get rid of control flow in loops which can then be processed by our software pipeliner (which works on single basic block loops only). In the course of our analyses, we have also realized the importance of having accurate register pressure heuristics for scheduling code across basic blocks. We will be enhancing the set of heuristics we have now, in order to achieve closer interactions with the register allocator.

Acknowledgements

The authors would like to thank Manoj Dadoo, Wei-Chung Hsu, Bob Rau, Vatsa Santhanam and Carol Thompson for their helpful suggestions during the implementation of this work and also during the preparation of this paper. We would also like to thank Linda Lawson and Richard Holman for their support of this effort.

References

1. J. Fisher. Trace Scheduling: A technique for global microcode compaction. *IEEE Trans. on Computers*, C-30, No. 7, pages 478-490, 1981

2. S.M. Freudenberger, T.R. Gross and P.G. Lowney. Avoidance and Suppression of Compensation Code in a Trace Scheduling Compiler. *Hewlett Packard Labs. Tech. Report, HPL-93-35*, May 1993.

3. W.W. Hwu, S.A. Mahlke, W.Y. Chen, P.P. Chang, N.J. Warter, R.A. Bringmann, R.O. Ouellette, R.E. Hank, T.Kiyohara, G.E. Haab, J.G. Holm, and D.M. Lavery. The Superblock: An Effective Technique for VLIW and Superscalar Compilation. *Journal of Supercomputing*, 7(1,2), March 1993.

4. D. Bernstein and M. Rodeh. Global Instruction Scheduling for Superscalar Machines. *Proceedings of the SIGPLAN Conference*, pages 241-255, 1991.

5. S. Moon and K. Ebcioglu. An Efficient Resource-Constrained Global Scheduling Technique for Superscalar and VLIW processors. *Proceedings of Micro25*, pages 55-71,1992

6. M.D. Smith, M.S. Lam, and M.A. Horowitz. Boosting beyond static scheduling in a superscalar processor. *IEEE Conference on Computer Architecture*, pages 344-354, 1990

7. R. Gupta and M.L. Soffa. Region Scheduling: An Approach for Detecting and Redistributing Parallelism. *Proceedings of the second International Conference on Supercomputing*, pages 3:141-148, May 1987.

8. D. Bernstein and M. Rodeh. Proving Safety of Speculative Load Instructions at Compile Time. *Fourth European Symposium on Programming*, 1992.

9. D. Bernstein, D. Cohen, and H. Krawcyzk. Code Duplication: An Assist for Global Instruction Scheduling. *Proceedings of MICRO24*, pages 103-113. IEEE Computer Society, Nov. 1991.

10. R. Cytron, J. Ferrante, B.K. Rosen, M.N. Wegman and F.K. Zadeck. Efficiently Computing Static Single Assignment Form and the Control Dependence Graph. *ACM TOPLAS*, Vol. 13, No. 4, pages 451-490, Oct. 1991.

11. J. Ferrante, K.J. Ottenstein, and J.D. Warren. The program dependence graph and its use in optimization. *ACM TOPLAS*, Vol. 9, No. 3, page 319-349, Jul. 1987.

12. J. Scott A. Mahlke, William Y. Chen, Wen-mei W. Hwu, B. Ramakrishna Rau, and Michael Schlansker. Sentinel Scheduling for VLIW and superscalar processors. *ASPLOS*, 1992.

Transport-Triggering vs. Operation-Triggering

Jan Hoogerbrugge and Henk Corporaal

Delft University of Technology
Department of Electrical Engineering
Section Computer Architecture and Digital Systems

Abstract. Transport-triggered architectures are a new class of architectures that provide more scheduling freedom and have unique compiler optimizations. This paper reports experiments that quantify the advantages of transport-triggered architectures with respect to traditional operation-triggered architectures.

For the experiments we use an extended basic block scheduler that is currently being developed. The paper gives an description of the scheduling techniques used.

The results of our experiments show that the extra scheduling freedom together with the new optimizations are very welcome when resource constraints are limiting the performance. This is the case when resources are scarce or when the application contains a lot of instruction level parallelism.

1 Introduction

Improvements in current computer architectures are obtained by higher clock frequencies, exploitation of instruction level parallelism (ILP), and improvements in compiler technology.

Higher clock frequencies are a result of better VLSI technology, better VLSI design techniques, and superpipelining which reduces the number of logic levels between pipeline stages.

ILP is made possible due to higher transistor densities which allows for duplication of function units and data paths. The exploitation of ILP consists of mapping the ILP of the application onto the ILP of the target architecture as efficiently as possible. This mapping, which consists of scheduling and resource allocation, can be done in hardware or in software. The hardware approach is used by superscalar architectures, which contain advanced hardware to detect dependences and resource conflicts between operations [Joh89]. A major problem of this approach is the scalability of the scheduling hardware. The software approach is used by Very Long Instruction Word (VLIW) architectures. These architectures have instructions with multiple operations that are issued simultaneously. It is the responsibility of the compiler to fill these instructions such that data dependence and resource conflicts will not occur. The major problem with this approach is that the static information used by the compiler is in some ways less powerful than the dynamic information used by the hardware scheduler.

The third factor that can improve performance significantly is compiler technology. By designing an architecture such that the compiler has more control and information about the target hardware it is possible to develop new compiler optimizations. An example of this are the exact specifications of function units. When the number of stages and the pipelining degree are known to the compiler, the compiler can generate code such that pipeline stalls and bubbles are minimized.

The class of transport-triggered architectures (TTAs) that we advocate fit nicely into these developments. It allows for superpipelining, exploitation of (VLIW) ILP, and more compiler control about the hardware. The major difference between TTAs and traditional operation-triggered architectures (OTAs) lies in the way they are programmed. OTAs are programmed by specifying operations which result in data-transports between internal registers and function units. TTAs are programmed at a lower level; a TTA program specifies the data-transports directly. This results in a number of advantages which together improve the total performance significantly.

The MOVE project researches a framework for the generation of application specific processors (ASPs) by means of TTAs. Central within the framework is a precisely specified architecture template and a set of architecture parameters. A compiler for this framework has been developed.

The purpose of this paper is to present an evaluation of both TTAs and the (scheduling) techniques used by the compiler. The next section will introduce TTAs and the advantages of TTAs. Section 3 discusses the developed compiler and the scheduling techniques it uses. Section 4 describes the performed experiments and evaluates their results. Finally, Sect. 5 gives conclusions and indications for further research.

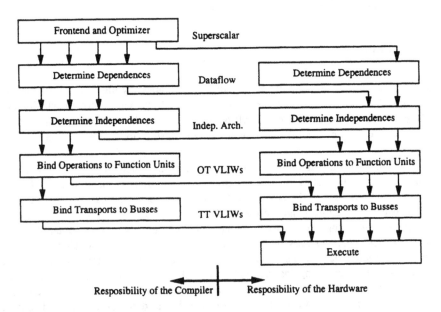

Fig. 1. The division of responsibilities between hardware and compiler.

2 Transport-Triggered Architectures

Transport-triggered architectures [CM91] trust the task of translating operations into data-transports to the compiler. This can be depicted as an extension of a scheme presented in [RF93]. Figure 1 shows a division between the responsibilities of the compiler and the hardware. It shows five classes of architectures: superscalar, data flow machines, independence architectures [TS88], operation-triggered (OT) VLIWs, and transport-triggered (TT) VLIWs. Superscalars shift most responsibilities to the hardware, while VLIWs shift most responsibilities to the compiler. The figure clearly shows that TT VLIWs depend even more on compilers than OT VLIWs.

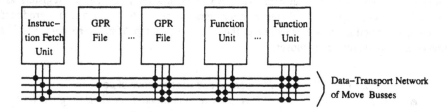

Fig. 2. The general structure of a TTA.

2.1 Principles

The compiler sees a TTA as a set of function units connected by a data-transport network of one or more move busses (see Fig. 2). To perform an operation the compiler generates moves to move the operands of the operation to registers of the function unit that will perform the operation, and a move to move the result of the operation from the function unit to a place where it will be stored or further processed. For example, an addition "$r4 = r2 + r3$" is translated into three moves:

$$r2 \rightarrow add\_o \qquad \text{/* Operand move from GPR file to FU */}$$
$$r3 \rightarrow add\_t \qquad \text{/* Trigger move from GPR file to FU */}$$
$$add\_r \rightarrow r4 \qquad \text{/* Result move from FU to GPR file */}$$

The first two moves specify that the contents of general purpose registers (GPRs) $r2$ and $r3$ are transported to input registers of the adder function unit. The third move transports the result of the addition to GPR $r4$.

One of the moves that move the operands to the function unit should signal the function unit that all operands are available and the operation can begin. This is called the *trigger move*, and the other moves that provide operands are called *operand moves*. The move that fetches the result is called a *result move*. A trigger move should be scheduled in the same or in a later cycle than the operand moves that belong to the same operation. The distance between a trigger and a corresponding result move should be at least the latency of the function unit.

A move instruction consists of multiple *move slots*; each slot specifies a separate transport. Immediate operands are provided by an (optional) immediate bit per move. This bit indicates whether the source field of the move is an immediate or it is a register specifier.

Longer immediates are provided by making the instruction register (partly) accessible. Long immediates may or may not take the place of one or more move slots.

Control flow is provided by making the program counter accessible. Writing to the program counter causes a (possible delayed) jump. Reading the program counter is necessary for saving the program counter during a function call.

Conditional execution is provided by means of predicated execution [AKPW83]. Moves can be predicated be a (simple) boolean expression of predicate registers. The move is only executed whenever the boolean expression evaluates to *true*. The predicate registers are stored in a special register file of single bit registers and are set by boolean values produced by compare function units. For example, the conditional jump "*if r2 = r3 goto label*" is translated into the following moves:

$r2 \rightarrow eq\_o; r3 \rightarrow eq\_t$ /* Operand and trigger move of compare */
$eq\_r \rightarrow b4$ /* Result move of compare to predicate register *b4* */
$b4 ? label \rightarrow pc$ /* Predicated jump to *label* */

2.2 Hybrid Pipelines

Transport-triggered architectures give the compiler more freedom to schedule moves from and to function units by means of *hybrid pipelines*. Each pipeline stage is accompanied with a valid bit that indicates whether the stage contains valid data or not. An operation proceeds to the next stage only when it does not overwrite data of a previous operation, i.e., the valid bit of the next stage is off. The first pipeline stage consists of operand and trigger registers, the last stage corresponds to the result register(s). Figure 3 shows the organization of a function unit with a four stage pipeline.

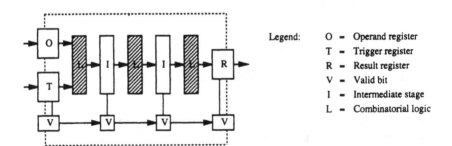

Legend:
O - Operand register
T - Trigger register
R - Result register
V - Valid bit
I - Intermediate stage
L - Combinatorial logic

Fig. 3. A function unit with a four stage pipeline.

Hybrid pipelines allow that operations stay longer in the pipeline than is strictly needed to perform the operation. This extra scheduling freedom is useful for operations that are not on the critical path and that can be performed by function units that are not fully utilized.

In order to be able to perform different operations on a single function unit (e.g., addition and subtraction on an integer unit), a trigger register may be mapped at multiple address locations. This makes it possible to select an operation depending on the used address by the trigger move.

2.3 Advantages

The main advantages of TTAs are its extreme simplicity and great flexibility, allowing short processor cycle times and a quick design. Apart from design advantages [CM91], TTAs also have advantages with respect to the following issues:

1. **More scheduling freedom:** Dividing operations into individual transports of operands and results allows for better scheduling opportunities and therefore speeding up execution.
2. **Transport capacity:** Because the required transport capacity is designed on desired performance instead of worst case usage (three busses per RISC type operation), its utilization can be significantly higher.
3. **Register usage:** Many values can be bypassed from one function unit to another without needing to be stored in GPRs.
4. **Operand swapping:** Operands of commutative operations can be swapped by the compiler whenever that turns out to be useful. The operand that is moved last to the function unit will trigger the operation.
5. **Software bypassing:** Bypassing is scheduled by the compiler instead of scheduled by a hardware bypass unit.
6. **Dead result move elimination:** When all usages of a value are in the same cycle as the value is defined by a result move the result move to a GPR becomes dead code and can be eliminated.

Section 4 describes experiments that quantify some of these advantages using an extended basic block scheduler that is described in the next section.

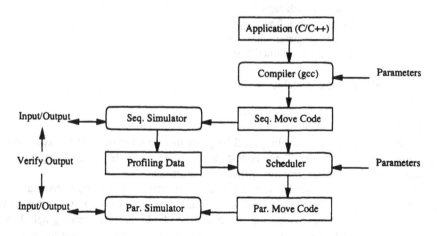

Fig. 4. The compiler trajectory.

3   The Extended Basic Block Scheduler

Our compiler trajectory consists of the GNU gcc compiler, a scheduler, and a simulator (see Fig. 4). The gcc compiler is ported to a generic sequential TTA. It has parameters that allow the user to strip the target operation set whenever that target ASP does not support certain operations (e.g., byte and half word loads and stores).

The scheduler is controlled by a machine description file that describes the target ASP. This description includes available function units, the operations that each function unit supports, latencies, GPR file sizes, and a description of the interconnection network.

A simulator for both sequential and parallel code is provided (1) to obtain profiling information, (2) to verify the compiler, (3) to verify the scheduler, and (4) to obtain application characteristics.

3.1 Scheduling an Executable

The input of our scheduler is a complete executable of generic MOVE code. The scheduler starts with reading the executable and its profiling data when present. After that the following steps are done to convert a sequential executable into a parallel executable:

```
schedule an executable
{
        perform inlining, unrolling, and loop peeling
        for each procedure do
        {
                perform data and control flow analysis
                perform memory reference disambiguation
                make a data dependence graph and determine regions
                schedule each region
                flatten control flow graph
                perform register allocation
                reschedule modified basic blocks
        }
        relocate the executable
}
```

Function inlining, loop unrolling, and loop peeling are done in order to expose more parallelism for the scheduler. These code expansions are controlled by profiling data, the amount of code duplication, and a user specified parameter.

The data and control flow analysis step is pretty standard. It partitions a procedure into natural loops [ASU85] which correspond to *regions*. It performs live-analysis to detect off-liveness during inter-basic block code motions and to build an interference graph during register allocation. The data flow analysis step also assigns each live-range to an unique GPR. This should eliminate most of the false data-dependences.

The currently used memory disambiguator is very limited by the choice of using gcc[1]. It consists of making address derivations by means of reaching definitions produced by the data flow analysis phase. These derivations are used for the gcd-test in order to try to proof independence between two memory references.

---

[1] A lot of information that can be used by the disambiguator is not available in the current backend of gcc. This will become better in future releases of gcc.

After building a data-dependences graph for the whole procedure, the scheduler schedules each region of the procedure individually. Scheduling a region will be discussed in the next section.

The intermediate representation of the procedure consists of a control flow graph that does not require that some control flow edges have to be fall through. This makes inlining, unrolling, peeling, and some control flow transformations during scheduling easier to perform. However the basic blocks of the final code have to be placed sequentially into memory. It is therefore necessary to flatten the control flow graph. This step may introduce extra jumps.

Since the procedure is fully renamed by assigning each live-range to a unique GPR a large number of GPRs are in use. The register allocation step maps these live-ranges back to physical GPRs. The register allocator inserts save/restore code whenever it runs out of GPRs. The basic blocks that are modified are rescheduled by a (simple) basic block scheduler. This scheduling before register allocation approach has the advantage that it decouples the two complex problems of scheduling and register allocation. The drawback is that it requires that all GPRs of the same type (integer, floating point, and predicate) should be in a single register file.

Since the size of the code is changed during scheduling, the executable has to be relocated. This consists of modifying addresses in the data and text segments of the executable.

3.2 Scheduling a Region

In order to find sufficient ILP to justify the cost of multiple function units and data paths, a scheduler should have a larger scope than a single basic block at a time. Various scheduling scope types that are larger than a single basic block are known from the literature:

1. **Trace:** A sequence of basic blocks that are likely to be executed after each other. A trace may have side entries/exits from/to other traces [Fis81].
2. **Superblock:** A trace with the limitation that only the first basic block is allowed to have entries from other superblocks [MLC+92].
3. **Hyperblock:** A superblock created from an acyclic control flow graph by means of predicated execution [HMC+93].
4. **Decision tree:** A tree of basic blocks. A decision tree may have side exits, however only the root of the decision tree is allowed to have entries from other decision trees [HD86].
5. **Region:** A set of basic blocks that corresponds to the body of a natural loop. Since loops can be nested, regions can also be nested in each other. Like natural loops, regions have a single entry point (the loop header) and may have multiple exits [BR91].

Our scheduler operates on regions which is the most general scheduling scope from the five mentioned above. More general means a larger scheduling scope, and potentially more and better exploitation of ILP.

The scheduler schedules a region by visiting the basic blocks of the region in a topological order. Each basic block is scheduled by means of a basic block list scheduling algorithm, and after that the basic blocks that are reachable from the current basic block are examined for operations that can be scheduled in the current basic block. Thus the global algorithm for scheduling a region looks like:

```
schedule a region
{
        for each basic block b of the region in topological order do
        {
                1: schedule b's operations by means of list scheduling
                2: try to import operations from reachable basic blocks into b
        }
}
```

The first step is basically list scheduling modified for TTAs. A data-dependence graph (DDG) and a set of *ready* operations are used. An operation is ready whenever all its predecessors in the DDG are scheduled. The list scheduler repeatedly takes an operation from the ready set and schedules it at the first cycle where data-dependences and resource constraints are satisfied. The selection from the ready list is based on the critical path heuristic used by almost every other list scheduler.

The second step examens all operations from basic blocks in the current region reachable from the current basic block. The priority function that is used to select a ready operation looks like:

$$global\_priority = probability * local\_priority - duplication\_cost$$

where $probability$ is the probability (estimated or based on profiling data) that the operation will be executed after the current basic block is executed, $local\_priority$ is the critical path priority[2] function scaled between 0 and 100, and $duplication\_cost$ is a parameter that is subtracted whenever the inter-basic block code motion requires code duplication. The scheduler tries to schedule the selected operation in the current basic block. This is repeated until all ready operations from reachable basic blocks have been tried.

Code motion from one basic block *source* to another basic block *destination* requires code duplication whenever *destination* does not dominate [ASU85] *source*, and requires off-lives checks whenever *source* does not post-dominate *destination*.

Figure 5 shows what needs to be done when an operation is taken from *source* and placed in *destination*. First the scheduler determines all intermediate basic blocks in the current region between *source* and *destination*. All immediate predecessors of *source* and of the intermediate basic blocks that are not reachable from *destination* require a duplication. This is the set of *entry basic blocks* in Fig. 5. Whenever it is not possible to place one of these duplications the whole code motion from *source* to *destination* is aborted.

The off-liveness checks consist of testing the immediate successors of *destination* and the immediate successors of the intermediate basic blocks from which *source* is not reachable. These blocks are shown in Fig. 5 as *exit basic blocks*. Whenever the value that an operation defines is live at the beginning of one of the exit basic blocks the operation needs to be predicated by the predicate register that controls the corresponding exit control flow edge. Since our scheduler assumes only predicate expressions of a single predicate register (b and $\bar{b}$), the number of exit basic blocks which require predicated execution is limited to one. If predicated execution is needed an extra (*flow*) dependence is introduced between the

---

[2] The local priority is based on data-dependences between moves within the same basic block.

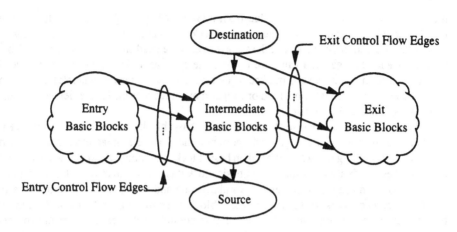

Fig. 5. A fragment of a region.

operation and the (compare) operation that defines the predicate. A memory store operation can be viewed as a normal operation that defines *memory*, which is always live.

3.3 Scheduling an Operation

Scheduling an operation[3] consists of scheduling the moves that perform the operation. Each operation consists of one trigger move, zero or more operand moves, and zero or one result moves (only a store has no result).

The scheduler starts with scheduling the trigger move. It has to find the first cycle where (1) a suitable function unit is available, (2) a suitable move bus is available, and (3) an immediate can be provided when needed.

After the trigger is scheduled the scheduler proceeds with scheduling the operand and result moves. This consists of finding a cycle where a suitable move bus is available and when needed an immediate for an operand move. During this step the scheduler has to make the following checks in order to use the hybrid pipelines correctly:

1. Trigger and result moves should be scheduled in first-in first-out order.
2. The number of outstanding operations on a function unit may not exceed the capacity of the function unit.
3. An operand register is in use until the operation proceeds to the second pipeline stage.

All these checks are verified by means of a resource table that keeps track of the state of each function unit. When one of the checks fails the (operand or result) move has to be placed in an earlier (in case of an operand move) or later cycle (in case of a result move). There are cases where this does not help. In these situations the scheduler has to unschedule the operation and delay the trigger move by one cycle.

Whenever the scheduler schedules an operand or trigger move the scheduler checks whether the value used by the move needs to be bypassed from the function unit that

---

[3] For example, an addition, multiply, load, or store. Jumps, function calls, OS calls, and copy operations are handled differently.

produced it instead of getting the value from a GPR. If bypassing is required the source field of the move is changed. Furthermore, a check is made to find out whether the result move of the operation that produced the value has become dead and can be eliminated. This happens when all usages of a value are in the same cycle as the result move that produced the value. A dead result move is marked as being dead and its move bus is released. When the scheduler has to delay the operand or trigger move it restores the source field and brings a killed result move back to live.

When an operation is imported from a reachable basic block into the current basic block it is not allowed to increase the length of the current basic block. This guarantees that extended basic block scheduling is always better than basic block scheduling. However, when a result move reaches the "bottom" of the current basic block it is allowed to move to the immediate successor(s) of the current basic block. Similarly, operand moves are allowed to move to immediate predecessor(s) of the current basic block when they hit the "top" of the current basic block. Due to these two code motions it is possible that operations are in progress during the transition of one basic block to another.

4 Experimental Results

The goal of our experiments is to measure the quality of (the current state of) our scheduler, and evaluate some aspects of transport-triggering. We shall perform three experiments. The first experiment will measure the difference between basic block and extended basic block scheduling, the second experiment will measure the effect of scheduling freedom, and the third experiment compares transport-triggering with operation-triggering.

We shall focus on workstation type applications, which are characterized by a limited amount of ILP and an irregular data driven control flow. For a discussion of scientific code and TTAs see [HCM91, HC92].

4.1 Architecture and Benchmarks

Since we are focussing on workstation code we shall assume an architecture with short latencies. Table 4.1 shows which function units are available in our experimental architecture together with their number and latency. Other assumed architecture parameters are:

1. A fully connected interconnection network. For our experiments we shall vary the number of move busses between one and eight.
2. No branch delay and predicate registers can be used in the same cycle as they are defined. This corresponds to similar conditional branch latencies as most RISC CPUs (e.g., MIPS R2000). For example, a branch-if-equal looks like:

$$r2 \rightarrow eq\_o; r3 \rightarrow eq\_t \qquad \text{/* Operand and trigger move of compare */}$$
$$eq\_r ? label \rightarrow pc \qquad \text{/* Predicated jump without delay slots */}$$

3. Sufficient GPRs. We have to assume this since our register allocator is not fully operational yet.
4. No base-offset memory addressing mode. Since many memory addresses are the sum of two components (about 40–60%), the actual load latency is about 2.5 cycles when compared with an architecture that supports base-offset addressing.

5. 6-bit short immediates and one 32-bit long immediate per instruction.

The following set of twenty benchmarks is used for our experiments. It should reflect a typical workstation load:

a68, bison, cksum, cmp, compress, cpp, dhrystone, diff, expand, flex, gnuplot, gunzip, gzip, od, sed, stanford, uncompress, unexpand, uniq, and *virtex.*

Most of the benchmarks are GNU utilities, the exceptions are *compress, uncompress, virtex, dhrystone,* and *stanford.*

Table 1. Assumed function unit parameters.

Function unit	Number	Latency
Load/Store	2	2
Integer	2	1
Shift, sign-extend	1	1
Integer compare	1	1
Logic	1	1
Floating point	1	3
Floating point compare	1	3
Floating point convert	1	3

4.2 Effect of Extended Basic Block Scheduling

Figure 6 shows the effect of a larger scheduling scope. The values plotted are the average speedups of the twenty benchmarks relative to basic block scheduling for a single move bus machine. The figure clearly shows that more ILP in the hardware requires extended basic block scheduling in order to use the hardware effectively. The difference between basic block and extended basic block is about 40% for an eight move bus machine. The main reasons we observed why the speedup is sub-linear are:

1. Due to speculative execution some moves are not always useful.
2. ILP of workstation code is limited [Wal91].
3. ILP of workstation code is not very smoothable [TGH92].
4. Memory references of workstation code are hard to disambiguate.

4.3 Effect of Scheduling Freedom

OTAs deliver all operands of an operation in the same cycle and fetch the result as soon as it is available. TTAs using hybrid function units have more scheduling freedom, a trigger move can be scheduled after an operand move and operations can stay longer in the pipeline if the scheduler "thinks" that is wise. To investigate the effect of the extra scheduling freedom of TTA we introduce four scheduling models:

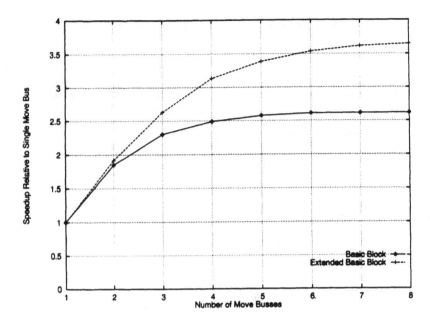

Fig. 6. Basic block vs. extended basic block scheduling.

1. **OTR:** The distances between all moves of the same operations are fixed.
2. **OT:** The distance between operand and trigger moves of the same operation is fixed.
3. **TR:** The distance between trigger and result moves of the same operation is fixed.
4. **FREE:** No restrictions on the distance between the moves of an operation.

Figure 7 shows the DDGs of a n cycle dyadic operation for the four different models. It shows that OTR has more dependences than OT and TR, and FREE has less dependences. Less dependences means more freedom and potentially better results.

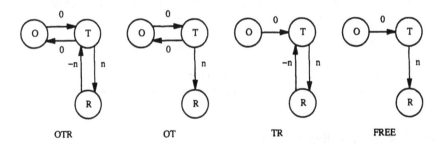

Fig. 7. The DDGs of a dyadic operation for the four scheduling models.

Figure 8 shows the result of scheduling the benchmarks according to the four scheduling models. It shows that the extra scheduling freedom is profitable when the transport capacity is small (less than five busses), in other words when resource constraints are limiting the performance. It can be expected that for applications with more parallelism, and when the scheduling techniques are improved, the point where the four lines of Fig. 8 merge will shift to the right. In other words, the extra scheduling freedom will become more important.

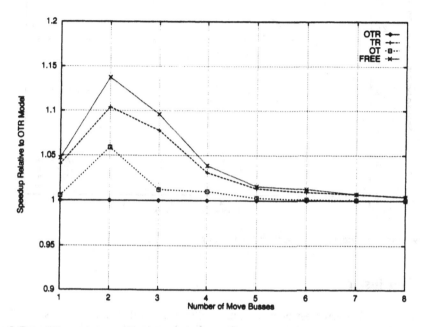

Fig. 8. Four different degrees of scheduling freedom.

4.4 Effect of Transport-Triggering vs. Operation-Triggering

Our last experiment will compare an n-issue TTA with an m-issue OTA for $1 \leq n \leq 8$ and $1 \leq m \leq 3$ (n is the number of concurrent transports, m is the number of concurrent operations). Since n-issue OTA needs $3n$ busses it is interesting to compare a $3n$-issue TTA with an n-issue OTA. We model an n-issue OTA for our scheduler as a TTA with an infinite number of busses and an extra restriction of at most n operations per cycle. Figure 9 shows the results. The three horizontal lines correspond to one, two, and three issue OTAs. It is interesting where they cross the curved line that represents an one to eight issue TTA. These crossing let us make the following conclusions:

1. A $3n$-issue TTA performs better than an n-issue OTA.
2. A TTA needs less than $3n$-issue to compete with an n-issue OTA.

As in Sect. 4.3 the benefit of transport-triggering is most expressive when resource constraints are limiting the performance.

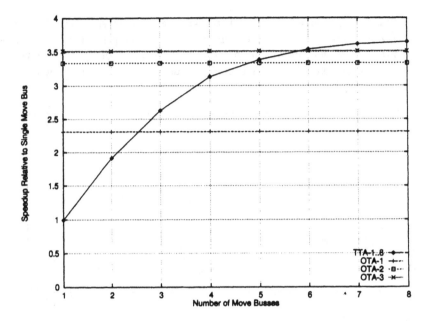

Fig. 9. Transport-Triggering vs. Operation-Triggering.

5 Conclusions

We described (1) a new class of architectures called TTAs with their advantages, and (2) an extended basic block scheduler for these TTAs. With this scheduler we did some experiments to measure how it compares to basic block scheduling and how TTAs compare to traditional OTAs.

We observed a 40% higher speedup for extended basic block scheduling instead of basic block scheduling for an eight move bus TTA. Further research should find out how this can be improved by better memory reference disambiguation, more flexible code motions, and software pipelining instead of loop unrolling.

We also observed significant better results due to transport-triggering instead of operation-triggering. This is especially true for the cases where resources are scarce and it is hard for the scheduler to map the ILP of the application on the ILP of the hardware. These are precisely the architectures that are most cost-effective and for which instruction scheduling is most challenging.

References

[AKPW83] J.R. Allen, K. Kennedy, C. Porterfield, and J. Warren. Conversion of Control Dependence to Data Dependence. In *Proceedings of the 10th ACM Symposium on Principles of Programming Languages*, pages 177–189, Januari 1983.

[ASU85] Alfred V. Aho, Ravi Sethi, and Jeffrey D. Ullman. *Compilers: Principles, Techniques and Tools*. Addison-Wesley Series in Computer Science. Addison-Wesley Publishing Company, Reading, Massachusetts, 1985.

[BR91] David Bernstein and Michael Rodey. Global Instruction Scheduling for Superscalar Machines. In *Proceedings of the SIGPLAN '91 Conference on Programming Language Design and Implementation*, pages 241–255, June 1991.

[CM91] Henk Corporaal and Hans (J.M.) Mulder. MOVE: A Framework for High-Performance Processor Design. In *Supercomputing-91, Albuquerque*, pages 692–701, November 1991.

[Fis81] Joseph A. Fisher. Trace Scheduling: A Technique for Global Microcode Compaction. *IEEE Transactions on Computers*, C-30(7):478–490, July 1981.

[HC92] Jan Hoogerbrugge and Henk Corporaal. Comparing Software Pipelining for an Operation-Triggered and a Transport-Triggered Architecture. In *International Workshop on Compiler Construction*, pages 219–228, Paderborn, Germany, October 1992.

[HCM91] Jan Hoogerbrugge, Henk Corporaal, and Hans Mulder. Software Pipelining for Transport-Triggered Architectures. In *Proceedings of the 24th Annual International Workshop on Microprogramming*, pages 74–81, Albuquerque, New Mexico, November 1991.

[HD86] Peter Y.T. Hsu and Edwards S. Davidson. Higly Concurrent Scalar Processing. In *Proceedings of ISCA 13*, pages 386–395, June 1986.

[HMC+93] Wen-Mei W. Hwu, Scott A. Mahlke, William Y. Chen, Pohua P. Chang, Nancy J. Warter, Roger A. Bringmann, Roland G. Ouellette, Richard E. Hank, Tokuzo Kiyohara, Grant E. Haab, John G. Holm, and Daniel M. Lavery. The Superblock: An Effective Technique fro VLIW and Superscalar Compilation. *The Journal of Supercomputing*, 7(1/2):229–249, May 1993.

[Joh89] William M. Johnson. Super-scalar processor design. Technical Report CSL-TR-89-383, Computer Systems Laboratory, Stanford University, June 1989.

[MLC+92] Scott A. Mahlke, David C. Lin, William Y. Chen, Richard E. Hank, and Roger A. Bringmann. Effective Compiler Support for Predicated Execution Using the Hyperblock. In *Proceedings of the 25th Annual International Workshop on Microprogramming*, pages 45–54, Portland, Oregon, December 1992.

[RF93] B. Ramakrishna Rau and Joseph A. Fisher. Instruction-Level Parallel Processing: History, Overview, and Perspective. *The Journal of Supercomputing*, 7(1/2):9–50, May 1993.

[TGH92] Kevin B. Theobald, Guang R. Gao, and Laurie J. Hendren. One the Limits of Program Parallelism and its Smoothability. In *Proceedings of the 25th Annual International Workshop on Microprogramming*, pages 10–19, Portland, Oregon, December 1992.

[TS88] M.R. Thistle and B.J Smith. A Processor Architecture fo Horizon. In *Proceedings of Supercomputing '88*, pages 35–41, Orlando, Florida, November 1988.

[Wal91] D.W. Wall. Limits of Instruction-Level Parallelism. In *Proc. 4th Int. Conf. on Architectural Support for Programming Languages and Operating Systems*, pages 176–188, April 1991.

Author Index

Springer-Verlag
and the Environment

We at Springer-Verlag firmly believe that an international science publisher has a special obligation to the environment, and our corporate policies consistently reflect this conviction.

We also expect our business partners – paper mills, printers, packaging manufacturers, etc. – to commit themselves to using environmentally friendly materials and production processes.

The paper in this book is made from low- or no-chlorine pulp and is acid free, in conformance with international standards for paper permanency.

Lecture Notes in Computer Science

For information about Vols. 1–709
please contact your bookseller or Springer-Verlag